Introduction to Business- Business 105

Brookdale Community College

12e

William M. Pride | Robert J. Hughes | Jack R. Kapoor

CENGAGE
Learning·

Australia • Brazil • Japan • Korea • Mexico • Singapore • Spain • United Kingdom • United States

CENGAGE
Learning·

Introduction to Business- Business 105: Brookdale Community College, 12e

Introduction to Business- Business 105, Brookdale Community College, 12e
Pride | Hughes | Kapoor

Senior Project Development Manager:
Linda deStefano

Market Development Manager:
Heather Kramer

Senior Production/Manufacturing Manager:
Donna M. Brown

Production Editorial Manager:
Kim Fry

Sr. Rights Acquisition Account Manager:
Todd Osborne

For product information and technology assistance, contact us at
Cengage Learning Customer & Sales Support, 1-800-354-9706

For permission to use material from this text or product,
submit all requests online at **cengage.com/permissions**
Further permissions questions can be emailed to
permissionrequest@cengage.com

This book contains select works from existing Cengage Learning resources and was produced by Cengage Learning Custom Solutions for collegiate use. As such, those adopting and/or contributing to this work are responsible for editorial content accuracy, continuity and completeness.

Compilation © 2013 Cengage Learning
ISBN-13: 978-1-285-91482-4

ISBN-10: 1-285-91482-1

Cengage Learning
5191 Natorp Boulevard
Mason, Ohio 45040
USA
Cengage Learning is a leading provider of customized learning solutions with office locations around the globe, including Singapore, the United Kingdom, Australia, Mexico, Brazil, and Japan. Locate your local office at:
international.cengage.com/region.

Cengage Learning products are represented in Canada by Nelson Education, Ltd.
For your lifelong learning solutions, visit **www.cengage.com/custom.**
Visit our corporate website at **www.cengage.com.**

Printed in the United States of America

Brief Contents

The Environment of Business

PART 1

In Part 1 of *Business*, we begin by examining the world of business and how the economy affects your life. Next, we discuss ethical and social responsibility issues that affect business firms and our society. Then we explore the increasing importance of international business.

1
Exploring the World of Business and Economics

LEARNING OBJECTIVES

What you will be able to do once you complete this chapter:

① Discuss what you must do to be successful in the world of business.

② Define *business* and identify potential risks and rewards.

③ Define *economics* and describe the two types of economic systems: capitalism and command economy.

④ Identify the ways to measure economic performance.

⑤ Examine the different phases in the typical business cycle.

⑥ Outline the four types of competition.

⑦ Summarize the factors that affect the business environment and the challenges that American businesses will encounter in the future.

Inside BUSINESS

Zynga Zooms into Business

Zynga, named for its founder's American bulldog, is the fast-growing business behind some of the social media world's fastest-growing games. If you've ever tended crops on FarmVille, you know how addictive a Zynga game can be. Even though FarmVille was developed and launched in only six weeks, it instantly captured the imagination of millions of players who eagerly logged onto their Facebook accounts to plant trees or exchange seeds with "neighbors." Other popular Zynga games include CityVille, CastleVille, and Words with Friends.

Founder and CEO Mark Pincus is a seasoned entrepreneur who earned an MBA from Harvard University. Before Zynga, he had started four other Internet businesses—and earned millions of dollars from their success. In 2007, he came up with the idea for a game business in which players could get ahead by connecting with friends (think "neighbors" in FarmVille) and buying special items (such as virtual tractors and cows) that would give them a competitive edge.

Now, when players worldwide buy digital tractors and cows in FarmVille, they can pay with real money, which is why Zynga's profits are real. So real, in fact, that on the basis of its track record, Zynga was able to go public and sell shares of its corporate stock in December, 2011.

As Zynga continues to grow, Pincus and his managers are keeping their workforce satisfied by offering benefits such as surprise vacations and by making the workplace as comfortable as possible. Like many other high-tech firms, Zynga offers free lunch and dinner. Dogs are welcome at the San Francisco headquarters (and they get free dog nibbles, too). Employees can grab a cup of fresh-brewed espresso at the office's gourmet coffee station, sip tea in the Zen-style tea garden, work out in the fitness center, or take a break to play arcade games in the company lounge.

In today's fast-paced business environment, the online games that get everyone talking and clicking right now can become has-beens as soon as the next new thing comes to market. That's why Pincus and his entire team are working hard to keep Zynga zooming ahead year after year.[1]

Wow! What a challenging world we live in. Just for a moment, think about the economic problems listed here and how they affect not only you, but also businesses in the United States and the global economy.

- U.S. unemployment rates hovering around 8 percent
- Reduced spending by worried consumers
- Increased government spending to stimulate a troubled economy that created the largest national debt in the nation's history
- A volatile stock market and concerns about banks and financial institutions
- Reform movements including the "Occupy Wall Street" movement that protest differences in wealth and income

In fact, just about every person around the globe was affected in some way by the economic crisis that began in late 2007. Despite the efforts of the U.S. government and other world governments to provide the economic stimulus needed to stabilize the economy, it took nearly four years before the economy began to improve. Today, even with signs of modest improvement, people still worry about their economic future and the future of the nation. Hopefully, by the time you read this material, the nation's economy will be much stronger. Still, it is important to remember the old adage, "History is a great teacher." Both the nation and individuals should take a look at what went wrong to avoid making the same mistakes in the future.

In addition, it helps to keep one factor in mind: Our economy continues to adapt and change to meet the challenges of an ever-changing world and to provide opportunities for those who want to achieve success. Our economic system provides an amazing amount of freedom that allows businesses like Zynga—the Internet gaming company profiled in the Inside Business opening case for this chapter—to adapt to changing business environments. Despite troubling economic times and a weak economy, Zynga—and its 3,000 employees—is a success because it was able to introduce new games that players love, earn a profit, and sell stock to the general public.

Within certain limits, imposed mainly to ensure public safety, the owners of a business can produce any legal good or service they choose and attempt to sell it at the price they set. This system of business, in which individuals decide what to produce, how to produce it, and at what price to sell it, is called **free enterprise**. Our free-enterprise system ensures, for example, that Amazon.com can sell everything from televisions, toys, and tools to computers, cameras, and clothing. Our system gives Amazon's owners and stockholders the right to make a profit from the company's success. It gives Amazon's management the right to compete with bookstore rival Barnes & Noble and electronics giant Sony. It also gives you the right to choose.

In this chapter, we look briefly at what business is and how it became that way. First, we discuss what you must do to be successful in the world of business and explore some important reasons for studying business. Then we define *business*, noting how business organizations satisfy their customers' needs and earn profits. Next, we examine how capitalism and command economies answer four basic economic questions. Then our focus shifts to how the nations of the world measure economic performance, the phases in a typical business cycle, and the four types of competitive situations. Next, we look at the events that helped shape today's business system, the current business environment, and the challenges that businesses face.

YOUR FUTURE IN THE CHANGING WORLD OF BUSINESS

Discuss what you must do to be successful in the world of business.
①

The key word in this heading is *changing*. When faced with both economic problems and increasing competition not only from firms in the United States but also from international firms located in other parts of the world, employees and managers began to ask the question: What do we do now? Although this is a fair question, it is difficult to answer. Certainly, for a college student taking business courses or an employee just starting a career, the question is even more difficult to answer. Yet there are still opportunities out there for people who are willing to work hard, continue to learn, and possess the ability to adapt to change. Let's begin our discussion in this section with three basic concepts.

- What do you want?
- Why do you want it?
- Write it down!

During a segment on a national television talk show, Joe Dudley, one of the world's most respected black business owners, gave the preceding advice to anyone who wanted to succeed in business. His advice can help you achieve success. What is so amazing about Dudley's success is that he started a manufacturing business in his own kitchen, with his wife and children serving as the new firm's only employees. He went on to develop his own line of hair-care and cosmetic products sold directly to cosmetologists, barbers, beauty schools, and consumers in the United States and 18 foreign countries. Today, Mr. Dudley has a multimillion-dollar empire—one of the

free enterprise the system of business in which individuals are free to decide what to produce, how to produce it, and at what price to sell it most successful minority-owned companies in the nation. He is not only a successful business owner but also a winner of the Horatio Alger Award—an award given to outstanding individuals who have succeeded in the face of adversity.[2]

Although many people would say that Joe Dudley was just lucky or happened to be in the right place at the right time, the truth is that he became a success because he had a dream and worked hard to turn his dream into a reality. Today, Dudley's vision is to see people succeed—to realize "The American Dream." He would be the first to tell you that you have the same opportunities that he had. According to Mr. Dudley, "Success is a journey, not just a destination."[3]

Whether you want to obtain part-time employment to pay college and living expenses, begin your career as a full-time employee, or start a business, you must *bring* something to the table that makes you different from the next person. Employers and our economic system are more demanding than ever before. Ask yourself: What can I do that will make employers want to pay me a salary? What skills do I have that employers need? With these two questions in mind, we begin the next section with another basic question: Why study business?

Why Study Business?

The potential benefits of higher education are enormous. To begin with, there are economic benefits. Over their lifetimes, college graduates on average earn much more than high school graduates. Although lifetime earnings are substantially higher for college graduates, so are annual income amounts (see Figure 1.1). In addition to higher income, you will find at least five compelling reasons for studying business.

For Help in Choosing a Career What do you want to do with the rest of your life? At some time in your life, someone probably has asked you this same question. Like many people, you may find it a difficult question to answer. This business course will introduce you to a wide array of employment opportunities. In private enterprise, these range from small, local businesses owned by one individual to large companies such as American Express and Marriott International that are owned by thousands of stockholders. There are also employment opportunities with federal, state, county, and local governments and with charitable organizations such as the Red Cross and Save the Children. For help in deciding which career might be right for you, read Appendix A: Careers in Business, which appears on the text Web site. To view this information:

1. Go to www.cengagebrain.com.
2. At the CengageBrain.com home page, search for the ISBN for your book (located on the back cover of your book) using the search box at the top of the page. This will take you to the product page where free companion resources can be found.

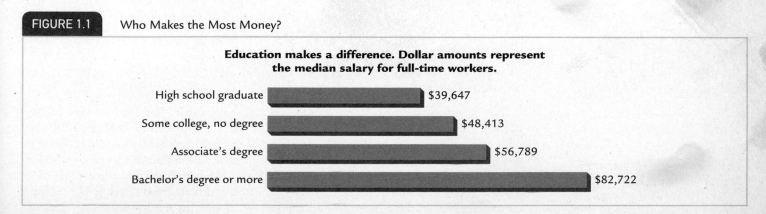

| FIGURE 1.1 | Who Makes the Most Money? |

Education makes a difference. Dollar amounts represent the median salary for full-time workers.

High school graduate	$39,647
Some college, no degree	$48,413
Associate's degree	$56,789
Bachelor's degree or more	$82,722

Source: The 2012 Statistical Abstract of the U.S. Web site at www.census.gov (accessed January 10, 2012). Salary amounts were obtained from Table 692.

Career SUCCESS

Show Off Your Skills with Digital Merit Badges

Made of pixels instead of fabric, the next generation of merit badges is on its way, bringing new possibilities for showing off your skills via digital badges on your Web site, blog, or Facebook page. The point is to encourage students, career-changers, veterans, and learners of all ages to acquire or polish skills that can be helpful in career moves and in life. Whether you're just entering the workforce or you want to branch out into a new field, take a look at what digital merit badges have to offer.

The MacArthur Foundation is partnering with organizations such as the Smithsonian and the U.S. Department of Veterans Affairs to encourage and recognize skill attainment in a variety of areas through its "Badges for Lifelong Learning" program.

In the works are badges for financial literacy, engineering design, filmmaking, mathematics proficiency, natural history, and military experience. "The badges are another way to tell the story of who you are and what you know," explains a MacArthur executive.

TopCoder, a Connecticut company, awards digital badges (and cash) to those who earn top scores in its international programming competitions. NASA has teamed up with the Boy Scouts of America and the Girl Scouts of America to offer badges in robotics. Is a digital merit badge in your future?

Sources: Based on information in Anne Eisenberg, "For Job Hunters, Digital Merit Badges," *New York Times*, November 20, 2011, p. BU-3; Sam Kilb, "Credentials, the Next Generation," *New York Times Education Life*, November 6, 2011, p. 10; Leslie Katz, "Boy Scouts Can Now Earn Robotics Merit Badge," *Cnet News*, April 10, 2011, http://news.cnet.com.

In addition to career information in Appendix A, a number of additional Web sites provide information about career development. For more information, visit the following sites:

- Career Builder at www.careerbuilder.com
- Career One Stop at www.careeronestop.org
- Monster at www.monster.com

To click your career into high gear, you can also use online networking to advance your career. Web sites like Facebook, Twitter, LinkedIn, and other social media sites can help you locate job openings, help prospective employers to find you, and make a good impression on current and future bosses. To make the most of online networking, begin by identifying and joining sites where you can connect with potential employers, former classmates, and others who may have or may hear of job openings. Next, be sure your online profiles, photographs, and posts communicate your abilities and interest without being offensive or overly revealing. Finally, be ready to respond quickly when you spot a job opening.

One thing to remember as you think about what your ideal career might be is that a person's choice of a career ultimately is just a reflection of what he or she values and holds most important. What will give one individual personal satisfaction may not satisfy another. For example, one person may dream of a career as a corporate executive and becoming a millionaire before the age of 30. Another may choose a career that has more modest monetary rewards but that provides the opportunity to help others. What you choose to do with your life will be based on what you feel is most important. And *you* are a very important part of that decision.

To Be a Successful Employee Deciding on the type of career you want is only the first step. To get a job in your chosen field and to be successful at it, you will have to develop a plan, or a road map, that ensures that you have the skills and knowledge the job requires. You will also be expected to have the ability to work well with many types of people in a culturally diverse workforce. **Cultural (or workplace) diversity** refers to the differences among people in a workforce owing to race, ethnicity, and

cultural (or workplace) diversity differences among people in a workforce owing to race, ethnicity, and gender

gender. These skills, together with a working knowledge of the American business system and an appreciation for a culturally diverse workplace, can give you an inside edge when you are interviewing with a prospective employer.

This course, your instructor, and all of the resources available at your college or university can help you to acquire the skills and knowledge you will need for a successful career. But do not underestimate your part in making your dream a reality. In addition to the job-related skills and knowledge you'll need to be successful in a specific job, employers will also look for the following characteristics when hiring a new employee or promoting an existing employee:

- Honesty and integrity
- Willingness to work hard
- Dependability
- Time management skills
- Self-confidence
- Motivation
- Willingness to learn
- Communication skills
- Professionalism

Employers will also be interested in any work experience you may have had in cooperative work/school programs, during summer vacations, or in part-time jobs during the school year. These things can make a difference when it is time to apply for the job you really want.

Personal APPS

Sometimes you have to reach for success! There's an old saying that if you choose a career you like, you never have to work a day in your life. For most people, the first decision is choosing a career. Then the material in the sections "To Be a Successful Employee" and "To Improve Your Management Skills" can help you achieve success.

To Improve Your Management Skills Often, employees become managers or supervisors. In fact, many employees want to become managers because managers often receive higher salaries. Although management obviously can be a rewarding career, what is not so obvious is the amount of time and hard work needed to achieve the higher salaries. For starters, employers expect more from managers and supervisors than ever before. Typically, the heavy workload requires that managers work long hours, and most do not get paid overtime. They also face increased problems created by the economic crisis, increased competition, employee downsizing, the quest for improved quality, and the need for efficient use of the firm's resources.

To be an effective manager, managers must be able to perform four basic management functions: planning, organizing, leading and motivating, and controlling. All four topics are discussed in Chapter 6, Understanding the Management Process. To successfully perform these management functions, managers must possess four very important skills.

- *Interpersonal skills*—The ability to deal effectively with individual employees, other managers within the firm, and people outside the firm.
- *Analytic skills*—The ability to identify problems correctly, generate reasonable alternatives, and select the "best" alternatives to solve problems.
- *Technical skills*—The skill required to accomplish a specific kind of work being done in an organization. Although managers may not actually perform the technical tasks, they should be able to train employees and answer technical questions.
- *Conceptual skills*—The ability to think in abstract terms in order to see the "big picture." Conceptual skills help managers understand how the various parts of an organization or idea can fit together.

In addition to the four skills just described, a successful manager will need many of the same characteristics that an employee needs to be successful.

To Start Your Own Business Some people prefer to work for themselves, and they open their own businesses. To be successful, business owners must possess many of the same characteristics that successful employees have, and they must be willing to work hard and put in long hours.

It also helps if your small business can provide a product or service that customers want. For example, Steve Demeter, the CEO and founder of the software development firm Demiforce, began his career by creating the *Trism* application for the Apple iPhone. *Trism* was an immediate sensation and sold 50,000 copies at $4.99 in its first two months on Apple's AppStore. Now Demeter and the employees at Demiforce are working with a number of promising ideas in the works all with one goal in mind: to provide games and applications that people want.[4]

Unfortunately, many small-business firms fail: Approximately 70 percent of them fail within the first ten years. Typical reasons for business failures include undercapitalization (not enough money), poor business location, poor customer service, unqualified or untrained employees, fraud, lack of a proper business plan, and failure to seek outside professional help. The material in Chapter 5, Small Business, Entrepreneurship, and Franchises, and selected topics and examples throughout this text will help you to decide whether you want to open your own business. This material will also help you to overcome many of these problems.

To Become a Better Informed Consumer and Investor The world of business surrounds us. You cannot buy a home, a new Ford Fusion Hybrid from the local Ford dealer, a pair of jeans at Gap Inc., or a hot dog from a street vendor without entering a business transaction. Because you no doubt will engage in business transactions almost every day of your life, one very good reason for studying business is to become a more fully informed consumer.

Many people also rely on a basic understanding of business to help them to invest for the future. According to Julie Stav, Hispanic stockbroker-turned-author/radio personality, "Take $25, add to it drive plus determination and then watch it multiply into an empire."[5] The author of *Get Your Share* believes that it is important to learn the basics about the economy and business, stocks, mutual funds, and other alternatives before investing your money. She also believes that it is never too early to start investing. Although this is an obvious conclusion, just dreaming of being rich does not make it happen. In fact, like many facets of life, it takes planning and determination to establish the type of investment program that will help you to accomplish your financial goals.

Special Note to Business Students

It is important to begin reading this text with one thing in mind: *This business course does not have to be difficult.* We have done everything possible to eliminate the problems that you encounter in a typical class. All of the features in each chapter have been evaluated and recommended by instructors with years of teaching experience. In addition, business students were asked to critique each chapter component. Based on this feedback, the text includes the following features:

- *Learning objectives* appear at the beginning of each chapter.
- *Inside Business* is a chapter-opening case that highlights how successful companies do business on a day-to-day basis.
- *Margin notes* are used throughout the text to reinforce both learning objectives and key terms.
- *Two boxed features* in each chapter chosen from Career Success, Entrepreneurial Success, Ethical Success or Failure?, and Going for Success highlight how both employees and entrepreneurs can be successful.

- *Two Personal Apps* in each chapter provide special student-centered examples and explanations that help you immediately grasp and retain the material.
- *Sustaining the Planet* features provide information about companies working to protect the environment.
- *Social Media* features provide examples of how businesses and individuals are using social networking and social media sites.
- *End-of-chapter materials* provide questions about the opening case, a chapter summary, a list of key terms, review and discussion questions, and two cases.
- The last section of every chapter is entitled Building Skills for Career Success and includes exercises devoted to enhancing your social media skills, building communication skills with a journal exercise, developing critical-thinking skills, building team skills, and researching different careers.
- *End-of-part materials* provide a continuing video case about Graeter's Ice Cream, a company that operates a chain of retail outlets in the Cincinnati, Ohio, area and sells to Kroger Stores throughout the country. Also, at the end of each major part is an exercise designed to help you to develop the components that are included in a typical business plan.

In addition to the text, a number of student supplements will help you to explore the world of business. We are especially proud of the Web site that accompanies this edition. There, you will find online study aids, such as interactive quizzes, key terms and definitions, student PowerPoint slides, crossword puzzles, and links to the videos for each chapter. If you want to take a look at the Internet support materials available for this edition of *Business*,

1. Go to www.cengagebrain.com.
2. At the CengageBrain.com home page, search for the ISBN for your book (located on the back cover of your book) using the search box at the top of the page. This will take you to the textbook Web site where free companion resources can be found.

As authors, we want you to be successful. We know that your time is valuable and that your schedule is crowded with many different activities. We also appreciate the fact that textbooks are expensive. Therefore, we want you to use this text and get the most out of your investment. To help you get off to a good start, a number of suggestions for developing effective study skills and using this text are provided in Table 1.1.

TABLE 1.1 Seven Ways to Use this Text and Its Resources

1. Prepare before you go to class.	Early preparation is the key to success in many of life's activities. Certainly, early preparation can help you to participate in class, ask questions, and improve your performance on examinations.
2. Read the chapter.	Although it may seem like an obvious suggestion, many students never take the time to really read the material. Find a quiet space where there are no distractions, and invest enough time to become a "content expert."
3. Underline or highlight important concepts.	Make this text yours. Do not be afraid to write on the pages of your text or highlight important material. It is much easier to review material if you have identified important concepts.
4. Take notes.	While reading, take the time to jot down important points and summarize concepts in your own words. Also, take notes in class.
5. Apply the concepts.	Learning is always easier if you can apply the content to your real-life situation. Think about how you could use the material either now or in the future.
6. Practice critical thinking.	Test the material in the text. Do the concepts make sense? To build critical-thinking skills, answer the questions that accompany the cases at the end of each chapter. Also, many of the exercises in the Building Skills for Career Success require critical thinking.
7. Prepare for the examinations.	Allow enough time to review the material before the examinations. Check out the summary and review questions at the end of the chapter. Then use the resources on the text Web site.

Why not take a look at these suggestions and use them to help you succeed in this course and earn a higher grade. Remember what Joe Dudley said, "Success is a journey, not just a destination."

Because a text should always be evaluated by the students and instructors who use it, we would welcome and sincerely appreciate your comments and suggestions. Please feel free to contact us by using one of the following e-mail addresses:

Bill Pride: w-pride@tamu.edu
Bob Hughes: bhughes@dcccd.edu
Jack Kapoor: kapoorj@cod.edu

Define *business* and identify potential risks and rewards.

BUSINESS: A DEFINITION

Business is the organized effort of individuals to produce and sell, for a profit, the goods and services that satisfy society's needs. The general term *business* refers to all such efforts within a society (as in "American business"). However, *a business* is a particular organization, such as Kraft Foods, Inc., or Cracker Barrel Old Country Stores. To be successful, a business must perform three activities. It must be organized, it must satisfy needs, and it must earn a profit.

The Organized Effort of Individuals

For a business to be organized, it must combine four kinds of resources: material, human, financial, and informational. *Material* resources include the raw materials used in manufacturing processes as well as buildings and machinery. For example, Sara Lee (now part of Hillshire Brands) needs flour, sugar, butter, eggs, and other raw materials to produce the food products it sells worldwide. In addition, this Illinois-based company needs human, financial, and informational resources. *Human* resources are the people who furnish their labor to the business in return for wages. The *financial* resource is the money required to pay employees, purchase materials, and generally keep the business operating. *Information* is the resource that tells the managers of the business how effectively the other three resources are being combined and used (see Figure 1.2).

business the organized effort of individuals to produce and sell, for a profit, the goods and services that satisfy society's needs

Today, businesses are usually organized as one of three specific types. *Service businesses* produce services, such as haircuts, legal advice, or tax preparation. H&R Block provides tax preparation, retail banking, and various business advisory and consulting services in the United States, Canada, and Australia. *Manufacturing businesses* process various materials into tangible goods, such as delivery trucks, towels, or computers. Intel, for example, produces computer chips that, in turn, are sold to companies that manufacture computers. Finally, some firms called *marketing intermediaries* buy products from manufacturers and then resell them. Sony Corporation is a manufacturer that produces stereo equipment, televisions, and other electronic products. These products may be sold to a marketing intermediary such as Best Buy or Walmart, which then resells the manufactured goods to consumers in their retail stores.

Satisfying Needs

The ultimate objective of every firm must be to satisfy the needs of its customers. People generally do not buy goods and services simply to own them; they buy goods and services to satisfy

© ANTON GVZDOKOV/SHUTTERSTOCK

Organization when it counts. Imagine what would happen if the medical professionals in a hospital operating room weren't organized—especially if you were the patient. Like a surgical operating room, a business must be organized in order to meet the needs of its customers and earn a profit.

FIGURE 1.2   Combining Resources

A business must combine all four resources effectively to be successful.

particular needs. Some of us may feel that the need for transportation is best satisfied by an air-conditioned BMW with navigation system, stereo system, heated and cooled seats, automatic transmission, power windows, and remote-control side mirrors. Others may believe that a Chevrolet Sonic with a stick shift will do just fine. Both products are available to those who want them, along with a wide variety of other products that satisfy the need for transportation.

When firms lose sight of their customers' needs, they are likely to find the going rough. However, when businesses understand their customers' needs and work to satisfy those needs, they are usually successful. Back in 1962, Sam Walton opened his first discount store in Rogers, Arkansas. Although the original store was quite different from the Walmart Superstores you see today, the basic ideas of providing customer service and offering goods that satisfied needs at low prices are part of the reason why this firm has grown to become the largest retailer in the world. Although Walmart has over 10,000 stores in the United States and 27 other countries, this highly successful discount-store organization continues to open new stores to meet the needs of its customers around the globe.[6]

Business Profit

A business receives money (sales revenue) from its customers in exchange for goods or services. It must also pay out money to cover the expenses involved in doing business. If the firm's sales revenues are greater than its expenses, it has earned a profit. More specifically, as shown in Figure 1.3, **profit** is what remains after all business expenses have been deducted from sales revenue.

A negative profit, which results when a firm's expenses are greater than its sales revenue, is called a *loss*. A business cannot continue to operate at a loss for an indefinite period of time. Management and employees must find some way to increase sales revenues and reduce expenses to return to profitability. If some

FIGURE 1.3   The Relationship Between Sales Revenue and Profit

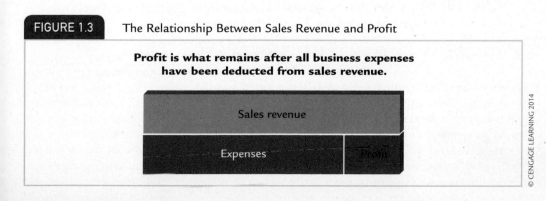

Profit is what remains after all business expenses have been deducted from sales revenue.

Sales revenue

Expenses

Profit

profit what remains after all business expenses have been deducted from sales revenue

Sustaining the PLANET

Honda: Not Just Another Automobile Manufacturer

When you hear the name Honda, you typically think about automobiles. But Honda is much more than that. Honda product lines include motorcycles, financial services, and even walk assist devices to help the disabled. The company continues to innovate and create products with a global perspective but they balance innovation with a commitment to the preservation of the environment both globally and in the local communities where they operate. Take a look at http://corporate. honda.com/innovation/ or http://corporate.honda. com/environment/.

specific actions are not taken to eliminate losses, a firm may be forced to close its doors or file for bankruptcy protection. Although many people—especially stockholders and business owners—believe that profit is literally the bottom line or most important goal for a business, many stakeholders may be just as concerned about a firm's social responsibility record. The term **stakeholders** is used to describe all the different people or groups of people who are affected by the policies, decisions, and activities made by an organization. Many corporations, for example, are careful to point out their efforts to sustain the planet, participate in the green ecological movement, and help people to live better lives in an annual social responsibility report. In its 86-page social responsibility report, General Mills describes how it contributed $100 million in 2010—a 10 percent increase when compared to 2009—to a wide variety of causes, including support for programs that feed the hungry and non-profit organizations in the United States and around the globe.[7] Although stockholders and business owners sometimes argue that the money that a business contributes to charitable causes could have been used to pay larger dividends to stockholders or increase the return on the owners' investment, the fact is that most socially responsible business firms feel social responsibility is the right thing to do and is good for business.

The profit earned by a business becomes the property of its owners. Thus, in one sense, profit is the reward business owners receive for producing goods and services that customers want. Profit is also the payment that business owners receive for assuming the considerable risks of business ownership. One of these is the risk of not being paid. Everyone else—employees, suppliers, and lenders—must be paid before the owners.

A second risk that owners undertake is the risk of losing whatever they have invested into the business. A business that cannot earn a profit is very likely to fail, in which case the owners lose whatever money, effort, and time they have invested.

To satisfy society's needs and make a profit, a business must operate within the parameters of a nation's economic system. In the next section, we define economics and describe two different types of economic systems.

Define *economics* and describe the two types of economic systems: capitalism and command economy.

③

stakeholders all the different people or groups of people who are affected by the policies and decisions made by an organization

TYPES OF ECONOMIC SYSTEMS

Economics is the study of how wealth is created and distributed. By *wealth*, we mean "anything of value," including the goods and services produced and sold by business. *How wealth is distributed* simply means "who gets what." Experts often use economics to explain the choices we make and how these choices change as we cope with the demands of everyday life. In simple terms, individuals, businesses, governments, and society must make decisions that reflect what is important to each group at a particular time. For example, suppose you want to take a weekend trip to some exotic vacation spot, and you also want to begin an investment program. Because of your

Entrepreneurial SUCCESS

Building a Million-Dollar App Business

Nick D'Aloisio, who lives in the south of London, England, created his first iPhone app when he was 12. Two apps later, teen entrepreneur D'Aloisio hit upon a new app idea that has brought him into the major leagues of the app business world.

D'Aloisio was searching the Internet for information for a term paper when he realized how much time it takes to determine the content of each web page. To speed things up, he developed an algorithm that summarizes the key points in a few words. He named this app Trimit, priced it at 99 cents per download, released it on Apple's App Store, and earned $1,600 within the first three days.

To accelerate Trimit's momentum, D'Aloisio decided to give it away instead of charging for it. The app's download numbers skyrocketed, bringing it to the attention of Horizon Ventures, a firm that invests in businesses when they're in the early stages of growth. Horizon invested $250,000 to commercialize the app, which was renamed Summly and relaunched a few months later. As Summly, the app was downloaded 30,000 times in the first week alone, putting D'Aloisio squarely on the path toward his goal of building a $1 million app business.

Sources: Based on information in Jane Wakefield, "British Teenage Designer of Summly App Hits Jackpot," *BBC News*, December 28, 2011, www.bbc.co.uk; Parmy Olson, "Teen Programmer Hopes to Make a Million from A.I. App," *Forbes*, September 1, 2011, www.forbes.com; Kit Eaton, "The 15-year-old Creator of the Trimit App Makes Regular Old Entrepreneurs Seem Like Slackers," *Fast Company*, August 11, 2011, www.fastcompany.com.

---

financial resources, though, you cannot do both, so you must decide what is most important. Business firms, governments, and to some extent society face the same types of decisions. Each group must deal with scarcity when making important decisions. In this case, *scarcity* means "lack of resources"—money, time, natural resources, and so on—that are needed to satisfy a want or need.

Today, experts often study economic problems from two different perspectives: micro-economics and macroeconomics. **Microeconomics** is the study of the decisions made by individuals and businesses. Microeconomics, for example, examines how the prices of homes affect the number of homes individuals will buy. On the other hand, **macroeconomics** is the study of the national economy and the global economy. Macroeconomics examines the economic effect of national income, unemployment, inflation, taxes, government spending, interest rates, and similar factors on a nation and society.

The decisions that individuals, business firms, government, and society make, and the way in which people deal with the creation and distribution of wealth determine the kind of economic system, or **economy**, that a nation has.

Over the years, the economic systems of the world have differed in essentially two ways: (1) the ownership of the factors of production and (2) how they answer four basic economic questions that direct a nation's economic activity.

Factors of production are the resources used to produce goods and services. There are four such factors:

- *Land and natural resources*—elements that can be used in the production process to make appliances, automobiles, and other products. Typical examples include crude oil, forests, minerals, land, water, and even air.
- *Labor*—the time and effort that we use to produce goods and services. It includes human resources such as managers and employees.
- *Capital*—the money, facilities, equipment, and machines used in the operation of organizations. Although most people think of capital as just money, it can also be the manufacturing equipment in a Pepperidge Farm production facility or a computer used in the corporate offices of McDonald's.

economics the study of how wealth is created and distributed

microeconomics the study of the decisions made by individuals and businesses

macroeconomics the study of the national economy and the global economy

economy the way in which people deal with the creation and distribution of wealth

factors of production resources used to produce goods and services

Saving natural resources one bus at a time.
While "green" used to refer to a color in a box of crayons, now it has taken on a whole new meaning. For consumers, the government, *and* businesses, green means a new way to save natural resources, to protect the environment, and often to reduce our dependence on oil from foreign countries.

- *Entrepreneurship*—the activity that organizes land, labor, and capital. It is the willingness to take risks and the knowledge and ability to use the other factors of production efficiently. An **entrepreneur** is a person who risks his or her time, effort, and money to start and operate a business.

A nation's economic system significantly affects all the economic activities of its citizens and organizations. This far-reaching impact becomes more apparent when we consider that a country's economic system determines how the factors of production are used to meet the needs of society. Today, two different economic systems exist: capitalism and command economies. The way each system answers the four basic economic questions listed here determines a nation's economy.

1. *What* goods and services—and how much of each—will be produced?
2. *How* will these goods and services be produced?
3. *For whom* will these goods and services be produced?
4. *Who* owns and who controls the major factors of production?

Capitalism

Capitalism is an economic system in which individuals own and operate the majority of businesses that provide goods and services. Capitalism stems from the theories of the 18th-century Scottish economist Adam Smith. In his book *Wealth of Nations*, published in 1776, Smith argued that a society's interests are best served when the individuals within that society are allowed to pursue their own self-interest. According to Smith, when individuals act to improve their own fortunes, they indirectly promote the good of their community and the people in that community. Smith went on to call this concept the "invisible hand." The **invisible hand** is a term created by Adam Smith to describe how an individual's own personal gain benefits others and a nation's economy. For example, the only way a small-business owner who produces shoes can increase personal wealth is to sell shoes to customers. To become even more prosperous, the small-business owner must hire workers to produce even more shoes. According to the invisible hand, people in the small-business owner's community not only would have shoes but also would have jobs working for the shoemaker. Thus, the success of people in the community and, to some extent, the nation's economy is tied indirectly to the success of the small-business owner.

Adam Smith's capitalism is based on the following fundamental issues—also see Figure 1.4.

1. The creation of wealth is properly the concern of private individuals, not the government.
2. Private individuals must own private property and the resources used to create wealth.
3. Economic freedom ensures the existence of competitive markets that allow both sellers and buyers to enter and exit the market as they choose.
4. The role of government should be limited to providing defense against foreign enemies, ensuring internal order, and furnishing public works and education.

entrepreneur a person who risks time, effort, and money to start and operate a business

capitalism an economic system in which individuals own and operate the majority of businesses that provide goods and services

invisible hand a term created by Adam Smith to describe how an individual's personal gain benefits others and a nation's economy

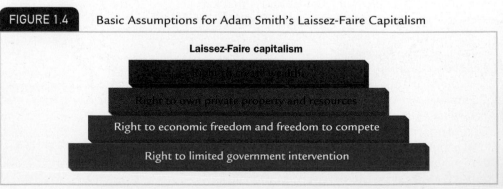

FIGURE 1.4   Basic Assumptions for Adam Smith's Laissez-Faire Capitalism

Laissez-Faire capitalism

Right to create wealth

Right to own private property and resources

Right to economic freedom and freedom to compete

Right to limited government intervention

© CENGAGE LEARNING 2014

One factor that Smith felt was extremely important was the role of government. He believed that government should act only as rule maker and umpire. The French term *laissez faire* describes Smith's capitalistic system and implies that there should be no government interference in the economy. Loosely translated, this term means "let them do" (as they see fit).

Adam Smith's laissez-faire capitalism is also based on the concept of a market economy. A **market economy** (sometimes referred to as a *free-market economy*) is an economic system in which businesses and individuals decide what to produce and buy, and the market determines prices and quantities sold. The owners of resources should be free to determine how these resources are used and also to enjoy the income, profits, and other benefits derived from ownership of these resources.

Capitalism in the United States

Our economic system is rooted in the laissez-faire capitalism of Adam Smith. However, our real-world economy is not as laissez-faire as Smith would have liked because government participates as more than umpire and rule maker. Our economy is, in fact, a **mixed economy**, one that exhibits elements of both capitalism and socialism.

In a mixed economy, the four basic economic questions discussed at the beginning of this section (*what, how, for whom,* and *who*) are answered through the interaction of households, businesses, and governments. The interactions among these three groups are shown in Figure 1.5.

© KATHERINE WELLES/SHUTTERSTOCK

An apple a day . . . Regarded as one of the most successful and profitable businesses in the very competitive technology industry, Apple has a history of introducing state-of-the-art consumer products like the iPhone and iPad. Although there are many ways to obtain Apple products, one way to "try out" the latest products is to visit one of their retail stores.

| FIGURE 1.5 | The Circular Flow in Our Mixed Economy |

Our economic system is guided by the interaction of buyers and sellers, with the role of government being taken into account.

Resource markets

Natural resources Labor Capital — Income

Natural resources Labor Capital — Wages Rent Interest

Govt. spending — Resources

Households — Taxes — Governments — Taxes — Businesses

Service — Service

Govt. spending — Products

Consumer spending — Goods Services

Sales revenue — Goods Services

Product markets

© CENGAGE LEARNING 2014

market economy an economic system in which businesses and individuals decide what to produce and buy, and the market determines quantities sold and prices

mixed economy an economy that exhibits elements of both capitalism and socialism

Households Households, made up of individuals, are the consumers of goods and services as well as owners of some of the factors of production. As *resource owners,* the members of households provide businesses with labor, capital, and other resources. In return, businesses pay wages, rent, and dividends and interest, which households receive as income.

As *consumers,* household members use their income to purchase the goods and services produced by business. Today, approximately 70 percent of our nation's total production consists of **consumer products**—goods and services purchased by individuals for personal consumption.[8] This means that consumers, as a group, are the biggest customers of American business.

Businesses Like households, businesses are engaged in two different exchanges. They exchange money for natural resources, labor, and capital and use these resources to produce goods and services. Then they exchange their goods and services for sales revenue. This sales revenue, in turn, is exchanged for additional resources, which are used to produce and sell more goods and services.

Along the way, of course, business owners would like to remove something from the circular flow in the form of profits. When business profits are distributed to business owners, these profits become household income. (Business owners are, after all, members of households.) Households try to retain some income as savings. But are profits and savings really removed from the flow? Usually not! When the economy is running smoothly, households are willing to invest their savings in businesses. They can do so directly by buying stocks issued by businesses, by purchasing shares in mutual funds that purchase stocks in businesses, or by lending money to businesses. They can also invest indirectly by placing their savings in bank accounts. Banks and other financial institutions then invest these savings as part of their normal business operations. Thus, business profits, too, are retained in the business system, and the circular flow in Figure 1.5 is complete. How, then, does government fit in?

Governments The Preamble to the Constitution sets forth the responsibility of the government to protect and promote public welfare. The numerous government services are important but they (1) would either not be produced by private business firms or (2) would be produced only for those who could afford them. Typical services include national defense, police, fire protection, education, and construction of roads and highways. To pay for all these services, governments collect a variety of taxes from households (such as personal income taxes and sales taxes) and from businesses (corporate income taxes).

Figure 1.5 shows this exchange of taxes for government services. It also shows government spending of tax dollars for resources and products required to provide these services.

Actually, with government included, our circular flow looks more like a combination of several flows. In reality, it is. The important point is that together the various flows make up a single unit—a complete economic system that effectively provides answers to the basic economic questions. Simply put, the system works.

Command Economies

Before we discuss how to measure a nation's economic performance, we look quickly at another economic system called a command economy. A **command economy** is an economic system in which the government decides *what* goods and services will be produced, *how* they will be produced, *for whom* available goods and services will be produced, and *who* owns and controls the major factors of production. The answers to all four basic economic questions are determined, at least to some degree, through centralized government planning. Today, two types of economic systems—*socialism* and *communism*—serve as examples of command economies.

Socialism In a socialist economy, the key industries are owned and controlled by the government. Such industries usually include transportation, utilities, communications, banking, and industries producing important materials such as steel. Land, buildings, and raw materials may also be the property of the state in a socialist economy. Depending on the country, private ownership of smaller businesses is permitted to varying degrees. Usually, people may choose their own occupations, although many work in state-owned industries.

What to produce and how to produce it are determined in accordance with national goals, which are based on projected needs and the availability of resources. The distribution of goods and services—who gets what—is also controlled by the state to the extent that it controls taxes, rents, and wages. Among the professed aims of socialist countries are the equitable distribution of income, the elimination of poverty, and the distribution of social services (such as medical care) to all who need them. The disadvantages of socialism include increased taxation and loss of incentive and motivation for both individuals and business owners.

Today, many of the nations that have been labeled as socialist nations traditionally, including France, Sweden, and India, are transitioning to a free-market economy. Currently, many countries that were once thought of as communist countries are now often referred to as socialist countries. Examples of former communist countries often referred to as socialists (or even capitalists) include most of the nations that were formerly part of the Union of Soviet Socialist Republics, China, and Vietnam.

Communism If Adam Smith was the father of capitalism, Karl Marx was the father of communism. In his writings during the mid-19th century, Marx advocated a classless society whose citizens together owned all economic resources. All workers would then contribute to this *communist* society according to their ability and would receive benefits according to their need.

Since the breakup of the Soviet Union and economic reforms in China and most of the Eastern European countries, the best remaining examples of communism are North Korea and Cuba. Today these so-called communist economies seem to practice a strictly controlled kind of socialism. The basic four economic questions are answered through centralized government plans. Emphasis is placed on the production of goods the government needs rather than on the products that consumers might want, so there are frequent shortages of consumer goods. Workers have little choice of jobs, but special skills or talents seem to be rewarded with special privileges.

MEASURING ECONOMIC PERFORMANCE

 Identify the ways to measure economic performance.

Today, it is hard to turn on the radio, watch the news on television, use the Internet, or read the newspaper without hearing or seeing something about the economy. Consider for just a moment the following questions:

- Is the gross domestic product for the United States increasing or decreasing?
- Why is the unemployment rate important?
- Are U.S. workers as productive as workers in other countries?

The information needed to answer these questions, along with the answers to other similar questions, is easily obtainable from many sources. More important, the answers to these and other questions can be used to gauge the economic health of the nation. For individuals, the health of the nation's economy can affect:

- the financing you need to continue your education;
- your ability to get a job; and
- the amount of interest you pay for credit card purchases, automobiles, homes, and other credit transactions.

One way to reduce costs is to manufacture products in a foreign country. In this photo, a Chinese worker assembles an electronic keyboard. To compete with foreign competition, manufacturers in the United States use sophisticated equipment and the latest technology to reduce costs, increase profits, *and* improve productivity.

© HE YUAN/EPA/LANDOV

The Importance of Productivity in the Global Marketplace

One way to measure a nation's economic performance is to assess its productivity. **Productivity** is the average level of output per worker per hour. An increase in productivity results in economic growth because a larger number of goods and services are produced by a given labor force. To see how productivity affects you and the economy, consider the following three questions:

Question: *How does productivity growth affect the economy?*

Answer: Because of increased productivity, it now takes fewer workers to produce more goods and services. As a result, employers have reduced costs, earned more profits, and sold their products for less. Finally, productivity growth helps American business to compete more effectively with other nations in a competitive world.

Question: *How does a nation improve productivity?*

Answer: Reducing costs and enabling employees to work more efficiently are at the core of all attempts to improve productivity. For example, productivity in the United States is expected to improve dramatically as more economic activity is transferred onto the Internet, reducing costs for customer service and handling routine ordering functions between businesses. Other methods that can be used to increase productivity are discussed in detail in Chapter 8, Producing Quality Goods and Services.

Question: *Is productivity growth always good?*

Answer: Fewer workers producing more goods and services can lead to higher unemployment rates. In this case, increased productivity is good for employers but not good for unemployed workers seeking jobs in a very competitive work environment. Because employers had been able to produce more goods and services with fewer employees during the recent economic crisis, they did not want to increase the firm's salary expense by hiring new employees after the economy began to improve.

The Nation's Gross Domestic Product

In addition to productivity, a measure called *gross domestic product* can be used to measure the economic well-being of a nation. **Gross domestic product (GDP)** is the total dollar value of all goods and services produced by all people within the boundaries of a country during a one-year period. For example, the values of automobiles produced by employees in an American-owned General Motors plant and a Japanese-owned Toyota plant in the United States are both included in the GDP for the United States. The U.S. GDP was $15.1 trillion in 2011.[9] (*Note:* At the time of publication, 2011 was the last year for which complete statistics were available.)

The GDP figure facilitates comparisons between the United States and other countries because it is the standard used in international guidelines for economic accounting. It is also possible to compare the GDP for one nation over several different time periods. This comparison allows observers to determine the extent to which a nation is experiencing economic growth. For example, government experts project that GDP will grow to $21.8 trillion by the year 2018.[10]

To make accurate comparisons of the GDP for different years, we must adjust the dollar amounts for inflation. **Inflation** is a general rise in the level of prices. (The opposite of inflation is deflation.) **Deflation** is a general decrease in the level of prices. By using inflation-adjusted figures, we are able to measure the *real* GDP for a nation. In effect, it is now possible to compare the products and services produced by a nation in constant dollars—dollars that will purchase the same amount of goods and services. Figure 1.6 depicts the GDP of the United States in current dollars and the real GDP in

productivity the average level of output per worker per hour

gross domestic product (GDP) the total dollar value of all goods and services produced by all people within the boundaries of a country during a one-year period

inflation a general rise in the level of prices

deflation a general decrease in the level of prices

FIGURE 1.6   GDP in Current Dollars and in Inflation-Adjusted Dollars

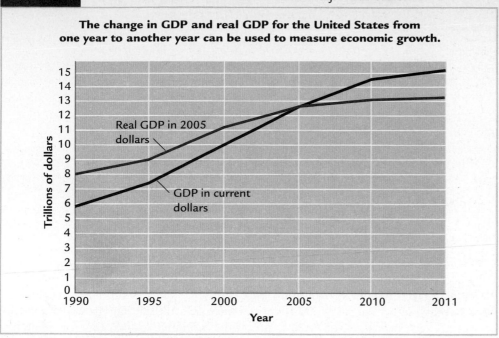

The change in GDP and real GDP for the United States from one year to another year can be used to measure economic growth.

Source: U.S. Bureau of Economic Analysis Web site at www.bea.gov (accessed January 30, 2012).

inflation-adjusted dollars. Note that between 1990 and 2011, America's real GDP grew from $8 trillion to $13.3 trillion.[11]

Important Economic Indicators that Measure a Nation's Economy

In addition to productivity, GDP, and real GDP, other economic measures exist that can be used to evaluate a nation's economy. Because of the recent economic crisis, one very important statistic that is in the news on a regular basis is the unemployment rate. The **unemployment rate** is the percentage of a nation's labor force unemployed at any time. According to the Bureau of Labor Statistics, when workers are unemployed, they, their families, and the country as a whole lose. Workers and their families lose wages, and the country loses the goods or services that could have been produced. In addition, the purchasing power of these workers is lost, which can lead to unemployment for yet other workers.[12] Although the unemployment rate for the United States is typically about 4 to 6 percent, it peaked during the recent economic crisis. Despite both federal and state programs to reduce the unemployment rate for the United States, it is still hovering around 8 percent at the time of publication. This is an especially important statistic—especially if you are unemployed.

The **consumer price index (CPI)** is a monthly index that measures the changes in prices of a fixed basket of goods purchased by a typical consumer in an urban area. Goods listed in the CPI include food and beverages, transportation, housing, clothing, medical care, recreation, education, communication, and other goods and services. Economists often use the CPI to determine the effect of inflation on not only the nation's economy but also individual consumers. Another monthly index is the producer price index. The **producer price index (PPI)** measures prices that producers receive for their finished goods. Because changes in the PPI reflect price increases or decreases at the wholesale level, the PPI is an accurate predictor of both changes in the CPI and prices that consumers will pay for many everyday necessities.

Some additional economic measures are described in Table 1.2. Like the measures for GDP, real GDP, unemployment rate, and price indexes, these measures can be used to compare one economic statistic over different periods of time.

unemployment rate the percentage of a nation's labor force unemployed at any time

consumer price index (CPI) a monthly index that measures the changes in prices of a fixed basket of goods purchased by a typical consumer in an urban area

producer price index (PPI) an index that measures prices that producers receive for their finished goods

TABLE 1.2   Common Measures Used to Evaluate a Nation's Economic Health

Economic Measure	Description
1. Balance of trade	The total value of a nation's exports minus the total value of its imports over a specific period of time.
2. Consumer confidence index	A measure of how optimistic or pessimistic consumers are about the nation's economy. This measure is usually reported on a monthly basis.
3. Corporate profits	The total amount of profits made by corporations over selected time periods.
4. Inflation rate	An economic statistic that tracks the increase in prices of goods and services over a period of time. This measure is usually calculated on a monthly or an annual basis.
5. National income ·	The total income earned by various segments of the population, including employees, self-employed individuals, corporations, and other types of income.
6. New housing starts	The total number of new homes started during a specific time period.
7. Prime interest rate	The lowest interest rate that banks charge their most credit-worthy customers.

© CENGAGE LEARNING 2014

 Examine the different phases in the typical business cycle.

THE BUSINESS CYCLE

All industrialized nations of the world seek economic growth, full employment, and price stability. However, a nation's economy fluctuates rather than grows at a steady pace every year. In fact, if you were to graph the economic growth rate for a country like the United States, it would resemble a roller coaster ride with peaks (high points) and troughs (low points). These fluctuations are generally referred to as the **business cycle,** that is, the recurrence of periods of growth and recession in a nation's economic activity. At the time of publication, many experts believed that the U.S. economy was showing signs of improvement. However, the recent economic crisis that began in fall 2007 caused a recession that will require more time before the nation experiences a complete recovery. The nation's unemployment rate is still high. People are reluctant to spend money on many consumer goods. Stock prices, although improving, are still below the record values experienced a few years ago. Although the federal government has enacted a number of stimulus plans designed to help unemployed workers, to shore up the nation's banks and Wall Street firms, to reduce the number of home foreclosures, and to free up credit for both individuals and businesses, many experts still believe that we have serious financial problems. For one, the size of the national debt—a topic described later in this section—is a concern. Another problem—the inequality of income and wealth—has also become evident as a result of the Occupy Wall Street protestors and similar groups of discontented people. To make matters worse, the recent economic crisis did not affect just the U.S. economy but also the economies of countries around the world.

The changes that result from either economic growth or economic downturn affect the amount of products and services that consumers are willing to purchase and, as a result, the amount of products and services produced by business firms. Generally, the business cycle consists of four phases: the peak (sometimes called prosperity), recession, the trough, and recovery (sometimes called expansion).

During the *peak period* (prosperity), the economy is at its highest point and unemployment is low. Total income is relatively high. As long as the economic outlook remains prosperous, consumers are willing to buy products and services. In fact, businesses often expand and offer new products and services during the peak period to take advantage of consumers' increased buying power.

Generally, economists define a **recession** as two or more consecutive three-month periods of decline in a country's GDP. Because unemployment rises during a recession, total buying power declines. The pessimism that accompanies a recession often stifles both consumer

business cycle the recurrence of periods of growth and recession in a nation's economic activity

recession two or more consecutive three-month periods of decline in a country's GDP

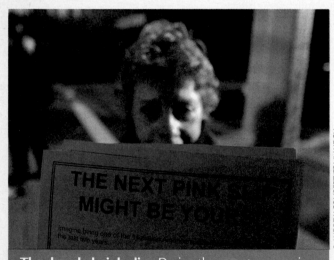

© ANDREW COMBERT/EPA/LANDOV

The dreaded pink slip. During the recent economic crisis, unemployment rates were over 10 percent and millions of Americans got a "pink slip" and lost their jobs. While economists still debate if we were in a recession or a depression, the economy is now improving and the unemployment rate is beginning to decline.

and business spending. As buying power decreases, consumers tend to become more value conscious and reluctant to purchase frivolous or nonessential items. And companies and government at all levels often postpone or go slow on major projects during a recession. In response to a recession, many businesses focus on producing the products and services that provide the most value to their customers. And yet, there are still opportunities out there for business firms that are well managed and provide goods and services that their customers need. For example, Caterpillar, a global company that produces earth moving and construction equipment has profited from the ongoing building boom in developing nations, where many basic infrastructure improvements move ahead regardless of what the economic conditions are in the rest of the world.

Economists define a **depression** as a severe recession that lasts longer than a typical recession and has a larger decline in business activity when compared to a recession. A depression is characterized by extremely high unemployment rates, low wages, reduced purchasing power, lack of confidence in the economy, lower stock values, and a general decrease in business activity.

The third phase of the business cycle is the *trough*. The trough of a recession or depression is the turning point when a nation's production and employment bottom out and reach their lowest levels. To offset the effects of recession and depression, the federal government uses both monetary and fiscal policies. **Monetary policies** are the Federal Reserve's decisions that determine the size of the supply of money in the nation and the level of interest rates. Through **fiscal policy**, the government can influence the amount of savings and expenditures by altering the tax structure and changing the levels of government spending.

Although the federal government collects approximately $2 trillion in annual revenues, the government usually spends more than it receives, resulting in a **federal deficit**. For example, the government had a federal deficit for each year between 2002 and 2011. The total of all federal deficits is called the **national debt**. Today, the U.S. national debt is $15.2 trillion or approximately $49,000 for every man, woman, and child in the United States.[13]

Since World War II, business cycles have lasted from three to five years from one peak period to the next peak period. During the same time period, the average length of recessions has been 11 months.[14] Some experts believe that effective use of monetary and fiscal policies can speed up recovery and reduce the amount of time the economy is in recession. *Recovery* (or *expansion*) is the movement of the economy from recession or depression to prosperity. High unemployment rates decline, income increases, and both the ability and the willingness to buy rise.

At the time of publication, many business leaders and politicians were debating whether the U.S. economy is still in recession, in the trough, or beginning recovery. Unfortunately, many of the problems that caused the recent economic crisis are still there, and they will take years to correct and resolve.

TYPES OF COMPETITION

Our capitalist system ensures that individuals and businesses make the decisions about what to produce, how to produce it, and what price to charge for the product. Mattel, Inc., for example, can introduce new versions of its famous Barbie doll, license the Barbie name, change the doll's price and method of distribution, and attempt to produce and market Barbie in other countries or over the Internet at www.mattel.com. Our system also allows customers the right to choose between Mattel's products and those produced by competitors.

As a consumer, you get to choose which products or services you want to buy. Competition like that between Mattel and other toy manufacturers is a necessary and extremely important by-product of capitalism. Business **competition** is essentially a rivalry among businesses for sales to potential customers. In a capitalistic economy, competition also ensures that a firm will survive only if it serves its customers well by providing products and services that meet needs. Economists recognize four different degrees of competition ranging from ideal, complete competition to no competition at all. These are perfect competition, monopolistic competition, oligopoly, and

depression a severe recession that lasts longer than a typical recession and has a larger decline in business activity when compared to a recession

monetary policies Federal Reserve decisions that determine the size of the supply of money in the nation and the level of interest rates

 Outline the four types of competition.

fiscal policy government influence on the amount of savings and expenditures; accomplished by altering the tax structure and by changing the levels of government spending

federal deficit a shortfall created when the federal government spends more in a fiscal year than it receives

national debt the total of all federal deficits

competition rivalry among businesses for sales to potential customers

Competition often gives consumers a choice. Often wonder why there are so many soap products? It's called competition. Different manufacturers use product differentiation to develop and promote the differences between their products and all similar products. Not only does product differentiation help their products stand out from the competition, it gives you—the consumer—a choice.

monopoly. For a quick overview of the different types of competition, including numbers of firms and examples for each type, look at Table 1.3.

Perfect Competition

Perfect (or pure) competition is the market situation in which there are many buyers and sellers of a product, and no single buyer or seller is powerful enough to affect the price of that product. For perfect competition to exist, there are five very important concepts.

- We are discussing the market for a single product, such as bushels of wheat.
- There are no restrictions on firms entering the industry.
- All sellers offer essentially the same product for sale.
- All buyers and sellers know everything there is to know about the market (including, in our example, the prices that all sellers are asking for their wheat).
- The overall market is not affected by the actions of any one buyer or seller.

When perfect competition exists, every seller should ask the same price that every other seller is asking. Why? Because if one seller wanted 50 cents more per bushel of wheat than all the others, that seller would not be able to sell a single bushel. Buyers could—and would—do better by purchasing wheat from the competition. On the other hand, a firm willing to sell below the going price would sell all its wheat quickly. However, that seller would lose sales revenue (and profit) because buyers are actually willing to pay more.

In perfect competition, then, sellers—and buyers as well—must accept the going price. The price of each product is determined by the actions of all buyers and all sellers together through the forces of supply and demand.

The Basics of Supply and Demand The **supply** of a particular product is the quantity of the product that producers are willing to sell at each of various prices. Producers are rational people, so we would expect them to offer more of a product for sale at higher prices and to offer less of the product at lower prices, as illustrated by the supply curve in Figure 1.7.

The **demand** for a particular product is the quantity that buyers are willing to purchase at each of various prices. Buyers, too, are usually rational, so we would expect them—as a group—to buy more of a product when its price is low and to buy less of the product when its price is high, as depicted by the demand curve in Figure 1.7.

The Equilibrium, or Market, Price There is always one certain price at which the demand for a product is exactly equal to the quantity of that product produced. Suppose that producers are willing to *supply* two million bushels of wheat at a price of $7 per bushel and that buyers are willing to *purchase* two million bushels at a price of $7 per bushel.

perfect (or pure) competition the market situation in which there are many buyers and sellers of a product, and no single buyer or seller is powerful enough to affect the price of that product

supply the quantity of a product that producers are willing to sell at each of various prices

demand the quantity of a product that buyers are willing to purchase at each of various prices

TABLE 1.3	Four Different Types of Competition	
The number of firms determines the degree of competition within an industry.		
Type of Competition	Number of Business Firms or Suppliers	Real-World Examples
1. Perfect	Many	Corn, wheat, peanuts
2. Monopolistic	Many	Clothing, shoes
3. Oligopoly	Few	Automobiles, cereals
4. Monopoly	One	Software protected by copyright, many local public utilities

© CENGAGE LEARNING 2014

In other words, supply and demand are in balance, or in equilibrium, at the price of $7. Economists call this price the *market price*. The **market price** of any product is the price at which the quantity demanded is exactly equal to the quantity supplied.

In theory and in the real world, market prices are affected by anything that affects supply and demand. The *demand* for wheat, for example, might change if researchers suddenly discovered that it offered a previously unknown health benefit. Then buyers would demand more wheat at every price. Or the *supply* of wheat might change if new technology permitted the production of greater quantities of wheat from the same amount of acreage. Other changes that can affect competitive prices are shifts in buyer tastes, the development of new products, fluctuations in income owing to inflation or recession, or even changes in the weather that affect the production of wheat.

Perfect competition is quite rare in today's world. Many real markets, however, are examples of monopolistic competition.

Monopolistic Competition

Monopolistic competition is a market situation in which there are many buyers along with a relatively large number of sellers. The various products available in a monopolistically competitive market are very similar in nature, and they are all intended to satisfy the same need. However, each seller attempts to make its product different from the others by providing unique product features, an attention-getting brand name, unique packaging, or services such as free delivery or a lifetime warranty.

Product differentiation is the process of developing and promoting differences between one's products and all competitive products. It is a fact of life for the producers of many consumer goods, from soaps to clothing to furniture to shoes. A furniture manufacturer such as Thomasville sees what looks like a mob of competitors, all trying to chip away at its share of the market. By differentiating each of its products from all

Personal APPS

Why do consumers choose one product instead of another? The next time you go to the discount store, supermarket, or drug store, notice all the products competing for your dollars. No two canned vegetables, shampoos, or candies are exactly alike. Thanks to product differentiation, you have a lot of choices when you shop.

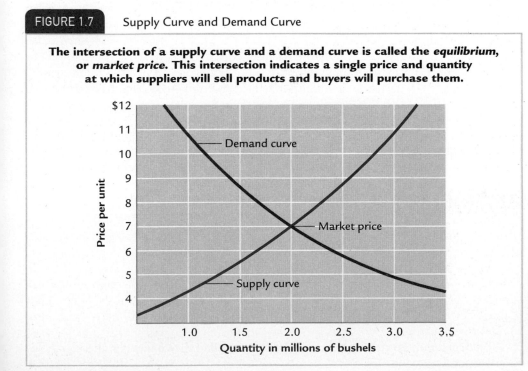

FIGURE 1.7   Supply Curve and Demand Curve

The intersection of a supply curve and a demand curve is called the *equilibrium*, or *market price*. This intersection indicates a single price and quantity at which suppliers will sell products and buyers will purchase them.

market price the price at which the quantity demanded is exactly equal to the quantity supplied

monopolistic competition a market situation in which there are many buyers along with a relatively large number of sellers who differentiate their products from the products of competitors

product differentiation the process of developing and promoting differences between one's products and all competitive products similar products produced by competitors, Thomasville obtains some limited control over the market price of its product.

Oligopoly

An **oligopoly** is a market (or industry) situation in which there are few sellers. Generally, these sellers are quite large, and sizable investments are required to enter into their market. Examples of oligopolies are the automobile, airline, car rental, cereal, and farm implement industries.

Because there are few sellers in an oligopoly, the market actions of each seller can have a strong effect on competitors' sales and prices. If General Motors, for example, reduces its automobile prices, Ford, Honda, Toyota, and Nissan usually do the same to retain their market shares. In the absence of much price competition, product differentiation becomes the major competitive weapon; this is very evident in the advertising of the major automobile manufacturers. For instance, when Toyota was faced with declining sales as a result of quality and safety issues, it began offering buyer incentives to attract new-car buyers. Quickly, both Ford and General Motors began offering similar incentives and for the same reason—to attract new-car buyers.

Monopoly

A **monopoly** is a market (or industry) with only one seller, and there are barriers to keep other firms from entering the industry. In a monopoly, there is no close substitute for the product or service. Because only one firm is the supplier of a product, it would seem that it has complete control over price. However, no firm can set its price at some astronomical figure just because there is no competition; the firm would soon find that it has no customers or sales revenue either. Instead, the firm in a monopoly position must consider the demand for its product and set the price at the most profitable level.

Classic examples of monopolies in the United States are public utilities, including companies that provide local gas, water, or electricity. Each utility firm operates in a **natural monopoly,** an industry that requires a huge investment in capital and within which any duplication of facilities would be wasteful. Natural monopolies are permitted to exist because the public interest is best served by their existence, but they operate under the scrutiny and control of various state and federal agencies. Although many public utilities are still classified as natural monopolies, there is increased competition in many areas of the country. For example, there have been increased demands for consumer choice when selecting a company that provides electrical service to both homes and businesses.

A legal monopoly—sometimes referred to as a *limited monopoly*—is created when a government entity issues a franchise, license, copyright, patent, or trademark. For example, a copyright exists for a specific period of time and can be used to protect the owners of written materials from unauthorized use by competitors that have not shared in the time, effort, and expense required for their development. Because Microsoft owns the copyright on its popular Windows software, it enjoys a legal-monopoly position. Except for natural monopolies and legal monopolies, federal antitrust laws prohibit both monopolies and attempts to form monopolies.

AMERICAN BUSINESS TODAY

Although our economic system is far from perfect, it provides Americans with a high standard of living compared with people in other countries throughout the world. **Standard of living** is a loose, subjective measure of how well off an individual or a society is, mainly in terms of want satisfaction through goods and services. Also, our economic system offers solutions to many of the problems that plague society and provides opportunities for people who are willing to work and to continue learning.

To understand the current business environment and the challenges ahead, it helps to understand how business developed.

oligopoly a market (or industry) in which there are few sellers

monopoly a market (or industry) with only one seller, and there are barriers to keep other firms from entering the industry

natural monopoly an industry requiring huge investments in capital and within which any duplication of facilities would be wasteful and thus not in the public interest

Summarize the factors that affect the business environment and the challenges that American businesses will encounter in the future.

standard of living a loose, subjective measure of how well off an individual or a society is, mainly in terms of want satisfaction through goods and services

Early Business Development

Our American business system has its roots in the knowledge, skills, and values that the earliest settlers brought to this country. The first settlers in the United States were concerned mainly with providing themselves with basic necessities—food, clothing, and shelter. Almost all families lived on farms, and the entire family worked at the business of surviving. They used their surplus for trading, mainly by barter, among themselves and with the English trading ships that called at the colonies. **Barter** is a system of exchange in which goods or services are traded directly for other goods or services without using money. As this trade increased, small businesses began to appear. Some settlers were able to use their skills and their excess time to work under the domestic system of production. The **domestic system** was a method of manufacturing in which an entrepreneur distributed raw materials to various homes, where families would process them into finished goods. The merchant entrepreneur then offered the goods for sale.

Then, in 1793, a young English apprentice mechanic named Samuel Slater set up a textile factory in Pawtucket, Rhode Island, to spin raw cotton into thread. Slater's ingenuity resulted in America's first use of the **factory system** of manufacturing, in which all the materials, machinery, and workers required to manufacture a product are assembled in one place. The Industrial Revolution in America was born. A manufacturing technique called *specialization* was used to improve productivity. **Specialization** is the separation of a manufacturing process into distinct tasks and the assignment of the different tasks to different individuals.

The years from 1820 to 1900 were the golden age of invention and innovation in machinery. At the same time, new means of transportation greatly expanded the domestic markets for American products. Certainly, many basic characteristics of our modern business system took form during this time period.

© AP PHOTO

Gas shortages—could it happen again? For an industrialized economy like the United States, crude oil is an essential natural resource. When the nation experienced a shortage of crude oil during the mid-1970s, it was common to see signs like the one in this photo. Even now, both the supply and price for a gallon of gasoline are still concerns as the nation begins to rebound from the recent economic crisis.

Business Development in the 1900s

Industrial growth and prosperity continued well into the 20th century. Henry Ford's moving automotive assembly line, which brought the work to the worker, refined the concept of specialization and helped spur on the mass production of consumer goods. Fundamental changes occurred in business ownership and management as well. No longer were the largest businesses owned by one individual; instead, ownership was in the hands of thousands of corporate shareholders who were willing to invest in—but not to operate—a business.

The Roaring Twenties ended with the sudden crash of the stock market in 1929 and the near collapse of the economy. The Great Depression that followed in the 1930s was a time of misery and human suffering. People lost their faith in business and its ability to satisfy the needs of society without government involvement. After Franklin D. Roosevelt became president in 1933, the federal government devised a number of programs to get the economy moving again. In implementing these programs, the government got deeply involved in business for the first time.

To understand the major events that shaped the United States during the remainder of the 20th century, it helps to remember that the economy was compared to a roller coaster ride earlier in this chapter—periods of economic growth followed by periods of economic slowdown. The following are major events that shaped the nation's economy during the period from 1940 to 2000:

- World War II, the Korean War, and the Vietnam War
- Rapid economic growth and higher standard of living during the 1950s and 1960s
- The social responsibility movement during the 1960s
- A shortage of crude oil and higher prices for most goods in the mid-1970s
- High inflation, high interest rates, and reduced business profits during the early 1980s
- Sustained economic growth in the 1990s

During the last part of the 20th century, the Internet became a major force in the economy. e-Business—a topic we will continue to explore throughout this text—became

barter a system of exchange in which goods or services are traded directly for other goods or services without using money

domestic system a method of manufacturing in which an entrepreneur distributes raw materials to various homes, where families process them into finished goods to be offered for sale by the merchant entrepreneur

factory system a system of manufacturing in which all the materials, machinery, and workers required to manufacture a product are assembled in one place

specialization the separation of a manufacturing process into distinct tasks and the assignment of the different tasks to different individuals an accepted method of conducting business. **e-Business** is the organized effort of individuals to produce and sell *through the Internet,* for a profit, the products and services that satisfy society's needs.

Unfortunately, by the last part of the 20th century, a larger number of business failures and declining stock values were initial signs that larger economic problems were on the way.

A New Century: 2000 and Beyond

According to many economic experts, the first part of the 21st century might be characterized as the best of times and the worst of times rolled into one package. On the plus side, technology became available at an affordable price. Both individuals and businesses could now access information with the click of a button. They also could buy and sell merchandise online.

In addition to information technology, the growth of service businesses also changed the way American firms do business in the 21st century. Because service businesses employ approximately 85 percent of the nation's workforce, we now have a service economy.[15] A **service economy** is an economy in which more effort is devoted to the production of services than to the production of goods. Typical service businesses include restaurants, laundries and dry cleaners, real estate, movie theaters, repair companies, and other services that we often take for granted. More information about how service businesses affect the economy is provided in Chapter 8, Producing Quality Goods and Services.

On the negative side, it is hard to watch television, surf the Web, listen to the radio, or read the newspaper without hearing some news about the economy. Because many of the economic indicators described in Table 1.2 on page 20 indicate troubling economic problems, there is still a certain amount of pessimism surrounding the economy.

The Current Business Environment

Before reading on, answer the following question:

In today's competitive business world, which of the following environments affects business?

a. The competitive environment
b. The global environment
c. The technological environment
d. The economic environment
e. All of the above

Correct Answer: e. All the environments listed affect business today.

The Competitive Environment Businesses operate in a competitive environment. As noted earlier in this chapter, competition is a basic component of capitalism. Every day, business owners must figure out what makes their businesses successful and how the goods and services they provide are different from the competition. Often, the answer is contained in the basic definition of business provided on page 10. Just for a moment, review the definition:

Business is the organized effort of individuals to produce and sell, for a profit, the goods and services that satisfy society's needs.

In the definition of business, note the phrase *satisfy society's needs*. These three words say a lot about how well a successful firm competes with competitors. If you meet customer needs, then you have a better chance at success.

The Global Environment Related to the competitive environment is the global environment. Not only do American businesses have to compete with other American businesses, but they also must compete with businesses from all over the globe. According to global experts, China is one of the fastest-growing economies in the world. And China is not alone. Other countries around the world also compete with U.S. firms. There was once

e-business the organized effort of individuals to produce and sell *through the Internet,* for a profit, the products and services that satisfy society's needs

service economy an economy in which more effort is devoted to the production of services than to the production of goods a time when the label "Made in the United States" gave U.S. businesses an inside edge both at home and in the global marketplace. Now, other countries manufacture and sell goods. According to Richard Haass, president of the Council on Foreign Relations, "There will be winners and losers from globalization. We win every time we go shopping because prices are lower. Choice is greater because of globalization. But there are losers. There are people who will lose their jobs either to foreign competition or [to] technological innovation."[16]

While many foreign firms are attempting to sell goods and services to U.S. customers, U.S. firms are also increasing both sales and profits by selling goods and services to customers in other countries. In fact there are many "potential" customers in developing nations that will buy goods and services manufactured by U.S. firms. For example, Procter & Gamble sells laundry detergent, soap, and diapers in Nigeria and has plans to do business in more than 50 African countries.[17] And Procter & Gamble is not alone. Unilever, DuPont, Johnson & Johnson, General Motors, and many more U.S. companies are also selling goods and services to customers in countries all over the globe. The world is, in fact, a much smaller place than many U.S. business leaders once thought.

The Technology Environment Although increased global competition and technological innovation has changed the way we do business, the technology environment for U.S. businesses has never been more challenging. Changes in manufacturing equipment, distribution of products, and communication with customers are all examples of how technology has changed everyday business practices. For example, many businesses are now using social media to provide customers with information about products and services. If you ask different people, you will often find different definitions for social media, but for our purposes **social media** is defined as online interaction that allows people and businesses to communicate and share ideas, personal information, and information about products or services. To illustrate how popular social media is, consider that Facebook with 800 million current users was launched in 2004 and Twitter with 300 million current users was launched in 2006. Because of rapid developments in social media and the increased importance of technology and information, businesses will need to spend additional money to keep abreast of an ever-changing technology environment and even more money to train employees to use the new technology.

The Economic Environment The economic environment must always be considered when making business decisions. This fact is especially important when the nation's economy takes a nosedive or an individual firm's sales revenue and profits are declining. For example, both small and large business firms reduced both spending and hiring new employees over the last four years because of the recent economic crisis.

In addition to economic pressures, today's socially responsible managers and business owners must be concerned about the concept of sustainability. According to the U.S. Environmental Protection Agency, **sustainability** means meeting the needs of the present without compromising the ability of future generations to meet their own needs.[18] Although the word *green* used to mean a color in a box of crayons, today green means a new way of doing business. As a result, a combination of forces, including economic factors, growth in population, increased energy use, and concerns for the environment, is changing the way individuals live and businesses operate.

When you look back at the original question we asked at the beginning of this section, clearly, each different type of environment—competitive, global, technological, and economic—affects the way a business does *business*. As a result, there are always opportunities for improvement and challenges that must be considered.

The Challenges Ahead

There it is—the American business system in brief.

When it works well, it provides jobs for those who are willing to work, a standard of living that few countries can match, and many opportunities for personal advancement. However, like every other system devised by humans, it is not perfect. Our business system may give us prosperity, but it also gave us the Great Depression of the

social media the online interaction that allows people and businesses to communicate and share ideas, personal information, and information about products or services

sustainability meeting the needs of the present without compromising the ability of future generations to meet their own needs

1930s, the economic problems of the 1970s and the early 1980s, and the economic crisis that began in the fall of 2007.

Obviously, the system can be improved. Certainly, there are plenty of people who are willing to tell us exactly what they think the American economy needs. However, these people often provide us only with conflicting opinions. Who is right and who is wrong? Even the experts cannot agree.

The experts do agree, however, that several key issues will challenge our economic system (and our nation) over the next decade. Some of the questions to be resolved include:

- How can we create a more stable economy and create new jobs for the unemployed?
- How can we regulate banks, savings and loan associations, credit unions, and other financial institutions to prevent the type of abuses that led to the recent economic crisis?
- How do we reduce the national debt and still maintain a healthy economy and stimulate business growth?
- How can we use technology to make American workers more productive and American firms more competitive in the global marketplace?
- How can we preserve the benefits of competition and small business in our American economic system?
- How can we encourage economic growth and at the same time continue to conserve natural resources and sustain our environment?
- How can we meet the needs of two-income families, single parents, older Americans, and the less fortunate who need health care and social programs to exist?
- How can we defeat terrorism and resolve conflict with Iran, North Korea, and other countries throughout the world?

The answers to these questions are anything but simple. In the past, Americans have always been able to solve their economic problems through ingenuity and creativity. Now, as we continue the journey through the 21st century, we need that same ingenuity and creativity not only to solve our current problems but also to compete in the global marketplace and build a nation and economy for future generations.

The American business system is not perfect by any means, but it does work reasonably well. We discuss some of its problems in Chapter 2 as we examine the topics of social responsibility and business ethics.

return to Inside BUSINESS

Zynga

Online games have become big business. In just a few years—and during a difficult economic period—founder Mark Pincus has transformed Zynga from a start-up game company into a profitable, 3,000-employee corporation with shares traded on the Nasdaq stock exchange. Social media games are about more than winning and losing: "We're giving a reliable 15 minutes a day that lets them not only play but also connect with people in their lives with some level of meaning," Pincus explains.

Competing against established rival firms such as Electronic Arts and Activision Blizzard, Zynga must continually introduce new games to retain player loyalty and keep revenues growing through the sale of virtual goods and advertising. Pincus and his management team keep a close eye on Zynga's business health by measuring how many people play each game, how many buy virtual goods, and which game features are the most popular. Can Zynga keep clicking ahead?

Questions

1. Of the four resources (material, human, informational, and financial) that businesses combine and organize to be successful, which have had the most significant effect on Zynga's growth—and why?

2. Of the four environments that affect business (competitive, global, technological, and economic), which do you think will help and hurt Zynga's long-term profitability?

Discuss what you must do to be successful in the world of business.

For many years, people in business—both employees and managers—assumed that prosperity would continue. When faced with both economic problems and increased competition, a large number of these people began to ask the question: What do we do now? Although this is a fair question, it is difficult to answer. Certainly, for a college student taking business courses or an employee just starting a career, the question is even more difficult to answer. And yet there are still opportunities out there for people who are willing to work hard, continue to learn, and possess the ability to adapt to change. The kind of career you choose ultimately will depend on your own values and what you feel is most important in life. By studying business, you can become a better employee or manager or you may decide to start your own business. You can also become a better consumer and investor.

 Define *business* and identify potential risks and rewards.

Business is the organized effort of individuals to produce and sell, for a profit, the goods and services that satisfy society's needs. Four kinds of resources—material, human, financial, and informational—must be combined to start and operate a business. The three general types of businesses are service businesses, manufacturers, and marketing intermediaries. Profit is what remains after all business expenses are deducted from sales revenue. It is the payment that owners receive for assuming the risks of business—primarily the risks of not receiving payment and of losing whatever has been invested in the firm. Although many people believe that profit is literally the bottom line or most important goal for a business, many corporations are careful to point out their efforts to sustain the planet, participate in the green ecological movement, and help people to live better lives.

 Define *economics* and describe the two types of economic systems: capitalism and command economy.

Economics is the study of how wealth is created and distributed. An economic system must answer four questions: *What* goods and services will be produced? *How* will they be produced? *For whom* will they be produced? *Who* owns and who controls the major factors of production? Capitalism (on which our economic system is based) is an economic system in which individuals own and operate the majority of businesses that provide goods and services. Capitalism stems from the theories of Adam Smith. Smith's pure laissez-faire capitalism is an economic system in which the factors of production are owned by private entities and all individuals are free to use their resources as they see fit; prices are determined by the workings of supply and demand in competitive markets; and the economic role of government is limited to rule maker and umpire.

Our economic system today is a mixed economy. In the circular flow that characterizes our business system (see Figure 1.5), households and businesses exchange resources for goods and services, using money as the medium of exchange. In a similar manner, the government collects taxes from businesses and households and purchases products and resources with which to provide services.

In a command economy, government, rather than individuals, owns many of the factors of production and provides the answers to the three other economic questions. Socialist and communist economies are—at least in theory—command economies.

 Identify the ways to measure economic performance.

One way to evaluate the performance of an economic system is to assess changes in productivity, which is the average level of output per worker per hour. Gross domestic product (GDP) can also be used to measure a nation's economic well-being and is the total dollar value of all goods and services produced by all people within the boundaries of a country during a one-year period. It is also possible to adjust GDP for inflation and thus to measure real GDP. In addition to GDP, other economic indicators include a nation's balance of trade, consumer confidence index, consumer price index (CPI), corporate profits, inflation rate, national income, new housing starts, prime interest rate, producer price index (PPI), and unemployment rate.

 Examine the different phases in the typical business cycle.

A nation's economy fluctuates rather than grows at a steady pace every year. These fluctuations are generally referred to as the business cycle. Generally, the business cycle consists of four states: the peak (sometimes called prosperity), recession, the trough, and recovery (sometimes called expansion). Some experts believe that effective use of monetary policy (the Federal Reserve's decisions that determine the size of the supply of money and the level of interest rates) and fiscal policy (the government's influence on the amount of savings and expenditures) can speed up recovery.

A federal deficit occurs when the government spends more than it receives in taxes and other revenues. At the time of publication, the national debt is over $15 trillion or approximately $49,000 for every man, woman, and child in the United States.

 Outline the four types of competition.

Competition is essentially a rivalry among businesses for sales to potential customers. In a capitalist economy, competition works to ensure the efficient and effective operation of business. Competition also ensures that a firm will survive only if it serves its customers well by providing products and services that meet their needs. Economists recognize four degrees of competition. Ranging from most to least competitive, the four degrees are perfect competition, monopolistic competition, oligopoly, and monopoly. The factors of supply and demand generally influence the price that customers pay producers for goods and services.

 Summarize the factors that affect the business environment and the challenges that American businesses will encounter in the future.

From the beginning of the Industrial Revolution to the phenomenal expansion of American industry in the 19th and early 20th centuries, our government maintained an essentially laissez-faire attitude toward business. However, during the Great Depression of the 1930s, the federal government began to provide a number of social services to its citizens.

To understand the major events that shaped the United States during the remainder of the 20th and 21st century, it helps to remember that the economy was compared to a roller coaster ride earlier in this chapter—periods of economic growth followed by periods of economic slowdown. Events and a changing business environment including wars, rapid economic growth, the social responsibility movement, a shortage of crude oil, high inflation, high interest rates, reduced business profits, increased use of technology, e-business, and social media all have shaped business and the economy.

Now more than ever before, the way a business operates is affected by the competitive environment, global environment, technological environment, and economic environment. As a result, business has a number of opportunities for improvement and challenges for the future.

KEY TERMS

You should now be able to define and give an example relevant to each of the following terms:

free enterprise (4)
cultural (or workplace) diversity (6)
business (10)
profit (11)
stakeholders (12)
economics (13)
microeconomics (13)
macroeconomics (13)
economy (13)
factors of production (13)
entrepreneur (14)
capitalism (14)
invisible hand (14)

market economy (15)
mixed economy (15)
consumer products (16)
command economy (16)
productivity (18)
gross domestic product (GDP) (18)
inflation (18)
deflation (18)
unemployment rate (19)
consumer price index (CPI) (19)
producer price index (PPI) (19)
business cycle (20)

recession (20)
depression (21)
monetary policies (21)
fiscal policy (21)
federal deficit (21)
national debt (21)
competition (21)
perfect (or pure) competition (22)
supply (22)
demand (22)
market price (23)
monopolistic competition (23)

product differentiation (23)
oligopoly (24)
monopoly (24)
natural monopoly (24)
standard of living (24)
barter (25)
domestic system (25)
factory system (25)
specialization (25)
e-business (26)
service economy (26)
social media (27)
sustainability (27)

REVIEW QUESTIONS

1. What reasons would you give if you were advising someone to study business?
2. What factors affect a person's choice of careers?
3. Describe the four resources that must be combined to organize and operate a business. How do they differ from the economist's factors of production?
4. Describe the relationship among profit, business risk, and the satisfaction of customers' needs.
5. What are the four basic economic questions? How are they answered in a capitalist economy?
6. Describe the four basic assumptions required for a laissez-faire capitalist economy.
7. Based on Figure 1.5, outline the economic interactions between business and households in our business system.
8. How does capitalism differ from socialism and communism?

9. How is productivity related to the unemployment rate?
10. Define gross domestic product. Why is this economic measure significant?
11. How is the producer price index related to the consumer price index?
12. What are the four phases in a typical business cycle? How are monetary and fiscal policies related to the business cycle?
13. Identify and compare the four forms of competition.
14. Explain how the equilibrium, or market, price of a product is determined.
15. Four different environments that affect business were described in this chapter. Choose one of the environments and explain how it affects a small electronics manufacturer located in Oregon. Why?

1. In what ways have the problems caused by the recent economic crisis affected business firms? In what ways have these problems affected employees and individuals?
2. What factors caused American business to develop into a mixed economic system rather than some other type of economic system?
3. Does an individual consumer really have a voice in answering the basic four economic questions?
4. Is gross domestic product a reliable indicator of a nation's economic health? What might be a better indicator?
5. Discuss this statement: "Business competition encourages efficiency of production and leads to improved product quality."
6. Is government participation in our business system good or bad? What factors can be used to explain your position.
7. Choose one of the challenges listed on page 28 and describe possible ways in which business and society could help to solve or eliminate the problem in the future.

Video Case 1.1

Entertainment Means Profits for Nederlander Concerts

Nederlander Concerts is based in Los Angeles, one of the two biggest markets in the U.S. concert industry (New York is the other). The company, which is one of the few remaining family-owned businesses in the entertainment industry, specializes in booking and promoting musical artists like the Goo Goo Dolls, Maroon 5, and Cyndi Lauper for events in the western United States. It owns or operates some of the theaters, amphitheaters, and arenas—including the Greek Theatre in Los Angeles, the Santa Barbara Bowl, and the Grove in Anaheim—and it rents space for concerts and events in other cities along the West Coast. Nederlander Concerts also partners with some of California's major cities such as Santa Monica and San Jose to manage or operate their civic theaters and present events there.

Since Nederlander Concerts deliberately focuses on small- to mid-sized events, it can offer a unique concert experience that brings audiences and performers closer together. It can therefore sell a high-quality experience at a higher price than seats in a bigger theater yield. Because of this high-quality experience, it can also count on selling out the house, which helps the company and the artists to profit. According to the concert company's chief operating officer, "The key areas or departments of the company include talent-buying and marketing, operations, finance, and business development. . . . I have a talent-buying team, I have a marketing team, we have a general manager of the building, we have a substantial team of people who take care of the fans, take care of the artist, and look after the shows that we buy. We're in a competitive market, and it's pretty interesting what we do."

Although it might seem odd that the concert business is a competitive one, in fact Nederlander Concerts competes with other promoters (like Live Nation) not just for audiences at its events but for bookings by popular artists. Therefore, it must keep both music lovers and performers happy. Musicians are especially concerned with the financial deal they are getting. As Nederlander's chief operating officer explains, "It's not always easy to get the show; there is competition. . . . We have a great reputation with the artist. But also there's one other factor, and

that's making the deal. That's making your best offer. That's trying to think about whether the agent is . . . telling you that your competition is paying more, willing to go more. You have to get your own 'I won't go above' number and stop bidding (for the act), or you have to say, 'Okay, I'll pay a little bit more and try to get the show.' So there's a real gamesmanship between agent and buyer. . . . The art of the deal is something we live with every day."

Given the talent, how does Nederlander get music lovers to its events? Says its vice president of marketing, "It's learning about the market, and picking up every newspaper you can find, listening to every radio station you can find, watching all of the TV, all the news programming. . . . It still comes back to, who is the artist, and who is their audience? And how do you find them? . . . The number one reason why people don't go to a show, so they say, is that they don't know about it. Which is infuriating. But we just try to make that percentage of people . . . smaller, and smaller, and smaller."

When everything is going well, the company profits. "Where we like to do most of our business, and in fact is where we probably do 90 percent of our business, is in the venues that we own or operate, so that the risk profile of those shows goes down . . . we have more revenues coming in to ensure that we're able to cover the cost, including the cost of talent, and then walk away with a greater profit."[19]

Questions

1. Nederlander Concerts competes for music lovers with other concert arenas and promoters. Do you think it also competes with TV, movies, CDs, DVDs, streaming video, and sports events? If yes, what implications does this type of competition have for Nederlander's business?
2. How many different groups can you think of whose needs Nederlander Concerts must satisfy in order to be a successful business?
3. Give an example showing how Nederlander Concerts uses each of the four factors of production.

The company that brought Mickey and Minnie Mouse into the public eye has been entertaining families for 90 years. Although animation was the Walt Disney Company's original focus, its entertainment empire now spans four main business groups: studio entertainment (including movies, stage shows, and recorded music), parks and resorts (such as Disney World and the Disney Cruise Line), consumer products (toys, books, and other merchandise), and media (including broadcast television, cable television, and online media). Disney has its headquarters in Burbank, California, but its operations are spread around the world, with $41 billion in annual revenues and a workforce of 156,000 employees.

Over the years, Disney has acquired other businesses and started new businesses to further strengthen its competitive position and its profits. It owns Pixar, the movie studio responsible for *Toy Story* and many other animated films, and it established Touchstone Pictures to produce and distribute movies for wider audiences. It acquired the ABC television networks and the ESPN sports channels as part of its drive for global growth in multiple media. To expand into interactive media for children, Disney bought the popular Club Penguin site and began creating online and video games, many featuring its popular movie and television characters.

Founder Walt Disney didn't invent the theme park, but he did transform the industry with the 1955 opening of Disneyland in California. The magic continued with the 1971 opening of Disney World in Florida. Both theme parks were drawing crowds from every continent when the company opened Tokyo Disneyland in 1983, at the height of the Japanese economic boom. Later, it worked with international partners to create Disneyland Paris and Hong Kong Disneyland. Shanghai Disney Resort will be the next to open, the result of a $3.7 billion joint business venture with a Chinese company. In all, more than 120 million people visit Disney theme parks and resorts over the course of one year.

Disney sees great growth potential in China. Thanks to economic and political changes, Chinese consumers have more disposable income than ever before and more opportunities to exercise their higher buying power. Box-office receipts from Chinese movie theaters are growing at double-digit rates, and many of Disney's Hollywood blockbusters have also been big hits in China. At the same time, competition to get movies into Chinese theaters is enormous, because the government limits the number of foreign movies that can be distributed nationwide. With an eye toward the future, Disney worked with a local partner to co-produce *Iron Man 3* with a Chinese plot twist. It has also been lending its movie-making expertise to help develop the Chinese animation industry.

All these years of serving customers with a smile have given Disney considerable insight into how to meet the needs of people of all ages. The company set up the Disney Institute in 1986 to teach businesses, schools, hospitals, and other organizations how to deliver good customer service with the famous Disney touch. Its experts have trained National Football League staff members in preparation for Super Bowl events and given Chevrolet dealer employees tips about working with car buyers. When Florida Hospital asked for help in improving patient satisfaction, Disney experts conducted studies and recommended a number of steps, such as having a friendly greeter to put young patients at ease and replacing the glare of fluorescent bulbs with recessed lighting. These and other changes helped push the hospital's patient satisfaction scores into the top 10 percent across America. The Disney Institute's revenues have doubled over the past few years and are yet another reason for the company's profit momentum.[20]

Questions

1. How is the Walt Disney Company combining human, informational, material, and financial resources for business success?
2. What is Disney's competitive situation, and what are the implications for its future expansion and profitability?
3. Which of the factors in the business environment seem to be exerting the most influence on Disney's ability to grow? Explain.

Building Skills for Career Success

① SOCIAL MEDIA EXERCISE

Today, many companies have a social media presence on Facebook, Twitter, Flickr, and other sites beyond their corporate Web site. Think of three of your favorite car companies and conduct a quick search using a search engine like Google or Yahoo! Answer the following:

1. Name the social networks for each company.
2. Compare each of their Facebook pages. How many "likes" does each company have? Are there multiple pages for the company? How much interaction (or engagement) is on each Facebook page?
3. What business goals do you think each company is trying to reach through their Facebook presence?

② JOURNALING FOR SUCCESS

Much of the information in this chapter was designed to get you to think about what it takes to be a successful employee in the competitive business world.

Assignment

Assume that you are now 25 years old and are interviewing for a position as a management trainee in a large corporation. Also assume that this position pays $45,000 a year.

1. Describe what steps you would take to prepare for this interview.
2. Assuming that you get the management trainee position, describe the personal traits or skills that you have that will help you to become successful.
3. Describe the one personal skill or trait that you feel needs improvement. How would you go about improving your weakness?

❸ DEVELOPING CRITICAL-THINKING SKILLS

With capitalism, competition is a driving force that allows the market economy to work. Let's see how competition works by pretending that you want to buy a new car.

Assignment

1. Brainstorm the following questions:
   a. Where would you go to get information about new cars?
   b. How will you decide on the make and model of car you want to buy, where to buy the car, and how to finance it?
   c. How is competition at work in this scenario?
   d. What are the pros and cons of competition as it affects the buyer?
2. Record your ideas.
3. Write a summary of the key points you learned about how competition works in the marketplace.

❹ BUILDING TEAM SKILLS

Over the past few years, employees have been expected to function as productive team members instead of working alone. People often believe that they can work effectively in teams, but many people find working with a group of people to be a challenge.

College classes that function as teams are more interesting and more fun to attend, and students generally learn more about the topics in the course. One way to begin creating a team is to learn something about each student in the class. This helps team members to feel comfortable with each other and fosters a sense of trust.

Assignment

1. Find a partner, preferably someone you do not know.
2. Each partner has two to three minutes to answer the following questions:
   a. What is your name, and where do you work?
   b. What interesting or unusual thing have you done in your life? (Do not talk about work or college; rather, focus on such things as hobbies, travel, family, and sports.)
   c. Why are you taking this course, and what do you expect to learn? (Satisfying a degree requirement is not an acceptable answer.)
3. Introduce your partner to the class. Use one to two minutes, depending on the size of the class.

❺ RESEARCHING DIFFERENT CAREERS

In this chapter, *entrepreneurship* is defined as the willingness to take risks and the knowledge and ability to use the other factors of production efficiently. An *entrepreneur* is a person who risks time, effort, and money to start and operate a business. Often, people believe that these terms apply only to small business. However, employees with entrepreneurial attitudes have recently advanced more rapidly in large companies as well.

Assignment

1. Go to the local library or use the Internet to research how large firms, especially corporations, are rewarding employees who have entrepreneurial skills.
2. Find answers to the following questions:
   a. Why is an entrepreneurial attitude important in large corporations today?
   b. What makes an entrepreneurial employee different from other employees?
   c. How are these employees being rewarded, and are the rewards worth the effort?
3. Write a two-page report that summarizes your findings.

ENDNOTES

1. Sources: Based on information from the Zynga Web site at www.zynga.com accessed January 12, 2012; Jon Swartz, "CEO Calls Zynga His 'Crowning Achievement,'" *USA Today*, December 18, 2011, www.usatoday.com; Evelyn M. Rusli, "Zynga's Tough Culture Risks a Talent Drain," *New York Times*, November 27, 2011, www.nytimes.com; Miguel Helft, "Check Out Zynga's Zany New Offices," *Fortune*, November 7, 2011, pp. 59–60; "The World's 50 Most Innovative Companies: #9, Zynga," *Fast Company*, n.d., www.fastcompany.com.
2. The Horatio Alger Web site at www.horatioalger.org (accessed January 5, 2012).
3. Ibid.
4. The 66Apps Web site at www.66apps.com (accessed January 11, 2012).
5. Idy Fernandez, "Julie Stav," *Hispanic*, June–July 2005, 204.
6. The Walmart stores Web site at www.walmartstores.com (accessed January 9, 2012).
7. The General Mills Web site at www.generalmills.com (accessed January 9, 2012).
8. The Bureau of Economic Analysis Web site at www.bea.gov (accessed January 9, 2012).
9. The Bureau of Economic Analysis Web site at www.bea.gov (accessed January 30, 2012).
10. The Bureau of Labor Statistics Web site at www.bls.gov (accessed January 9, 2011).
11. The Bureau of Economic Analysis Web site at www.bea.gov (accessed January 30, 2012).
12. The Bureau of Labor Statistics Web site at www.bls.gov (accessed January 8, 2012).
13. The Treasury Direct Web site at www.treasurydirect.gov (accessed January 9, 2012) and the U.S. Census Bureau Web site at www.census.gov (accessed January 9, 2012).
14. The Investopedia Web site at www.investopedia.com (accessed January 9, 2012).
15. The Bureau of Labor Statistics Web site at www.bls.gov (accessed January 12, 2011).
16. Bill Weir, "Made in China: Your Job, Your Future, Your Fortune," ABC News Web site at www.abcnews.com (accessed September 20, 2005).

17. Les Dlabay, "The Future of Global Business at 'Base of the Pyramid,'" *The Daily Herald Business Ledger*, November 29, 2011, p. 22.

18. The Environmental Protection Agency Web site at www.epa.gov (accessed January 9, 2012).

19. Company Web site www.nederlanderconcerts.com (accessed January 14, 2012); "Nederlander Organization company overview," *BusinessWeek*, August 20, 2010, www.businessweek.com; Hannah Heineman, "Moving Forward on Capital Improvement Projects," *Santa Monica Mirror*, July 28, 2010, www.smmirror.com; Steve Knopper, "Tour Biz Strong in Weak Economy," *Rolling Stone*, October 2, 2008, 11–12; Ray Waddell, "Nederlander/Viejas Deal Offers Touring Opportunities," *Billboard*, January 10, 2008, www.billboard.com; interviews with Nederlander employees and the video "For Nederlander Concerts, Entertainment Is a Profitable Business."

20. Sources: Based on information in Brooks Barnes, "In Customer Service Consulting, Disney's Small World Is Growing," *New York Times*, April 23, 2012, www.nytimes.com; David Pierson and Richard Verrier, "Disney to Join Animation Initiative," *Los Angeles Times*, April 11, 2012, www.latimes.com; "Disney Making 'Iron Man 3' with Chinese Partner as Hollywood Expands China Ties," *Washington Post*, April 16, 2012, www.washingtonpost.com; Jason Garcia, "Cruise Line, Theme Parks Propel Disney Profit," *Orlando Sentinel*, February 7, 2012, www.orlandosentinel.com; http://corporate.disney.go.com.

Being Ethical and Socially Responsible

2

LEARNING OBJECTIVES

Once you complete this chapter, you will be able to:

1 Understand what is meant by *business ethics*.

2 Identify the types of ethical concerns that arise in the business world.

3 Discuss the factors that affect the level of ethical behavior in organizations.

4 Explain how ethical decision making can be encouraged.

5 Describe how our current views on the social responsibility of business have evolved.

6 Explain the two views on the social responsibility of business and understand the arguments for and against increased social responsibility.

7 Discuss the factors that led to the consumer movement and list some of its results.

8 Analyze how present employment practices are being used to counteract past abuses.

9 Describe the major types of pollution, their causes, and their cures.

10 Identify the steps a business must take to implement a program of social responsibility.

Panera Cares About Its Communities

Out of 1,500 Panera bakery-cafés spread across the United States and Canada, a handful are slightly different from the rest of the chain. These Panera Cares cafés are owned by the nonprofit division of Panera Bread, and the posted menus show "suggested funding levels" rather than specific prices. After customers place their orders, they don't pay at the cash register. Instead, they drop money into a donation box, contributing whatever amount they wish to pay for their meals. People who can't afford to pay are encouraged to do their part by volunteering some time at the café.

Welcome to Panera Cares, the next phase of an ongoing effort to "make a contribution to the community in a real, substantive way," says Ron Shaich, Panera's founder. Although his company has a long history of donating money and food to charitable causes, Shaich wanted to do more. His idea was to open pay-what-you-wish cafés where people struggling to make ends meet could enjoy a regular restaurant meal with dignity.

When the first three cafés opened (in Clayton, Missouri; Dearborn, Michigan; and Portland, Oregon), Shaich wasn't sure whether customers who could afford to pay would donate as much as expected or how many people with money to spend would take advantage by paying too little or not at all. The goal is for Panera Cares to be self-supporting so it can give back to the community with more than meals. So far, approximately 60 percent of the customers are donating the suggested amount, 20 percent are donating more, and 20 percent are donating less. The largest single donation ever made for a meal was $500.

As long as each location brings in about 80 percent of the suggested funding level, the cafes will generate enough profit to keep going and pay for extras such as providing job training for teenagers in the local area. "This is not about a handout," Shaich explains. "This is about a hand up, and every one of us has a need for that at some point in our lives."[1]

O bviously, organizations like Panera want to be recognized as responsible corporate citizens. Such companies recognize the need to harmonize their operations with environmental demands and other vital social concerns. Not all firms, however, have taken steps to encourage a consideration of social responsibility and ethics in their decisions and day-to-day activities. Some managers still regard such business practices as a poor investment, in which the cost is not worth the return. Other managers—indeed, most managers—view the cost of these practices as a necessary business expense, similar to wages or rent.

Most managers today, like those at Panera, are finding ways to balance a growing agenda of socially responsible activities with the drive to generate profits. This also happens to be a good way for a company to demonstrate its values and to attract like-minded employees, customers, and stockholders. In a highly competitive business environment, an increasing number of companies are, like Panera, seeking to set themselves apart by developing a reputation for ethical and socially responsible behavior.

We begin this chapter by defining *business ethics* and examining ethical issues. Next, we look at the standards of behavior in organizations and how ethical behavior can be encouraged. We then turn to the topic of social responsibility. We compare and contrast two present-day models of social responsibility and present arguments for and against increasing the social responsibility of business. We then examine the major elements of the consumer movement. We discuss how social responsibility in business has affected employment practices and environmental concerns. Finally, we consider the commitment, planning, and funding that go into a firm's program of social responsibility.

BUSINESS ETHICS DEFINED

1 Understand what is meant by *business ethics*.

Ethics is the study of right and wrong and of the morality of the choices individuals make. An ethical decision or action is one that is "right" according to some standard of behavior. **Business ethics** is the application of moral standards to business situations. Recent court cases involving unethical behavior have helped to make business ethics a matter of public concern. In one such case, Copley Pharmaceutical, Inc., pled guilty to federal criminal charges (and paid a $10.65 million fine) for falsifying drug manufacturers' reports to the Food and Drug Administration. In another much-publicized case, lawsuits against tobacco companies have led to $246 billion in settlements, although there has been only one class-action lawsuit filed on behalf of all smokers. The case, *Engle v. R. J. Reynolds*, could cost tobacco companies an estimated $500 billion. In yet another case, Adelphia Communications Corp., the nation's fifth-largest cable television company, agreed to pay $715 million to settle federal investigations stemming from rampant earnings manipulation by its founder John J. Rigas, and his son, Timothy J. Rigas. Prosecutors and government regulators charged that both father and son had misappropriated $2.3 billion of Adelphia funds for their own use and had failed to pay the corporation for securities they controlled. Consequently, investors lost more than $60 billion when Adelphia declared bankruptcy. The tax evasion charge against the Rigases was dismissed in early 2012. John Rigas and Timothy Rigas are serving 12 years and 17 years in prison, respectively. John Rigas applied for a presidential pardon in January 2009, but George W. Bush left office without making a decision on Rigas's request. Mr. Rigas is scheduled to be released from federal prison in 2018. The Rigases have appealed their convictions to the Second Court of Appeals and they are awaiting a date from the court for oral arguments.[2]

Personal APPS

Business ethics apply to customers as well as to managers and employees. In some buying situations, the "right" thing to do isn't always clear, is it? For example, should you buy from a retail store that has been found to be unfair to its employees? Read on for tips about recognizing and resolving ethical issues.

ETHICAL ISSUES

2 Identify the types of ethical concerns that arise in the business world.

Ethical issues often arise out of a business's relationship with investors, customers, employees, creditors, or competitors. Each of these groups has specific concerns and usually exerts pressure on the organization's managers. For example, investors want management to make sensible financial decisions that will boost sales, profits, and returns on their investments. Customers expect a firm's products to be safe, reliable, and reasonably priced. Employees demand to be treated fairly in hiring, promotion, and compensation decisions. Creditors require accounts to be paid on time and the accounting information furnished by the firm to be accurate. Competitors expect the firm's competitive practices to be fair and honest. Consider TAP Pharmaceutical Products, Inc., whose sales representatives offered every urologist in the United States a big-screen TV, computers, fax machines, and golf vacations if the doctors prescribed TAP's new prostate cancer drug Lupron. Moreover, the sales representatives sold Lupron at cut-rate prices or gratis while defrauding Medicare. Recently, the federal government won an $875 million judgment against TAP when a former TAP vice president of sales, Douglas Durand, and Dr. Joseph Gerstein blew the whistle.[3]

In late 2006, Hewlett-Packard Co.'s chairman, Patricia Dunn, and general counsel, Ann Baskins, resigned amid allegations that the company used intrusive tactics in observing the personal lives of journalists and the company's directors, thus tarnishing

ethics the study of right and wrong and of the morality of the choices individuals make

business ethics the application of moral standards to business situations

Hewlett-Packard's reputation for integrity. According to Congressman John Dingell of Michigan, "We have before us witnesses from Hewlett-Packard to discuss a plunderers' operation that would make (former president) Richard Nixon blush were he still alive." Alternatively, consider Bernard Madoff, former stockbroker, financial advisor, and chairman of the NASDAQ stock exchange. In 2009, he was convicted of securities and other frauds including a Ponzi scheme that defrauded clients of $65 billion. Madoff was sentenced to 150 years in prison.

Businesspeople face ethical issues every day, and some of these issues can be difficult to assess. Although some types of issues arise infrequently, others occur regularly. Let's take a closer look at several ethical issues.

Fairness and Honesty

Fairness and honesty in business are two important ethical concerns. Besides obeying all laws and regulations, businesspeople are expected to refrain from knowingly deceiving, misrepresenting, or intimidating others. The consequences of failing to do so can be expensive. Recently, for example, Keith E. Anderson and Wayne Anderson, the leaders of an international tax shelter scheme known as Anderson's Ark and Associates, were sentenced to as many as 20 years in prison. The Andersons; Richard Marks, their chief accounting officer; and Karolyn Grosnickle, the chief administrative officer, were ordered to pay more than $200 million in fines and restitution.[4] More than 1,500 clients of Anderson's Ark and Associates lost about $31 million. In yet another case, the accounting firm PricewaterhouseCoopers LLP agreed to pay the U.S. government $42 million to resolve allegations that it made false claims in connection with travel reimbursements it collected for several federal agencies.[5]

Deere & Company requires each employee to deal fairly with its customers, suppliers, competitors, and employees. "No employee should take unfair advantage of anyone through manipulation, concealment, abuse of privileged information, misrepresentation of material facts or any other unfair dealing practice." Employees are encouraged to report possible violations of company ethics policies using a 24-hour hotline or anonymous e-mails. Reporting is not only encouraged; it is an accepted and protected behavior.[6]

Personal data security breaches have become a major threat to personal privacy in the new millennium. Can businesses keep your personal data secure?

Organizational Relationships

A businessperson may be tempted to place his or her personal welfare above the welfare of others or the welfare of the organization. For example, in late 2002, former CEO of Tyco International, Ltd, Leo Dennis Kozlowski, was indicted for misappropriating $43 million in corporate funds to make philanthropic contributions in his own name, including $5 million to Seton Hall University, which named its new business-school building Kozlowski Hall. Furthermore, according to Tyco, the former CEO took $61.7 million in interest-free relocation loans without the board's permission. He allegedly used the money to finance many personal luxuries, including a $15 million yacht and a $3.9 million Renoir painting, and to throw a $2 million party for his wife's birthday. Mr. Kozlowski, currently serving up to 25 years in prison, paid $134 million in restitution to Tyco and criminal fines of $70 million. In 2009, the U.S. Supreme Court denied his petition for a judicial review.[7]

Relationships with customers and co-workers often create ethical problems. Unethical behavior in these areas includes taking credit for others' ideas or work, not meeting one's commitments in a mutual agreement, and pressuring others to behave unethically.

© GUS CHAN/THE PLAIN DEALER/LANDOV

Violating ethics can be humiliating and costly.
Former Cuyahoga County Sheriff Gerald McFaul listens to his attorney after McFaul pleaded guilty to theft in office and ethics violation.

Conflict of Interest

Conflict of interest results when a businessperson takes advantage of a situation for his or her own personal interest rather than for the employer's interest. Such conflict may occur when payments and gifts make their way into business deals. A wise rule to remember is that anything given to a person that might unfairly influence that person's business decision is a bribe, and all bribes are unethical.

For example, Nortel Networks Corporation does not permit its employees, officers, and directors to accept any gifts or to serve as directors or officers of any organization that might supply goods or services to Nortel Networks. However, Nortel employees may work part-time with firms that are not competitors, suppliers, or customers. At AT&T, employees are instructed to discuss with their supervisors any investments that may seem improper. Verizon Communications forbids its employees and executives from holding a "significant" financial stake in vendors, suppliers, or customers.

At Procter & Gamble Company (P&G), all employees are obligated to act at all times solely in the best interests of the company. A conflict of interest arises when an employee has a personal relationship or financial or other interest that could interfere with this obligation, or when an employee uses his or her position with the company for personal gain. P&G requires employees to disclose all potential conflicts of interest and to take prompt actions to eliminate a conflict when the company asks them to do so. Generally, it is not acceptable to receive gifts, entertainment, or other gratuities from people with whom P&G does business because doing so could imply an obligation on the part of the company and potentially pose a conflict of interest.

Communications

Business communications, especially advertising, can present ethical questions. False and misleading advertising is illegal and unethical, and it can infuriate customers. Sponsors of advertisements aimed at children must be especially careful to avoid misleading messages. Advertisers of health-related products also must take precautions to guard against deception when using such descriptive terms as *low fat*, *fat free*, and *light*. In fact, the Federal Trade Commission has issued guidelines on the use of these labels.

FACTORS AFFECTING ETHICAL BEHAVIOR

 Discuss the factors that affect the level of ethical behavior in organizations.

Is it possible for an individual with strong moral values to make ethically questionable decisions in a business setting? What factors affect a person's inclination to make either ethical or unethical decisions in a business organization? Although the answers to these questions are not entirely clear, three general sets of factors do appear to influence the standards of behavior in an organization. As shown in Figure 2.1, the sets consist of individual factors, social factors, and opportunities.

FIGURE 2.1   Factors that Affect the Level of Ethical Behavior in an Organization

Source: Based on O. C. Ferrell and Larry Gresham, "A Contingency Framework for Understanding Ethical Decision Making in Marketing," *Journal of Marketing* (Summer 1985), 89.

Individual Factors Affecting Ethics

Several individual factors influence the level of ethical behavior in an organization.

- *Individual knowledge of an issue.* How much an individual knows about an issue is one factor. A decision maker with a greater amount of knowledge regarding a situation may take steps to avoid ethical problems, whereas a less-informed person may take action unknowingly that leads to an ethical quagmire.
- *Personal values.* An individual's moral values and central, value-related attitudes also clearly influence his or her business behavior. Most people join organizations to accomplish personal goals.
- *Personal goals.* The types of personal goals an individual aspires to and the manner in which these goals are pursued have a significant impact on that individual's behavior in an organization. The actions of specific individuals in scandal-plagued companies, such as Adelphia, Arthur Anderson, Enron, Halliburton, Qwest, and WorldCom, often raise questions about individuals' personal character and integrity.

Social Factors Affecting Ethics

- *Cultural norms.* A person's behavior in the workplace, to some degree, is determined by cultural norms, and these social factors vary from one culture to another. For example, in some countries it is acceptable and ethical for customs agents to receive gratuities for performing ordinary, legal tasks that are a part of their jobs, whereas in other countries these practices would be viewed as unethical and perhaps illegal.
- *Co-workers.* The actions and decisions of co-workers constitute another social factor believed to shape a person's sense of business ethics. For example, if your co-workers make long-distance telephone calls on company time and at company expense, you might view that behavior as acceptable and ethical because everyone does it.
- *Significant others.* The moral values and attitudes of "significant others"—spouses, friends, and relatives, for instance—also can affect an employee's perception of what is ethical and unethical behavior in the workplace.
- *Use of the Internet.* Even the Internet presents new challenges for firms whose employees enjoy easy access to sites through convenient high-speed connections at work. An employee's behavior online can be viewed as offensive to co-workers and possibly lead to lawsuits against the firm if employees engage in unethical behavior on controversial Web sites not related to their job. Interestingly, one recent survey of employees found that most workers assume that their use of technology at work will be monitored. A large majority of employees approved of most monitoring methods such as monitoring faxes and e-mail, tracking Web use, and even recording telephone calls.

"Opportunity" as a Factor Affecting Ethics

- *Presence of opportunity.* *Opportunity* refers to the amount of freedom an organization gives an employee to behave unethically if he or she makes that choice. In some organizations, certain company policies and procedures reduce the opportunity to be unethical. For example, at some fast-food restaurants, one employee takes your order and receives your payment, and another fills the order. This procedure reduces the opportunity to be unethical because the person handling the money is not dispensing the product, and the person giving out the product is not handling the money.
- *Ethical codes.* The existence of an ethical code and the importance management places on this code are other determinants of opportunity (codes of ethics are discussed in more detail in the next section).

- *Enforcement.* The degree of enforcement of company policies, procedures, and ethical codes is a major force affecting opportunity. When violations are dealt with consistently and firmly, the opportunity to be unethical is reduced.

Do you make personal telephone calls on company time? Many individuals do. Although most employees limit personal calls to a few minutes, some make personal calls in excess of 30 minutes. Whether you use company time and equipment to make personal calls is an example of a personal ethical decision.

Now that we have considered some of the factors believed to influence the level of ethical behavior in the workplace, let us explore what can be done to encourage ethical behavior and to discourage unethical behavior.

ENCOURAGING ETHICAL BEHAVIOR

④ Explain how ethical decision making can be encouraged.

Most authorities agree that there is room for improvement in business ethics. A more problematic question is: Can business be made more ethical in the real world? The majority opinion on this issue suggests that government, trade associations, and individual firms indeed can establish acceptable levels of ethical behavior.

Government's Role in Encouraging Ethics

The government can encourage ethical behavior by legislating more stringent regulations. For example, the landmark **Sarbanes–Oxley Act of 2002** provides sweeping new legal protection for those who report corporate misconduct. At the signing ceremony, President George W. Bush stated, "The act adopts tough new provisions to deter and punish corporate and accounting fraud and corruption, ensure justice for wrongdoers, and protect the interests of workers and shareholders." Among other things, the law deals with corporate responsibility, conflicts of interest, and corporate accountability. However, rules require enforcement, and the unethical businessperson frequently seems to "slip something by" without getting caught. Increased regulation may help, but it surely cannot solve the entire ethics problem.

Sarbanes–Oxley Act of 2002 provides sweeping new legal protection for employees who report corporate misconduct

code of ethics a guide to acceptable and ethical behavior as defined by the organization

Trade Associations' Role in Encouraging Ethics

Trade associations can and often do provide ethical guidelines for their members. These organizations, which operate within particular industries, are in an excellent position to exert pressure on members who stoop to questionable business practices. For example, recently, a pharmaceutical trade group adopted a new set of guidelines to halt the extravagant dinners and other gifts sales representatives often give to physicians. However, enforcement and authority vary from association to association. Because trade associations exist for the benefit of their members, harsh measures may be self-defeating.

Individual Companies' Role in Encouraging Ethics

Codes of ethics that companies provide to their employees are perhaps the most effective way to encourage ethical behavior. A **code of ethics** is a written guide to acceptable and ethical behavior as defined by an organization; it outlines uniform policies, standards, and punishments for violations. Because employees know what is expected of them and what will happen if they violate the rules, a code of ethics goes a long way toward encouraging ethical behavior. However, codes cannot possibly

© CONGRESSIONAL QUARTERLY PHOTO BY SCOTT J. FERRELL/NEWSCOM

Meet Senators Sarbanes and Oxley. The Sarbanes–Oxley Act of 2002 adopted tough new provisions to deter and punish corporate and accounting fraud and corruption. Here, Senator Paul S. Sarbanes and John LaFalce congratulate each other as Senator Michael J. Oxley (center) looks on. The legislation passed with near unanimous support.

cover every situation. Companies also must create an environment in which employees recognize the importance of complying with the written code. Managers must provide direction by fostering communication, actively modeling and encouraging ethical decision making, and training employees to make ethical decisions.

During the 1980s, an increasing number of organizations created and implemented ethics codes. In a recent survey of *Fortune* 1000 firms, 93 percent of the companies that responded reported having a formal code of ethics. Some companies are now even taking steps to strengthen their codes. For example, to strengthen its accountability, the Healthcare Financial Management Association recently revised its code to designate contact persons who handle reports of ethics violations, to clarify how its board of directors should deal with violations of business ethics, and to guarantee a fair hearing process. S. C. Johnson & Son, makers of Pledge®, Drano®, Windex®, and many other household products, is another firm that recognizes that it must behave in ways the public perceives as ethical; its code includes expectations for employees and its commitment to consumers, the community, and society in general. As shown in Figure 2.2, the ethics code of electronics giant Texas Instruments (TI) includes issues relating to policies and procedures; laws and regulations; relationships with customers, suppliers, and competitors; conflicts of interest; handling of proprietary information; and code enforcement.

Assigning an ethics officer who coordinates ethical conduct gives employees someone to consult if they are not sure of the right thing to do. An ethics officer meets with employees and top management to provide ethical advice, establishes and maintains an anonymous confidential service to answer questions about ethical issues, and takes action on ethics code violations.

Sometimes even employees who want to act ethically may find it difficult to do so. Unethical practices can become ingrained in an organization. Employees with high personal ethics may then take a controversial step called *whistle-blowing*. **Whistle-blowing** is informing the press or government officials about unethical practices within one's organization.

The year 2002 was labeled as the "Year of the Whistle-Blower." Consider Joe Speaker, a 40-year-old acting chief financial officer (CFO) at Rite Aid Corp. in 1999. He discovered that inventories at Rite Aid had been overvalued and that millions in expenses had not been reported properly. Further digging into Rite Aid's books revealed that $541 million in earnings over the previous two years was really $1.6 billion in losses. Mr. Speaker was a main government witness when former Rite Aid Corp. Chairman and CEO Martin L. Grass went on trial. Mr. Speaker is among dozens of corporate managers who have blown the whistle. Enron's Sherron S. Watkins and WorldCom's Cynthia Cooper are now well-known whistle-blowers and *Time* magazine's persons of the year 2002. According to Linda Chatman Thomsen, deputy director for enforcement at the Securities and Exchange Commission, "Whistle-blowers give us an insider's perspective and have advanced our investigation immeasurably."

Whistle-blowing could have averted disaster and prevented needless deaths in the *Challenger* space shuttle disaster, for example. How could employees have known about life-threatening problems and let them pass? Whistle-blowing, however, can have serious repercussions for employees: Those who "blow whistles" sometimes lose their jobs. However, the Sarbanes–Oxley Act of 2002 protects whistle-blowers who report corporate misconduct. Any executive who retaliates against a whistle-blower can be held criminally liable and imprisoned for up to ten years.

Retaliations do occur, however. For example, in 2005, the U.S. Court of Appeals for the 8th Circuit unanimously upheld the right of Jane Turner, a 25-year veteran FBI agent, to obtain monetary damages and a jury trial against the FBI. The court held that Ms. Turner presented sufficient facts to justify a trial by jury based on the FBI's retaliatory transfer of Ms. Turner from her investigatory position in Minot, North Dakota, to a demeaning desk job in Minneapolis. Kris Kolesnik, executive director of the National Whistle Blower Center, said, "Jane Turner is an American hero. She refused to be silent when her co-agents committed misconduct in a child rape case. She refused to be silent when her co-agents stole property from Ground Zero. She paid the price and lost her job. The 8th Circuit Court did the right thing and insured

whistle-blowing informing the press or government officials about unethical practices within one's organization

Texas Instruments encourages ethical behavior through an extensive training program and a written code of ethics and shared values.

TEXAS INSTRUMENTS CODE OF ETHICS

"Integrity is the foundation on which TI is built. There is no other characteristic more essential to a TIer's makeup. It has to be present at all levels. Integrity is expected of managers and individuals when they make commitments. They are expected to stand by their commitments to the best of their ability.

One of TI's greatest strengths is its values and ethics. We had some early leaders who set those values as the standard for how they lived their lives. And it is important that TI grew that way. It's something that we don't want to lose. At the same time, we must move more rapidly. But we don't want to confuse that with the fact that we're ethical and we're moral. We're very responsible, and we live up to what we say."

Tom Engibous, President and CEO
Texas Instruments, 1997

We Respect and Value People By:

Treating others as we want to be treated.

- Exercising the basic virtues of respect, dignity, kindness, courtesy and manners in all work relationships.
- Recognizing and avoiding behaviors that others may find offensive, including the manner in which we speak and relate to one another and the materials we bring into the workplace, both printed and electronically.
- Respecting the right and obligation of every TIer to resolve concerns relating to ethics questions in the course of our duties without retribution and retaliation.
- Giving all TIers the same opportunity to have their questions, issues and situations fairly considered while understanding that being treated fairly does not always mean that we will all be treated the same.
- Trusting one another to use sound judgment in our use of TI business and information systems.
- Understanding that even though TI has the obligation to monitor its business information systems activity, we will respect privacy by prohibiting random searches of individual TIers' communications.
- Recognizing that conduct socially and professionally acceptable in one culture and country may be viewed differently in another.

We Are Honest By:

Representing ourselves and our intentions truthfully.

- Offering full disclosure and withdrawing ourselves from discussions and decisions when our business judgment appears to be in conflict with a personal interest.
- Respecting the rights and property of others, including their intellectual property. Accepting confidential or trade secret information only after we clearly understand our obligations as defined in a nondisclosure agreement.
- Competing fairly without collusion or collaboration with competitors to divide markets, set prices, restrict production, allocate customers or otherwise restrain competition.
- Assuring that no payments or favors are offered to influence others to do something wrong.
- Keeping records that are accurate and include all payments and receipts.
- Exercising good judgment in the exchange of business courtesies, meals and entertainment by avoiding activities that could create even the appearance that our decisions could be compromised.
- Refusing to speculate in TI stock through frequent buying and selling or through other forms of speculative trading.

Source: Courtesy of Texas Instruments, www.ti.com/corp/docs/csr/corpgov/downloads/CCR_Summary.pdf (accessed February 15, 2012).

that justice will take place in her case." In 2008, the U.S. government was ordered to pay $1 million in legal fees to Turner's lawyers. The Whistleblower Protection Act of 1989 protects federal employees who report an agency's misconduct. The Obama administration is attempting to pass a law that would further protect the government whistle-blowers.[8]

TABLE 2.1	Guidelines for Making Ethical Decisions
1. Listen and learn.	Recognize the problem or decision-making opportunity that confronts your company, team, or unit. Don't argue, criticize, or defend yourself—keep listening and reviewing until you are sure that you understand others.
2. Identify the ethical issues.	Examine how co-workers and consumers are affected by the situation or decision at hand. Examine how you feel about the situation, and attempt to understand the viewpoint of those involved in the decision or in the consequences of the decision.
3. Create and analyze options.	Try to put aside strong feelings such as anger or a desire for power and prestige and come up with as many alternatives as possible before developing an analysis. Ask everyone involved for ideas about which options offer the best long-term results for you and the company. Then decide which option will increase your self-respect even if, in the long run, things don't work out the way you hope they will.
4. Identify the best option from your point of view.	Consider it and test it against some established criteria, such as respect, understanding, caring, fairness, honesty, and openness.
5. Explain your decision and resolve any differences that arise.	This may require neutral arbitration from a trusted manager or taking "time out" to reconsider, consult, or exchange written proposals before a decision is reached.

Source: Based on information in Tom Rusk with D. Patrick Miller, "Doing the Right Thing," *Sky* (Delta Airlines), August 1993, 18–22.

When firms set up anonymous hotlines to handle ethically questionable situations, employees actually may be more likely to engage in whistle-blowing. When firms instead create an environment that educates employees and nurtures ethical behavior, fewer ethical problems arise. Ultimately, the need for whistle-blowing is greatly reduced.

It is difficult for an organization to develop ethics codes, policies, and procedures to deal with all relationships and every situation. When no company policies or procedures exist or apply, a quick test to determine if a behavior is ethical is to see if others—co-workers, customers, and suppliers—approve of it. Ethical decisions will always withstand scrutiny. Openness and communication about choices will often build trust and strengthen business relationships. Table 2.1 provides some general guidelines for making ethical decisions.

SOCIAL RESPONSIBILITY

Social responsibility is the recognition that business activities have an impact on society and the consideration of that impact in business decision making. In the first few days after Hurricane Katrina hit New Orleans, Walmart delivered $20 million in cash (including $4 million to employees displaced by the storm), 100 truckloads of free merchandise, and food for 100,000 meals. The company also promised a job elsewhere for every one of its workers affected by the catastrophe. Obviously, social responsibility costs money. It is perhaps not so obvious—except in isolated cases—that social responsibility is also good business. Customers eventually find out which firms act responsibly and which do not. Just as easily as they can purchase a product made by a company that is socially responsible, they can choose against buying from the firm that is not.

Consider the following examples of organizations that are attempting to be socially responsible:

social responsibility the recognition that business activities have an impact on society and the consideration of that impact in business decision making

- Social responsibility can take many forms—including flying lessons. Through Young Eagles, underwritten by S. C. Johnson, Phillips Petroleum, Lockheed Martin, Jaguar, and other corporations, 22,000 volunteer pilots have taken a half million youngsters on free flights designed to teach flying basics and inspire excitement about flying careers. Young Eagles is just one of the growing number of education projects undertaken by businesses building solid records as good corporate citizens.

- The General Mills Foundation, created in 1954, is one of the nation's largest company-sponsored foundations. Since the General Mills Foundation was created, it has awarded more than $535 million to its communities.

  In the Twin Cities, the General Mills Foundation provides grants for youth nutrition and fitness, education, arts and culture, social services, and the United Way. Beyond financial resources, the General Mills Foundation also supports organizations with volunteers and mentors who share their expertise and talents. For example, General Mills plays a leadership role in supporting education, arts, and cultural organizations by matching employee and retiree contributions dollar for dollar. Recently, the Foundation donated $28.2 million in food to Feeding America, the largest hunger-relief organization in the United States. Food is also donated following natural disasters such as, devastating earthquakes in Haiti and Chile, and flood relief in Pakistan.[9]

- As part of Dell's commitment to the community, the Dell Foundation contributes significantly to the quality of life in communities where Dell employees live and work. The Dell Foundation supports innovative and effective programs that provide fundamental prerequisites to equip youth to learn and excel in a world driven by the digital economy. The Dell Foundation supports a wide range of programs that benefit children from newborn to 17 years of age in Dell's principal U.S. locations and welcomes proposals from non-profit organizations that address health and human services, education, and technology access for youth.

  Globally, the Michael and Susan Dell Foundation has contributed more than $700 million to improve student performance and increase access to education so that all children have the opportunity to achieve their dreams.[10]

- Improving public schools around the world continues to be IBM's top social priority. Its efforts are focused on preparing the next generation of leaders and workers. Through Reinventing Education and other strategic efforts, IBM is solving education's toughest problems with solutions that draw on advanced information technologies and the best minds IBM can apply. Its programs are paving the way for reforms in school systems around the world.

  IBM launched the World Community Grid in November 2004. It combines excess processing power from thousands of computers into a virtual supercomputer. This grid enables researchers to gather and analyze unprecedented quantities of data aimed at advancing research on genomics, diseases, and natural disasters. The first project, the Human Proteome Folding Project, assists in identifying cures for diseases such as malaria and tuberculosis and has registered 85,000 devices around the world to date.

  Recently, as IBM celebrated its centennial, the company announced that Africa is the destination for is 100th team and 1,000th employee involved in the company's Corporate Service Corps. Often called a "corporate version" of the Peace Corps, this program has made a direct economic impact in many of the 20 countries it has helped. Participants, who are selected from among IBM's highest performing employees, provide technology-related assistance to both local governments and community organizations. Issues they tackle include local economic development, entrepreneurship, transportation, education, citizen services, health care, and disaster recovery. Stanley S. Litow, IBM's vice president of Corporate Citizenship and Corporate Affairs, and president of IBM's Foundation stated, "Our Corporate Service Corps program epitomizes the progressive ethics of IBM's employees, both today and 100 years ago."[11]

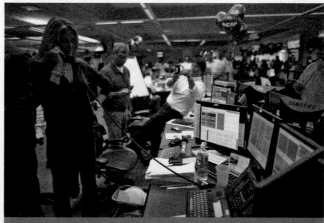

© JACOB SILBERG/REUTERS/LANDOV

Social responsibility is good business. ICAP, the world's largest interdealer broker in Jersey City, New Jersey, hosts its 16th annual global Charity Day during which the company revenues are donated to over 100 charities around the world.

- General Electric Company (GE) has a long history of supporting the communities where its employees work and live through GE's unique combination of resources, equipment, and employees' and retirees' hearts and souls. Today GE's responsibility extends to communities around the world.

  GE applies its long-standing spirit of innovation and unique set of capabilities to take on tough challenges in its communities. For example, recently, GE awarded a five-year grant of $20 million to Milwaukee Public Schools to improve academic achievement and better prepare students for college and career opportunities, with a focus on math and science programs. This grant is a part of the GE Foundation Developing Futures™ in Education program, an initiative to ensure that U.S. students are prepared to compete in an increasingly competitive global economy.[12]

- With the help of dedicated Schwab volunteers, the Charles Schwab Foundation provides programs and funding to help individuals fill the information gap. For example, Schwab MoneyWise helps adults teach—and children learn—the basics of financial literacy. Interactive tools are available at http://schwabmoneywise.com, and local workshops cover topics such as getting kids started on a budget. In addition to these efforts, widely distributed publications and news columns by foundation President Carrie Schwab Pomerantz promote financial literacy on a wide range of topics—from saving for a child's education to bridging the health insurance gap for retirees. Since its founding in 1993, Charles Schwab Foundation has made contributions averaging $4 million a year to more than 2,300 nonprofit organizations.[13]

- Improving basic literacy skills in the United States is among the Verizon Foundation's major priorities because of its enormous impact on education, health, and economic development. Here in the United States, more than 30 million American adults have basic or below-average literacy skills. Thinkfinity.org is designed to improve education and literacy achievement. This comprehensive free Web site delivers online resources to advance student achievement. Thinkfinity delivers top-quality K–12 lesson plans, student materials, interactive tools, and connections to educational Web sites. It gives teachers, instructors, and parents the tools they need to increase student performance.

  Recently, Verizon employees and retirees donated more than 608,000 hours of service and, with the Verizon Foundation, contributed more than $25 million in combined matching gift funds, making Verizon Volunteers one of the largest corporate volunteer incentive programs in the United States.

- ExxonMobil's commitment to education spans all levels of achievement. One of its corporate primary goals is to support basic education and literacy programs in the developing world. In areas of the world where basic education levels have been met, ExxonMobil supports education programs in science, technology, engineering, and mathematics.

  ExxonMobil recognizes the essential role that proficiency in math and science plays not only in the energy business but also in fostering innovation and facilitating human progress. The company encourages new generations to pursue studies and careers in fields involving mathematics and science. Toward this goal, it supports programs focused on laying the foundation for long-term educational improvements, such as the National Math and Science Initiative and the Mickelson ExxonMobil Teachers Academy.

  In recognition of 2011 International Women's Day, ExxonMobil granted $6 million to support economic opportunities for women around the world. In announcing the grant, Suzanne McCarron, president of ExxonMobil Foundation said, "Research tells us that the success of women entrepreneurs is key to building communities. When women thrive economically, entire societies are transformed by becoming healthier, more stable and more prosperous." Recently, ExxonMobil, its employees, and retirees provided $238 million in contributions worldwide.[14]

- AT&T has built a tradition of supporting education, health and human services, the environment, public policy, and the arts in the communities it serves since Alexander Graham Bell founded the company over a century ago. Since 1984, AT&T has invested more than $600 million in support of education. Currently, more than half the company's contribution dollars, employee volunteer time, and community-service activities are directed toward education. Since 1911, AT&T has been a sponsor to the Telephone Pioneers of America, the world's largest industry-based volunteer organization consisting of nearly 750,000 employees and retirees from the telecommunications industry. Each year, the Pioneers volunteer millions of hours and raise millions of dollars for health and human services and the environment. In schools and neighborhoods, the Pioneers strengthen connections and build communities.

To respond to the high school drop-out crisis, AT&T launched Aspire, a $100 million philanthropic program that focuses on the crisis. It is the biggest and most significant investment in education in the company's history. The job shadowing program had reached more than 23,000 students in more than 200 cities. By summer of 2013, the program will provide 100,000 students with the opportunity to learn more about career options and what it takes to be successful in today's workforce.[15]

- At Merck & Co., Inc., the Patient Assistance Program makes the company's medicines available to low-income Americans and their families at no cost. When patients do not have health insurance or a prescription drug plan and are unable to afford the Merck medicines their doctors prescribe, they can work with their physicians to contact the Merck Patient Assistance Program. For more than 50 years, Merck has provided its medicines completely free of charge to people in need through this program. Patients can get information through www.merck.com; by calling a toll-free number, 1-800-727-5400; or from their physician's office. For eligible patients, the medicines are shipped directly to their home or the prescribing physician's office. Each applicant may receive up to one year of medicines, and patients may reapply to the program if their need continues.

Established in 1957, the Merck Company Foundation has contributed more than $560 million to develop and initiate programs that help improve the health and well-being of people around the world. According to Richard T. Clark, chairman, president, and CEO, "Merck established the Foundation more than 50 years ago because we knew that along with corporate success comes social responsibility."

Education programs often link social responsibility with corporate self-interest. For example, Bayer and Merck, two major pharmaceuticals firms, promote science education as a way to enlarge the pool of future employees. Students who visit the Bayer Science Forum in Elkhart, Indiana, work alongside scientists conducting a variety of experiments. Workshops created by the Merck Institute for Science Education show teachers how to put scientific principles into action through hands-on experiments.

These are just a few illustrations from the long list of companies, big and small, that attempt to behave in socially responsible ways. In general, people are more likely to want to work for and buy from such organizations.

THE EVOLUTION OF SOCIAL RESPONSIBILITY IN BUSINESS

 5 Describe how our current views on the social responsibility of business have evolved.

Business is far from perfect in many respects, but its record of social responsibility today is much better than that in past decades. In fact, present demands for social responsibility have their roots in outraged reactions to the abusive business practices of the early 1900s.

Historical Evolution of Business Social Responsibility

During the first quarter of the 20th century, businesses were free to operate pretty much as they chose. Government protection of workers and consumers was minimal. As a result, people either accepted what business had to offer or they did without. Working conditions often were deplorable by today's standards. The average workweek in most industries exceeded 60 hours, no minimum-wage law existed, and employee benefits were almost nonexistent. Work areas were crowded and unsafe, and industrial accidents were the rule rather than the exception. To improve working conditions, employees

Breaking away from fossil fuels. Today's consumers are more open to transportation alternatives, such as the electric car, because they are concerned about the negative impact of gasoline-run vehicles.

organized and joined labor unions. During the early 1900s, however, businesses—with the help of government—were able to use court orders, brute force, and even the few existing antitrust laws to defeat union attempts to improve working conditions.

During this period, consumers generally were subject to the doctrine of **caveat emptor**, a Latin phrase meaning "let the buyer beware." In other words, "what you see is what you get," and if it is not what you expected, too bad. Although victims of unscrupulous business practices could take legal action, going to court was very expensive, and consumers rarely won their cases. Moreover, no consumer groups or government agencies existed to publicize their consumers' grievances or to hold sellers accountable for their actions.

Before the 1930s, most people believed that competition and the action of the marketplace would, in time, correct abuses. Government, therefore, became involved in day-to-day business activities only in cases of obvious abuse of the free-market system. Six of the more important business-related federal laws passed between 1887 and 1914 are described in Table 2.2. As you can see, these laws were aimed more at encouraging competition than at correcting abuses, although two of them did deal with the purity of food and drug products.

The collapse of the stock market on October 29, 1929, triggered the Great Depression and years of dire economic problems for the United States. Factory production fell by almost half, and up to 25 percent of the nation's workforce was unemployed. Before long, public pressure mounted for the government to "do something" about the economy and about worsening social conditions.

Soon after Franklin D. Roosevelt became president in 1933, he instituted programs to restore the economy and improve social conditions. The government passed laws to correct what many viewed as the monopolistic abuses of big business, and provided various social services for individuals. These massive federal programs became the foundation for increased government involvement in the dealings between business and society.

As government involvement has increased, so has everyone's awareness of the social responsibility of business. Today's business owners are concerned about the return on their investment, but at the same time most of them demand ethical behavior from employees. In addition, employees demand better working conditions, and consumers want safe, reliable products. Various advocacy groups echo these concerns and also call for careful consideration of Earth's delicate ecological balance. Therefore, managers must operate in a complex business environment—one in which they are just as responsible for their managerial actions as for their actions as individual citizens. Interestingly, today's high-tech and Internet-based firms fare relatively well when it comes to environmental issues, worker conditions, the representation of minorities and women in upper management, animal testing, and charitable donations.

caveat emptor a Latin phrase meaning "let the buyer beware"

TABLE 2.2	Early Government Regulations that Affected American Business
	Six of the important business-related federal laws passed between 1887 and 1914 were aimed more at encouraging competition than at correcting abuses.

Government Regulation	Major Provisions
Interstate Commerce Act (1887)	First federal act to regulate business practices; provided regulation of railroads and shipping rates
Sherman Antitrust Act (1890)	Prevented monopolies or mergers where competition was endangered
Pure Food and Drug Act (1906)	Established limited supervision of interstate sales of food and drugs
Meat Inspection Act (1906)	Provided for limited supervision of interstate sales of meat and meat products
Federal Trade Commission Act (1914)	Created the Federal Trade Commission to investigate illegal trade practices
Clayton Antitrust Act (1914)	Eliminated many forms of price discrimination that gave large businesses a competitive advantage over smaller firms

TWO VIEWS OF SOCIAL RESPONSIBILITY

6 Explain the two views on the social responsibility of business and understand the arguments for and against increased social responsibility.

Government regulation and public awareness are *external* forces that have increased the social responsibility of business. However, business decisions are made within the firm—there, social responsibility begins with the attitude of management. Two contrasting philosophies, or models, define the range of management attitudes toward social responsibility.

The Economic Model

According to the traditional concept of business, a firm exists to produce quality goods and services, earn a reasonable profit, and provide jobs. In line with this concept, the **economic model of social responsibility** holds that society will benefit most when business is left alone to produce and market profitable products that society needs. The economic model has its origins in the 18th century, when businesses were owned primarily by entrepreneurs or owner-managers. Competition was vigorous among small firms, and short-run profits and survival were the primary concerns.

To the manager who adopts this traditional attitude, social responsibility is someone else's job. After all, stockholders invest in a corporation to earn a return on their investment, not because the firm is socially responsible, and the firm is legally obligated to act in the economic interest of its stockholders. Moreover, profitable firms pay federal, state, and local taxes that are used to meet the needs of society. Thus, managers who concentrate on profit believe that they fulfill their social responsibility indirectly through the taxes paid by their firms. As a result, social responsibility becomes the problem of the government, various environmental groups, charitable foundations, and similar organizations.

The Socioeconomic Model

In contrast, some managers believe that they have a responsibility not only to stockholders but also to customers, employees, suppliers, and the general public. This broader view is referred to as the **socioeconomic model of social responsibility**, which places emphasis not only on profits but also on the impact of business decisions on society.

Recently, increasing numbers of managers and firms have adopted the socioeconomic model, and they have done so for at least three reasons. First, business is dominated by the corporate form of ownership, and the corporation is a creation of society. If a corporation does not perform as a good citizen, society can and will demand changes. Second, many firms have begun to take pride in their social responsibility records, among them Starbucks Coffee, Hewlett-Packard, Colgate-Palmolive, and Coca-Cola. Each of these companies is a winner of a Corporate Conscience Award in the areas of environmental concern, responsiveness to employees, equal opportunity, and community involvement. Of course, many other corporations are much more socially responsible today than they were ten years ago. Third, many businesspeople believe that it is in their best interest to take the initiative in this area. The alternative may be legal action brought against the firm by some special-interest group; in such a situation, the firm may lose control of its activities.

The Pros and Cons of Social Responsibility

Business owners, managers, customers, and government officials have debated the pros and cons of the economic and socioeconomic models for years. Each side seems to have four major arguments to reinforce its viewpoint.

economic model of social responsibility the view that society will benefit most when business is left alone to produce and market profitable products that society needs

socioeconomic model of social responsibility the concept that business should emphasize not only profits but also the impact of its decisions on society

Arguments for Increased Social Responsibility Proponents of the socioeconomic model maintain that a business must do more than simply seek profits. To support their position, they offer the following arguments:

1. Because business is a part of our society, it cannot ignore social issues.
2. Business has the technical, financial, and managerial resources needed to tackle today's complex social issues.
3. By helping resolve social issues, business can create a more stable environment for long-term profitability.
4. Socially responsible decision making by firms can prevent increased government intervention, which would force businesses to do what they fail to do voluntarily.

These arguments are based on the assumption that a business has a responsibility not only to its stockholders but also to its customers, employees, suppliers, and the general public.

Arguments Against Increased Social Responsibility Opponents of the socioeconomic model argue that business should do what it does best: earn a profit by manufacturing and marketing products that people want. Those who support this position argue as follows:

1. Business managers are responsible primarily to stockholders, so management must be concerned with providing a return on owners' investments.
2. Corporate time, money, and talent should be used to maximize profits, not to solve society's problems.
3. Social problems affect society in general, so individual businesses should not be expected to solve these problems.
4. Social issues are the responsibility of government officials who are elected for that purpose and who are accountable to the voters for their decisions.

These arguments obviously are based on the assumption that the primary objective of business is to earn profits and that government and social institutions should deal with social problems.

Table 2.3 compares the economic and socioeconomic viewpoints in terms of business emphasis. Today, few firms are either purely economic or purely socioeconomic in outlook; most have chosen some middle ground between the two extremes. However, our society generally seems to want—and even to expect—some degree of social responsibility from business. Thus, within this middle ground, businesses are leaning toward the socioeconomic view. In the next several sections, we look at some results of this movement in four specific areas: consumerism, employment practices, concern for the environment, and implementation of social responsibility programs.

TABLE 2.3	A Comparison of the Economic and Socioeconomic Models of Social Responsibility as Implemented in Business	
Economic Model Primary Emphasis		**Socioeconomic Model Primary Emphasis**
1. Production		1. Quality of life
2. Exploitation of natural resources		2. Conservation of natural resources
3. Internal, market-based decisions	Middle ground	3. Market-based decisions, with some community controls
4. Economic return (profit)		4. Balance of economic return and social return
5. Firm's or manager's interest		5. Firm's and community's interests
6. Minor role for government		6. Active government

Source: Adapted from Keith Davis, William C. Frederick, and Robert L. Blomstron, *Business and Society: Concepts and Policy Issues* (New York: McGraw-Hill, 1980), 9. Used by permission of The McGraw-Hill Companies, Inc.

CONSUMERISM

7 Discuss the factors that led to the consumer movement and list some of its results.

Consumerism consists of all activities undertaken to protect the rights of consumers. The fundamental issues pursued by the consumer movement fall into three categories: environmental protection, product performance and safety, and information disclosure. Although consumerism has been with us to some extent since the early 19th century, the consumer movement became stronger in the 1960s. It was then that President John F. Kennedy declared that the consumer was entitled to a new "Bill of Rights."

The Six Basic Rights of Consumers

President Kennedy's Consumer Bill of Rights asserted that consumers have a right to safety, to be informed, to choose, and to be heard. Two additional rights added since 1975 are the right to consumer education and the right to courteous service. These six rights are the basis of much of the consumer-oriented legislation passed during the last 45 years. These rights also provide an effective outline of the objectives and accomplishments of the consumer movement.

The Right to Safety The consumers' right to safety means that the products they purchase must be safe for their intended use, must include thorough and explicit directions for proper use, and must be tested by the manufacturer to ensure product quality and reliability. There are several reasons why American business firms must be concerned about product safety.

Corrective Actions Can Be Expensive. Federal agencies, such as the Food and Drug Administration and the Consumer Product Safety Commission, have the power to force businesses that make or sell defective products to take corrective actions. Such actions include offering refunds, recalling defective products, issuing public warnings, and reimbursing consumers—all of which can be expensive.

Increasing Number of Lawsuits. Business firms also should be aware that consumers and the government have been winning an increasing number of product-liability lawsuits against sellers of defective products. Moreover, the amount of the awards in these suits has been increasing steadily. Fearing the outcome of numerous lawsuits filed around the nation, tobacco giants Philip Morris and R. J. Reynolds, which for decades had denied that cigarettes cause illness, began negotiating in 1997 with state attorneys general, plaintiffs' lawyers, and antismoking activists. The tobacco giants proposed sweeping curbs on their sales and advertising practices and the payment of hundreds of billions of dollars in compensation.

Consumer Demand. Yet another major reason for improving product safety is consumers' demand for safe products. People simply will stop buying a product they believe is unsafe or unreliable.

The Right to Be Informed The right to be informed means that consumers must have access to complete information about a product before they buy it. Detailed information about ingredients and nutrition must be provided on food containers, information about fabrics and laundering methods must be attached to clothing,

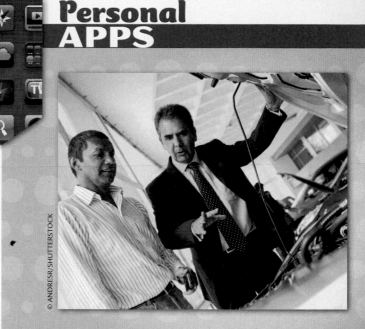

© VJOM/SHUTTERSTOCK

© ANDRESR/SHUTTERSTOCK

Personal APPS

Keep these consumer rights in mind when you shop around for goods or services, buy something, or have a problem with a purchase. You're entitled to be informed, to have choices, to be heard, to buy safe products, to have responsive service, and to know your rights.

consumerism all activities undertaken to protect the rights of consumers and lenders must disclose the true cost of borrowing the money they make available to customers who purchase merchandise on credit.

In addition, manufacturers must inform consumers about the potential dangers of using their products. Manufacturers that fail to provide such information can be held responsible for personal injuries suffered because of their products. For example, Maytag provides customers with a lengthy booklet that describes how they should use an automatic clothes washer. Sometimes such warnings seem excessive, but they are necessary if user injuries (and resulting lawsuits) are to be avoided.

The right to safety. The Consumer Bill of Rights asserts consumers' basic rights. The right to safety means that products must be safe for their intended use and must be tested by the processor to ensure product quality and safety.

© PICSFIVE/SHUTTERSTOCK

The Right to Choose The right to choose means that consumers must have a choice of products, offered by different manufacturers and sellers, to satisfy a particular need. The government has done its part by encouraging competition through antitrust legislation. The greater the competition, the greater is the choice available to consumers.

Competition and the resulting freedom of choice provide additional benefits for customers by reducing prices. For example, when personal computers were introduced, they cost more than $5,000. Thanks to intense competition and technological advancements, personal computers today can be purchased for less than $500.

The Right to Be Heard This fourth right means that someone will listen and take appropriate action when customers complain. Actually, management began to listen to consumers after World War II, when competition between businesses that manufactured and sold consumer goods increased. One way that firms got a competitive edge was to listen to consumers and provide the products they said they wanted and needed. Today, businesses are listening even more attentively, and many larger firms have consumer relations departments that can be contacted easily via toll-free telephone numbers. Other groups listen, too. Most large cities and some states have consumer affairs offices to act on citizens' complaints.

Additional Consumer Rights In 1975, President Gerald Ford added to the Consumer Bill of Rights the right to consumer education, which entitles people to be fully informed about their rights as consumers. In 1994, President Bill Clinton added a sixth right, the right to service, which entitles consumers to convenience, courtesy, and responsiveness from manufacturers and sellers of consumer products.

Major Consumerism Forces

The major forces in consumerism are individual consumer advocates and organizations, consumer education programs, and consumer laws. Consumer advocates, such as Ralph Nader, take it on themselves to protect the rights of consumers. They band together into consumer organizations, either independently or under government sponsorship. Some organizations, such as the National Consumers' League and the Consumer Federation of America, operate nationally, whereas others are active at state and local levels. They inform and organize other consumers, raise issues, help businesses to develop consumer-oriented programs, and pressure lawmakers to enact consumer protection laws. Some consumer advocates and organizations encourage consumers to boycott products and businesses to which they have objections. Today, the consumer movement has adopted corporate-style marketing and addresses a broad range of issues. Current campaigns include efforts (1) to curtail the use of animals for

Ethical
SUCCESS OR FAILURE?

Is Personal Data *Really* Private?

Nearly everything you do online—from the Web sites you visit to the Facebook pages you "like"—is being tracked by a business. Advertisers want to know about your activities so they can show you appropriate online ads; retailers want to know what you buy so they can send you targeted e-mails and catalogs. But are your personal details really private?

Although privacy policies are supposed to explain which details each Web site collects and who will have access to your private data, these policies may not tell the whole story. After Facebook changed its privacy policy and then reset users' privacy controls on its own, the Federal Trade Commission charged the firm with making "deceptive privacy claims." Users believed their personal details were private, yet advertisers and others were allowed access. Now, in a settlement with the FTC, Facebook has tightened its privacy controls, and its privacy program must be monitored for the next 20 years to ensure compliance. The FTC also thinks Internet users should be able to opt out of online tracking if they choose. Meanwhile, millions of individuals have already installed anti-tracking software such as Ghostery and Do Not Track Plus for added online privacy.

Sources: Based on information in Byron Acohido, "Consumers Turn to Do-Not-Track Software to Maintain Privacy," *USA Today*, December 29, 2011, www.usatoday.com; Joel Stein, "Your Data, Yourself," *Time*, March 21, 2011, pp. 40-46; Fahmida Y. Rashid, "Facebook Settles FTC Charges about Privacy Policy Changes, Misleading Users," *EWeek*, November 29, 2011, www.eweek.com.

testing purposes, (2) to reduce liquor and cigarette billboard advertising in low-income, inner-city neighborhoods, and (3) to encourage recycling.

Educating consumers to make wiser purchasing decisions is perhaps one of the most far-reaching aspects of consumerism. Increasingly, consumer education is becoming a part of high school and college curricula and adult-education programs. These programs cover many topics—for instance, what major factors should be considered when buying specific products, such as insurance, real estate, automobiles, appliances and furniture, clothes, and food; the provisions of certain consumer-protection laws; and the sources of information that can help individuals become knowledgeable consumers.

Major advances in consumerism have come through federal legislation. Some laws enacted in the last 50 years to protect your rights as a consumer are listed and described in Table 2.4.

Here is the 2009 list of proposed legislation to protect consumers and investors:[16]

- Accountability and Transparency in Rating Agencies Act of 2009
- Consumer Financial Protection Agency Act of 2009
- Corporate and Financial Institution Compensation Fairness Act of 2009
- Credit Risk Retention Act of 2009
- Dissolution Authority for Large, Interconnected Financial Companies Act of 2009
- Federal Insurance Office Act of 2009
- Financial Stability Improvement Act of 2009
- Investor Protection Act of 2009
- Over-the-Counter Derivatives Markets Act of 2009
- Private Fund Investment Advisers Registration Act of 2009

Most businesspeople now realize that they ignore consumer issues only at their own peril. Managers know that improper handling of consumer complaints can result in lost sales, bad publicity, and lawsuits.

TABLE 2.4   Major Federal Legislation Protecting Consumers Since 1960

Legislation	Major Provisions
Federal Hazardous Substances Labeling Act (1960)	Required warning labels on household chemicals if they were highly toxic
Kefauver–Harris Drug Amendments (1962)	Established testing practices for drugs and required manufacturers to label drugs with generic names in addition to trade names
Cigarette Labeling Act (1965)	Required manufacturers to place standard warning labels on all cigarette packages and advertising
Fair Packaging and Labeling Act (1966)	Called for all products sold across state lines to be labeled with net weight, ingredients, and manufacturer's name and address
Motor Vehicle Safety Act (1966)	Established standards for safer cars
Truth in Lending Act (1968)	Required lenders and credit merchants to disclose the full cost of finance charges in both dollars and annual percentage rates
Credit Card Liability Act (1970)	Limited credit-card holder's liability to $50 per card and stopped credit-card companies from issuing unsolicited cards
Fair Credit Reporting Act (1971)	Required credit bureaus to provide credit reports to consumers regarding their own credit files; also provided for correction of incorrect information
Consumer Product Safety Commission Act (1972)	Established an abbreviated procedure for registering certain generic drugs
Fair Credit Billing Act (1974)	Amended the Truth in Lending Act to enable consumers to challenge billing errors
Equal Credit Opportunity Act (1974)	Provided equal credit opportunities for males and females and for married and single individuals
Magnuson–Moss Warranty–Federal Trade Commission Act (1975)	Provided for minimum disclosure standards for written consumer-product warranties for products that cost more than $15
Amendments to the Equal Credit Opportunity Act (1976, 1994)	Prevented discrimination based on race, creed, color, religion, age, and income when granting credit
Fair Debt Collection Practices Act (1977)	Outlawed abusive collection practices by third parties
Nutrition Labeling and Education Act (1990)	Required the Food and Drug Administration to review current food labeling and packaging focusing on nutrition label content, label format, ingredient labeling, food descriptors and standards, and health messages
Telephone Consumer Protection Act (1991)	Prohibited the use of automated dialing and prerecorded-voice calling equipment to make calls or deliver messages
Consumer Credit Reporting Reform Act (1997)	Placed more responsibility for accurate credit data on credit issuers; required creditors to verify that disputed data are accurate and to notify a consumer before reinstating the data
Children's Online Privacy Protection Act (2000)	Placed parents in control over what information is collected online from their children younger than 13 years; required commercial Web site operators to maintain the confidentiality, security, and integrity of personal information collected from children
Do Not Call Implementation Act (2003)	Directed the FCC and the FTC to coordinate so that their rules are consistent regarding telemarketing call practices including the Do Not Call Registry and other lists, as well as call abandonment
Credit Card Accountability, Responsibility, and Disclosure Act (2009)	Provided the most sweeping changes in credit card protections since the Truth in Lending Act of 1968
Dodd–Frank Wall Street Reform and Consumer Protection Act of 2010	Promoted the financial stability of the United States by improving accountability and responsibility in the financial system; established a new Consumer Financial Protection Agency to regulate home mortgages, car loans, and credit cards; became Public Law on July 21, 2010

EMPLOYMENT PRACTICES

8 Analyze how present employment practices are being used to counteract past abuses.

Managers who subscribe to the socioeconomic view of a business's social responsibility, together with significant government legislation enacted to protect the buying public, have broadened the rights of consumers. The last five decades have seen similar progress in affirming the rights of employees to equal treatment in the workplace.

Everyone should have the opportunity to land a job for which he or she is qualified and to be rewarded on the basis of ability and performance. This is an important issue for society, and it also makes good business sense. Yet, over the years, this opportunity has been denied to members of various minority groups. A **minority** is a racial, religious, political, national, or other group regarded as different from the larger group of which it is a part and that is often singled out for unfavorable treatment.

The federal government responded to the outcry of minority groups during the 1960s and 1970s by passing a number of laws forbidding discrimination in the workplace. (These laws are discussed in Chapter 9 in the context of human resources management.) Now, almost 50 years after passage of the first of these (the Civil Rights Act of 1964), abuses still exist. An example is the disparity in income levels for whites, blacks, Hispanics, and Asians, as illustrated in Figure 2.3. Lower incomes and higher unemployment rates also characterize Native Americans, handicapped persons, and women. Responsible managers have instituted a number of programs to counteract the results of discrimination.

Affirmative Action Programs

An **affirmative action program** is a plan designed to increase the number of minority employees at all levels within an organization. Employers with federal contracts of more than $50,000 per year must have written affirmative action plans. The objective of such programs is to ensure that minorities are represented within the organization in approximately the same proportion as in the surrounding community. If 25 percent of the electricians in a geographic area in which a company is located are African-Americans,

---

FIGURE 2.3 Comparative Income Levels

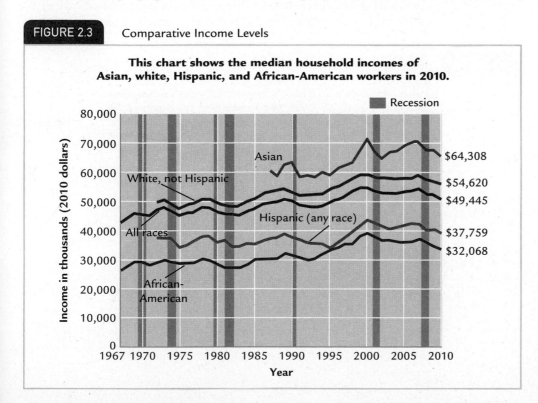

This chart shows the median household incomes of Asian, white, Hispanic, and African-American workers in 2010.

Source: U.S. Census Bureau, Current Population Survey, 1968 to 2010 Annual Social and Economic Supplements, *Income, Poverty, and Health Insurance Coverage in the United States: 2010*, issued September 2011, U.S. Census Bureau, U.S. Department of Commerce, 8, www.census.gov/prod/2011pubs/p60-239pdf (accessed March 4, 2012).

minority a racial, religious, political, national, or other group regarded as different from the larger group of which it is a part and that is often singled out for unfavorable treatment

affirmative action program a plan designed to increase the number of minority employees at all levels within an organization

Meet Sam's Club president and CEO. In early 2012, Rosalind Brewer became the first African-American woman to hold a CEO position at one of the company's business units.

then approximately 25 percent of the electricians it employs also should be African-Americans. Affirmative action plans encompass all areas of human resources management: recruiting, hiring, training, promotion, and pay.

Unfortunately, affirmative action programs have been plagued by two problems. The first involves quotas. In the beginning, many firms pledged to recruit and hire a certain number of minority members by a specific date. To achieve this goal, they were forced to consider only minority applicants for job openings; if they hired nonminority workers, they would be defeating their own purpose. However, the courts have ruled that such quotas are unconstitutional even though their purpose is commendable. They are, in fact, a form of discrimination called *reverse discrimination*.

The second problem is that although most such programs have been reasonably successful, not all businesspeople are in favor of affirmative action programs. Managers not committed to these programs can "play the game" and still discriminate against workers. To help solve this problem, Congress created (and later strengthened) the **Equal Employment Opportunity Commission (EEOC)**, a government agency with the power to investigate complaints of employment discrimination and sue firms that practice it.

The threat of legal action has persuaded some corporations to amend their hiring and promotional policies, but the discrepancy between men's and women's salaries still exists, as illustrated in Figure 2.4. For more than 50 years, women have consistently earned only about 77 cents for each dollar earned by men.

Training Programs for the Hard-Core Unemployed

For some firms, social responsibility extends far beyond placing a help-wanted advertisement in the local newspaper. These firms have assumed the task of helping the **hard-core unemployed**, workers with little education or vocational training and a long history of unemployment. For example, a few years ago, General Mills helped establish Siyeza, a frozen soul-food processing plant in North Minneapolis. Through the years, Siyeza has provided stable, high-quality full-time jobs for a permanent core of 80 unemployed or underemployed minority inner-city residents. In addition, groups of up

Equal Employment Opportunity Commission (EEOC) a government agency with the power to investigate complaints of employment discrimination and the power to sue firms that practice it

hard-core unemployed workers with little education or vocational training and a long history of unemployment

| FIGURE 2.4 | Relative Earnings of Male and Female Workers |

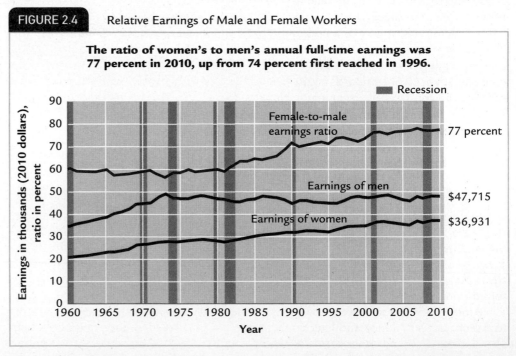

Source: U.S. Census Bureau, Current Population Survey, 1960 to 2010 Annual Social and Economic Supplements, *Income, Poverty, and Health Insurance Coverage in the United States: 2010,* issued September 2011, U.S. Census Bureau, U.S. Department of Commerce, 12, www.census.gov/prod/2011pubs/p60-239.pdf (accessed March 4, 2012).

to 100 temporary employees are called in when needed. In the past, such workers often were turned down routinely by personnel managers, even for the most menial jobs.

Obviously, such workers require training; just as obviously, this training can be expensive and time-consuming. To share the costs, business and community leaders have joined together in a number of cooperative programs. One particularly successful partnership is the **National Alliance of Business (NAB)**, a joint business–government program to train the hard-core unemployed. The alliance's 5,000 members include companies of all sizes and industries, their CEOs and senior executives, as well as educators and community leaders. NAB, founded in 1968 by President Lyndon Johnson and Henry Ford II, is a major national business organization focusing on education and workforce issues.

CONCERN FOR THE ENVIRONMENT

 Describe the major types of pollution, their causes, and their cures.

The social consciousness of responsible business managers, the encouragement of a concerned government, and an increasing concern on the part of the public have led to a major effort to reduce environmental pollution, conserve natural resources, and reverse some of the worst effects of past negligence in this area. **Pollution** is the contamination of water, air, or land through the actions of people in an industrialized society. For several decades, environmentalists have been warning us about the dangers of industrial pollution. Unfortunately, business and government leaders either ignored the problem or were not concerned about it until pollution became a threat to life and health in America. Today, Americans expect business and government leaders to take swift action to clean up our environment—and to keep it clean.

Effects of Environmental Legislation

As in other areas of concern to our society, legislation and regulations play a crucial role in pollution control. The laws outlined in Table 2.5 reflect the scope of current environmental legislation: laws to promote clean air, clean water, and even quiet work and living environments. Of major importance was the creation of the Environmental Protection Agency (EPA), the federal agency charged with enforcing laws designed to protect the environment.

When they are aware of a pollution problem, many firms respond to it rather than wait to be cited by the EPA. Other owners and managers, however, take the position that environmental standards are too strict. (Loosely translated, this means that compliance with present standards is too expensive.) Consequently, it often has been necessary for the EPA to take legal action to force firms to install antipollution equipment and to clean up waste storage areas.

Experience has shown that the combination of environmental legislation, voluntary compliance, and EPA action can succeed in cleaning up the environment and keeping it clean. However, much still remains to be done.

Water Pollution The Clean Water Act has been credited with greatly improving the condition of the waters in the United States. This success comes largely from the control of pollutant discharges from industrial and wastewater treatment plants. Although the quality of our nation's rivers, lakes, and streams has improved significantly in recent years, many of these surface waters remain severely polluted. Currently, one of the most serious water-quality problems results from the high level of toxic pollutants found in these waters.

Among the serious threats to people posed by water pollutants are respiratory irritation, cancer, kidney and liver damage, anemia, and heart failure. Toxic pollutants also damage fish and other forms of wildlife. In fish, they cause tumors or reproductive problems; shellfish and wildlife living in or drinking from toxin-laden waters also have suffered genetic defects. Recently, the Pollution Control Board of Kerala in India

National Alliance of Business (NAB) a joint business–government program to train the hard-core unemployed

pollution the contamination of water, air, or land through the actions of people in an industrialized society

TABLE 2.5   Summary of Major Environmental Laws

Legislation	Major Provisions
National Environmental Policy Act (1970)	Established the Environmental Protection Agency (EPA) to enforce federal laws that involve the environment
Clean Air Amendment (1970)	Provided stringent automotive, aircraft, and factory emission standards
Water Quality Improvement Act (1970)	Strengthened existing water pollution regulations and provided for large monetary fines against violators
Resource Recovery Act (1970)	Enlarged the solid-waste disposal program and provided for enforcement by the EPA
Water Pollution Control Act Amendment (1972)	Established standards for cleaning navigable streams and lakes and eliminating all harmful waste disposal by 1985
Noise Control Act (1972)	Established standards for major sources of noise and required the EPA to advise the Federal Aviation Administration on standards for airplanes
Clean Air Act Amendment (1977)	Established new deadlines for cleaning up polluted areas; also required review of existing air-quality standards
Resource Conservation and Recovery Act (1984)	Amended the original 1976 act and required federal regulation of potentially dangerous solid-waste disposal
Clean Air Act Amendment (1987)	Established a national air-quality standard for ozone
Oil Pollution Act (1990)	Expanded the nation's oil-spill prevention and response activities; also established the Oil Spill Liability Trust Fund
Clean Air Act Amendments (1990)	Required that motor vehicles be equipped with onboard systems to control about 90 percent of refueling vapors
Food Quality Protection Act (1996)	Amended the Federal Insecticide, Fungicide and Rodenticide Act and the Federal Food Drug and Cosmetic Act; the requirements included a new safety standard—reasonable certainty of no harm—that must be applied to all pesticides used on foods
American Recovery and Reinvestment Act (2009)	Provided $7.22 billion to the EPA to protect and promote "green" jobs and a healthier environment

© CENGAGE LEARNING 2014

ordered Coca-Cola to close its major bottling plant. For years, villagers in the nearby areas had accused Coke of depleting local groundwater and producing other local pollution. The village council president said, "We are happy that the government is finally giving justice to the people who are affected by the plant."

One of the worst environmental disasters in 2010 was the explosion of the *Deepwater Horizon*, during which 11 people died. The British Petroleum (BP) catastrophe led to an oil spill in the Gulf of Mexico that contaminated a vast area of the United States marine environment. It caused a serious impact on wildlife, the local fishing industry, and regional tourism. British Petroleum was held liable for property damaged by the oil spill and the cleanup efforts; loss of income or earning capacity; loss of income to boat owners, hotel owners, and restaurant owners; removal and cleanup costs of property; and claims of bodily injury caused by the spill. Under the settlement in early 2012, British Petroleum expected to pay out $7.8 billion to settle the claims.

The task of water cleanup has proved to be extremely complicated and costly because of pollution runoff and toxic contamination. Yet, improved water quality is not only necessary, it is also achievable. Consider Cleveland's Cuyahoga River. A few years ago, the river was so contaminated by industrial wastes that it burst into flames one hot summer day! Now, after a sustained community cleanup effort, the river is pure enough for fish to thrive in.

Another serious issue is acid rain, which is contributing significantly to the deterioration of coastal waters, lakes, and marine life in the eastern United States. Acid rain forms when sulfur emitted by smokestacks in industrialized areas combines with moisture in the atmosphere to form acids that are spread by winds. The acids eventually fall to Earth in rain, which finds its way into streams, rivers, and lakes. The acid-rain problem has spread rapidly in recent years, and experts fear that the situation will worsen if the nation begins to burn more coal to generate electricity. To solve the problem, investigators first must determine where the sulfur is being emitted. The costs of this vital investigation and cleanup are going to be high. The human costs of having ignored the problem so long may be higher still.

Air Pollution Aviation emissions are a potentially significant and growing percentage of greenhouse gases that contribute to global warming. Aircraft emissions are significant for several reasons. First, jet aircraft are the main source of human emissions deposited directly into the upper atmosphere, where they may have a greater warming effect than if they were released at Earth's surface. Second, carbon dioxide—the primary aircraft emission—is the main focus of international concern. For example, it survives in the atmosphere for nearly 100 years and contributes to global warming, according to the Intergovernmental Panel on Climate Change. The carbon dioxide emissions from worldwide aviation roughly equal those of some industrialized countries. Third, carbon dioxide emissions combined with other gases and particles emitted by jet aircraft could have two to four times as great an effect on the atmosphere as carbon dioxide alone. Fourth, the Intergovernmental Panel recently concluded that the rise in aviation emissions owing to the growing demand for air travel would not be fully offset by reductions in emissions achieved solely through technological improvements.

Usually, two or three factors combine to form air pollution in any given location. The first factor is large amounts of carbon monoxide and hydrocarbons emitted by motor vehicles concentrated in a relatively small area. The second is the smoke and other pollutants emitted by manufacturing facilities. These two factors can be eliminated in part through pollution control devices on cars, trucks, and smokestacks.

A third factor that contributes to air pollution—one that cannot be changed—is the combination of weather and geography. The Los Angeles Basin, for example, combines just the right weather and geographic conditions for creating dense smog. Los Angeles has strict regulations regarding air pollution. Even so, Los Angeles still struggles with air pollution problems because of uncontrollable conditions.

How effective is air pollution control? The EPA estimates that the Clean Air Act and its amendments will eventually result in the removal of 56 billion pounds of pollution from the air each year, thus measurably reducing lung disease, cancer, and other serious health problems caused by air pollution. Other authorities note that we have already seen improvement in air quality. A number of cities have cleaner air today than they did 30 years ago. Even in southern California, bad air-quality days have dropped to less than 40 days a year, about 60 percent lower than that observed just a decade ago. Numerous chemical companies have recognized that

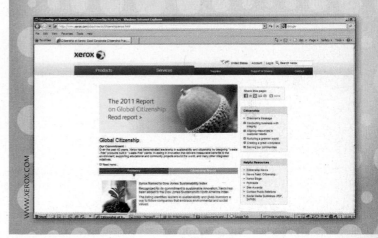

Sustaining the PLANET

Social Responsibility at Xerox

Over the past 40 years, Xerox has demonstrated leadership in sustainability and corporate citizenship by designing waste-free products built in waste-free plants, investing in innovations that benefit the environment, supporting community projects, and many other initiatives. Take a look at its 2011 Report on Global Citizenship, which details its environmental sustainability initiatives, corporate donations, volunteerism and more.

www.xerox.com/about-xerox/citizenship/enus.html

WWW.XEROX.COM

Worsening water and land pollution problem. Land pollution is still a serious problem in many parts of the country. It is not just the manufacturers and service businesses that produce millions of tons of waste! We, the individuals in the United States, contribute to the waste-disposal problem, too.

they must take responsibility for operating their plants in an environmentally safe manner; some now devote considerable capital to purchasing antipollution devices. For example, 3M's pioneering Pollution Prevention Pays (3P) program, designed to find ways to avoid the generation of pollutants, marked its 30th anniversary in 2005. Since 1975, more than 5,600 employee-driven 3P projects have prevented the generation of more than 2.2 billion pounds of pollutants and produced first-year savings of nearly $1 billion.

Land Pollution Air and water quality may be improving, but land pollution is still a serious problem in many areas. The fundamental issues are (1) how to restore damaged or contaminated land at a reasonable cost and (2) how to protect unpolluted land from future damage.

The land pollution problem has been worsening over the past few years because modern technology has continued to produce increasing amounts of chemical and radioactive waste. U.S. manufacturers produce an estimated 40 to 60 million tons of contaminated oil, solvents, acids, and sludge each year. Service businesses, utility companies, hospitals, and other industries also dump vast amounts of wastes into the environment.

Individuals in the United States contribute to the waste-disposal problem, too. A shortage of landfills, owing to stricter regulations, makes garbage disposal a serious problem in some areas. Incinerators help to solve the landfill-shortage problem, but they bring with them their own problems. They reduce the amount of garbage but also leave tons of ash to be buried—ash that often has a higher concentration of toxicity than the original garbage. Other causes of land pollution include strip mining of coal, nonselective cutting of forests, and development of agricultural land for housing and industry.

To help pay the enormous costs of cleaning up land polluted with chemicals and toxic wastes, Congress created a $1.6 billion Superfund in 1980. Originally, money was to flow into the Superfund from a tax paid by 800 oil and chemical companies that produce toxic waste. The EPA was to use the money in the Superfund to finance the cleanup of hazardous waste sites across the nation. To replenish the Superfund, the EPA had two options: It could sue companies guilty of dumping chemicals at specific waste sites, or it could negotiate with guilty companies and thus completely avoid the legal system. During the 1980s, officials at the EPA came under fire because they preferred negotiated settlements. Critics referred to these settlements as "sweetheart deals" with industry. They felt that the EPA should be much more aggressive in reducing land pollution. Of course, most corporate executives believe that cleanup efficiency and quality might be improved if companies were more involved in the process. Many firms, including Delphi Automotive Systems Corporation and 3M, have modified or halted the production and sale of products that have a negative impact on the environment. For example, after tests showed that ScotchGard™ does not decompose in the environment, 3M announced a voluntary end to production of the 40-year-old product, which had generated $300 million in sales.

Noise Pollution Excessive noise caused by traffic, aircraft, and machinery can do physical harm to human beings. Research has shown that people who are exposed to loud noises for long periods of time can suffer permanent hearing loss. The Noise Control Act of 1972 established noise emission standards for aircraft and airports, railroads, and interstate motor carriers. The act also provided funding for noise research at state and local levels.

Noise levels can be reduced by two methods. The source of noise pollution can be isolated as much as possible. (Thus, many metropolitan airports are located outside the cities.) Engineers can also modify machinery and equipment to reduce noise levels. If it is impossible to reduce industrial noise to acceptable levels, workers should be required to wear earplugs to guard them against permanent hearing damage.

Who Should Pay for a Clean Environment?

Governments and businesses are spending billions of dollars annually to reduce pollution—more than $45 billion to control air pollution, $33 billion to control water pollution, and $12 billion to treat hazardous wastes. To make matters worse, much of the money required to purify the environment is supposed to come from already depressed industries, such as the chemical industry. A few firms have discovered that it is cheaper to pay a fine than to install expensive equipment for pollution control.

Who, then, will pay for the environmental cleanup? Many business leaders offer one answer—tax money should be used to cleanup the environment and to keep it clean. They reason that business is not the only source of pollution, so business should not be forced to absorb the entire cost of the cleanup. Environmentalists disagree. They believe that the cost of proper treatment and disposal of industrial wastes is an expense of doing business. In either case, consumers probably will pay a large part of the cost—either as taxes or in the form of higher prices for goods and services.

IMPLEMENTING A PROGRAM OF SOCIAL RESPONSIBILITY

 Identify the steps a business must take to implement a program of social responsibility.

A firm's decision to be socially responsible is a step in the right direction—but only the first step. The firm then must develop and implement a program to reach this goal. The program will be affected by the firm's size, financial resources, past record in the area of social responsibility, and competition. Above all, however, the program must have the firm's total commitment or it will fail.

Developing a Program of Social Responsibility

An effective program for social responsibility takes time, money, and organization. In most cases, developing and implementing such a program will require four steps:

securing the commitment of top executives, planning, appointing a director, and preparing a social audit.

Commitment of Top Executives Without the support of top executives, any program will soon falter and become ineffective. For example, the Boeing Company's Ethics and Business Conduct Committee is responsible for the ethics program. The committee is appointed by the Boeing board of directors, and its members include the company chairman and CEO, the president and chief operating officer, the presidents of the operating groups, and senior vice presidents. As evidence of their commitment to social responsibility, top managers should develop a policy statement that outlines key areas of concern. This statement sets a tone of positive support and later will serve as a guide for other employees as they become involved in the program.

Planning Next, a committee of managers should be appointed to plan the program. Whatever form their plan takes, it should deal with each of the issues described in the top managers' policy statement. If necessary, outside consultants can be hired to help develop the plan.

Appointment of a Director After the social responsibility plan is established, a top-level executive should be appointed to implement the organization's plan. This individual should be charged with recommending specific policies and helping individual departments to understand and live up to the social responsibilities the firm has assumed. Depending on the size of the firm, the director may require a staff to handle the program on a day-to-day basis. For example, at the Boeing Company, the director of ethics and business conduct administers the ethics and business conduct program.

The Social Audit At specified intervals, the program director should prepare a social audit for the firm. A **social audit** is a comprehensive report of what an organization has done and is doing with regard to social issues that affect it. This document provides the information the firm needs to evaluate and revise its social responsibility program. Typical subject areas include human resources, community involvement, the quality and safety of products, business practices, and efforts to reduce pollution and improve the environment. The information included in a social audit should be as accurate and as quantitative as possible, and the audit should reveal both positive and negative aspects of the program.

Today, many companies listen to concerned individuals within and outside the company. For example, the Boeing Ethics Line listens to and acts on concerns expressed by employees and others about possible violations of company policies, laws, or regulations, such as improper or unethical business practices, as well as health, safety, and environmental issues. Employees are encouraged to communicate their concerns, as well as ask questions about ethical issues. The Ethics Line is available to all Boeing employees, including Boeing subsidiaries. It is also available to concerned individuals outside the company.

Funding the Program

We have noted that social responsibility costs money. Thus, just like any other corporate undertaking, a program to improve social responsibility must be funded. Funding can come from three sources:

1. Management can pass the cost on to consumers in the form of higher prices.
2. The corporation may be forced to absorb the cost of the program if, for example, the competitive situation does not permit a price increase. In this case, the cost is treated as a business expense, and profit is reduced.
3. The federal government may pay for all or part of the cost through tax reductions or other incentives.

social audit a comprehensive report of what an organization has done and is doing with regard to social issues that affect it

Panera Cares

Panera Cares is very much like every other Panera bakery-café, offering the same seasonal menu, the same fresh-baked bread, and the same comfortable ambiance. At Panera Cares, however, customers pay what they can afford. A mother with a toddler in tow may donate $5 for a pastry while a homeless person pays nothing for the same type of pastry. It's Panera's way of doing something for local communities, and it's starting to catch on.

Panera Cares must receive 80 percent of the suggested funding level to continue as a viable venture. Some of the cafés consistently achieve that level, while others fall short on some days. As word spreads and more customers understand what Panera is trying to achieve, the cafés are building a loyal and generous following. "The lesson here is that most people are fundamentally good," notes Panera's founder. "People step up and they do the right thing."

Questions

1. How does Panera Cares fit into the socioeconomic model of social responsibility?
2. What ethical issues are raised by the idea of expecting some people to pay more for a Panera meal so that others can pay less?

SUMMARY

Looking for Success?
Get Flashcard, Quizzes, Games, and more
@ www.cengagebrain.com

 Understand what is meant by *business ethics.*

Ethics is the study of right and wrong and of the morality of choices. Business ethics is the application of moral standards to business situations.

 Identify the types of ethical concerns that arise in the business world.

Ethical issues arise often in business situations out of relationships with investors, customers, employees, creditors, or competitors. Businesspeople should make every effort to be fair, to consider the welfare of customers and others within the firm, to avoid conflicts of interest, and to communicate honestly.

3 **Discuss the factors that affect the level of ethical behavior in organizations.**

Individual, social, and opportunity factors all affect the level of ethical behavior in an organization. Individual factors include knowledge level, moral values and attitudes, and personal goals. Social factors include cultural norms and the actions and values of co-workers and significant others. Opportunity factors refer to the amount of leeway that exists in an organization for employees to behave unethically if they choose to do so.

 Explain how ethical decision making can be encouraged.

Governments, trade associations, and individual firms can establish guidelines for defining ethical behavior. Governments can pass stricter regulations. Trade associations provide ethical guidelines for their members. Companies provide codes of ethics—written guides to acceptable and ethical behavior as defined by an organization—and create an atmosphere in which ethical behavior is encouraged. An ethical employee working in an unethical environment may resort to whistle-blowing to bring a questionable practice to light.

 Describe how our current views on the social responsibility of business have evolved.

In a socially responsible business, management realizes that its activities have an impact on society and considers that impact in the decision-making process. Before the 1930s, workers, consumers, and government had very little influence on business activities; as a result, business leaders gave little thought to social responsibility. All this changed with the Great Depression. Government regulations, employee demands, and consumer awareness combined to create a demand that businesses act in socially responsible ways.

 Explain the two views on the social responsibility of business and understand the arguments for and against increased social responsibility.

The basic premise of the economic model of social responsibility is that society benefits most when business is left alone to produce profitable goods and services.

According to the socioeconomic model, business has as much responsibility to society as it has to its owners. Most managers adopt a viewpoint somewhere between these two extremes.

 Discuss the factors that led to the consumer movement and list some of its results.

Consumerism consists of all activities undertaken to protect the rights of consumers. The consumer movement generally has demanded—and received—attention from business in the areas of product safety, product information, product choices through competition, and the resolution of complaints about products and business practices. Although concerns over consumer rights have been around to some extent since the early 19th century, the movement became more powerful in the 1960s when President John F. Kennedy initiated the Consumer Bill of Rights. The six basic rights of consumers include the right to safety, the right to be informed, the right to choose, the right to be heard, and the rights to consumer education and courteous service.

 Analyze how present employment practices are being used to counteract past abuses.

Legislation and public demand have prompted some businesses to correct past abuses in employment practices—mainly with regard to minority groups. Affirmative action and training of the hard-core unemployed are two types of programs that have been used successfully.

 Describe the major types of pollution, their causes, and their cures.

Industry has contributed to noise pollution and pollution of our land and water through the dumping of wastes, and to air pollution through vehicle and smokestack emissions. This contamination can be cleaned up and controlled, but the big question is: Who will pay? Present cleanup efforts are funded partly by government tax revenues, partly by business, and in the long run by consumers.

 Identify the steps a business must take to implement a program of social responsibility.

A program to implement social responsibility in a business begins with total commitment by top management. The program should be planned carefully, and a capable director should be appointed to implement it. Social audits should be prepared periodically as a means of evaluating and revising the program. Programs may be funded through price increases, reduction of profit, or federal incentives.

KEY TERMS

You should now be able to define and give an example relevant to each of the following terms:

ethics (37)
business ethics (37)
Sarbanes–Oxley Act of 2002 (41)
code of ethics (41)
whistle-blowing (42)

social responsibility (44)
caveat emptor (48)
economic model of social responsibility (49)
socioeconomic model of social responsibility (49)

consumerism (51)
minority (55)
affirmative action program (55)
Equal Employment Opportunity Commission (EEOC) (56)

hard-core unemployed (56)
National Alliance of Business (NAB) (57)
pollution (57)
social audit (62)

REVIEW QUESTIONS

1. Why might an individual with high ethical standards act less ethically in business than in his or her personal life?
2. How would an organizational code of ethics help to ensure ethical business behavior?
3. How and why did the American business environment change after the Great Depression?
4. What are the major differences between the economic model of social responsibility and the socioeconomic model?
5. What are the arguments for and against increasing the social responsibility of business?
6. Describe and give an example of each of the six basic rights of consumers.

7. There are more women than men in the United States. Why, then, are women considered a minority with regard to employment?
8. What is the goal of affirmative action programs? How is this goal achieved?
9. What is the primary function of the Equal Employment Opportunity Commission?
10. How do businesses contribute to each of the four forms of pollution? How can they avoid polluting the environment?
11. Our environment can be cleaned up and kept clean. Why haven't we simply done so?
12. Describe the steps involved in developing a social responsibility program within a large corporation.

1. When a company acts in an ethically questionable manner, what types of problems are caused for the organization and its customers?
2. How can an employee take an ethical stand regarding a business decision when his or her superior already has taken a different position?
3. Overall, would it be more profitable for a business to follow the economic model or the socioeconomic model of social responsibility?

4. Why should business take on the task of training the hard-core unemployed?
5. To what extent should the blame for vehicular air pollution be shared by manufacturers, consumers, and government?
6. Why is there so much government regulation involving social responsibility issues? Should there be less?

Video Case 2.1

Scholfield Honda—Going Green with Honda

Signs of green marketing can be found everywhere today: reusable shopping bags are the rule rather than the exception, organic and natural products fill grocers' shelves, and socially responsible companies are increasing their efforts to reduce pollution, conserve water and energy, and recycle waste paper, plastic, and other reusable materials.

Of course, some companies have always been ahead of the curve. Since the early 1970s, Honda has been producing the low-emissions, fuel-efficient Civic model, and the company has never strayed from its roots. Today's Honda line consists of four classes of vehicles: Good, Better, Best, and Ultimate. Its regular gas cars are Good, with about 30 mpg; hybrids are Better at about 45 mpg; and its Best solution is a natural gas-powered Civic GX, which gets about 220 miles to a tank. Honda also has Ultimate solutions in the works, such as the new Honda FCX Clarity—a hydrogen fuel-cell car that uses hydrogen and oxygen to create electricity. Although the Civic GX and Clarity models are available to consumers, neither vehicle is practical for the average driver as fueling stations are scarce.

Alternative energy vehicles are making their way to the Midwest. Lee Lindquist, an alternative fuels specialist at Scholfield Honda in Wichita, Kansas, was researching alternative fuel vehicles for a local Sierra Club meeting when he learned that municipalities in New York and California used the natural gas Civic GX to address air-quality issues. Although Lee recognized that his own Wichita market was not teeming with green consumers, he knew that people needed ways to combat rising fuel prices—so he proposed the Civic GX for use at his dealership.

Lee's boss was skeptical of the idea. Although management was open to clever ways to promote the dealership, owner Roger Scholfield did not want to risk muddying the waters with a new and somewhat impractical vehicle. Nevertheless, he agreed to offer the car to his fleet and corporate customers, and in time fate offered another opportunity for Scholfield Honda to go green.

In May 2007, a devastating tornado hit the nearby town of Greensburg, Kansas, leveling the area. Once again Lee Lindquist approached his boss. This time, he proposed donating both a Honda Civic GX and a natural-gas fueling station to Greensburg as a way of helping the town rebuild. Upon careful reflection, Roger realized that Lee's idea would benefit his dealership through good publicity and higher awareness of alternative fuel vehicles. Scholfield made the Civic model and fuel station available to Greensburg residents free of charge, and the dealership has been on the green bandwagon ever since.

Although there are more cost-effective ways of advertising, Roger Scholfield notes that customers are becoming more interested in alternative fuel vehicles since he donated the Civic GX. In addition, his dealership has generated plenty of goodwill in the press and among local residents—Scholfield Honda has developed a good reputation for its commitment to the environment and the people of Greensburg, even opening a "Honda Green Zone" conference room on the premises. The room can hold several hundred people. It includes a digital projector, sound system, and kitchenette and is available free to local firms and organizations for meetings and conferences. Its chairs, tables, tiles, and flooring are all made from recycled materials.[17]

Questions

1. How would you rate Scholfield Honda's sense of social responsibility? Does the dealership meet all the criteria for a socially responsible company?
2. What is Scholfield Honda's primary ethical responsibility in situations where a proposed green initiative is cost-prohibitive or even detrimental to the company's bottom line?
3. Should the government regulate companies' claims that their products are green? Should official classifications for environmental friendliness be defined?

Can a corporate giant build its business on the basis of being green and clean? By 2020, Unilever aims to double its revenues while cutting its environmental footprint in half and educating one billion people about how to live healthier lives. Although these are aggressive goals, the Anglo-Dutch company has considerable resources available to implement its plans. Unilever rings up $62 billion in annual sales of a wide range of foods, household cleaners, and personal care products under such well-known brands as Axe, Ben & Jerry's, Dove, Lipton, Lifebuoy, Skippy, Suave, and Surf. It has 170,000 employees and operates in 100 countries, with more than half of its revenues coming from developing nations. Every day, all over the world, 2 billion people use one (or more) of its products.

Unilever's managers see great profit potential in actively managing the environmental and social impacts of its products to meet the needs of consumers in all markets and at all income levels. "We are advocating a business model that gives to the environment and society," explains CEO Paul Polman. "That is the essence of sustainable growth."

Before setting specific green and clean goals, Unilever's managers spent years studying the eco-effects of its products and talking with customers, suppliers, government officials, and non-profit specialists about population growth, natural resources, and human health. They set up programs to develop and test efficient, eco-friendly ways of manufacturing products and obtaining raw materials. They also took a close look at how they might address challenges such as providing clean drinking water for billions of people and preventing the spread of disease.

Out of this research came a comprehensive plan called the Unilever Sustainable Living Plan. It included a detailed timeline for dramatically reducing Unilever's energy and water usage, getting raw materials from sustainable sources, and slashing emissions and waste. As one example, the company set a deadline for obtaining all of its palm oil from certified sustainable sources (and achieved that goal three years early). Meanwhile, Unilever's product development experts began devising new products to address common consumer needs in earth-friendly ways. For example, for areas where water is scarce, they developed a shampoo to be used without water and laundry products that clean with a single rinse.

Unilever's research also pointed to the need for educating consumers about simple steps they can take to stay healthy, such as washing their hands. The company found that the first step is to explain why people should take a particular action (wash with soap to stop disease from spreading). Next, show them how easy it is to take action (by buying and using soap), outline the benefits (keeping families safe from germs), and make them feel good about taking action (to keep family members healthy). Finally, encourage people to continue this action over and over again (for example, by reminding children to wash before meals). Following these five steps, Unilever has already educated 35 million people in developing nations about the benefits of washing hands—while promoting the company's Lifebuoy soap brand at the same time.

In the process of moving toward its sustainability goals, Unilever has developed tools and techniques that it is now sharing with other companies and with suppliers. Its free, downloadable Cool Farm Tool, for instance, enables farmers to calculate the level of greenhouse gas emissions from their farming and livestock activities. Using this calculation as a baseline, farmers can then experiment with different ways of reducing emissions while improving agricultural yield. This is yet another way that the company's plan "can unleash innovation which will help us grow," says the head of Unilever's business in India.[18]

Questions

1. Every year, Unilever posts on its web site and distributes to the media a report detailing its progress toward the 2020 sustainability goals. Why would the public be interested in such a report?
2. Is Unilever applying the economic or the socioeconomic model of social responsibility? How do you know?
3. Do you agree with Unilever's approach of promoting its Lifebuoy soap brand in programs to teach consumers about handwashing? Explain your answer.

Building Skills for Career Success

① SOCIAL MEDIA EXERCISE

In 2010, Pepsi decided to develop a new social media–based project, called Pepsi Refresh Project, aimed at Millennials and allowing consumers to post ideas for improving their communities. This replaced the $20 million they spent on Superbowl advertising. The project received more than 57 million votes. However, the general consensus was this was not a successful program for Pepsi. Using the Internet for research, answer the following questions:

1. Why do you think the Pepsi Refresh Project was not as successful as the company hoped?
2. Do you think this is a good example of corporate social responsibility (CSR)? Why or why not?
3. How does this CSR example for Pepsi compare with that of its main rival Coca-Cola (see www.thecoca-colacompany.com/citizenship/index.html)?

② JOURNALING FOR SUCCESS

Discovery statement: This chapter was devoted mostly to business ethics, ethical concerns that arise in the business world, personal ethics, and social responsibility of business.

Assume that you are an accountant at ABC Corporation, where you question the company's accounting practices. What legal and managerial changes would you suggest to prevent the use of accounting tricks to manipulate corporate earnings?

Assignment

1. Assume that your manager refuses to incorporate any of your suggestions. Would you blow the whistle? Why or why not?
2. Suppose that you blow the whistle and get fired. Which law might protect your rights, and how would you proceed to protect yourself?

③ DEVELOPING CRITICAL-THINKING SKILLS

Recently, an article entitled "Employees Coming to Terms with Moral Issues on the Job" appeared in a big-city newspaper. It posed the following situations:

- You are asked to work on a project you find morally wrong.
- Important tasks are left undone because a co-worker spends more time planning a social event than working on a proposal.
- Your company is knowingly selling defective merchandise to customers.

Unfortunately, many employees currently are struggling with such issues. The moral dilemmas that arise when employees find their own ethical values incompatible with the work they do every day are causing a lot of stress in the workplace, and furthermore, these dilemmas are not being discussed. There exists an ethics gap. You already may have faced a similar situation in your workplace.

Assignment

1. In small groups with your classmates, discuss your answers to the following questions:
   a. If you were faced with any of the preceding situations, what would you do?
   b. Would you complete work you found morally unacceptable, or would you leave it undone and say nothing?
   c. If you spoke up, what would happen to you or your career? What would be the risk?
   d. What are your options?

   e. If you were a manager rather than a lower-level employee, would you feel differently and take a different approach to the issue? Why?
2. In a written report, summarize what you learned from this discussion.

④ BUILDING TEAM SKILLS

A firm's code of ethics outlines the kinds of behaviors expected within the organization and serves as a guideline for encouraging ethical behavior in the workplace. It reflects the rights of the firm's workers, shareholders, and consumers.

Assignment

1. Working in a team of four, find a code of ethics for a business firm. Start the search by asking firms in your community for a copy of their codes, by visiting the library, or by searching and downloading information from the Internet.
2. Analyze the code of ethics you have chosen, and answer the following questions:
   a. What does the company's code of ethics say about the rights of its workers, shareholders, consumers, and suppliers? How does the code reflect the company's attitude toward competitors?
   b. How does this code of ethics resemble the information discussed in this chapter? How does it differ?
   c. As an employee of this company, how would you personally interpret the code of ethics? How might the code influence your behavior within the workplace? Give several examples.

⑤ RESEARCHING DIFFERENT CAREERS

Business ethics has been at the heart of many discussions over the years and continues to trouble employees and shareholders. Stories about dishonesty and wrongful behavior in the workplace appear on a regular basis in newspapers and on the national news.

Assignment

Prepare a written report on the following:

1. Why can it be so difficult for people to do what is right?
2. What is your personal code of ethics? Prepare a code outlining what you believe is morally right. The document should include guidelines for your personal behavior.
3. How will your code of ethics affect your decisions about:
   a. The types of questions you should ask in a job interview?
   b. Selecting a company in which to work?

ENDNOTES

1. Sources: Based on information in Peter Korn, "A Gentle Nudge Helps Panera Cares Fulfill Mission, Get Paid," *Portland Tribune (OR)*, December 29, 2011, www.portlandtribune.com; Peter Korn, "Panera Lets People Pay What They Can," *Portland Tribune (OR)*, April 21, 2011, www.portlandtribune.com; Sarah Skidmore, "Panera Opens Pay-What-You-Wish Location in Oregon," *Associated Press*, January 12, 2011, http://abcnews.go.com; "Year Later, Pay-What-You-Want Panera a Success," *Cleveland Plain Dealer*, May 16, 2011, www.cleveland.com.
2. Official John Rigas Web site, johnrigas.com/AdelphiaLitigation.html (accessed April 24, 2012), www.time.com/time/specials/packages/articles/0,288 (accessed

April 24, 2012), and the U.S. Department of Justice Web site at www.justice.gov/usao/pam/news/2012/Rigas_01_25 (accessed April 24, 2012).
3. The U.S. Department of Justice Web site at www.justice.gov/opa/pr/2001/October/513civ.htm, and www.justice.gov/opa/pr/2003/June/03_civ_371.htm (accessed April 24, 2012).
4. The U.S. Department of Justice Web site at www.usdoj.gov (accessed April 20, 2012).
5. *Frontlines* (Washington, DC: U.S. Agency for International Development, September 2005), 16.

6. Deere & Company Corporate Governance—Code of Ethics Web site at http://search.deere.com/DDC/en_US/?query=business+conduct (accessed February 6, 2012).

7. U.S. Securities and Exchange Commission Web site at www.sec.gov/litigation/litre-leases/2009/lr211129.htm (accessed April 5, 2010).

8. The Politico Web site at www.politico.com/news/stories/0310/3410/34105.html (accessed April 17, 2010).

9. The General Mills Web site at www.generalmills.com/Responsibility/Community_ (accessed February 5, 2012).

10. The Michael and Susan Dell Foundation Web site at www.msdf.org/about-us (accessed March 1, 2012).

11. The IBM Web site at www.ibm.com/ibm/responsibility/corporateservicecorps/progr (accessed March 6, 2012).

12. GE *Press Release*, January 19, 2011, www.genewscenter.com/content/detail.aspx? (accessed March 6, 2012).

13. The Charles Schwab Foundation Web site at www.aboutschwab.com/about/over-view/charles_schwab/ (accessed March 4, 2012).

14. The ExxonMobil Web site at www.exxonmobil.com/Corporate/community_women.aspx (accessed February 29, 2012).

15. The AT&T Web site at www.att.com/gen/corporate-citizenship?pid=17884 (accessed March 1, 2012).

16. Wall Street Reform and Consumer Protection Act of 2010, www.govtrack.us/congress/bill.xpd?bill=h111-4173 (accessed March 9, 2011).

17. www.sholfieldhonda.com (accessed May 13, 2010); Adam Knapp, "Scholfield Honda Trying to Turn Green Movement into Good Business," *Wichita Business Journal*, http://wichita.bizjournals.com, March 7, 2008, and information provided through inter-views with Scholfield Honda personnel and in the video "Scholfield Honda."

18. Based on information in Namrata Singh, "Unilever Reports on First Year's Progress Against Sustainable Living Plan Targets," *Times of India*, April 24, 2012, http://timeso-findia.indiatimes.com; Loulla-Mae Eleftheriou-Smith, "Unilever to Mark Sustainability Efforts Through Corporate Campaign," *Marketing*, April 25, 2012, www.marketing-magazine.co.uk; Ian Quinn, "Unilever Shares Cool Farm Emissions Tool," *Grocer*, March 17, 2012, p. 11; Louise Lucas, "Changing Lives," *Financial Times*, March 20, 2012, www.ft.com; Louise Jack, "Unilever CEO Paul Polman on the Packaged Goods Giant's Creative Shift," *Fast Company*, January 12, 2012, www.fastcocreate.com; www.unilever.com.

Exploring Global Business

3

LEARNING OBJECTIVES

Once you complete this chapter, you will be able to:

1. Explain the economic basis for international business.

2. Discuss the restrictions nations place on international trade, the objectives of these restrictions, and their results.

3. Outline the extent of international business and the world economic outlook for trade.

4. Discuss international trade agreements and international economic organizations working to foster trade.

5. Define the methods by which a firm can organize for and enter into international markets.

6. Describe the various sources of export assistance.

7. Identify the institutions that help firms and nations finance international business.

Volkswagen Speeds Along on Global Sales

Volkswagen is shifting into high gear to become the world's largest and most profitable automaker by 2018. The company, based in Germany, sells vehicles in 150 nations under many brands, including Audi, Bentley, Bugatti, Lamborghini, Porsche, Scania, Seat, Skoda, and Volkswagen. Although Volkswagen is strongest on its home continent of Europe, it's been steering toward higher sales in Asia and the Americas for years.

Nearly 30 years ago, Volkswagen was among the first major automakers to do business in China. It has joined forces with two local partners, SAIC and FAW, to build and market cars all around the country. Originally, the cars Volkswagen made with its Chinese partners were no-frills, low-price models. Now, in addition to these basic cars, Volkswagen is introducing larger, more stylish (and more profitable) cars designed especially for China, such as the VW Lavida.

Volkswagen imports some of its cars from Germany and makes some in its new high-tech factory in Chattanooga, Tennessee. Having most of the parts supplied by United States–based companies or German firms with U.S. divisions allows Volkswagen to keep costs down, so it can price its made-in-America cars more competitively. Having a strong U.S. presence will help Volkswagen achieve its goal of becoming the industry leader by 2018, despite aggressive moves by U.S. rivals such as General Motors and global rivals such as Toyota and Hyundai. "You have to be successful in the United States if you want to be the number one in the industry," says Volkswagen's chief executive officer. "Trends are set in America, not just for consumer behavior but also for communication technology, computers, and software."

Sales are also growing in South America, where Volkswagen operates eight factories to make the compact Gol car, a popular line of minibuses, and other vehicles. The firm has an engine factory and an assembly plant in Mexico, as well, as part of its long-term plan to increase production and boost sales in both North and South America.

Two factors that might slow Volkswagen's drive for global growth are economic uncertainties and intense competition. Can the company continue accelerating toward higher sales?[1]

Volkswagen is just one of a growing number of foreign companies, large and small, that are doing business with firms in other countries. Some companies, such as Coca-Cola, sell to firms in other countries; others, such as Pier 1 Imports, buy goods around the world to import into the United States. Whether they buy or sell products across national borders, these companies are all contributing to the volume of international trade that is fueling the global economy.

Theoretically, international trade is every bit as logical and worthwhile as interstate trade between, say, California and Washington. Yet, nations tend to restrict the import of certain goods for a variety of reasons. For example, in the early 2000s, the United States restricted the import of Mexican fresh tomatoes because they were undercutting price levels of domestic fresh tomatoes.

Despite such restrictions, international trade has increased almost steadily since World War II. Many of the industrialized nations have signed trade agreements intended to eliminate problems in international business and to help less-developed nations participate in world trade. Individual firms around the world have seized the opportunity to compete in foreign markets by exporting products and increasing foreign production, as well as by other means.

Signing the Trade Act of 2002, President George W. Bush remarked, "Trade is an important source of good jobs for our workers and a source of higher growth for our economy. Free trade is also a proven strategy for building global prosperity and adding to the momentum of political freedom. Trade is an engine of economic growth. In our lifetime, trade has helped lift millions of people and whole nations out of poverty and put them on the path of prosperity."[2] In his national best seller, *The World Is Flat,* Thomas L. Friedman states, "The flattening of the world has presented us with new opportunities, new challenges, new partners but, also, alas new dangers, particularly as Americans it is imperative that we be the best global citizens that we can be—because in a flat world, if you don't visit a bad neighborhood, it might visit you."

We describe international trade in this chapter in terms of modern specialization, whereby each country trades the surplus goods and services it produces most efficiently for products in short supply. We also explain the restrictions nations place on products and services from other countries and present some of the possible advantages and disadvantages of these restrictions. We then describe the extent of international trade and identify the organizations working to foster it. We describe several methods of entering international markets and the various sources of export assistance available from the federal government. Finally, we identify some of the institutions that provide the complex financing necessary for modern international trade.

THE BASIS FOR INTERNATIONAL BUSINESS

 Explain the economic basis for international business.

International business encompasses all business activities that involve exchanges across national boundaries. Thus, a firm is engaged in international business when it buys some portion of its input from, or sells some portion of its output to, an organization located in a foreign country. (A small retail store may sell goods produced in some other country. However, because it purchases these goods from American distributors, it is not engaged in international trade.)

Absolute and Comparative Advantage

Some countries are better equipped than others to produce particular goods or services. The reason may be a country's natural resources, its labor supply, or even customs or a historical accident. Such a country would be best off if it could specialize in the production of such products so that it can produce them most efficiently. The country could use what it needed of these products and then trade the surplus for products it could not produce efficiently on its own.

Saudi Arabia thus has specialized in the production of crude oil and petroleum products; South Africa, in diamonds; and Australia, in wool. Each of these countries is said to have an absolute advantage with regard to a particular product. An **absolute advantage** is the ability to produce a specific product more efficiently than any other nation.

One country may have an absolute advantage with regard to several products, whereas another country may have no absolute advantage at all. Yet it is still worthwhile for these two countries to specialize and trade with each other. To see why this is so, imagine that you are the president of a successful manufacturing firm and that you can accurately type 90 words per minute. Your assistant can type 80 words per minute but would run the business poorly. Thus, you have an absolute advantage over your assistant in both typing and managing. However, you cannot afford to type your own letters because your time is better spent in managing the business. That is, you have a **comparative advantage** in managing. A comparative advantage is the ability to produce a specific product more efficiently than any other product.

international business all business activities that involve exchanges across national boundaries

absolute advantage the ability to produce a specific product more efficiently than any other nation

comparative advantage the ability to produce a specific product more efficiently than any other product

© KLETR/SHUTTERSTOCK

Exploiting an American advantage. The United States has long specialized in the production of wheat. Because of its natural resource, the United States and some other countries enjoy an absolute advantage— their ability to produce wheat more efficiently than countries in other parts of the world.

Your assistant, on the other hand, has a comparative advantage in typing because he or she can do that better than managing the business. Thus, you spend your time managing, and you leave the typing to your assistant. Overall, the business is run as efficiently as possible because you are each working in accordance with your own comparative advantage.

The same is true for nations. Goods and services are produced more efficiently when each country specializes in the products for which it has a comparative advantage. Moreover, by definition, every country has a comparative advantage in some product. The United States has many comparative advantages—in research and development, high-technology industries, and identifying new markets, for instance.

Exporting and Importing

Suppose that the United States specializes in producing corn. It then will produce a surplus of corn, but perhaps it will have a shortage of wine. France, on the other hand, specializes in producing wine but experiences a shortage of corn. To satisfy both needs—for corn and for wine—the two countries should trade with each other. The United States should export corn and import wine. France should export wine and import corn.

Exporting is selling and shipping raw materials or products to other nations. The Boeing Company, for example, exports its airplanes to a number of countries for use by their airlines. Figure 3.1 shows the top ten merchandise-exporting states in this country.

Importing is purchasing raw materials or products in other nations and bringing them into one's own country. Thus, buyers for Macy's department stores may purchase rugs in India or raincoats in England and have them shipped back to the United States for resale.

exporting selling and shipping raw materials or products to other nations

importing purchasing raw materials or products in other nations and bringing them into one's own country

FIGURE 3.1   The Top Ten Merchandise-Exporting States

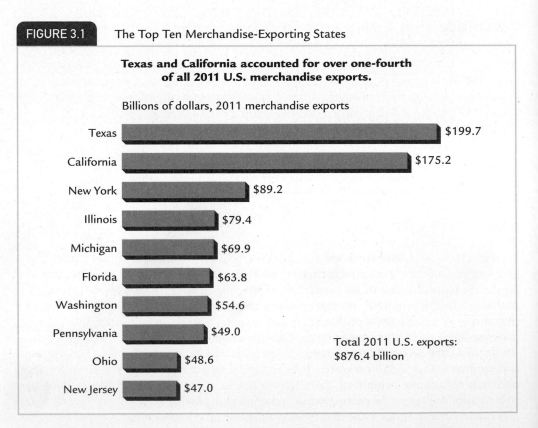

Texas and California accounted for over one-fourth of all 2011 U.S. merchandise exports.

Billions of dollars, 2011 merchandise exports

State	
Texas	$199.7
California	$175.2
New York	$89.2
Illinois	$79.4
Michigan	$69.9
Florida	$63.8
Washington	$54.6
Pennsylvania	$49.0
Ohio	$48.6
New Jersey	$47.0

Total 2011 U.S. exports: $876.4 billion

Source: www.census.gov/foreign-trade/statistics/state/zip/2011/12/zipstate.pdf (accessed March 7, 2012).

FIGURE 3.2   U.S. International Trade in Goods and Services

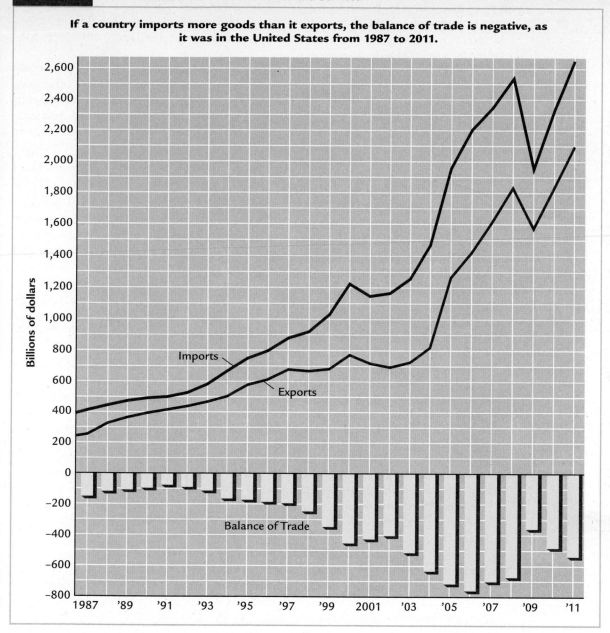

If a country imports more goods than it exports, the balance of trade is negative, as it was in the United States from 1987 to 2011.

Source: U.S. Department of Commerce, International Trade Administration, U.S. Bureau of Economic Analysis, www.census.gov/foreign-trade/Press-Release/curent_press_release/ft900.pdf (accessed March 8, 2012).

Importing and exporting are the principal activities in international trade. They give rise to an important concept called the *balance of trade*. A nation's **balance of trade** is the total value of its exports minus the total value of its imports over some period of time. If a country imports more than it exports, its balance of trade is negative and is said to be *unfavorable*. (A negative balance of trade is unfavorable because the country must export money to pay for its excess imports.)

In 2011, the United States imported $2,661 billion worth of goods and services and exported $2,103 billion worth. It thus had a trade deficit of $558 billion. A **trade deficit** is a negative balance of trade (see Figure 3.2). However, the United States has consistently enjoyed a large and rapidly growing surplus in services. For example, in 2011, the United States imported $426 billion worth of services and exported $605 billion worth, thus creating a favorable balance of $179 billion.[3]

balance of trade the total value of a nation's exports minus the total value of its imports over some period of time

trade deficit a negative balance of trade

Career SUCCESS

Want to Work Overseas? Get Ready Now!

If you'd like to work abroad for part or all of your career, start now to prepare for a successful experience by:

- *Focusing.* Which region or country do you want to work in—and why? Focusing will help you organize your job search and research the business environment in your chosen area.
- *Thinking global.* Broaden your perspective by learning more about international events as well as political trends, economic issues, and social influences in the area where you want to work.
- *Sharpening your skills.* Potential employers "will be especially interested in your language skills, either languages you already speak or your willingness and ability to learn quickly," says one expert. What other skills can you polish to show overseas employers?

- *Networking.* Talk with the professionals in your school's career office and with others who may be able to offer ideas or suggest leads to follow in locating potential jobs.

Although landing a job abroad takes time and effort, it's a worthwhile investment in your future. "Global experience is becoming more important and more valuable in the workplace," advises a human resources consultant, "and it can give employees an advantage when it comes to long-term career development."

Sources: Based on information in Anne Fisher, "Can You Get Hired for a Job Overseas?" *Fortune*, October 21, 2011, www.fortune.com; Michael Morella, "How to Find a Job Abroad," *U.S. News & World Report*, November 22, 2010, http://usnews.com/money; Michelle Goodman, "How to Find Work Outside the U.S.," ABC News, May 20, 2010, www.abcnews.go.com; Eve Tahmincioglu, "In Tough Market, Some Job Seekers Look Abroad," MSNBC, March 29, 2010, www.msnbc.msn.com.

Question: *Are trade deficits bad?*

Answer: In testimony before the Senate Finance Committee, Daniel T. Griswold, associate director of the Center for Trade Policy at the Cato Institute, remarked, "The trade deficit is not a sign of economic distress, but of rising domestic demand and investment. Imposing new trade barriers will only make Americans worse off while leaving the trade deficit virtually unchanged."

On the other hand, when a country exports more than it imports, it is said to have a favorable balance of trade. This has consistently been the case for Japan over the last two decades or so.

A nation's **balance of payments** is the total flow of money into a country minus the total flow of money out of that country over some period of time. Balance of payments, therefore, is a much broader concept than balance of trade. It includes imports and exports, of course. However, it also includes investments, money spent by foreign tourists, payments by foreign governments, aid to foreign governments, and all other receipts and payments.

A continual deficit in a nation's balance of payments (a negative balance) can cause other nations to lose confidence in that nation's economy. Alternatively, a continual surplus may indicate that the country encourages exports but limits imports by imposing trade restrictions.

Discuss the restrictions nations place on international trade, the objectives of these restrictions, and their results. ②

balance of payments the total flow of money into a country minus the total flow of money out of that country over some period of time

RESTRICTIONS TO INTERNATIONAL BUSINESS

Specialization and international trade can result in the efficient production of want-satisfying goods and services on a worldwide basis. As we have noted, international business generally is increasing. Yet the nations of the world continue to erect barriers to free trade. They do so for reasons ranging from internal political and economic pressures to simple mistrust of other nations. We examine first the types of restrictions that are applied and then the arguments for and against trade restrictions.

Types of Trade Restrictions

Nations generally are eager to export their products. They want to provide markets for their industries and to develop a favorable balance of trade. Hence, most trade restrictions are applied to imports from other nations.

Tariffs Perhaps the most commonly applied trade restriction is the customs (or import) duty. An **import duty** (also called a **tariff**) is a tax levied on a particular foreign product entering a country. For example, the United States imposes a 2.2 percent import duty on fresh Chilean tomatoes, an 8.7 percent duty if tomatoes are dried and packaged, and nearly 12 percent if tomatoes are made into ketchup or salsa. The two types of tariffs are revenue tariffs and protective tariffs; both have the effect of raising the price of the product in the importing nations, but for different reasons. *Revenue tariffs* are imposed solely to generate income for the government. For example, the United States imposes a duty on Scotch whiskey solely for revenue purposes. *Protective tariffs*, on the other hand, are imposed to protect a domestic industry from competition by keeping the price of competing imports level with or higher than the price of similar domestic products. Because fewer units of the product will be sold at the increased price, fewer units will be imported. The French and Japanese agricultural sectors would both shrink drastically if their nations abolished the protective tariffs that keep the price of imported farm products high. Today, U.S. tariffs are the lowest in history, with average tariff rates on all imports under 3 percent.

Some countries rationalize their protectionist policies as a way of offsetting an international trade practice called *dumping*. **Dumping** is the exportation of large quantities of a product at a price lower than that of the same product in the home market.

Thus, dumping drives down the price of the domestic item. Recently, for example, the Pencil Makers Association, which represents eight U.S. pencil manufacturers, charged that low-priced pencils from Thailand and the People's Republic of China were being sold in the United States at less than fair value prices. Unable to compete with these inexpensive imports, several domestic manufacturers had to shut down. To protect themselves, domestic manufacturers can obtain an antidumping duty through the government to offset the advantage of the foreign product. Recently, for example, the U.S. Department of Commerce imposed antidumping duties of up to 99 percent on a variety of steel products imported from China, following allegations by U.S. Steel Corp. and other producers that the products were being dumped at unfair prices.

Nontariff Barriers A **nontariff barrier** is a nontax measure imposed by a government to favor domestic over foreign suppliers. Nontariff barriers create obstacles to the marketing of foreign goods in a country and increase costs for exporters. The following are a few examples of government-imposed nontariff barriers:

- An **import quota** is a limit on the amount of a particular good that may be imported into a country during a given period of time. The limit may be set in terms of either quantity (so many pounds of beef) or value (so many dollars' worth of shoes). Quotas also may be set on individual products imported from specific countries. Once an import quota has been reached, imports are halted until the specified time has elapsed.
- An **embargo** is a complete halt to trading with a particular nation or of a particular product. The embargo is used most often as a political weapon. At present, the United States has import embargoes against Iran and North Korea—both as a result of extremely poor political relations.

import duty (tariff) a tax levied on a particular foreign product entering a country

dumping exportation of large quantities of a product at a price lower than that of the same product in the home market

nontariff barrier a nontax measure imposed by a government to favor domestic over foreign suppliers

import quota a limit on the amount of a particular good that may be imported into a country during a given period of time

embargo a complete halt to trading with a particular nation or in a particular product

Restricting the trade: The Russian style. In early 2012, Russian foreign minister Sergey Lavrov speaks at a news conference in Moscow, Russia. Mr. Lavrov threatens that Moscow will not abide by its World Trade Organization's commitments in trade with the United States unless it scraps a Cold War trade law.

Personal APPS

PARTS CONTENT INFORMATION

FOR VEHICLES IN THIS CARLINE:
U.S./CANADIAN PARTS CONTENT: 82%

NOTE: PARTS CONTENT DOES NOT INCLUDE FINAL
ASSEMBLY, DISTRIBUTION, OR OTHER NON-PARTS COSTS.

FOR THIS VEHICLE:
FINAL ASSEMBLY POINT:
WENTZVILLE, MO   U.S.A.
COUNTRY OF ORIGIN:
ENGINE: UNITED STATES
TRANSMISSION: MEXICO

ORDER NO ODGFM2   SALES CODE E
SALES MODEL CODE TG13405
DEALER NO 06149
FINAL ASSEMBLY:
WENTZVILLE, MO   U.S.A.

VIN 1GTS7AFX2C1148938

DEALER TO WHOM DELIVERED
SUDBAY CHEVROLET-BUICK-CADILLAC-GMC, INC.
88 CAUSEWAY ST
GLOUCESTER, MA 01930-2132

What's your reaction when you see "Made in America" on a pickup truck? Would your reaction be the same if the truck had been made elsewhere? Clearly, cultural attitudes can influence how people feel about goods in the global marketplace.

- A **foreign-exchange control** is a restriction on the amount of a particular foreign currency that can be purchased or sold. By limiting the amount of foreign currency importers can obtain, a government limits the amount of goods importers can purchase with that currency. This has the effect of limiting imports from the country whose foreign exchange is being controlled.
- A nation can increase or decrease the value of its money relative to the currency of other nations. **Currency devaluation** is the reduction of the value of a nation's currency relative to the currencies of other countries.

Devaluation increases the cost of foreign goods, whereas it decreases the cost of domestic goods to foreign firms. For example, suppose that the British pound is worth $2. In this case, an American-made $2,000 computer can be purchased for £1,000. However, if the United Kingdom devalues the pound so that it is worth only $1, that same computer will cost £2,000. The increased cost, in pounds, will reduce the import of American computers—and all foreign goods—into England.

On the other hand, before devaluation, a £500 set of English bone china will cost an American $1,000. After the devaluation, the set of china will cost only $500. The decreased cost will make the china—and all English goods—much more attractive to U.S. purchasers. Bureaucratic red tape is more subtle than the other forms of nontariff barriers. Yet it can be the most frustrating trade barrier of all. A few examples are the unnecessarily restrictive application of standards and complex requirements related to product testing, labeling, and certification.

Cultural Barriers Another type of nontariff barrier is related to cultural attitudes. Cultural barriers can impede acceptance of products in foreign countries. For example, illustrations of feet are regarded as despicable in Thailand. Even so simple a thing as the color of a product or its package can present a problem. In Japan, black and white are the colors of mourning, so they should not be used in packaging. In Brazil, purple is the color of death. And in Egypt, green is never used on a package because it is the national color. When customers are unfamiliar with particular products from another country, their general perceptions of the country itself affect their attitude toward the product and help to determine whether they will buy it. Because Mexican cars have not been viewed by the world as being quality products, Volkswagen, for example, may not want to advertise that some of its models sold in the United States are made in Mexico. Many retailers on the Internet have yet to come to grips with the task of designing an online shopping site that is attractive and functional for all global customers.

Gifts to authorities—sometimes quite large ones—may be standard business procedure in some countries. In others, including the United States, they are called bribes or payoffs and are strictly illegal.

Reasons for Trade Restrictions

Various reasons are given for trade restrictions either on the import of specific products or on trade with particular countries. We have noted that political considerations usually are involved in trade embargoes. Other frequently cited reasons for restricting trade include the following:

- *To equalize a nation's balance of payments.* This may be considered necessary to restore confidence in the country's monetary system and in its ability to repay its debts.

foreign-exchange control a restriction on the amount of a particular foreign currency that can be purchased or sold

currency devaluation the reduction of the value of a nation's currency relative to the currencies of other countries

- *To protect new or weak industries.* A new, or infant, industry may not be strong enough to withstand foreign competition. Temporary trade restrictions may be used to give it a chance to grow and become self-sufficient. The problem is that once an industry is protected from foreign competition, it may refuse to grow, and "temporary" trade restrictions will become permanent. For example, a recent report by the Government Accountability Office (GAO), the congressional investigative agency, has accused the federal government of routinely imposing quotas on foreign textiles without "demonstrating the threat of serious damage" to U.S. industry. The GAO said that the Committee for the Implementation of Textile Agreements sometimes applies quotas even though it cannot prove the textile industry's claims that American companies have been hurt or jobs have been eliminated.
- *To protect national security.* Restrictions in this category generally apply to technological products that must be kept out of the hands of potential enemies. For example, strategic and defense-related goods cannot be exported to unfriendly nations.
- *To protect the health of citizens.* Products may be embargoed because they are dangerous or unhealthy (e.g., farm products contaminated with insecticides).
- *To retaliate for another nation's trade restrictions.* A country whose exports are taxed by another country may respond by imposing tariffs on imports from that country.
- *To protect domestic jobs.* By restricting imports, a nation can protect jobs in domestic industries. However, protecting these jobs can be expensive. For example, protecting 9,000 jobs in the U.S. carbon-steel industry costs $6.8 billion, or $750,000 per job. In addition, Gary Hufbauer and Ben Goodrich, economists at the Institute for International Economics, estimate that the tariffs could temporarily save 3,500 jobs in the steel industry, but at an annual cost to steel users of $2 billion, or $584,000 per job saved. Yet recently the United States imposed tariffs of up to 616 percent on steel pipes imported from China, South Korea, and Mexico. Similarly, it is estimated that we spent more than $100,000 for every job saved in the apparel manufacturing industry—jobs that seldom paid more than $35,000 a year.

Reasons Against Trade Restrictions

Trade restrictions have immediate and long-term economic consequences—both within the restricting nation and in world trade patterns. These include the following:

- *Higher prices for consumers.* Higher prices may result from the imposition of tariffs or the elimination of foreign competition, as described earlier. For example, imposing quota restrictions and import protections adds $25 billion annually to U.S. consumers' apparel costs by directly increasing costs for imported apparel.
- *Restriction of consumers' choices.* Again, this is a direct result of the elimination of some foreign products from the marketplace and of the artificially high prices that importers must charge for products that are still imported.
- *Misallocation of international resources.* The protection of weak industries results in the inefficient use of limited resources. The economies of both the restricting nation and other nations eventually suffer because of this waste.
- *Loss of jobs.* The restriction of imports by one nation must lead to cutbacks—and the loss of jobs—in the export-oriented industries of other nations. Furthermore, trade protection has a significant effect on the composition of employment. U.S. trade restrictions—whether on textiles, apparel, steel, or automobiles—benefit only a few industries while harming many others. The gains in employment accrue to the protected industries and their primary suppliers, and the losses are spread across all other industries. A few states gain employment, but many other states lose employment.

Outline the extent of international business and the world economic outlook for trade.

THE EXTENT OF INTERNATIONAL BUSINESS

Restrictions or not, international business is growing. Although the worldwide recessions of 1991 and 2001–2002 slowed the rate of growth, and the 2008–2009 global economic crisis caused the sharpest decline in more than 75 years, globalization is a reality of our time. In the United States, international trade now accounts for over one-fourth of GDP. As trade barriers decrease, new competitors enter the global marketplace, creating more choices for consumers and new opportunities for job seekers. International business will grow along with the expansion of commercial use of the Internet.

The World Economic Outlook for Trade

Although the global economy continued to grow robustly until 2007 economic performance was not equal: growth in the advanced economies slowed and then stopped in 2009, whereas emerging and developing economies continued to grow. Looking ahead, the International Monetary Fund (IMF), an international bank with 187 member nations, expected a gradual global growth to continue in 2012 and 2013 in both advanced and emerging developing economies.[4]

Although the U.S. economy had been growing steadily since 2000 and recorded the longest peacetime expansion in the nation's history, the worldwide recession which began in December 2007 has slowed the rate of growth. The IMF estimated that the U.S. economy grew by less than half of 1 percent in 2008 and, because of subprime mortgage lending and other global financial problems, declined 2.5 percent in 2009. However, international experts expected global economic growth of 3.3 percent in 2012 and 3.9 percent in 2013, despite the high oil prices and financial crises in the euro area economies.

Canada and Western Europe Our leading export partner, Canada, is projected to show a growth rate of 1.7 percent in 2012 and 2.0 percent in 2013. The euro area, which was projected to decline by 0.5 percent in 2012 is expected to grow 0.8 percent in 2013. The United Kingdom is expected to grow 0.6 percent and 2.0 percent in 2012 and 2013, respectively.

Mexico and Latin America Our second-largest export customer, Mexico, suffered its sharpest recession ever in 1995, and experienced another major setback in 2009. However, its growth rate in 2012 and 2013 is expected to be 3.5 percent. Brazil escaped the recent global economic crisis with only minor setbacks: Its growth in 2010 was more than 7.5 percent, and in 2011 it declined to 2.9 percent. Growth of about 3 percent and 4 percent is expected in 2012 and 2013, respectively. In general, the Latin American and the Caribbean economies are recovering at a robust pace.

Japan Japan's economy is regaining some momentum after suffering from an earthquake, tsunami, and nuclear plant disaster in 2011. Stronger consumer demand and business investment make Japan less reliant on exports for growth. The IMF estimates the growth for Japan at 1.7 percent in 2012 and 1.8 percent in 2013.

Other Asian Countries The economic growth in Asia remained strong in 2010 and 2011 despite the global recession. Growth was led by China, where its economy expanded by 9.2 percent in 2011, and is expected to grow at 8.2 percent and 8.8 percent in 2012 and 2013, respectively. Growth in India was 7.4 percent in 2011, and is predicted to grow at 7 percent and 7.3 percent in 2012 and 2013, respectively. Growth in ASEAN-5 countries—Indonesia, Malaysia, the Philippines, Thailand, and Vietnam—is expected at 5.2 percent and 5.6 percent in 2012 and 2013, respectively. In short, the key emerging economies in Asia are leading the global recovery.

China's emergence as a global economic power has been among the most dramatic economic developments of recent decades. From 1980 to

COURTESY, CATERPILLAR CORPORATION

Caterpillar in Saudi Arabia. Restrictions or not, international business is booming. Globalization is the reality of our time. As trade barriers decrease, ever increasing number of U.S. companies, such as Caterpillar, are selling in the global marketplace.

2004, China's economy averaged a real GDP growth rate of 9.5 percent and became the world's sixth-largest economy. By 2004, China had become the third-largest trading nation in dollar terms, behind the United States and Germany and just ahead of Japan. Today, China, the world's second-largest economy, generates 10 to 15 percent of world GDP, and in 2011, accounted for about 25 percent of world GDP growth. The United States now imports more goods from China than any other nation in the world. In fact, China, with almost $1.9 trillion in exports, is the world's number-one exporter. In 2012, China took steps to promote the international use of its currency, the renminbi.[5]

Commonwealth of Independent States The growth in this region is expected to be 3.7 percent in 2012 and 3.8 percent in 2013. Strong growth is expected to continue in Azerbaijan and Armenia, whereas growth is projected to remain stable in Moldova, Tajikistan, and Uzbekistan.

After World War II, trade between the United States and the communist nations of Central and Eastern Europe was minimal. The United States maintained high tariff barriers on imports from most of these countries and also restricted their exports. However, since the disintegration of the Soviet Union and the collapse of communism, trade between the United States and Central and Eastern Europe has expanded substantially.

The countries that made the transition from communist to market economies quickly have recorded positive growth for several years—those that did not continue to struggle. Among the nations that have enjoyed several years of positive economic growth are the member countries of the Central European Free Trade Association: Hungary, the Czech Republic, Poland, Slovenia, and Slovakia.

U.S. exports to Central and Eastern Europe and Russia will increase, as will U.S. investment in these countries, as demand for capital goods and technology opens new markets for U.S. products. There already has been a substantial expansion in trade between the United States and the Czech Republic, Slovakia, Hungary, and Poland. Table 3.1 shows the growth rates from 2010 to 2013 for most regions of the world.

Exports and the U.S. Economy In 2008, U.S. exports supported more than 10.3 million full- and part-time jobs during a historic time, when exports as a percentage of GDP reached the highest levels since 1916. The new record, 13.8 percent of GDP in 2011, shows that U.S. businesses have great opportunities in the global marketplace.

TABLE 3.1	Global Growth Is Picking Up Gradually			
Growth has been led by developing countries and emerging markets.				
			Annual Percent Change	
	2010	2011	Projected 2012	Projected 2013
World	5.2	3.8	3.3	3.9
United States	3.0	1.8	1.8	2.2
Euro area	1.9	1.6	−0.5	0.8
United Kingdom	2.1	0.9	0.6	2.0
Japan	4.4	−0.9	1.7	1.8
Canada	3.2	2.3	1.7	2.0
Other advanced economies	5.8	3.3	2.6	3.4
Newly industrialized Asian economies	8.4	4.2	3.3	4.1
Developing countries and emerging markets	7.3	6.2	5.4	5.9
Developing Asia	9.5	7.9	7.3	7.8
Commonwealth of Independent States	4.6	4.5	3.7	3.8
Middle East and North Africa	4.3	3.1	3.2	3.6
Latin America and the Caribbean	6.1	4.6	3.6	3.9

Source: *International Monetary Fund: World Economic Outlook* by International Monetary Fund. Copyright 2012 by International Monetary Fund. Reproduced with permission of International Monetary Fund via Copyright Clearance Center. www.imf.org/external/pubs/ft/weo/2012/update/01/index.htm (accessed March 10, 2012).

TABLE 3.2	Value of U.S. Merchandise Exports and Imports, 2011		
Rank/Trading Partner	**Exports ($ billions)**	**Rank/Trading Partner**	**Imports ($ billions)**
1) Canada	280.9	1) China	399.3
2) Mexico	197.5	2) Canada	316.5
3) China	103.9	3) Mexico	263.1
4) Japan	66.2	4) Japan	128.8
5) United Kingdom	55.9	5) Germany	98.4
6) Germany	49.1	6) South Korea	56.6
7) South Korea	43.5	7) United Kingdom	51.5
8) Brazil	42.9	8) Saudi Arabia	47.5
9) Netherlands	42.8	9) Venezuela	43.3
10) Hong Kong	36.5	10) Taiwan	41.3

Source: U.S. Department of Commerce, International Trade Administration, http://trade.gov/mas/ian/build/group/public/@tg_ian/documents/webcontent/tg_ian_003364.pdf (accessed March 9, 2012).

Even though the global economic crisis caused the number of jobs supported by exports to decline sharply to 8.5 million in 2009, globalization represents a huge opportunity for all countries—rich or poor. Indeed, in 2011, for the first time, the U.S. exports exceeded $2.1 trillion and supported 9.7 million jobs, an increase of $1.2 million since 2009.[6] The 15-fold increase in trade volume over the past 60 years has been one of the most important factors in the rise of living standards around the world. During this time, exports have become increasingly important to the U.S. economy. Exports as a percentage of U.S. GDP have increased steadily since 1985, except in the 2001 and 2008 recessions. Our exports to developing and newly industrialized countries are on the rise. Table 3.2 shows the value of U.S. merchandise exports to, and imports from, each of the nation's ten major trading partners. Note that Canada and Mexico are our best partners for our exports; China and Canada, for imports.

Figure 3.3 shows the U.S. goods export and import shares in 2011. Major U.S. exports and imports are manufactured goods, agricultural products, and mineral fuels.

FIGURE 3.3	U.S. Goods Export and Import Shares in 2011

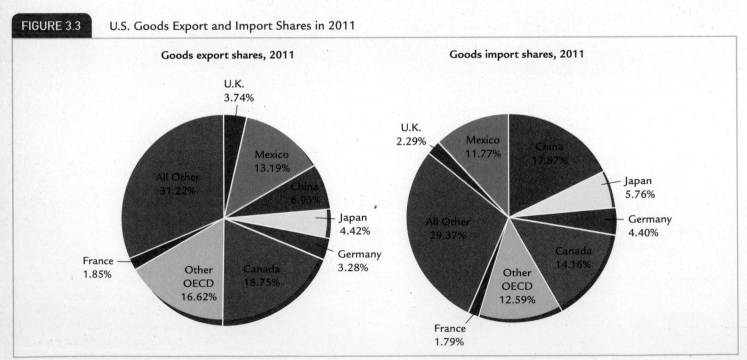

Goods export shares, 2011

U.K. 3.74%
Mexico 13.19%
All Other 31.22%
China 6.93%
Japan 4.42%
Germany 3.28%
France 1.85%
Other OECD 16.62%
Canada 18.75%

Goods import shares, 2011

U.K. 2.29%
Mexico 11.77%
China 17.87%
Japan 5.76%
Germany 4.40%
All Other 29.37%
Canada 14.16%
Other OECD 12.59%
France 1.79%

Source: Federal Reserve Bank of St. Louis, *National Economic Trends*, March 2012, 18.

INTERNATIONAL TRADE AGREEMENTS

 Discuss international trade agreements and international economic organizations working to foster trade.

The General Agreement on Tariffs and Trade and the World Trade Organization

At the end of World War II, the United States and 22 other nations organized the body that came to be known as GATT. The **General Agreement on Tariffs and Trade (GATT)** was an international organization of 153 nations dedicated to reducing or eliminating tariffs and other barriers to world trade. These 153 nations accounted for more than 97 percent of the world's merchandise trade (see Figure 3.4). GATT, headquartered in Geneva, Switzerland, provided a forum for tariff negotiations and a means for settling international trade disputes and problems. Most-favored-nation status (MFN) was the famous principle of GATT. It meant that each GATT member nation was to be treated equally by all contracting nations. Therefore, MFN ensured that any tariff reductions or other trade concessions were extended automatically to all GATT members. From 1947 to 1994, the body sponsored eight rounds of negotiations to reduce trade restrictions. Three of the most fruitful were the Kennedy Round, the Tokyo Round, and the Uruguay Round.

The Kennedy Round (1964–1967) In 1962, the United States Congress passed the Trade Expansion Act. This law gave President John F. Kennedy the authority to negotiate reciprocal trade agreements that could reduce U.S. tariffs by as much as 50 percent. Armed with this authority, which was granted for a period of five years, President Kennedy called for a round of negotiations through GATT.

These negotiations, which began in 1964, have since become known as the Kennedy Round. They were aimed at reducing tariffs and other barriers to trade in

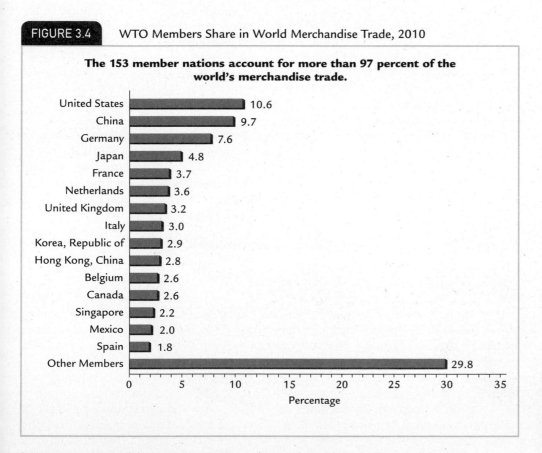

| FIGURE 3.4 | WTO Members Share in World Merchandise Trade, 2010 |

The 153 member nations account for more than 97 percent of the world's merchandise trade.

Country	Percentage
United States	10.6
China	9.7
Germany	7.6
Japan	4.8
France	3.7
Netherlands	3.6
United Kingdom	3.2
Italy	3.0
Korea, Republic of	2.9
Hong Kong, China	2.8
Belgium	2.6
Canada	2.6
Singapore	2.2
Mexico	2.0
Spain	1.8
Other Members	29.8

Source: www.wto.org/english/res_e/Statis_e/its2011_e/charts_e/chart07.xls (accessed on March 7, 2012).

General Agreement on Tariffs and Trade (GATT) an international organization of 153 nations dedicated to reducing or eliminating tariffs and other barriers to world trade both industrial and agricultural products. The participants succeeded in reducing tariffs on these products by an average of more than 35 percent. However, they were less successful in removing other types of trade barriers.

The Tokyo Round (1973–1979) In 1973, representatives of approximately 100 nations gathered in Tokyo for another round of GATT negotiations. The *Tokyo Round* was completed in 1979. The participants negotiated tariff cuts of 30 to 35 percent, which were to be implemented over an eight-year period. In addition, they were able to remove or ease such nontariff barriers as import quotas, unrealistic quality standards for imports, and unnecessary red tape in customs procedures.

The Uruguay Round (1986–1993) In 1986, the *Uruguay Round* was launched to extend trade liberalization and widen the GATT treaty to include textiles, agricultural products, business services, and intellectual-property rights. This most ambitious and comprehensive global commercial agreement in history concluded overall negotiations on December 15, 1993, with delegations on hand from 109 nations. The agreement included provisions to lower tariffs by greater than one-third, to reform trade in agricultural goods, to write new rules of trade for intellectual property and services, and to strengthen the dispute-settlement process. These reforms were expected to expand the world economy by an estimated $200 billion annually.

The Uruguay Round also created the **World Trade Organization (WTO)** on January 1, 1995. The WTO was established by GATT to oversee the provisions of the Uruguay Round and resolve any resulting trade disputes. Membership in the WTO obliges 153 member nations to observe GATT rules. The WTO has judicial powers to mediate among members disputing the new rules. It incorporates trade in goods, services, and ideas and exerts more binding authority than GATT. Its main function is to ensure that trade flows as smoothly, predictably, and freely as possible.

The Doha Round (2001) On November 14, 2001, in Doha, Qatar, the WTO members agreed to further reduce trade barriers through multilateral trade negotiations over the next three years. This new round of negotiations focuses on industrial tariffs and nontariff barriers, agriculture, services, and easing trade rules. U.S. exporters of industrial and agricultural goods and services should have improved access to overseas markets. The Doha Round has set the stage for WTO members to take an important step toward significant new multilateral trade liberalization. It is a difficult task, but the rewards—lower tariffs, more choices for consumers, and further integration of developing countries into the world trading system—are sure to be worth the effort. Some experts suggest that U.S. exporters of industrial and agricultural goods and services should have improved access to overseas markets, whereas others disagree. Negotiations between the developed and developing countries continued in 2012.

World Trade and the Global Economic Crisis

After the sharpest decline in more than 72 years, world trade was set to rebound in 2010 by growing at 9.5 percent, according to the WTO economists. In a 2012 speech, WTO Director-General Pascal Lamy stated, "The multilateral trading system has been instrumental in maintaining trade openness during the crisis, thereby avoiding even worse outcomes. Members must remain vigilant. This is not the time for go-it-alone measures. This is the time to strengthen and preserve the global trading system so that it keeps performing this vital function in the future."[7]

Exports from developed economies increased nearly 13 percent in 2010, compared to a 16.5 percent increase in the rest of the world. China's exports increased in 2010 by a massive 28 percent. Furthermore, the higher prices and extraordinary growth of trade in developing Asia increased the combined share of developing economies and the Commonwealth of Independent States in world exports to 45 percent in 2010, its highest ever.

World Trade Organization (WTO) powerful successor to GATT that incorporates trade in goods, services, and ideas

FIGURE 3.5 The Evolving European Union

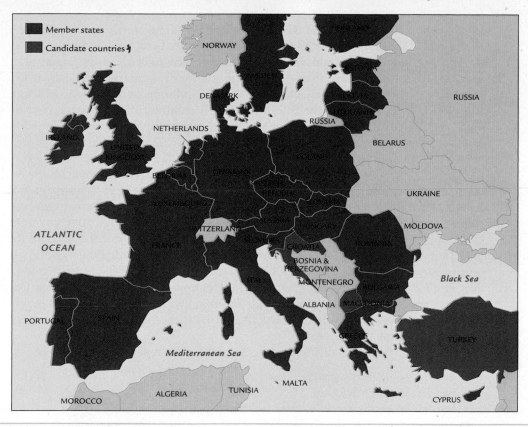

The Evolving European Union: The European Union is now an economic force, with a collective economy larger than that of the United States or Japan.

Source: http://europa.eu/abc/european_countries/index_en.htm (accessed March 14, 2012).

International Economic Organizations Working to Foster Trade

The primary objective of the WTO is to remove barriers to trade on a worldwide basis. On a smaller scale, an **economic community** is an organization of nations formed to promote the free movement of resources and products among its members and to create common economic policies. A number of economic communities now exist.

The European Union The European Union (EU), also known as the European Economic Community and the Common Market, was formed in 1957 by six countries—France, the Federal Republic of Germany, Italy, Belgium, the Netherlands, and Luxembourg. Its objective was freely conducted commerce among these nations and others that might later join. As shown in Figure 3.5, many more nations have joined the EU since then.

On January 1, 2007, the 25 nations of the EU became the EU27 as Bulgaria and Romania became new members. The EU, with a population of nearly half a billion, is now an economic force with a collective economy larger than much of the United States or Japan.

In celebrating the EU's 50th anniversary in 2007, the president of the European Commission, Jose Manuel Durao Barraso, declared, "Let us first recognize 50 years of achievement. Peace, liberty, and prosperity, beyond the dreams of even the most optimistic founding fathers of Europe. In 1957, 15 of our 27 members were either under dictatorship or were not allowed to exist as independent countries. Now we are all prospering democracies. The EU of today is around 50 times more prosperous and with three times the population of the EU of 1957."

economic community an organization of nations formed to promote the free movement of resources and products among its members and to create common economic policies

Since January 2002, 15 member nations of the EU have been participating in the new common currency, the euro. The euro is the single currency of the European Monetary Union nations. However, three EU members, Denmark, the United Kingdom, and Sweden, still maintain their own currencies.

The North American Free Trade Agreement The North American Free Trade Agreement (NAFTA) joined the United States with its first- and second-largest export trading partners, Canada and Mexico. Implementation of NAFTA on January 1, 1994, created a market of more than 462 million people. This market consists of Canada (population 34 million), the United States (313 million), and Mexico (115 million). According to the Office of the U.S. Trade Representative, after 18 years, NAFTA has achieved its core goals of expanding trade and investment between the United States, Canada, and Mexico. For example, from 1993 to 2011, trade among the NAFTA nations more than tripled, from $297 billion to $1,058 billion.

NAFTA is built on the Canadian Free Trade Agreement, signed by the United States and Canada in 1989, and on the substantial trade and investment reforms undertaken by Mexico since the mid-1980s. Initiated by the Mexican government, formal negotiations on NAFTA began in June 1991 among the three governments. The support of NAFTA by President Bill Clinton, past U.S. Presidents Ronald Reagan and Jimmy Carter, and Nobel Prize–winning economists provided the impetus for U.S. congressional ratification of NAFTA in November 1993. By 2008, NAFTA had gradually eliminated all tariffs and quotas on goods produced and traded among Canada, Mexico, and the United States to provide for a totally free-trade area. Chile is expected to become the fourth member of NAFTA, but political forces may delay its entry into the agreement for several years.

However, NAFTA is not without its critics. Critics maintain that NAFTA:

- has not achieved its goals
- has resulted in job losses
- hurts workers by eroding labor standards and lowering wages
- undermines national sovereignty and independence
- does nothing to help the environment, and
- hurts the agricultural sector

The proponents of NAFTA call the agreement a remarkable economic success story for all three partners. They maintain that NAFTA:

- has contributed to significant increases in trade and investment
- has benefited companies in all three countries
- has resulted in increased sales, new partnerships, and new opportunities
- has created high-paying export-related jobs, and
- better prices and selection in consumer goods

The Central American Free Trade Agreement The Central American Free Trade Agreement (CAFTA) was created in 2003 by the United States and four Central American countries—El Salvador, Guatemala, Honduras, and Nicaragua. The CAFTA became CAFTA-DR when the Dominican Republic joined the group in 2007. On January 1, 2009, Costa Rica joined CAFTA-DR as the sixth member. CAFTA-DR creates the third-largest U.S. export market in Latin America, behind only Mexico and Brazil.

The Association of Southeast Asian Nations The Association of Southeast Asian Nations, with headquarters in Jakarta, Indonesia, was established in 1967 to promote political, economic, and social cooperation among its seven member countries: Indonesia, Malaysia, the Philippines, Singapore, Thailand, Brunei, and Vietnam. With the three new members, Cambodia, Laos, and Myanmar, this region of 600 million people is already our fifth-largest trading partner.

The Commonwealth of Independent States The Commonwealth of Independent States was established in December 1991 by the newly independent states as an association of 11 republics of the former Soviet Union.

Trans-Pacific Partnership (TPP) On November 12, 2011, the leaders of the nine countries—Australia, Brunei Darussalam, Chile, Malaysia, New Zealand, Peru, Singapore, Vietnam, and the United States—formed the Trans-Pacific Partnership. This partnership will boost economies of the member countries, lower barriers to trade and investment, increase exports, and create more jobs. Together, these eight economies would be America's fifth-largest trading partner. According to President Obama, "We already do more than $200 billion in trade with them every year, and with nearly 500 million consumers between us, there's so much more that we can do together." The Asia-Pacific region is one of the fastest growing areas in the world and TPP will open more markets to American businesses and exports.[8]

The Common Market of the Southern Cone (MERCOSUR) The Common Market of the Southern Cone (MERCOSUR) was established in 1991 under the Treaty of Asuncion to unite Argentina, Brazil, Paraguay, and Uruguay as a free-trade alliance; Colombia, Ecuador, Peru, Bolivia, and Chile joined later as associates. The alliance represents more than 267 million consumers—67 percent of South America's population, making it the third-largest trading block behind NAFTA and the EU. Like NAFTA, MERCOSUR promotes "the free circulation of goods, services and production factors among the countries" and established a common external tariff and commercial policy.

The Organization of Petroleum Exporting Countries The Organization of Petroleum Exporting Countries was founded in 1960 in response to reductions in the prices that oil companies were willing to pay for crude oil. The organization was conceived as a collective bargaining unit to provide oil-producing nations with some control over oil prices.

Sustaining the PLANET

2degrees: A Global Community

A new organization called 2degrees is now the world's largest community for sustainable business with around 30,000 professional members from over 90 countries. The online platform helps members (individual professionals and organizations) to improve their resource efficiency by sharing best practices and enabling them to solve common business problems together.

2degrees features webinars hosted by top experts; working groups on topics such as energy management, renewable power, greener health care and waste management; white papers; blogs; and the latest news on sustainability. Explore the site to learn more about how this organization is helping to make business more sustainable worldwide.

www.2degreesnetwork.com

METHODS OF ENTERING INTERNATIONAL BUSINESS

A firm that has decided to enter international markets can do so in several ways. We will discuss several different methods. These different approaches require varying degrees of involvement in international business. Typically, a firm begins its international operations at the simplest level. Then, depending on its goals, it may progress to higher levels of involvement.

⑤ Define the methods by which a firm can organize for and enter into international markets.

Licensing

Licensing is a contractual agreement in which one firm permits another to produce and market its product and use its brand name in return for a royalty or other compensation. For example, Yoplait yogurt is a French yogurt licensed for production in the United States. The Yoplait brand maintains an appealing French image, and in return, the U.S. producer pays the French firm a percentage of its income from sales of the product.

licensing a contractual agreement in which one firm permits another to produce and market its product and use its brand name in return for a royalty or other compensation

Celebrating OPEC's 50th anniversary. Secretary General of OPEC Abdalla Salem El-Badri and Iranian Oil Minister Masoud Mir Kazemi attend a ceremony to celebrate the 50th anniversary of the founding of OPEC, in Tehran, Iran, on April 19th, 2011.

Licensing is especially advantageous for small manufacturers wanting to launch a well-known domestic brand internationally. For example, all Spalding sporting products are licensed worldwide. The licensor, the Questor Corporation, owns the Spalding name but produces no goods itself. Licensing thus provides a simple method for expanding into a foreign market with virtually no investment. On the other hand, if the licensee does not maintain the licensor's product standards, the product's image may be damaged. Another possible disadvantage is that a licensing arrangement may not provide the original producer with any foreign marketing experience.

Exporting

A firm also may manufacture its products in its home country and export them for sale in foreign markets. As with licensing, exporting can be a relatively low-risk method of entering foreign markets. Unlike licensing, however, it is not a simple method; it opens up several levels of involvement to the exporting firm.

At the most basic level, the exporting firm may sell its products outright to an *export–import merchant*, which is essentially a merchant wholesaler. The merchant assumes all the risks of product ownership, distribution, and sale. It may even purchase the goods in the producer's home country and assume responsibility for exporting the goods. An important and practical issue for domestic firms dealing with foreign customers is securing payment. This is a two-sided issue that reflects the mutual concern rightly felt by both parties to the trade deal: The exporter would like to be paid before shipping the merchandise, whereas the importer obviously would prefer to know that it has received the shipment before releasing any funds. Neither side wants to take the risk of fulfilling its part of the deal only to discover later that the other side has not. The result would lead to legal costs and complex, lengthy dealings that would waste everyone's resources. This mutual level of mistrust, in fact, makes good business sense and has been around since the beginning of trade centuries ago. The solution then was the same as it still is today—for both parties to use a mutually trusted go-between who can ensure that the payment is held until the merchandise is in fact delivered according to the terms of the trade contract. The go-between representatives employed by the importer and exporter are still, as they were in the past, the local domestic banks involved in international business.

Exporting to International Markets American companies may manufacture their products in the United States and export them for sale in foreign markets. Exporting can be a relatively low-risk method of entering foreign markets.

Here is a simplified version of how it works. After signing contracts detailing the merchandise sold and terms for its delivery, an importer will ask its local bank to issue a **letter of credit** for the amount of money needed to pay for the merchandise. The letter of credit is issued "in favor of the exporter," meaning that the funds are tied specifically to the trade contract involved. The importer's bank forwards the letter of credit to the exporter's bank, which also normally deals in international transactions. The exporter's bank then notifies the exporter that a letter of credit has been received in its name, and the exporter can go ahead with the shipment. The carrier transporting the merchandise provides the exporter with evidence of the shipment in a document called a **bill of lading**. The exporter signs over title to the merchandise (now in transit) to its bank by delivering signed copies of the bill of lading and the letter of credit.

In exchange, the exporter issues a **draft** from the bank, which orders the importer's bank to pay for the merchandise. The draft, bill of lading, and letter of credit are sent from the exporter's bank to the importer's bank. Acceptance by the importer's bank leads to return of the draft and its sale by the exporter to its bank, meaning that the exporter receives cash and the bank assumes the risk of collecting the funds from the

letter of credit issued by a bank on request of an importer stating that the bank will pay an amount of money to a stated beneficiary

bill of lading document issued by a transport carrier to an exporter to prove that merchandise has been shipped

draft issued by the exporter's bank, ordering the importer's bank to pay for the merchandise, thus guaranteeing payment once accepted by the importer's bank foreign bank. The importer is obliged to pay its bank on delivery of the merchandise, and the deal is complete.

In most cases, the letter of credit is part of a lending arrangement between the importer and its bank. Of course, both banks earn fees for issuing letters of credit and drafts and for handling the import–export services for their clients. Furthermore, the process incorporates the fact that both importer and exporter will have different local currencies and might even negotiate their trade in a third currency. The banks look after all the necessary exchanges. For example, the vast majority of international business is negotiated in U.S. dollars, even though the trade may be between countries other than the United States. Thus, although the importer may end up paying for the merchandise in its local currency and the exporter may receive payment in another local currency, the banks involved will exchange all necessary foreign funds in order to allow the deal to take place.

Alternatively, the exporting firm may ship its products to an *export–import agent*, which arranges the sale of the products to foreign intermediaries for a commission or fee. The agent is an independent firm—like other agents—that sells and may perform other marketing functions for the exporter. The exporter, however, retains title to the products during shipment and until they are sold.

An exporting firm also may establish its own *sales offices*, or *branches*, in foreign countries. These installations are international extensions of the firm's distribution system. They represent a deeper involvement in international business than the other exporting techniques we have discussed—and thus they carry a greater risk. The exporting firm maintains control over sales, and it gains both experience in and knowledge of foreign markets. Eventually, the firm also may develop its own sales force to operate in conjunction with foreign sales offices.

Exporting to international markets. American companies may manufacture their products in the United States and export them for sale in foreign markets. Exporting can be a relatively risk-free method of entering foreign markets.

Joint Ventures

A *joint venture* is a partnership formed to achieve a specific goal or to operate for a specific period of time. A joint venture with an established firm in a foreign country provides immediate market knowledge and access, reduced risk, and control over product attributes. However, joint-venture agreements established across national borders can become extremely complex. As a result, joint-venture agreements generally require a very high level of commitment from all the parties involved.

A joint venture may be used to produce and market an existing product in a foreign nation or to develop an entirely new product. Recently, for example, Archer Daniels Midland Company (ADM), one of the world's leading food processors, entered into a joint venture with Gruma SA, Mexico's largest corn flour and tortilla company. Besides a 22 percent stake in Gruma, ADM also received stakes in other joint ventures operated by Gruma. One of them will combine both companies' U.S. corn flour operations, which account for about 25 percent of the U.S. market. ADM also has a 40 percent stake in a Mexican wheat flour mill. ADM's joint venture increased its participation in the growing Mexican economy, where ADM already produces corn syrup, fructose, starch, and wheat flour.

Totally Owned Facilities

At a still deeper level of involvement in international business, a firm may develop *totally owned facilities,* that is, its own production and marketing facilities in one or more foreign nations. This *direct investment* provides complete control over operations, but it carries a greater risk than the joint venture. The firm is really establishing a subsidiary in a foreign country. Most firms do so only after they have acquired some knowledge of the host country's markets.

Going for SUCCESS

Services Team Up to Enter India

A growing number of U.S.-based service firms are expanding into India by forming joint ventures with local firms. Both partners bring specific strengths to the joint venture, not just their brands but also the Indian firm's in-depth knowledge of customers and the U.S. firm's service concepts.

For example, Cigna, which markets health insurance, has teamed up with TTK Group to sell insurance policies in India. TTK Group operates 1,500 retail stores and sells a variety of goods and services, including insurance. The joint venture will enable Cigna to reach consumers without creating a separate network of insurance agents—and TTK Group gains another product line to diversify its offerings.

CBS and its partner in India, Reliance Broadcast Networks, recently launched English-language channels to tap into the country's burgeoning market for television entertainment. CBS provides the content (including hit programs such as CSI) and Reliance provides its expertise in distribution and advertising sales for this joint venture, known as Big CBS.

Dunkin' Donuts has a joint venture with Jubilant Foodworks to open shops featuring an all-day menu of coffee, donuts, and other foods adapted to Indian tastes. In this partnership, "Dunkin' provides flexibility in localizing recipes, and we have strengths in food and culinary which we intend to leverage," explains Jubilant's chairman.

Sources: Based on information in Vikas Bajaj, "Cigna in Deal to Sell Health Insurance in India," *New York Times*, November 21, 2011, www.nytimes.com; Sanjeev Choudhary, "Dunkin' Donuts to Enter India with Jubilant Foodworks," *Reuters*, February 25, 2011, www.reuters.com; Nyay Bhushan, "Reliance, RTL Group Plan Joint Venture for English, Local-Language Channels," *Hollywood Reporter*, March 11, 2011, www.hollywoodreporter.com.

Direct investment may take either of two forms. In the first, the firm builds or purchases manufacturing and other facilities in the foreign country. It uses these facilities to produce its own established products and to market them in that country and perhaps in neighboring countries. Firms such as General Motors, Union Carbide, and Colgate-Palmolive are multinational companies with worldwide manufacturing facilities. Colgate-Palmolive factories are becoming *Eurofactories*, supplying neighboring countries as well as their own local markets.

A second form of direct investment in international business is the purchase of an existing firm in a foreign country under an arrangement that allows it to operate independently of the parent company. When Sony Corporation (a Japanese firm) decided to enter the motion picture business in the United States, it chose to purchase Columbia Pictures Entertainment, Inc., rather than start a new motion picture studio from scratch.

strategic alliance a partnership formed to create competitive advantage on a worldwide basis

Strategic Alliances

A **strategic alliance**, the newest form of international business structure, is a partnership formed to create competitive advantage on a worldwide basis. Strategic alliances are very similar to joint ventures. The number of strategic alliances is growing at an estimated rate of about 20 percent per year. In fact, in the automobile and computer industries, strategic alliances are becoming the predominant means of competing. International competition is so fierce and the costs of competing on a global basis are so high that few firms have all the resources needed to do it alone. Thus, individual firms that lack the internal resources essential for international success may seek to collaborate with other companies.

An example of such an alliance is the New United Motor Manufacturing, Inc. (NUMMI), formed by Toyota and General Motors to make automobiles of both firms. This enterprise united the quality engineering of Japanese cars with the marketing expertise and market access of General Motors.

Strategic alliance for mutual benefits. Chairman and Managing Director of Air India, V. Thulasidas, and Chairman of Lufthansa AG, Wolfgang Mayrhuber, sign a strategic alliance agreement in Mumbai, India. The alliance improves their market leadership position on India–Europe–U.S. routes.

Trading Companies

A **trading company** provides a link between buyers and sellers in different countries. A trading company, as its name implies, is not involved in manufacturing or owning assets related to manufacturing. It buys products in one country at the lowest price consistent with quality and sells to buyers in another country. An important function of trading companies is taking title to products and performing all the activities necessary to move the products from the domestic country to a foreign country. For example, large grain-trading companies operating out of home offices both in the United States and overseas control a major portion of the world's trade in basic food commodities. These trading companies sell homogeneous agricultural commodities that can be stored and moved rapidly in response to market conditions.

Countertrade

In the early 1990s, many developing nations had major restrictions on converting domestic currency into foreign currency. Therefore, exporters had to resort to barter agreements with importers. **Countertrade** is essentially an international barter transaction in which goods and services are exchanged for different goods and services. Examples include Saudi Arabia's purchase of ten 747 jets from Boeing with payment in crude oil and Philip Morris's sale of cigarettes to Russia in return for chemicals used to make fertilizers.

Multinational Firms

A **multinational enterprise** is a firm that operates on a worldwide scale without ties to any specific nation or region. The multinational firm represents the highest level of involvement in international business. It is equally "at home" in most countries of the world. In fact, as far as the operations of the multinational enterprise are concerned, national boundaries exist only on maps. It is, however, organized under the laws of its home country.

Table 3.3 shows the ten largest foreign and U.S. public multinational companies; the ranking is based on a composite score reflecting each company's best three out of four rankings for sales, profits, assets, and market value. Table 3.4 describes steps in entering international markets.

trading company provides a link between buyers and sellers in different countries

countertrade an international barter transaction

multinational enterprise a firm that operates on a worldwide scale without ties to any specific nation or region

TABLE 3.3	The Ten Largest Foreign and U.S. Multinational Corporations			
2011 Rank	Company	Business	Country	Revenue ($ millions)
1	Walmart Stores	General merchandiser	United States	421,849
2	Royal Dutch Shell	Energy	Netherlands/ United Kingdom	378,152
3	ExxonMobil	Energy	United States	354,674
4	BP	Energy	United Kingdom	308,928
5	Sinopec Group	Energy	China	273,422
6	China Natural Petroleum	Energy	China	240,192
7	State Grid	Power grids	China	226,294
8	Toyota Motor	Automobiles	Japan	221,760
9	Japan Post Holdings	Financial services	Japan	203,958
10	Chevron	Energy	United States	196,337

Source: From *Fortune Magazine*, "Global 500 Our Annual Ranking of the World's Largest Corporations," July 25, 2011, © 2011 Time Inc. Used under license. Fortune and Time Inc. are not affiliated with, and do not endorse products or services of, Licensee.

TABLE 3.4 Steps in Entering International Markets

Step	Activity	Marketing Tasks
1	Identify exportable products.	Identify key selling features. Identify needs that they satisfy. Identify the selling constraints that are imposed.
2	Identify key foreign markets for the products.	Determine who the customers are. Pinpoint what and when they will buy. Do market research. Establish priority, or "target," countries.
3	Analyze how to sell in each priority market (methods will be affected by product characteristics and unique features of country/market).	Locate available government and private-sector resources. Determine service and backup sales requirements.
4	Set export prices and payment terms, methods, and techniques.	Establish methods of export pricing. Establish sales terms, quotations, invoices, and conditions of sale. Determine methods of international payments, secured and unsecured.
5	Estimate resource requirements and returns.	Estimate financial requirements. Estimate human resources requirements (full- or part-time export department or operation?). Estimate plant production capacity. Determine necessary product adaptations.
6	Establish overseas distribution network.	Determine distribution agreement and other key marketing decisions (price, repair policies, returns, territory, performance, and termination). Know your customer (use U.S. Department of Commerce international marketing services).
7	Determine shipping, traffic, and documentation procedures and requirements.	Determine methods of shipment (air or ocean freight, truck, rail). Finalize containerization. Obtain validated export license. Follow export-administration documentation procedures.
8	Promote, sell, and be paid.	Use international media, communications, advertising, trade shows, and exhibitions. Determine the need for overseas travel (when, where, and how often?). Initiate customer follow-up procedures.
9	Continuously analyze current marketing, economic, and political situations.	Recognize changing factors influencing marketing strategies. Constantly re-evaluate.

Source: U.S. Department of Commerce, International Trade Administration, Washington, DC.

According to the chairman of the board of Dow Chemical Company, a multinational firm of U.S. origin, "The emergence of a world economy and of the multinational corporation has been accomplished hand in hand." He sees multinational enterprises moving toward what he calls the "anational company," a firm that has no nationality but belongs to all countries. In recognition of this movement, there already have been international conferences devoted to the question of how such enterprises would be controlled.

Describe the various sources of export assistance.

6

SOURCES OF EXPORT ASSISTANCE

In August 2010, President Obama announced the *National Export Initiative* (NEI) to revitalize U.S. exports. Under the NEI, many federal agencies assist U.S. firms in developing export-promotion programs. The export services and programs of these

TABLE 3.5	U.S. Government Export Assistance Programs	
1	U.S. Export Assistance Centers, www.sba.gov/oit/export/useac.html	Provides assistance in export marketing and trade finance
2	International Trade Administration, www.ita.doc.gov/	Offers assistance and information to exporters through its domestic and overseas commercial officers
3	U.S. and Foreign Commercial Services, www.export.gov/	Helps U.S. firms compete more effectively in the global marketplace and provides information on foreign markets
4	Advocacy Center, www.ita.doc.gov/advocacy	Facilitates advocacy to assist U.S. firms competing for major projects and procurements worldwide
5	Trade Information Center, www.ita.doc.gov/td/tic/	Provides U.S. companies information on federal programs and activities that support U.S. exports
6	STAT-USA/Internet, www.stat-usa.gov/	Offers a comprehensive collection of business, economic, and trade information on the Web
7	Small Business Administration, www.sba.gov/oit/	Publishes many helpful guides to assist small- and medium-sized companies
8	National Trade Data Bank, www.stat-usa.gov/tradtest.nsf	Provides international economic and export-promotion information supplied by more than 20 U.S. agencies

© CENGAGE LEARNING 2014

agencies can help American firms to compete in foreign markets and create new jobs in the United States. For example, in 2011 the International Trade Administration coordinated 77 trade missions to 38 countries. More than 1,120 companies secured over $1.25 billion in export sales during these missions. Table 3.5 provides an overview of selected export assistance programs.

These and other sources of export information enhance the business opportunities of U.S. firms seeking to enter expanding foreign markets. Another vital energy factor is financing.

FINANCING INTERNATIONAL BUSINESS

 7 Identify the institutions that help firms and nations finance international business.

International trade compounds the concerns of financial managers. Currency exchange rates, tariffs and foreign exchange controls, and the tax structures of host nations all affect international operations and the flow of cash. In addition, financial managers must be concerned both with the financing of their international operations and with the means available to their customers to finance purchases.

Fortunately, along with business in general, a number of large banks have become international in scope. Many have established branches in major cities around the world. Thus, like firms in other industries, they are able to provide their services where and when they are needed. In addition, financial assistance is available from U.S. government and international sources.

Several of today's international financial organizations were founded many years ago to facilitate free trade and the exchange of currencies among nations. Some, such as the Inter-American Development Bank, are supported internationally and focus on developing countries. Others, such as the Export-Import Bank, are operated by one country but provide international financing.

The Export-Import Bank of the United States

The **Export-Import Bank of the United States**, created in 1934, is an independent agency of the U.S. government whose function is to assist in financing the exports of American firms. *Ex-Im Bank*, as it is commonly called, extends and guarantees credit to overseas buyers of American goods and services and guarantees short-term financing for exports. It also cooperates with commercial banks in helping American exporters to offer credit to their overseas customers.

Export-Import Bank of the United States an independent agency of the U.S. government whose function is to assist in financing the exports of American firms

If you're interested in doing business outside the United States, you'll need to know something about international finance. Currency exchange rates will affect anything you buy or sell, for example, and you'll probably want to deal with a bank experienced in global business.

According to Fred P. Hochberg, chairman and president of Ex-Im Bank, "Working with private lenders we are helping U.S. exporters put Americans to work producing the high quality goods and services that foreign buyers prefer. As part of President Obama's National Export Initiative, Ex-Im Bank's export financing is contributing to the goal of doubling of U.S. exports within the next five years."

Multilateral Development Banks

A **multilateral development bank (MDB)** is an internationally supported bank that provides loans to developing countries to help them grow. The most familiar is the World Bank, a cooperative of 187 member countries, which operates worldwide. Established in 1944 and headquartered in Washington, DC, the bank provides low-interest loans, interest-free credits, and grants to developing countries. The loans and grants help these countries to:

- supply safe drinking water
- build schools and train teachers
- increase agricultural productivity
- expand citizens' access to markets, jobs, and housing
- improve health care and access to water and sanitation
- manage forests and other natural resources
- build and maintain roads, railways, and ports, and
- reduce air pollution and protect the environment.[9]

Four other MDBs operate primarily in Central and South America, Asia, Africa, and Eastern and Central Europe. All five are supported by the industrialized nations, including the United States.

The Inter-American Development Bank The Inter-American Development Bank (IDB), the oldest and largest regional bank, was created in 1959 by 19 Latin American countries and the United States. The bank, which is headquartered in Washington, DC, makes loans and provides technical advice and assistance to countries. Today, the IDB is owned by 48 member states.

The Asian Development Bank With 67 member nations, the Asian Development Bank (ADB), created in 1966 and headquartered in the Philippines, promotes economic and social progress in Asian and Pacific regions. The U.S. government is the second-largest contributor to the ADB's capital, after Japan.

The African Development Bank The African Development Bank (AFDB), also known as *Banque Africaines de Development*, was established in 1964 with headquarters in Abidjan, Ivory Coast. Its members include 53 African and 24 non-African countries from the Americas, Europe, and Asia. The AFDB's goal is to foster the economic and social development of its African members. The bank pursues this goal through loans, research, technical assistance, and the development of trade programs.

European Bank for Reconstruction and Development Established in 1991 to encourage reconstruction and development in the Eastern and Central European countries, the London-based *European Bank for Reconstruction and Development* is owned by 61 countries and 2 intergovernmental institutions. Its loans are geared toward developing market-oriented economies and promoting private enterprise.

© EXPORT-IMPORT BANK OF THE UNITED STATES (WWW.EXIM.GOV)

Mission possible. The Export-Import Bank of the United States (Ex-Im Bank) is the official export credit agency of the United States. Ex-Im Bank's mission is to assist in financing U.S. goods and services to international markets. With more than 78 years of experience, Ex-Im Bank has supported more than $400 billion of U.S. exports, primarily to developing markets worldwide.

The International Monetary Fund

The **International Monetary Fund (IMF)** is an international bank with 188 member nations that makes short-term loans to developing countries experiencing balance-of-payment deficits. This financing is contributed by member nations, and it must be repaid with interest. Loans are provided primarily to fund international trade. Created in 1945 and headquartered in Washington, DC, the bank's main goals are to:

- promote international monetary cooperation,
- facilitate the expansion and balanced growth of international trade,
- promote exchange rate stability,
- assist in establishing a multilateral system of payments, and
- make resources available to members experiencing balance-of-payment difficulties.

The Challenges Ahead

In a 2012 speech at Oxford University, Pascal Lamy, Director-General of the World Trade Organiztion stated, "We live in a world of ever-growing independence and interconnectedness. Our interdependence has grown beyond anyone's imagination.

multilateral development bank (MDB) an internationally supported bank that provides loans to developing countries to help them grow

International Monetary Fund (IMF) an international bank with 188 member nations that makes short-term loans to developing countries experiencing balance-of-payment deficits

The world of today is virtually unrecognizable from the world in which we lived one generation ago." The most striking example of globalization is Apple. Apple's iPod is designed in the United States, manufactured with components from Japan, Korea, and several other Asian countries, and assembled in China by a company from Chinese Taipei. Nowadays, most products are not "Made in the UK" or "Made in France"; they are in fact "Made in the World."[10]

In 2012, the global economic recovery remained sluggish. Financial challenges in some euro-area economies slowed the economic growth. However, WTO rules and principles have assisted governments in keeping markets open and they now provide a platform for which the trade can grow as the global economy improves. According to Mr. Lamy, "We see the light at the end of the tunnel and trade promises to be an important part of the recovery. But we must avoid derailing any economic revival through protectionism."

return to Inside BUSINESS

Volkswagen

If Volkswagen achieves its goal of manufacturing and selling 10 million vehicles yearly by 2018, it will move into first place as the world's largest automaker. With this in mind, Volkswagen is redesigning its vehicles so more parts fit more models, an important consideration for a company with facilities in so many countries. "We're creating a system that enables us to produce vehicles based on this architecture at any factory," explains a Volkswagen executive.

The company's joint ventures in China are also a key advantage in its expansion plans. China has the potential to be Volkswagen's largest market within just a few years because of higher demand from the ever-growing middle class. Volkswagen is already the top-selling foreign car brand in China, and building on that success will only add momentum to the company's global growth.

Questions

1. Can Volkswagen be considered a multinational firm? Explain your answer.
2. Do you agree with Volkswagen's CEO's statement that a car company has to be successful in the United States if it wants to be number one in the industry? Why or why not?

SUMMARY

Looking for Success?
Get Flashcards, Quizzes, Games, Crosswords, and more @ www.cengagebrain.com.

 Explain the economic basis for international business.

International business encompasses all business activities that involve exchanges across national boundaries. International trade is based on specialization, whereby each country produces the goods and services that it can produce more efficiently than any other goods and services. A nation is said to have a comparative advantage relative to these goods. International trade develops when each nation trades its surplus products for those in short supply.

A nation's balance of trade is the difference between the value of its exports and the value of its imports. Its balance of payments is the difference between the flow of money into and out of the nation. Generally, a negative balance of trade is considered unfavorable.

 Discuss the restrictions nations place on international trade, the objectives of these restrictions, and their results.

Despite the benefits of world trade, nations tend to use tariffs and nontariff barriers (import quotas, embargoes, and other restrictions) to limit trade. These restrictions typically are justified as being needed to protect a nation's economy, industries, citizens, or security. They can result in the loss of jobs, higher prices, fewer choices in the marketplace, and the misallocation of resources.

 Outline the extent of international business and the world economic outlook for trade.

World trade is generally increasing. Trade between the United States and other nations is increasing in dollar value but decreasing in terms of our share of the world market. Exports as a percentage of U.S. GDP have increased steadily since 1985, except in the 2001 and 2008 recessions.

 Discuss international trade agreements and international economic organizations working to foster trade.

The General Agreement on Tariffs and Trade (GATT) was formed to dismantle trade barriers and provide an environment in which international business can grow. Today, the World Trade Organization (WTO) and various economic communities carry on this mission. These world economic communities include the European Union, the NAFTA, the CAFTA, the Association of Southeast Asian Nations, the Pacific Rim, the Commonwealth of Independent States, the Caribbean Basin Initiative, the Common Market of the Southern Cone, the Organization of Petroleum Exporting Countries, and the Organization for Economic Cooperation and Development.

 Define the methods by which a firm can organize for and enter into international markets.

A firm can enter international markets in several ways. It may license a foreign firm to produce and market its products. It may export its products and sell them through foreign intermediaries or its own sales organization abroad, or it may sell its exports outright to an export–import merchant. It may enter into a joint venture with a foreign firm. It may establish its own foreign subsidiaries, or it may develop into a multinational enterprise.

Generally, each of these methods represents an increasingly deeper level of involvement in international business, with licensing being the simplest and the development of a multinational corporation the most involved.

 Describe the various sources of export assistance.

Many government and international agencies provide export assistance to U.S. and foreign firms. The export services and programs of the 19 agencies of the U.S. Trade Promotion Coordinating Committee (TPCC) can help U.S. firms to compete in foreign markets and create new jobs in the United States. Sources of export assistance include U.S. Export Assistance Centers, the International Trade Administration, U.S. and Foreign Commercial Services, Export Legal Assistance Network, Advocacy Center, National Trade Data Bank, and other government and international agencies.

 Identify the institutions that help firms and nations finance international business.

The financing of international trade is more complex than that of domestic trade. Institutions such as the Ex-Im Bank and the International Monetary Fund have been established to provide financing and ultimately to increase world trade for American and international firms.

KEY TERMS

You should now be able to define and give an example relevant to each of the following terms:

international business (71)	dumping (75)	World Trade Organization (WTO) (82)	countertrade (89)
absolute advantage (71)	nontariff barrier (75)		multinational enterprise (89)
comparative advantage (71)	import quota (75)	economic community (83)	Export-Import Bank of the United States (91)
exporting (72)	embargo (75)	licensing (85)	
importing (72)	foreign-exchange control (76)	letter of credit (86)	multilateral development bank (MDB) (93)
balance of trade (73)	currency devaluation (76)	bill of lading (86)	
trade deficit (73)	General Agreement on Tariffs and Trade (GATT) (81)	draft (86)	International Monetary Fund (IMF) (93)
balance of payments (74)		strategic alliance (88)	
import duty (tariff) (75)		trading company (89)	

REVIEW QUESTIONS

1. Why do firms engage in international trade?
2. What is the difference between an absolute and a comparative advantage in international trade? How are both types of advantages related to the concept of specialization?
3. What is a favorable balance of trade? In what way is it "favorable"?

4. List and briefly describe the principal restrictions that may be applied to a nation's imports.
5. What reasons are generally given for imposing trade restrictions?
6. What are the general effects of import restrictions on trade?

7. Define and describe the major objectives of the WTO and the international economic communities.
8. Which nations are the principal trading partners of the United States? What are the major U.S. imports and exports?
9. The methods of engaging in international business may be categorized as either direct or indirect. How would you classify each of the methods described in this chapter? Why?

10. In what ways is a multinational enterprise different from a large corporation that does business in several countries?
11. List some key sources of export assistance. How can these sources be useful to small business firms?
12. In what ways do the Ex-Im Bank, multilateral development banks, and the IMF enhance international trade?

DISCUSSION QUESTIONS

1. The United States restricts imports but, at the same time, supports the WTO and international banks whose objective is to enhance world trade. As a member of Congress, how would you justify this contradiction to your constituents?
2. What effects might the devaluation of a nation's currency have on its business firms, its consumers, and the debts it owes to other nations?
3. Should imports to the United States be curtailed by, say, 20 percent to eliminate our trade deficit? What might happen if this were done?

4. When should a firm consider expanding from strictly domestic trade to international trade? When should it consider becoming further involved in international trade? What factors might affect the firm's decisions in each case?
5. How can a firm obtain the expertise needed to produce and market its products in, for example, the EU?

Video Case 3.1   Keeping Brazil's Economy Hot

It's been hot in Brazil. No, we're not talking about the country's temperature: We're talking about its economy, which has been growing at a heated pace. In 2010, the country's GDP grew by 7.5 percent. That's a growth rate developed countries such as the United States haven't experienced for years, if not decades. Although Brazil's growth rate slowed considerably in 2011 and 2012 due to the global economic crisis, it has fared better than many other nations. Recently it surpassed the United Kingdom as the sixth-largest economy in the world.

Why has Brazil done so well economically? Increased world trade is one reason why. The country has an abundant amount of natural resources firms in other countries around the world are eager to buy—especially companies in the fast-growing nation of China. Greater exports have also helped 40 million Brazilians rise up out of poverty and into the middle class. Their massive spending power is creating new markets for multinational companies ranging from McDonald's and Whirlpool to Nestlé, Avon, and Volkswagen. Brazil has become Avon's largest market. Volkswagen now sells more cars in Brazil than it does Germany, where the company is headquartered. "China may have over a billion inhabitants, but Brazil has 200,000 consumers," explains Ivan Zurita, the president of Nestle's Brazil division.

Clouds on the horizon threaten to cool off Brazil's growth, however. To begin with, the country is concerned that its trade with China is out of balance. Although China purchases more natural resources from Brazil than any other nation, it doesn't purchase near as many manufactured goods from Brazil as it exports to it.

A bigger issue is the appreciation of Brazil's currency, the real. Massive amounts of money have been flowing into Brazil to take advantage of the nation's high interest rates and growth opportunities. This has increased the demand for the real, causing its value to rise by nearly 50 percent relative to other currencies. The good news is that the stronger real has made imported products cheaper for Brazilians to buy. The bad news is that products made in Brazil have become more expensive for the rest of the world to purchase, slowing the country's exports and growth.

Businesses in Brazil have lobbied the government to weaken the real so their products are better able to compete against imports. Their efforts appear to have paid off. Recently, Guido Mantega, Brazil's minister of finance, said the country will take steps "as needed" to weaken the real. The government has also imposed tariffs on a number of imported products, including cars, shoes, chemicals, and textiles, and signed a trade deal with Mexico that put a quota on the number of automobiles imported from that country.

Imports and the value of the real are not the only clouds threatening Brazil, though. Businesses in the country face a great deal of bureaucratic red tape, heavy regulations, and tax rates that are some of the highest in the world. To deal with these problems, Brazilian President Dilma Rousseff has announced that her administration will eliminate payroll taxes for employers in industries hardest hit by imports. To further ease the nation's growing pains, Brazil's development bank, BDM, will subsidize business loans to boost the production of many products, including tablets and off-shore oil rigs. The goal is to stimulate technological innovations that will enable manufacturers to produce higher-value products so Brazil doesn't have to rely on natural resources to fuel its growth. "Look, a government isn't made on the second or third day," Rousseff has said about her administration's incremental efforts to keep Brazil's emerging economy moving forward. "It's made over time. Things mature."[11]

Questions

1. Do you think the efforts of Brazil's government to keep the economy growing will be successful? Why or why not?
2. What downsides might Brazil experience by implementing quotas, tariffs, and measures to devalue its currency?

Case 3.2

Global Profits Are a Menu Mainstay at McDonald's

Few U.S. businesses are as international as McDonald's, the Illinois-based fast-food giant that began as an all-American hamburger place. With $22 billion in annual revenue, McDonald's now rings the world with 32,400 restaurants and serves 60 million customers every day. Although the United States accounts for 35 percent of McDonald's global revenue, Europe accounts for 41 percent and the Asia/Pacific, Middle East, and Africa regions account for 19 percent.

Hamburgers are, of course, the main attraction in many McDonald's restaurants: Worldwide, the company sells more than four million burgers every day. However, one of McDonald's key strengths is its ability to adapt to local tastes. In Japan, McDonald's sells Cheese Katsu sandwiches, featuring fried pork and cheese. In the Middle East, it sells McArabia pita sandwiches filled with grilled chicken or spiced beef. In France, it sells Croque McDo sandwiches with melted cheese and ham. In India, it sells vegetarian McAloo Tikki burgers. In Mexico, it sells McMolletes sandwiches made with refried beans and cheese.

Being a global business also helps McDonald's weather the economic ups and downs of different regions. At one point during the recent recession, its Asian revenue grew almost twice as quickly as its European revenue, both of which balanced the smaller increase in U.S. sales. Worldwide, McDonald's owns some of its restaurants and also sells franchise licenses to firms that open restaurants under the McDonald's brand name. In some markets, the company operates restaurants in joint ventures with local firms. For example, in India, it has one joint venture with a local firm to operate restaurants in the west and south and a second joint venture with a different company to operate restaurants in the east and the north.

The company is also building its global business by attracting more customers during different "dayparts," such as at breakfast time and in the late-night hours. A growing number of its global units stay open 24 hours a day for customer convenience. McDonald's has introduced a steady stream of breakfast, beverage, snack, and sandwich items to encourage repeat visits from customers at all income levels.

On the high end, McDonald's is doing well with its McCafés, which serve mochas and other gourmet coffees in a separate area of selected McDonald's units. As the company opens new restaurants and remodels existing restaurants, it is adding more McCafés in U.S. and European markets. The Angus Burger is another popular premium menu item. Both McCafé coffees and Angus Burgers appeal to customers willing to pay a little more to splurge on high quality. At the same time, the items on McDonald's budget menus are priced to appeal to customers who keep a close rein on their wallets.

Being a major power in global business means McDonald's must think carefully about the value of the different currencies its restaurants take in. Outside the United States, much of its revenue is rung up in euros, British pounds, Australian dollars, and Canadian dollars. As a result, McDonald's pays close attention to swings in foreign-exchange rates as it manages its financial affairs.

McDonald's is stepping up its involvement in sustainability all around the world. It has increased its use of packaging made from renewable materials and boosted recycling efforts to keep waste out of landfills. It has also been building eco-friendly restaurants in North and South America as well as in Europe to test green construction methods and cut back on energy and water usage. The company's social responsibility menu includes supporting the Ronald McDonald House charities and offering a range of organic foods and beverages plus healthy snack choices.

From India to Ireland, Argentina to Australia, McDonald's is poised for continued growth in sales and profits as it expands its restaurant empire and cooks up new products for customers to enjoy around the clock and around the world.[12]

Questions

1. What are the advantages and disadvantages of McDonald's ringing up sales in so many foreign currencies worldwide?
2. Why would McDonald's use two joint ventures to operate restaurants in different regions of India?
3. Discuss how being a multinational enterprise, with a presence in more than 170 countries, helps McDonald's build its business regardless of the short-term global economic outlook.

4 Choosing a Form of Business Ownership

LEARNING OBJECTIVES

Once you complete this chapter, you will be able to:

(1) Describe the advantages and disadvantages of sole proprietorships.

(2) Explain the different types of partners and the importance of partnership agreements.

(3) Describe the advantages and disadvantages of partnerships.

(4) Summarize how a corporation is formed.

(5) Describe the advantages and disadvantages of a corporation.

(6) Examine special types of corporations, including S-corporations, limited-liability companies, and not-for-profit corporations.

(7) Discuss the purpose of a cooperative, joint venture, and syndicate.

(8) Explain how growth from within and growth through mergers can enable a business to expand.

Kimpton Hotel & Restaurant Group Strives for Perfection!

When investment banker Bill Kimpton traveled to Europe, he liked staying in small hotels with personality and personalized service rather than big hotels owned by big chains. Adapting the "boutique" hotel idea, he bought and renovated an older San Francisco hotel with architectural charm and a central location. It reopened in 1981 as the Clarion Bedford Hotel and featured each room decorated in an individual style rather than all being identical, as in most hotel chains. It also offered a complimentary wine-tasting hour to bring guests together in the lobby for a bit of socializing every evening.

Little by little, Kimpton and his investment partners bought and renovated other hotels on the West Coast and, later, across the country. Now, more than 30 years later, the company that Kimpton founded has grown to more than 100 boutique hotels and trendy restaurants in North America. It employs more than 7,200 employees and rings up annual revenue of more than $700 million.

Kimpton Hotel & Restaurant Group is a limited-liability company (LLC), a form of business ownership that allows it the financial and management flexibility to work with different investment partners on different hotel and restaurant properties. The company also partners with different chefs to create specialty restaurants where the chef, not the hotel manager, is in charge. This unconventional approach led to Kimpton partnering with Wolfgang Puck, among other well-known chefs, to open restaurants inside or alongside Kimpton hotels.

Kimpton's boutique hotels are always adding special touches to make guests feel pampered. For example, under the "Guppy Love" program, the hotels will put a fish bowl stocked with goldfish in a guest room by request. The idea is to "provide little fish friends to anyone who [wants] a pet companion," explains Niki Leondakis, Kimpton's president. Employees further personalize the hotel experience by helping guests "live like a local, offering tailored recommendations from staff picks to one-of-a-kind experiences," Leondakis adds. Whether they're talking about a unique historical site or giving directions to a local art gallery, Kimpton's employees are "proud to be the cultural ambassadors of their city."[1]

Bill Kimpton started the Kimpton Hotel and Restaurant Group—the company profiled in the Inside Business feature for this chapter—with one goal in mind: He wanted customers to have a unique and memorable experience. Over the next 30 years, with the help of investors and partners, Kimpton created more than 100 boutique hotels and restaurants that ring up annual revenue of more than $700 million and employ more than 7,200 employees. Pretty impressive achievements for a company that must compete with larger corporate hotel and restaurant chains.

For Bill Kimpton, deciding to start a business was only the first step. It takes hard work, and there are many decisions that you must make to build a successful business. For example, you must choose the right type of business ownership. Kimpton chose the limited liability company (LLC) form of ownership because it allows the financial and management flexibility to work with different investment partners on different hotels and restaurant properties. And yet, as you will see in this chapter, there are other popular forms of ownership including sole proprietorships, partnerships, and corporations.

We begin this chapter by describing the three common forms of business ownership: sole proprietorships, partnerships, and corporations. We discuss how these types of businesses are formed and note the advantages and disadvantages of each. Next, we consider several types of business ownership usually chosen for special purposes, including S-corporations, limited-liability companies, not-for-profit corporations, cooperatives, joint ventures, and syndicates. We conclude the chapter with a discussion of how businesses can grow through internal expansion or through mergers with other companies.

Describe the advantages and disadvantages of sole proprietorships.

SOLE PROPRIETORSHIPS

A **sole proprietorship** is a business that is owned (and usually operated) by one person. Although a few sole proprietorships are large and have many employees, most are small. Sole proprietorship is the simplest form of business ownership and the easiest to start. In most instances, the owner (the *sole* proprietor) simply decides that he or she is in business and begins operations. Some of today's largest corporations, including Walmart, JCPenney, H.J. Heinz Company, and Procter & Gamble Company, started out as tiny—and in many cases, struggling—sole proprietorships.

Often entrepreneurs with a promising idea choose the sole proprietorship form of ownership. Annie Withey, for example, created a cheddar cheese–flavored popcorn snack food. Annie's popcorn, called Smartfood, became one of the fastest-selling snack foods in U.S. history. After a few years, PepsiCo Inc.'s Frito-Lay division bought the brand for about $15 million. Ms. Withey, an organic farmer and mother of two children, went on to develop an all-natural white-cheddar macaroni and cheese product. This venture was also a success. Today even though her firm, Annie's Homegrown, has grown and become part of a larger conglomerate, Annie remains the entrepreneurial heart of the company and still thinks like a sole proprietor.

As you can see in Figure 4.1, there are approximately 23 million nonfarm sole proprietorships in the United States. They account for 72 percent of the country's business firms. Although the most popular form of ownership when compared with partnerships and corporations, they rank last in total sales revenues. As shown in Figure 4.2, sole proprietorships account for about $1.3 trillion, or about 4 percent of total annual sales.

Sole proprietorships are most common in retailing, service, and agriculture. Thus, the clothing boutique, corner grocery, television-repair shop down the street, and small, independent farmers are likely to be sole proprietorships.

sole proprietorship a business that is owned (and usually operated) by one person

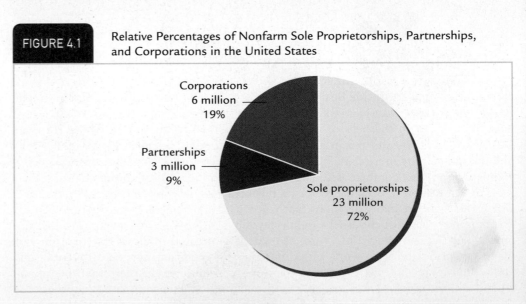

FIGURE 4.1 Relative Percentages of Nonfarm Sole Proprietorships, Partnerships, and Corporations in the United States

Corporations
6 million
19%

Partnerships
3 million
9%

Sole proprietorships
23 million
72%

Source: U.S. Bureau of the Census, *Statistical Abstract of the United States* (Washington, DC: Bureau of the Census, 2012), table 744 (www.census.gov).

FIGURE 4.2　Total Sales Receipts of American Businesses

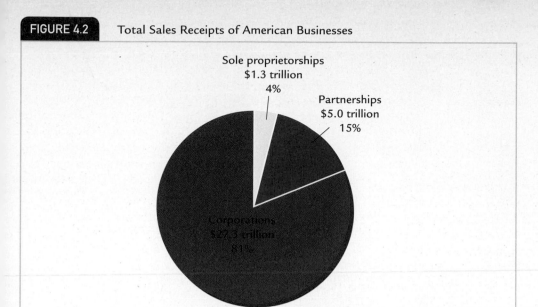

Sole proprietorships
$1.3 trillion
4%

Partnerships
$5.0 trillion
15%

Corporations
$27.3 trillion
81%

Source: U.S. Bureau of the Census, *Statistical Abstract of the United States* (Washington, DC: Bureau of the Census, 2012), table 744 (www.census.gov).

Advantages of Sole Proprietorships

Most of the advantages of sole proprietorships arise from the two main characteristics of this form of ownership: simplicity and individual control.

Ease of Start-Up and Closure Sole proprietorship is the simplest and cheapest way to start a business. Often, start-up requires no contracts, agreements, or other legal documents. Thus, a sole proprietorship can be, and most often is, established without the services of an attorney. The legal requirements often are limited to registering the name of the business and obtaining any necessary licenses or permits.

If the enterprise does not succeed, the firm can be closed as easily as it was opened. Creditors must be paid, of course, but generally, the owner does not have to go through any legal procedure before hanging up an "Out of Business" sign.

Pride of Ownership A successful sole proprietor is often very proud of her or his accomplishments—and rightfully so. In almost every case, the owner deserves a great deal of credit for solving the day-to-day problems associated with operating a sole proprietorship. Unfortunately, the reverse is also true. When the business fails, it is often the sole proprietor who is to blame.

Retention of All Profits Because all profits become the personal earnings of the owner, the owner has a strong incentive to succeed. This direct financial reward attracts many entrepreneurs to the sole proprietorship form of business and, if the business succeeds, is a source of great satisfaction.

No Special Taxes Profits earned by a sole proprietorship are taxed as the personal income of the owner. As a result, sole proprietors must report certain financial information for the business on their personal income tax returns and make estimated quarterly tax

© AP PHOTO/KATHY WILLENS

An entrepreneur with a sweet tooth! Hail a taxi anywhere in New York City and tell the driver, "Take me to the best cheesecake in New York." Odds are you will end up at a Junior's Restaurant. Founded in 1950 by Harry Rosen, the restaurant remains a family-owned business today. In this photo, Alan, a member of the Rosen family, displays some of the products that made this restaurant a New York tradition.

Do you dream of being your own boss? If you become a sole proprietor, you'll have all the flexibility that comes with making your own decisions. But remember: Although you'll have the final say, you'll also be responsible if something goes wrong.

payments to the federal government. Thus, a sole proprietorship does not pay the special state and federal income taxes that corporations pay.

Flexibility of Being Your Own Boss A sole proprietor is completely free to make decisions about the firm's operations. Without asking or waiting for anyone's approval, a sole proprietor can switch from retailing to wholesaling, move a shop's location, open a new store, or close an old one. Suppose that the sole proprietor of an appliance store finds that many customers now prefer to shop on Sunday afternoons. He or she can make an immediate change in business hours to take advantage of this information (provided that state laws allow such stores to open on Sunday). The manager of a store in a large corporate chain such as Best Buy Company may have to seek the approval of numerous managers and company officials before making such a change.

Disadvantages of Sole Proprietorships

The disadvantages of a sole proprietorship stem from the fact that these businesses are owned by one person. Some capable sole proprietors experience no problems. Individuals who start out with few management skills and little money are most at risk for failure.

Unlimited Liability Unlimited liability is a legal concept that holds a business owner personally responsible for all the debts of the business. There is legally no difference between the debts of the business and the debts of the proprietor. If the business fails, or if the business is involved in a lawsuit and loses, the owner's personal property—including savings and other assets—can be seized (and sold if necessary) to pay creditors.

Unlimited liability is perhaps the major factor that tends to discourage would-be entrepreneurs with substantial personal wealth from using the sole proprietor form of business organization.

Lack of Continuity Legally, the sole proprietor *is* the business. If the owner retires, dies, or is declared legally incompetent, the business essentially ceases to exist. In many cases, however—especially when the business is a profitable enterprise—the owner's heirs take it over and either sell it or continue to operate it. The business also can suffer if the sole proprietor becomes ill and cannot work for an extended period of time. If the owner, for example, has a heart attack, there is often no one who can step in and manage the business. An illness can be devastating if the sole proprietor's personal skills are what determine if the business is a success or a failure.

Lack of Money Banks, suppliers, and other lenders usually are unwilling to lend large sums of money to sole proprietorships. Only one person—the sole proprietor—can be held responsible for repaying such loans, and the assets of most sole proprietors usually are limited. Moreover, these assets may have been used already as security or collateral for personal borrowing (a home mortgage or car loan) or for short-term credit from suppliers. Lenders also worry about the lack of continuity of sole proprietorships: Who

unlimited liability a legal concept that holds a business owner personally responsible for all the debts of the business

Entrepreneurial SUCCESS

© ELNUR/SHUTTERSTOCK

Why Sell a Small Business to a Big Business?

Corey Capasso and Andrew Ferenci started Spinback in 2010 to help companies determine how social media connections were influencing sales. A year later, they had several large e-business customers and were ready for a major expansion, which meant raising more money. After discussing an alliance with Buddy Media, the co-founders realized that being acquired by Buddy Media was "a perfect fit," Ferenci says. "We would be able to focus more on the nuts and bolts of the business" without having to spend time looking for additional financing. But, he cautions, entrepreneurs "need to make sure the acquiring company has a solid corporate culture and will be a good place to work."

Aaron Patzer is another entrepreneur who let a big business acquire his small business, Mint.com, so he could keep improving operations and serving customers. Mint.com helps consumers manage their money online, and Patzer already had a million customers to consider when competitor Intuit approached him with an acquisition offer. The entrepreneur decided to sell, and became not only a millionaire but also a vice president at Intuit, bringing his employees to Intuit to keep running the business he had started. "They sort of left us alone to continue what we're doing," Patzer says of the post-acquisition situation.

Sources: Based on information in Aaron Shapiro, "The User-First Initiative," *Forbes*, January 4, 2012, www.forbes.com; Andrew Ferenci, "Spinback Founder: Why We Sold to Buddy Media Instead of Taking VC," *Business Insider*, June 3, 2011, www.businessinsider.com; Judith Messina, "Why Google Is the New Exit Strategy," *Crain's New York Business*, July 20, 2011, www.crainsnewyork.com; J.P. Mangalindan, "Aaron Patzer's Startups," *Fortune*, April 1, 2011, http://tech.fortune.cnn.com.

will repay a loan if the sole proprietor dies? Finally, many lenders are concerned about the large number of sole proprietorships that fail—a topic discussed in Chapter 5.

The limited ability to borrow money can prevent a sole proprietorship from growing. It is the main reason that many business owners, when in need of relatively large amounts of capital, change from a sole proprietorship to a partnership or corporate form of ownership.

Limited Management Skills The sole proprietor is often the sole manager—in addition to being the only salesperson, buyer, accountant, and, on occasion, janitor. Even the most experienced business owner is unlikely to have expertise in all these areas. Unless he or she obtains the necessary expertise by hiring employees, assistants, or consultants, the business can suffer in the areas in which the owner is less knowledgeable. For the many sole proprietors who cannot hire the help they need, there just are not enough hours in the day to do everything that needs to be done.

Difficulty in Hiring Employees The sole proprietor may find it hard to attract and keep competent help. Potential employees may feel that there is no room for advancement in a firm whose owner assumes all managerial responsibilities. And when those who *are* hired are ready to take on added responsibility, they may find that the only way to do so is to quit the sole proprietorship and go to work for a larger firm or start up their own businesses. The lure of higher salaries and increased benefits (especially health insurance) also may cause existing employees to change jobs.

Beyond the Sole Proprietorship

Like many others, you may decide that the major disadvantage of a sole proprietorship is the limited amount that one person can do in a workday. One way to reduce the effect of this disadvantage (and retain many of the advantages) is to have more than one owner.

Explain the different types of partners and the importance of partnership agreements.

PARTNERSHIPS

A person who would not think of starting and running a sole proprietorship business alone may enthusiastically seize the opportunity to form a business partnership. The U.S. Uniform Partnership Act defines a **partnership** as a voluntary association of two or more persons to act as co-owners of a business for profit. For example, in 1990, two young African-American entrepreneurs named Janet Smith and Gary Smith started IVY Planning Group—a company that provides strategic planning and performance measurement for clients. Today, more than 20 years later, the company has evolved into a multimillion-dollar company that has hired a diverse staff of employees and provides cultural diversity training for *Fortune* 1000 firms, large not-for-profit organizations, and government agencies. In recognition of its efforts, IVY Planning Group has been recognized by DiversityBusiness.com as one of the top 50 minority-owned companies. And both Janet Smith and Gary Smith have been named "1 of 50 Influential Minorities in Business" by Minority Business and Professionals Network.[2]

As shown in Figures 4.1 and 4.2, there are approximately 3 million partnerships in the United States, and this type of ownership accounts for about $5 trillion in sales receipts each year. Note, however, that this form of ownership is much less common than the sole proprietorship or the corporation. In fact, as Figure 4.1 shows, partnerships represent only about 9 percent of all American businesses. Although there is no legal maximum on the number of partners a partnership may have, most have only two. Regardless of the number of people involved, a partnership often represents a pooling of special managerial skills and talents; at other times, it is the result of a sole proprietor taking on a partner for the purpose of obtaining more capital.

Types of Partners

All partners are not necessarily equal. Some may be active in running the business, whereas others may have a limited role.

General Partners A **general partner** is a person who assumes full or shared responsibility for operating a business. General partners are active in day-to-day business operations, and each partner can enter into contracts on behalf of the other partners. He or she also assumes unlimited liability for all debts, including debts incurred by any other general partner without his or her knowledge or consent. A *general partnership* is a business co-owned by two or more general partners who are liable for everything the business does. To avoid future liability, a general partner who withdraws from the partnership must give notice to creditors, customers, and suppliers.

Limited Partners A **limited partner** is a person who invests money in a business but who has no management responsibility or liability for losses beyond his or her investment in the partnership. A *limited partnership* is a business co-owned by one or more general partners who manage the business and limited partners who invest money in it. Limited partnerships, for example, may be formed to finance real estate, oil and gas, motion picture, and other business ventures. Typically, the general partner or partners collect management fees and receive a percentage of profits. Limited partners receive a portion of profits and tax benefits.

Because of potential liability problems, special rules apply to limited partnerships. These rules are intended to protect customers and creditors who deal with limited partnerships. For example, prospective partners in a limited partnership must file a formal declaration, usually with the secretary of state, that describes the essential details of the partnership and the liability status of each partner involved in the business. At least one general partner must

partnership a voluntary association of two or more persons to act as co-owners of a business for profit

general partner a person who assumes full or shared responsibility for operating a business

limited partner a person who invests money in a business but has no management responsibility or liability for losses beyond the amount he or she invested in the partnership

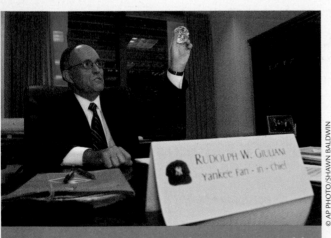

Sometimes it helps to have a famous partner with a proven track record. After leaving public office, former New York City Mayor Rudy Giuliani formed Giuliani Partners—a partnership with the accounting firm Ernst & Young. The objective of this partnership is to help business clients deal with the risks that stem from terrorism, crime, natural disasters, and other factors that threaten an organization's ability to survive.

© AP PHOTO/SHAWN BALDWIN

be responsible for the debts of the limited partnership. Also, some states prohibit the use of the limited partner's name in the partnership's name.

A special type of partnership is referred to as a *master limited partnership*. A **master limited partnership (MLP)** (sometimes referred to as a *publicly traded partnership*, or *PTP*) is a limited partnership that has units of ownership that can be traded on security exchanges much like shares of ownership in a corporation. Generally, both general partners and limited partners are involved in an MLP. The general partners manage the business; the limited partners provide investment capital. This special ownership arrangement has two major advantages. First, units of ownership in MLPs can be sold to investors to raise capital. Because MLP units can be traded on an exchange, investors can sell their units of ownership at any time, hopefully for a profit. While there are exceptions, most MLPs typically are in natural resources, energy, or real estate-related businesses.[3] Kinder Morgan Energy Partners, for example, is one of the largest publicly traded pipeline master limited partnerships in America. For Kinder Morgan Energy Partners, ownership units are traded on the New York Stock Exchange. Second, income from MLPs is generally reported as the personal income of the owners. MLPs thus avoided the double taxation paid on corporate income. For more information on the advantages and disadvantages of the MLP form of ownership, visit the National Association of Publicly Traded Partnerships Web site at www.naptp.org.

The Partnership Agreement

Articles of partnership refers to an agreement listing and explaining the terms of the partnership. Although both oral and written partnership agreements are legal and can be enforced in the courts, a written agreement has an obvious advantage. It is not subject to lapses of memory.

Figure 4.3 shows a typical partnership agreement. The partnership agreement should state

- Who will make the final decisions
- What each partner's duties will be
- The investment each partner will make
- How much profit or loss each partner receives or is responsible for
- What happens if a partner wants to dissolve the partnership or dies

Although the people involved in a partnership can draft their own agreement, most experts recommend consulting an attorney.

When entering into a partnership agreement, partners would be wise to let a neutral third party—a consultant, an accountant, a lawyer, or a mutual friend—assist with any disputes that might arise.

ADVANTAGES AND DISADVANTAGES OF PARTNERSHIPS

 Describe the advantages and disadvantages of partnerships.

When compared to sole proprietorships and corporations, partnerships are the least popular form of business ownership. Still there are situations when forming a partnership makes perfect sense. Before you make a decision to form a partnership, all the people involved should consider both the advantages and disadvantages of a partnership.

Advantages of Partnerships

Partnerships have many advantages. The most important are described as follows.

Ease of Start-Up Partnerships are relatively easy to form. As with a sole proprietorship, the legal requirements often are limited to registering the name of the business

master limited partnership (MLP) a limited partnership that has units of ownership that can be traded on security exchanges much like shares of ownership in a corporation

FIGURE 4.3   Articles of Partnership

The articles of partnership is a written or oral agreement that lists and explains the terms of a partnership.

PARTNERSHIP AGREEMENT

Names of partners — This agreement, made June 20, 2012, between Penelope Wolfburg of 783A South Street, Hazelton, Idaho, and Ingrid Swenson of RR 5, Box 96, Hazelton, Idaho.

Nature, name, and address of business —
1. The above named persons have this day formed a partnership that shall operate under the name of W-S Jewelers, located at 85 Broad Street, Hazelton, Idaho 83335, and shall engage in jewelry sales and repairs.

Duration of partnership —
2. The duration of this agreement will be for a term of fifteen (15) years, beginning June 20, 2012, or for a shorter period if agreed upon in writing by both partners.

Contribution of capital —
3. The initial investment by each partner will be as follows: Penelope Wolfburg, assets and liabilities of Wolfburg's Jewelry Store, valued at a capital investment of $40,000; Ingrid Swenson, cash of $20,000. These investments are partnership property.

Duties of each partner —
4. Each partner will give her time, skill, and attention to the operation of this partnership and will engage in no other business enterprise unless permission is granted in writing by the other partner.

Salaries, withdrawals, and distribution of profits —
5. The salary for each partner will be as follows: Penelope Wolfburg, $40,000 per year; Ingrid Swenson, $30,000 per year. Neither partner may withdraw cash or other assets from the business without express permission in writing from the other partner. All profits and losses of the business will be shared as follows: Penelope Wolfburg, 60 percent; Ingrid Swenson, 40 percent.

Termination —
6. Upon the dissolution of the partnership due to termination of this agreement, or to written permission by each of the partners, or to the death or incapacitation of one or both partners, a new contract may be entered into by the partners or the sole continuing partner has the option to purchase the other partner's interest in the business at a price that shall not exceed the balance in the terminating partner's capital account. The payment shall be made in cash in equal quarterly installments from the date of termination.

7. At the conclusion of this contract, unless it is agreed by both partners to continue the operation of the business under a new contract, the assets of the partnership, after the liabilities are paid, will be divided in proportion to the balance in each partner's capital account on that date.

Signatures —
Penelope Wolfburg   *Ingrid Swenson*

Penelope Wolfburg   Ingrid Swenson

Date —
June 20, 2012   *June 20, 2012*

Date   Date

Source: Adapted from Goldman and Sigismond, *Cengage Advantage Books: Business Law 8E.* © 2011 Cengage Learning.

and obtaining any necessary licenses or permits. It may not even be necessary to prepare written articles of partnership, although doing so is generally a good idea.

Availability of Capital and Credit   Because partners can pool their funds, a partnership usually has more capital available than a sole proprietorship does. This additional capital, coupled with the general partners' unlimited liability, may encourage banks and suppliers to extend more credit or approve larger loans to a partnership than to a sole proprietor. This does not mean that partnerships can borrow all the money they need. Many partnerships have found it hard to get long-term financing simply because lenders worry about the possibility of management disagreements and lack of continuity.

Personal Interest   General partners are very concerned with the operation of the firm—perhaps even more so than sole proprietors. After all, they are responsible for the actions of all other general partners, as well as for their own. The pride of ownership from solving the day-to-day problems of operating a business—with the help of another person(s)—is a strong motivating force and often makes all the people involved in the partnership work harder to become more successful.

Combined Business Skills and Knowledge Partners often have complementary skills. The weakness of one partner—in manufacturing, for example—may be offset by another partner's strength in that area. Moreover, the ability to discuss important decisions with another concerned individual often relieves some pressure and leads to more effective decision making.

Retention of Profits As in a sole proprietorship, all profits belong to the owners of the partnership. The partners share directly in the financial rewards and therefore are highly motivated to do their best to make the firm succeed. As noted, the partnership agreement should state how much profit or loss each partner receives or is responsible for.

Two entrepreneurs with one goal. There is a special pride of ownership that takes place when two people are solving problems and working together for the same purpose. Being responsible for what happens to the company—as well as your business partner—can be a motivating force for working that much harder to be successful.

No Special Taxes Although a partnership pays no income tax, the Internal Revenue Service requires partnerships to file an annual information return that states the names and addresses of all partners involved in the business. The return also must provide information about income and expenses and distributions made to each partner. Then each partner is required to report his or her share of profit (or loss) from the partnership on his or her individual tax return. Ultimately each partner's share of the partnership profit is taxed in the same way a sole proprietor is taxed.

Disadvantages of Partnerships

Although partnerships have many advantages when compared with sole proprietorships and corporations, they also have some disadvantages, which anyone thinking of forming a partnership should consider.

Unlimited Liability As we have noted, each *general* partner has unlimited liability for all debts of the business. Each partner is legally and personally responsible for the debts, taxes, and actions of any other partner conducting partnership business, even if that partner did not incur those debts or do anything wrong. General partners thus run the risk of having to use their personal assets to pay creditors. *Limited* partners, however, risk only their original investment.

Today, many states allow partners to form a *limited-liability partnership* (LLP), in which a partner may have limited-liability protection from legal action resulting from the malpractice or negligence of the other partners. Many states that allow LLPs restrict this type of ownership to certain types of professionals such as accountants, architects, attorneys, and similar professionals. (Note the difference between a limited partnership and a limited-liability partnership. A limited partnership must have at least one general partner that has unlimited liability. On the other hand, all partners in a limited-liability partnership may have limited liability *for the malpractice of the other partners*.)

Management Disagreements What happens to a partnership if one of the partners brings a spouse or a relative into the business? What happens if a partner wants to withdraw more money from the business? Notice that each of these situations—and for that matter, most of the other problems that can develop in a partnership—involves one partner doing something that disturbs the other partner(s). This human factor is especially important because business partners—with egos, ambitions, and money on the line—are especially susceptible to friction. When partners begin to disagree about decisions, policies, or ethics, distrust may build and get worse as time passes—often to the point where it is impossible to operate the business successfully.

Lack of Continuity Partnerships are terminated if any one of the general partners dies, withdraws, or is declared legally incompetent. However, the remaining partners can purchase that partner's ownership share. For example, the partnership agreement may permit surviving partners to continue the business after buying a deceased partner's interest from his or her estate. However, if the partnership loses an owner whose specific management or technical skills cannot be replaced, it is not likely to survive.

Frozen Investment It is easy to invest money in a partnership, but it is sometimes quite difficult to get it out. This is the case, for example, when remaining partners are unwilling to buy the share of the business that belongs to a partner who retires or wants to relocate to another city. To avoid such difficulties, the partnership agreement should include some procedure for buying out a partner.

In some cases, a partner must find someone outside the firm to buy his or her share. How easy or difficult it is to find an outsider depends on how successful the business is and how willing existing partners are to accept a new partner.

Beyond the Partnership

The main advantages of a partnership over a sole proprietorship are increased availability of capital and credit and the combined business skills and knowledge of the partners. However, some of the basic disadvantages of the sole proprietorship also plague the general partnership. One disadvantage in particular—unlimited liability—can cause problems for a partner with substantial personal wealth. A third form of business ownership, the corporation, overcomes this disadvantage.

Summarize how a corporation is formed.

CORPORATIONS

Back in 1837, William Procter and James Gamble—two sole proprietors—formed a partnership called Procter & Gamble (P&G) and set out to compete with 14 other soap and candle makers in Cincinnati, Ohio. Then, in 1890, Procter & Gamble incorporated to raise additional capital for expansion that eventually allowed the company to become a global giant. Today, P&G brands serve over 4 billion of the 7 billion people in the world today because the corporation operates in 180 countries around the globe.[4] Like many large corporations, P&G's market capitalization is greater than the gross domestic product of many countries. Although this corporation is a corporate giant, the firm's executives and employees believe it also has a responsibility to be an ethical corporate citizen. For example, P&G's purpose statement (or mission) is

> *We will provide branded products and services of superior quality and value that improve the lives of the world's consumers, now and for generations to come. As a result, consumers will reward us with leadership sales, profit and value creation, allowing our people, our shareholders and the communities in which we live and work to prosper.*[5]

In today's competitive environment, it's common to hear of large companies that are profitable. It is less common to hear of profitable companies that are held in high regard because they are good corporate citizens.

While not all sole proprietorships and partnerships become corporations, there are reasons why business owners choose the corporate form of ownership. Let's begin with a definition of a corporation. Perhaps the best definition of a corporation was given by Chief Justice John Marshall in a famous Supreme Court decision in 1819.

A corporation, he said, "is an artificial person, invisible, intangible, and existing only in contemplation of the law." In other words, a **corporation** (sometimes referred to as a *regular* or *C-corporation*) is an artificial person created by law, with most of the legal rights of a real person. These include:

- The right to start and operate a business
- The right to buy or sell property
- The right to borrow money
- The right to sue or be sued
- The right to enter into binding contracts

Unlike a real person, however, a corporation exists only on paper. There are approximately 6 million corporations in the United States. They comprise about 19 percent of all businesses, but they account for 81 percent of sales revenues (see Figures 4.1 and 4.2).

© AP PHOTO/AL BEHRMAN

Procter & Gamble: Once a sole proprietorship, then a partnership, and now a very large corporation. Although one of the largest corporations in the world, P&G was started when two sole proprietors formed a partnership to sell soap and candles. Today the corporation's product line has expanded and it now operates in 180 different countries around the globe.

Corporate Ownership

The shares of ownership of a corporation are called **stock**. The people who own a corporation's stock—and thus own part of the corporation—are called **stockholders**. Once a corporation has been formed, it may sell its stock to individuals or other companies that want to invest in the corporation. It also may issue stock as a reward to key employees in return for certain services or as a return to investors in place of cash payments.

A **closed corporation** is a corporation whose stock is owned by relatively few people and is not sold to the general public. As an example, Mars—the company famous for M&Ms, Snickers, Dove, Milky Way, Twix, and other chocolate candy—is a privately held, family-owned, closed corporation. Although many people think that a closed corporation is a small company, there are exceptions. Mars, for example, has annual sales of more than $30 billion, employs more than 65,000 associates worldwide, and operates in 70 different countries.[6]

An **open corporation** is one whose stock can be bought and sold by any individual. Examples of open corporations include General Electric, Microsoft, Apple, and Sony.

Forming a Corporation

Although you may think that incorporating a business guarantees success, it does not. There is no special magic about placing the word *Incorporated* or the abbreviation *Inc.* after the name of a business. Unfortunately, like sole proprietorships or partnerships, corporations can go broke. The decision to incorporate a business therefore should be made only after carefully considering whether the corporate form of ownership suits your needs better than the sole proprietorship or partnership forms.

If you decide that the corporate form is the best form of organization for you, most experts recommend that you begin the incorporation process by consulting a lawyer to be sure that all legal requirements are met. While it may be possible to incorporate a business without legal help, it is well to keep in mind the old saying, "A man who acts as his own attorney has a fool for a client." Table 4.1 lists some aspects of starting and running a business that may require legal help.

Where to Incorporate A business is allowed to incorporate in any state that it chooses. Most small- and medium-sized businesses are incorporated in the state where they do the most business. The founders of larger corporations or of those that will do business nationwide often compare the benefits that various states provide to corporations. The decision on where to incorporate usually is based on two factors: (1) the cost of incorporating in one state compared with the cost in another state and

corporation an artificial person created by law with most of the legal rights of a real person, including the rights to start and operate a business, to buy or sell property, to borrow money, to sue or be sued, and to enter into binding contracts

stock the shares of ownership of a corporation

stockholder a person who owns a corporation's stock

closed corporation a corporation whose stock is owned by relatively few people and is not sold to the general public

open corporation a corporation whose stock can be bought and sold by any individual

TABLE 4.1	Ten Aspects of Business That May Require Legal Help
1.	Choosing either the sole proprietorship, partnership, corporate, or some special form of ownership
2.	Constructing a partnership agreement
3.	Incorporating a business
4.	Registering a corporation's stock
5.	Obtaining a trademark, patent, or copyright
6.	Filing for licenses or permits at the local, state, and federal levels
7.	Purchasing an existing business or real estate
8.	Creating valid contracts
9.	Hiring employees and independent contractors
10.	Extending credit and collecting debts

© CENGAGE LEARNING 2014

(2) the advantages and disadvantages of each state's corporate laws and tax structure. Some states are more hospitable than others, and some offer fewer restrictions, lower taxes, and other benefits to attract new firms. Delaware, Nevada, and Wyoming are often chosen by corporations that do business in more than one state because of their corporation-friendly laws and pro-business climate.[7]

An incorporated business is called a **domestic corporation** in the state in which it is incorporated. In all other states where it does business, it is called a **foreign corporation**. Sears Holdings Corporation, the parent company of Sears and Kmart, is incorporated in Delaware, where it is a domestic corporation. In the remaining 49 states, Sears is a foreign corporation. Sears must register in all states where it does business and also pay taxes and annual fees to each state. A corporation chartered by a foreign government and conducting business in the United States is an **alien corporation**. Volkswagen AG, Sony Corporation, and the Royal Dutch/Shell Group are examples of alien corporations.

The Corporate Charter Once a home state has been chosen, the incorporator(s) submits *articles of incorporation* to the secretary of state. When the articles of incorporation are approved, they become a contract between a corporation and the state in which the state recognizes the formation of the artificial person that is the corporation. Usually, the articles of incorporation include the following information:

- The firm's name and address
- The incorporators' names and addresses
- The purpose of the corporation
- The maximum amount of stock and types of stock to be issued
- The rights and privileges of stockholders
- The length of time the corporation is to exist

To help you to decide if the corporate form of organization is the right choice, you may want to visit the library for more information on the incorporation process. You can also use an Internet search engine and enter the term "business incorporation" for useful Web sites. In addition, before making a decision to organize your business as a corporation, you may want to consider two additional areas: stockholders' rights and the importance of the organizational meeting.

Stockholders' Rights There are two basic types of stock. Owners of **common stock** may vote on corporate matters. Generally, an owner of common stock has one vote for each share owned. However, any claims of common-stock owners on profits, dividends, and assets of the corporation are paid after the claims of others. The owners

domestic corporation a corporation in the state in which it is incorporated

foreign corporation a corporation in any state in which it does business except the one in which it is incorporated

alien corporation a corporation chartered by a foreign government and conducting business in the United States

common stock stock owned by individuals or firms who may vote on corporate matters but whose claims on profits and assets are subordinate to the claims of others

preferred stock stock owned by individuals or firms who usually do not have voting rights but whose claims on dividends are paid before those of common-stock owners of **preferred stock** usually have no voting rights, but their claims on dividends are paid before those of common-stock owners. Although large corporations may issue both common and preferred stock, generally small corporations issue only common stock.

Perhaps the most important right of owners of both common and preferred stock is to share in the profit earned by the corporation through the payment of dividends. A **dividend** is a distribution of earnings to the stockholders of a corporation. Other rights include receiving information about the corporation, voting on changes to the corporate charter, and attending the corporation's annual stockholders' meeting, where they may exercise their right to vote.

Because common stockholders usually live all over the nation, very few actually may attend a corporation's annual meeting. Instead, they vote by proxy. A **proxy** is a legal form listing issues to be decided at a stockholders' meeting and enabling stockholders to transfer their voting rights to some other individual or individuals. The stockholder can register a vote and transfer voting rights simply by signing and returning the form. Today, most corporations also allow stockholders to exercise their right to vote by proxy by accessing the Internet or using a toll-free phone number.

Organizational Meeting As the last step in forming a corporation, the incorporators and original stockholders meet to adopt corporate by-laws and elect their first board of directors. (Later, directors will be elected or reelected at the corporation's annual meetings by the firm's stockholders.) The board members are directly responsible to the stockholders for the way they operate the firm.

Corporate Structure

The organizational structure of most corporations is more complicated than that of a sole proprietorship or partnership. In a corporation, both the board of directors and the corporate officers are involved in management.

Board of Directors As an artificial person, a corporation can act only through its directors, who represent the corporation's stockholders. The **board of directors** is the top governing body of a corporation and is elected by the stockholders. In theory, then, the stockholders are able to control the activities of the entire corporation through its directors because they are the group that elects the board of directors (see Figure 4.4)

Board members can be chosen from within the corporation or from outside it. *Note:* For a small corporation, only one director is required in many states although you can choose to have more. Directors who are elected from within the corporation are usually its top managers—the president and executive vice presidents, for

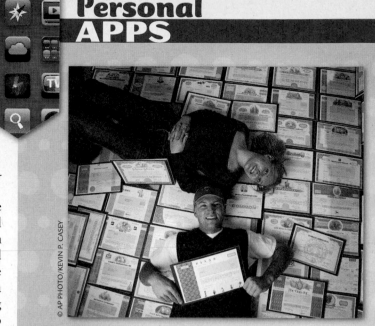

Personal APPS

Even if you own a single share of common stock, you're legally a part-owner of the corporation. You're entitled to receive any dividends paid to shareholders and you can vote on important matters such as electing the board of directors. Your vote is counted—and it counts.

dividend a distribution of earnings to the stockholders of a corporation

proxy a legal form listing issues to be decided at a stockholders' meeting and enabling stockholders to transfer their voting rights to some other individual or individuals

board of directors the top governing body of a corporation, the members of which are elected by the stockholders

| FIGURE 4.4 | Hierarchy of Corporate Structure |

Stockholders exercise a great deal of influence through their right to elect the board of directors.

Stockholders (owners) → *Elect* → Board of directors → *Appoints* → Officers → *Hire* → Employees

Social MEDIA

Going Social with Score

As "Counselors to America's Small Business," SCORE (formerly known as the Service Corps of Retired Executives) offers four ways for entrepreneurs to go social with peers and experts:

- *Facebook* SCORE's Facebook page (www.facebook.com/SCOREFans) is a hub for Q&A about starting a business.

- *YouTube* On SCORE's YouTube channel (www.youtube.com/SCORESmallBusiness), business owners can view and comment on brief videos highlighting tips for business success.
- *Blog* The SCORE blog (http://blog.score.org/) features timely articles about vital aspects of business ownership and operations.
- *Twitter* In 140 characters or less, SCORE mentors offer business advice and links to more info via Twitter (http://twitter.com/SCOREMentors).

The costs of incorporating, in terms of both time and money, discourage many owners of smaller businesses from forming corporations.

Government Regulation and Increased Paperwork A corporation must meet various government standards before it can sell its stock to the public. Then it must file many reports on its business operations and finances with local, state, and federal governments. In addition, the corporation must make periodic reports to its stockholders about various aspects of the business. To prepare all the necessary reports, even small corporations often need the help of an attorney, certified public accountant, and other professionals on a regular basis. In addition, a corporation's activities are restricted by law to those spelled out in its charter.

Conflict Within the Corporation Because a large corporation may employ thousands of employees, some conflict is inevitable. For example, the pressure to increase sales revenue, reduce expenses, and increase profits often leads to increased stress and tension for both managers and employees. This is especially true when a corporation operates in a competitive industry, attempts to develop and market new products, or must downsize the workforce to reduce employee salary expense during an economic crisis.

Double Taxation Corporations must pay a tax on their profits. In addition, stockholders must pay a personal income tax on profits received as dividends. Corporate profits thus are taxed twice—once as corporate income and a second time as the personal income of stockholders. *Note:* Both the S-corporation and the limited-liability company discussed in the next section eliminate the disadvantage of double taxation because they are taxed like a partnership.

Lack of Secrecy Because open corporations are required to submit detailed reports to government agencies and to stockholders, they cannot keep their operations confidential. Competitors can study these corporate reports and then use the information to compete more effectively. In effect, every public corporation has to share some of its secrets with its competitors.

TABLE 4.2	Some Advantages and Disadvantages of a Sole Proprietorship, Partnership, and Corporation		
	Sole Proprietorship	**General Partnership**	**Regular C-Corporaton**
Protecting against liability for debts	Difficult	Difficult	Easy
Raising money	Difficult	Difficult	Easy
Ownership transfer	Difficult	Difficult	Easy
Preserving continuity	Difficult	Difficult	Easy
Government regulations	Few	Few	Many
Formation	Easy	Easy	Difficult
Income taxation	Once	Once	Twice

© CENGAGE LEARNING 2014

SPECIAL TYPES OF BUSINESS OWNERSHIP

6 Examine special types of corporations, including S-corporations, limited-liability companies, and not-for-profit corporations.

In addition to the sole proprietorship, partnership, and the regular corporate form of organization, some entrepreneurs choose other forms of organization that meet their special needs. Additional organizational options include S-corporations, limited-liability companies, and not-for-profit corporations.

S-Corporations

If a corporation meets certain requirements, its directors may apply to the Internal Revenue Service for status as an S-corporation. An **S-corporation** is a corporation that is taxed as though it were a partnership. In other words, the corporation's income is taxed only as the personal income of its stockholders. Corporate profits or losses "pass through" the business and are reported on the owners' personal income tax returns.

To qualify for the special status of an S-corporation, a firm must meet the following criteria:[9]

1. No more than 100 stockholders are allowed.
2. Stockholders must be individuals, estates, or certain trusts.
3. There can be only one class of outstanding stock.
4. The firm must be a domestic corporation eligible to file for S-corporation status.
5. There can be no partnerships, corporations, or nonresident-alien stockholders.
6. All stockholders must agree to the decision to form an S-corporation.

Becoming an S-corporation can be an effective way to avoid double taxation while retaining the corporation's legal benefit of limited liability.

Limited-Liability Companies

A new form of ownership called a *limited-liability company* has been approved in all 50 states—although each state's laws may differ. A **limited-liability company (LLC)** is a form of business ownership that combines the benefits of a corporation and a partnership while avoiding some of the restrictions and disadvantages of those forms of ownership. Chief advantages of an LLC are as follows:

1. Like a sole proprietorship or partnership, an LLC enjoys pass-through taxation. This means that owners report their share of profits or losses in the company on their individual tax returns and avoid the double taxation imposed on most corporations. LLCs with at least two members are taxed like a partnership. LLCs with just one member are taxed like a sole proprietorship. LLCs can even elect to be taxed as a corporation if there are benefits to offset the corporate double taxation.
2. Like a corporation, it provides limited-liability protection for acts and debts of the LLC. An LLC thus extends the concept of personal-asset protection to small business owners.
3. The LLC type of organization provides more management flexibility when compared with corporations. A corporation, for example, is required to hold annual meetings and record meeting minutes; an LLC is not.

Although many experts believe that the LLC is nothing more than a variation of the S-corporation, there is a difference. An LLC is not restricted to 100 stockholders—a common drawback of the S-corporation. LLCs are also less restricted and have more flexibility than S-corporations in terms of who can become an owner. Although the owners of an LLC may file the required articles of organization in any state, most choose to file in their home state— the state where they do most of their business.

S-corporation a corporation that is taxed as though it were a partnership

limited-liability company (LLC) a form of business ownership that combines the benefits of a corporation and a partnership while avoiding some of the restrictions and disadvantages of those forms of ownership

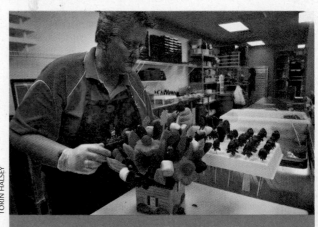

© AP PHOTO/WICHITA FALLS TIMES RECORD NEWS, TORIN HALSEY

Edible Arrangements: A limited-liability company. A limited-liability company doesn't have to be small. Edible Arrangements has over 1,100 stores around the world and is ranked as one of America's top 5,000 fastest growing private companies. It chose the limited-liability form of ownership to avoid some of the restrictions and disadvantages of other forms of business ownership.

Even though most LLCs are small to medium-sized businesses, a limited-liability company doesn't have to be small. American Girl Brands—a limited-liability company that sells dolls, clothing, furniture, books, and magazines for the popular American Girl product lines—chose the LLC type of business ownership because it provided limited liability for investors and avoided some of the restrictions and disadvantages of other forms of business ownership.

Because of the increased popularity of the LLC form of organization, experts are predicting that LLCs may become one of the most popular forms of business ownership available. For more information about the benefits of forming an LLC, go to www.llc.com/LLC_Benefits.html. For help in understanding the differences between a regular corporation, S-corporation, and limited-liability company, see Table 4.3.

Not-for-Profit Corporations

A **not-for-profit corporation** (sometimes referred to as *non-profit*) is a corporation organized to provide a social, educational, religious, or other service rather than to earn a profit. Various charities, museums, private schools, colleges, and charitable organizations are organized in this way, primarily to ensure limited liability.

While the process used to organize a not-for-profit corporation is similar to the process used to create a regular corporation, each state does have different laws. In fact, many of the requirements are different than the requirements for establishing a regular corporation. Once approved by state authorities, not-for-profit corporations must meet specific Internal Revenue Service guidelines in order to obtain tax-exempt status.

Today, there is a renewed interest in not-for-profits because these organizations are formed to improve communities and change lives. For example, Habitat for Humanity is a not-for-profit corporation and was formed to provide homes for qualified lower income people who cannot afford housing. Even though this corporation may receive more money than it spends, any surplus funds are "reinvested" in building activities to provide low-cost housing to qualified individuals. Other examples of not-for-profit corporations include the SeaWorld and Busch Gardens Conservation Fund, the Girl Scouts, the Bill and Melinda Gates Foundation, and many local not-for-profits designed to meet specific needs within a community.

not-for-profit corporation a corporation organized to provide a social, educational, religious, or other service rather than to earn a profit

TABLE 4.3	Some Advantages and Disadvantages of a Regular Corporation, S-Corporation, and Limited-Liability Company		
	Regular C-Corporations	S-Corporation	Limited-Liability Company
Double taxation	Yes	No	No
Limited liability and personal asset protection	Yes	Yes	Yes
Management flexibility	No	No	Yes
Restrictions on the number of owners/ stockholders	No	Yes	No
Internal Revenue Service tax regulations	Many	Many	Fewer

© CENGAGE LEARNING 2014

Many not-for-profit corporations operate in much the same way as for-profit businesses. Employees of not-for-profit businesses are responsible for making sure the organization achieves its goals and objectives, ensuring accountability for finances and donations, and monitoring activities to improve performance of both paid employees and volunteers. If you are interested in a business career, don't rule out the non-profit sector. You might consider volunteering your time and effort in a local not-for-profit organization to see if you enjoy this type of challenge.

COOPERATIVES, JOINT VENTURES, AND SYNDICATES

 7 Discuss the purpose of a cooperative, joint venture, and syndicate.

Today, three additional types of business organizations—cooperatives, joint ventures, and syndicates—are used for special purposes. Each of these forms of organization is unique when compared with more traditional forms of business ownership.

Cooperatives

A **cooperative** is an association of individuals or firms whose purpose is to perform some business function for its members. The cooperative can perform its function more effectively than any member could by acting alone. For example, cooperatives purchase goods in bulk and distribute them to members; thus, the unit cost is lower than it would be if each member bought the goods in a much smaller quantity.

Although cooperatives are found in all segments of our economy, they are most prevalent in agriculture. Farmers use cooperatives to purchase supplies, to buy services such as trucking and storage, and to process and market their products. Ocean Spray Cranberries, Inc., for example, is a cooperative of some 700 cranberry growers and about 50 citrus growers spread throughout the country and is North America's leading producer of canned and bottled juices and juice drinks.[10]

Joint Ventures

A **joint venture** is an agreement between two or more groups to form a business entity in order to achieve a specific goal or to operate for a specific period of time. Both the scope of the joint venture and the liabilities of the people or businesses involved usually are limited to one project. Once the goal is reached, the period of time elapses, or the project is completed, the joint venture is dissolved.

Corporations, as well as individuals, may enter into joint ventures. Major oil producers often have formed a number of joint ventures to share the extremely high cost of exploring for offshore petroleum deposits. And many U.S. companies are forming joint ventures with foreign firms in order to enter new markets around the globe. For example, Walmart has joined forces with India's Bharti Enterprises to establish wholesale cash-and-carry stores that sell directly to local retailers in different cities and towns in India. Plans are for each store to offer an assortment of approximately 6,000 items including food and nonfood items at competitive wholesale prices, allowing retailers and small business owners to lower their cost of operation. By the beginning of 2012, the Bharti Walmart joint venture had opened 14 cash-and-carry stores and employed over 3,000 associates.[11]

Syndicates

A **syndicate** is a temporary association of individuals or firms organized to perform a specific task that requires a large amount of capital. The syndicate is formed because no one person or firm is willing to put up the entire amount required for the undertaking. Like a joint venture, a syndicate is dissolved as soon as its purpose has been accomplished.

cooperative an association of individuals or firms whose purpose is to perform some business function for its members

joint venture an agreement between two or more groups to form a business entity in order to achieve a specific goal or to operate for a specific period of time

syndicate a temporary association of individuals or firms organized to perform a specific task that requires a large amount of capital

Syndicates are used most commonly to underwrite large insurance policies, loans, and investments. To share the risk of default, banks have formed syndicates to provide loans to developing countries. Stock brokerage firms usually join together in the same way to market a new issue of stock. In May 2012 and after years of anticipation in the investment world, Facebook sold stock to investors. Facebook—the world's leading social media Web site—raised $16 billion with the help of a syndicate of Wall Street firms including Bank of America Merrill Lynch, JPMorgan Chase & Co., Morgan Stanley, and Goldman Sachs.[12] This initial public offering, often referred to as an IPO, is one of the largest in recent history. (An *initial public offering* is the term used to describe the first time a corporation sells stock to the general public.)

Explain how growth from within and growth through mergers can enable a business to expand.

8

CORPORATE GROWTH

Growth seems to be a basic characteristic of business. One reason for seeking growth has to do with profit: A larger firm generally has greater sales revenue and thus greater profit. Another reason is that in a growing economy, a business that does not grow is actually shrinking relative to the economy. A third reason is that business growth is a means by which some executives boost their power, prestige, and reputation.

Growth poses new problems and requires additional resources that first must be available and then must be used effectively. The main ingredient in growth is capital—and as we have noted, capital is most readily available to corporations.

Growth from Within

Most corporations grow by expanding their present operations. Some introduce and sell new but related products. Others expand the sale of present products to new geographic markets or to new groups of consumers in geographic markets already served. Although Walmart was started by Sam Walton in 1962 with one discount store, today Walmart has over 10,000 stores in the United States and 27 other countries and has long-range plans for expanding into additional international markets.[13]

Growth from within, especially when carefully planned and controlled, can have relatively little adverse effect on a firm. For the most part, the firm continues to do what it has been doing, but on a larger scale. For instance, Larry Ellison, co-founder and CEO of Oracle Corporation of Redwood Shores, California, built the firm's annual revenues up from a mere $282 million in 1988 to approximately $36 billion today.[14] Much of this growth has taken place over the last 15 years as Oracle capitalized on its global leadership in information management software.

Growth Through Mergers and Acquisitions

merger the purchase of one corporation by another

hostile takeover a situation in which the management and board of directors of a firm targeted for acquisition disapprove of the merger

tender offer an offer to purchase the stock of a firm targeted for acquisition at a price just high enough to tempt stockholders to sell their shares

proxy fight a technique used to gather enough stockholder votes to control a targeted company

Another way a firm can grow is by purchasing another company. The purchase of one corporation by another is called a **merger**. An *acquisition* is essentially the same thing as a merger, but the term usually is used in reference to a large corporation's purchases of other corporations. Although most mergers and acquisitions are friendly, hostile takeovers also occur. A **hostile takeover** is a situation in which the management and board of directors of a firm targeted for acquisition disapprove of the merger.

When a merger or acquisition becomes hostile, a corporate raider—another company or a wealthy investor—may make a tender offer or start a proxy fight to gain control of the target company. A **tender offer** is an offer to purchase the stock of a firm targeted for acquisition at a price just high enough to tempt stockholders to sell their shares. Corporate raiders also may initiate a proxy fight. A **proxy fight** is a technique used to gather enough stockholder votes to control a targeted company.

If the corporate raider is successful and takes over the targeted company, existing management usually is replaced. Faced with this probability, existing management may take specific actions, sometimes referred to as "poison pills," "shark repellents," or "porcupine provisions," to maintain control of the firm and avoid the hostile takeover. Whether mergers are friendly or hostile, they are generally classified as *horizontal, vertical,* or *conglomerate* (see Figure 4.5).

Growth through global joint ventures. General Electric, which owns many businesses that fortify the world's infrastructure, recently formed two joint ventures in Russia. Here is Russian president Vladimir Putin meeting with GE executives.

Horizontal Mergers A *horizontal merger* is a merger between firms that make and sell similar products or services in similar markets. The proposed merger between AT&T and T-Mobile was an example of a horizontal merger because both firms provide cell phone service to their customers. This type of merger tends to reduce the number of firms in an industry—and thus may reduce competition. As a result most horizontal mergers are reviewed carefully by federal agencies before they are approved in order to protect competition in the marketplace. In fact, the AT&T merger with T-Mobile was effectively blocked when the U.S. Department of Justice filed a law suit to block the merger. According to the Department of Justice, the main reason behind the government's legal action was to protect the competitive environment and the consumers' right to choose. Rather than fight the government's attempt to block the merger, AT&T withdrew its offer to acquire T-Mobile.

Vertical Mergers A *vertical merger* is a merger between firms that operate at different but related levels in the production and marketing of a product. Generally, one of the merging firms is either a supplier or a customer of the other. A vertical

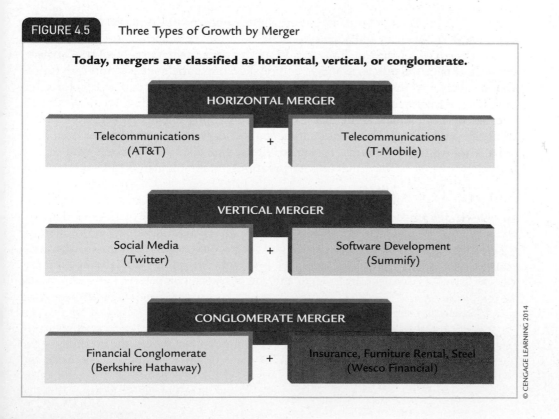

| FIGURE 4.5 | Three Types of Growth by Merger |

Today, mergers are classified as horizontal, vertical, or conglomerate.

HORIZONTAL MERGER

Telecommunications (AT&T) + Telecommunications (T-Mobile)

VERTICAL MERGER

Social Media (Twitter) + Software Development (Summify)

CONGLOMERATE MERGER

Financial Conglomerate (Berkshire Hathaway) + Insurance, Furniture Rental, Steel (Wesco Financial)

© CENGAGE LEARNING 2014

merger occurred when social media giant Twitter acquired Summify. At the time of the 2012 merger, Summify, based in Vancouver, was a startup technology company in the process of building the next generation of news-reader software that had a unique approach to summarizing the most important information from social media feeds from Google, Facebook, and Twitter. Rather than develop its own software to summarize the most important information, Twitter simply purchased the Summify company.[15]

Conglomerate Mergers A *conglomerate* merger takes place between firms in completely different industries. A conglomerate merger occurred when financial conglomerate Berkshire Hathaway acquired Wesco Financial Corporation. While both companies were recognized as successful companies that have a history of increasing sales revenues and profits, they operate in different industries. Berkshire Hathaway, led by its CEO Warren Buffett, has a long history of acquiring firms that have great financial potential. Wesco, on the other hand, is a smaller company with its main business interests in insurance, furniture rental, and steel.[16] The Berkshire Hathaway–Wesco merger was friendly because it was beneficial for both firms. (Note: For more information on the Berkshire Hathaway Corporation and its merger activities, read Case 4.2 on page 130.)

Merger and Acquisition Trends for the Future

While there have always been mergers and acquisitions, the recent economic crisis has changed the dynamics of how and why firms merge. Recently, mergers and acquisitions have been fueled by the desire of financially secure firms to take over firms in financial trouble. For a firm experiencing financial difficulties, a merger or acquisition is often a better option than bankruptcy. During the recent economic crisis, this trend was especially evident in the financial services and banking industry. For example, Wachovia was purchased by Wells Fargo in order to avoid a Wachovia bank failure or a government takeover of Wachovia's assets and loan portfolio. In other situations, a financially secure firm will purchase a company experiencing financial problems because it is a good investment.

Economists, financial analysts, corporate managers, and stockholders still hotly debate whether mergers and acquisitions are good for the economy—or for individual companies—in the long run. Takeover advocates argue that for companies that have been taken over, the purchasers have been able to make the company more profitable and productive by installing a new top-management team, by reducing expenses, and by forcing the company to concentrate on one main business.

Takeover opponents argue that takeovers do nothing to enhance corporate profitability or productivity. These critics argue that the only people who benefit from takeovers are investment bankers, brokerage firms, and takeover "artists," who receive financial rewards by manipulating corporations rather than by producing tangible products or services.

Most experts now predict that mergers and acquisitions after the economic crisis will be the result of cash-rich companies looking to acquire businesses that will enhance their position in the marketplace. Analysts also anticipate more mergers that involve companies or investors from other countries. Regardless of the companies involved or where the companies are from, future mergers and acquisitions will be driven by solid business logic and the desire to compete in the international marketplace.

Whether they are sole proprietorships, partnerships, corporations, or some other form of business ownership, most U.S. businesses are small. In the next chapter, we focus on these small businesses. We examine, among other things, the meaning of the word *small* as it applies to business and the place of small business in the American economy.

Kimpton Hotel & Restaurant Group

While Kimpton's chef partners use their culinary talents to build the restaurant side of the business, its hotel experts focus on delivering personalized customer service, which requires a knowledgeable, dedicated workforce. Kimpton grooms future managers through a formal training program and matches promising employees with experienced mentors to further develop their skills. Based on its many employee development and motivation programs, it has twice been named to the *Fortune* magazine list of "Best Companies to Work For."

The company has also made environmental protection one of its top priorities. Following its Kimpton EarthCare plan, it has installed water-conservation systems in its hotels, expanded its recycling programs, and invested in energy-efficient equipment to save power. Going further,

Kimpton works with the Nature Conservancy and the Trust for Public Land to raise money for environmental projects. The company isn't finished growing—watch for more boutique hotels and restaurants to open in the coming years.

Questions

1. Do you think Kimpton should switch from the LLC form of ownership to an open corporation to be able to raise money by selling shares of stock? Explain your answer.

2. Kimpton sometimes buys individual hotels from other companies, renovates them, and reopens them under a new name. Why would Kimpton do this rather than grow through a merger with a larger, more recognized hotel?

SUMMARY

Looking for Success?

Get Flashcards, Quizzes, Games, Crosswords, and more @ www.cengagebrain.com.

Describe the advantages and disadvantages of sole proprietorships.

In a sole proprietorship, all business profits become the property of the owner, but the owner is also personally responsible for all business debts. A successful sole proprietorship can be a great source of pride for the owner. When comparing different types of business ownership, the sole proprietorship is the simplest form of business to enter, control, and leave. It also pays no special taxes. Perhaps for these reasons, 72 percent of all American business firms are sole proprietorships. Sole proprietorships nevertheless have disadvantages, such as unlimited liability and limits on one person's ability to borrow or to be an expert in all fields. As a result, this form of ownership accounts for only 4 percent of total revenues when compared with partnerships and corporations.

Explain the different types of partners and the importance of partnership agreements.

Like sole proprietors, general partners are responsible for running the business and for all business debts. Limited partners receive a share of the profit in return for investing in the business. However, they are not responsible for

business debts beyond the amount they have invested. It is also possible to form a master limited partnership (MLP) and sell units of ownership to raise capital. Regardless of the type of partnership, it is always a good idea to have a written agreement (or articles of partnership) setting forth the terms of a partnership.

Describe the advantages and disadvantages of partnerships.

Although partnership eliminates some of the disadvantages of sole proprietorship, it is the least popular of the major forms of business ownership. The major advantages of a partnership include ease of start-up, availability of capital and credit, personal interest, combined skills and knowledge, retention of profits, and possible tax advantages. The effects of management disagreements are one of the major disadvantages of a partnership. Other disadvantages include unlimited liability (in a general partnership), lack of continuity, and frozen investment. By forming a limited partnership, the disadvantage of unlimited liability may be eliminated for the limited partner(s). This same disadvantage may be eliminated for partners that form a limited-liability partnership (LLP). Of course, special requirements must be met if partners form either the limited partnership or the limited-liability partnership.

Summarize how a corporation is formed.

A corporation is an artificial person created by law, with most of the legal rights of a real person, including the right to start and operate a business, to buy or sell property, to borrow money, to be sued or sue, and to enter into contracts. With the corporate form of ownership, stock can be sold to individuals to raise capital. The people who own a corporation's common or preferred stock are called stockholders. Stockholders are entitled to receive any dividends paid by the corporation, and common stockholders can vote either in person or by proxy. Generally, corporations are classified as closed corporations (few stockholders) or open corporations (many stockholders).

The process of forming a corporation is called incorporation. Most experts believe that the services of a lawyer are necessary when making decisions about where to incorporate and about obtaining a corporate charter, issuing stock, holding an organizational meeting, and all other legal details involved in incorporation. In theory, stockholders are able to control the activities of the corporation because they elect the board of directors who appoint the corporate officers.

 Describe the advantages and disadvantages of a corporation.

Perhaps the major advantage of the corporate form is limited liability—stockholders are not liable for the corporation's debts beyond the amount they paid for its stock. Other important advantages include ease of raising capital, ease of transfer of ownership, perpetual life, and specialized management. A major disadvantage of a large corporation is double taxation: All profits are taxed once as corporate income and again as personal income because stockholders must pay a personal income tax on the profits they receive as dividends. Other disadvantages include difficulty and expense of formation, government regulation, conflict within the corporation, and lack of secrecy.

 Examine special types of corporations, including S-corporations, limited-liability companies, and not-for-profit corporations.

S-corporations are corporations that are taxed as though they were partnerships but that enjoy the benefit of limited liability. To qualify as an S-corporation, a number of criteria must be met. A limited-liability company (LLC) is a form of business ownership that provides limited liability and has fewer restrictions when compared to a regular corporation or an S-corporation. LLCs with at least two members are taxed like a partnership and thus avoid the double taxation imposed on most corporations. LLCs with just one member are taxed like a sole proprietorship. When compared with a regular corporation or an S-corporation, an LLC is more flexible. Not-for-profit corporations are formed to provide social services and to improve communities and change lives rather than to earn profits.

 Discuss the purpose of a cooperative, joint venture, and syndicate.

Three additional forms of business ownership—the cooperative, joint venture, and syndicate—are used by their owners to meet special needs. A cooperative is an association of individuals or firms whose purpose is to perform some business function for its members. A joint venture is formed when two or more groups form a business entity in order to achieve a specific goal or to operate for a specific period of time. Once the goal is reached, the period of time elapses, or the project is completed, the joint venture is dissolved. A syndicate is a temporary association of individuals or firms organized to perform a specific task that requires large amounts of capital. Like a joint venture, a syndicate is dissolved as soon as its purpose has been accomplished.

 Explain how growth from within and growth through mergers can enable a business to expand.

A corporation may grow by expanding its present operations or through a merger or an acquisition. Although most mergers are friendly, hostile takeovers also occur. A hostile takeover is a situation in which the management and board of directors of a firm targeted for acquisition disapprove of the merger. Mergers generally are classified as horizontal, vertical, or conglomerate.

During the recent economic crisis, mergers and acquisitions have been fueled by the desire of financially secure firms to take over firms in financial trouble. For a firm experiencing financial trouble, a merger or acquisition is often a better option than bankruptcy. In other situations, a financially secure firm will purchase a company experiencing financial problems because it is a good investment.

While economists, financial analysts, corporate managers, and stockholders debate the merits of mergers, some trends should be noted. First, experts predict that future mergers will be the result of cash-rich companies looking to acquire businesses that will enhance their position in the marketplace. Second, more mergers are likely to involve foreign companies or investors. Third, mergers will be driven by business logic and the desire to compete in the international marketplace.

KEY TERMS

You should now be able to define and give an example relevant to each of the following terms:

sole proprietorship (106)	limited partner (110)	stock (115)	domestic corporation (116)
unlimited liability (108)	master limited partnership	stockholder (115)	foreign corporation (116)
partnership (110)	(MLP) (111)	closed corporation (115)	alien corporation (116)
general partner (110)	corporation (115)	open corporation (115)	common stock (116)

preferred stock (116)	limited liability (119)	not-for-profit corporation	merger (124)
dividend (117)	S-corporation (121)	(122)	hostile takeover (124)
proxy (117)	limited-liability company	cooperative (123)	tender offer (124)
board of directors (117)	(LLC) (121)	joint venture (123)	proxy fight (125)
corporate officers (118)		syndicate (123)	

REVIEW QUESTIONS

1. What is a sole proprietorship? What are the major advantages and disadvantages of this form of business ownership?
2. How does a partnership differ from a sole proprietorship? Which disadvantages of sole proprietorship does the partnership tend to eliminate or reduce?
3. What is the difference between a general partner and a limited partner?
4. What issues should be included in a partnership agreement? Why?
5. Explain the difference between
   a. an open corporation and a closed corporation.
   b. a domestic corporation, a foreign corporation, and an alien corporation.
6. Outline the incorporation process, and describe the basic corporate structure.

7. What rights do stockholders have?
8. What are the primary duties of a corporation's board of directors? How are directors selected?
9. What are the major advantages and disadvantages associated with the corporate form of business ownership?
10. How do an S-corporation and a limited-liability company differ?
11. Why are not-for-profit corporations and cooperatives formed? Explain how they operate.
12. In what ways are joint ventures and syndicates alike? In what ways do they differ?
13. What is a hostile takeover? How is it related to a tender offer and a proxy fight?
14. Describe the three types of mergers.

DISCUSSION QUESTIONS

1. If you were to start a business, which ownership form would you choose? What factors might affect your choice?
2. Why might an investor choose to become a partner in a limited partnership instead of purchasing the stock of an open corporation?
3. Discuss the following statement: "Corporations are not really run by their owners."

4. What kinds of services do not-for-profit corporations provide? Would a career in a not-for-profit corporation appeal to you?
5. Is growth a good thing for all firms? How does management know when a firm is ready to grow?

Video Case 4.1

AT&T and T-Mobile: What Went Wrong with Their Merger?

When it tried to buy T-Mobile for $39 billion in 2011, AT&T went so far as to offer the company a "break up" fee of $4 billion if the deal fell through. Why was AT&T so determined to purchase T-Mobile? AT&T was no. 2 in the wireless phone-service market. T-Mobile was no. 4. By merging, they would have become the nation's largest wireless provider, surpassing Verizon. The deal would also have given AT&T access to the spectrum (airwaves) T-Mobile owned but couldn't afford to upgrade to 4G (state-of-the art, fourth-generation technology).

Executives at the companies said that in addition to creating jobs, the merger would result in fewer dropped calls and faster connection times for customers. The merged company would also be able to immediately expand wireless service to rural areas that lacked it. "AT&T will immediately gain cell sites

equivalent to what would have taken on average five years to build without the transaction," the two companies said in their merger announcement. The announcement also referred to a government report that showed that despite many mergers in the industry over the past decade, the price of wireless service had declined.

Investors cheered when they heard about the merger. However, many consumers, the Department of Justice, and the Federal Communications Commission (FCC) were wary of the deal. The merged company would have controlled nearly half of the market. The only remaining big players in the industry would have been Verizon and Sprint. Some industry experts thought Sprint might get forced out of the market because it held the least market share. They also believed few new companies would enter the market. Competing against a combined AT&T and T-Mobile would make it too difficult.

What would the merger have meant for consumers? Dan Gillmor, the director of the Knight Center for Digital Media Entrepreneurship at Arizona State University, said he thought the deal would be bad for consumers. They would have fewer wireless providers to choose from, Gillmor said. He also predicted consumers could end up paying higher prices. "T-Mobile is the only company that's now competing seriously on price," he explained.

Researchers at the magazine *Consumer Reports* also concluded that T-Mobile charged less than many of its competitors for different types of plans. What firm would keep AT&T and its prices in check if it were to swallow up T-Mobile? Another issue was that a number of surveys had found that AT&T's service quality was uneven. Would it get worse following the merger? Or better?

As you learned earlier in the chapter, the Department of Justice ultimately filed a lawsuit to block the merger. "The combination of AT&T and T-Mobile would result in tens of millions of consumers all across the United States facing higher prices, fewer choices, and lower-quality products for mobile wireless services," said Department of Justice Deputy Attorney General James M. Cole. And even though AT&T and T-Mobile claimed

the merger would produce more jobs, an investigation by the FCC came to a different conclusion. The internal records of the two companies showed that the firms planned to lay off personnel by combining duplicate functions in their organizations such as their sales, management, and customer service departments. The FCC also disputed the companies' claim that the merger would immediately expand wireless service to rural areas. Why? Because T-Mobile serviced mostly urban areas—not rural ones.

Acquiring T-Mobile became such an upward battle that AT&T eventually abandoned the effort and paid T-Mobile the $4 billion breakup fee. A few months later, T-Mobile announced it was spending $4 billion to expand and upgrade its network to 4G.[17]

Questions

1. Did the Department of Justice make the right decision when it blocked the merger of T-Mobile and AT&T? Why or why not?
2. What do you think the pros and cons of acquiring a competing company are? Create a list of each.
3. Name some other examples of horizontal, vertical, and conglomerate mergers you're aware of. Considering the impact of mergers on competition, what are the advantages and disadvantages of each type of merger?

Case 4.2   The Conglomerate Success of Berkshire Hathaway

When Warren Buffett started his first partnership more than 50 years ago, he never dreamed he would wind up putting together a wildly diverse collection of businesses under one corporate umbrella. Originally, Buffett set up a series of partnerships with family and friends to pool cash for buying big blocks of stock in companies he had researched. Not all of Buffett's stock picks paid off, but many were so successful that Buffett quickly earned a worldwide reputation for savvy investing.

Always looking for a good investment, Buffett turned his attention to the prospects of Berkshire Hathaway, a struggling textile manufacturer based in New Bedford, Massachusetts. Seeing value in the company's heritage and its plans for making synthetic fibers, Buffett began buying its stock. Once he controlled the mills, Buffett put one of Berkshire Hathaway's executives in charge. This was Buffett's pattern over and over as he built a conglomerate by adding to his company's portfolio of businesses. He provided the financial backing, but he didn't meddle in the day-to-day management decisions of the corporations he purchased.

Berkshire Hathaway became the corporate vehicle through which Buffett acquired a variety of companies. In the early days, he pursued insurance firms, banks, and publishing companies. He continued buying year after year, adding See's Candies to his conglomerate and, later, GEICO insurance, sticking to his tried-and-true formula of investing in companies with long-term profit potential and strong competitive positions.

Living in Omaha, Buffett couldn't help but notice the success of the Nebraska Furniture Mart, a superstore that annually sold $100 million worth of furniture. The family-owned business was a fierce competitor and a major regional power in furniture retailing. Although Buffett had tried, unsuccessfully, to buy the store, he never gave up. During the 1980s, he again approached the retailer. This time he pointed out all the financial benefits of being part of Berkshire Hathaway and emphasized his hands-off approach to ownership. Berkshire Hathaway won the deal.

Today Berkshire Hathaway has more than six dozen companies in its diverse portfolio. Although it still owns some of the companies it acquired decades ago, the portfolio has changed a bit over the years. GEICO, the third-largest U.S. auto insurance firm, has been a member of the conglomerate since 1996. Berkshire Hathaway also owns the General Re insurance firm. Among the retailing businesses it owns are Jordan Furniture, Star Furniture, Helzberg Diamonds, and the Pampered Chef direct-seller of kitchen tools. In addition, it owns the ice-cream franchising company Dairy Queen; Benjamin Moore paint; Johns Manville building products; and Shaw Industries, which makes tufted broadloom carpeting and distributes other flooring products.

Berkshire Hathaway has expanded into transportation, as well. Its NetJets was a pioneer in offering companies and individuals the opportunity to own a fraction of a private jet, so they can enjoy the convenience of flying whenever and wherever they want. In 2010, the conglomerate paid $26 billion for Burlington Northern Santa Fe Corp., a railroad that serves western and southwestern states. This acquisition, labeled "brilliant" by a railway competitor because it was completed just as the industry began to rebound from recession, gave Buffett access to years of details about the size, volume, and destination of train shipments. By analyzing this information, Buffett spotted clues that helped him fine-tune his investments.

The annual meeting held by Berkshire Hathaway is unlike any stockholder gathering on Earth. The more-than-35,000 people in attendance spend hours browsing and buying from exhibits set up by the conglomerate's companies. Stockholders are encouraged to bring the details of their car insurance and let GEICO give them quotes on the spot, including a small ownership discount. Nebraska Furniture Mart promotes a special stockholders' weekend of sales,

as do other Berkshire Hathaway-owned retailers in the area. The annual meeting is such a high-profile event that it merits coverage by the *New York Times*, CNBC, and *Fortune* magazine, among many other major media outlets. What will Berkshire Hathaway's next acquisition target be?[18]

Questions

1. Why would Berkshire Hathaway own a number of furniture retailers? Outline the possible advantages and disadvantages.
2. Do you think Berkshire Hathaway should allow stockholders to suggest or vote on potential acquisitions via proxy or at the annual meeting? Why or why not?
3. How much influence are Berkshire Hathaway's stockholders likely to have (or want) over the management of the conglomerate or one of the conglomerate's companies? Explain.

Building Skills for Career Success

① SOCIAL MEDIA EXERCISE

Not-for-profit organizations have used social media to redefine how they can get funding for their missions. There are even a few that exist totally online. Check out www.donorschoose.org and www.kiva.org. Both of these depend on crowds (called crowdfunding) to either fund educational projects (Donors Choose) or lend money to support projects all over the world (Kiva) using the microfinancing model.

a. Take a minute to explore these sites and view some of the projects up for funding. How are these projects organized? Do you think these models are effective? Why or why not?
b. Both Donors Choose and Kiva are for not-for-profits; do you think these models are useful for "for-profit" businesses? Why or why not?

② JOURNALING FOR SUCCESS

Today, many people work for a sole proprietorship, partnership, or corporation. Still others decide to become entrepreneurs and start their own business.

Assignment

Assume that you are now age 25 and have graduated from college. Would you prefer to work in someone else's business or one that you would start? Explain your answer.

Assuming that you have decided to start your own small business, what type of business will you start? What special skills and experience will you need to be successful? (*Note:* You may want to talk with someone who owns a business before answering this question.)

Now describe where and how you could obtain the skills and experience you need to be successful.

What type of business ownership would you choose for your business? Record your ideas and responses to the preceding questions.

③ DEVELOPING CRITICAL-THINKING SKILLS

Suppose that you are a person who has always dreamed of owning a business but never had the money to open one. Since you were old enough to read a recipe, your mother allowed you to help in the kitchen. Most of all, you enjoyed baking and decorating cakes. You liked using your imagination to create cakes for special occasions. By the time you were in high school, you were baking and decorating wedding cakes for a fee. Also assume that after high school you started working full time as an adjuster for an insurance company. Your schedule now allows little time for baking and decorating cakes. Finally, assume that you inherited $250,000 and that changes at your job have created undue stress in your life. What should you do?

Assignment

Discuss the following points:

a. What career options are available to you?
b. If you decide to open your own business, what form of ownership would be best for your business?
c. What advantages and disadvantages apply to your preferred form of business ownership?

Prepare a two-page report summarizing your findings.

④ BUILDING TEAM SKILLS

Using the scenario in Exercise 3, suppose that you have decided to quit your job as an insurance adjuster and open a bakery. Your business is now growing, and you have decided to add a full line of catering services. This means more work and responsibility. You will need someone to help you, but you are undecided about what to do. Should you hire an employee or find a partner? If you add a partner, what type of decisions should be made to create a partnership agreement?

Assignment

In a group, discuss the following questions:

a. What are the advantages and disadvantages of adding a partner versus hiring an employee?

b. Assume that you have decided to form a partnership. What articles should be included in a partnership agreement?

c. How would you go about finding a partner?

Summarize your group's answers to these questions, and present them to your class. As a group, prepare an articles-of-partnership agreement. Be prepared to discuss the pros and cons of your group's agreement with other groups from your class, as well as to examine their agreements.

⑤ RESEARCHING DIFFERENT CAREERS

Many people spend their entire lives working in jobs that they do not enjoy. Why is this so? Often, it is because they have taken the first job they were offered without giving it much thought.

How can you avoid having this happen to you? First, you should determine your "personal profile" by identifying and analyzing your own strengths, weaknesses, things you enjoy, and things you dislike. Second, you should identify the types of jobs that fit your profile. Third, you should identify and research the companies that offer those jobs.

Assignment

a. Take two sheets of paper and draw a line down the middle of each sheet, forming two columns on each page. Label column 1 "Things I Enjoy or Like to Do," column 2 "Things I Do Not Like Doing," column 3 "My Strengths," and column 4 "My Weaknesses."

b. Record data in each column over a period of at least one week. You may find it helpful to have a relative or friend give you input.

c. Summarize the data, and write a profile of yourself.

d. Take your profile to a career counselor at your college or to the public library and ask for help in identifying jobs that fit your profile. Your college may offer testing to assess your skills and personality. The Internet is another resource.

e. Research the companies that offer the types of jobs that fit your profile.

f. Write a report on your findings.

ENDNOTES

1. Sources: Based on information from the Kimpton Hotel and Restaurant Group, LLC Web site at www.kimptonhotels.com (accessed February 9, 2012); Tim McKeough, "Putting Nemo to Work," *New York Times*, November 17, 2011, p. D4; Robert Klara, "Boutique Chic," *Adweek*, September 26, 2011, p. 32; "5 Questions for Niki Leondakis," *Hospitality Design*, July 2011, p. 76; Len Vermillion, "Kimpton's 30-Year Journey," *Lodging*, April 13, 2011, www.lodgingmagazine.com; Paris Wolfe, "Kimpton Reaches 51 Hotels in 30 Years," *Lodging Hospitality Online*, June 15, 2011, http://lhon-line.com; Lisa Fickenscher, "Crain's 2011 Best Places to Work in NYC," *Crain's New York Business*, December 5, 2011, p. 22.

2. The IVY Planning Group Web site at www.ivygroupllc.com (accessed February 2, 2012).

3. The National Association of Publicly Traded Partnerships Web site at www.naptp.com (accessed February 5, 2012).

4. The Procter & Gamble Web site at www.pg.com (accessed February 5, 2012).

5. Ibid.

6. The Mars Corporate Web site at www.mars.com (accessed February 5, 2012).

7. The My New Company Web site at www.mynewcompany.com (accessed February 2, 2012).

8. The Hispanic PR Wire Web site at www.hispanicprwire.com (accessed February 3, 2012).

9. The Internal Revenue Service Web site at www.irs.gov (accessed February 2, 2012).

10. The Ocean Spray Cranberries, Inc. Web site at www.oceanspray.com (accessed January 30, 2012).

11. The Walmart Corporate Web site at www.walmartstores.com (accessed December 31, 2011).

12. "Facebook, Banks Sued Over Pre-IPO Analyst Calls," The Reuters Web site at www.reuters.com (accessed May 23, 2012).

13. The Walmart Corporate Web site at www.walmartstores.com (accessed February 4, 2012).

14. The Oracle Web site at www.oracle.com (accessed June 23, 2011).

15. "Twitter Acquires Social Media Feed Condenser Summify," The Tech World Web site at www.techworld.com (accessed February 4, 2012).

16. Maria Aspen, "Berkshire Hathaway to Buy Rest of Wesco," The Thomson Reuters Web site at www.reuters.com (accessed February 4, 2012).

17. Based on information from Amy Schatz and Greg Bensinger, "FCC Blasts AT&T Deal," *Wall Street Journal*, November 30, 2011; http://online.wsj.com; David Goldman, "DOJ Files Antitrust Suit to Block AT&T Merger with T-Mobile," *CNNMoney*, August 31, 2011, http://money.cnn.com; Russ Wiles, "AT&T Merger with T-Mobile May Cut Competition," *Arizona Republic*, March 11, 2011, www.azcentral.com/arizonarepublic.

18. Based on information from the Berkshire Hathaway Corporate Web site at www.berkshirehathaway.com (accessed February 6, 2012); Becky Quick, "Who Says the Economy Is Rebounding?" *Fortune*, May 3, 2010, www.fortune.com; Angela Greiling Keane and Ed Dufner, "CSX's Ward Calls Buffett's Rail Purchase 'Brilliant,'" *BusinessWeek*, April 14, 2010, www.businessweek.com; Alice Schroeder, *The Snowball: Warren Buffett and the Business of Life* (New York: Bantam Dell, 2008), Chapters 22 and 44, www.BerkshireHathaway.com.

Small Business, Entrepreneurship, and Franchises

5

Once you complete this chapter, you will be able to:

① Define what a small business is and recognize the fields in which small businesses are concentrated.

② Identify the people who start small businesses and the reasons why some succeed and many fail.

③ Assess the contributions of small businesses to our economy.

④ Describe the advantages and disadvantages of operating a small business.

⑤ Explain how the Small Business Administration helps small businesses.

⑥ Explain the concept and types of franchising.

⑦ Analyze the growth of franchising and its advantages and disadvantages.

Did You Know?

Two mothers founded Locker Lookz after their daughters couldn't find ready-made accessories to decorate their middle-school lockers.

Locker Lookz Looks for Higher Sales

Texas entrepreneurs Christi Sterling and JoAnn Brewer started Locker Lookz in 2008 with $50,000 in personal savings and an idea based on their daughters' interest in personalizing their school lockers. Shopping for fun accessories before the start of school, the mothers and their daughters found very little ready-made for dressing up a locker, in stores or online. Eventually, they bought materials at local craft stores to create wallpaper and carpeting for the girls' lockers. When friends started asking where they could buy these decorations, "We had a light-bulb moment," Brewer says. "There's a real need for something that's cute, easy, and one-stop shopping."

The co-founders designed a limited line of locker decorations, all styled for middle-school tastes, and priced at $10 and up. Next, they connected with a sales expert who specializes in distributing products through local and national retailers. With his help, Sterling and Brewer arranged for overseas manufacturers to produce the items, found a packager to ready the products for retail display, and completed a successful sales test in several dozen stores. Soon, JCPenney and Hallmark were placing orders, followed by Learning Express and other retail chains.

By mid-2011, more than 1,200 stores were signed up to carry Locker Lookz accessories for the back-to-school selling season. Now Sterling and Brewer had a few weeks to raise $1 million to pay for manufacturing and shipping the goods from factories in China to stores across the United States. Just in time, they raised cash from relatives and from a church investment group. The containers filled with Locker Lookz merchandise arrived on schedule, and soon the co-founders began crisscrossing the country to publicize their expanding product line.

Today, Locker Lookz is an entrepreneurial multimillion-dollar company facing increased competition from other firms that see locker decor as a profitable business opportunity. Although the preferences of preteen girls can change rapidly and without warning, Brewer and Sterling are paying close attention to fashion trends and asking their daughters' advice about new product ideas. How much room does Locker Lookz have to grow?[1]

As is in the case of Christie Sterling's and JoAnn Brewer's Locker Lookz, most businesses start small and those that survive usually stay small. They provide a solid foundation for our economy—as employers, as suppliers and purchasers of goods and services, and as taxpayers.

In this chapter, we do not take small businesses for granted. Instead, we look closely at this important business sector—beginning with a definition of small business, a description of industries that often attract small businesses, and a profile of some of the people who start small businesses. Next, we consider the importance of small businesses in our economy. We also present the advantages and disadvantages of smallness in business. We then describe services provided by the Small Business Administration, a government agency formed to assist owners and managers of small businesses. We conclude the chapter with a discussion of the pros and cons of franchising, an approach to small-business ownership that has become very popular in the last 50 years.

SMALL BUSINESS: A PROFILE

 Define what a small business is and recognize the fields in which small businesses are concentrated.

The Small Business Administration (SBA) defines a **small business** as "one which is independently owned and operated for profit and is not dominant in its field." How small must a firm be not to dominate its field? That depends on the particular industry it is in. The SBA has developed the following specific "smallness" guidelines for the various industries, as shown in Table 5.1.[2] The SBA periodically revises and simplifies its small-business size regulations.

Annual sales in millions of dollars may not seem very small. However, for many firms, profit is only a small percentage of total sales. Thus, a firm may earn only $40,000 or $50,000 on yearly sales of $1 million—and that is small in comparison with the profits earned by most medium-sized and large firms. Moreover, most small firms have annual sales well below the maximum limits in the SBA guidelines.

Small businesses are very important to the U.S. economy. For example, small businesses

- represent 99.7 percent of all employer firms;
- employ about half of all private sector employees;
- pay 43 percent of total U.S. private payroll;
- have generated 65 percent of net new jobs over the past 17 years;
- create more than half of the nonfarm private GDP;
- hire 43 percent of high-tech workers (scientists, engineers, computer programmers, and others);
- are 52 percent home-based and 2 percent franchises;
- made up 97.5 percent of all identified exporters and produced 31 percent of export value in FY 2008; and
- produced 16.5 times more patents per employee than large patenting firms.[3]

The Small-Business Sector

In the United States, it typically takes less than a week and $500 to establish a business as a legal entity. The steps include registering the name of the business, applying for

TABLE 5.1	Industry Group-Size Standards
Small-business size standards are usually stated in number of employees or average annual sales. In the United States, 99.7 percent of all businesses are considered small.	
Industry Group	**Size Standard**
Manufacturing, mining industries	500 employees
Wholesale trade	100 employees
Agriculture	$750,000
Retail trade	$7 million
General and heavy construction (except dredging)	$33.5 million
Dredging	$20 million
Special trade contractors	$14 million
Travel agencies	$3.5 million (commissions and other income)
Business and personal services except	$7 million
• Architectural, engineering, surveying, and mapping services	$4.5 million
• Dry cleaning and carpet cleaning services	$4.5 million

Source: www.sba.gov/content/summary-size-standards-industry (accessed March 19, 2012).

small business one that is independently owned and operated for profit and is not dominant in its field

Sometime in your career, you're likely to have a job in a small business. You might work in a store, in a service business, or in production. If you're thinking of starting your own business, be sure to watch how these entrepreneurs manage their companies.

tax IDs, and setting up unemployment and workers' compensation insurance. In Japan, however, a typical entrepreneur spends more than $3,500 and 31 days to follow 11 different procedures.

A surprising number of Americans take advantage of their freedom to start a business. There are, in fact, about 27.5 million businesses in this country. Only just 18,469 of these employ more than 500 workers—enough to be considered large.

Interest in owning or starting a small business has never been greater than it is today. During the last decade, the number of small businesses in the United States has increased 49 percent. For the last few years, new-business formation in the United States has broken successive records, except during the 2001–2002 and 2008 recessions. Recently, nearly 552,600 new businesses were incorporated. Furthermore, part-time entrepreneurs have increased fivefold in recent years; they now account for one-third of all small businesses.[4]

According to a recent study, 69 percent of new businesses survive at least two years, about 50 percent survive at least five years, and 31 percent survive at least ten years.[5] The primary reason for these failures is mismanagement resulting from a lack of business know-how. The makeup of the small-business sector thus is constantly changing. Despite the high failure rate, many small businesses succeed modestly. Some, like Apple Computer, Inc., are extremely successful—to the point where they can no longer be considered small. Taken together, small businesses are also responsible for providing a high percentage of the jobs in the United States. According to some estimates, the figure is well over 50 percent.

Industries That Attract Small Businesses

Some industries, such as auto manufacturing, require huge investments in machinery and equipment. Businesses in such industries are big from the day they are started—if an entrepreneur or group of entrepreneurs can gather the capital required to start one.

By contrast, a number of other industries require only a low initial investment and some special skills or knowledge. It is these industries that tend to attract new businesses. Growing industries, such as outpatient-care facilities, are attractive because of their profit potential. However, knowledgeable entrepreneurs choose areas with which they are familiar, and these are most often the more established industries.

Small enterprise spans the gamut from corner newspaper vending to the development of optical fibers. The owners of small businesses sell gasoline, flowers, and coffee to go. They publish magazines, haul freight, teach languages, and program computers. They make wines, movies, and high-fashion clothes. They build new homes and restore old ones. They fix appliances, recycle metals, and sell used cars. They drive cabs and fly planes. They make us well when we are ill, and they sell us the products of corporate giants. In fact, 74 percent of real estate, rental, and leasing industries; 61 percent of the businesses in the leisure and hospitality services; and 86 percent of the construction industries are dominated by small businesses. The various kinds of businesses generally fall into three broad categories of industry: distribution, service, and production.

Distribution Industries This category includes retailing, wholesaling, transportation, and communications—industries concerned with the movement of goods from producers to consumers. Distribution industries account for approximately 33 percent of all small businesses. Of these, almost three-quarters are involved in retailing, that is, the sale of goods directly to consumers. Clothing and jewelry stores, pet shops, bookstores, and grocery stores, for example, are all retailing firms. Slightly less than one-quarter of the small distribution firms are wholesalers. Wholesalers purchase products in quantity from manufacturers and then resell them to retailers.

Service Industries This category accounts for more than 48 percent of all small businesses. Of these, about three-quarters provide such nonfinancial services as medical and dental care; watch, shoe, and TV repairs; haircutting and styling; restaurant meals; and dry cleaning. About 8 percent of the small service firms offer financial services, such as accounting, insurance, real estate, and investment counseling. An increasing number of self-employed Americans are running service businesses from home.

Production Industries This last category includes the construction, mining, and manufacturing industries. Only about 19 percent of all small businesses are in this group, mainly because these industries require relatively large initial investments. Small firms that do venture into production generally make parts and subassemblies for larger manufacturing firms or supply special skills to larger construction firms.

THE PEOPLE IN SMALL BUSINESSES: THE ENTREPRENEURS

 Identify the people who start small businesses and the reasons why some succeed and many fail.

The entrepreneurial spirit is alive and well in the United States. One study revealed that the U.S. population is quite entrepreneurial when compared with those of other countries. More than 70 percent of Americans would prefer being an entrepreneur to working for someone else. This compares with 46 percent of adults in Western Europe and 58 percent of adults in Canada. Another study on entrepreneurial activity for 2002 found that of 36 countries studied, the United States was in the top third in entrepreneurial activity and was the leader when compared with Japan, Canada, and Western Europe.[6]

Small businesses typically are managed by the people who started and own them. Most of these people have held jobs with other firms and still could be so employed if they wanted. Yet owners of small businesses would rather take the risk of starting and operating their own firms, even if the money they make is less than the salaries they otherwise might earn.

Researchers have suggested a variety of personal factors as reasons why people go into business for themselves. These are discussed next.

Characteristics of Entrepreneurs

Entrepreneurial spirit is the desire to create a new business. For example, Nikki Olyai always knew that she wanted to create and develop her own business. Her father, a successful businessman in Iran, was her role model. She came to the United States at the age of 17 and lived with a host family in Salem, Oregon, attending high school there. Undergraduate and graduate degrees in computer science led her to start Innovision Technologies while she held two other jobs to keep the business going and took care of her four-year-old son. Recently, Nikki Olyai's business was honored by the Women's Business Enterprise National Council's "Salute to Women's Business Enterprises" as one of 11 top successful firms. For three consecutive years, her firm was selected as a "Future 50 of Greater Detroit Company."

Other Personal Factors

Other personal factors in small-business success include

- independence;
- a desire to determine one's own destiny;

©AP PHOTO/NATI HARNIK

Meet Sam Altman, co-founder and CEO of Loopt. In 2004, Altman co-founded a location-based social networking mobile application when he was a sophomore majoring in computer science at Stanford University. *BusinessWeek* named him one of the "Best Young Entrepreneurs in Technology" and *Inc.* magazine ranked him number 4 among the top 30 entrepreneurs under the age of 30. In 2012, prepaid money card issuer Green Dot Corp. agreed to acquire Loopt Inc. for $43.4 million.

- a willingness to find and accept a challenge;
- family background (in particular, researchers think that people whose families have been in business, successfully or not, are most apt to start and run their own businesses); and
- age (those who start their own businesses also tend to cluster around certain ages—more than 70 percent are between 24 and 44 years of age; see Figure 5.1).

Motivation

There must be some motivation to start a business. A person may decide that he or she simply has "had enough" of working and earning a profit for someone else. Another may lose his or her job for some reason and decide to start the business he or she has always wanted rather than to seek another job. Still another person may have an idea for a new product or a new way to sell an existing product. Or the opportunity to go into business may arise suddenly, perhaps as a result of a hobby. For example, Cheryl Strand started baking and decorating cakes from her home while working full time as a word processor at Clemson University. Her cakes became so popular that she soon found herself working through her lunch breaks and late into the night to meet customer demand.

Women as Small-Business Owners

According to the latest 2012 data available from the Small Business Administration:

- Women are 51 percent of the U.S. population, and according to the SBA, they owned at least 50 percent of all small businesses in 2008.
- Women already own 66 percent of the home-based businesses in this country, and the number of men in home-based businesses is growing rapidly.
- About 7.8 million women-owned businesses in the United States provide almost 7.6 million jobs and generate $1.2 trillion in sales.
- Women-owned businesses in the United States have proven that they are more successful; more than 40 percent have been in business for 12 years or more.
- Women-owned businesses are financially sound and credit-worthy, and their risk of failure is lower than average.
- Compared to other working women, self-employed women are older, better educated, and have more managerial experience.
- Just over one-half of small businesses are home based, and 91 percent have no employees. About 60 percent of home-based businesses are in service industries, 16 percent in construction, 14 percent in retail trade, and the rest in manufacturing, finance, transportation, communications, wholesaling, and other industries.[7]

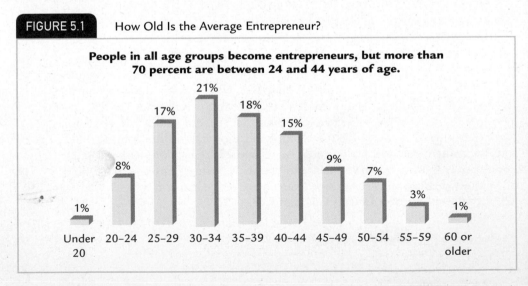

| FIGURE 5.1 | How Old Is the Average Entrepreneur? |

People in all age groups become entrepreneurs, but more than 70 percent are between 24 and 44 years of age.

Under 20: 1%
20–24: 8%
25–29: 17%
30–34: 21%
35–39: 18%
40–44: 15%
45–49: 9%
50–54: 7%
55–59: 3%
60 or older: 1%

Source: Data developed and provided by the National Federation of Independent Business Foundation and sponsored by the American Express Travel Related Services Company, Inc.

Part 2 Business Ownership and Entrepreneurship

Career SUCCESS

Is Entrepreneurship in Your Future?

Some entrepreneurs realize early that they want to start a business. Others become entrepreneurs after working for other people. You can take a number of tests to assess whether you have the drive, temperament, and attitude to be your own boss. No test can tell whether your business will be successful, but you can get a sense of your own skills and capabilities as a future entrepreneur.

Stop by the career center on campus, which may offer an entrepreneurship self-test. For another perspective on your entrepreneurial potential, take at least one more test. For example, the informal questions on the Isenberg Entrepreneur Test, created by Professor Daniel Isenberg of Babson College, are designed to get you thinking about what you like and why.

Do you like to challenge yourself? Would you prefer to fail at something you've chosen rather than succeed at something chosen by someone else?

The U.S. Small Business Administration (www.sba.gov) offers an online self-assessment to determine whether you're ready to start your own business. In addition, compare what you know about yourself to the SBA's listing of entrepreneur characteristics to see how well you match up. Similarly, the Business Development Bank of Canada's online test shows whether your attitudes, aptitudes, and motivations would be a good fit with the entrepreneurial life.

Sources: Based on information in Daniel Isenberg, "Should You Be an Entrepreneur? Take This Test," Harvard Business Review, February 12, 2010, www.hbr.org; U.S. Small Business Administration, www.sba.gov; Business Development Bank of Canada, www.bdc.ca.

Teenagers as Small-Business Owners

High-tech teen entrepreneurship is definitely exploding. "There's not a period in history where we've seen such a plethora of young entrepreneurs," comments Nancy F. Koehn, associate professor of business administration at Harvard Business School. Still, teen entrepreneurs face unique pressures in juggling their schoolwork, their social life, and their high-tech workload. Some ultimately quit school, whereas others quit or cut back on their business activities. Consider Brian Hendricks at Winston Churchill High School in Potomac, Maryland. He is the founder of StartUpPc and VB Solutions, Inc. StartUpPc, founded in 2001, sells custom-built computers and computer services for home users, home offices, small businesses, and students. Brian's services include design, installation of systems, training, networking, and on-site technical support. In October 2002, Brian founded VB Solutions, Inc., which develops and customizes Web sites and message boards. The firm sets up advertising contracts and counsels Web site owners on site improvements. The company has designed corporate ID kits, logos, and Web sites for clients from all over the world. Brian learned at a very young age that working for yourself is one of the best jobs available. According to Brian, a young entrepreneur must possess "the five P's of entrepreneurship"— planning, persistence, patience, people, and profit. Brian knows what it takes to be a successful entrepreneur. His accolades include Junior Achievement's "National Youth Entrepreneur of the Year" and SBA's 2005 "Young Entrepreneur of the Year" awards.[8]

In some people, the motivation to start a business develops slowly as they gain the knowledge and ability required for success as a business owner. Knowledge and ability—especially, management ability—are probably the most important factors involved. A new firm is very much built around the entrepreneur. The owner must be able to manage the firm's finances, its personnel (if there are any employees), and its day-to-day operations. He or she must handle sales, advertising, purchasing, pricing, and a variety of other business functions. The knowledge and ability to do so are acquired most often through experience working for other firms in the same area of business.

Mary Rodas, a child entrepreneur. At age 13, Mary scored an instant success with the 'Balzac,' a ball made by blowing up a balloon inside a fabric sack, jazzed up with vivid colors and designs. At Catco, Inc., she became vice president of marketing at age 14, earning $200,000 a year. Balzac Balloon Ball sales have exceeded $100 million per year.

© AP PHOTO/ED BAILEY

TABLE 5.2	U.S. Business Start-ups, Closures, and Bankruptcies		
	New	Closures	Bankruptcies
2010	NA	NA	56,282
2009	552,600ᵉ	660,990ᵉ	60,837
2008	597,074	641,400	43,546
2007	668,395	592,410	28,322
2006	670,058	599,333	19,695
2005	644,122	565,745	39,201

ᵉ = Advocacy estimate. For a discussion of methodology, see Brian Headd, 2005 (www.sba.gov/advo/research/rs258tot.pdf).

NA = Not available.

Source: U.S. Small Business Administration, Office of Advocacy, *Small Business Economy 2011*, www.sba.gov/advocacy (accessed March 21, 2012).

Why Some Entrepreneurs and Small Businesses Fail

Small businesses are prone to failure. Capital, management, and planning are the key ingredients in the survival of a small business, as well as the most common reasons for failure. Businesses can experience a number of money-related problems. It may take several years before a business begins to show a profit. Entrepreneurs need to have not only the capital to open a business but also the money to operate it in its possibly lengthy start-up phase. One cash flow obstacle often leads to others. Moreover, a series of cash flow predicaments usually ends in a business failure. This scenario is played out all too often by small and not-so-small start-up Internet firms that fail to meet their financial backers' expectations and so are denied a second wave of investment dollars to continue their drive to establish a profitable online firm. According to Maureen Borzacchiello, co-owner of Creative Display Solutions, a trade show products company, "Big businesses such as Bear Stearns, Fannie Mae and Freddie Mac, and AIG can get bailouts, but small-business owners are on their own when times are tough and credit is tight."

Many entrepreneurs lack the management skills required to run a business. Money, time, personnel, and inventory all need to be managed effectively if a small business is to succeed. Starting a small business requires much more than optimism and a good idea.

Success and expansion sometimes lead to problems. Frequently, entrepreneurs with successful small businesses make the mistake of overexpansion. Fast growth often results in dramatic changes in a business. Thus, the entrepreneur must plan carefully and adjust competently to new and potentially disruptive situations.

Every day, and in every part of the country, people open new businesses. For example, 552,600 new businesses recently opened their doors. At the same time, however, 660,900 businesses closed their business and 60,837 businesses (in 2009) declared bankruptcy (see Table 5.2).[9] Although many fail, others represent well-conceived ideas developed by entrepreneurs who have the expertise, resources, and determination to make their businesses succeed. As these well-prepared entrepreneurs pursue their individual goals, our society benefits in many ways from their work and creativity. Billion-dollar companies such as Apple Computer, McDonald's Corporation, and Procter & Gamble are all examples of small businesses that expanded into industry giants.

THE IMPORTANCE OF SMALL BUSINESSES IN OUR ECONOMY

Assess the contributions of small businesses to our economy.

③

This country's economic history abounds with stories of ambitious men and women who turned their ideas into business dynasties. The Ford Motor Company started as a one-man operation with an innovative method for industrial production. L.L.Bean, Inc., can trace its beginnings to a basement shop in Freeport, Maine. Both Xerox and Polaroid began as small firms with a better way to do a job. Indeed, every year since 1963, the President of the United States has proclaimed National Small Business Week to recognize the contributions of small businesses to the economic well-being of America.

Providing Technical Innovation

Invention and innovation are part of the foundations of our economy. The increases in productivity that have characterized the past 200 years of our history are all rooted in one principal source: new ways to do a job with less effort for less money. Studies show that the incidence of innovation among small-business workers is significantly higher than among workers in large businesses. Small firms produce two-and-a-half times as many innovations as large firms relative to the number of persons employed. In fact, small firms employ 40 percent of all high-tech workers such as scientists, engineers, and computer specialists. No wonder small firms produce 13 to 14 times more patents per employee than large patenting firms.

Consider Waymon Armstrong, the owner of a small business that uses computer simulations to help government and other clients prepare for and respond to natural disasters, medical emergencies, and combat. In presenting the 2010 National Small Business Person of the Year award, Karen Mills, Administrator of the U.S. Small Business Administration, said, "Waymon Armstrong is a perfect example of the innovation, inspiration, and determination that exemplify America's most successful entrepreneurs. He believed in his brainchild to the point where he deferred his own salary for three years to keep it afloat. When layoffs loomed for his staff after 9/11, their loyalty and belief in the company was so great that they were willing to work without pay for four months.

"Waymon's commitment to his employees and to his business—Engineering & Computer Simulations, Inc.—demonstrates the qualities that make small businesses such a powerful force for job creation in the American economy and in their local communities," said Mills. "It's the same qualities that will lead us to economic recovery. We are especially proud that his company benefited from two grants under SBA's Small Business Innovation and Research Program."[10]

According to the U.S. Office of Management and Budget, more than half the major technological advances of the 20th century originated with individual inventors and small companies. Even just a sampling of those innovations is remarkable:

- Air conditioning
- Airplane
- Automatic transmission
- FM radio
- Heart valve
- Helicopter
- Instant camera
- Insulin
- Jet engine
- Penicillin
- Personal computer
- Power steering

Perhaps even more remarkable—and important—is that many of these inventions sparked major new U.S. industries or contributed to an established industry by adding some valuable service.

Providing Employment

Small firms traditionally have added more than their proportional share of new jobs to the economy. Seven out of the ten industries that added the most new jobs were small-business-dominated industries. Small businesses creating the most new jobs recently included business services, leisure and hospitality services, and special trade

Providing technical innovation. Meet *Time* magazine's 2010 Person of the Year, entrepreneur Mark Zuckerberg, who founded Facebook while still a student at Harvard. In 2008, Zuckerberg became the world's youngest billionaire at age 25.

©WIREIMAGE/GETTY IMAGES

contractors. Small firms hire a larger proportion of employees who are younger workers, older workers, women, or workers who prefer to work part time.

Furthermore, small businesses provide 67 percent of workers with their first jobs and initial on-the-job training in basic skills. According to the SBA, small businesses represent 99.7 percent of all employers, employ more than 50 percent of the private workforce, and provide about two-thirds of the net new jobs added to our economy.[11] Small businesses thus contribute significantly to solving unemployment problems.

The business cycle, as discussed in Chapter 1, is an important factor in the net creation or loss of jobs. During the 2008–2009 recession, businesses with fewer than 20 employees began losing jobs as early as mid-2007. From 2008 to mid-2009, these smallest businesses accounted for 24 percent of the net job losses, while those with 20–499 employees accounted for 36 percent; the remaining 40 percent of job losses were in larger firms with more than 500 employees.[12]

Providing Competition

Small businesses challenge larger, established firms in many ways, causing them to become more efficient and more responsive to consumer needs. A small business cannot, of course, compete with a large firm in all respects. However, a number of small firms, each competing in its own particular area and its own particular way, together have the desired competitive effect. Thus, several small janitorial companies together add up to reasonable competition for the no-longer-small ServiceMaster.

Filling Needs of Society and Other Businesses

Small firms also provide a variety of goods and services to each other and to much larger firms. Sears, Roebuck & Co. purchases merchandise from approximately 12,000 suppliers—and most of them are small businesses. General Motors relies on more than 32,000 companies for parts and supplies and depends on more than 11,000 independent dealers to sell its automobiles and trucks. Large firms generally buy parts and assemblies from smaller firms for one very good reason: It is less expensive than manufacturing the parts in their own factories. This lower cost eventually is reflected in the price that consumers pay for their products.

It is clear that small businesses are a vital part of our economy and that, as consumers and as members of the labor force, we all benefit enormously from their existence. Now let us look at the situation from the viewpoint of the owners of small businesses.

Describe the advantages and disadvantages of operating a small business.

THE PROS AND CONS OF SMALLNESS

Do most owners of small businesses dream that their firms will grow into giant corporations—managed by professionals—while they serve only on the board of directors? Or would they rather stay small, in a firm where they have the opportunity (and the responsibility) to do everything that needs to be done? The answers depend on the personal characteristics and motivations of the individual owners. For many, the advantages of remaining small far outweigh the disadvantages.

Advantages of Small Business

Small-business owners with limited resources often must struggle to enter competitive new markets. They also have to deal with increasing international competition. However, they enjoy several unique advantages.

Personal Relationships with Customers and Employees

For those who like dealing with people, small business is the place to be. The owners of retail shops get to know many of their customers by name and deal with them on a personal basis. Through such relationships, small-business owners often become involved in the social, cultural, and political life of the community.

Getting personal. For those who like dealing with people, small business is the place to be. Here a business owner provides personalized service to a happy customer.

Relationships between owner-managers and employees also tend to be closer in smaller businesses. In many cases, the owner is a friend and counselor as well as the boss.

These personal relationships provide an important business advantage. The personal service small businesses offer to customers is a major competitive weapon—one that larger firms try to match but often cannot. In addition, close relationships with employees often help the small-business owner to keep effective workers who might earn more with a larger firm.

Ability to Adapt to Change Being his or her own boss, the owner-manager of a small business does not need anyone's permission to adapt to change. An owner may add or discontinue merchandise or services, change store hours, and experiment with various price strategies in response to changes in market conditions. And through personal relationships with customers, the owners of small businesses quickly become aware of changes in people's needs and interests, as well as in the activities of competing firms.

Simplified Record Keeping Many small firms need only a simple set of records. Record keeping might consist of a checkbook, a cash-receipts journal in which to record all sales, and a cash-disbursements journal in which to record all amounts paid out. Obviously, enough records must be kept to allow for producing and filing accurate tax returns.

Independence Small-business owners do not have to punch in and out, bid for vacation times, take orders from superiors, or worry about being fired or laid off. They are the masters of their own destinies—at least with regard to employment. For many people, this is the prime advantage of owning a small business.

Other Advantages According to the SBA, the most profitable companies in the United States are small firms that have been in business for more than ten years and employ fewer than 20 people. Small-business owners also enjoy all the advantages of sole proprietorships, which were discussed in Chapter 4. These include being able to keep all profits, the ease and low cost of going into business and (if necessary) going out of business, and being able to keep business information secret.

Disadvantages of Small Business

Personal contacts with customers, closer relationships with employees, being one's own boss, less cumbersome record-keeping chores, and independence are the bright side of small business. In contrast, the dark side reflects problems unique to these firms.

Risk of Failure As we have noted, small businesses (especially new ones) run a heavy risk of going out of business—about 50 percent survive at least five years.

Older, well-established small firms can be hit hard by a business recession mainly because they do not have the financial resources to weather an extended difficult period.

Limited Potential Small businesses that survive do so with varying degrees of success. Many are simply the means of making a living for the owner and his or her family. The owner may have some technical skill—as a hair stylist or electrician, for example—and may have started a business to put this skill to work. Such a business is unlikely to grow into big business. In addition, employees' potential for advancement is limited.

Limited Ability to Raise Capital Small businesses typically have a limited ability to obtain capital. Figure 5.2 shows that most small-business financing comes out of the owner's pocket. Personal loans from lending institutions provide only about one-fourth of the capital required by small businesses. About 50 percent of all new firms begin with less than $30,000 in total capital, according to Census Bureau and Federal Reserve surveys. In fact, almost 36 percent of new firms begin with less than $20,000, usually provided by the owner or family members and friends.[13]

Although every person who considers starting a small business should be aware of the hazards and pitfalls we have noted, a well-conceived business plan may help to avoid the risk of failure. The U.S. government is also dedicated to helping small businesses make it. It expresses this aim most actively through the SBA.

The Importance of a Business Plan

Lack of planning can be as deadly as lack of money to a new small business. Planning is important to any business, large or small, and never should be overlooked or taken lightly. A **business plan** is a carefully constructed guide for the person starting a business. Consider it as a tool with three basic purposes: communication, management,

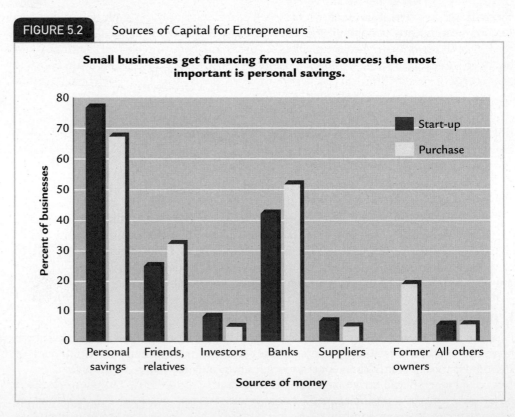

| FIGURE 5.2 | Sources of Capital for Entrepreneurs |

Source: Data developed and provided by the National Federation of Independent Business Foundation and sponsored by the American Express Travel Related Services Company, Inc.

business plan a carefully constructed guide for the person starting a business

Entrepreneurial SUCCESS

Students by Day, Entrepreneurs by Night

A growing number of students are becoming entrepreneurs even before they graduate, gaining valuable business experience and taking advantage of the many resources on campus. Brandt Page, who started a company while at Brigham Young University and has since founded or co-founded two more, explains that as a student entrepreneur, "you have free access to libraries, free access to mentors, to professors, to business competitions, to really being recognized and mentored."

Corinne Prevot had already earned $8,000 from her ski apparel business, Skida, before she entered college. After taking an entrepreneurship course as a freshman at Middlebury College, she rethought her approach to business. She researched competitors, looked at distribution, repriced her products, and formalized her branding. Now Skida's yearly sales are more than $100,000, and Prevot is ready to expand.

Partners Noah Chilton, Harry Kelley, Jackson Kroopf, and Misha Epstein like gourmet coffee, so they created a rolling cart to bring their favorite brews to classmates at Vassar through a business they called Tree City. The entrepreneurs buy from growers who use eco-friendly agricultural methods and they discuss good coffee while they brew a fresh cup for each customer. "Part of what we love about coffee is the way it brings people together," Kroopf says.

Sources: Based on information in Rebecca Palmer, "The College of Hard Knocks," *Utah Business*, January 11, 2012, www.utahbusiness.com; Joanna Hamer, "Tree City Serves Up Ethical Coffee, Enticing Conversation," *Miscellany News* (Poughkeepsie, New York), October 25, 2011, www.miscellanynews.com; Helen Coster, "All Star Student Entrepreneurs," *Forbes*, August 3, 2011, www.forbes.com; Brian Nichols, "Know-How for Hire," *New York Times Education Life*, November 6, 2011, p. 34.

and planning. As a communication tool, a business plan serves as a concise document that potential investors can examine to see if they would like to invest or assist in financing a new venture. It shows whether a business has the potential to make a profit. As a management tool, the business plan helps to track, monitor, and evaluate the progress. The business plan is a living document; it is modified as the entrepreneur gains knowledge and experience. It also serves to establish time lines and milestones and allows comparison of growth projections against actual accomplishments. Finally, as a planning tool, the business plan guides a businessperson through the various phases of business. For example, the plan helps to identify obstacles to avoid and to establish alternatives. According to Robert Krummer, Jr., chairman of First Business Bank in Los Angeles, "The business plan is a necessity. If the person who wants to start a small business can't put a business plan together, he or she is in trouble."

Personal APPS

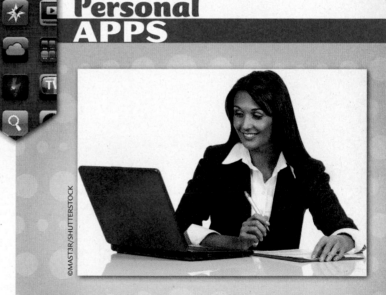

Although writing a business plan won't guarantee your success, it will help you think through many of the issues that can trip up entrepreneurs. And if you work for a big company, you may find yourself writing a kind of business plan for a product or project.

Components of a Business Plan

Table 5.3 shows the 12 sections that a business plan should include. Each section is further explained at the end of each of the seven major parts in the text. The goal of each end-of-the-part exercise is to help a businessperson create his or her own business plan. When constructing a business plan, the businessperson should strive to keep it easy to read, uncluttered, and complete. Like other busy executives, officials of financial institutions do not have the time to wade through pages of extraneous data. The business plan should answer the four questions banking officials and investors are most interested in: (1) What exactly is the nature

TABLE 5.3	Components of a Business Plan

1. *Introduction.* Basic information such as the name, address, and phone number of the business; the date the plan was issued; and a statement of confidentiality to keep important information away from potential competitors.

2. *Executive Summary.* A one- to two-page overview of the entire business plan, including a justification why the business will succeed.

3. *Benefits to the Community.* Information on how the business will have an impact on economic development, community development, and human development.

4. *Company and Industry.* The background of the company, choice of the legal business form, information on the products or services to be offered, and examination of the potential customers, current competitors, and the business's future.

5. *Management Team.* Discussion of skills, talents, and job descriptions of management team, managerial compensation, management training needs, and professional assistance requirements.

6. *Manufacturing and Operations Plan.* Discussion of facilities needed, space requirements, capital equipment, labor force, inventory control, and purchasing requirement.

7. *Labor Force.* Discussion of the quality of skilled workers available and the training, compensation, and motivation of workers.

8. *Marketing Plan.* Discussion of markets, market trends, competition, market share, pricing, promotion, distribution, and service policy.

9. *Financial Plan.* Summary of the investment needed, sales and cash flow forecasts, breakeven analysis, and sources of funding.

10. *Exit Strategy.* Discussion of a succession plan or going public. Who will take over the business?

11. *Critical Risks and Assumptions.* Evaluation of the weaknesses of the business and how the company plans to deal with these and other business problems.

12. *Appendix.* Supplementary information crucial to the plan, such as résumés of owners and principal managers, advertising samples, organization chart, and any related information.

Source: From HATTEN, *Small Business Management*, 5E. © 2012 Cengage Learning.

and mission of the new venture? (2) Why is this new enterprise a good idea? (3) What are the businessperson's goals? (4) How much will the new venture cost?

The great amount of time and consideration that should go into creating a business plan probably will end up saving time later. For example, Sharon Burch, who was running a computer software business while earning a degree in business administration, had to write a business plan as part of one of her courses. Burch has said, "I wish I'd taken the class before I started my business. I see a lot of things I could have done differently. But it has helped me since because I've been using the business plan as a guide for my business." Table 5.4 provides a business plan checklist. Accuracy and realistic expectations are crucial to an effective business plan. It is unethical to deceive loan officers, and it is unwise to deceive yourself.

TABLE 5.4	Business Plan Checklist

1. Does the executive summary grab the reader's attention and highlight the major points of the business plan?

2. Does the business-concept section clearly describe the purpose of the business, the customers, the value proposition, and the distribution channel and convey a compelling story?

3. Do the industry and market analyses support acceptance and demand for the business concept in the marketplace and define a first customer in depth?

4. Does the management team plan persuade the reader that the team could implement the business concept successfully? Does it assure the reader that an effective infrastructure is in place to facilitate the goals and operations of the company?

5. Does the product/service plan clearly provide details on the status of the product, the time line for completion, and the intellectual property that will be acquired?

6. Does the operations plan prove that the product or service could be produced and distributed efficiently and effectively?

7. Does the marketing plan successfully demonstrate how the company will create customer awareness in the target market and deliver the benefit to the customer?

8. Does the financial plan convince the reader that the business model is sustainable—that it will provide a superior return on investment for the investor and sufficient cash flow to repay loans to potential lenders?

9. Does the growth plan convince the reader that the company has long-term growth potential and spin-off products and services?

10. Does the contingency and exit-strategy plan convince the reader that the risk associated with this venture can be mediated? Is there an exit strategy in place for investors?

Source: From ALLEN, *Launching New Ventures*, 6E. © 2012 Cengage Learning.

THE SMALL BUSINESS ADMINISTRATION

 Explain how the Small Business Administration helps small businesses.

The **Small Business Administration (SBA)**, created by Congress in 1953, is a governmental agency that assists, counsels, and protects the interests of small businesses in the United States. It helps people get into business and stay in business. The agency provides assistance to owners and managers of prospective, new, and established small businesses. Through more than 1,000 offices and resource centers throughout the nation, the SBA provides both financial assistance and management counseling. Recently, the SBA provided training, technical assistance, and education to more than 3 million small businesses. It helps small firms to bid for and obtain government contracts, and it helps them to prepare to enter foreign markets.

SBA Management Assistance

Statistics show that most failures in small business are related to poor management. For this reason, the SBA places special emphasis on improving the management ability of the owners and managers of small businesses. The SBA's Management Assistance Program is extensive and diversified. It includes free individual counseling, courses, conferences, workshops, and a wide range of publications. Recently, the SBA provided management and technical assistance to nearly 1 million small businesses through its

Small Business Administration (SBA) a governmental agency that assists, counsels, and protects the interests of small businesses in the United States

1,100 Small Business Development Centers and 13,000 volunteers from the Service Corps of Retired Executives.[14]

Management Courses and Workshops The management courses offered by the SBA cover all the functions, duties, and roles of managers. Instructors may be teachers from local colleges and universities or other professionals, such as management consultants, bankers, lawyers, and accountants. Fees for these courses are quite low. The most popular such course is a general survey of eight to ten different areas of business management. In follow-up studies, businesspeople may concentrate in depth on one or more of these areas depending on their particular strengths and weaknesses. The SBA occasionally offers one-day conferences. These conferences are aimed at keeping owner-managers up-to-date on new management developments, tax laws, and the like. The Small Business Training Network (SBTN) is an online training network consisting of 83 SBA-run courses, workshops, and resources. Some of the most requested courses include Entrepreneurship, Starting and Managing Your Own Business, Developing a Business Plan, Managing the Digital Enterprise, Identify Your Target Market, and Analyze Profitability. Find out more at www.sba.gov/training. Recently, more than 240,000 small-business owners benefited from SBA's free online business courses.

SCORE The **Service Corps of Retired Executives (SCORE)**, created in 1964, is a group of more than 13,000 retired and active businesspeople including more than 2,000 women who volunteer their services to small businesses through the SBA. The collective experience of SCORE volunteers spans the full range of American enterprise. These volunteers have worked for such notable companies as Eastman Kodak, General Electric, IBM, and Procter & Gamble. Experts in areas of accounting, finance, marketing, engineering, and retailing provide counseling and mentoring to entrepreneurs.

A small-business owner who has a particular problem can request free counseling from SCORE. An assigned counselor visits the owner in his or her establishment and, through careful observation, analyzes the business situation and the problem. If the problem is complex, the counselor may call on other volunteer experts to assist. Finally, the counselor offers a plan for solving the problem and helping the owner through the critical period.

Consider the plight of Elizabeth Halvorsen, a mystery writer from Minneapolis. Her husband had built up the family advertising and graphic arts firm for 17 years when he was called in 1991 to serve in the Persian Gulf War. The only one left behind to run the business was Mrs. Halvorsen, who admittedly had no business experience. Enter SCORE. With a SCORE management expert at her side, she kept the business on track. Recently, SCORE volunteers served more than 523,800 small-business people like Mrs. Halvorsen through its 389 offices. The 13,000 counselors provided 203,000 face-to-face counseling sessions, 119,000 online counseling sessions, and more than 49,500 online workshops to more than 201,000 workshop participants. Since its inception, SCORE has assisted more than 9 million small-business people with online and face-to-face small business counseling.[15]

Service Corps of Retired Executives (SCORE) a group of businesspeople who volunteer their services to small businesses through the SBA

© AP PHOTO/WACO TRIBUNE-HERALD, DUANE A. LAVERTY

Banking on the Banks. Meet Marilyn and Dwayne Banks, owners of Marilyn's Gift Gallery and Sound World Music, in their East Waco, TX, gift shop. Since opening their business in 1989, they have helped start many community projects including an association to help minority business owners in the area.

Help for Minority-Owned Small Businesses

Americans who are members of minority groups have had difficulty entering the nation's economic mainstream. Raising money is a nagging problem for minority business owners, who also may lack adequate training. Members of minority groups are, of course, eligible for all SBA programs, but the SBA makes a special effort to assist those minority groups who want to start small businesses or expand existing ones. For example, the Minority Business Development Agency awards grants to develop and increase business opportunities for members of racial and ethnic minorities.

Helping women become entrepreneurs is also a special goal of the SBA. Emily Harrington, one of nine children, was born in Manila, the Philippines. She arrived in the United States in 1972 as a foreign-exchange student. Convinced that there was a market for hard-working, dedicated minorities and women, she launched Qualified Resources, Inc., a professional staffing services firm. *Inc.* magazine selected her firm as one of "America's Fastest Growing Private Companies" just six years later. Harrington credits the SBA with giving her the technical support that made her first loan possible. Finding a SCORE counselor to work directly with her, she refined her business plan until she got a bank loan. Before contacting the SBA, Harrington was turned down for business loans "by all the banks I approached," even though she worked as a manager of loan credit and collection for a bank. Later, Emily Harrington was SBA's winner of the local, regional, and national Small Business Entrepreneurial Success Award for Rhode Island, the New England region, and the nation! For several years in a row, Qualified Resources, Inc., was named one of the fastest growing private companies in Rhode Island. Now with more than 100 Women's Business Centers, entrepreneurs like Harrington can receive training and technical assistance, access to credit and capital, federal contracts, and international markets. The SBA's Online Women's Business Center (www.sba.gov/aboutsba/sbaprograms/onlinewbc/index.html) is a state-of-the-art Internet site to help women expand their businesses. This free, interactive Web site offers women information about business principles and practices, management techniques, networking, industry news, market research and technology training, online counseling, and hundreds of links to other sites, as well as information about the many SBA services and resources available to them.

Small-Business Institutes Small-business institutes (SBIs), created in 1972, are groups of senior and graduate students in business administration who provide management counseling to small businesses. SBIs have been set up on more than 520 college campuses as another way to help business owners. The students work in small groups guided by faculty advisers and SBA management-assistance experts. Like SCORE volunteers, they analyze and help solve the problems of small-business owners at their business establishments.

Small-Business Development Centers Small-business development centers (SBDCs) are university-based groups that provide individual counseling and practical training to owners of small businesses. SBDCs draw from the resources of local, state, and federal governments, private businesses, and universities. These groups can provide managerial and technical help, data from research studies, and other types of specialized assistance of value to small businesses. In 2011, there were more than 1,000 SBDC locations, primarily at colleges and universities, assisting people such as Kathleen DuBois. After scribbling a list of her abilities and the names of potential clients on a napkin in a local restaurant, Kathleen DuBois decided to start her own marketing firm. Beth Thornton launched her engineering firm after a discussion with a colleague in the ladies room of the Marriott. When Richard Shell was laid off after 20 years of service with Nisource (Columbia Gas), he searched the Internet tirelessly before finding the right franchise option. Introduced by mutual friends, Jim Bostic and Denver McMillion quickly connected, built a high level of trust, and combined their diverse professional backgrounds to form a manufacturing company. Although these entrepreneurs took different routes in starting their new businesses in West Virginia, all of them turned to the West Virginia Small Business Development Center for the technical assistance to make their dreams become a reality.

SBA Publications The SBA issues management, marketing, and technical publications dealing with hundreds of topics of interest to present and prospective managers of small firms. Most of these publications are available from the SBA free of charge. Others can be obtained for a small fee from the U.S. Government Printing Office.

small-business institutes (SBIs) groups of senior and graduate students in business administration who provide management counseling to small businesses

small-business development centers (SBDCs) university-based groups that provide individual counseling and practical training to owners of small businesses

SBA Financial Assistance

Small businesses seem to be constantly in need of money. An owner may have enough capital to start and operate the business. But then he or she may require more money to finance increased operations during peak selling seasons, to pay for required pollution control equipment, to finance an expansion, or to mop up after a natural disaster such as a flood or a terrorist attack. For example, the Supplemental Terrorist Activity Relief program has made $3.7 billion in loans to 8,202 small businesses harmed or disrupted by the September 11 terrorist attacks. In October 2005, the SBA guaranteed loans of up to $150,000 to small businesses affected by Hurricanes Katrina and Rita. Since the 2005 hurricanes, SBA has made more than $4.9 billion in disaster loans to 102,903 homeowners and renters in the Gulf region. Businesses in the area received 16,828 business disaster loans with disbursements worth $1.5 billion.[16] In 2010, the SBA offered economic injury loans to fishing and fishing-dependent small businesses as a result of the Deepwater BP spill that shut down commercial and recreational fishing waters. According to the SBA Administrator Karen Mills, "SBA remains committed to taking every step to help small businesses deal with the financial challenges they are facing as a result of the Deepwater BP oil spill."[17] The SBA offers special financial-assistance programs that cover all these situations. However, its primary financial function is to guarantee loans to eligible businesses.

Regular Business Loans Most of the SBA's business loans are actually made by private lenders such as banks, but repayment is partially guaranteed by the agency. That is, the SBA may guarantee that it will repay the lender up to 90 percent of the loan if the borrowing firm cannot repay it. Guaranteed loans approved on or after October 1, 2002, may be as large as $1.5 million (this loan limit may be increased in the future). The average size of an SBA-guaranteed business loan is about $300,000, and its average duration is about eight years.

Small-Business Investment Companies Venture capital is money that is invested in small (and sometimes struggling) firms that have the potential to become very successful. In many cases, only a lack of capital keeps these firms from rapid and solid growth. The people who invest in such firms expect that their investments will grow with the firms and become quite profitable.

The popularity of these investments has increased over the past 30 years, but most small firms still have difficulty obtaining venture capital. To help such businesses, the SBA licenses, regulates, and provides financial assistance to **small-business investment companies (SBICs)**.

An SBIC is a privately owned firm that provides venture capital to small enterprises that meet its investment standards. Such firms as America Online, Apple Computer, Federal Express, Compaq Computer, Intel Corporation, Outback Steakhouse, and Staples, Inc., all were financed through SBICs during their initial growth period. SBICs are intended to be profit-making organizations. The aid that SBA offers allows them to invest in small businesses that otherwise would not attract venture capital. Since Congress created the program in 1958, SBICs have financed more than 107,000 small businesses for a total of about $60 billion. Recently, SBIC benefited 1,477 businesses, and 24 percent of these firms were less than two years old.[18]

State of Small Business During the Recession

Celebrating the 47th annual observance of National Small Business Week in May 2010, President Obama stated,

> *Our nation is still emerging from one of the worst recessions in our history, and small businesses were among the hardest hit. From mom-and-pop stores to high tech start-ups, countless small businesses have been forced to lay off employees or shut their doors entirely. In these difficult times, we must do all we can to help these firms recover from the recession and put Americans back to work. Our*

venture capital money that is invested in small (and sometimes struggling) firms that have the potential to become very successful

small-business investment companies (SBICs) privately owned firms that provide venture capital to small enterprises that meet their investment standards *government cannot guarantee a company's success, but it can help create market conditions that allow small businesses to thrive.*

My Administration is committed to helping small businesses drive our economy toward recovery and long-term growth. The American Recovery and Reinvestment Act has supported billions of dollars in loans and Federal contracts for small businesses across the country. The Affordable Care Act makes it easier for small business owners to provide health insurance to their employees, and gives entrepreneurs the security they need to innovate and take risks. We have enacted new tax cuts and tax credits for small firms. Still, we must do more to empower these companies. Small businesses are the engine of our prosperity and a proud reflection of our character. A healthy small business sector will give us vibrant communities, cutting-edge technology, and an American economy that can compete and win in the 21st century.[19]

As if the recession was not enough, in the states near the Gulf of Mexico, many small businesses suffered financial losses following the April 20, 2010, Deepwater Horizon BP oil spill that shut down commercial and recreational fishing along the coasts. According to the SBA Administrator Karen Mills, "With the region still recovering from previous devastation and the national recession of the last couple of years, it's critical that we take every step we can to provide small businesses with resources to make it through this latest crisis so that they can continue to drive local economic growth and provide good-paying jobs." The SBA offered working capital loans up to $2 million at an interest rate of 4 percent with terms up to 30 years.[20]

We have discussed the importance of the small-business segment of our economy. We have weighed the advantages and drawbacks of operating a small business as compared with a large one. But is there a way to achieve the best of both worlds? Can one preserve one's independence as a business owner and still enjoy some of the benefits of "bigness"? Let's take a close look at franchising.

FRANCHISING

6 Explain the concept and types of franchising.

A **franchise** is a license to operate an individually owned business as if it were part of a chain of outlets or stores. Often, the business itself is also called a *franchise*. Among the most familiar franchises are McDonald's, H&R Block, AAMCO Transmissions, GNC (General Nutrition Centers), and Dairy Queen. Many other franchises carry familiar names; this method of doing business has become very popular in the last 30 years or so. It is an attractive means of starting and operating a small business.

What Is Franchising?

Franchising is the actual granting of a franchise. A **franchisor** is an individual or organization granting a franchise. A **franchisee** is a person or organization purchasing a franchise. The franchisor supplies a known and advertised business name, management skills, the required training and materials, and a method of doing business. The franchisee supplies labor and capital, operates the franchised business, and agrees to abide by the provisions of the franchise agreement. Table 5.5 lists the basic franchisee rights and obligations that would be covered in a typical franchise agreement.

Types of Franchising

Franchising arrangements fall into three general categories. In the first approach, a manufacturer authorizes a number of retail stores to sell a certain brand-name item. This type of franchising arrangement, one of the oldest, is prevalent in sales of passenger cars and trucks, farm equipment, shoes, paint, earth-moving equipment, and petroleum. About 90 percent of all gasoline is sold through franchised, independent retail service stations, and franchised dealers handle virtually all sales of new cars and trucks. In the second type of franchising arrangement, a producer licenses distributors to sell a

franchise a license to operate an individually owned business as though it were part of a chain of outlets or stores

franchising the actual granting of a franchise

franchisor an individual or organization granting a franchise

franchisee a person or organization purchasing a franchise

TABLE 5.5 Basic Rights and Obligations Delineated in a Franchise Agreement

Franchisee rights include:

1. use of trademarks, trade names, and patents of the franchisor;

2. use of the brand image and the design and decor of the premises developed by the franchisor;

3. use of the franchisor's secret methods;

4. use of the franchisor's copyrighted materials;

5. use of recipes, formulae, specifications, processes, and methods of manufacture developed by the franchisor;

6. conducting the franchised business upon or from the agreed premises strictly in accordance with the franchisor's methods and subject to the franchisor's directions;

7. guidelines established by the franchisor regarding exclusive territorial rights; and

8. rights to obtain supplies from nominated suppliers at special prices.

Franchisee obligations include:

1. to carry on the business franchised and no other business upon the approved and nominated premises;

2. to observe certain minimum operating hours;

3. to pay a franchise fee;

4. to follow the accounting system laid down by the franchisor;

5. not to advertise without prior approval of the advertisements by the franchisor;

6. to use and display such point-of-sale advertising materials as the franchisor stipulates;

7. to maintain the premises in good, clean, and sanitary condition and to redecorate when required to do so by the franchisor;

8. to maintain the widest possible insurance coverage;

9. to permit the franchisor's staff to enter the premises to inspect and see if the franchisor's standards are being maintained;

10. to purchase goods or products from the franchisor or his designated suppliers;

11. to train the staff in the franchisor's methods to ensure that they are neatly and appropriately clothed; and

12. not to assign the franchise contract without the franchisor's consent.

Source: Excerpted from the SBA's "Is Franchising for Me?" www.sba.gov (accessed March 12, 2012).

given product to retailers. This arrangement is common in the soft drink industry. Most national manufacturers of soft drink syrups—The Coca-Cola Company, Dr. Pepper/ Seven-Up Companies, PepsiCo, Royal Crown Companies, Inc.—franchise independent bottlers who then serve retailers. In a third form of franchising, a franchisor supplies brand names, techniques, or other services instead of a complete product. Although the franchisor may provide certain production and distribution services, its primary role is the careful development and control of marketing strategies. This approach to franchising, which is the most typical today, is used by Holiday Inns, Howard Johnson Company, AAMCO Transmissions, McDonald's, Dairy Queen, Avis, Hertz Corporation, KFC (Kentucky Fried Chicken), and SUBWAY, to name but a few.

THE GROWTH OF FRANCHISING

7 Analyze the growth of franchising and its advantages and disadvantages.

Franchising, which began in the United States around the time of the Civil War, was used originally by large firms, such as the Singer Sewing Company, to distribute their products. Franchising has been increasing steadily in popularity since the early 1900s, primarily for filling stations and car dealerships; however, this retailing strategy has experienced enormous growth since the mid-1970s. The franchise proliferation generally has paralleled the expansion of the fast-food industry.

Of course, franchising is not limited to fast foods. Hair salons, tanning parlors, and dentists and lawyers are expected to participate in franchising arrangements in growing numbers. Franchised health clubs, pest exterminators, and campgrounds are already widespread, as are franchised tax preparers and travel agencies. The real estate industry also has experienced a rapid increase in franchising.

Also, franchising is attracting more women and minority business owners in the United States than ever before. One reason is that special outreach programs designed to encourage franchisee diversity have developed. Consider Angela Trammel, a young mother of two. She had been laid off from her job at the Marriott after 9/11. Since she was a member of a Curves Fitness Center and liked the concept of empowering women to become physically fit, she began researching the cost of purchasing a Curves franchise and ways to finance the business. "I was online looking for financing, and I linked to Enterprise Development Group in Washington, DC. I knew that they had diverse clients." The cost for the franchise was $19,500, but it took $60,000 to open the doors to her fitness center. "Applying for a loan to start the business was much harder than buying a house," said Trammel. Just three years later, Angela and her husband, Ernest, own three Curves Fitness Centers with 12 employees. Recently, since giving birth to her third child, she has found the financial freedom and flexibility needed to care for her busy family. In fact, within a three-year period, the Trammels grew their annual household income from $80,000 to $250,000.[21] Franchisors such as Wendy's, McDonald's, Burger King, and Church's Chicken all have special corporate programs to attract minority and women franchisees. Just as important, successful women and minority franchisees are willing to get involved by offering advice and guidance to new franchisees.

Herman Petty, the first African-American McDonald's franchisee, remembers that the company provided a great deal of help while he worked to establish his first units. In turn, Petty traveled to help other black franchisees, and he invited new franchisees to gain hands-on experience in his Chicago restaurants before starting their own establishments. In 1972, Petty also organized a support group, the National Black McDonald's Operators Association, to help black franchisees in other areas. Today, members of this association own nearly 1,400 McDonald's restaurants throughout the United States, South Africa, and the Caribbean with annual sales of more than $3.2 billion. "We are really concentrating on helping our operators to be successful both operationally and financially," says Craig Welburn, the McDonald's franchisee who leads the group.

Dual-branded franchises, in which two franchisors offer their products together, are a new small-business trend. For example, in 1993, pleased with the success of its first cobranded restaurant with Texaco in Beebe, Arkansas, McDonald's now has more than 400 cobranded restaurants in the United States. Also, an agreement between franchisors Doctor's Associates, Inc., and TCBY Enterprises, Inc., now allows franchisees to sell SUBWAY sandwiches and TCBY yogurt in the same establishment.

Are Franchises Successful?

Franchising is designed to provide a tested formula for success, along with ongoing advice and training. The success rate for businesses

PR NEWSFOTO/SIGNS BY TOMORROW

Getting ad value from your car. Joe McGuinness founded Signs By Tomorrow in 1986. Today, with over 180 locations nationwide, the Columbia, Md.-based franchise company turns hundreds of autos into rolling billboards each year, much like this one for 1-800-GOT-JUNK. Some companies may compensate your gas costs to use your car.

owned and operated by franchisees is significantly higher than the success rate for other independently owned small businesses. In a recent nationwide Gallup poll of 944 franchise owners, 94 percent of franchisees indicated that they were very or somewhat successful, only 5 percent believed that they were very unsuccessful or somewhat unsuccessful, and 1 percent did not know. Despite these impressive statistics, franchising is not a guarantee of success for either franchisees or franchisors. Too rapid expansion, inadequate capital or management skills, and a host of other problems can cause failure for both franchisee and franchisor. Thus, for example, the Dizzy Dean's Beef and Burger franchise is no longer in business. Timothy Bates, a Wayne State University economist, warns, "Despite the hype that franchising is the safest way to go when starting a new business, the research just doesn't bear that out." Just consider Boston Chicken, which once had more than 1,200 restaurants before declaring bankruptcy in 1998.

Advantages of Franchising

Franchising plays a vital role in our economy and soon may become the dominant form of retailing. Why? Because franchising offers advantages to both the franchisor and the franchisee.

To the Franchisor The franchisor gains fast and well-controlled distribution of its products without incurring the high cost of constructing and operating its own outlets. The franchisor thus has more capital available to expand production and to use for advertising. At the same time, it can ensure, through the franchise agreement, that outlets are maintained and operated according to its own standards.

The franchisor also benefits from the fact that the franchisee—a sole proprietor in most cases—is likely to be very highly motivated to succeed. The success of the franchise means more sales, which translate into higher royalties for the franchisor.

To the Franchisee The franchisee gets the opportunity to start a business with limited capital and to make use of the business experience of others. Moreover, an outlet with a nationally advertised name, such as RadioShack, McDonald's, or Century 21, has guaranteed customers as soon as it opens.

If business problems arise, the franchisor gives the franchisee guidance and advice. This counseling is primarily responsible for the very high degree of success enjoyed by franchises. In most cases, the franchisee does not pay for such help.

The franchisee also receives materials to use in local advertising and can take part in national promotional campaigns sponsored by the franchisor. McDonald's and its franchisees, for example, constitute one of the nation's top 20 purchasers of advertising. Finally, the franchisee may be able to minimize the cost of advertising, supplies, and various business necessities by purchasing them in cooperation with other franchisees.

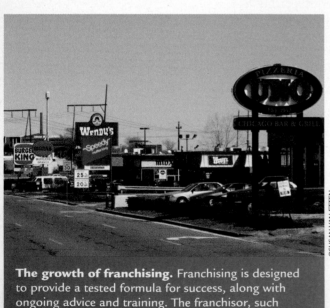

The growth of franchising. Franchising is designed to provide a tested formula for success, along with ongoing advice and training. The franchisor, such as Wendy's or Burger King, supplies a known and advertised business name, management skills, the required training and materials, and a method of doing business. Franchising, however, is not a guarantee of success for either franchisees or franchisors.

Disadvantages of Franchising

The main disadvantage of franchising affects the franchisee, and it arises because the franchisor retains a great deal of control. The franchisor's contract can dictate every aspect of the business: decor, design of employee uniforms, types of signs, and all the details of business operations. All Burger King French fries taste the same because all Burger King franchisees have to make them the same way.

Contract disputes are the cause of many lawsuits. For example, Rekha Gabhawala, a Dunkin' Donuts franchisee in Milwaukee, alleged that the franchisor was forcing her out of business so that the company could profit by reselling the downtown franchise to someone else; the company, on the other hand, alleged that

Gabhawala breached the contract by not running the business according to company standards. In another case, Dunkin' Donuts sued Chris Romanias, its franchisee in Pennsylvania, alleging that Romanias intentionally underreported gross sales to the company. Romanias, on the other hand, alleged that Dunkin' Donuts, Inc., breached the contract because it failed to provide assistance in operating the franchise. Other franchisees claim that contracts are unfairly tilted toward the franchisors. Yet others have charged that they lost their franchise and investment because their franchisor would not approve the sale of the business when they found a buyer.

To arbitrate disputes between franchisors and franchisees, the National Franchise Mediation Program was established in 1993 by 30 member firms, including Burger King Corporation, McDonald's Corporation, and Wendy's International, Inc. Negotiators have since resolved numerous cases through mediation. Recently, Carl's Jr. brought in one of its largest franchisees to help set its system straight, making most franchisees happy for the first time in years. The program also helped PepsiCo settle a long-term contract dispute and renegotiate its franchise agreements.

Because disagreements between franchisors and franchisees have increased in recent years, many franchisees have been demanding government regulation of franchising. In 1997, to avoid government regulation, some of the largest franchisors proposed a new self-policing plan to the Federal Trade Commission.

Franchise holders pay for their security, usually with a one-time franchise fee and continuing royalty and advertising fees, collected as a percentage of sales. A SUBWAY franchisee pays an initial franchise fee of $15,000 and an annual fee of 8 percent of gross sales. In some fields, franchise agreements are not uniform. One franchisee may pay more than another for the same services.

Even success can cause problems. Sometimes a franchise is so successful that the franchisor opens its own outlet nearby, in direct competition—although franchisees may fight back. For example, a court recently ruled that Burger King could not enter into direct competition with the franchisee because the contract was not specific on the issue. A spokesperson for one franchisor contends that the company "gives no geographical protection" to its franchise holders and thus is free to move in on them. Franchise operators work hard. They often put in 10- and 12-hour days, six days a week. The International Franchise Association advises prospective franchise purchasers to investigate before investing and to approach buying a franchise cautiously. Franchises vary widely in approach as well as in products. Some, such as Dunkin' Donuts and Baskin-Robbins, demand long hours. Others, such as Great Clips hair salons and Albert's Family Restaurants, are more appropriate for those who do not want to spend many hours at their stores.

GLOBAL PERSPECTIVES IN SMALL BUSINESS

For small American businesses, the world is becoming smaller. National and international economies are growing more and more interdependent as political leadership and national economic directions change and trade barriers diminish or disappear. Globalization and instant worldwide communications are rapidly shrinking distances at the same time that they are expanding business opportunities. According to a recent study, the Internet is increasingly important to small-business strategic thinking, with more than 50 percent of those surveyed indicating that the Internet represented their most favored strategy for growth. This was more than double the next-favored choice, strategic alliances reflecting the opportunity to reach both global and domestic customers. The Internet and online payment systems enable even very small businesses to serve international customers. In fact, technology now gives small businesses the leverage and power to reach markets that were once limited solely to large corporations. No wonder the number of businesses exporting their goods and services has tripled since 1990, with two-thirds of that boom coming from companies with fewer than 20 employees.[22]

The SBA offers help to the nation's small-business owners who want to enter the world markets. The SBA's efforts include counseling small firms on how and where to market overseas, matching U.S. small-business executives with potential overseas customers, and helping exporters to secure financing. The agency brings small U.S. firms into direct contact with potential overseas buyers and partners. The SBA International Trade Loan program provides guarantees of up to $5 million in loans to small-business owners. These loans help small firms in expanding or developing new export markets. The U.S. Commercial Service, a Commerce Department division, aids small and medium-sized businesses in selling overseas. The division's global network includes more than 100 offices in the United States and 151 others in 75 countries around the world.[23]

Consider Daniel J. Nanigian, President of Nanmac Corporation in Framingham, Massachusetts. This company manufactures temperature sensors used in a wide range of industrial applications. With an export strategy aimed at growing revenues in diverse foreign markets including China, the Nanmac Corporation experienced explosive growth in 2009. The company nearly doubled its sales from $2.7 million in 2008 to $5.1 million in 2009. The company's international sales, at $300,000 in 2004, reached $700,000 in 2009 and $1.7 million in 2010. Its administrative, sales, and manufacturing employees have increased by 80 percent.

The company has a strong presence in China and is expanding in other markets, as well, including Latin America, Singapore, and Russia. Under Nanigian's guidance, the company has developed creative solutions and partnerships to help maximize its presence internationally. As part of its China strategy, Nanmac partners with distributors, recruits European and in-country sales representatives, uses a localized Chinese Web site, and relies for advice on the export assistance programs of the Massachusetts Small Business Development Center Network's Massachusetts Export Center. The strategy, along with travel to China to conduct technical training seminars and attend trade shows and technical conferences, has helped to grow Nanmac's Chinese client list from 1 in 2003 to more than 30 accounts today. Mr. Nanigian received SBA's 2010 Small Business Exporter of the Year Award.[24]

International trade will become more important to small-business owners as they face unique challenges in the new century. Small businesses, which are expected to remain the dominant form of organization in this country, must be prepared to adapt to significant demographic and economic changes in the world marketplace.

This chapter ends our discussion of American business today. From here on, we shall be looking closely at various aspects of business operations. We begin, in the next chapter, with a discussion of management—what management is, what managers do, and how they work to coordinate the basic economic resources within a business organization.

return to Inside BUSINESS

Locker Lookz

JoAnn Brewer and Christi Sterling had never run a company before they teamed up to found Locker Lookz. After helping their preteen daughters create accessories to dress up their school lockers as a way to show off their personal style, they recognized a viable business opportunity. "Self-expression is such a huge, huge thing at this age," explains Sterling. "Not everybody gets to see your bedroom at home, but everyone gets to see your locker."

Part of the fun for customers is mixing and matching products for a unique look. For this reason, Locker Lookz's Web site has an interactive design feature to help girls visualize how different products go together. The site also offers instructional videos so customers know how to install and remove accessories without damaging the locker. Coming soon: Accessories to personalize boys' lockers.

Questions

1. When Locker Lookz needed to raise money quickly, why do you think the founders sought financing from family, friends, and a church investment group rather than talking with banks?

2. If you were writing a business plan for Locker Lookz, what would you recommend as an exit strategy? Explain your answer.

Looking for Success?

Get Flashcards, Quizzes, Games, Crosswords, and more @ www.cengagebrain.com.

1 Define what a small business is and recognize the fields in which small businesses are concentrated.

A small business is one that is independently owned and operated for profit and is not dominant in its field. There are about 27.5 million businesses in this country, and more than 99.7 percent of them are small businesses. Small businesses employ more than half the nation's workforce. About 69 percent of small businesses survive at least two years and about 50 percent survive at least five years. More than half of all small businesses are in retailing and services.

2 Identify the people who start small businesses and the reasons why some succeed and many fail.

Such personal characteristics as independence, desire to create a new enterprise, and willingness to accept a challenge may encourage individuals to start small businesses. Various external circumstances, such as special expertise or even the loss of a job, also can supply the motivation to strike out on one's own. Poor planning and lack of capital and management experience are the major causes of small-business failures.

3 Assess the contributions of small businesses to our economy.

Small businesses have been responsible for a wide variety of inventions and innovations, some of which have given rise to new industries. Historically, small businesses have created the bulk of the nation's new jobs. Further, they have mounted effective competition to larger firms. They provide things that society needs, act as suppliers to larger firms, and serve as customers of other businesses, both large and small.

4 Describe the advantages and disadvantages of operating a small business.

The advantages of smallness in business include the opportunity to establish personal relationships with customers and employees, the ability to adapt to changes quickly, independence, and simplified record keeping. The major disadvantages are the high risk of failure, the limited potential for growth, and the limited ability to raise capital.

5 Explain how the Small Business Administration helps small businesses.

The Small Business Administration (SBA) was created in 1953 to assist and counsel the nation's millions of small-business owners. The SBA offers management courses and workshops; managerial help, including one-to-one counseling through SCORE; various publications; and financial assistance through guaranteed loans and SBICs. It places special emphasis on aid to minority-owned businesses, including those owned by women.

6 Explain the concept and types of franchising.

A franchise is a license to operate an individually owned business as though it were part of a chain. The franchisor provides a known business name, management skills, a method of doing business, and the training and required materials. The franchisee contributes labor and capital, operates the franchised business, and agrees to abide by the provisions of the franchise agreement. There are three major categories of franchise agreements.

7 Analyze the growth of franchising and its advantages and disadvantages.

Franchising has grown tremendously since the mid-1970s. The franchisor's major advantage in franchising is fast and well-controlled distribution of products with minimal capital outlay. In return, the franchisee has the opportunity to open a business with limited capital, to make use of the business experience of others, and to sell to an existing clientele. For this, the franchisee usually must pay both an initial franchise fee and a continuing royalty based on sales. He or she also must follow the dictates of the franchise with regard to operation of the business.

Worldwide business opportunities are expanding for small businesses. The SBA assists small-business owners in penetrating foreign markets. The next century will present unique challenges and opportunities for small-business owners.

KEY TERMS

You should now be able to define and give an example relevant to each of the following terms:

small business (135)
business plan (144)
Small Business Administration (SBA) (147)
Service Corps of Retired Executives (SCORE) (148)

small-business institutes (SBIs) (149)
small-business development centers (SBDCs) (149)
venture capital (150)
small-business investment companies (SBICs) (150)

franchise (151)
franchising (151)
franchisor (151)
franchisee (151)

1. What information would you need to determine whether a particular business is small according to SBA guidelines?
2. Which two areas of business generally attract the most small businesses? Why are these areas attractive to small business?
3. Distinguish among service industries, distribution industries, and production industries.
4. What kinds of factors encourage certain people to start new businesses?
5. What are the major causes of small-business failure? Do these causes also apply to larger businesses?
6. Briefly describe four contributions of small business to the American economy.
7. What are the major advantages and disadvantages of smallness in business?
8. What are the major components of a business plan? Why should an individual develop a business plan?
9. Identify five ways in which the SBA provides management assistance to small businesses.
10. Identify two ways in which the SBA provides financial assistance to small businesses.
11. Why does the SBA concentrate on providing management and financial assistance to small businesses?
12. What is venture capital? How does the SBA help small businesses to obtain it?
13. Explain the relationships among a franchise, the franchisor, and the franchisee.
14. What does the franchisor receive in a franchising agreement? What does the franchisee receive? What does each provide?
15. Cite one major benefit of franchising for the franchisor. Cite one major benefit of franchising for the franchisee.

1. Most people who start small businesses are aware of the high failure rate and the reasons for it. Why, then, do some take no steps to protect their firms from failure? What steps should they take?
2. Are the so-called advantages of small business really advantages? Wouldn't every small-business owner like his or her business to grow into a large firm?
3. Do average citizens benefit from the activities of the SBA, or is the SBA just another way to spend our tax money?
4. Would you rather own your own business independently or become a franchisee? Why?

Video Case 5.1

Murray's Cheese: More Cheese Please

Murray's Cheese began in New York's Greenwich Village in 1940, as a wholesale butter and egg shop owned by a Jewish veteran of the Spanish Civil War named Murray Greenberg. When the current president Rob Kaufelt purchased the shop in 1991, it was little more than a local hole-in-the-wall. Kaufelt and his staff made the decision to focus on high-quality gourmet cheeses from around the world. Today, people come from all over to sample Murray's cheeses and to take classes or attend its Cheese U boot camp to learn about cheese. Although Murray's has extended its product line to include gourmet meats, crackers, olives, and dried fruit, cheese remains its core product. In fact, Murray's Cheese has been voted by *Forbes* as "the best cheese shop" and it is expanding to three other stores. Its success prompted Kroger to seek it out as a partner in its chain of supermarkets, a step that included intensively training Kroger employees in the fine points of selling Murray's products and the creation of a 300-page cheese service guide for them.

"We are little and they are very big," says Murray's managing director, Liz Thorpe, in speaking of Kroger. "So it's a very interesting model for us. We've begun operating cheese shops in Kroger delis that are similar to our New York shops. This allows us to bring our knowledge and expertise on sourcing, production selection, education, and customer service to a different format. . . . We're actually going to be opening 50 of these shops in the next 36 months."

Murray's is still small, with about 70 employees, and has an advertising budget of zero dollars. Instead of advertising, Murray's relies on providing great customer service and creating positive word of mouth to promote its products and to secure its reputation. Personal selling is key. The company recruits salespeople who are passionate about both cheese and people and trains them carefully. The key is to inform customers about the store's many unique products and persuade them to taste and then purchase. The staff enjoys listening to customers, gaining an understanding of their interests, and trying to find the right product to satisfy their needs. Their efforts often succeed in getting customers to purchase more and to make repeat buys.

All customers get to taste free samples of cheese before they buy it. "We like knowing the folks who walk in our door and having everyone taste the cheese," said the managing director. "It's part of the shopping experience. That said, we are getting more sophisticated about how we communicate with people. E-mail marketing continues to be really critical, and we're starting to take advantage of social networking outlets like Twitter. For people who are into cheese and into Murray's, it's a great way for them to be directly tapped into knowing what's going on right this second."

What continues to appeal to sophisticated shoppers about Murray's is that cheese is an affordable luxury. A wine and cheese party for a dozen people, for instance, can fit almost any budget, and Murray's salespeople are happy to provide suggestions and samples to assist in the selection. Murray's manager also credits popular media like the Food Network with helping to popularize food in general, and cheese in particular. After all, he says, cheeses "don't have to be improved upon or fortified. They are naturally good for you."[25]

Questions

1. How does Murray's overcome one of the most common limitations facing small companies: its nonexistent advertising budget?

2. What are some of the advantages of being a small business that Murray's can (or does) take advantage of? What disadvantages might it face as a small firm?

3. Do you think the partnership with Kroger will have a negative or a positive effect on the unique experience customers expect from Murray's? Why?

Case 5.2   Warby Parker's Business Vision

Fashionable, affordable prescription eyeglasses sold directly to customers—that's the business vision of Warby Parker, a fast-growing small firm based in New York City. Founded by four friends from the Wharton business school, Warby Parker uses easy-on-the-eyes styling and easy-on-the-budget pricing to compete with national chains such as LensCrafters as well as with neighborhood optical shops. Its exclusive retro-style prescription glasses are priced under $100, with prescription sunglasses priced at $150. Warby Parker's affordable prices include extras such as free shipping, free in-home frame try-ons, and a money-back guarantee. Just as important is that, for every pair of glasses purchased, the company donates one pair to someone in need.

Rather than pay to license famous brand names for its frames, Warby Parker designs its own, inspired by styles from the 1950s and 1960s and manufactured in China. Based on each customer's individual prescription, the company has the optical lenses made to order by a U.S. lab. After the lenses are set in place, the finished product is inspected twice before glasses are shipped to customers.

Because Warby Parker's prices are significantly lower than those of traditional eyeglass providers, customers can afford to buy frames as fashion accessories, not just for vision correction. Co-founder David Gilboa points out that while U.S. consumers typically buy new eyeglasses every other year, many Warby Parker customers "are buying six, seven, eight pairs at a time." They choose different frames for different occasions, such as one pair for going to work and another pair for going out with friends, and they buy frames to fit with particular outfits. The largest single order Warby Parker ever received was from a customer who ordered 14 pairs at once.

Warby Parker operates a showroom at its headquarters in the hip SoHo section of New York, plus seven other showrooms inside fashion boutiques across the country. It also invites customers to call a toll-free number for information and ordering. The main focus, however, is on the interactive Web site, where customers can browse more than two dozen frames, narrow down the choice by color, shape, and size, and upload a digital headshot for a virtual "try on" before ordering. Customers can order up to five frames and try them on at home for five days—enough time to post photos on Warby Parker's Facebook page, if they choose, and ask for feedback on which frames are the most flattering. Shipping and returns are paid by the company, which takes the risk out of trying and buying.

Customers feel good about buying from Warby Parker because they save money and they know each purchase covers a donation of eyeglasses. The company's "buy one, give one" policy allows it to donate more than 100,000 pairs of eyeglasses a year to people in need worldwide through a connection with the nonprofit organization VisionSpring. Now, with the help of venture capital funding, Warby Parker is expanding. It has more than 50 employees and uses social media such as Twitter, Tumblr, and Pinterest to publicize its business vision. Because satisfied customers tell friends and relatives about their experiences, "over 50 percent of our sales are driven by word of mouth," says co-founder Neil Blumenthal.[26]

Questions

1. If you were writing a business plan for Warby Parker, what critical risks and challenges would you mention? What are the business implications of each risk or challenge?

2. Why would Warby Parker have eyeglass frames made in China but optical lenses made in America?

3. Do you agree with Warby Parker's decision to open showrooms inside trendy boutiques in addition to operating on the Internet? Explain your answer.

① SOCIAL MEDIA EXERCISE

American Express's "Open Forum" is a Web site that is designed for small business owners (www.openforum.com). Do a search using a search engine like Google or Bing and you will also find its presence on Tumblr and Pinterest. Take a look at the Open Forum Web site and answer the following questions.

1. What questions can Open Forum answer for business owners?
2. Develop a list of five issues or topics that you feel illustrates how American Express does an effective job of presenting information on this Web site.

② JOURNALING FOR SUCCESS

Discovery statement: One of the objectives in this chapter was to make you aware of the advantages and disadvantages of owning a franchise.

Assignment

1. Assume that after evaluating your skills, experience, and financial situation, you have decided to purchase a franchise in your community. Identify and describe sources where you can obtain information on what the franchise package should contain.
2. List at least five reasons why you should choose franchising rather than starting a new, independent business.
3. Identify issues you need to be aware of as a franchisee.
4. Make a list of possible advantages and disadvantages of the franchise you are considering. What are your rights and your obligations as a franchisee?

③ DEVELOPING CRITICAL-THINKING SKILLS

Small businesses play a vital role in our economy. They not only contribute to technological innovation and to the creation of many new jobs but also ensure that customers have an alternative to the products and services offered by large firms. In addition, by making parts for large firms at a lower cost than the large firms could make the parts themselves, they help to keep the lid on consumer prices. Regardless of our need for them, many small businesses fail within their first five years. Why is this so?

Assignment

1. Identify several successful small businesses in your community.
2. Identify one small business that has failed.
3. Gather enough information about those businesses to answer the following questions:
   a. What role do small businesses play in your community?
   b. Why are they important?
   c. Why did the business fail?
   d. What was the most important reason for its failure?
   e. How might the business have survived?
4. Summarize what you have learned about the impact of small businesses on your community. Give the summary to your instructor.

④ BUILDING TEAM SKILLS

A business plan is a written statement that documents the nature of a business and how that business intends to achieve its goals. Although entrepreneurs should prepare a business plan *before* starting a business, the plan also serves as an effective guide later on. The plan should concisely describe the business's mission, the amount of capital it requires, its target market, competition, resources, production plan, marketing plan, organizational plan, assessment of risk, and financial plan.

Assignment

1. Working in a team of four students, identify a company in your community that would benefit from using a business plan, or create a scenario in which a hypothetical entrepreneur wants to start a business.
2. Using the resources of the library or the Internet and/or interviews with business owners, write a business plan incorporating the information in Table 5.3.
3. Present your business plan to the class.

⑤ RESEARCHING DIFFERENT CAREERS

Many people dream of opening and operating their own businesses. Are you one of them? To be successful, entrepreneurs must have certain characteristics; their profiles generally differ from those of people who work for someone else. Do you know which personal characteristics make some entrepreneurs succeed and others fail? Do you fit the successful entrepreneur's profile? What is your potential for opening and operating a successful small business?

Assignment

1. Use the resources of the library or the Internet to establish what a successful entrepreneur's profile is and to determine whether your personal characteristics fit that profile. Internet addresses that can help you are www.smartbiz.com/sbs/arts/ieb1.html and www.sba.gov (see "Start your Business" and "FAQ"). These sites have quizzes online that can help you to assess your personal characteristics. The SBA also has helpful brochures.
2. Interview several small-business owners. Ask them to describe the characteristics they think are necessary for being a successful entrepreneur.
3. Using your findings, write a report that includes the following:
   a. A profile of a successful small-business owner
   b. A comparison of your personal characteristics with the profile of the successful entrepreneur
   c. A discussion of your potential as a successful small-business owner

A Fourth-Generation Family Business

Independent and family-owned for more than 140 years, Graeter's has successfully made the transition from a 19th-century mom-and-pop ice cream business to a 21st-century corporation with three manufacturing facilities, dozens of ice cream shops, and hundreds of employees. Much of the company's success over the years has been due to the family's strong and enduring entrepreneurial spirit.

SMALL BUSINESS, BIG AMBITIONS

The road to small-business success started with cofounder Louis Charles Graeter, who developed the startup's first flavors, insisted on only the finest ingredients, and made all his ice cream by hand in small batches to ensure freshness and quality. After his death, his wife and cofounder Regina maintained the same high level of quality as she led the company through three decades of aggressive growth. Her great-grandson, CEO Richard Graeter II, says that "without her strength, fortitude, and foresight, there would be no Graeter's ice cream today."

Richard, Bob, and Chip, great-grandsons of the founders, are the fourth generation to own and operate Graeter's. They grew up in the business, and now they share responsibility for the firm's day-to-day management and for determining its future direction. Bob worked his way up to vice president of operations, starting with a management position in one of the Graeter's ice-cream shops. Chip, currently vice president of retail operations, handled all kinds of jobs in Graeter's stores as a teenager. He uses this first-hand knowledge of customer relations to fine-tune every store function.

Richard Graeter became the company's CEO in 2007. "Even though I have the title of CEO, in a family business titles don't mean a whole lot," he comments. "The functions that I am doing now as CEO, I was doing as executive vice president for years . . . It really was and remains a partnership with my two cousins . . . Our fathers brought us into the business at an early age . . . I think most important is we saw our fathers and their dedication and the fact that, you know, they came home later, they came home tired, they got up early and went to work before we ever got up to go to school in the morning, and you see that dedication and appreciate that—that is what keeps your business going."

Graeter continues, "It can be challenging to work with your family. My father and I didn't always see things the same way. But on the other hand, there is a lot of strength in the family relationship . . . we certainly had struggles, and family businesses do struggle, especially with transition . . . but we found people to help us, including lawyers, accountants, and a family-business psychologist."

GROWING BEYOND CINCINNATI

To expand beyond Cincinnati without diverting resources from the existing stores and factory, the third generation of Graeter's family owners decided to license a handful of franchise operators. One franchise operation was so successful that it even opened its own factory. A few years ago, however, the fourth generation switched gears on growth and repurchased all the stores of its last remaining franchisee. "When you think about Graeter's," says the CEO, "the core of Graeter's is the quality of the product. You can't franchise your core. So by franchising our manufacturing, that created substantial risk for the organization, because the customer doesn't know that it is a franchise. . . . They know it is Graeter's. . . . You really have to rely on the intention and good-will of the individual franchisees to make the product the way you would make it, and that is not an easy thing to guarantee."

After working with consultants to carefully analyze the situation and evaluate alternative paths to future growth, the founder's great-grandsons decided against further franchising. Instead, they pursued nationwide distribution through a large network of grocery stores and supermarket chains. They also built a new facility to increase production capacity and hired experienced executives to help manage the expanded business.

As a private company, Graeter's can take actions like these without worrying about the reaction of the stock market. Specifically, Graeter's is an S-corporation, which allows it limited liability protection coupled with the benefit of not being taxed as a corporation. Instead, the three owners—who are the stockholders—pay only personal income taxes on the corporation's profits. In the event of significant legal or tax code changes, Graeter's owners do have the option of choosing a different form of corporate organization.[27]

Questions

1. Graeter's current management team bought the business from their parents, who did not have a formal succession plan in place to indicate who would do what. Do you think the current team should have such a plan specifying who is to step into the business, when, and with what responsibilities? Why or why not?

2. Graeter's hired management consultants to help improve its training procedures and expand distribution. "I think my cousins and I all have come to realize we can't do it alone," says the CEO. Why do you think the management team made this decision? Does the involvement of outside consultants move Graeter's further from its roots as a family business?

3. Do you agree with Graeter's decision to stop franchising? Explain your answer.

After reading Part 2, "Business Ownership and Entrepreneurship," you should be ready to tackle the company and industry component of your business plan. In this section, you will provide information about the background of the company, choice of the legal business form, information on the product or services to be offered, and descriptions of potential customers, current competitors, and the business's future. Chapter 4 in your textbook, "Choosing a Form of Business Ownership," and Chapter 5, "Small Business, Entrepreneurship, and Franchises," can help you to answer some of the questions in this part of the business plan.

THE COMPANY AND INDUSTRY COMPONENT

The company and industry analysis should include the answers to at least the following questions:

2.1. What is the legal form of your business? Is your business a sole proprietorship, a partnership, or a corporation?

2.2. What licenses or permits will you need, if any?

2.3. Is your business a new independent business, a takeover, an expansion, or a franchise?

2.4. If you are dealing with an existing business, how did your company get to the point where it is today?

2.5. What does your business do, and how does it satisfy customers' needs?

2.6. How did you choose and develop the products or services to be sold, and how are they different from those currently on the market?

2.7. What industry do you operate in, and what are the industry-wide trends?

2.8. Who are the major competitors in your industry?

2.9. Have any businesses recently entered or exited? Why did they leave?

2.10. Why will your business be profitable, and what are your growth opportunities?

2.11. Does any part of your business involve e-business?

REVIEW OF BUSINESS PLAN ACTIVITIES

Make sure to check the information you have collected, make any changes, and correct any weaknesses before beginning Part 3.

Reminder: Review the answers to questions in the preceding part to make sure that all your answers are consistent throughout the business plan. Finally, write a summary statement that incorporates all the information for this part of the business plan.

ENDNOTES

1. Sources: Based on information in Elissa Gootman, "Middle School Girls Unlock a Room of Their Own, in Miniature," *New York Times*, October 10, 2011, pp. A1, A3; Alaina Raftis, "Students Prepping to Deck Out Lockers," *Pittsburgh Tribune-Review*, August 19, 2011, www.pittsburghlive.com; Barry Shlachter, "Texas Moms Create Hallway Hit," *Fort Worth Star Telegram*, May 9, 2011, pp. 1D, 10D; Colleen Diskin, "Dress Your Locker with the Perfect Combination of Accessories," *NorthJersey.com*, August 29, 2011, www.northjersey.com.

2. U.S. Small Business Administration Web site at www.sba.gov/content/summary-size-standards-industry (accessed March 18, 2012).

3. U.S. Small Business Administration, Office of Advocacy, *Frequently Asked Questions*, updated January 2011, www.sba.gov/advo (accessed March 19, 2012).

4. Ibid.

5. Ibid.

6. Thomas A. Garrett, "Entrepreneurs Thrive in America," *Bridges*, Federal Reserve Bank of St. Louis, Spring 2005, 2.

7. U.S. Small Business Administration, Office of Advocacy, *Frequently Asked Questions*, updated January 2011, www.sba.gov/advo (accessed March 15, 2012).

8. U.S. Small Business Administration, *News Release*, Number 05–53, September 13, 2005, www.sba.gov/teens/brian_hendricks.html (accessed March 19, 2012).

9. U.S. Small Business Administration, Office of Advocacy, *Frequently Asked Questions*, updated January 2011, www.sba.gov/advo (accessed March 19, 2012).

10. SBA Press Release, "Computer Simulation Company from Florida Is National Small Business of the Year," May 25, 2010, www.sba.gov/news (accessed March 15, 2012).

11. U.S. Small Business Administration, Office of Advocacy, *Frequently Asked Questions*, September 2009, www.sba.gov/advo (accessed March 15, 2011).

12. U.S. Small Business Administration, Office of Advocacy, *News Release*, Number 10-03 ADVO, March 3, 2010, www.sba.gov/advo/press/10-03.html (accessed March 15, 2011).

13. Timothy S. Hatten, *Small Business Management: Entrepreneurship and Beyond*, 4th ed., Copyright © 2009 by Houghton Mifflin Company, 238. Reprinted with permission.

14. SCORE Web site at www.score.org/about-score (accessed March 19, 2012).

15. Ibid.

16. SBA Press Release, *Fact Sheet*, September 11, 2008, 2.

17. U.S. Small Business Administration, *News Release*, Release Number 10-33, May 26, 2010, www.sba.gov/news (accessed March 18, 2012).

18. SBIC Program Overview, Web site at http://archive.sba.gov/idc/groups/public/documents/sba_program_office/inv_sbic; and Small Business Investor Alliance Web site at www.nabic.org (accessed March 23, 2012).

19. SBA Press Release, "President Obama Proclaims National Small Business Week," May 21, 2010, www.sba.gov/news (accessed March 7, 2012).

20. SBA Press Release Number 10–414, *News Release*, May 14, 2010, www.sba.gov/news (accessed March 12, 2012).

21. Cindy Elmore, "Putting the Power into the Hands of Small Business Owners," *Marketwise*, Federal Reserve Bank of Richmond, Issue II, 2005, 13.

22. U.S. Small Business Administration, www.sba.gov/managing/marketing/intlsales.html (accessed October 4, 2008).

23. SBA Press Release 12-12, "SBA Announces a New Partnership to Connect Small Businesses With Corporate Supply Chains," March 22, 2012, www.sba.gov/news (accessed March 23, 2012); and International Trade Web site at www.trade.gov/CS/ (accessed March 23, 2012).

24. SBA Press Release, "SBA 2010 Small Business Exporter of the Year," www.sba.gov/news (accessed March 20, 2012); and NANMAC Corporation Web site at http://nanmac.com/press-sba.html (accessed March 23, 2012).

25. Based on information from company Web site www.murrayscheese.com (accessed April 23, 2010); www.murrayscheese.com/images_global/murrays_kroger_press_release.pdf (accessed April 23, 2010); Kelsey Blackwell, "Liz Thorpe," *Natural Foods Merchandiser*, March 2010; Kim Severson, "Murray's Cheese Will Open 50 Locations in Kroger Markets," *The New York Times*, November 24, 2009, http://dinersjournal.blogs.nytimes.com/tag/murrays-cheese/; Rosalind Resnick, "Market with Meaning," *Entrepreneur*, November 6, 2009, www.entrepreneur.com/marketing/marketingideas/article203938.html#.

26. Based on information in Shira Lazar, "Warby Parker's Grand Vision," *Entrepreneur*, April 10, 2012, www.entrepreneur.com; Alex Williams, "On Spec: Vintage-Style Glasses Online," *New York Times*, January 18, 2012, www.nytimes.com; "Warby Parker Revolutionizes Eyewear Market by Borrowing from Apple, Zappos," *Advertising Age*, November 27, 2011, www.adage.com; and Andrew Maclean, "Warby Parker," *Inc.*, November 24, 2011, www.inc.com; www.warbyparker.com.

27. Sources: Based on information from Kimberly L. Jackson, "Graeter's Premium Chocolate Chip Ice Cream Lands at Stop & Shop," *Newark Star-Ledger (NJ)*, April 4, 2012, www.nj.com; "Graeter's Ice Cream Debuts in Bay Area," *Tampa Bay Times (St. Petersburg, FL)*, January 10, 2012, p. 4B; Jim Carper, "Graeter's Runs a Hands-on Ice Cream Plant," *Dairy Foods*, August 2011, pp. 36+; Jim Carper, "The Greater Good," *Dairy Foods*, August 2011, pp. 95+; "Graeter's Unveils New 'Mystery Flavor,'" *Dayton Daily News*, March 29, 2012, www.daytondailynews.com; Bob Driehaus, "A Cincinnati Ice Cream Maker Aims Big," *New York Times*, September 11, 2010, www.nytimes.com; Lucy May, "Graeter's Northern Kentucky Franchisee Puts Stores on the Block," *Business Courier*, August 6, 2010, http://cincinnati.bizjournals.com; www.graeters.com; interviews with company staff and Cengage videos about Graeter's.

Management and Organization

PART 3

This Part of the book deals with the organization—the "thing" that is a business. We begin with a discussion of the management functions involved in developing and operating a business. Next, we analyze the organization's elements and structure. Then we consider a firm's operations that are related to the production of goods and services.

42-30300813©DAVID J. PHILLIP/AP CORBIS

6

Understanding the Management Process

Once you complete this chapter, you will be able to:

1. Define what management is.

2. Describe the four basic management functions: planning, organizing, leading and motivating, and controlling.

3. Distinguish among the various kinds of managers in terms of both level and area of management.

4. Identify the key management skills of successful managers.

5. Explain the different types of leadership.

6. Discuss the steps in the managerial decision-making process.

7. Describe how organizations benefit from total quality management.

IBM's New CEO Feels Technological Leadership Is Key

IBM had just begun its second century of business when it appointed Virginia Rometty as its first female CEO. IBM made technology history throughout its first century, with innovations such as the automatic tabulating machine, FORTRAN programming language, the personal computer, and the speedy Watson supercomputer that scored decisive wins on the television show *Jeopardy*. During the decade before Rometty became CEO, IBM sharpened its focus on serving business customers by acquiring PricewaterhouseCoopers Consulting and selling its consumer-oriented PC business to China's Lenovo.

When Rometty took over in 2012, IBM was already aiming to achieve the ambitious goal of generating an additional $20 billion in new revenue by 2015. She had joined IBM 30 years before and managed the team that integrated PricewaterhouseCoopers Consulting into the IBM organization. Later, heading up part of IBM's services division, she gained senior-level experience in marketing and strategy. All these experiences have prepared Rometty for her responsibilities as CEO of a $100 billion company that employs nearly 400,000 employees worldwide.

With the global economy in trouble, ongoing technological shifts, and increasingly intense competition, Rometty's top priority is to keep reinventing the company. "We are different today than we were a decade ago," she says, and moving quickly to adapt to the ever-changing business environment will help IBM extend its record of success. The company now makes more money from the sale of technology services and business software than from the sale of computers, the result of lucrative, long-term contracts with business and government customers. Because a significant amount of IBM's future revenue will come from overseas customers, Rometty has appointed a senior vice president to head the Growth Markets unit and moved that unit's headquarters to Shanghai, China. She continues to invest heavily in research and development activities for future growth, and is on the lookout for potential acquisitions that will give IBM an even bigger edge in delivering the services and software that business customers need to solve their most pressing problems.[1]

FYI

Did You Know?

Founded in 1911, IBM rings up more than $100 billion in annual revenue from global sales of software, services, and computers.

The leadership employed at IBM illustrates that management can be one of the most exciting and rewarding professions available today. Depending on its size, a firm may employ a number of specialized managers who are responsible for particular areas of management, such as marketing, finance, and operations. That same organization also includes managers at several levels within the firm. In this chapter, we define *management* and describe the four basic management functions of planning, organizing, leading and motivating, and controlling. Then we focus on the types of managers with respect to levels of responsibility and areas of expertise. Next, we focus on the skills of effective managers and the different roles managers must play. We examine several styles of leadership and explore the process by which managers make decisions. We also describe how total quality management can improve customer satisfaction.

WHAT IS MANAGEMENT?

Management is the process of coordinating people and other resources to achieve the goals of an organization. As we saw in Chapter 1, most organizations make use of four kinds of resources: material, human, financial, and informational (see Figure 6.1).

 Define what management is.

management the process of coordinating people and other resources to achieve the goals of an organization

Personal APPS

Maybe you've never thought of yourself as a manager. But if you've ever headed a committee or organized a new school club, you've actually been involved in management. Understanding more about the way management works can make you more successful in the daily business of *your* life.

Material resources are the tangible, physical resources an organization uses. For example, General Motors uses steel, glass, and fiberglass to produce cars and trucks on complex machine-driven assembly lines. A college or university uses books, classroom buildings, desks, and computers to educate students. And the Mayo Clinic uses operating room equipment, diagnostic machines, and laboratory tests to provide health care.

Perhaps the most important resources of any organization are its *human resources*—people. In fact, some firms live by the philosophy that their employees are their most important assets. Some managers believe that the way employees are developed and managed may have more impact on an organization than other vital components such as marketing, sound financial decisions about large expenditures, production, or use of technology. One such firm that takes pride in its employees is Southwest Airlines. Southwest treats its employees with the same respect and attention it gives its passengers. Southwest selectively seeks employees with upbeat attitudes and promotes from within 80 percent of the time. In decision making, everyone who will be affected is encouraged to get involved in the process. In an industry in which deregulation, extreme price competition, and fluctuating fuel costs have eliminated several major competitors, Southwest keeps growing and making a profit because of its employees. Many experts would agree with Southwest's emphasis on employees.

Financial resources are the funds an organization uses to meet its obligations to investors and creditors. A 7-Eleven convenience store obtains money from customers at the checkout counter and uses a portion of that money to pay its suppliers. Your college obtains money in the form of tuition, income from its endowments, and state and federal grants. It uses the money to pay utility bills, insurance premiums, and professors' salaries.

Finally, many organizations increasingly find that they cannot afford to ignore *information*. External environmental conditions—including the economy, consumer markets, technology, politics, and cultural forces—are all changing so rapidly that a business that does not adapt probably will not survive. To adapt to change, the business must know what is changing and how it is changing. Most companies gather information about their competitors to increase their knowledge about changes in their industry and to learn from other companies' failures and successes.

It is important to realize that the four types of resources described earlier are only general categories of resources. Within each category are hundreds or thousands of more specific resources. It is this complex mix of specific resources—and not simply "some of each" of the four general categories—that managers must coordinate to produce goods and services.

Another interesting way to look at management is in terms of the different functions managers perform. These functions have been identified as planning, organizing, leading and motivating employees, and controlling. We look at each of these management functions in the next section.

| FIGURE 6.1 | The Four Main Resources of Management |

Managers coordinate an organization's resources to achieve the organization's goals.

BASIC MANAGEMENT FUNCTIONS

When pharmaceutical company Eli Lilly decided to focus on the emerging market of China, the company reorganized its structure so that one of its six units would handle emerging markets, doubled its employee count from 1,100 to 2,200, and began construction on a second manufacturing plant in Suzhou, China. The company also implemented a partnering strategy in China to handle research and development. Eli Lilly's key strategies include maximizing their core assets, accelerating new product launches, capitalizing on longer product life-cycles in areas like China, and establishing local alliances to access fast-growing market segments.[2]

Management functions such as those just described do not occur according to some rigid, preset timetable. Managers do not plan in January, organize in February, lead and motivate in March, and control in April. At any given time, managers may engage in a number of functions simultaneously. However, each function tends to lead naturally to others. Figure 6.2 provides a visual framework for a more detailed discussion of the four basic management functions. How well managers perform these key functions determines whether a business is successful.

© KURHAN/SHUTTERSTOCK

Superior human resources management can set a firm apart. Do you have a great business plan or product? A competitor can easily copy both. Great employees, however, are much harder to duplicate. That's why being able to attract, train, and retain talented workers can give a firm a competitive advantage over its rivals.

Planning

Planning, in its simplest form, is establishing organizational goals and deciding how to accomplish them. It is often referred to as the "first" management function because all other management functions depend on planning. Organizations such as Starbucks, Houston Community College system, and Facebook begin the planning process by developing a mission statement.

An organization's **mission** is a statement of the basic purpose that makes that organization different from others. Starbucks' mission statement, for example, is "to inspire and nurture the human spirit—one person, one cup, and one neighborhood at a time." Houston Community College's mission is to provide an education for local citizens. Facebook's mission statement is "to give people the power to share and make the world more open and connected."[3] Once an organization's mission has been described in a mission statement, the next step is to engage in strategic planning.

Strategic Planning Process The **strategic planning process** involves establishing an organization's major goals and objectives and allocating resources to achieve them. Top management is responsible for strategic planning, although customers, products, competitors, and company resources are some of the factors that are analyzed in the strategic planning process.

planning establishing organizational goals and deciding how to accomplish them

mission a statement of the basic purpose that makes an organization different from others

strategic planning process the establishment of an organization's major goals and objectives and the allocation of resources to achieve them

---

FIGURE 6.2 The Management Process

Note that management is not a step-by-step procedure but a process with a feedback loop that represents a flow.

Planning → Organizing → Leading and motivating → Controlling

Review and modify

© CENGAGE LEARNING 2014

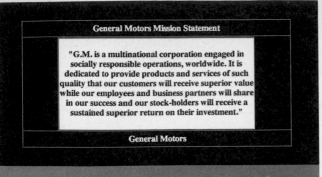

General Motors Mission Statement

"G.M. is a multinational corporation engaged in socially responsible operations, worldwide. It is dedicated to provide products and services of such quality that our customers will receive superior value while our employees and business partners will share in our success and our stock-holders will receive a sustained superior return on their investment."

General Motors

What is your organization's purpose? How is it different than other organizations? Those are the questions a firm's mission statement like the one shown here should answer. Mission statements are meant for multiple audiences, including a company's customers, investors, the general public, and employees. Most firms familiarize their personnel with their mission statements so they know what's expected of them and what they should strive for.

In today's rapidly changing business environment, constant internal or external changes may necessitate changes in a company's goals, mission, or strategy. The time line for strategic plans is generally one to two years and can be as long as ten years. Strategic plans should be flexible and include action items, such as outlining how plans will be implemented.

Establishing Goals and Objectives A **goal** is an end result that an organization is expected to achieve over a one- to ten-year period. An **objective** is a specific statement detailing what the organization intends to accomplish over a shorter period of time.

Goals and objectives can deal with a variety of factors, such as sales, company growth, costs, customer satisfaction, and employee morale. Whereas a small manufacturer may focus primarily on sales objectives for the next six months, a large firm may be more interested in goals that impact several years in the future. Starbucks, for example, has established several goals under its "Shared Planet" program to be completed in the next few years, specifically in the areas of ethical sourcing, environmental stewardship, and community involvement. By 2015, Starbucks hopes to purchase 100 percent of its coffee from ethical sources or farmers who grow their coffee responsibly without permanently harming the environment. The company also hopes to combat climate change by encouraging farmers to prevent deforestation through the use of incentive programs. Starbucks hopes to make 100% of its cups reusable or recyclable by 2015. Also, the company hopes to use their stores to lead volunteer programs in each store's community.[4] Finally, goals are set at every level of an organization. Every member of an organization—the president of the company, the head of a department, and an operating employee at the lowest level—has a set of goals that he or she hopes to achieve.

The goals developed for these different levels must be consistent. However, it is likely that some conflict will arise. A production department, for example, may have a goal of minimizing costs. One way to do this is to produce only one type of product and offer "no frills." Marketing may have a goal of maximizing sales. One way to implement this goal is to offer customers a wide range of products and options. As part of goal setting, the manager who is responsible for *both* departments must achieve some sort of balance between conflicting goals. This balancing process is called *optimization*.

The optimization of conflicting goals requires insight and ability. Faced with the marketing-versus-production conflict just described, most managers probably would not adopt either viewpoint completely. Instead, they might decide on a reasonably diverse product line offering only the most widely sought-after options. Such a compromise would seem to be best for the whole organization.

SWOT Analysis SWOT analysis is the identification and evaluation of a firm's strengths, weaknesses, opportunities, and threats. Strengths and weaknesses are internal factors that affect a company's capabilities. Strengths refer to a firm's favorable characteristics and core competencies. **Core competencies** are approaches and processes that a company performs well that may give it an advantage over its competitors. These core competencies may help the firm attract financial and human resources and be more capable of producing products that better satisfy customers. Weaknesses refer to any internal limitations a company faces in developing or implementing plans. At times, managers have difficulty identifying and understanding the negative effects of weaknesses in their organizations.

External opportunities and threats exist independently of the firm. Opportunities refer to favorable conditions in the environment that could produce rewards for the organization. That is, opportunities are situations that exist but must be exploited for

goal an end result that an organization is expected to achieve over a one- to ten-year period

objective a specific statement detailing what an organization intends to accomplish over a shorter period of time

SWOT analysis the identification and evaluation of a firm's strengths, weaknesses, opportunities, and threats

core competencies approaches and processes that a company performs well that may give it an advantage over its competitors

Ethical
SUCCESS OR FAILURE?

Digging Deep to Research Competitors

When preparing a SWOT analysis, how far can companies go in researching their competition? Many firms carefully monitor social media comments in search of tidbits about their rivals, for example. What are the ethical limits of competitive research?

In general, companies are going too far when they rummage through a competitor's trash cans, tap its phone lines, hack into its computer systems, or try to obtain proprietary information such as customer lists and product blueprints. On the other hand, visiting competitors' publicly-available Web sites and Facebook pages, shopping their stores or showrooms, and watching for announcements of new products and price changes are all good ways to map the competitive landscape. One biotechnology firm pays close attention to how quickly competitors' pharmaceutical products are moving through regulatory channels, clues that help it plan the timing of its own introductions and its marketing campaigns.

No matter how much a company learns about its competitors' strengths and weaknesses, the information is useless unless the right people see it. That's why Egencia, a travel agency that serves business customers, maintains a "Know Your Enemy" internal site where employees can post and review competitive details. Then, when salespeople meet with customers, they can emphasize Egencia's competitive strengths.

Sources: Based on information in Robert L. Scheier, "Why Social Tech's Real Value Is Inside the Business," *InfoWorld*, December 19, 2011, http:// infoworld.com/d/applications/why-social-techs-real-value-inside-the-business-178336; "Crash Course in Competitive Intelligence (CI)," *Management Today*, May 1, 2011, p. 18; Judith Lamont, "Gaining Insight to Enhance Decision-Making," *KMWorld*, November–December 2011, p. 12.

the firm to benefit from them. Threats, on the other hand, are conditions or barriers that may prevent the firm from reaching its objectives. Opportunities and threats can stem from many sources within the business environment. For example, a competitor's actions, new laws, economic changes, or new technology can be threats. Threats for some firms may be opportunities for others. Examples of strengths, weaknesses, opportunities, and threats are shown in Figure 6.3.

FIGURE 6.3 Elements and Examples of SWOT Analysis

STRENGTHS
- Efficient distribution channels
- Employee education and experience
- Protected patents
- Core competencies
- Excellent facilities/equipment
- Proven management
- Economies of scale
- Cost advantages

WEAKNESSES
- High turnover, absenteeism
- Lack of strategic direction
- Obsolete production facilities
- Labor grievances
- Lack of managerial depth
- Negative public image

SWOT Analysis

OPPORTUNITIES
- New markets opening up
- New technologies
- Increased demand for new products
- Potential strategic alliances
- More favorable trade regulations in desirable foreign markets
- Competitor complacency

THREATS
- Entry of lower-cost foreign competitors
- Unfavorable changes in buyer needs and tastes
- Rising sales of substitute products
- Slowing market growth
- Costly regulatory requirements
- Vulnerability to business cycle changes
- Sole sourcing

© CENGAGE LEARNING 2014

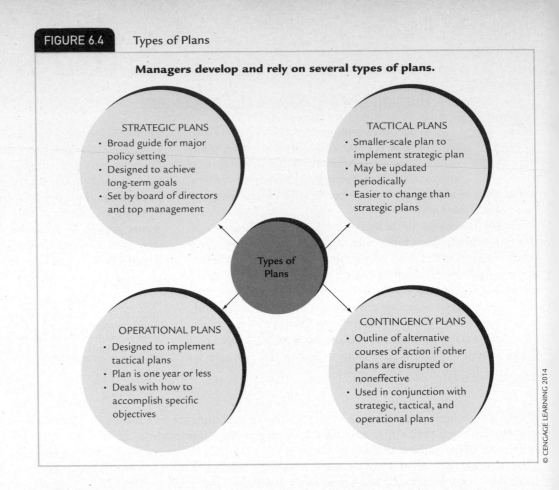

FIGURE 6.4   Types of Plans

Managers develop and rely on several types of plans.

STRATEGIC PLANS
- Broad guide for major policy setting
- Designed to achieve long-term goals
- Set by board of directors and top management

TACTICAL PLANS
- Smaller-scale plan to implement strategic plan
- May be updated periodically
- Easier to change than strategic plans

Types of Plans

OPERATIONAL PLANS
- Designed to implement tactical plans
- Plan is one year or less
- Deals with how to accomplish specific objectives

CONTINGENCY PLANS
- Outline of alternative courses of action if other plans are disrupted or noneffective
- Used in conjunction with strategic, tactical, and operational plans

Types of Plans Once goals and objectives have been set for the organization, managers must develop plans for achieving them. A **plan** is an outline of the actions by which an organization intends to accomplish its goals and objectives. Just as it has different goals and objectives, the organization also develops several types of plans, as shown in Figure 6.4.

Resulting from the strategic planning process, an organization's **strategic plan** is its broadest plan, developed as a guide for major policy setting and decision making. Strategic plans are set by the board of directors and top management and are generally designed to achieve the organization's long-term goals. Thus, a firm's strategic plan defines what business the company is in or wants to be in and the kind of company it is or wants to be. Gannett, a major publisher of 82 different newspapers, revamped its strategic plan in the face of a prolonged advertising slump. The firm's plan involved increasing sports coverage and revamping its subscriber model in an effort to boost revenues. The new strategic plan recognizes that subscribers increasingly obtain their news online in a digital format and implemented an online subscriber system. Customers can read between 5 and 15 articles per month for free, after which they have to pay.[5]

In addition to strategic plans, most organizations also employ several narrower kinds of plans. A **tactical plan** is a smaller scale plan developed to implement a strategy. Most tactical plans cover a one- to three-year period. If a strategic plan will take five years to complete, the firm may develop five tactical plans, one covering each year. Tactical plans may be updated periodically as dictated by conditions and experience. Their more limited scope permits them to be changed more easily than strategies. IKEA has a tactical plan that involves opening three stores per year in China through 2016. These stores must be located in urban areas near transit, such as train or light rail. Because Chinese infrastructure, income levels, lifestyles, and living spaces all differ from those of its customers in the west, IKEA must utilize a different tactical plan for its Chinese expansion.[6]

plan an outline of the actions by which an organization intends to accomplish its goals and objectives

strategic plan an organization's broadest plan, developed as a guide for major policy setting and decision making

tactical plan a smaller scale plan developed to implement a strategy

An **operational plan** is a type of plan designed to implement tactical plans. Operational plans are usually established for one year or less and deal with how to accomplish the organization's specific objectives.

Regardless of how hard managers try, sometimes business activities do not go as planned. Today, most corporations also develop contingency plans along with strategies, tactical plans, and operational plans. A **contingency plan** is a plan that outlines alternative courses of action that may be taken if an organization's other plans are disrupted or become ineffective. For instance, Air Canada was forced to enact its contingency plan for servicing aircraft after its normal supplier, Aveos Fleet Performance, suspended operations. Without warning, Aveos locked out 2,300 workers, filed for credit protection, and announced that it permanently closed its airframe maintenance operation. Luckily, Air Canada had a contingency plan in place to reroute aircraft to a supplier in Quebec for repairs.[7]

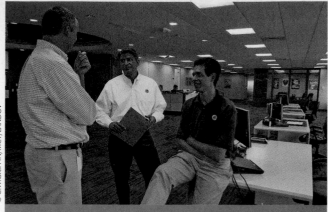

Tearing down the walls at Burger King. Burger King's top-level executives no longer have closed door offices, and employees no longer work in cubicles. The new physical arrangement facilitates better communication and collaboration among employees at all levels.

Organizing the Enterprise

After goal setting and planning, the manager's second major function is organization. **Organizing** is the grouping of resources and activities to accomplish some end result in an efficient and effective manner. Consider the case of an inventor who creates a new product and goes into business to sell it. At first, the inventor will do everything on his or her own—purchase raw materials, make the product, advertise it, sell it, and keep business records. Eventually, as business grows, the inventor will need help. To begin with, he or she might hire a professional sales representative and a part-time bookkeeper. Later, it also might be necessary to hire sales staff, people to assist with production, and an accountant. As the inventor hires new personnel, he or she must decide what each person will do, to whom each person will report, and how each person can best take part in the organization's activities. We discuss these and other facets of the organizing function in much more detail in Chapter 7.

Leading and Motivating

The leading and motivating function is concerned with the human resources within an organization. Specifically, **leading** is the process of influencing people to work toward a common goal. **Motivating** is the process of providing reasons for people to work in the best interests of an organization. Together, leading and motivating are often referred to as **directing**.

We have already noted the importance of an organization's human resources. Because of this importance, leading and motivating are critical activities. Obviously, different people do things for different reasons—that is, they have different *motivations*. Some are interested primarily in earning as much money as they can. Others may be spurred on by opportunities to get promoted. Part of a manager's job, then, is to determine what factors motivate workers and to try to provide those incentives to encourage effective performance. Jeffrey R. Immelt, GE's chairperson and CEO, has worked to transform GE into a leader in essential themes tied to world development, such as emerging markets, environmental solutions, demographics, and digital connections. He believes in giving freedom to his teams and wants them to come up with their own solutions. However, he does not hesitate to intervene if the situation demands. He believes that a leader's primary role is to teach, and he makes people feel that he is willing to share what he has learned. Immelt also laid the vision for GE's ambitious "ecomagination initiative" and has been named one of the "World's Best CEOs" three times by *Barron's*.[8] A lot of research has been done on both motivation and leadership. As you will see in Chapter 10, research on motivation has yielded very useful information. However, research on leadership has been less successful. Despite decades of study, no one has discovered a general set of personal traits or characteristics that makes a good leader. Later in this chapter, we discuss leadership in more detail.

operational plan a type of plan designed to implement tactical plans

contingency plan a plan that outlines alternative courses of action that may be taken if an organization's other plans are disrupted or become ineffective

organizing the grouping of resources and activities to accomplish some end result in an efficient and effective manner

leading the process of influencing people to work toward a common goal

motivating the process of providing reasons for people to work in the best interests of an organization

directing the combined processes of leading and motivating

FIGURE 6.5   The Control Function

The control function includes three steps: setting standards, measuring actual performance, and taking corrective action.

© CENGAGE LEARNING 2014

Controlling Ongoing Activities

Controlling is the process of evaluating and regulating ongoing activities to ensure that goals are achieved. To see how controlling works, consider a rocket launched by NASA to place a satellite in orbit. Do NASA personnel simply fire the rocket and then check back in a few days to find out whether the satellite is in place? Of course not. The rocket is monitored constantly, and its course is regulated and adjusted as needed to get the satellite to its destination.

The control function includes three steps (see Figure 6.5). The first is *setting standards* with which performance can be compared. The second is *measuring actual performance* and comparing it with the standard. The third is *taking corrective action* as necessary. Notice that the control function is circular in nature. The steps in the control function must be repeated periodically until the goal is achieved. For example, suppose that Southwest Airlines establishes a goal of increasing profits by 12 percent. To ensure that this goal is reached, Southwest's management might monitor its profit on a monthly basis. After three months, if profit has increased by 3 percent, management might be able to assume that plans are going according to schedule. In this case, it is likely that no action will be taken. However, if profit has increased by only 1 percent after three months, some corrective action is needed to get the firm on track. The particular action that is required depends on the reason for the small increase in profit.

KINDS OF MANAGERS

③ Distinguish among the various kinds of managers in terms of both level and area of management.

Managers can be classified in two ways: according to their level within an organization and according to their area of management. In this section, we use both perspectives to explore the various types of managers.

Levels of Management

For the moment, think of an organization as a three-story structure (as illustrated in Figure 6.6). Each story corresponds to one of the three general levels of management: top managers, middle managers, and first-line managers.

controlling the process of evaluating and regulating ongoing activities to ensure that goals are achieved

top manager an upper-level executive who guides and controls the overall fortunes of an organization

Top Managers A **top manager** is an upper-level executive who guides and controls an organization's overall fortunes. Top managers constitute a small group. In terms of planning, they are generally responsible for developing the organization's mission. They also

FIGURE 6.6 Management Levels Found in Most Companies

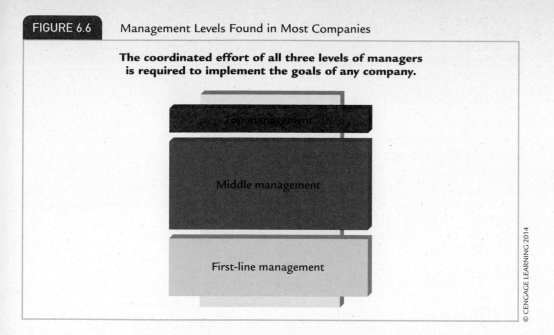

The coordinated effort of all three levels of managers is required to implement the goals of any company.

Top management

Middle management

First-line management

© CENGAGE LEARNING 2014

determine the firm's strategy. It takes years of hard work, long hours, and perseverance, as well as talent and no small share of good luck, to reach the ranks of top management in large companies. Common job titles associated with top managers are president, vice president, chief executive officer (CEO), and chief operating officer (COO).

Middle Managers Middle managers probably make up the largest group of managers in most organizations. A **middle manager** is a manager who implements the strategy and major policies developed by top management. Middle managers develop tactical plans and operational plans, and they coordinate and supervise the activities of first-line managers. Titles at the middle-management level include division manager, department head, plant manager, and operations manager.

First-Line Managers A **first-line manager** is a manager who coordinates and supervises the activities of operating employees. First-line managers spend most of their time working with and motivating their employees, answering questions, and solving day-to-day problems. Most first-line managers are former operating employees who, owing to their hard work and potential, were promoted into management. Many of today's middle and top managers began their careers on this first management level. Common titles for first-line managers include office manager, supervisor, and foreman.

Areas of Management Specialization

Organizational structure can also be divided into areas of management specialization (see Figure 6.7). The most common areas are finance, operations, marketing, human resources, and administration. Depending on its mission, goals, and objectives, an organization may include other areas as well—research and development (R&D), for example.

Financial Managers A **financial manager** is primarily responsible for an organization's financial resources. Accounting and investment are specialized areas within financial management. Because

middle manager a manager who implements the strategy and major policies developed by top management

first-line manager a manager who coordinates and supervises the activities of operating employees

financial manager a manager who is primarily responsible for an organization's financial resources

© AP PHOTO/MARK LENNIHAN

A top manager's out-of-this world business strategy. At the age of 16, Richard Branson, the CEO and founder of the Virgin Group, started his first business venture: a magazine called *The Student*. Today, the Virgin Group consists of over 400 companies, including Virgin Telecommunications, Virgin Radio, Virgin Cola, Virgin Wine, Virgin Spa, Virgin Airlines—and the list goes on. By 2014, Virgin Galactic, one of Branson's newest companies, aims to launch paying customers into space.

Going for SUCCESS

Steve Jobs: Futurist Extraordinaire

The late Steve Jobs was not just an inspiring leader within Apple, the company he cofounded—he was also an inspiration to many other business leaders, including Virgin Group's entrepreneur-in-chief, Richard Branson. Observing that "all true leaders go about things in their own way," Branson observes that Jobs's success as CEO was due to his ability to envision things that others could not.

With Jobs as its visionary CEO, Apple introduced now-iconic products such as the iPhone, the iPad, and iTunes. Jobs was creative, charismatic, and autocratic. He made quick and confident decisions, pushing Apple to be the very best at what it does. At his insistence, any product carrying the company logo of an apple minus a bite had to be aesthetically distinctive, intuitive to use, and top quality.

To the outside world, Jobs was the face of Apple, introducing every new product with personal pride. Inside the company, he was a relentless innovator, always thinking about the next new thing and pushing for the next breakthrough. Over the years, Jobs changed the way people use computers, make phone calls, and listen to music. His leadership legacy is a strong, successful company with can-do spirit.

Sources: Based on information in Steve Lohr, "The Yin and Yang of Corporate Innovation," *New York Times*, January 26, 2012, p. BU-3; Frederick E. Allen, "Steve Jobs Broke Every Leadership Rule. Don't Try It Yourself," *Forbes*, August 27, 2011, http://forbes.com/sites/frederickallen/2011/08/27/steve-jobs-broke-every-leadership-rule-dont-try-that-yourself/; Joe Nocera, "What Makes Steve Jobs Great," *New York Times*, August 26, 2011, http://nytimes.com/2011/08/27/opinion/nocera-what-makes-steve-jobs-great.html; Richard Branson, "Apple Boss Steve Jobs Was the Entrepreneur I Most Admired," *Telegraph (U.K.)*, October 6, 2011, http://telegraph.co.uk/technology/steve-jobs/8811232/Virgins-Richard-Branson-Apple-boss-Steve-Jobs-was-the-entrepreneur-I-most-admired.html.

financing affects the operation of the entire firm, many of the CEOs and presidents of this country's largest companies are people who got their "basic training" as financial managers.

Operations Managers An **operations manager** manages the systems that convert resources into goods and services. Traditionally, operations management has been equated with manufacturing—the production of goods. However, in recent years, many of the techniques and procedures of operations management have been applied to the production of services and to a variety of nonbusiness activities. As with financial management, operations management has produced a large percentage of today's company CEOs and presidents.

Marketing Managers A **marketing manager** is responsible for facilitating the exchange of products between an organization and its customers or clients. Specific areas within marketing are marketing research, product management, advertising, promotion, sales, and distribution. A sizable number of today's company presidents have risen from the ranks of marketing management.

Human Resources Managers A **human resources manager** is charged with managing an organization's human resources programs. He or she engages in human resources planning; designs systems for hiring, training, and evaluating the performance of employees; and ensures that the organization follows government

operations manager a manager who manages the systems that convert resources into goods and services

marketing manager a manager who is responsible for facilitating the exchange of products between an organization and its customers or clients

human resources manager a person charged with managing an organization's human resources programs

FIGURE 6.7   Areas of Management Specialization

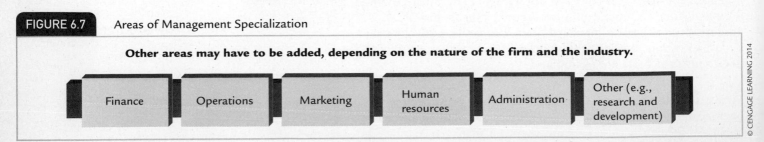

Other areas may have to be added, depending on the nature of the firm and the industry.

Finance   Operations   Marketing   Human resources   Administration   Other (e.g., research and development)

© CENGAGE LEARNING 2014

regulations concerning employment practices. Some human resources managers make effective use of technology. For example, more than 1 million job openings are posted on Monster.com, which attracts about 23 million visitors monthly.[9]

Administrative Managers An **administrative manager** (also called a *general manager*) is not associated with any specific functional area but provides overall administrative guidance and leadership. A hospital administrator is an example of an administrative manager. He or she does not specialize in operations, finance, marketing, or human resources management but instead coordinates the activities of specialized managers in all these areas. In many respects, most top managers are really administrative managers.

Whatever their level in the organization and whatever area they specialize in, successful managers generally exhibit certain key skills and are able to play certain managerial roles. However, as we shall see, some skills are likely to be more critical at one level of management than at another.

© AUREMAR/SHUTTERSTOCK

Harnessing the cooperation of an organization's specialized managers. Imagine the managers of different departments as a team of horses. If they—and their employees—don't all work together and pull in the same direction, the organization won't get to the destination it's trying to reach.

KEY SKILLS OF SUCCESSFUL MANAGERS

Identify the key management skills of successful managers.

As shown in Figure 6.8, managers need a variety of skills, including conceptual, analytic, interpersonal, technical, and communication skills.

Conceptual Skills

Conceptual skills involve the ability to think in abstract terms. Conceptual skills allow a manager to see the "big picture" and understand how the various parts of an organization or idea can fit together. For example, Jim Whitehurst of Red Hat, an open-source technology company, strongly believes in the advantage offered by conceptual thinkers. He believes that managers should solicit creative ideas from all levels of the

| FIGURE 6.8 | Key Skills of Successful Managers |

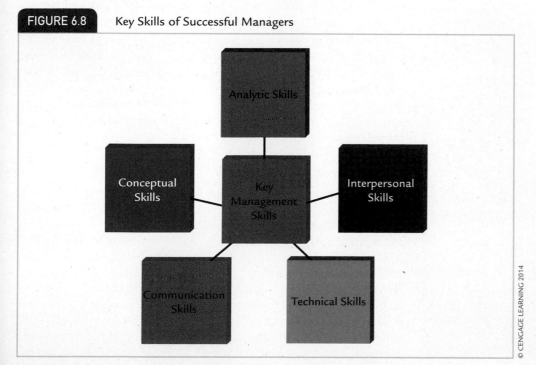

© CENGAGE LEARNING 2014

administrative manager a manager who is not associated with any specific functional area but who provides overall administrative guidance and leadership

conceptual skills the ability to think in abstract terms organization in order to help them see the big picture better and to obtain a wide variety of creative viewpoints.[10] These skills are useful in a wide range of situations, including the optimization of goals described earlier.

Analytic Skills

Employers expect managers to use **analytic skills** to identify problems correctly, generate reasonable alternatives, and select the "best" alternatives to solve problems. Top-level managers especially need these skills because they need to discern the important issues from the less important ones, as well as recognize the underlying reasons for different situations. Managers who use these skills not only address a situation but also correct the initial event or problem that caused it to occur. Thus, these skills are vital to run a business efficiently and logically.

Interpersonal Skills

Interpersonal skills involve the ability to deal effectively with other people, both inside and outside an organization. Examples of interpersonal skills are the ability to relate to people, understand their needs and motives, and show genuine compassion. Howard Schultz, founder and CEO of Starbucks, used his knowledge of interpersonal communication to save the company recently. Schultz quickly shut down 800 poorly performing stores, laid off 4,000 employees, retrained staff, modernized technology, and improved operations. Despite these drastic changes, employees are still loyal to the company and motivated for change because of Schultz's commitment to community and employee growth. For example, he refused to reduce employee health coverage because this would "sap the reservoir of trust" that employees have. While it may be obvious that a CEO such as Schultz must be able to work with employees throughout the organization, it's not so obvious that middle and first-line managers must also possess these interpersonal skills.[11]

Technical Skills

Technical skills involve specific skills needed to accomplish a specialized activity. For example, the skills engineers and machinists need to do their jobs are technical skills. First-line managers (and, to a lesser extent, middle managers) need the technical skills relevant to the activities they manage. Although these managers may not perform the technical tasks themselves, they must be able to train subordinates, answer questions, and otherwise provide guidance and direction. A first-line manager in the accounting department of the Hyatt Corporation, for example, must be able to perform computerized accounting transactions and help employees complete the same accounting task. In general, top managers do not rely on technical skills as heavily as managers at other levels. Still, understanding the technical side of a business is an aid to effective management at every level.

Communication Skills

Communication skills, both oral and written, involve the ability to speak, listen, and write effectively. Managers need both oral and written communication skills. Because a large part of a manager's day is spent conversing with others, the ability to speak *and* listen is critical. Oral communication skills are used when a manager makes sales presentations, conducts interviews, and holds press conferences. Written communication skills are important because a manager's ability to prepare letters, e-mails, memos, sales reports, and other written documents may spell the difference between success and failure. Computers, smartphones, and other high-tech devices make communication in today's business world both easier and more

analytic skills the ability to identify problems correctly, generate reasonable alternatives, and select the "best" alternatives to solve problems

interpersonal skills the ability to deal effectively with other people

technical skills specific skills needed to accomplish a specialized activity

communication skills the ability to speak, listen, and write effectively

© BLEND IMAGES/SHUTTERSTOCK

How good are your managerial skills? To be successful, managers must master and simultaneously utilize a number of skills, including: technical skills that aid with specialized work; conceptual skills that foster abstract thinking; and interpersonal skills to help manage and motivate their employees. Which of these skills will you need to work on as you build your career?

complex. To effectively manage an organization and to stay adequately informed, it is very important that managers understand how to use and maximize the potential of digital communication devices.

LEADERSHIP

⑤ Explain the different types of leadership.

Leadership has been defined broadly as the ability to influence others. A leader can use his or her power to affect the behavior of others. Leadership is different from management in that a leader strives for voluntary cooperation, whereas a manager may have to depend on coercion to change employee behavior.

Formal and Informal Leadership

Some experts make distinctions between formal leadership and informal leadership. Formal leaders have legitimate power of position. They have *authority* within an organization to influence others to work for the organization's objectives. Informal leaders usually have no such authority and may or may not exert their influence in support of the organization. Both formal and informal leaders make use of several kinds of power, including the ability to grant rewards or impose punishments, the possession of expert knowledge, and personal attraction or charisma. Informal leaders who identify with the organization's goals are a valuable asset to any organization. However, a business can be brought to its knees by informal leaders who turn work groups against management.

leadership the ability to influence others

autocratic leadership task-oriented leadership style in which workers are told what to do and how to accomplish it; workers have no say in the decision-making process

participative leadership leadership style in which all members of a team are involved in identifying essential goals and developing strategies to reach those goals

Styles of Leadership

For many years, leadership was viewed as a combination of personality traits, such as self-confidence, concern for people, intelligence, and dependability. Achieving a consensus on which traits were most important was difficult, however, so attention turned to styles of leadership behavior. In recent years, several styles of leadership have emerged, including *autocratic, participative,* and *entrepreneurial.*

Autocratic leadership is very task-oriented. Decisions are made confidently, with little concern about employee opinions. Employees are told exactly what is expected from them and given specific guidelines, rules, and regulations on how to achieve their tasks. Managers at Hyundai USA successfully employ the autocratic leadership style.[12]

Participative leadership is common in today's business organizations. Participative leaders consult workers before making decisions. This helps workers understand which goals are important and fosters a sense of ownership and commitment to reach those goals. Participative leaders can be classified into three groups: consultative, consensus, and democratic. *Consultative leaders* discuss issues with workers but retain the final authority for decision making. *Consensus leaders* seek input from almost all workers and make final decisions based on their support. *Democratic leaders* give final authority to the group. They collect opinions and base their decisions on the vote of the group. Google co-founders Larry Page and Sergey Brin are known for their democratic decision-making styles.[13] Communication is active upward and downward in participative organizations. Coaching, collaborating, and negotiating are important skills for participative leaders.

© VJOM/SHUTTERSTOCK

© TERRY SCHMITT/UPI/LANDOV

Personal APPS

Think of a leader you admire—someone in the business world or an entertainer raising awareness for a social cause, for example. Why does this person inspire you or make you want to take action? What can you learn from his or her leadership that will help you become a leader in *your* life?

A CEO who leads by example. Bill Gates's leadership style and technological know-how have helped him foster an environment at Microsoft in which top-notch products can be created. Gates's leadership style includes dimensions of both autocratic and participative leadership.

Entrepreneurial leadership is personality dependent. Although each entrepreneur is different, this leadership style is generally task-oriented, driven, charismatic, and enthusiastic.[14] The entrepreneurial personality tends to take initiative, venture into new areas, be visionary, and focus on the next deal. Their enthusiasm energizes and inspires their people. Entrepreneurial leaders tend to be very invested in their businesses, working extremely long hours trying to ensure the success of their firm. They may not understand why their employees do not have the same level of passion for their work. Steve Jobs, former CEO of Apple, was probably the preeminent example of an entrepreneurial leader. He was highly charismatic and worked tirelessly and passionately for his organization.[15]

Which Leadership Style Is the Best?

Today, most management experts agree that no "best" managerial leadership style exists. Each of the styles described—autocratic, participative, and entrepreneurial—has advantages and disadvantages. Participative leadership can motivate employees to work effectively because they are implementing their own decisions. However, the decision-making process in participative leadership takes time that subordinates could be devoting to the work itself. Table 6.1 presents tips for effective leadership. Most of these tips are consistent with the participative leadership style.

Although hundreds of research studies have been conducted to prove which leadership style is best, there are no definite conclusions. The "best" leadership seems to occur when the leader's style matches the situation. Each of the leadership styles can be effective in the right situation. The *most* effective style depends on interaction among employees, characteristics of the work situation, and the manager's personality.

TABLE 6.1	Tips for Successful Leadership
1.	Walk the talk. Make your actions consistent with your words.
2.	Be truthful, fair, and respectful, and honor confidences.
3.	Demonstrate a vision and values worth following.
4.	Co-workers make mistakes. So do you. Admit to them and learn from them.
5.	Be open to what others have to offer. Ask questions and take time to listen to co-workers.
6.	Know your weaknesses, so that you can build a team to make up for them.
7.	All work and no fun can reduce productivity.
8.	Help workers do their best by encouraging them to grow and learn.
9.	Never publicly blame anyone but yourself.
10.	Stay positive and expect it of your people. Negativity leads downhill fast.
11.	Involve people in decisions—especially those regarding change.
12.	Be open to new ways of doing things. Embrace change—it's inevitable.
13.	Recognize and celebrate individual and team successes, both big and not so big.
14.	Embrace and benefit from diversity.
15.	Empower your workers. They will have greater self-respect, responsibility, and accountability.
16.	Take your work, but not yourself, seriously.

© CENGAGE LEARNING 2014

entrepreneurial leadership personality-based leadership style in which the manager seeks to inspire workers with a vision of what can be accomplished to benefit all stakeholders

MANAGERIAL DECISION MAKING

6 Discuss the steps in the managerial decision-making process.

Decision making is the act of choosing one alternative from a set of alternatives.[16] In ordinary situations, decisions are made casually and informally. We encounter a problem, mull it over, settle on a solution, and go on. Managers, however, require a more systematic method for solving complex problems. As shown in Figure 6.9, managerial decision making involves four steps: (1) identifying the problem or opportunity, (2) generating alternatives, (3) selecting an alternative, and (4) implementing and evaluating the solution.

Identifying the Problem or Opportunity

A **problem** is the discrepancy between an actual condition and a desired condition—the difference between what is occurring and what one wishes would occur. For example, a marketing manager at Campbell's Soup Company has a problem if sales revenues for Campbell's Hungry Man frozen dinners are declining (the actual condition). To solve this problem, the marketing manager must take steps to increase sales revenues (desired condition). Most people consider a problem to be "negative"; however, a problem also can be "positive." A positive problem should be viewed as an "opportunity."

Although accurate identification of a problem is essential before it can be solved or turned into an opportunity, this stage of decision making creates many difficulties for managers. Sometimes managers' preconceptions of the problem prevent them from seeing the actual situation. They produce an answer before the proper question has been asked. In other cases, managers overlook truly significant issues by focusing on unimportant matters. Also, managers may mistakenly analyze problems in terms of symptoms rather than underlying causes.

Effective managers learn to look ahead so that they are prepared when decisions must be made. They clarify situations and examine the causes of problems, asking whether the presence or absence of certain variables alters a situation. Finally, they consider how individual behaviors and values affect the way problems or opportunities are defined.

Generating Alternatives

After a problem has been defined, the next task is to generate alternatives. The more important the decision, the more attention must be devoted to this stage. Managers should be open to fresh, innovative ideas as well as obvious answers.

Certain techniques can aid in the generation of creative alternatives. Brainstorming, commonly used in group discussions, encourages participants to produce many new ideas. During brainstorming, other group members are not permitted to criticize or ridicule. Another approach, developed by the U.S. Navy, is called "Blast! Then Refine." Group members tackle a recurring problem by erasing all previous solutions and procedures. The group then re-evaluates its original objectives, modifies them if necessary, and devises new solutions. Other techniques—including trial and error—are also useful in this stage of decision making.

Selecting an Alternative

Final decisions are influenced by a number of considerations, including financial constraints, human and informational resources, time limits, legal obstacles, and political

---

FIGURE 6.9   Major Steps in the Managerial Decision-Making Process

Managers require a systematic method for solving problems in a variety of situations.

Identifying the problem or opportunity → Generating alternatives → Selecting an alternative → Implementing and evaluating the solution

© CENGAGE LEARNING 2014

decision making the act of choosing one alternative from a set of alternatives

problem the discrepancy between an actual condition and a desired condition

Through Social Media, Do Workers Create Problems for Their Employers?

How should managers handle employee use of social media? Despite the growing popularity of Facebook, LinkedIn, Twitter, and other sites, some companies are concerned that employees will disclose proprietary information or become involved in controversial conversations that could harm the company's image. They also worry that employees will be distracted during the workday.

Employers in a few industries—such as financial services—are required to monitor business-related messages posted by employees to ensure compliance with government regulations. In most cases, however, companies are free to set their own policies. For example, IBM's policy requires employees to use respectful language, obey copyright laws, and indicate that their views are personal.

Sources: Melinda J. Caterine, "Your Business: Make Your Social Media Policy Clear," *Portland Press Herald* (Maine), January 25, 2011, www.pressherald.com; Tamara Schweitzer, "Do You Need a Social Media Policy?" *Inc.*, January 25, 2010, www.inc. com; David Scheer, "Brokers' Facebook, Twitter Posts Must Be Tracked by Employers," *BusinessWeek*, January 25, 2010, www. businessweek.com.

A growing number of firms are encouraging employees to interact with each other and with customers and suppliers using social media, as long as they follow specific guidelines. Kodak's employees must disclose their affiliation when discussing anything related to the company's business and are not allowed to reveal any confidential information. The social-media policy of online retailer Zappos is short and to the point: "Be real and use your best judgment."

Sources: Tamara Schweitzer, "Do You Need a Social Media Policy?" *Inc.*, January 25, 2010, www.inc.com/ articles/2010/01/need-a-social-media-policy.html; David Scheer, "Brokers' Facebook, Twitter Posts Must Be Tracked by Employers," *BusinessWeek*, January 25, 2010, www.businessweek.com; Charlene Li, *Open Leadership* (San Francisco, CA: Jossey-Bass, 2010), chap. 5; Stephen Baker, "Beware Social Media Snake Oil," *BusinessWeek*, December 14, 2009, 48–51.

factors. Managers must select the alternative that will be most effective and practical. Long known for its simple menu of fast food, McDonald's has been forced recently to choose between different alternatives in order to accommodate changing consumer tastes. A few years ago, McDonald's was faced with a problem of slumping sales and had to make decisions regarding business structure and the type of food offerings that would attract customers. Management outlined its alternatives selection in the "Plan to Win," which involved changing the fast food chain's menu to include more salads, smoothies, and other healthier items; as well as acquiring other companies, such as Chipotle, which offers healthy Mexican fast food. Management also implemented a careful leadership succession plan in order to make leadership transfers as smooth as possible.[17]

At times, two or more alternatives or some combination of alternatives will be equally appropriate. Managers may choose solutions to problems on several levels. The coined word *satisfice* describes solutions that are only adequate and not ideal. When lacking time or information, managers often make decisions that "satisfice." Whenever possible, managers should try to investigate alternatives carefully and select the ideal solution.

Implementing and Evaluating the Solution

Implementation of a decision requires time, planning, preparation of personnel, and evaluation of results. Managers usually deal with unforeseen consequences even when they have carefully considered the alternatives.

The final step in managerial decision making entails evaluating a decision's effectiveness. If the alternative that was chosen removes the difference between the actual condition and the desired condition, the decision is considered effective. If the problem still exists, managers may select one of the following choices:

- Decide to give the chosen alternative more time to work.
- Adopt a different alternative.
- Start the problem identification process all over again.

Failure to evaluate decisions adequately may have negative consequences. After the recent Wall Street financial meltdown, stakeholders and regulators spent years debating what happened and how to prevent a similar financial system breakdown in the future. Derivatives were largely blamed for the meltdown. At the time, organizational management, gatekeepers, and regulators all failed to adequately assess the risks of using derivatives. Recently, regulators came together to approve new rules that they hope will reduce the likelihood of widespread derivatives problems in the future.[18]

MANAGING TOTAL QUALITY

 Describe how organizations benefit from total quality management.

The management of quality is a high priority in some organizations today. Major reasons for a greater focus on quality include foreign competition, more demanding customers, and poor financial performance resulting from reduced market shares and higher costs. Over the last few years, several U.S. firms have lost the dominant competitive positions they had held for decades.

Total quality management is a much broader concept than just controlling the quality of the product itself (which is discussed in Chapter 8). **Total quality management (TQM)** is the coordination of efforts directed at improving customer satisfaction, increasing employee participation, strengthening supplier partnerships, and facilitating an organizational atmosphere of continuous quality improvement. For TQM programs to be effective, management must address each of the following components:

- *Customer satisfaction.* Ways to improve include producing higher-quality products, providing better customer service, and showing customers that the company cares.
- *Employee participation.* This can be increased by allowing employees to contribute to decisions, develop self-managed work teams, and assume responsibility for improving the quality of their work.
- *Strengthening supplier partnerships.* Developing good working relationships with suppliers can ensure that the right supplies and materials will be delivered on time at lower costs.
- *Continuous quality improvement.* A program based on continuous improvement has proven to be the most effective long-term approach.

One tool that is used for TQM is called benchmarking. **Benchmarking** is the process of evaluating the products, processes, or management practices of another organization for the purpose of improving quality. The focal organization may be superior in safety, customer service, productivity, innovativeness, or in some other way.

For example, competitors' products might be disassembled and evaluated, or wage and benefit plans might be surveyed to measure compensation packages against the labor market. The four basic steps of benchmarking are identifying objectives, forming a benchmarking team, collecting data, analyzing data, and acting on the results. Best practices may be discovered in any industry or organization.

Although many factors influence the effectiveness of a TQM program, two issues are crucial. First, top management must make a strong commitment to a TQM program by treating quality improvement as a top priority and giving it frequent attention. Firms that establish a TQM program but then focus on other priorities will find that their quality-improvement initiatives will fail.

total quality management (TQM) the coordination of efforts directed at improving customer satisfaction, increasing employee participation, strengthening supplier partnerships, and facilitating an organizational atmosphere of continuous quality improvement

benchmarking a process used to evaluate the products, processes, or management practices of another organization that is superior in some way in order to improve quality

Total quality management accelerates Toyota's competitiveness. Prior to the 1970s, products "Made in Japan" were often considered shoddy. Not anymore. Toyota Motor Company worked hard to change that image by pioneering the use of total quality management practices. As a part of its total quality management practices, Toyota meticulously inspects its products and continuously strives to improve them.

Second, management must coordinate the specific elements of a TQM program so that they work in harmony with each other.

Although not all U.S. companies have TQM programs, these programs provide many benefits. Overall financial benefits include lower operating costs, higher return on sales and on investments, and an improved ability to use premium pricing rather than competitive pricing. Firms that do not implement TQM are sometimes afraid that the costs of doing so will be prohibitive. While implementing TQM can be high initially, the savings from preventing future problems and integrating systems usually make up for the expense. The long-term costs of not implementing TQM can involve damage to a company's reputation and lost productivity and time from fixing mistakes after they have happened.[19]

return to Inside BUSINESS

IBM

As Virginia Rometty rose through the ranks of IBM, she earned the experience and skills needed to head this pioneering technology company. She worked closely with the previous CEO on implementing the current strategic plan, which aims to accelerate growth of IBM's global sales and profits. On her first day as CEO, she announced top-management changes to support IBM's international activities and its services division, two key groups important to the company's future.

Although IBM is more than 100 years old, its CEO wants it to be as innovative as a young start-up. For more than 15 years, IBM has been awarded more U.S. patents than any other company, and Rometty plans to maintain this technological leadership as she positions the company for aggressive growth in the years ahead.

Questions

1. Virginia Rometty worked for IBM for more than 30 years before she was named CEO. How do you think this experience affects her ability to plan, organize, lead, and control as CEO? Explain your answer.

2. Would you recommend that IBM use its closest competitors as the models for benchmarking technological innovation? Why or why not?

SUMMARY

Looking for Success?
Get Flashcards, Quizzes, Games, and more at @ www.cengagebrain.com.

① Define what management is.

Management is the process of coordinating people and other resources to achieve an organization's goals. Managers are concerned with four types of resources—material, human, financial, and informational.

② Describe the four basic management functions: planning, organizing, leading and motivating, and controlling.

Managers perform four basic functions. Management functions do not occur according to some rigid, preset timetable, though. At any time, managers may engage in a number of functions simultaneously. However, each function tends to lead naturally to others. First, managers engage in planning—determining where the firm should be going and how best to get there. One method of planning that can be used is SWOT analysis, which identifies and evaluates a firm's strengths, weaknesses, opportunities, and threats. Three types of plans, from the broadest to the most specific, are strategic plans, tactical plans, and operational plans. Managers also organize resources and activities to accomplish results in an efficient and effective manner, and they lead and motivate others to work in the best interests of the organization. In addition, managers control ongoing activities to keep the organization on course. There are three steps in the control function: setting standards, measuring actual performance, and taking corrective action.

③ Distinguish among the various kinds of managers in terms of both level and area of management.

Managers—or management positions—may be classified from two different perspectives. From the perspective of level within the organization, there are top managers, who control the fortunes of the organization; middle managers, who implement strategies and major policies; and first-line managers, who supervise the activities of operating employees. From the viewpoint of area of management, managers most often deal with the areas of finance, operations, marketing, human resources, and administration.

 Identify the key management skills of successful managers.

Managers need a variety of skills in order to run a successful and efficient business. Conceptual skills are used to think in abstract terms or see the "big picture." Analytic skills are used to identify problems correctly, generate reasonable alternatives, and select the "best" alternatives to solve problems. Interpersonal skills are used to deal effectively with other people, both inside and outside an organization. Technical skills are needed to accomplish a specialized activity, whether they are used to actually do the task or used to train and assist employees. Communication skills are used to speak, listen, and write effectively.

 Explain the different types of leadership.

Managers' effectiveness often depends on their styles of leadership—that is, their ability to influence others, either formally or informally. Autocratic leaders are very task oriented; they tell their employees exactly what is expected from them and give them specific instructions on how to do their assigned tasks. Participative leaders consult their employees before making decisions and can be classified into three groups: consultative, consensus, and democratic. Entrepreneurial leaders are different depending on their personalities, but they are generally enthusiastic and passionate about their work and tend to take initiative.

 Discuss the steps in the managerial decision-making process.

Decision making, an integral part of a manager's work, is the process of developing a set of possible alternative solutions to a problem and choosing one alternative from among the set. Managerial decision making involves four steps: Managers must accurately identify problems, generate several possible solutions, choose the solution that will be most effective under the circumstances, and implement and evaluate the chosen course of action.

 Describe how organizations benefit from total quality management.

Total quality management (TQM) is the coordination of efforts directed at improving customer satisfaction, increasing employee participation, strengthening supplier partnerships, and facilitating an organizational atmosphere of continuous quality improvement. Another tool used for TQM is benchmarking, which is used to evaluate the products, processes, or management practices of another organization that is superior in some way in order to improve quality. The five basic steps in benchmarking are identifying objectives, forming a benchmarking team, collecting data, analyzing data, and acting on the results. To have an effective TQM program, top management must make a strong, sustained commitment to the effort and must be able to coordinate all the program's elements so that they work in harmony. Overall financial benefits of TQM include lower operating costs, higher return on sales and on investment, and an improved ability to use premium pricing rather than competitive pricing.

KEY TERMS

You should now be able to define and give an example relevant to each of the following terms:

REVIEW QUESTIONS

1. Define the term *manager* without using the word *management* in your definition.
2. Identify and describe the basic management functions.
3. What are the major elements of SWOT analysis?

4. How do a strategic plan, a tactical plan, and an operational plan differ? What do they all have in common?
5. What exactly does a manager organize and for what reason?

6. Why are leadership and motivation necessary in a business in which people are paid for their work?
7. Explain the steps involved in the control function.
8. How are the two perspectives on kinds of managers—that is, level and area—different from each other?
9. What skills should a manager possess in order to be successful?
10. Compare and contrast the major styles of leadership.
11. Discuss what happens during each of the four steps of the managerial decision-making process.
12. What are the major benefits of a total quality management program?

DISCUSSION QUESTIONS

1. Does a healthy firm (one that is doing well) have to worry about effective management? Explain.
2. What might be the mission of a neighborhood restaurant? Of the Salvation Army? What might be reasonable objectives for these organizations?
3. Which of the management functions and skills do not apply to the owner-operator of a sole proprietorship?
4. Which leadership style might be best suited to each of the three general levels of management within an organization?
5. According to this chapter, the leadership style that is *most* effective depends on interaction among the employees, characteristics of the work situation, and the manager's personality. Do you agree or disagree? Explain your answer.
6. Do you think that people are really as important to an organization as this chapter seems to indicate?
7. As you learned in this chapter, managers often work long hours at a hectic pace. Would this type of career appeal to you? Explain your answer.

Video Case 6.1

L.L.Bean Relies on Its Core Values and Effective Leadership

L.L.Bean's first product was a waterproof boot, designed by Maine outdoorsman Leon Leonwood Bean, who promised complete customer satisfaction. One hundred pairs were sold—and 90 pairs were returned because of a defect. Bean refunded the customers' money and went to work perfecting the product, now one of the most popular in the firm's long and successful history.

L.L.Bean began in 1912 as a tiny mail-order company and has grown to include 14 retail stores in ten states, an online store, and a popular catalog showcasing many of the company's 20,000 items, including high-quality clothing, accessories, outdoor gear, luggage, linens, and furniture. It is still privately owned and family run and has had just three presidents in its history—L.L.Bean himself, his grandson Leon Gorman, and now Chris McCormick, the first nonfamily member to lead the firm. New England is the core of L.L.Bean's market, and its selling cycle accelerates sharply every year around the winter holidays. Headquartered in Freeport, Maine, near its original store, the company reports annual sales of over $1.5 billion.

Managers at L.L.Bean today have many opportunities for using their planning, organizing, leading, and controlling skills. During the preholiday selling season, for instance, temporary workers hired to handle the increased workload bring the regular staff of about 4,600 to almost double its size, so managers have to reorganize the teams of 25 to 30 front-line employees who work in the call centers. Regular employees not currently in leadership positions are asked to head the teams

of temps, ensuring they have an experienced person to help them develop their skills and perform to expectations. This organizing strategy works so well that many temps return year after year.

Planning skills come to the fore when top management decides when and where to open new retail stores, whether to expand the number of outlet stores offering discontinued items and overstocks, and how much to invest in ensuring that L.L.Bean buildings meet the highest standards of environmental stewardship. One recent strategic planning project resulted in the creation of a new clothing and accessories collection called L.L.Bean Signature, featuring updated versions of classic items from the company's 100-year heritage.

With respect to the control function, managers assess employee performance with a continuous evaluation process. Corporate-level goals are broken down to the level of the individual store and employee. If something isn't on track, the supervisor is expected to let the employee know and help figure out a solution. However, control at L.L.Bean is not entirely a top-down process. Employees are encouraged to develop their own personal goals, such as learning a new skill or gaining a better appreciation of the way L.L.Bean makes business decisions. Managers help them find ways to meet these personal objectives as well, through a temporary reassignment within the firm or participation in a special company project.

L.L.Bean has a strong collaborative work culture in which it is equally important to work through your supervisor, your co-workers, and your subordinates. That means everyone is a leader to some extent. Formal management candidates are asked to demonstrate both analytical and interpersonal skills and to model the company's six core values: outdoor heritage, integrity, service, respect, perseverance, and safe and healthy living. In the early days of the company, L.L.Bean lived above the store and would come downstairs in the middle of the night to help a customer who rang the bell. "A customer is the most important person ever in this office—in person or by mail," he was fond of saying. So, true to his beliefs, leadership style continues to revolve around serving the customer's needs. As one L.L.Bean manager said, the company is all about salespeople and customer service representatives so that they can better serve customers.[20]

Questions

1. What style of leadership do you think most L.L.Bean managers probably employ?
2. To produce hot water in L.L.Bean's flagship store, the company recently installed a solar hot water system that will offset almost 11,000 pounds of carbon dioxide emissions every year. Suggest some of the questions the company's managers might have asked at each level of planning (strategic, tactical, operational, and contingency) for this project.
3. Which managerial role or roles do you think the leaders of L.L.Bean's temp teams fill?

Case 6.2

What's Next for "Earth's Biggest Bookstore"?

When CEO Jeff Bezos founded the pioneering online retailer Amazon.com in 1995, his goal was to build "Earth's biggest bookstore." Amazon now rings up $48 billion in annual sales and offers "Earth's biggest selection" of merchandise, everything from cameras and clothing to lamps and luggage. What began as a virtual bookstore has become a multifaceted, multinational business serving 164 million consumers and business customers, thanks to the founder's visionary leadership and relentless focus on customer satisfaction.

Sitting around the conference table with his top managers, Bezos often leaves one chair empty to represent "the most important person in the room"—the customer. Although many CEOs keep a close eye on the earnings they must report to shareholders every three months, Bezos has always paid more attention to long-term customer needs than to short-term financial results. Amazon's strategic plans look ahead a decade or more, and cover innovations that take advantage of the company's technology strengths. "We are comfortable planting seeds and waiting for them to grow into trees," he says. Bezos and his executives have the patience and conviction to make far-reaching decisions about future investments and actions, watch how things unfold during implementation, and adjust the plans as needed while the world catches up.

The Kindle is a good example of how Amazon's strategic planning pays off. When electronic book readers were in their infancy, Bezos was convinced that Amazon could upend the market by making an easy-to-use device capable of downloading and displaying any book in one minute or less. Company engineers invested years (and millions of dollars) inventing the original Kindle, which immediately sold out when introduced in 2007. Since then, newer models with additional features and functionality, including the Kindle Fire, have attracted a huge wave of new customers as well as new "content creators"—authors who use the Kindle platform to publish their own books. Electronic books now outsell printed books, a development that has driven Borders and other book stores into bankruptcy while Amazon profits from the surge in digital downloads that its Kindle helped to stimulate.

To ensure that Amazon is doing what it should be doing to satisfy customers, management sets standards for hundreds of everyday activities and constantly measures actual performance. For example, it times how quickly its web pages load and finds ways to speed things up, because it has learned that even a split-second delay can cause customers to click away. The company maintains minimum inventory levels to avoid running out of merchandise, presorts packages to add to its shipping partners' efficiency, and tracks down the cause of any delivery delays so customers will know they can rely on Amazon's delivery promises. No wonder Amazon routinely comes out on top in customer-satisfaction surveys.

Today, the company's Web site serves as an online marketplace where individuals and businesses can sell their products, paying Amazon a small percentage every time they make a sale. Major corporations like Netflix pay for access to Amazon's sophisticated Internet software and data storage systems. Still, because Amazon's roots are in retailing, Bezos continues his habit of reading customers' letters to see what they like and what they don't like, seeking clues that will lead him to the next big opportunity.[21]

Questions

1. Knowing that Amazon.com's strength is technology, which can change rapidly and unpredictably, do you agree with Jeff Bezos's method of looking up to a decade ahead for strategic planning purposes? Explain your answer.
2. Does Jeff Bezos appear to be an autocratic, a participative, or an entrepreneurial leader? What are the implications for Amazon.com?
3. How does Amazon.com apply total quality management, and why?

① SOCIAL MEDIA EXERCISE

Crowdsourcing is a set of principles, processes, and platforms to get things done that includes putting out an open call to a group and managing the responses and output. Crowdsourcing can be like outsourcing in a bigger way because instead of contracting to one known entity, you are putting a call out to a bigger group, often a global online community, to either get many to participate or to find the person you need by casting a much wider net.

There are crowdsourcing companies that perform specific types of work such as translations (MyGengo, Smartling), transcription (CastingWords), keyword marketing (Trada), even design and marketing work (Prova, 99Designs, CrowdSpring). Each company operates differently. In the case of transcription or translation, you give work to a company like CastingWords or MyGengo, and they in turn put the job out to their "crowd" of workers from around the world. They are like the middleman to helping you get the work done, and their distributed workforce can be less costly to them so they pass on their savings to your organization.

1. Check out a few of these crowdsourcing companies. What are your thoughts? Do you think they are effective? Why or why not?
2. Which type of leadership is most likely to include the use of crowdsourcing?
3. Can you think of other areas in businesses that can benefit from the use of crowdsourcing? What are they?

② JOURNALING FOR SUCCESS

Discovery statement: This chapter discussed the critical management function of leading and motivating others to work in the best interests of an organization. Think about your current job or a job that you had previously.

Assignment

1. Who is the most outstanding leader with whom you have worked?
2. What was his or her position and in what capacity did you work with the person?
3. What are this person's outstanding leadership qualities?
4. Select the most outstanding leadership quality from question 3 and provide an example that demonstrates this quality.
5. Do most of your co-workers view this person as being an outstanding leader, too? Explain.

③ DEVELOPING CRITICAL-THINKING SKILLS

As defined in the chapter, an organization's mission is a statement of the basic purpose that makes the organization different from others. Clearly, a mission statement, by indicating the purpose of a business, directly affects the company's employees, customers, and stockholders.

Assignment

1. Find the mission statements of three large corporations in different industries. The Internet is one source of mission statements. For example, you might search these sites:

    www.apple.com
    www.benjerry.com
    www.walmart.com
    Compare the mission statements on the basis of what each reflects about the company's philosophy and its concern for employees, customers, and stockholders.
2. Which company would you like to work for and why?
3. Prepare a report on your findings.

④ BUILDING TEAM SKILLS

Over the past few years, an increasing number of employees, stockholders, and customers have been demanding to know what their companies are about. As a result, more companies have been taking the time to analyze their operations and to prepare mission statements that focus on the purpose of the company. The mission statement is becoming a critical planning tool for successful companies. To make effective decisions, employees must understand the purpose of their company.

Assignment

1. Divide into teams and write a mission statement for one of the following types of businesses:

    Food service, restaurant
    Banking
    Airline
    Auto repair
    Cabinet manufacturing
2. Discuss your mission statement with other teams. How did the other teams interpret the purpose of your company? What is the mission statement saying about the company?
3. Write a one-page report on what you learned about developing mission statements.

⑤ RESEARCHING DIFFERENT CAREERS

A successful career requires planning. Without a plan, or roadmap, you will find it very difficult, if not impossible, to reach your desired career destination. The first step in planning is to establish your career goal. You then must set objectives and develop plans for accomplishing those objectives. This kind of planning takes time, but it will pay off later.

Assignment

Complete the following statements:
1. My career objective is to:
    -
    -
    -
    -

This statement should encapsulate what you want to accomplish over the long run. It may include the type of job you want and the type of business or industry you want to work in. Examples include the following:

- My career goal is to work as a top manager in the food industry.
- My career goal is to supervise aircraft mechanics.
- My career goal is to win the top achievement award in the advertising industry.

2. My career objectives are to
-
-
-
-

Objectives are benchmarks along the route to a career destination. They are more specific than a career goal. A statement about a career objective should specify what you want to accomplish, when you will complete it, and any other details that will serve as criteria against which you can measure your progress. Examples include the following:

- My objective is to enroll in a management course at Main College in the spring semester 2014.
- My objective is to earn an A in the management course at Main College in the spring semester 2014.
- My objective is to be promoted to supervisor by January 1, 2016.
- My objective is to prepare a status report by September 30 covering the last quarter's activities by asking Charlie in Quality Control to teach me the procedures.

3. Exchange your goal and objectives statements with another class member. Can your partner interpret your objectives correctly? Are the objectives concise and complete? Do they include criteria against which you can measure your progress? If not, discuss the problem and rewrite the objective.

ENDNOTES

1. Based on information in "IBM Keeps Top Patent Spot for 19th Year as Asian Rivals Gain," *Bloomberg BusinessWeek*, January 11, 2012, http://news.businessweek.com/article.asp?documentKey=1376-LXMW751A74E901-39IF2F50723L13O-T62AKFA8GSQ; Nicola Leske, "IBM's Plain Vanilla Flavor Leaves Investors Satisfied," *Reuters*, January 20, 2012, http://reuters.com/article/2012/01/21/us-ibm-idUSTRE80K01G20120121; Spencer E. Ante and Joann S. Lublin, "IBM Names Rometty as Next CEO," *Wall Street Journal*, October 26, 2011, http://online.wsj.com/article/SB1000142405297020477790457665351267101 2304.html; Darryl K. Taft, "New IBM CEO Rometty Makes Key Management Changes," *eWeek*, January 3, 2012, http://eweek.com/c/a/IT-Management/New-IBM-CEO-Rometty-Makes-Key-Management-Changes-296800/.

2. "Eli Lilly Made China Pharma Market a Top Priority," *Transmedia.com*, January 1, 2010, http://transmedia-china.com/default.aspx?portalid5442&tabid50&mid55606&ctl5news&iid53561.

3. Starbucks, http://starbucks.com/about-us/company-information/mission-statement (accessed February 15, 2012); Facebook, http://facebook.com/facebook#!/facebook?v=info (accessed February 15, 2012).

4. Starbucks, http://starbucks.com/responsibility (accessed February 15, 2012).

5. Amy Chozick, "Gannet Pushes its Pay Wall Plan to Investors," *New York Times*, February 22, 2012, http://mediadecoder.blogs.nytimes.com/2012/02/22/gannett-pushes-its-pay-wall-plan-to-investors.

6. Jens Hansegard, "IKEA Taking China by Storm," *The Wall Street Journal*, March 20, 2012, http://online.wsj.com/article/SB10001424052702304636404577293083481821536.html.

7. Staff reporter, "Air Canada Uses Contingency Plan to Service Planes," *Reuters*, March 21, 2012, www.reuters.com/article/2012/03/21/aircanada-idUSL1E8ELL3F20120321.

8. http://fastcompany.com/tag/Ecomagination (accessed February 15, 2012); http://ge.com/company/leadership/ceo.html (accessed February 15, 2012).

9. http://quantcast.com/monster.com (accessed February 14, 2012).

10. Adam Bryant, "The Memo List: Where Everyone Has an Opinion," New York Times, March 10, 2012, www.nytimes.com/2012/03/11/business/jim-whitehurst-of-red-hat-on-merits-of-an-open-culture.html.

11. David A. Kaplan, "The 2011 Business Person of the Year: Howard Schultz, Strong Coffee," *Fortune*, December 12, 2011, pp. 101–116.

12. http://kwikiblog.blogspot.com/2008/03/korean-management-practices-at-hyundai.html (accessed February 5, 2012).

13. www.flatworldknowledge.com/pub/1.0/principles-management/32395; www.google.com/intl/en/corporate/culture.html (accessed January 5, 2012).

14. Andrew J. Dubrin, *Leadership: Research Findings, Practice and Skills*, 7th ed. (Mason, OH: South-Western/Cengage Learning, 2013).

15. Walter Isaacson, "The Real Leadership Lessons of Steve Jobs," *Harvard Business Review*, April 2012, http://hbr.org/2012/04/the-real-leadership-lessons-of-steve-jobs/ar/1.

16. Ricky Griffin, *Management*, 11th ed. (Mason, OH: South-Western Cengage, 2012), 7.

17. Deborah L. Jacobs, "McDonald's Recipe for Success Brought New CEO to the Table," *Forbes*, March 22, 2012, www.forbes.com/sites/deborahljacobs/2012/03/22/mcdonalds-recipe-for-success-brought-new-ceo-to-the-table/.

18. Ben Protess, "Regulators Approve New Derivatives Rules," *New York Times Dealbook*, March 20, 2012, http://dealbook.nytimes.com/2012/03/20/regulators-approve-new-derivatives-rule.

19. Martin Murray, "Total Quality Management (TQM)," http://logistics.about.com/od/qualityinthesupplychain/a/TQM.htm (accessed March 23, 2012).

20. Based on information on the company Web site www.llbean.com (accessed January 20, 2011); company news release, "L.L.Bean Installs a Solar Hot Water System to Its Flagship Store in Freeport," www.llbean.com, June 15, 2010; interviews with L.L.Bean employees, and the video, "L.L.Bean Relies on Its Core Values and Effective Leadership."

21. Based on information in George Anders, "Inside Amazon's Idea Machine," *Forbes*, April 4, 2012, www.forbes.com; James B. Stewart, "Amazon Says Long Term and Means It," *New York Times*, December 17, 2011, p. B1; Steven Levy, "CEO of the Internet," *Wired*, December 2011, p. 208.

©MATREE LAIPITAKSIN, SHUTTERSTOCK

12 Building Customer Relationships Through Effective Marketing

LEARNING OBJECTIVES

Once you complete this chapter, you will be able to:

1 Understand the meaning of *marketing* and the importance of management of customer relationships.

2 Explain how marketing adds value by creating several forms of utility.

3 Trace the development of the marketing concept and understand how it is implemented.

4 Understand what markets are and how they are classified.

5 Identify the four elements of the marketing mix and be aware of their importance in developing a marketing strategy.

6 Explain how the marketing environment affects strategic market planning.

7 Understand the major components of a marketing plan.

8 Describe how market measurement and sales forecasting are used.

9 Distinguish between a marketing information system and marketing research.

10 Identify the major steps in the consumer buying decision process and the sets of factors that may influence this process.

Inside BUSINESS

At $62 a Pound, Single-Serve Coffee is Hot!

Nespresso knows that what makes single-serve coffee so hot is the ability to brew one very good cup of coffee in a very short time. Owned by the Swiss food giant Nestlé, Nespresso focuses on convenience and quality when it markets machines and coffee capsules to consumers and businesses. Now its annual sales of $3 billion are growing at a rate of nearly 20 percent per year as the company introduces dozens of new coffeemakers and compatible capsules for consumers, small businesses, and corporate use.

Although Nespresso's machines and capsules are especially popular in Europe, where they were first introduced, the firm also targets coffee lovers in other countries where the "coffee culture" is strong. Customers view single-serve coffee or espresso as an affordable luxury, whether the economy is up or down. Nespresso makes it easy to reorder replacement capsules online, by phone, or in one of 300 branded boutiques in 50 countries. For the convenience of premeasured, premium coffee in their choice of flavors and strengths, customers pay about 55 cents per capsule. This works out to about $62 per pound, and earns Nespresso a healthy profit margin from every cup.

As the single-serve coffee market heats up, Nespresso faces an increasingly competitive marketing environment. For example, Vermont's Green Mountain Coffee Roasters holds a sizable share of the U.S. market, thanks to its fast-selling Keurig coffee machines and individual K-Cup portions. In addition to marketing a variety of flavors under its own brand, Green Mountain makes K-Cups prefilled with Starbucks, Dunkin' Donuts, and Newman's Own coffees.

The competitive stakes are particularly high because Nespresso's capsules don't work in Keurig machines, and K-Cups don't work in Nespresso machines. This is generally the case for other brands, as well. So when customers buy a single-serve coffeemaker, they're also making a choice about the replacement capsules they will buy in the future. As a result, Nespresso's marketers aren't just selling a machine—they're vying for the opportunity to sell each customer thousands of coffee, tea, and cocoa capsules at a sizable profit, year after year after year.[1]

FYI
Did You Know?

Nespresso has sold more than 100 million single-serve coffee capsules since being founded in 1986.

Numerous organizations, like Nepresso, use marketing efforts to provide customer satisfaction and value. Understanding customers' needs, such as "what's cool," is crucial to provide customer satisfaction. Although marketing encompasses a diverse set of decisions and activities, marketing always begins and ends with the customer. The American Marketing Association defines **marketing** as "The activity, set of institutions, and processes for creating, communicating, delivering, and exchanging offerings that have value for customers, clients, partners, and society at large."[2] The marketing process involves eight major functions and numerous related activities (see Table 12.1). All of these are essential if the marketing process is to be effective.

In this chapter, we examine marketing activities that add value to products. We trace the evolution of the marketing concept and describe how organizations practice it. Next, our focus shifts to market classifications and marketing strategy. We analyze the four elements of a marketing mix and discuss uncontrollable factors in the marketing environment. Then we examine the major components of a marketing plan. We consider tools for strategic market planning, including market measurement, sales forecasts, marketing information systems, and marketing research. Last, we look at the forces that influence consumer and organizational buying behavior.

marketing the activity, set of institutions, and processes for creating, communicating, delivering, and exchanging offerings that have value for customers, clients, partners, and society at large

TABLE 12.1 Eight Major Marketing Functions

Exchange functions: All companies—manufacturers, wholesalers, and retailers—buy and sell to market their merchandise.

1. Buying includes obtaining raw materials to make products, knowing how much merchandise to keep on hand, and selecting suppliers.

2. Selling creates possession utility by transferring the title of a product from seller to customer.

Physical distribution functions: These functions involve the flow of goods from producers to customers. Transportation and storage provide time utility and place utility and require careful management of inventory.

3. Transporting involves selecting a mode of transport that provides an acceptable delivery schedule at an acceptable price.

4. Storing goods is often necessary to sell them at the best selling time.

Facilitating functions: These functions help the other functions to take place.

5. Financing helps at all stages of marketing. To buy raw materials, manufacturers often borrow from banks or receive credit from suppliers. Wholesalers may be financed by manufacturers, and retailers may receive financing from the wholesaler or manufacturer. Finally, retailers often provide financing to customers.

6. Standardization sets uniform specifications for products or services. Grading classifies products by size and quality, usually through a sorting process. Together, standardization and grading facilitate production, transportation, storage, and selling.

7. Risk taking—even though competent management and insurance can minimize risks—is a constant reality of marketing because of such losses as bad-debt expense, obsolescence of products, theft by employees, and product-liability lawsuits.

8. Gathering market information is necessary for making all marketing decisions.

 Understand the meaning of *marketing* and the importance of management of customer relationships.

MANAGING CUSTOMER RELATIONSHIPS

Marketing relationships with customers are the lifeblood of all businesses. Maintaining positive relationships with customers is an important goal for marketers. The term **relationship marketing** refers to "marketing decisions and activities focused on achieving long-term, satisfying relationships with customers." Relationship marketing continually deepens the buyer's trust in the company, which, as the customer's loyalty grows, increases a company's understanding of the customer's needs and desires. Successful marketers respond to customers' needs and strive to continually increase value to buyers over time. Eventually, this interaction becomes a solid relationship that allows for cooperation and mutual trust. The Internet has expanded and improved relationship marketing options for many firms by making targeted communication faster, cheaper, and easier. New digital technologies allow firms to connect to consumers and have a dialogue with them in real-time. This not only improves the speed at which firms can innovate, but it gives consumers a feeling that they are being listened to. Some firms specialize in cultivating this relationship. Sparks and Honey, for example, is a trend-spotting agency started by advertising holding company Omnicom Group. Sparks and Honey seeks to take advantage of the technological forces that are remaking the advertising industry through utilizing social media, Twitter, and YouTube to identify and market the products that consumers currently like and want.[3]

To build long-term customer relationships, marketers are increasingly turning to marketing research and information technology. **Customer relationship management (CRM)** focuses on using information about customers to create marketing strategies that develop and sustain desirable customer relationships. By increasing customer value over time, organizations try to retain and increase long-term profitability through customer loyalty. Because CRM is such an important part of creating and building customer loyalty, many companies offer high-tech products aimed at helping firms to identify good customers and to manage relations with them over the long-term. The accessibility of technology has contributed to a more even playing field for firms of all

Who do customers want? Like many other organizations, airline companies spend a considerable amount of money on marketing programs to develop and maintain long-term relationships with their customers—especially the valuable ones. Sometimes it's more profitable to retain these customers by offering them big rewards than attracting new customers who may never develop the same loyalty.

© SUSAN VAN ETTEN

Ethical
SUCCESS OR FAILURE?

The Customer Is Always Right—Or Not

Is the customer *always* right? When customers return a broken product to Kohler, which makes kitchen and bathroom fixtures, the company nearly always offers a replacement, to maintain good customer relations. Still, "there are times you've got to say 'no,'" explains a Kohler warranty expert, such as when a product is undamaged or has been abused. Entrepreneur Lauren Thorp, who owns the e-commerce company Umba Box, says, "While the customer is 'always' right, sometimes you just have to fire a customer." When Thorp has tried everything to resolve a complaint and realizes that the customer will be dissatisfied no matter what, she returns her attention to the rest of her customers, who she says are "the reason for my success."

What about customers who hurt other customers? On Black Friday, at the start of the Christmas gift-buying season, some customers waiting for bargains have started fights or broken store fixtures. What about customers who abuse marketers' policies? Costco traditionally offered a money-back guarantee on everything. A few years ago, however, the retailer noticed that some customers were returning older televisions, receiving refunds, and then buying newer models at lower prices. To stop these practices, Costco now offers a 90-day return policy on electronics and invites customers to call a toll-free hotline for technical assistance.

Sources: Based on information in Leslie Bradshaw, "Lauren Thorp on Taking the Plunge," *Forbes*, March 6, 2012, www.forbes.com; "Warranty Success Stories," *Warranty Week*, March 1, 2012, www.warrantyweek.com; Laarni A. Ragaza, "Costco Laptops and Desktops for the Holidays," *PC Magazine*, November 19, 2010, www.pcmag.com; Nick Carbone, "Black and Blue Friday," *Time*, November 26, 2011, www.time.com; www.costco.com.

---

sizes. Software and programs such as Batchbook and Mailchimp allow even very small companies to manage customers and maintain consistent communication with them.[4]

Managing customer relationships requires identifying patterns of buying behavior and using this information to focus on the most promising and profitable customers. Companies must be sensitive to customers' requirements and desires and establish communication to build customers' trust and loyalty. In some instances, it may be more profitable for a company to focus on satisfying a valuable existing customer than to attempt to attract a new one who may never develop the same level of loyalty. This involves determining how much the customer will spend over his or her lifetime. The **customer lifetime value** (CLV) is a measure of a customer's worth (sales minus costs) to a business during one's lifetime.[5] However, there are also intangible benefits of retaining lifetime-value customers, such as their ability to provide feedback to a company and refer new customers of similar value. The amount of money a company is willing to spend to retain such customers is also a factor. In general, when marketers focus on customers chosen for their lifetime value, they earn higher profits in future periods than when they focus on customers selected for other reasons.[6] Thanks to technological innovations and improved research, it is a fairly straightforward task to calculate CLV these days. In fact there are many online calculators that companies can utilize, including one created by Harvard University.[7] Because the loss of a potential lifetime customer can result in lower profits, managing customer relationships has become a major focus of marketers.

relationship marketing establishing long-term, mutually satisfying buyer–seller relationships

customer relationship management (CRM) using information about customers to create marketing strategies that develop and sustain desirable customer relationships

customer lifetime value a measure of a customer's worth (sales minus costs) to a business over one's lifetime

utility the ability of a good or service to satisfy a human need

UTILITY: THE VALUE ADDED BY MARKETING

 ② Explain how marketing adds value by creating several forms of utility.

As defined in Chapter 8, **utility** is the ability of a good or service to satisfy a human need. The latest iPad, Nike Zoom running shoes, or Mercedes Benz luxury car all satisfy human needs. Thus, each possesses utility. There are four kinds of utility.

Form utility is created by converting production inputs into finished products. Marketing efforts may influence form utility indirectly because the data gathered as part of marketing research are frequently used to determine the size, shape, and features of a product.

The three kinds of utility that are created directly by marketing are place, time, and possession utility. **Place utility** is created by making a product available at a location

form utility utility created by converting production inputs into finished products

place utility utility created by making a product available at a location where customers wish to purchase it

@GETTY IMAGES

Putting products at the customer's fingertips. Firms try to provide customers with products whenever and wherever they need them.

time utility utility created by making a product available when customers wish to purchase it

possession utility utility created by transferring title (or ownership) of a product to a buyer

Trace the development of the marketing concept and understand how it is implemented.

③

marketing concept a business philosophy that a firm should provide goods and services that satisfy customers' needs through a coordinated set of activities that allow the firm to achieve its objectives

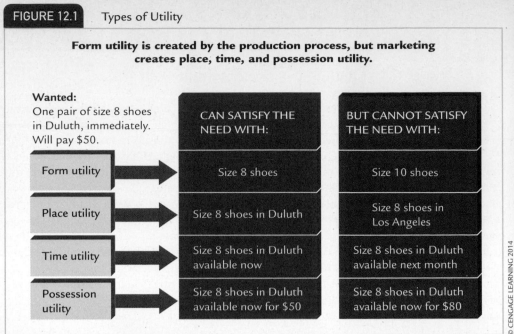

© CENGAGE LEARNING 2014

FIGURE 12.1 Types of Utility

Form utility is created by the production process, but marketing creates place, time, and possession utility.

Wanted: One pair of size 8 shoes in Duluth, immediately. Will pay $50.

	CAN SATISFY THE NEED WITH:	BUT CANNOT SATISFY THE NEED WITH:
Form utility	Size 8 shoes	Size 10 shoes
Place utility	Size 8 shoes in Duluth	Size 8 shoes in Los Angeles
Time utility	Size 8 shoes in Duluth available now	Size 8 shoes in Duluth available next month
Possession utility	Size 8 shoes in Duluth available now for $50	Size 8 shoes in Duluth available now for $80

where customers wish to purchase it. A pair of shoes is given place utility when it is shipped from a factory to a department store.

Time utility is created by making a product available when customers wish to purchase it. For example, Halloween costumes may be manufactured in April but not displayed until late September, when consumers start buying them. By storing the costumes until they are wanted, the manufacturer or retailer provides time utility.

Possession utility is created by transferring title (or ownership) of a product to a buyer. For a product as simple as a pair of shoes, ownership usually is transferred by means of a sales slip or receipt. For such products as automobiles and homes, the transfer of title is a more complex process. Along with the title to its products, the seller transfers the right to use that product to satisfy a need (see Figure 12.1).

Place, time, and possession utility have real value in terms of both money and convenience. This value is created and added to goods and services through a wide variety of marketing activities—from research indicating what customers want to product warranties ensuring that customers get what they pay for. Overall, these marketing activities account for about half of every dollar spent by consumers. When they are part of an integrated marketing program that delivers maximum utility to the customer, many would agree that they are worth the cost.

Place, time, and possession utility are only the most fundamental applications of marketing activities. In recent years, marketing activities have been influenced by a broad business philosophy known as the *marketing concept*.

THE MARKETING CONCEPT

The **marketing concept** is a business philosophy that a firm should provide goods and services that satisfy customers' needs through a coordinated set of activities that allow the firm to achieve its objectives. Thus, initially, the firm must communicate with potential customers to assess their product needs. Then, the firm must develop a good or service to satisfy those needs. Finally, the firm must continue to seek ways to provide customer satisfaction. This process is an application of the marketing concept or marketing orientation. After years of declining sales related to poor product quality and not satisfying customers' demands adequately, Captain D's fast-food seafood chain overhauled its marketing approach and implemented the marketing concept. Under new management, the restaurant spent years investing in future success and increased customer loyalty though improved products, improved service, hiring new management talent, and even new decor for its restaurants. The investments have paid off with increased sales and improved customer satisfaction and loyalty.[8]

Evolution of the Marketing Concept

From the start of the Industrial Revolution until the early 20th century, business effort was directed mainly toward the production of goods. Consumer demand for manufactured products was so great that manufacturers could almost bank on selling everything they produced. Business had a strong *production orientation*, in which emphasis was placed on increased output and production efficiency. Marketing was limited to taking orders and distributing finished goods.

Tell us what you *really* think. Customer satisfaction is a major element of the marketing concept. Many businesses attempt to measure customer satisfaction through surveys. Surveys can be conducted in a variety of ways: in-person, by mail or fax, or online. Online surveys have made it very inexpensive for firms to gather customer feedback.

In the 1920s, production caught up with and began to exceed demand. Now producers had to direct their efforts toward selling goods rather than just producing goods that consumers readily bought. This new *sales orientation* was characterized by increased advertising, enlarged sales forces, and, occasionally, high-pressure selling techniques. Manufacturers produced the goods they expected consumers to want, and marketing consisted primarily of promoting products through personal selling and advertising, taking orders, and delivering goods.

During the 1950s, however, businesspeople started to realize that even enormous advertising expenditures and the most thoroughly proven sales techniques were not enough. Something else was needed if products were to sell as well as expected. It was then that business managers recognized that they were not primarily producers or sellers but rather were in the business of satisfying customers' needs. Marketers realized that the best approach was to adopt a customer orientation—in other words, the organization had to first determine what customers need and then develop goods and services to fill those particular needs (see Table 12.2).

All functional areas—research and development, production, finance, human resources, and, of course, marketing—are viewed as playing a role in providing customer satisfaction.

Implementing the Marketing Concept

To implement the marketing concept, a firm first must obtain information about its present and potential customers. The firm must determine not only what customers' needs are but also how well these needs are being satisfied by products currently in the market—both its own products and those of competitors. It must ascertain how its products might be improved and what opinions customers have about the firm and its marketing efforts.

TABLE 12.2 Evolution of Customer Orientation

Business managers recognized that they were not primarily producers or sellers but were rather in the business of satisfying customers' wants.		
Production Orientation	**Sales Orientation**	**Customer Orientation**
Take orders	Increase advertising	Determine customer needs
Distribute goods	Enlarge sales force	Develop products to fill these needs
	Intensify sales techniques	Achieve the organization's goals

© CENGAGE LEARNING 2014

Think about the purchases you've made this year. From books and beverages to movies and music, you're part of the consumer market for many types of products. You want these products, and you also have the ability, authority, and money to buy them.

The firm then must use this information to pinpoint the specific needs and potential customers toward which it will direct its marketing activities and resources. Next, the firm must mobilize its marketing resources to (1) provide a product that will satisfy its customers, (2) price the product at a level that is acceptable to buyers and that will yield an acceptable profit, (3) promote the product so that potential customers will be aware of its existence and its ability to satisfy their needs, and (4) ensure that the product is distributed so that it is available to customers where and when needed.

Finally, the firm must again obtain marketing information—this time regarding the effectiveness of its efforts. Can the product be improved? Is it being promoted properly? Is it being distributed efficiently? Is the price too high or too low? The firm must be ready to modify any or all of its marketing activities based on information about its customers and competitors. Sears' Kenmore brand, for example, has become an iconic American brand of appliances. However, as the brand neared its 85-year mark, managers noticed that the aging brand was not in high demand among the younger generation. Sears decided to rebrand Kenmore, modernizing it with a focus on sophisticated, contemporary styling and increased energy efficiency. Sears launched a new advertising campaign that featured real customers and used the tagline "Kenmore, That's Genius." This campaign was launched through advertisements on television and online at Facebook, YouTube, and Twitter. Sears hopes that this rebranding will help Kenmore appeal to the younger generations as the market adjusts.[9]

MARKETS AND THEIR CLASSIFICATION

Understand what markets are and how they are classified.

A **market** is a group of individuals or organizations, or both, that need products in a given category and that have the ability, willingness, and authority to purchase such products. Markets are broadly classified as consumer or business-to-business markets because marketing efforts vary depending on the intended market. Marketers should understand the general characteristics of these two groups.

Consumer markets consist of purchasers and/or household members who intend to consume or benefit from the purchased products and who do not buy products to make profits. *Business-to-business markets,* also called *industrial markets,* are grouped broadly into producer, reseller, governmental, and institutional categories. These markets purchase specific kinds of products for use in making other products for resale or for day-to-day operations. *Producer markets* consist of individuals and business organizations that buy certain products to use in the manufacture of other products. *Reseller markets* consist of intermediaries such as wholesalers and retailers, who buy finished products and sell them for a profit. *Governmental markets* consist of federal, state, county, and local governments. They buy goods and services to maintain internal operations and to provide citizens with such products as highways, education, water, energy, and national defense. Governmental purchases total billions of dollars each year. *Institutional markets* include churches, not-for-profit private schools and hospitals, civic clubs, fraternities and sororities, charitable organizations, and foundations. Their goals are different from such typical business goals as profit, market share, or return on investment.

market a group of individuals or organizations, or both, that need products in a given category and that have the ability, willingness, and authority to purchase such products

DEVELOPING MARKETING STRATEGIES

A **marketing strategy** is a plan that will enable an organization to make the best use of its resources and advantages to meet its objectives. A marketing strategy consists of (1) the selection and analysis of a target market and (2) the creation and maintenance of an appropriate **marketing mix,** a combination of product, price, distribution, and promotion developed to satisfy a particular target market.

Target Market Selection and Evaluation

A **target market** is a group of individuals or organizations, or both, for which a firm develops and maintains a marketing mix suitable for the specific needs and preferences of that group. In selecting a target market, marketing managers examine potential markets for their possible effects on the firm's sales, costs, and profits. The managers attempt to determine whether the organization has the resources to produce a marketing mix that meets the needs of a particular target market and whether satisfying these needs is consistent with the firm's overall objectives. They also analyze the strengths and number of competitors already marketing to people in this target market. Marketing managers may define a target market as a sizable number of people or a relatively small group. The Nissan Cube, for example, has features designed to attract teenagers and early 20-somethings, and the company ensured that the Cube's promotion, price, and distribution were appropriate for this target market. Ideas for promoting this vehicle came straight from U.S. college students who competed to have their marketing strategy adopted by Nissan and are part of this vehicle's target market.[10] On the other hand, Rolls-Royce targets its automobiles toward a small, very exclusive market: wealthy people who want the ultimate in prestige in an automobile. Other companies target multiple markets with different products, prices, distribution systems, and promotion for each one. For example, some high-end clothing designers target multiple markets through developing affordable lines distributed at mass market retail outlets, such as Target, Kmart, and Walmart. This strategy allows designers to target customers with different needs and levels of disposable income. High-end fashion houses like Rodarte and Jason Wu, whose haute couture designs sell for thousands of dollars, offered designs at Target that retailed for much lower prices. Discount clothing retailer H&M has pursued a similar tactic, offering reasonably priced items by pricey designers, such as Karl Lagerfeld. Such collaborations between high and low end help to broadcast a designer's name among a large audience and provide positive publicity for both the retailers and the designer.[11]

Undifferentiated Approach A company that designs a single marketing mix and directs it at the entire market for a particular product is using an **undifferentiated approach** (see Figure 12.2). This approach assumes that individual customers in the target market for a specific kind of product have similar needs and that the organization therefore can satisfy most customers with a single marketing mix. This single marketing mix consists of one type of product with little or no variation, one price, one promotional program aimed at everyone, and one distribution system to reach all customers in the total market. Products that can be marketed successfully with the undifferentiated approach include staple food items, such as sugar and salt, and certain kinds of farm produce. An undifferentiated approach is useful in only a limited number of situations because for most product categories buyers have different needs. When customers' needs vary, a company should use the market segmentation approach.

COURTESY OF THE ADVERTISING ARCHIVES

Reaching the right market segments. The market for moisturizers is segmented based on gender. Some skin care products are aimed at women, while others, such as the LAB Series, are aimed at men. There are very few brands of moisturizers that are aimed at both men and women.

marketing strategy a plan that will enable an organization to make the best use of its resources and advantages to meet its objectives

marketing mix a combination of product, price, distribution, and promotion developed to satisfy a particular target market

target market a group of individuals or organizations, or both, for which a firm develops and maintains a marketing mix suitable for the specific needs and preferences of that group

undifferentiated approach directing a single marketing mix at the entire market for a particular product

FIGURE 12.2   General Approaches for Selecting Target Markets

The undifferentiated approach assumes that individual customers have similar needs and that most customers can be satisfied with a single marketing mix. When customers' needs vary, the market segmentation approach—either concentrated or differentiated—should be used.

UNDIFFERENTIATED APPROACH

CONCENTRATED MARKET SEGMENTATION APPROACH

DIFFERENTIATED MARKET SEGMENTATION APPROACH

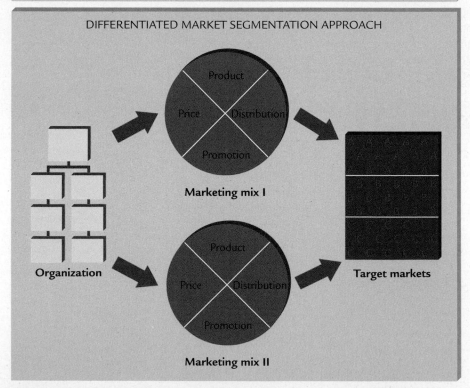

NOTE: The letters in each target market represent potential customers. Customers that have the same letters have similar characteristics and similar product needs.

Source: William M. Pride and O. C. Ferrell, *Marketing: Concepts and Strategies*, 17th ed. (Mason, OH: South-Western/Cengage Learning, 2014). Adapted with permission.

Market Segmentation Approach A firm that is marketing 40-foot yachts would not direct its marketing effort toward every person in the total boat market. Some might want a sailboat or a canoe. Others might want a speedboat or an outboard-powered fishing boat. Still others might be looking for something resembling a small ocean liner. Marketing efforts directed toward such boat buyers would be wasted.

Instead, the firm would direct its attention toward a particular portion, or segment, of the total market for boats. A **market segment** is a group of individuals or organizations within a market that shares one or more common characteristics. The process of dividing a market into segments is called **market segmentation**. As shown in Figure 12.2, there are two types of market segmentation approaches: concentrated and differentiated. When an organization uses *concentrated* market segmentation, a single marketing mix is directed at a single market segment. If *differentiated* market segmentation is used, multiple marketing mixes are focused on multiple market segments.

In our boat example, one common characteristic, or *basis*, for segmentation might be "end use of a boat." The firm would be interested primarily in the market segment whose uses for a boat could lead to the purchase of a 40-foot yacht. Another basis for segmentation might be income, still another might be geographic location. Each of these variables can affect the type of boat an individual might purchase. When choosing a basis for segmentation, it is important to select a characteristic that relates to differences in people's needs for a product. The yacht producer, for example, would not use religion to segment the boat market because people's needs for boats do not vary based on religion.

Marketers use a wide variety of segmentation bases. Bases most commonly applied to consumer markets are shown in Table 12.3. Each may be used as a single basis for market segmentation or in combination with other bases. OfficeMax, for example, is typically considered to be in a not-so-dazzling industry with a very broad definition for its target market (people and businesses that need office supplies). Therefore, the company recently decided to completely reposition itself. Driven by new research on consumers' shopping experiences and expectations, OfficeMax launched a national campaign called "Life Is Beautiful, Work Can Be Too," which featured stylish new private-label product

COURTESY OF THE ADVERTISING ARCHIVES; © J GROUP PHOTO

Two pens, two different concentrated targeting strategies. Both Mont Blanc pens, which are expensive, and Bic pens, which are not, are marketed using a concentrated targeting strategy. Each one is aimed at a different market segment. They do not compete for the same customers. Which do you buy and why?

market segment a group of individuals or organizations within a market that share one or more common characteristics

market segmentation the process of dividing a market into segments and directing a marketing mix at a particular segment or segments rather than at the total market

TABLE 12.3	Common Bases of Market Segmentation		
Demographic	**Psychographic**	**Geographic**	**Behavioristic**
Age	Personality attributes	Region	Volume usage
Gender	Motives	Urban, suburban, rural	End use
Race	Lifestyles	Market density	Benefit expectations
Ethnicity		Climate	Brand loyalty
Income		Terrain	Price sensitivity
Education		City size	
Occupation		County size	
Family size		State size	
Family life cycle			
Religion			
Social class			

Source: William M. Pride and O. C. Ferrell, *Marketing: Concepts and Strategies,* 17th ed. (Mason, OH: South-Western/Cengage Learning, 2014). Adapted with permission.

lines and a spiced-up catalog. OfficeMax has made a huge effort to separate itself from other office supply stores by further defining its target market based on research data that women are responsible for over 85 percent of office purchases.[12]

Identify the four elements of the marketing mix and be aware of their importance in developing a marketing strategy.

⑤

Creating a Marketing Mix

A business firm controls four important elements of marketing that it combines in a way that reaches the firm's target market. These are the *product* itself, the *price* of the product, the means chosen for its *distribution*, and the *promotion* of the product. When combined, these four elements form a marketing mix (see Figure 12.3). Marketers for Toyota's Scion brand automobiles developed a marketing mix to target consumers who are young and hip. Scion aims much of its marketing efforts at the 18 to 34 demographic. Around 75% of Scion purchasers are new to the Scion brand. Many Scion customers are buying a car for the first time. Scion's most recent advertising campaign, called iQ Therefore I Am, surrounded the release of the new Scion model, the iQ, and included a variety of online content, such as racy videos, an interactive car brochure to highlight features of the vehicle, and even an online museum of underground cultural movements. Also included in the Scion iQ marketing mix is a test drive program in major cities around the country and collaborative events with artists to underscore Scion's affiliation with arts and music.[13]

A firm can vary its marketing mix by changing any one or more of these ingredients. Thus, a firm may use one marketing mix to reach one target market and a second, somewhat different, marketing mix to reach another target market. For example, most automakers produce several different types and models of vehicles and aim them at different market segments based on the potential customers' age, income, and other factors.

The *product* ingredient of the marketing mix includes decisions about the product's design, brand name, packaging, warranties, and the like. When McDonald's decides on brand names, package designs, sizes of orders, flavors of sauces, and recipes, these choices are all part of the product ingredient.

The *pricing* ingredient is concerned with both base prices and discounts of various kinds. Pricing decisions are intended to achieve particular goals, such as to maximize profit or even to make room for new models. The rebates offered by automobile manufacturers are a pricing strategy developed to boost low auto sales. Product and pricing are discussed in detail in Chapter 13.

The *distribution* ingredient involves not only transportation and storage but also the selection of intermediaries. How many levels of intermediaries should be used

FIGURE 12.3   The Marketing Mix and the Marketing Environment

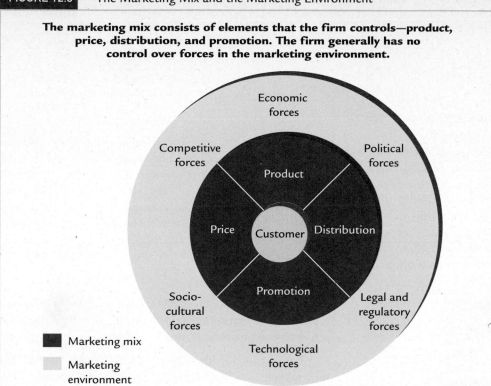

The marketing mix consists of elements that the firm controls—product, price, distribution, and promotion. The firm generally has no control over forces in the marketing environment.

Economic forces

Competitive forces

Political forces

Product

Price — Customer — Distribution

Promotion

Socio-cultural forces

Legal and regulatory forces

Technological forces

■ Marketing mix

■ Marketing environment

Source: William M. Pride and O. C. Ferrell, *Marketing: Concepts and Strategies,* 17th ed. (Mason, OH: South-Western/ Cengage Learning, 2014). Adapted with permission.

in the distribution of a particular product? Should the product be distributed as widely as possible or should distribution be restricted to a few specialized outlets in each area? Video rental retailers have had to make numerous decisions regarding distribution. Currently, Redbox, owned by Coinstar, has 24 percent of the video rental market share, Dish Network Corporation, who recently took over Blockbuster, has 14 percent, and Netflix has 5 percent.[14] Fifteen years ago, almost all videos were distributed through brick-and-mortar stores. Distribution decisions and activities are discussed in more detail in Chapter 14.

The *promotion* ingredient focuses on providing information to target markets. The major forms of promotion are advertising, personal selling, sales promotion, and public relations. These four forms are discussed in Chapter 15.

These ingredients of the marketing mix are controllable elements. A firm can vary each of them to suit its organizational goals, marketing goals, and target markets. As we extend our discussion of marketing strategy, we will see that the marketing environment includes a number of *uncontrollable* elements.

Developing the right marketing mix. Firms have little control over the marketing environment. However, they *can* control the marketing mixes for their products—that is, the nature of the products themselves and how they are priced, distributed, and promoted. The maker of All Small & Mighty has developed a specific marketing mix for the detergent. Who do you think the product is aimed at?

MARKETING STRATEGY AND THE MARKETING ENVIRONMENT

6 Explain how the marketing environment affects strategic market planning.

The marketing mix consists of elements that a firm controls and uses to reach its target market. In addition, the firm has control over such organizational resources as finances and information. These resources may be used to accomplish marketing goals,

Online Videos Add Vitality to Marketing Mix

Online videos can add vitality to any marketing mix, helping companies engage, educate, and persuade customers. Whether a video shows a product demonstration or a customer testimonial, it can capture attention, build buzz, and highlight key features and benefits. Ford, for example, posts videos on YouTube, Facebook, and its Web site to spotlight its vehicles' innovative features. Blendtec demonstrates the power of its blenders through its popular "Will it blend?" videos. Viewers can't take their eyes off the screen as the CEO puts an iPod and other unlikely objects into a blender, turns it on, and the item is pulverized in just a few seconds.

Sources: Andrew Hampp, "Super Bowl Buzz Wears Off the Viral Video Chart," *Advertising Age*, March 3, 2011, www.adage.com; Erik Bratt, "Social Media: Adding Video to Your Digital Marketing Plan," *San Diego Union-Tribune*, February 6, 2011, www.signonsandiego.com; David Kiley, "Ford Kicks Off Social-Media Push for Explorer," *Advertising Age*, February 9, 2011, www.adage.com www.youtube.com/user/Honda#p/c/1F2F88164C76470D/11/5gmzECyp7nA.

too. However, the firm's marketing activities are also affected by a number of external—and generally uncontrollable—forces. As Figure 12.3 illustrates, the following forces make up the external *marketing environment:*

- *Economic forces*—the effects of economic conditions on customers' ability and willingness to buy
- *Sociocultural forces*—influences in a society and its culture that result in changes in attitudes, beliefs, norms, customs, and lifestyles
- *Political forces*—influences that arise through the actions of elected and appointed officials
- *Competitive forces*—the actions of competitors, who are in the process of implementing their own marketing plans
- *Legal and regulatory forces*—laws that protect consumers and competition and government regulations that affect marketing
- *Technological forces*—technological changes that can create new marketing opportunities or cause products to become obsolete almost overnight

These forces influence decisions about marketing-mix ingredients. Changes in the environment can have a major impact on existing marketing strategies. In addition, changes in environmental forces may lead to abrupt shifts in customers' needs. Consider the effect technological forces have had on printed newspapers: Years ago, very few people would have predicted that consumers would one day have no need for their daily newspaper. However, that day has come. Consumers want today's news now and are able to access it online at any time.

Understand the major components of a marketing plan.

DEVELOPING A MARKETING PLAN

A **marketing plan** is a written document that specifies an organization's resources, objectives, marketing strategy, and implementation and control efforts to be used in marketing a specific product or product group. The marketing plan describes the firm's current position or situation, establishes marketing objectives for the product, and specifies how the organization will attempt to achieve these objectives. Marketing plans vary with respect to the time period involved. Short-range plans are for one year or less, medium-range plans cover from over one year to five years, and long-range plans cover periods of more than five years.

Although time-consuming, developing a clear, well-written marketing plan is important. The plan will be used for communication among the firm's employees. It covers the assignment of responsibilities, tasks, and schedules for implementation. It specifies how resources are to be allocated to achieve marketing objectives. It helps marketing managers monitor and evaluate the performance of the marketing strategy. Because the forces of the marketing environment are subject to change, marketing plans have to be updated frequently. For instance, in spite of overtaking Burger King as the second-largest hamburger chain in the United States, Wendy's has undertaken a mission

marketing plan a written document that specifies an organization's resources, objectives, strategy, and implementation and control efforts to be used in marketing a specific product or product group

TABLE 12.4   Components of the Marketing Plan

Plan Component	Component Summary	Highlights
Executive summary	One- to two-page synopsis of the entire marketing plan	
Environmental analysis	Information about the company's current situation with respect to the marketing environment	1. Assessment of marketing environment factors 2. Assessment of target market(s) 3. Assessment of current marketing objectives and performance
SWOT analysis	Assessment of the organization's strengths, weaknesses, opportunities, and threats	1. Strengths 2. Weaknesses 3. Opportunities 4. Threats
Marketing objectives	Specification of the firm's marketing objectives	Qualitative measures of what is to be accomplished
Marketing strategies	Outline of how the firm will achieve its objectives	1. Target market(s) 2. Marketing mix
Marketing implementation	Outline of how the firm will implement its marketing strategies	1. Marketing organization 2. Activities and responsibilities 3. Implementation timetable
Evaluation and control	Explanation of how the firm will measure and evaluate the results of the implemented plan	1. Performance standards 2. Financial controls 3. Monitoring procedures (audits)

Source: William M. Pride and O. C. Ferrell, *Marketing: Concepts and Strategies,* 17th ed. (Mason, OH: South-Western/Cengage Learning, 2014). Reprinted with permission.

to remake its marketing plan and revamp its image in order to gain market share and increase revenues. Wendy's announced plans to reposition the restaurant chain as a more high-end competitor as it struggles to gain ground on McDonald's, which brings in roughly four times as much annual revenue as either Wendy's or Burger King. McDonald's has experienced success through releasing healthier and more upscale menu items and Wendy's hopes to make similar changes that respond to the marketing environment and consumer preferences. To helm this revamp of its marketing plan, the chain hired a new chief of marketing, a former Procter & Gamble executive.[15]

The major components of a marketing plan are shown in Table 12.4.

MARKET MEASUREMENT AND SALES FORECASTING

 8 Describe how market measurement and sales forecasting are used.

Measuring the sales potential of specific types of market segments helps an organization to make some important decisions, such as the feasibility of entering new segments. The organization can also decide how best to allocate its marketing resources and activities among market segments in which it is already active. All such estimates should identify the relevant time frame. As with marketing plans, these estimates may be short-range plans, covering periods of less than one year; medium-range plans, covering one to five years; or long-range plans, covering more than five years. The estimates should also define the geographic boundaries of the forecast. For example, sales potential can be estimated for a city, county, state, or group of nations. Finally, analysts should indicate whether their estimates are for a specific product item, a product line, or an entire product category.

A **sales forecast** is an estimate of the amount of a product that an organization expects to sell during a certain period of time based on a specified level of marketing effort. Managers in different divisions of an organization rely on sales forecasts when they purchase raw materials, schedule production, secure financial resources, consider

sales forecast an estimate of the amount of a product that an organization expects to sell during a certain period of time based on a specified level of marketing effort

marketing information system a system for managing marketing information that is gathered continually from internal and external sources

marketing research the process of systematically gathering, recording, and analyzing data concerning a particular marketing problem

Distinguish between a marketing information system and marketing research. ⑨

plant or equipment purchases, hire personnel, and plan inventory levels. Because the accuracy of a sales forecast is so important, organizations often use several forecasting methods, including executive judgments, surveys of buyers or sales personnel, time-series analyses, correlation analyses, and market tests. The specific methods used depend on the costs involved, type of product, characteristics of the market, time span of the forecast, purposes for which the forecast is used, stability of historical sales data, availability of the required information, and expertise and experience of forecasters. A number of companies utilize sales forecasting software to help with predictions. IBM, for example, uses economic and demographic data from the U.S. Census Bureau combined with sales forecasting software to make its complicated short-term and long-term sales forecasting predictions.[16]

MARKETING INFORMATION

The availability and use of accurate and timely information are critical to make effective marketing decisions. A wealth of marketing information is obtainable. There are two general ways to obtain it: through a marketing information system and through marketing research.

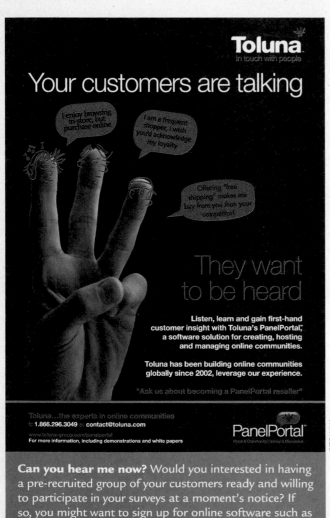

Can you hear me now? Would you interested in having a pre-recruited group of your customers ready and willing to participate in your surveys at a moment's notice? If so, you might want to sign up for online software such as PortalPanel, produced the marketing research company Toluna. Keep in mind that good marketing research can be invaluable. But bad marketing research can be disastrous if it leads to the wrong decisions.

Marketing Information Systems

A **marketing information system** is a system for managing marketing information that is gathered continually from internal and external sources. Most of these systems are computer based because of the amount of data the system must accept, store, sort, and retrieve. *Continual* collection of data is essential if the system is to incorporate the most up-to-date information.

In concept, the operation of a marketing information system is simple. Data from a variety of sources are fed into the system. Data from *internal* sources include sales figures, product and marketing costs, inventory levels, and activities of the sales force. Data from *external* sources relate to the organization's suppliers, intermediaries, and customers; competitors' marketing activities; and economic conditions. All these data are stored and processed within the marketing information system. Its output is a flow of information in the form that is most useful for making marketing decisions. This information might include daily sales reports by territory and product, forecasts of sales or buying trends, and reports on changes in market share for the major brands in a specific industry. Both the information outputs and their form depend on the requirements of the personnel in the organization. No matter what the industry and its needs; marketers must be well versed in the latest technology in order to maximize the efficiency of MIS. Companies like Adobe, IBM, Google, Acxiom, and Merkle all offer high-tech tools to help marketers collect and process information, manage marketing initiatives, and generate reports.[17]

Marketing Research

Marketing research is the process of systematically gathering, recording, and analyzing data concerning a particular marketing problem. Thus, marketing research is used in specific situations to obtain information not otherwise available to decision makers. Marketing research is an important step of the marketing process because it involves collecting and analyzing data on what consumers want and need; their consumption habits; trends; and anticipating changes in the marketing environment. For example, a recent study of car buyers suggests that there is a correlation between political party affiliation and automobile model preference. The study demonstrates that Democrats prefer smaller more affordable cars, like the Honda Civic, while Republicans opt for larger, pricier models, such as the Ford Mustang. Such information can help marketers to determine target markets, marketing mixes, and other factors.[18]

Table 12.5 outlines a six-step procedure for conducting marketing research. This procedure is particularly well-suited to test new products, determine various characteristics of consumer markets, and evaluate promotional activities. Food-processing companies, such as Kraft Foods and Kellogg's, use a variety of marketing research methods to avoid costly mistakes in introducing the wrong products, not to mention introducing products in the wrong way or at the wrong time. They have been particularly interested in using marketing research to learn more about the African-American and Hispanic markets. Understanding of the food preferences, loyalties, and purchase motivators of these groups enables companies to serve them better.

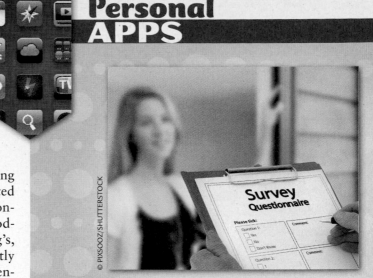

Personal APPS

If you're ever asked to participate in a survey, remember that by responding, you're helping a marketer understand your needs and do a better job of giving you what you want. Your answers and comments can make a real difference.

TABLE 12.5	The Six Steps of Marketing Research
1. Define the problem.	In this step, the problem is stated clearly and accurately to determine what issues are involved in the research, what questions to ask, and what types of solutions are needed. This is a crucial step that should not be rushed.
2. Make a preliminary investigation.	The objective of preliminary investigation is to develop both a sharper definition of the problem and a set of tentative answers. The tentative answers are developed by examining internal information and published data and by talking with persons who have some experience with the problem. These answers will be tested by further research.
3. Plan the research.	At this stage, researchers know what facts are needed to resolve the identified problem and what facts are available. They make plans on how to gather needed but missing data.
4. Gather factual information.	Once the basic research plan has been completed, the needed information can be collected by mail, telephone, or personal interviews; by observation; or from commercial or government data sources. The choice depends on the plan and the available sources of information.
5. Interpret the information.	Facts by themselves do not always provide a sound solution to a marketing problem. They must be interpreted and analyzed to determine the choices available to management.
6. Reach a conclusion.	Sometimes the conclusion or recommendation becomes obvious when the facts are interpreted. However, in other cases, reaching a conclusion may not be so easy because of gaps in the information or intangible factors that are difficult to evaluate. If and when the evidence is less than complete, it is important to say so.

Going for SUCCESS

Using Neuroscience for Marketing Research

Marketers are beginning to use neuroscience—studying the brain and the nervous system—to learn more about the inner workings of consumer behavior. For example, when Frito-Lay wanted to dig deeper into consumers' reactions to its Cheetos, it hired a company to measure the brain waves of consumers as they snacked on the cheese puffs. The research showed that consumers enjoyed the messy orange cheese crumbs that Cheetos leave all over their fingers. Based on this research, Frito-Lay has used messy-fingers visuals in its ads and Facebook messages.

The Nabisco cookie brand Chips Ahoy! used insights from neuroscience when redesigning a package. Previous research showed that consumers placed a high value on resealable packaging, so researchers tested different ways to highlight the new design's resealability tab. They also tested package images and, based on response, chose an image featuring chocolate chips "flying" off the cookie.

Magazines are also using neuroscience for marketing research. *New Scientist* magazine measured the brainwaves of readers to understand how they react to cover art. Putting the results into practice, one issue with a specially-designed cover enjoyed 12 percent higher newsstand sales compared with the previous year. Also, *Time* magazine is using neuroscience to gauge consumer involvement in the ads that accompany its iPad apps. Although neuroscience won't replace traditional research techniques, it's another tool for collecting data for marketing decisions.

Sources: Based on information in Carmen Nobel, "What Neuroscience Tells Us About Consumer Desire, *Harvard Business School Working Knowledge*, March 26, 2012, http://hbswk.hbs.edu; "Marketing on the Brain," *Marketing*, November 2, 2011, p. 24; Scott Young, "Neuroscience Explains the Emotional Buy," *Brand Packaging*, July 2011, p. 16; Deena Higgs Nenad, "Emotional Marketing," *Editor & Publisher*, January 2011, p. 7.

Using Technology to Gather and Analyze Marketing Information

Technology is making information for marketing decisions increasingly accessible. The ability of firms to track the purchase behaviors of customers electronically and to better determine what they want is changing the nature of marketing. The integration of telecommunications with computing technology provides marketers with access to accurate information not only about customers and competitors but also about industry forecasts and business trends.

A *database* is a collection of information arranged for easy access and retrieval. Using databases, marketers tap into internal sales reports, newspaper articles, company news releases, government economic reports, bibliographies, and more. Many marketers use commercial databases, such as LEXIS-NEXIS, to obtain useful information for marketing decisions. The Internet has made available a great deal of information that used to be obtainable only for a high price from companies specializing in producing commercial databases. However, sometimes firms still need to access the broad and in-depth information contained in large commercial databases, such as Dun & Bradstreet's Global Commercial database, with 205 million business records.[19]

Information provided by a single firm on household demographics, purchases, television viewing behavior, and responses to promotions such as coupons and free samples is called *single-source data*. For example, Behavior Scan, offered by Information Resources, Inc., screens about 60,000 households in 26 U.S. markets. This single-source information service monitors household televisions and records the programs and commercials viewed. When buyers from these households shop in stores equipped with scanning registers, they present Hotline cards (similar to credit cards) to cashiers. This enables each customer's identification to be coded electronically so that the firm can track each product purchased and store the information in a database.

Online information services offer subscribers access to e-mail, Web sites, downloadable files, news, databases, and research materials. By subscribing to mailing lists,

TABLE 12.6 Sources of Secondary Information

Government sources	
Economic census	www.census.gov/econ/census07/
Export.gov—country and industry market research	www.export.gov/mrktresearch/index.asp
National Technical Information Services	www.ntis.gov/
Strategis—Canadian trade	http://strategis.ic.gc.ca/engdoc/main.html
Trade associations and shows	
American Society of Association Executives	www.asaecenter.org/
Directory of Associations	www.marketingsource.com/associations/
Trade Show News Network	www.tsnn.com/
Magazines, newspapers, video, and audio news programming	
Blinkx	www.blinkx.com/
FindArticles.com	http://findarticles.com/p/articles/tn_bus/?tag=trunk
Google Video Search	http://video.google.com/
Media Jumpstation	www.directcontactpr.com/jumpstation/
Google News Directory	www.google.com/Top/News/
Yahoo! Video Search	http://video.search.yahoo.com/
Corporate information	
Annual Report Service	www.annualreportservice.com/
Bitpipe	www.bitpipe.com/
Business Wire—press releases	www.businesswire.com/
Hoover's Online	www.hoovers.com/
Open Directory Project	http://dmoz.org/
PR Newswire—press releases	www.prnewswire.com/

Source: Adapted from "Data Collection: Low-Cost Secondary Research," KnowThis.com, www.knowthis.com/principles-of-marketing-tutorials/data-collection-low-cost-secondary-research/ (accessed January 6, 2012).

marketers can receive electronic newsletters and participate in online discussions with other network users. This ability to communicate online with customers, suppliers, and employees improves the capability of a firm's marketing information system and helps the company track its customers' changing desires and buying habits.

The *Internet* has evolved as a powerful communication medium, linking customers and companies around the world. Growth in Internet use has given rise to an entire industry that makes marketing information easily accessible to both companies and customers. Among the many Web pages useful for marketing research are the home pages of Nielsen marketing research and *Advertising Age*. While most Web pages are open to all Internet users, some companies, such as U.S. West and Turner Broadcasting System, also maintain internal Web pages, called *intranets,* which allow employees to access internal data and facilitate communication among departments.

Table 12.6 contains a variety of sources of secondary information, which is existing information that has been gathered by other organizations. Many of these sources are available through Web sites. As can be seen in Table 12.6, secondary information can be obtained from a variety of sources including government sources, trade associations, general publications and news sources, and corporate information.

A tool that has recently gained popularity as a means of marketing research is social media. Many companies have begun using various social media outlets to solicit

A buyer goes through some or all of these steps when making a purchase.

POSSIBLE INFLUENCES ON THE DECISION PROCESS

Situational influences	Psychological influences	Social influences
• Physical surroundings	• Perception	• Family
• Social surroundings	• Motives	• Roles
• Time	• Learning	• Peer groups
• Purchase reason	• Attitudes	• Social class
• Buyer's mood and condition	• Personality	• Culture and subcultures
	• Lifestyles	

CONSUMER BUYING DECISION PROCESS

Recognize problem → Search for information → Evaluate alternatives → Purchase → Evaluate after purchase

Source: William M. Pride and O. C. Ferrell, *Marketing: Concepts and Strategies*, 17th ed. (Mason, OH: South-Western/Cengage Learning, 2014). Adapted with permission.

feedback from customers on the company's existing or upcoming products. However, a risk of being involved in social media is exposing your company to unwanted or negative information from the general public. Nevertheless, these comments need to be regarded as useful and viable information from a marketing research standpoint. Customer complaints are opportunities for improvement; if handled correctly, they can be an invaluable source of data.

Identify the major steps in the consumer buying decision process and the sets of factors that may influence this process.

TYPES OF BUYING BEHAVIOR

Buying behavior may be defined as the decisions and actions of people involved in buying and using products.[20] **Consumer buying behavior** refers to the purchasing of products for personal or household use, not for business purposes. **Business buying behavior** is the purchasing of products by producers, resellers, governmental units, and institutions. Because a firm's success depends greatly on buyers' reactions to a particular marketing strategy, it is important to understand buying behavior. Marketing managers are better able to predict customer responses to marketing strategies and to develop a satisfying marketing mix if they are aware of the factors that affect buying behavior.

Consumer Buying Behavior

buying behavior the decisions and actions of people involved in buying and using products

consumer buying behavior the purchasing of products for personal or household use, not for business purposes

business buying behavior the purchasing of products by producers, resellers, governmental units, and institutions

Consumers' buying behaviors differ when they buy different types of products. For frequently purchased low-cost items, a consumer uses routine response behavior involving very little search or decision-making effort. The buyer uses limited decision making for purchases made occasionally or when more information is needed about an unknown product in a well-known product category. When buying an unfamiliar, expensive item or one that is seldom purchased, the consumer engages in extended decision making. Increasingly, consumers are empowered by information found on the Internet. It allows consumers to compare prices and features and read reviews about products before they even step in a store. In situations where they would have relied on salespeople in the past, consumers feel informed enough by online research to make purchasing decisions themselves. In this new environment, marketing and customer service are increasingly important.[21]

A person deciding on a purchase goes through some or all of the steps shown in Figure 12.4. First, the consumer acknowledges that a problem exists. A problem is usually the lack of a product or service that is desired or needed. Then, the buyer looks for information, which may include brand names, product characteristics, warranties, and other features. Next, the buyer weighs the various alternatives he or she has discovered and then finally makes a choice and acquires the item. In the after-purchase stage, the consumer evaluates the suitability of the product. This judgment will affect future purchases. As Figure 12.4 shows, the buying process is influenced by situational factors (physical surroundings, social surroundings, time, purchase reason, and buyer's mood and condition), psychological factors (perception, motives, learning, attitudes, personality, and lifestyle), and social factors (family, roles, reference groups, online social networks, social class, culture, and subculture).

Consumer buying behavior is also affected by the ability to buy or one's buying power, which is largely determined by income. As every taxpayer knows, not all income is available for spending. For this reason, marketers consider income in three different ways. **Personal income** is the income an individual receives from all sources *less* the Social Security taxes the individual must pay. **Disposable income** is personal income *less* all additional personal taxes. These taxes include income, estate, gift, and property taxes levied by local, state, and federal governments. Historically, about 3 percent of disposable income in the United States is saved, but that percentage has gone up to about 4.5 percent of disposable income in recent years.[22] **Discretionary income** is disposable income *less* savings and expenditures on food, clothing, and housing. Discretionary income is of particular interest to marketers because consumers have the most choice in spending it. Consumers use their discretionary income to purchase items ranging from automobiles and vacations to movies and pet food.

How many trees can your toilet paper save in just 4 weeks?

TAKE THE 4 WEEK TEST DRIVE

If we all used Scott Naturals® paper products, we'd save over 2 million trees. That's because Scott Naturals® are the world's first line of hybrid™ paper products. They combine the green benefits of recycled fiber with the quality you need – so only our forests will notice the difference. That's Green Done Right™.

Start your test drive at ScottBrand.com/Naturals

SCOTT BATHROOM TISSUE

Recognizing a problem. Problem recognition is the first stage of the consumer buying decision process. This ad makes consumers aware of an environmental problem they might not have known they were contributing to. The ad then provides more information about the solution—which is to buy Scott Naturals bathroom tissue.

Business Buying Behavior

Business buyers consider a product's quality, its price, and the service provided by suppliers. Business buyers are usually better informed than consumers about products and generally buy in larger quantities. In a business, a committee or a group of people, rather than just one person, often decides on purchases. Committee members must consider the organization's objectives, purchasing policies, resources, and personnel. Business buying occurs through description, inspection, sampling, or negotiation. Because business transactions can be more complicated and orders tend to be larger, information on buyers and sellers is important. Credit rating agency Experian recently announced a partnership with the online marketplace Fedbid®, which will provide business and government buyers with access to sellers' and contractors' credit histories so that they can make more informed decisions regarding their supply chains and smart purchasing. This partnership should help save business buyers money while reducing fraud and wasted spending.[23]

personal income the income an individual receives from all sources *less* the Social Security taxes the individual must pay

disposable income personal income *less* all additional personal taxes

discretionary income disposable income *less* savings and expenditures on food, clothing, and housing

Nespresso

As the market for single-serve coffee heats up, Nespresso and its rivals are competing to start long-term customer relationships and profit from the lifetime value of each buyer's purchases. Selling a coffeemaker is the first step in serving a customer who will buy compatible coffee capsules for years to come. The Nespresso Club (now 10 million members strong) is the company's way of keeping these customers satisfied and loyal. Members can consult with coffee experts, request service for their machines, order capsules for express delivery, and get early word about new products.

Nespresso, like Green Mountain Coffee Roasters and others in the industry, has patented its machines and cap-

sules to protect against unauthorized copying. However, these patents will soon start to expire, which means the company must be ready with new and improved products to meet customers' needs and maintain market share.

Questions

1. How do Nespresso's coffeemakers and capsules provide short-term and long-term utility for customers?
2. Of the six forces in the marketing environment, which do you think have the most effect on Nespresso's ability to start and continue long-term customer relationships?

SUMMARY

Looking for Success?
Get Flashcards, Quizzes, Games, Crosswords, and more @ www.cengagebrain.com.

 Understand the meaning of *marketing* and the importance of management of customer relationships.

Marketing is an organizational function and a set of processes for creating, communicating, and delivering value to customers and for managing customer relationships in ways that benefit the organization and its stakeholders. Maintaining positive relationships with customers is crucial. Relationship marketing is establishing long-term, mutually satisfying buyer–seller relationships. Customer relationship management uses information about customers to create marketing strategies that develop and sustain desirable customer relationships. Managing customer relationships requires identifying patterns of buying behavior and focusing on the most profitable customers. Customer lifetime value is a combination of purchase frequency, average value of purchases, and brand-switching patterns over the entire span of a customer's relationship with the company.

 Explain how marketing adds value by creating several forms of utility.

Marketing adds value in the form of utility or the power of a product or service to satisfy a need. It creates place utility by

making products available where customers want them, time utility by making products available when customers want them, and possession utility by transferring the ownership of products to buyers.

 Trace the development of the marketing concept and understand how it is implemented.

From the Industrial Revolution until the early 20th century, businesspeople focused on the production of goods; from the 1920s to the 1950s, the emphasis moved to the selling of goods. During the 1950s, however, businesspeople recognized that their enterprises involved not only producing and selling products but also satisfying customers' needs. They began to implement the marketing concept, a business philosophy that involves the entire organization in the dual processes of meeting the customers' needs and achieving the organization's goals.

Implementation of the marketing concept begins and ends with customers—first to determine what customers' needs are and then to evaluate how well the firm is meeting these needs.

 Understand what markets are and how they are classified.

A market consists of people with needs, the ability to buy, and the desire and authority to purchase. Markets are classified as consumer and industrial (producer, reseller, governmental, and institutional) markets.

Identify the four elements of the marketing mix and be aware of their importance in developing a marketing strategy.

A marketing strategy is a plan for the best use of an organization's resources to meet its objectives. Developing a marketing strategy involves selecting and analyzing a target market and creating and maintaining a marketing mix that will satisfy the target market. A target market is chosen through either the undifferentiated approach or the market segmentation approach. A market segment is a group of individuals or organizations within a market that have similar characteristics and needs. Businesses that use an undifferentiated approach design a single marketing mix and direct it at the entire market for a particular product. The market segmentation approach directs a marketing mix at a segment of a market.

The four elements of a firm's marketing mix are product, price, distribution, and promotion. The product ingredient includes decisions about the product's design, brand name, packaging, and warranties. The pricing ingredient is concerned with both base prices and various types of discounts. Distribution involves not only transportation and storage but also the selection of intermediaries. Promotion focuses on providing information to target markets. The elements of the marketing mix can be varied to suit broad organizational goals, marketing objectives, and target markets.

 Explain how the marketing environment affects strategic market planning.

To achieve a firm's marketing objectives, marketing-mix strategies must begin with an assessment of the marketing environment, which, in turn, will influence decisions about marketing-mix ingredients. Marketing activities are affected by a number of external forces that make up the marketing environment. These forces include economic forces, sociocultural forces, political forces, competitive forces, legal and regulatory forces, and technological forces. Economic forces affect customers' ability and willingness to buy. Sociocultural forces are societal and cultural factors, such as attitudes, beliefs, and lifestyles, that affect customers' buying choices. Political forces and legal and regulatory forces influence marketing planning through laws that protect consumers and regulate competition. Competitive forces are the actions of competitors who are implementing their own marketing plans. Technological forces can create new marketing opportunities or quickly cause a product to become obsolete.

 Understand the major components of a marketing plan.

A marketing plan is a written document that specifies an organization's resources, objectives, strategy, and implementation and control efforts to be used in marketing a specific product or product group. The marketing plan describes a firm's current position, establishes marketing objectives, and specifies the methods the organization will use to achieve these objectives. Marketing plans can be short-range plans, covering one year or less; medium-range plans, covering two to five years; or long-range plans, covering periods of more than five years.

 Describe how market measurement and sales forecasting are used.

Market measurement and sales forecasting are used to estimate sales potential and predict product sales in specific market segments.

 Distinguish between a marketing information system and marketing research.

Strategies are monitored and evaluated through marketing research and the marketing information system that stores and processes internal and external data in a form that aids marketing decision making. A marketing information system is a system for managing marketing information that is gathered continually from internal and external sources. Marketing research is the process of systematically gathering, recording, and analyzing data concerning a particular marketing problem. It is an intermittent rather than a continual source of marketing information. Technology is making information for marketing decisions more accessible. Electronic communication tools can be very useful for accumulating accurate information with minimal customer interaction. Information technologies that are changing the way marketers obtain and use information are databases, online information services, and the Internet. Some companies are using social media to obtain feedback from customers.

 Identify the major steps in the consumer buying decision process and the sets of factors that may influence this process.

Buying behavior consists of the decisions and actions of people involved in buying and using products. Consumer buying behavior refers to the purchase of products for personal or household use. Organizational buying behavior is the purchase of products by producers, resellers, governments, and institutions. Understanding buying behavior helps marketers to predict how buyers will respond to marketing strategies. The consumer buying decision process consists of five steps, that is, recognizing the problem, searching for information, evaluating alternatives, purchasing, and evaluating after purchase. Factors affecting the consumer buying decision process fall into three categories: situational influences, psychological influences, and social influences.

KEY TERMS

You should now be able to define and give an example relevant to each of the following terms:

marketing (331)
relationship marketing (332)
customer relationship management (CRM) (332)
customer lifetime value (333)
utility (333)
form utility (333)
place utility (333)

time utility (334)
possession utility (334)
marketing concept (334)
market (336)
marketing strategy (337)
marketing mix (337)
target market (337)

undifferentiated approach (337)
market segment (339)
market segmentation (339)
marketing plan (342)
sales forecast (343)
marketing information system (344)

marketing research (344)
buying behavior (348)
consumer buying behavior (348)
business buying behavior (348)
personal income (349)
disposable income (349)
discretionary income (349)

REVIEW QUESTIONS

1. How, specifically, does marketing create place, time, and possession utility?
2. What is relationship marketing?
3. How is a marketing-oriented firm different from a production-oriented firm or a sales-oriented firm?
4. What are the major requirements for a group of individuals and organizations to be a market? How does a consumer market differ from a business-to-business market?
5. What are the major components of a marketing strategy?
6. What is the purpose of market segmentation? What is the relationship between market segmentation and the selection of target markets?
7. What are the four elements of the marketing mix? In what sense are they "controllable"?
8. Describe the forces in the marketing environment that affect an organization's marketing decisions.

9. What is a marketing plan, and what are its major components?
10. What major issues should be specified before conducting a sales forecast?
11. What is the difference between a marketing information system and a marketing research project? How might the two be related?
12. What new information technologies are changing the ways that marketers keep track of business trends and customers?
13. What are the major sources of secondary information?
14. Why do marketers need to understand buying behavior?
15. How are personal income, disposable income, and discretionary income related? Which is the best indicator of consumer purchasing power?

DISCUSSION QUESTIONS

1. What problems might face a company that focuses mainly on its most profitable customers?
2. In what way is each of the following a marketing activity?
   a. The provision of sufficient parking space for customers at a suburban shopping mall.
   b. The purchase by a clothing store of seven dozen sweaters in assorted sizes and colors.
   c. The inclusion of a longer and more comprehensive warranty on an automobile.

3. How might adoption of the marketing concept benefit a firm? How might it benefit the firm's customers?
4. Is marketing information as important to small firms as it is to larger firms? Explain.
5. How does the marketing environment affect a firm's marketing strategy?

Video Case 12.1

Raleigh Wheels Out Steel Bicycle Marketing

From its 19th-century roots as a British bicycle company, Raleigh has developed a worldwide reputation for marketing sturdy, comfortable, steel-frame bicycles. The firm, named for the street in Nottingham, England, where it was originally located, was a trend-setter in designing and manufacturing bicycles. When Raleigh introduced steel-frame bicycles equipped with three-speed gear hubs in 1903, it revolutionized the industry and set off a never-ending race to improve the product's technology. In the pre-auto era, its bicycles became a two-wheeled status symbol for British consumers, and the brand maintained its cachet for decades. Although Raleigh's chopper-style bicycles were hugely popular in the 1970s, international competition and changing consumer tastes have taken a toll during the past few decades.

Now Raleigh markets a wide variety of bicycles to consumers in Europe, Canada, and the United States. Its U.S. division, based in Kent, Washington, has been researching new bicycles for contemporary consumers and developing models that are lighter, faster, and better. Inspired by the European lifestyle and tradition of getting around on bicycles, and its long history in the business, Raleigh is looking to reinvigorate sales and capture a larger share of the $6 billion U.S. bicycle market.

Raleigh's U.S. marketers have been observing the "messenger market," customers who ride bicycles through downtown streets to deliver documents and small packages to businesses and individuals. They have also noted that many everyday bicycle riders dress casually, in T-shirts and jeans, rather than in special racing outfits designed for speed. Targeting consumers who enjoy riding bicycles as a lifestyle, Raleigh's marketers are focusing on this segment's specific needs and preferences as they develop, price, promote, and distribute new models.

In recent years, Raleigh's marketers have stepped up the practice of bringing demonstration fleets to public places where potential buyers can hop on one of the company's bicycles and pedal for a few minutes. The idea is to allow consumers who enjoy bicycling to actually experience the fun feeling of riding a Raleigh. The marketers are also fanning out to visit bicycle races and meet bicyclists in cities and towns across America, encouraging discussions about Raleigh and about bicycling in general and seeking feedback about particular Raleigh products.

Listening to consumers, Raleigh's marketers recognized that many had misperceptions about the weight of steel-frame bicycles. Although steel can be quite heavy, Raleigh's bicycles are solid yet light, nimble, and easy to steer. Those who have been on bicycles with steel frames praise the quality of the ride, saying that steel "has a soul," according to market research.

To stay in touch with its target market, Raleigh is increasingly active in social media. It has several thousand fans who visit its Facebook page to see the latest product concepts and post their own photos and comments about Raleigh bicycles. It also uses Twitter to keep customers informed and answer questions about its bicycles and upcoming demonstration events. The company's main blog communicates the latest news about everything from frame design and new bike colors under consideration to product awards and racing activities. It has a separate blog about both the fun and the challenges of commuting on bicycle, a topic in which its customers are intensely interested because so many do exactly that. By listening to customers and showing that it understands the daily life of its target market, Raleigh is wheeling toward higher sales in a highly competitive marketplace.[24]

Questions for Discussion

1. Is Raleigh using the marketing concept? Explain.
2. What type of approach does Raleigh use to select target markets?
3. Of the four categories of segmentation variables, which is most important to Raleigh's segmentation strategy, and why?

Case 12.2

PepsiCo Tailors Tastes to Tantalize Tastebuds of Target Markets

PepsiCo, the world's leading snack marketer, aims to gobble up more market share through careful targeting and creative marketing. Most of PepsiCo's sales come from North and South America, where it has traditionally been a strong competitor. Among its ever-expanding pantry of brands, 19 are already billion-dollar businesses, including Pepsi-Cola, Diet Pepsi, and Mountain Dew soft drinks; Lay's, Doritos, and Tostitos chips; Lipton teas; Tropicana fruit drinks; Gatorade sports drinks; Quaker foods; and Aquafina bottled waters.

The company faces aggressive competition from Coca-Cola and Draft Foods, both of which are making marketing waves in the Americas, across Europe, and in Asia. It must also deal with a variety of local brands that, in some cases, have large and loyal customer bases. Therefore, PepsiCo's marketers constantly research customers' needs and study the influence of environmental forces so that they can develop the right marketing mix for the right market.

One global trend that PepsiCo's marketers have identified is increased interest in healthier eating. Several years ago, the U.K. government mounted a campaign warning consumers of the dangers of high salt intake and urged them to change their diets. In response, PepsiCo slashed the amount of sodium in its locally popular Walkers snacks by 25 percent. With U.S. health experts also calling for lower salt in processed foods, PepsiCo is now reducing the level of salt in many other snacks worldwide. It is also lightening up on fats and sugar and making nutrition labeling more prominent so that consumers can make educated choices. "What we want to do with our 'fun for you' products is to make them the healthiest 'fun for you' products," says the CEO.

Another trend that PepsiCo's marketers noticed is sharply higher use of digital media among teenagers and young adults, a large and lucrative target market for snacks and beverages. As a result, PepsiCo has stepped up its use of the Internet, blogs, Twitter, Facebook, and YouTube to communicate with and influence these consumers. Its Dewmocracy campaigns, for example, invite customers to vote online for their favorite new Mountain Dew flavors. It has also run contests asking customers to create and submit homemade television commercials for Doritos chips. After posting the finalists online for public viewing and voting, PepsiCo airs the winning advertisements during the Super Bowl, giving winners cash prizes and their 30 seconds of fame.

PepsiCo's recent Refresh Project, one of its more unusual marketing efforts, combined digital marketing with social responsibility.

During the year-long program, PepsiCo invited consumers to apply online for grants to make a difference in their community. Every month, the public voted on which grants they thought were most deserving of funding. In all, PepsiCo awarded nearly $20 million in grants, got tens of thousands of customers interested in the project, and earned positive publicity for its good works. Of course, PepsiCo hoped that customers would also notice and respond to its social responsibility when they were making buying decisions about snacks and beverages.

These days, PepsiCo is keeping up a steady stream of new product introductions, based on marketing research that helps it understand the preferences of customers in each country. For example, catering to Russian palates, it offers Lay's chips flavored with red caviar. In China, its Cao Ben Le drinks feature herb flavors that local customers favor. In Japan, knowing that its customers look forward to seasonal variety, the company has launched a series of limited-edition soft drinks such as Pepsi Baobab (with the tang of African fruit flavor). In India, it markets Nimbooz by 7Up, its unique twist on a traditional lemon drink. What will PepsiCo do next in its quest to satisfy its global customer base?[25]

Questions

1. What is PepsiCo's approach to target marketing?
2. How are forces in the marketing environment affecting PepsiCo's marketing strategy?
3. Which influences on consumer buying behavior should PepsiCo pay particular attention to, and why?

Building Skills for Career Success

① SOCIAL MEDIA EXERCISE

Building customer relationships through effective marketing

Comcast, the cable and communications provider, was one of the first companies to use Twitter for customer service. Frank Eliason was the first director of digital care and the first to develop ComcastCares on Twitter. Essentially the Comcast team scans Twitter for people complaining about service and then contacts them to see if they can help. This has changed the entire culture of the organization, as well as prompted other companies to use Twitter for customer service. Visit the site at Comcastcares on Twitter (do a search in a search engine like Bing or Google).

1. After reviewing Comcastcares on Twitter, do you think that this helps with customer service? Why or why not?
2. Do you see other applications for Twitter for a communications giant like Comcast?

② JOURNALING FOR SUCCESS

Discovery statement: This chapter emphasized the importance of keeping the customer at the core of every marketing decision.

Assignment

1. Think about the businesses from which you have purchased goods or services. Select the organization that you believe has adopted the marketing concept. Discuss the reasons why you believe that this company has adopted the marketing concept.
2. Describe the marketing mix this company has created for the brand that you purchase from this company.
3. Which two companies are the strongest competitors of this organization? Explain why.
4. Besides competition, which environmental forces have the greatest impact on this company for which you are a customer?
5. Calculate your customer lifetime value to this company. After recording your customer lifetime value, describe how you calculated it.

③ DEVELOPING CRITICAL-THINKING SKILLS

Market segmentation is the process of breaking down a larger target market into smaller segments. One common base of market segmentation is demographics. Demographics for the consumer market, which consists of individuals and household members who buy goods for their own use, include criteria such as age, gender, race, religion, income, family size, occupation, education, social class, and marital status. Liz Claiborne, Inc., retailer of women's apparel, uses demographics to target a market it calls *Liz Lady*. The company knows Liz Lady's age, income range, professional status, and family status, and it uses this profile to make marketing decisions.

Assignment

1. Identify a company that markets to the consumer.
2. Identify the company's major product.
3. Determine the demographics of one of the company's markets.
   a. From the list that follows, choose the demographics that apply to this market. (Remember that the demographics chosen must relate to the interest, need, and ability of the customer to purchase the product.)
   b. Briefly describe each demographic characteristic.

Consumer	Market	Description
Age		
Gender		
Race		
Ethnicity		
Income		
Occupation		
Family size		
Education		
Religion		
Homeowner		
Marital status		
Social class		

4. Summarize your findings in a statement that describes the target market for the company's product.

④ BUILDING TEAM SKILLS

Review the text definitions of *market* and *target market*. Markets can be classified as consumer or industrial. Buyer behavior consists of the decisions and actions of those involved in buying and using products or services. By examining aspects of a company's products, you usually can determine the company's target market and the characteristics important to members of that target market.

Assignment

1. Working in teams of three to five, identify a company and its major products.
2. List and discuss characteristics that customers may find important. These factors may include price, quality, brand name, variety of services, salespeople, customer service, special offers, promotional campaign, packaging, convenience of use, convenience of purchase, location, guarantees, store/office decor, and payment terms.

3. Write a description of the company's primary customer (target market).

⑤ RESEARCHING DIFFERENT CAREERS

Before interviewing for a job, you should learn all you can about the company. With this information, you will be prepared to ask meaningful questions about the firm during the interview, and the interviewer no doubt will be impressed with your knowledge of the business and your interest in it. To find out about a company, you can conduct some market research.

Assignment

1. Choose at least two local companies for which you might like to work.
2. Contact your local Chamber of Commerce. (The Chamber of Commerce collects information about local businesses, and most of its services are free.) Ask for information about the companies.
3. Call the Better Business Bureau in your community and ask if there are any complaints against the companies.
4. Prepare a report summarizing your findings.

ENDNOTES

1. Based on information in Haig Simonian and Louise Lucas, "Starbucks Takes Coffee Wars to Nespresso," *Financial Times,* March 5, 2012, www.ft.com; Dermot Doherty, "Nestle Forecasts 2012 Earnings as Sales Beat Estimates," *Bloomberg BusinessWeek,* February 16, 2012, www.businessweek.com; Joshua Levine, "Pod of Gold," *Time,* March 7, 2011, www.time.com; www.nespresso.com; Tom Mulier, "Nespresso Will Survive 'Plethora' of Knock-Offs, Inventor Says," *Bloomberg BusinessWeek,* January 30, 2011, www.businessweek.com.
2. "Definition of Marketing," American Marketing Association, www.marketingpower.com/AboutAMA/Pages/DefinitionofMarketing.aspx, accessed March 19, 2012.
3. Stuart Elliot, "Spotting the Trends, Before They Break Out," *New York Times,* March 11, 2012, www.nytimes.com/2012/03/12/business/media/spotting-the-trends-before-they-break-out-advertising.html.
4. Eilene Zimmerman, "A Small Business Made to Seem Bigger," *New York Times,* March 2, 2011, www.nytimes.com/2011/03/03/business/smallbusiness/03sbiz.html, accessed March 19, 2012; "Batchbook: Your Social CRM," BatchBlue, http://batchblue.com/socialcrm/, accessed March 19, 2012.
5. V. Kumar, *Customer Lifetime Value* (Hanover, MA: now Publishers, 2008), 5.
6. Rajkumar Venkatesan and V. Kumar, "A Customer Lifetime Value Framework for Customer Selection and Resource Selection and Resource Allocation Strategy," *Journal of Marketing 68* (October 2004), 106–125.
7. Dennis Price, "How Much is a Customer REALLY Worth?" *Insider Retailing,* March 18, 2012, www.insideretailing.com.au/IR/IRNews/How-much-is-a-customer-REALLY-worth--4454.aspx; Customer Lifetime Value Calculator, http://hbsp.harvard.edu/multimedia/flashtools/cltv/index.html, accessed March 19, 2012.
8. Press release, "Captain D's Continues Brand Rejuvenation—Generates an 8.5 Percent Same-Store Sales Increase in Q1," March 28, 2012, www.prweb.com/releases/Ds/Q1/prweb9338053.htm.
9. Sears, press release, January 19, 2010, http://searsmedia.com/tools/press/content.jsp?id=2010-01-19-0005167078; Elaine Wong, "Why Sears Is Rebranding Kenmore," *Adweek,* February 24, 2010, http://adweek.com/news/advertising-branding/why-sears-rebranding-kenmore-107086.
10. "Nissan Announces U.S. Pricing on 2010 Cube," *PR Newswire,* January 28, 2010, http://prnewswire.com/news-releases/nissan-announces-us-pricing-on-2010-cube-70613072.html.
11. "Marni for H&M; Versace for H&M," *Vogue,* January 23, 2012, www.vogue.co.uk/news/2011/06/21/versace-collaborates-with-handm, accessed April 6, 2012; Karen

Talley, "Target to Test In-Store Boutiques," *Wall Street Journal,* January 12, 2012, http://online.wsj.com/article/SB10001424052970204409004577156691858884500.html, accessed April 6, 2012.
12. Paula Andruss, "New OfficeMax Catalog Courts Women Consumers," *Deliver Magazine,* June 29, 2009, www.delivermagazine.com/2009/06/new-officemax-catalog-courts-women-consumers/.
13. Elizabeth Olson, "Scion Aims Online Videos at Young Buyers," *New York Times,* March 4, 2012, www.nytimes.com/2012/03/05/business/media/scion-aims-online-videos-from-wry-to-racy-directly-at-young-buyers.html.
14. "DVD, Game & Video Rental in the US," IBISWorld, http://clients.ibisworld.com/industryus/majorcompanies.aspx?indid=1370 (accessed February 21, 2012).
15. Candace Choi, "Wendy's Takes No. 2 Spot from Burger King," *BusinessWeek,* March 19, 2012, www.businessweek.com/ap/2012-03/D9TJLUH00.htm; Tim Feran, "Wendy's Hires New Chief of Marketing," *The Columbus Dispatch,* March 29, 2012, www.dispatch.com/content/stories/business/2012/03/29/wendys-hires-new-chief-of-marketing.html.
16. Press Release, "IBM Forecasts Robust Gains in 2Q Home Furnishing Sales," Market Watch, April 6, 2012, www.marketwatch.com/story/ibm-forecasts-robust-gains-in-2q-home-furnishings-sales-2012-04-06.
17. David Cooperstein, "Why Marketers Have No Choice But to Adopt Marketing Technology," *Forbes,* April 3, 2012, www.forbes.com/sites/davidcooperstein/2012/04/03/why-marketers-have-no-choice-but-to-adopt-marketing-technology/.
18. Mary Chapman Party Affiliations in Car-Buying Choices: A Thorny Patch of Consumer Analysis," *New York Times,* March 30, 2012, http://wheels.blogs.nytimes.com/2012/03/30/party-affiliations-in-car-buying-choices-a-thorny-patch-of-consumer-analysis/.
19. "D&B Enhances Portfolio Risk Manager for DNBi with Greater Analytics Capabilities," Market Watch, March 21, 2012, www.marketwatch.com/story/db-enhances-portfolio-risk-manager-for-dnbi-with-deeper-analytic-capabilities-2012-03-21.
20. William M. Pride and O. C. Ferrell, *Foundations of Marketing,* 4th ed. (Mason, OH: South-Western/Cengage Learning, 2011), 128.
21. Christine Crandell, "The New Corporate Power Couple," *Forbes,* February 25, 2012, www.forbes.com/sites/christinecrandell/2012/02/25/the-new-corporate-power-couple/.

22. Press release, "Personal Income and Outlays, January 2012," U.S. Department of Commerce, Bureau of Economic Analysis, www.bea.gov/newsreleases/national/pi/pinewsrelease.htm

23. Press release, "Experian and FedBid Provide Government and Commercial Buyers with Indicators of Seller Business Health," Market Watch, March 29, 2012, www.marketwatch.com/story/experian-and-fedbid-provide-government-and-commercial-buyers-with-indicators-of-seller-business-health-2012-03-29.

24. "BRAINy Awards Honor Individuals," *Bicycle Retailer and Industry News*, April 15, 2010, www.bicycleretailer.com/news/newsDetail/3961.html; Francis Lawell, "Raleigh: Cycling to Success?" *Business Review (UK)* (February 2009): pp. 16ff; "Industry Overview 2008," *National Bicycle Dealers Association*, http://nbda.com/articles/industry-overview-2008-pg34.htm; www.raleigh.co.uk/; www.raleighusa.com.

25. Based on information from Betsy McKay, "PepsiCo Develops 'Designer Salt' to Chip Away at Sodium Intake," *Wall Street Journal*, March 22, 2010, http://online.wsj.com/article/SB10001424052748704534904575131602283791566.html; Natalie Zmuda and Emily Bryson York, "Cause Effect: Brands Rush to Save World One Deed at a Time," *Advertising Age*, March 1, 2010, 1, http://adage.com/article/news/effect-brands-rush-save-world-deed-a-time/142338/; Natalie Zmuda, "Pass or Fail, Pepsi's Refresh Will Be Case for Marketing Textbooks," *Advertising Age*, February 8, 2010, http://adage.com/article/digital/marketing-pepsi-refresh-case-marketing-textbooks/141973/; Sarah Theodore and Elizabeth Fuhrman, "The Best Packages of 2009," *Beverage Industry*, December 9, 2009, http://bevindustry.com/articles/the-best-packages-of-2009; http://pepsico.com accessed February 21, 2012.

Social Media, e-Business, and Accounting

PART 6

In this part of *Business*, we focus on social media, e-Business, and accounting. In Chapter 16, we discuss how business firms use social media to build relationships with customers and promote their products and services. We also investigate how companies use e-business to reduce expenses and increase sales and profits. Then in Chapter 17, we examine the role of management information and how accounting is used to improve managerial decisions.

16 Exploring Social Media and e-Business

LEARNING OBJECTIVES

Once you complete this chapter, you will be able to:

1 Examine why it is important for a business to use social media.

5 Explain the meaning of e-business.

2 Discuss how businesses use social media tools.

6 Understand the fundamental models of e-business.

3 Explain the business objectives for using social media.

7 Identify the factors that will affect the future of the Internet, social media, and e-business.

4 Describe how businesses develop a social media plan.

Inside BUSINESS

The Big Business of Angry Birds

A game that didn't exist until 2009 has rocketed its parent company into the big time with $100 million in annual revenue and millions of fans worldwide. Rovio Entertainment, based in Finland, created Angry Birds as a game application in which players use slingshots to send red birds hurtling toward green pigs. The company also started a Facebook page to spread the word and, a few months later, a blog to announce its news and connect with fans.

Within a year, 50 million people had downloaded Angry Birds to smartphones, iPads, and other electronic gadgets, playing either the free version (surrounded by ads) or paying to upgrade to premium versions. For less than the price of a latte, many players were happy to buy access to the game's highest levels. Before the game's third anniversary, the number of players had soared to 500 million, earning Rovio a healthy profit and a global fan base eager for more games and game-related merchandise.

To make the most of the game's popularity, Rovio developed a line of shirts and toys for sale through its e-business online store. Soon it was selling 1 million stuffed pigs and birds plus 1 million branded T-shirts every month through its Web site, along with seasonal items such as Halloween costumes. Then Rovio licensed its brand so that authorized products could be marketed through Amazon.com and other online businesses, as well as in traditional stores. Several times a year, Rovio released new Angry Birds games, some geared to seasonal events (such as the Chinese New Year) and some taking the birds-versus-pigs rivalry to new heights (outer space). Social media helped fuel the frenzy as players compared notes online about their triumphs and frustrations with the latest game variations.

Now, with nearly 1 billion downloads, Angry Birds has transformed the way Rovio makes money, allowing it to move beyond games into other goods and services. "We only care about two things, our fans and our brand," says the chief marketing officer, who views Angry Birds as an entertainment brand for movies, theme parks, and clothing, just like the Disney animated movie characters.[1]

FYI

Did You Know?

Rovio Entertainment, the parent company of Angry Birds, rings up more than $100 million every year from global sales of game-related goods and services.

For Rovio Entertainment, the company profiled in the Inside Business feature for this chapter, Angry Birds is big business! With nearly 1 billion downloads and $100 million in annual revenue from global sales of stuffed animals, T-shirts, and other game-related merchandise, Angry Birds and its parent company Rovio Entertainment provide a good example of how fast social media and e-business have developed and the degree to which they are changing the way people live their lives. Take a moment to think about how social media and technology affect your own life. In just a few short years, it has changed the way we communicate with each other, it has changed the way we meet people, and it has changed the way we shop. In this chapter, we explore how these trends affect both individuals and businesses.

We begin this chapter by examining why social media is important for both individuals and business firms. Next, we discuss how companies can use social media to build relationships with customers, the goals for social media usage, and the steps required to build a social media plan and measure the effectiveness of a firm's social media activities. In the last part of this chapter, we take a close look at how firms use technology to conduct business on the Internet and what growth opportunities and challenges affect both social media and e-businesses.

Examine why it is important for a business to use social media.

WHY IS SOCIAL MEDIA IMPORTANT?

If you are a "digital native" (anyone under the age of 32), you know exactly what social media is because you have grown up with technology and are very comfortable sharing information about yourself. If you are anyone else, social media seems like a strange (but exciting) phenomenon where millions of people freely share, create, vote, and connect with other people effortlessly using Internet-based technologies.

What Is Social Media and How Popular Is It?

Today, there are many definitions of social media because it is still developing and continually changing. For our purposes, **social media** represents the online interactions that allow people and businesses to communicate and share ideas, personal information, and information about products and services. Simply put: Social media is about people. It is about a culture of participation, meaning that people can now discuss, vote, create, connect, and advocate much easier than ever before. For

| FIGURE 16.1 | Timeline of Major Technology Events and Social Media |

Like computer technology, developments in social media have been not only rapid, they have also changed the way people connect.

TECHNOLOGY BREAKTHROUGH

Year	Technology Breakthrough
1966	• E-mail
1969	• Advanced Research Projects Agency Network (ARPANET), Compuserve
1979	• USENET
1986	• LISTSERV
1991	• AOL
1995	• Classmates.com; Yahoo
1996	• AOL instant messenger
1998	• MoveOn.org, Google
1999	• Napster, Blogger, Epinions, LiveJournal
2001	• Wikipedia, StumbleUpon
2002	• Friendster, Technorati
2003	• LinkedIn, Wordpress, MySpace, Hi5, Photobucket, Delicious
2004	• Gmail, Flickr, Facebook, Yelp, Digg, Orkut
2005	• YouTube, Mashable, Reddit, Bebo
2006	• Twitter, Ustream
2007	• Tumblr
2008	• Apple's App Store
2009	• Foursquare, Google Wave
2010	• Pinterest,
2011	• Google +
2012	• Facebook sells stock to the public
The Future	• Who knows what the next generation of social media will mean for both individuals and business?

© CENGAGE LEARNING 2014

social media the online interactions that allow people and businesses to communicate and share ideas, personal information, and information about products and services example, you can post your plans for a weekend trip on Facebook. Then you can share a travel itinerary and chronicle your trip through videos, photos, and ratings on Facebook. People can also use Twitter to raise awareness about bone-marrow donations in order to help a friend find a match. While it's hard to imagine, many popular social media sites like Facebook and Twitter were just created in the past decade (see Figure 16.1).

So how popular is social media? A recent Pew Internet Research study showed that more than two-thirds of online adults use some sort of social media platform like Facebook, LinkedIn, or Twitter. Most of them say staying in touch with family and friends is their primary reason for using social media and roughly half say that reconnecting with old friends is a major reason why they use social media. Other reasons like connecting with people who share interests, making new friends, and reading comments by public figures are less important.[2]

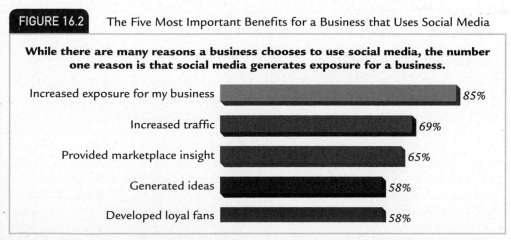

©YURI ARCURS/SHUTTERSTOCK

A new kind of family time. Today, technology has changed the way people communicate and share ideas, personal information, and information about products and services. In this photo, mom, dad, and the kids could be looking at pictures of relatives or reading movie reviews or sending an email to grandma—all social media activities.

Why Businesses Use Social Media

Social media has completely changed the business environment. Early on, companies saw potential in the sheer number of people using social media and that made using social media a top priority for many business firms. By using social media, companies could share information about their products and services and improve customer service. To date (and by the time you read this, the number will be higher), Facebook has not only one of the largest social networks with more than 850 million users, but also one of the "stickiest" Web sites, meaning that a lot of people spend a lot of time on Facebook.[3] As a result, many companies have flocked to build Facebook pages, develop contests, create Facebook ads, and find ways to get as many people as possible to "like" them on Facebook. Coca-Cola, for example, is one of the most effective marketers using Facebook, with more than 41 million likes to date.[4] For more information about why businesses use social media (and the benefits for a business), see Figure 16.2.

The fact that so many people are actively sharing information about themselves and their likes and dislikes online for all to see was a driving force behind many companies' attempts to develop a social media presence. Unlike social media, traditional marketing messages were top down—meaning that companies used television and magazine ads to promote their product to a large audience without any opportunity for feedback. Discussions about products were limited to consumers'

FIGURE 16.2 The Five Most Important Benefits for a Business that Uses Social Media

While there are many reasons a business chooses to use social media, the number one reason is that social media generates exposure for a business.

Increased exposure for my business	85%
Increased traffic	69%
Provided marketplace insight	65%
Generated ideas	58%
Developed loyal fans	58%

Source: Michael A. Stelzner, "2012 Social Media Marketing Industry Report," The SocialMediaExaminer.com Web site at www.socialmediaexaminer.com, accessed August 14, 2012.

Personal APPS

Although marketing may not be the first thing that comes to mind when you use social media, lots of companies want you to "like" them and spread the word about their products or services. Keep your eyes open for companies on social networking sites, and you just might grab a special deal.

immediate circle of friends and family. With social media, this is no longer the case. If a person has a bad experience with a product or service, they tend to post it on their blog or on Facebook, or tweet about it. A few years ago, Dell, Inc., experienced the wrath of a customer when blogger Jeff Jarvis posted a series of rants called "Dell Hell" after purchasing a Dell laptop. The post caught the attention of others who experienced similar problems; these consumers then proceeded to voice their own Dell Hell stories. As a result, more people knew about the company's mistakes than ever before. Jarvis continued to voice his experience with Dell's customer service department, which at the time was not very effective or responsive. After the story hit the mainstream press and their customer service ratings began to suffer, Dell finally developed a corporate initiative aimed at listening to customers and fixing its customer service problems.[5] Now Dell is considered a leader in monitoring social media and listening to customers. The bottom line: Because of social media, companies no longer have much control over what is said about their products or services, and many are not yet comfortable with the new roles set forth by a consumer-dominated culture.

 Discuss how businesses use social media tools.

SOCIAL MEDIA TOOLS FOR BUSINESS USE

For a business, part of what makes social media so challenging is the sheer number of ways to interact with other businesses and both existing and potential consumers. Companies are using social media because it allows the company to

- connect with customers;
- listen to its main stakeholders (including but not limited to customers);
- provide another means of customer service;
- develop content that is valuable to customers; and
- engage customers in product development and formulation.

Social content sites allow companies to create and share information about their products and services via blogs, videos, photos, and podcasts. For businesses selling to other businesses, social content sites can also include webinars and online informational promotional materials. For an overview of how businesses can use social media tools, take another look at Figure 16.2.

Business Use of Blogs

For businesses, blogs have become one of the most widely used tools for the effective use of social media. A **blog** is a Web site that allows a company to share information in order to increase customers' knowledge about its products and services, as well as to build trust. Once a story or information is posted, customers can provide feedback through comments, which is one of the most important ways of creating a conversation between business firms and consumers. Some experts believe that every company should have a blog that speaks to current and potential customers, not as customers, but as people.[6]

Blogs are effective at developing better relationships with customers, attracting new customers, telling stories about the company's products or services, and providing an active forum for testing new ideas. For example, Southwest Airlines' *Nuts about Southwest* blog (www.blogsouthwest.com) provides information about the company and allows customers to interact with company employees. By including information

social content sites allow companies to create and share information about their products and services

blog a Web site that allows a company to share information in order to not only increase the customer's knowledge about its products and services, but also to build trust about webinars and promotional materials, blogs are also effective for businesses that are selling to other businesses.

Photos, Videos, and Podcasts

In addition to blogs, another tool for social content is **media sharing sites**, which allow users to upload multimedia content including photos, videos, and podcasts. Before participating in media sharing, consider the following three factors.

- Who will create the photos, videos, and podcasts that will be used?
- How will the content be distributed to interested businesses and consumers?
- How much will it cost to create and distribute the material?

Today, photo sharing provides a method for companies to tell a compelling story about its products or services through postings on either the company's Web site or a social media site.

Videos have also gained popularity because of their inherent ability to tell stories. Entertainment companies, for example, now traditionally use YouTube as a way to showcase movie trailers. And Home Depot has also posted great do-it-yourself videos on its YouTube channel. Companies know that YouTube, Flickr, and others sites are useful because they are already recognized by other businesses and consumers as a source of both entertainment and information. YouTube is the largest video site and one of the largest general sites in the United States. YouTube is not only large (in terms of visitors), but the characteristics of its users are evenly split among different age groups and sexes.

Podcasts are digital audio or video files that people listen to or watch online on tablets, computers, MP3 players, or smartphones. Think of podcasts as radio shows that are distributed through various means (like iTunes) and not linked to a scheduled time period. The great thing about podcasts is that they are available for download at any time. Both National Public Radio (NPR) and the *New York Times* have used podcasts to share news and information.

Podcasts can be not only informative, but also inspirational. As the wife of a retired army sergeant and an army veteran herself, Victoria Parham knows what it is like to experience long separations, job instability, and single parenthood that come with the military lifestyle. Today she shares her experiences and solutions to everyday problems in a free twice-monthly podcast created to inspire, educate, and entertain military spouses.

Social Media Ratings

Social media enables shoppers to access opinions, recommendations, and referrals from others within and outside of their own social circles. This type of information is available via a social media site and can include reviews and ratings, as well as information on sales promotions programs like Groupon and LivingSocial. Both of these sites provide information about companies that offer deep discounts to customers that redeem an offer.

Sites for ratings and reviews are based on the idea that consumers trust the opinions of others when it comes to purchasing products and services. According to Nielsen Media Research, more than 70 percent of consumers said that they trust online consumer opinions.[7] This statistic was much higher when compared with the same type of research for traditional advertising. Based on the early work of Amazon and eBay, new sites have sprung up allowing consumers to rate local businesses or compare products and services. One of the most popular, Yelp, combines customer ratings with social networking and is now the largest local review directory on the Web.

Social Games

Social games are another area of growth in social media. A **social game** is "a multiplayer, competitive, goal-oriented activity with defined rules of engagement and online connectivity among a community of players."[8] One of the most important aspects of social media is entertainment and games like Angry Birds and FarmVille serve that purpose. Indeed, research shows that the "gamification" of social media is a huge trend because people like the competition, social status, and rewards that they can earn through social gaming.[9] For businesses that create games, it can be very profitable. As mentioned in the Inside Business

media sharing sites allow users to upload multimedia content including photos, videos, and podcasts

podcasts digital audio or video files that people listen to or watch online on tablets, computers, MP3 players, or smartphones

social game a multiplayer, competitive, goal-oriented activity with defined rules of engagement and online connectivity among a community of players feature for this chapter, Rovio Entertainment, the parent company of Angry Birds, rings up more than $100 million every year from global sales of game-related goods and services. While some businesses elect to create their own games, others choose to place advertising into a game. For example, the search engine Bing placed ads within the Facebook game FarmVille and gained several hundred thousand Facebook fans as a result.[10]

Explain the business objectives for using social media.

3

ACHIEVING BUSINESS OBJECTIVES THROUGH SOCIAL MEDIA

Although the popularity of social media is a recent phenomenon, many businesses are already using it to achieve important objectives. Some of these goals are long-term—such as building brand awareness and brand reputation—while others are more short-term—such as increasing Web site traffic or generating sales leads. Regardless of how social media is used, there are a lot of business opportunities. In this section, we explore a few ways that companies have used social media effectively to achieve business objectives.

Social Media Communities

For a business, social media can be used to build a community. **Social media communities** are social networks based on the relationships among people.[11] These electronic communities encourage two-way communication, allow for people to develop profiles, and identify other people to connect with by using technology and the Internet. People in each community can be called friends, fans, followers, or connections. Popular social networking sites include Facebook (the largest), LinkedIn (for professionals), Twitter, Google+, YouTube, Pinterest, and many others. To see how many businesses use the top four social media community sites, see Figure 16.3.

There are social communities for every interest, ethnic group, and lifestyle. Different types of social communities include forums and wikis. Forums were perhaps the earliest form of social community. A **forum** is an interactive version of a community bulletin board that focuses on threaded discussions. These are particularly popular with people who share a common interest such as video games. Another community based on social media is a wiki. A **wiki** is a collaborative online working space that enables members to contribute content that is then sharable with other people. With wikis, members of the community are the editors and gatekeepers ensuring that the content is correct and updated. Wikipedia—the free online encyclopedia—is the best example of a wiki. A community of unpaid experts voluntarily keeps the content on the Wikipedia Web site as updated and accurate as possible.

The whole purpose of social networks is to build communities and develop connections. Today, many companies are using social media to build communities with other businesses and consumers in order to achieve business objectives. Recently, Pepsi used social media to showcase its commitment to real-world communities by shifting the $20 million typically spent on Super Bowl advertising to a Web site that allowed customers to post

social media communities social networks based on the relationships among people

forum an interactive version of a community bulletin board that focuses on threaded discussions

wiki a collaborative online working space that enables members to contribute content that is then sharable with other people

FIGURE 16.3 The Top Four Social Media Networking Sites Used by Businesses

For businesses using social media, the most popular social networking sites are Facebook, Twitter, LinkedIn, and blogs.

Facebook	92%
Twitter	82%
LinkedIn	73%
Blogs	61%

Source: Michael A. Stelzner, "2012 Social Media Marketing Industry Report," The SocialMediaExaminer.com Web site at www.socialmediaexaminer.com, accessed August 14, 2012.

ideas for helping their own communities in areas like education and the environment. The driving force behind its "Refresh Everything" campaign was the belief that the company needed to "walk the walk" and really do something to make an impact. The Pepsi Refresh Project allowed people to upload their ideas or vote for their favorites. Pepsi then funded projects with the most votes. More than 57 million customers voted on different ideas—all designed to improve communities. For Pepsi, this social media project enabled the soft-drink giant to engage its customers who are heavy social media users.[12]

Crisis and Reputation Management

One of the most important reasons for listening to stakeholders is to determine whether there is a crisis brewing. A majority of companies believe that their company is less than a year away from some potential crisis moment and monitor social media for conversations that may predict a crisis.[13] Recently, the organization Susan G. Komen for the Cure decided to withdraw its funding for Planned Parenthood. Immediately, Planned Parenthood sent out an e-mail to its donors in an effort to replace the lost funding. As the news traveled from e-mail to social media, many people expressed their outrage that Komen for the Cure was playing a "political card." According to social media experts, the response from the Komen organization to negative publicity was inadequate. The Komen organization failed to address the issue on Facebook or Twitter even after mainstream media began reporting its controversial decision. It was not until the next day when Nancy Brinker, founder of Susan G. Komen for the Cure, talked about the issue, but by then the organization's public image had already been tarnished.

Social media: A new way to handle a crisis. For years, Walmart—the world's largest retailer—has tried to repair a reputation that's been damaged by decades of criticism and legal problems. Now Walmart has a new public relations tool—social media—to not only monitor what people are saying about the company, but also to tell its side of the story when controversies develop.

©AP PHOTO/EVAN VUCCI

United Airlines also found out the hard way what happens when customers complain to social networks. Guitarist Dave Carroll accused United Airlines of breaking his guitar during baggage handling in Chicago. After months of moving through the traditional channels and getting nowhere, Dave wrote a song, filmed a video, and posted it on YouTube. He also had friends send out the link to their networks. Soon the video had thousands of views and people started sharing their own negative United Airlines stories. United did try to control the damage on Twitter, but most people saw it as an empty promise to improve customer service. Soon the company was embroiled in bad press (in social media as well as mainstream media), which eventually caused their stock price to fall 10 percent. In the end, it is estimated that neglecting to attend to customer needs cost United Airlines about $180 million.[14]

Listening to Stakeholders

Listening to people, whether they are customers or not, is always an important aspect of a company's social media plan. Indeed, listening is often the first step when developing a social media strategy. Listening to the conversations unfolding on Facebook or Twitter, for example, can be important to understanding just what people think about a company's products and services. By monitoring Facebook, Twitter, and other social media sites, Domino's Pizza found out that people were not very happy with its product quality. Customers described the sauce as "tasting like ketchup" and the crust as "tasting like cardboard." Unfortunately, there were enough comments of a similar nature for the company to use traditional marketing research to verify this information. They found the sentiment to be true and the company then developed a plan to reinvent every aspect of the company—and its pizza products. Did the plan work? Same store sales increased more than 14 percent.[15]

Targeting Customers

Many companies are using social media to increase awareness and build their brand among customers. It is especially valuable in targeting the Millennials. **Millennials** are tech-savvy digital natives born after 1980. When Ford wanted to introduce its

Millennials tech-savvy digital natives born after 1980

subcompact car, the Fiesta, to Millennials, it used social media. Ford chose to target Millennials because, as a group, they are also more likely than older consumers to purchase a subcompact car. For this social media promotion, Ford recruited 100 social media users, dubbed "agents," who were given a Ford Fiesta to drive for six months. The only requirement was that each agent talked about the car on social media—using video, posts on Facebook and Twitter, and other social media sites. Initially, Ford set a goal of attracting 144,000 Web site visitors, but by the end of the promotion more than 300,000 people had viewed the Web site. Additional results showed that Ford's social media marketing promotion for the Fiesta worked well and social media could be used to build brand recognition with a specific group of people.[16]

In some cases, awareness is not a problem, but the ability to connect with the customer is. Social media can be used to build that connection. Consider the case of Old Spice. Once thought of as an "old man's" cologne, Old Spice struggled to gain attention for its body wash product in an industry dominated by newcomers like Axe—a brand that had done a very good job of connecting with Millennial men. Old Spice decided to use social media to reposition its body wash with a video launched on YouTube. The video was launched online during the Super Bowl, and then on network television later. The results were so positive that Old Spice followed up with a campaign using online videos based on comments from customers posted on Twitter and Facebook.[17]

Social Media Marketing

According to a survey by eMarketer, 80 percent of U.S. companies with more than 100 employees are using social media tools for marketing. Among small business, the rate of social media use for marketing is closer to 40 percent, and among businesses selling to other businesses, the rate is around 24 percent.[18] **Social media marketing** is the "utilization of social media technologies, channels, and software to create, communicate, deliver and exchange offerings that have value for an organization."[19] As companies become more comfortable with social media, we can expect even more companies to use social media to market products and services to their customers. Already, research indicates that companies are shifting their advertising money from traditional marketing (like television and magazines) to digital marketing (like Internet search engines and social media). Experts now predict that social media will account for 26 percent of all online spending by 2016.[20] The primary reason is simple. People are spending more time online.[21] Often the first step for a business that wants to use social media is to go to LinkedIn, Facebook, or Twitter. As you can tell from the information in Figure 16.4, companies like LinkedIn make using their technology as easy as possible to connect with potential or existing customers.

Today, many companies have been quite successful using social media marketing not only to develop customer awareness, but also to obtain sales leads and increase actual sales. HubSpot, for example, is a software company that helps small and medium-sized companies develop inbound marketing programs. **Inbound marketing** is a marketing term that describes new ways of gaining attention, and ultimately, customers, by creating content on a Web site that pulls customers in. Tools used for inbound marketing programs include search engine optimization, blogging, videos, and social media. In order to market its software products, the software company HubSpot shunned traditional advertising and began to practice what it preached. First, the company developed its own inbound marketing program by creating valuable content and marketing information that was then distributed through social media and search engine Web sites. Companies interested in HubSpot's software were required to enter contact information (name, phone number, and e-mail address) in order to view the information. People provided contact information because they believed the company's software could help them improve their marketing activities. As a result of HubSpot's inbound marketing program, the cost of generating new sales leads was five to seven times less than leads generated by more traditional marketing activities and as a bonus they gained thousands of new customers.[22]

social media marketing the utilization of social media technologies, channels, and software to create, communicate, deliver, and exchange offerings that have value for an organization

inbound marketing a marketing term that describes new ways of gaining attention and ultimately customers by creating content on a Web site that pulls customers in

FIGURE 16.4 LinkedIn's Marketing Solutions for Other Businesses

Like many popular social media communities, LinkedIn's marketing tools make it easy to connect with potential or existing customers.

Dell also uses social media to sell its computer and technology products. Unlike other companies experimenting with social media, Dell decided to be more visible and actively use social media to increase sales by using Twitter. The company has sold computers valued at more than $6.5 million by including links in its Twitter account to the DellOutlet Web site. While this represents a tiny percentage of total sales, it does show that products can be sold through social media.[23]

As important as social media is, it is only one aspect of digital marketing. Indeed, digital marketing or online marketing is comprised of several areas, including

- online public relations—developing social media press kits;
- search engine optimization—using keywords in the Web site in order to rank higher in search engine results;
- search engine marketing—buying ads like Google's AdWords to increase traffic to a company's Web site;
- display advertising—buying banner ads;
- e-mail marketing—targeting customers through opt-in email campaigns; and
- content marketing—developing photos, videos, podcasts, blog posts, and other tools to increase the value to the customer.

crowdsourcing outsourcing tasks to a group of people in order to tap into the ideas of the crowd

Generating New Product Ideas

Companies can use social media to conduct much of their consumer-based research. Using insight gained from Facebook or Twitter, for example, allows a company to modify existing products and services and develop new ones. **Crowdsourcing** involves outsourcing tasks to a group of people in order to tap into the ideas of the crowd. In some cases valuable information can be obtained by crowd voting. Frito Lay, for example, has used crowd voting for the last few years when they allowed

The face of social media. While many people use Facebook to connect with friends and relatives, the world's largest social media site is so much more! For many businesses, Facebook has created new ways to market their products and services and connect with potential or existing customers. Experts predict that the use of social media sites like Facebook will only increase in the future because people are spending more time online.

Career SUCCESS

Make a Good Impression Using Social Media

When you use social media to promote yourself to potential employers, what you post and how often you post can affect your ability to make a good impression.

- *Do: Show your professional side.* The first thing a visitor will notice is your photo—so be sure you look as professional as you would at an interview. Consider posting a brief "interview" video in which you answer a few questions that employers typically ask, such as what your career goals are or why you're interested in a particular industry. Include a contact link, with an e-mail address that matches the image you want to project.

- *Don't: Post inappropriate material.* One recruiter says he and his colleagues don't judge applicants based on their personal posts, but "we will judge their judgment for putting it on the Internet" if text or photos are offensive or racy. The head of a marketing research agency warns about using a lot of profanity online. An executive at the Hill Holliday ad agency doesn't like to "see a lot of posts about nothing or points of view that are judgmental or not open-minded. Inappropriate pictures can also [make] a bad impression."

- *Don't: Post too often.* Although many employers welcome active users of social media, they steer clear of applicants who post too often. "Too many Twitter posts from 9 to 5 might make us wonder how you find time for your real job," says the CEO of Zipcar.

Sources: Based on information in Rachel Barsky, "Career Tip Tuesday: How to Leverage Social Media in Your Job Search," *Fox News,* April 3, 2012, www.foxnews.com; Megan Marrs, "The First Step to Building Your Personal Brand," *Forbes,* February 14, 2012, www.forbes.com; Gerrit Hall, "4 Tips for Optimizing Your Resume with Social Media," *Mashable,* November 20, 2011, www.mashable.com; Scott Kirsner, "Social Media Advice for Job-Seekers," *Boston Globe,* September 9, 2011, www.boston.com.

people to create and then vote for their favorite television spots for its popular Doritos brand. The winners are then featured during the Super Bowl. Their effort "Crash the Super Bowl" has been wildly successful.[24]

Companies can even build communities for specific brands in order to obtain information and new ideas from consumers. A few years ago, Starbucks built a network called Mystarbucksidea.com that allowed customers to post ideas about how the company could improve. Since the creation of the Web site, thousands of ideas have been posted about Starbucks products, the customer's store experience, and the company's community involvement. The site also enables people to vote on the best ideas, many of which Starbucks has already implemented. For example, getting a free coffee on your birthday if you are a Gold Member or developing a VIP program were both originally customer ideas. In cases such as this one, customers appreciate the ability to share their ideas with a company to whom they are loyal, only to receive reciprocal loyalty when the company implements their ideas.[25]

Recruiting Employees

For years, companies have used current employees to recruit new employees based on the theory that "birds of a feather flock together." The concept is simple: Current employees' friends and family may prove to be good job candidates. Social media takes that concept to a whole new level. LinkedIn, the largest social network for professionals, has been used quite effectively by both large and small companies to recruit employees. Indeed, more than half of *Fortune* 100 companies use LinkedIn to recruit future employees. Using LinkedIn is beneficial for companies because it saves time and lowers recruiting costs. And using a site like LinkedIn also allows employers to see more information about candidates. Companies like Accenture, Home Depot, IBM, and Oracle have all had success with LinkedIn.

How do companies find the right employee?
Answer: More and more companies are using social media sites to recruit employees. Sites like LinkedIn, the largest social network for professionals, are often used by both large and small companies to advertise current job openings and reach out to potential employees located not only in the United States, but also in other parts of the world.

©VICHIE81/SHUTTERSTOCK

DEVELOPING A SOCIAL MEDIA PLAN

4 Describe how businesses develop a social media plan.

Before developing a plan to use social media, it is important to determine how social media can improve the organization's overall performance and how it "fits" with a company's other operational and promotional activities. For example, if a social media plan attempts to improve customer service, it needs to link to the company's overall organizational efforts to improve customer service.

Steps to Build a Social Media Plan

Once it is determined how social media links to the company's other activities, there are several steps that should be considered.

Step 1: Listen to Determine Opportunities Often social media is used to "listen" to what customers like and don't like about a company's products or services. For example, reading comments on social media sites can yield some insight into how consumers are reacting to a price increase or decrease for an existing product or service. Monitoring social media sites also allows managers and employees to enter the conversation and tell the company's side of the story. In addition, companies can monitor social media sites to gather information about competitors as well as what is being said about the industry.

After the listening phase, it is important to analyze the information to identify the company's strengths and weaknesses. For a company, it is also important to identify opportunities and threats before taking the next step—setting objectives.

Step 2: Establish Social Media Objectives After listening to and analyzing the information obtained from social media sites, it is important to use that information to develop specific objectives. For social media, an objective is a specific statement about what a social media plan should accomplish. Each objective should be specific, measurable, achievable, realistic, and oriented toward the future.

For most companies, the most popular objectives are increasing brand awareness, acquiring new customers, introducing new products, retaining current customers, and gaining customer insight.[26] Other objectives that are often important include improving search engine ranking, showcasing public relations activities, increasing Web site traffic, and generating sales leads.[27] All objectives need to be clear and linked to specific actions that can be used to accomplish each objective.

Step 3: Segment and Target the Social Customer Ideally, a company will have developed a customer profile that describes a typical customer in terms of age, income, gender, ethnicity, etc. When segmenting or targeting customers, it also helps to know how they think, how they spend their time, how much they buy, and how often they buy. In fact, more information about potential customers will help you develop a social media plan to achieve a company's objectives. Lack of information about customers can lead to wasted time and money and the inability to successfully achieve the firm's social media objectives. For example, most companies feel that they must use Facebook and Twitter. But if their core customer does not use these social media sites, then it does not make sense to use them. Additionally it is important to really understand how customers use social media.

- Do they create content like photos, videos, blog posts, etc?
- Do they use social media for ratings and reviews?
- Do they post product reviews and ratings on Facebook accounts?
- Do they spend a lot of time using social media?

According to Forrester Research, there are six types of individuals that use social media. Individuals can be classified as creators, critics, collectors, joiners, spectators, or inactives. In addition to the Forrester classifications of social media users, additional information that can help you target just the "right" social media customer is illustrated in Figure 16.5.

The more information you have about social media customers, the easier it is to develop a social media plan that targets the "right" customer.

General Information
- Age, income, gender, ethnicity, education, occupation, family size, religion, etc.

Identifying Factors
- What do they consider important?
- How do they spend their time?
- What do they buy and how often do they buy?

Social Media Usage
- How often do they use social media?
- Do they use Facebook, Twitter, YouTube, and other social media sites?
- Do they create videos, Web pages, or other content?
- Do they read ratings and reviews?
- What other factors can help you identify potential social customers?

POTENTIAL SOCIAL MEDIA CUSTOMERS

© CENGAGE LEARNING 2014

Step 4: Select Social Media Tools The search for the right social media tool(s) usually begins with the company's objectives, outlined in Step 2. It also helps to review the target customer or segment of the market the company is trying to reach (Step 3). With this information, the next step is to choose the right social media tools to reach the right customers. A company can use social communities, blogs, photos, videos, podcasts, or games to reach potential or existing customers. For example, if the goal is to recruit college students for college entry-level jobs, LinkedIn may be a good choice. Remember, it is not necessary (or even advisable) to use all of the above tools. It also helps to remember that social media is not free and can be quite expensive because it costs both time and money.

Step 5: Implement and Integrate the Plan Once social media tools have been identified, a company can implement and integrate the social media plan. Because a social media plan doesn't necessarily have a start and stop date, it is different from traditional advertising campaigns. Some social media activities continue and have a life of their own. For example, Zappos, a very successful and well-respected online retailer, is a company who is always "on" in terms of its social media. Indeed, they do very little traditional advertising and instead rely on social media to promote products, monitor customer service, and enhance the company's reputation. Some companies, on the other hand, feel that it is important to have a mix of short- and long-term social media promotion. In this case, it is important to develop each social media activity to make sure that it is as effective as it can be. For example, if a company is running a Facebook promotion, it is important to consider issues like developing a branded page, updating the page frequently, and providing fresh content to keep customers coming back to the Facebook site. If the same or similar social media activity is used on Twitter, the company must make changes to make sure it works on the Twitter site.

To increase the effectiveness of social media, companies will often integrate online promotions with more traditional or offline promotions. For example, it is not unusual to see the Twitter icon at the end of a television commercial. This signals to consumers that more information about the product or service is provided on Twitter. Indeed, as companies increase the amount of money spent on digital marketing and social media, they will attempt to tie online and offline promotions together in order to get "more bang for the buck."

©DAVID J. GREEN-LIFESTYLE 2/ALAMY

Technology that satisfies needs online. Both large and small businesses are using social media to sell products and services to customers 24 hours a day and seven days a week. As an added bonus, today's technology can reach potential and existing customers any place in the world as long as customers have access to the Internet.

Measuring and Adapting a Social Media Plan

Because social media is a relatively new method of reaching customers, many companies struggle when attempting to measure social media. Often companies use the same measurements that have been used with long-established media channels like television and radio to determine the effect of social media on the customer's awareness of the company or a specific brand and if sales (and profits) are increasing. Based on this information, the company may try to determine if it is getting a positive return on its investment in social media. Generally, there are two types of social media measurement. While both quantitative and qualitative measurements can be used, most companies tend to use quantitative measurements.

Quantitative Social Media Measurement Quantitative social media measurement consists of using numerical measurements, such as counting the number of Web site visitors, number of fans and followers, number of leads generated, and the number of new customers. For example, Coke has 41 million likes on its Facebook page and Dell Computer increases sales revenue by more than $6.5 million by using Twitter. Table 16.1 shows a few popular quantitative ways to measure social media.

Because a company must invest both time and money when it uses social media, it is important to measure the success and make adjustments if needed. In addition to the quantitative measurements already mentioned, a number of companies are using key performance indicators. **Key performance indicators (KPIs)** are measurements that define and measure the progress of an organization toward achieving its objectives. Generally, KPIs are *quantitative* (based on numbers like the number of Twitter followers).

TABLE 16.1	Quantitative Measurements for Selected Social Media Web Sites
Type of Social Media	**Typical Measuremens**
Blogs	• Unique visitors • Number of views • Ratio of visitors to posted comments
Twitter	• Number of followers • Number of tweets and retweets • Click through rate (CTR) of tweeted links • Visits to Web site from tweeted links
Facebook	• Number of fans • Number of likes • Number of comments • Growth of wall response • Visits to Web sites from Facebook links
YouTube	• Number of videos • Number of visitors • Ratio of comments to the number of videos uploaded • Number of embedded links

© CENGAGE LEARNING 2014

quantitative social media measurement using numerical measurements, such as counting the number of Web site visitors, number of fans and followers, number of leads generated, and the number of new customers

key performance indicators (KPIs) measurements that define and measure the progress of an organization toward achieving its objectives

If measuring the success or failure of social media activities with KPIs, the first step is to connect KPIs with objectives. The second step is to set a benchmark—a number that shows what success should look like. For example, Ford said that if 144,000 people visited the Ford Fiesta Web site within a specified time, it would indicate that the company's social media plan to introduce the new subcompact car to Millennials was successful. When measured, more than 300,000 people had visited the Web site. Simply put: The company's social media plan was successful because it surpassed the original benchmark. It is also possible to compare the company's social media KPIs to its benchmarks over time. When trend comparison is used to measure the effectiveness of social media, the trend may be more important than the actual percentage of increase or decrease for just one measurement period.

Qualitative Social Media Measurement Qualitative social media measurement is the process of accessing the opinions and beliefs about a brand. This process primarily uses sentiment analysis to categorize what is being said about a company. **Sentiment analysis** is a measurement that uses technology to detect the mood, attitudes, or emotions of people who experience a social media activity. Other measurements for determining customer sentiment include:

- *Customer satisfaction score*—defined as the relative satisfaction of customers.
- *Issue resolution rate*—the percentage of customer service inquiries resolved satisfactorily using social media.
- *Resolution time*—defined as the amount of time taken to resolve customer service issues.

When compared to quantitative measurement, it should be noted that many of these qualitative social media measurements are more subjective in nature.

Regardless of the type of measurement used, one of the most powerful aspects of social media—and indeed digital marketing—is the ability to tie the objectives of a social media plan to the results that were achieved. After reviewing results for social media activities against pre-established benchmarks and analyzing trends, changes can be made to increase the effectiveness of social media activities.

Social media is particularly important to businesses that use e-business to sell their products and services online. In the next section, we take a close look at how e-business firms are organized, satisfy needs online, and earn profits.

DEFINING E-BUSINESS

In Chapter 1, we defined *business* as the organized effort of individuals to produce and sell, for a profit, the products and services that satisfy society's needs. In a simple sense, then, **e-business**, or **electronic business**, can be defined as the organized effort of individuals to produce and sell, for a profit, the products and services that satisfy society's needs *through the facilities available on the Internet*. Sometimes people use the term *e-commerce* instead of *e-business*. In a strict sense, e-business is used when you're talking about all business activities and practices conducted on the Internet by an individual firm or industry. On the other hand, e-commerce is a part of e-business and usually refers only to buying and selling activities conducted online. In this chapter, we generally use the term *e-business* because of its broader definition and scope. As you will see in the remainder of this chapter, e-business is transforming key business activities.

Organizing e-Business Resources

As noted in Chapter 1, to be organized, a business must combine *human, material, informational,* and *financial resources*. This is true of e-business, too (see Figure 16.6), but in this case, the resources may be more specialized than in a typical business. For example, people who can design, create, and maintain Web sites are only a fraction of the specialized human resources required by e-businesses. Material resources must include specialized computers, sophisticated equipment and software, and high-speed

qualitative social media measurement the process of accessing the opinions and beliefs about a brand and primarily uses sentiment analysis to categorize what is being said about a company

sentiment analysis a measurement that uses technology to detect the moods, attitudes, or emotions of people who experience a social media activity

e-business (electronic business) the organized effort of individuals to produce and sell, for a profit, the products and services that satisfy society's needs *through the facilities available on the Internet*

FIGURE 16.6   Combining e-Business Resources

While all businesses use four resources (human, material, informational, and financial), these resources are typically more specialized when used in an e-business.

HUMAN RESOURCES
- Web site designers
- Programmers
- Web masters

INFORMATIONAL RESOURCES
- Customer tracking systems
- Order fulfillment and tracking systems
- Online content-monitoring systems

BUSINESS

MATERIAL RESOURCES
- Computers
- Software
- High-speed Internet connection lines

FINANCIAL RESOURCES
- Investors interested in supporting e-business firms
- Electronic payment from customers

© CENGAGE LEARNING 2014

outsourcing the process of finding outside vendors and suppliers that provide professional help, parts, or materials at a lower cost

Internet connections. Computer programs that track the number of customers who view a firm's Web site are generally among the specialized informational resources required. Financial resources, the money required to start and maintain the firm and allow it to grow, usually reflect greater participation by individual entrepreneurs, venture capitalists, and investors willing to invest in a high-tech firm instead of conventional financial sources such as banks.

In an effort to reduce the cost of specialized resources that are used in e-business, many firms have turned to outsourcing. **Outsourcing** is the process of finding outside vendors and suppliers that provide professional help, parts, or materials at a lower cost. For example, a firm that needs specialized software to complete a project may turn to an outside firm located in another part of the United States, India, or an Eastern European country.

Satisfying Needs Online

Think for a moment about this question: "Why do people use the Internet?" As pointed out in the first part of this chapter, more and more people are using computers, the Internet, and social media as a way to connect with people. The Internet can also be used to purchase products or services. Today, more people use the Internet to satisfy these needs than ever before. Let's start with two basic assumptions.

- The Internet has created some new customer needs that did not exist before the creation of the Internet.
- e-Businesses can satisfy those needs, as well as more traditional ones.

Restoration Hardware (www.restorationhardware.com), for instance, gives customers anywhere in the world access to the same virtual store of hardware and decorative items. And at eBay's global auction site (www.ebay.com), customers can, for a small fee, buy and sell almost anything. In each of these examples, customers can use the Internet to purchase a product or service.

In addition to purchasing products, the Internet can be used by both individuals and business firms to obtain information. For example:

- Internet users can access newspapers, magazines, and radio and television programming at a time and place convenient to them.
- The Internet provides the opportunity for two-way interaction between an Internet firm and the viewer. For example, the CNN news site (www.cnn.com)

©BLOOMBERG VIA GETTY IMAGES

Google—the number 1 search engine. When Google created its now-famous Web site, the developers chose a rather simple opening screen with just the Google name, a search box, and very little else. Users loved the simple format and used the search engine to find information about products and services, investment research, new movies, the current weather, and the latest news stories. Now Google has used its early success to develop new services, including Google Earth, Google+, and mobile apps.

Personal APPS

These days, you can find e-businesses that sell almost anything. Many will help you recognize a new need by offering free trials of apps, games, or other digital products. This is a great way to find out whether the digital product is useful, convenient, and worth buying.

revenue stream a source of revenue flowing into a firm

Using Facebook to reach online customers.
Today many retailers like The Container Store are using Facebook and other social network sites to reach consumers. It's just one more way to provide information to consumers that may want to purchase the firm's products or services.

and other news-content sites encourage dialogue among users.
- Customers can respond to information on the Internet by requesting more information or posing specific questions, which may lead to purchasing a product or service.
- Finally, the Internet allows customers to choose the content they are offered. Knowing the interests of a customer allows an Internet firm to direct appropriate, smart advertising to a specific customer. For the advertiser, knowing that its advertisements are being directed to the most likely customers represents a better way to spend advertising dollars.

Creating e-Business Profit

Business firms can increase profits either by increasing sales revenue or by reducing expenses through a variety of e-business activities.

Increasing Sales Revenue Each source of sales revenue flowing into a firm is referred to as a **revenue stream**. One way to increase revenues is to sell merchandise on the Internet. Online merchants can reach a global customer base 24 hours a day, seven days a week, because the opportunity to shop on the Internet is virtually unrestricted. However, shifting revenues earned from customers inside a real store to revenues earned from these same customers online does not create any real new revenue for a firm. The goal is to find *new customers* and generate *new sales* so that *total revenues are increased*.

Intelligent information systems also can help to generate sales revenue for Internet firms such as Amazon.com (www.amazon.com). Such systems store information about each customer's purchases, along with a variety of other information about the buyer's preferences. Using this information, the system can assist the customer the next time he or she visits the Web site. For example, if the customer has bought a Carrie Underwood CD in the past, the system might suggest CDs by similar artists who have either appeared on *American Idol* or won Country Music Awards.

Although some customers may not make a purchase online, the existence of the firm's Web site and the services and information it provides may lead to increased sales in the firm's physical stores. For example, Honda's Web site (www.honda.com) can provide basic comparative information for shoppers so that they are better prepared for their visit to an automobile showroom.

In addition to selling products or services online, e-business revenue streams are created by advertising placed on Web pages and by subscription fees charged for access to online services and content. For example, Hoover's (www.hoovers.com), a comprehensive source for company and industry information, makes some of its online content free for anyone who visits the site, but more detailed information is available only by paid subscription. In addition, Hoover's receives revenue from companies acting as sponsors who advertise their products and services on the site.

Many Internet firms that distribute news, magazine and newspaper articles, and similar content generate revenue from commissions earned from sellers of products linked to the site. Online shopping malls, for example, now provide groups of related vendors of electronic equipment and computer hardware and software with a new method of selling their products and services. In many cases, the vendors share online sales revenues with the site owners.

Reducing Expenses Reducing expenses is the second major way in which e-business can help to increase profitability. Providing online access to information that customers want can reduce the cost of dealing with customers. Sprint Nextel (www.sprint.com), for instance, is just one company that maintains an extensive Web site where potential customers can learn more about products and services, and where current customers can access personal account information, send questions to customer service, and purchase additional products or services. With such extensive online services, Sprint Nextel does not have to maintain as many physical store locations as it would without these online services. We examine more examples of how e-business contributes to profitability throughout this chapter, especially as we focus on some of the business models for activity on the Internet.

FUNDAMENTAL MODELS OF E-BUSINESS

6 Understand the fundamental models of e-business.

One way to get a better sense of how businesses are adapting to the opportunities available on the Internet is to identify e-business models. A **business model** represents a group of common characteristics and methods of doing business to generate sales revenues and reduce expenses. Each of the models discussed in the following text represents a primary e-business model. Regardless of the type of business model, planning often depends on if the e-business is a new firm or an existing firm adding an online presence—see Figure 16.7. It also helps to keep in mind that in order to generate sales revenues and earn profits, a business—especially an e-business—must meet the needs of its customers.

| FIGURE 16.7 | Planning for a New Internet Business or Building an Online Presence for an Existing Business |

The approach taken to creating an e-business plan will depend on whether you are establishing a new Internet business or adding an online component to an existing business.

SUCCESSFUL E-BUSINESS PLANNING

Starting a new Internet business

Building an online presence for an existing business

- Will the new e-business provide a product or service that meets customer needs?
- Who are the new firm's potential customers?
- How do promotion, pricing, and distribution affect the new e-business?
- Will the potential market generate enough sales and profits to justify the risk of starting an e-business?

- Is going online a logical way to increase sales and profits for the existing business?
- Are potential online customers different from the firm's traditional customers?
- Will the new e-business activities complement the firm's traditional activities?
- Does the firm have the time, talent, and financial resources to develop an online presence?

© CENGAGE LEARNING 2014

business model represents a group of common characteristics and methods of doing business to generate sales revenues and reduce expenses

Going for SUCCESS

Macy's and m-Commerce

Through *m-commerce*—mobile commerce, via smartphones and other mobile devices— Macy's is connecting with digital natives who like both fashion and bargains. The retailer operates 800 department stores in 45 states and rings up a total of $26 billion in annual sales. In the past few years, it has stepped up efforts to engage tech-savvy consumers between the ages of 13 and 30.

Macy's created a special version of its popular Web site to fit the size of phone screens, so that customers can browse, look up product details, and buy at any time from any location. It also began inviting customers to subscribe to text messages announcing sales and delivering coupons. Response was so positive that Macy's doubled the size of its text-message

subscriber list in just six months. In addition, the retailer includes QR (quick response) codes—boxy, pixilated codes packed with information—in its ads and product displays. Customers use a free QR app to decode the code and access information such as product specifications, demonstration videos, and designer interviews. In one of the store's most popular QR promotions, customers were treated to an exclusive video of beauty expert Bobbi Brown giving a brief makeup lesson. "We're using mobile in every way possible to really complete a customer's experience," explains a Macy's executive.

Sources: Based on information in Sarah Mahoney, "Macy's Revamping Its Bid for Gen Y," *MediaPost*, March 22, 2012, www.mediapost.com; Rimma Kats, "Macy's Mobile Spend Up 70pc: FirstLook Keynote," *Mobile Marketer*, January 20, 2012, www.mobilemarketer.com; Giselle Tsirulnik, "Macy's Is 2011 Mobile Marketer of the Year," *Mobile Marketer*, December 9, 2011, www.mobilemarketer.com.

A new way to reach business customers around the globe. Alibaba.com is a business-to-business (B2B) global trade site that makes it easy for millions of importers and exporters to buy and sell products and services online. Because it meets the needs of its customers, Alibaba.com has become a successful company with offices in more than 70 cities around the globe.

business-to-business (or B2B) model a model used by firms that conduct business with other businesses

Business-to-Business (B2B) Model

Many e-businesses can be distinguished from others simply by their customer focus. For instance, some firms use the Internet mainly to conduct business with other businesses. These firms are generally referred to as having a **business-to-business (or B2B) model**.

When examining B2B firms, two clear types emerge. In the first type, the focus is simply on facilitating sales transactions between businesses. For example, Dell manufactures computers to specifications that customers enter on the Dell Web site (www.dell.com). A large portion of Dell's online orders are from corporate clients who are well informed about the products they need and are looking for fairly priced, high-quality computer products that will be delivered quickly. Basically, by building only what is ordered, Dell reduces storage and carrying costs and rarely is stuck with unsold inventory. By dealing directly with Dell, customers eliminate costs associated with wholesalers and retailers, thereby helping to reduce the price they pay for equipment.

A second, more complex type of B2B model involves a company and its suppliers. Today, suppliers use the Internet to bid on products and services they wish to sell to a customer and learn about the customer's rules and procedures that must be followed. For example, Ford has developed a B2B model to link thousands of suppliers that sell the automobile maker parts, supplies, and raw materials worth millions of dollars each year. Although the B2B site is expensive to start and maintain, there are significant savings for Ford. Given the potential savings, it is no wonder that many other manufacturers and their suppliers are beginning to use the same kind of B2B systems that are used by the automaker. In fact, suppliers know that to be a "preferred" supplier for a large firm that may purchase large quantities of parts, supplies, or raw materials, they must be tied into the purchaser's B2B system.

TABLE 16.2	Other Business Models that Perform Specialized e-Business Activities
Although modified versions of B2B or B2C, these business models perform specialized e-business activities to generate revenues.	
Advertising e-business model	Advertisements that are displayed on a firm's Web site in return for a fee. Examples include pop-up and banner advertisements on search engines and other popular Internet sites.
Brokerage e-business model	Online marketplaces where buyers and sellers are brought together to facilitate an exchange of goods and services. One example is eBay (www.ebay.com), which provides a site for buying and selling virtually anything.
Consumer-to-consumer model	Peer-to-peer software that allows individuals to share information over the Internet. Examples include Bit Torrent (www.bittorrent.com), which allows users to exchange digital media files.
Subscription and pay-per-view e-business models	Content that is available only to users who pay a fee to gain access to a Web site. Examples include investment information provided by Standard & Poor's (www.netadvantage.standardandpoors.com) and business research provided by Forrester Research, Inc. (www.forrester.com).

© CENGAGE LEARNING 2014

Business-to-Consumer (B2C) Model

In contrast with the B2B model, firms such as Barnes and Noble (www.barnesandnoble.com) and online retailer Lands' End (www.landsend.com) clearly are focused on individual consumers. These companies are referred to as having a **business-to-consumer (or B2C) model.** In a B2C situation, understanding how consumers behave online is critical to a firm's success. Typically, a business firm that uses a B2C model must answer the following questions:

- Will consumers use Web sites merely to simplify and speed up comparison shopping?
- Will consumers purchase services and products online or end up buying at a traditional retail store?
- What sorts of products and services are best suited for online consumer shopping?

In addition to providing round-the-clock global access to all kinds of products and services, B2C firms often attempt to build long-term relationships with their customers. Often, firms will make a special effort to make sure that the customer is satisfied and that problems, if any, are solved quickly. Specialized software also can help build good customer relationships. Tracking the decisions and buying preferences as customers navigate a Web site, for instance, helps management to make well-informed decisions about how best to serve online customers. In essence, this is Orbitz's (www.orbitz.com) online selling approach. By tracking and analyzing customer data, the online travel company can provide individualized service to its customers. Although a "little special attention" may increase the cost of doing business for a B2C firm, the customer's repeated purchases will repay the investment many times over.

Today, B2B and B2C models are the most popular business models for e-business. And yet, there are other business models that perform specialized e-business activities to generate revenues. Most of the business models described in Table 16.2 are modified versions of the B2B and B2C models.

THE FUTURE OF THE INTERNET, SOCIAL MEDIA, AND E-BUSINESS

 Identify the factors that will affect the future of the Internet, social media, and e-business.

business-to-consumer (or B2C) model a model used by firms that focus on conducting business with individual consumers

Since the beginning of commercial activity on the Internet, developments in computer technology, social media, and e-business have been rapid and formidable with spectacular successes such as Google, eBay, and Pinterest. However, a larger-than-usual number of technology companies struggled or even failed during the economic crisis. Today, most firms involved in the Internet, social media, and e-business use a more intelligent approach to development. The long-term view held by the vast majority of analysts is that the Internet, social media, and e-business will continue to expand to meet the needs of businesses and consumers.

Internet Growth Potential

To date, only a small percentage of the global population uses the Internet. At the beginning of 2012, estimates suggest that about 2.3 billion of the nearly 7 billion people in the world use the Web. [28] Clearly, there is much more growth opportunity. Americans comprise 11 percent of all Internet users.[29] Of the 310 million people making up the American population, 239 million use the Internet. With approximately 77 percent of the American population already using the Internet, potential growth in the United States is limited.[30] On the other hand, the number of Internet users in the world's developing countries is expected to increase dramatically.

Although the number of global Internet users is expected to increase, that's only part of the story. Perhaps the more important question is why people are using the Internet. Primary reasons for using the Internet include the ability to connect with other people, to obtain information, or to purchase a firm's products or services. Of particular interest to business firms is the growth of social media. The number of Facebook users, for example, increased from 664 million to 835 million in the 12-month period from March 2011 to March 2012. And because only 12 percent of the world population currently uses Facebook, the number of Facebook users is expected to continue to increase for years to come.[31] And the number of users for other social media sites like LinkedIn, Twitter, Pinterest, are also expected to increase.

Experts also predict that the number of companies using e-business to increase sales and reduce expenses will continue to increase. Firms that adapt existing business models to an online environment will continue to dominate development. For example, books, CDs, clothing, hotel accommodations, car rentals, and travel reservations are products and services well suited to online buying and selling. These products or services will continue to be sold in the traditional way, as well as in a more cost-effective and efficient fashion over the Internet.

Ethical and Legal Concerns

The social and legal concerns for the Internet, social media, and e-business extend beyond those shared by all businesses. Essentially, the Internet is a new "frontier" without borders and without much control by governments or other organizations.

Ethics and Social Responsibility Socially responsible and ethical behavior by individuals and businesses on the Internet are major concerns. For example, an ethically questionable practice in cyberspace is the unauthorized access and use of information discovered through computerized tracking of users once they are connected to the Internet. Essentially, a user may visit a Web site and unknowingly receive a small piece of software code called a **cookie.** This cookie can track where the user goes on the Internet and measure how long the user stays at any particular Web site. Although this type of software may produce valuable customer information, it also can be viewed as an invasion of privacy, especially since users may not even be aware that their movements are being monitored.

Besides the unauthorized use of cookies to track online behavior, there are several other threats to users' privacy and confidentiality. Monitoring an employee's computer usage may be intended to help employers police unauthorized Internet use on company time. However, the same records can also give a firm the opportunity to observe what otherwise might be considered private and confidential information. Today, legal experts suggest that, at the very least, employers need to disclose the level of surveillance to their employees and consider the corporate motivation for monitoring employees' behavior.

Some firms also practice data mining. **Data mining** refers to the practice of searching through data records looking for useful information. Customer registration forms typically require a variety of information before a user is given access to a site. Based

cookie a small piece of software sent by a Web site that tracks an individual's Internet use

data mining the practice of searching through data records looking for useful information

Part 6 Social Media, e-Business, and Accounting

on an individual's information, data mining analysis can then provide what might be considered private and confidential information about individuals. For instance, assume an individual frequents a Web site that provides information about a life-threatening disease. If this information is sent to an insurance company, the company might refuse to insure this individual, thinking that there is a higher risk associated with someone who wants more information about this disease.

Internet Crime Because the Internet is often regarded as an unregulated frontier, both individuals and business users must be particularly aware of online risks and dangers. For example, a general term that describes software designed to infiltrate a computer system without the user's consent is **malware**. Malware is often based on the creator's criminal or malicious intent and can include computer viruses, spyware, deceptive adware, and other software capable of criminal activities. A more specific term used to describe disruptive software is computer virus. A **computer virus**, which can originate anywhere in the world, is a software code designed to disrupt normal computer activities. The potentially devastating effects of both malware and computer viruses have given rise to a software security industry.

In addition to the risk of computer viruses, identity theft is one of the most common computer crimes that impacts both individuals and business users. A recent study conducted by Javelin Strategy and Research determined that more than 11.6 million Americans were victims of identity theft in just one year.[32] Most consumers are also concerned about fraud. Because the Internet allows easy creation of Web sites, access from anywhere in the world, and anonymity for the creator, it is almost impossible to know with certainty that the Web site, organization, or individuals that you believe you are interacting with are what they seem. As always, caveat emptor ("let the buyer beware") is a good suggestion to follow whether on the Internet or not.

Sustaining the PLANET

Lululemon Develops Lasting Legacies

Lululemon has built an online presence based on demand for their technical athletic apparel for yoga, dancing, and running. Their product line, coupled with the company's social responsibility perspective—which they refer to as Community Legacies—has created a loyal customer base. Viewing efficiency and waste reduction as good business, the company is focused on eliminating waste in their factories, stores, and support centers. Lululemon has an embedded core culture, "Personal responsibility creates global change," that reaches every aspect of the business. For more information, go to www.lululemon.com/community/legacies/focus.

Future Challenges for Computer Technology, Social Media, and e-Business

Today, more information is available than ever before. Although individuals and business users may think we are at the point of information overload, the amount of information will only increase in the future. In order to obtain more information in the future, both individuals and business users must consider the cost of obtaining information and computer technology. For a business, the ability to obtain information or sell products or services with a simple click or touch is expensive. In an effort to reduce expenses and improve accessibility, some companies and individuals are now using cloud computing. **Cloud computing** is a type of computer usage in which services stored on the Internet are provided to users on a temporary basis. When cloud computing is used, a third party makes processing power, software applications, databases, and storage available for on-demand use from anywhere. Instead of running software and storing data on their employer's computer network or their individual computers, employees log onto the third party's system and use (and pay for) only the applications and data storage they actually need. In addition to just cost, there are a number of external and internal factors that a business must consider.

Although the environmental forces at work are complex, it is useful to think of them as either *internal* or *external* forces that affect how a business uses computer

malware a general term that describes software designed to infiltrate a computer system without the user's consent

computer virus a software code designed to disrupt normal computer operations

cloud computing a type of computer usage in which services stored on the Internet is provided to users on a temporary basis

FIGURE 16.8   Internal and External Forces that Affect an e-Business

Today, managers and employees of an e-business must respond to internal forces within the organization and external forces outside the organization.

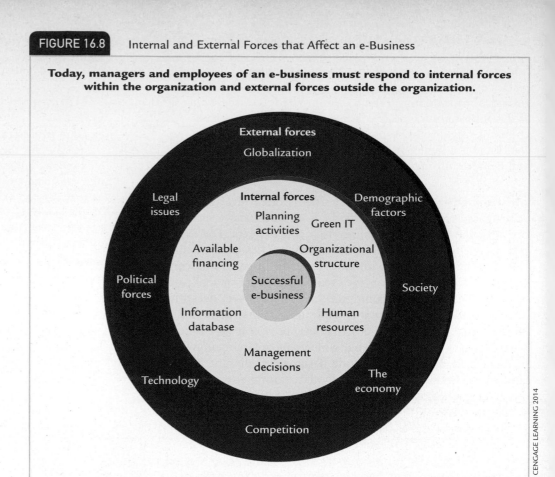

technology. Internal environmental forces are those that are closely associated with the actions and decisions taking place within a firm. As shown in Figure 16.8, typical internal forces include a firm's planning activities, organizational structure, human resources, management decisions, information database, and available financing. A shortage of skilled employees needed for a specialized project, for instance, can undermine a firm's ability to sell its services to clients. Unlike the external environmental forces affecting the firm, internal forces such as this one are more likely to be under the direct control of management. In this case, management can either hire the needed staff or choose to pass over a prospective project. In addition to the obvious internal factors that affect how a company operates, a growing number of firms are concerned about how their use of technology affects the environment. The term **green IT** is now used to describe all of a firm's activities to support a healthy environment and sustain the planet. Many offices, for example, are reducing the amount of paper they use by storing data and information on computers.

In contrast, external environmental forces affect a company's use of technology and originate outside the organization. These forces are unlikely to be controllable by a company. Instead, managers and employees of a company generally will react to these forces, attempting to shield the organization from any undue negative effects and finding ways to take advantage of opportunities in an ever-changing technology environment. The primary external environmental forces affecting a company's use of technology include globalization, demographic, societal, economic, competitive, technological, and political and legal forces.

In this chapter, we have explored how both individuals and businesses use social media. We also examined how e-business is changing the way that firms do business. In Chapter 17, we examine a business firm's need for information and why accounting is a major source of information for business.

green IT a term used to describe all of a firm's activities to support a healthy environment and sustain the planet

Angry Birds

Every time Rovio uses Facebook, Twitter, and blogs to announce the release of a new Angry Birds game, it sets the social media world buzzing. Angry Birds Space took social games to new heights when the product introduction featured a NASA astronaut on the International Space Station using an Angry Bird toy and a balloon "pig" to demonstrate the principle of trajectory. Fans downloaded the new space game 10 million times in its first three days, a new record that also helped boost Rovio's e-business revenue for the year.

Now that Angry Birds is an international download phenomenon, Rovio is planning Angry Birds theme parks in Europe, Angry Birds stores in China, and an Angry Birds movie for global release. How long will Rovio's revenues be flying high?

Questions

1. If you were a corporate executive, how could you measure the effectiveness of Rovio's use of social media?
2. Of the environmental forces affecting e-business, which seem to have had the most influence on Rovio's success with Angry Birds?

SUMMARY

Looking for Success?

Get Flashcards, Quizzes, Games, Crosswords, and More @ **www.cengagebrain.com**.

 Examine why it is important for a business to use social media.

Millions of people of all ages use social media to interact with people and share ideas, personal information, and information about products and services. Today, more than two-thirds of online adults use some sort of social media platform like Facebook, LinkedIn, or Twitter, according to a recent Pew Internet Research Study. The primary reason for using social media is to stay in touch with family and friends. Other reasons include reconnecting with friends, connecting with people who share interests, making new friends, and reading comments by public figures. Early on, companies saw the potential in the sheer numbers of people using social media. Even though companies have used social media to share information about their products and services and improve customer service, many are still uncomfortable with this new method of communicating with customers because they do not have complete control over what is said about their products or services.

 Discuss how businesses use social media tools.

Companies use social media to connect with customers, listen to stakeholders, provide customer service, provide information to customers, and engage customers in product development and formulation. To share social content (information about products and services), companies can use blogs, photos, videos, and podcasts. In addition, social media also enables shoppers to access opinions, recommendations, and referrals from others within and outside their own social circle. Rating and review sites are based on the idea that people trust the opinions of others when it comes to purchasing products and services. Social games are another area of growth in social media. A social game (like Angry Birds or FarmVille) is a multiplayer, competitive, goal-oriented activity with defined rules of engagement and online connectivity among a community of players. While some businesses elect to create their own game, others choose to place advertising into a game.

 Explain the business objectives for using social media.

Although its popularity is a recent phenomenon, many businesses are already using social media to achieve important goals and objectives. In fact, there are many ways for businesses to use social media to take advantage of business opportunities to build connections with other businesses and consumers. For example, businesses can use social media to build a community. Social media communities are social networks based on the relationships among people. Today, there are social communities for every interest, ethnic group, and lifestyle. Different types of communities include both forums and wikis. Other reasons for using social media include crisis and reputation management, listening to stakeholders, targeting customers, social media marketing, generating new product ideas, and recruiting employees. For a business, social media marketing is especially important because it can not only develop customer awareness, but also obtain sales leads and increase actual sales.

 Describe how businesses develop a social media plan.

Before developing a plan to use social media, it is important to determine how social media can improve the organization's overall performance and how it "fits" with a company's other operational and promotional activities. Once it is determined how social media links to the company's other activities, the first step is to listen to what customers like and don't like about a company's products or services. Typically, the second step is to establish social media objectives that are specific, measurable, achievable, realistic, and time oriented. After listening and establishing objectives, the third step is to identify the customer or market segment a business is trying to reach with a social media promotion. The fourth step is to select the social media tool that will be used to reach customers. While it is not necessary (or even advisable) to use all of the available tools, a company can use social media communities, blogs, photos, videos, podcasts, or games to reach potential or existing customers. Once social media tools have been identified, a company can implement and integrate the social media plan.

Both quantitative and qualitative measurements can be used to determine the effectiveness of a social media plan. Quantitative social media measurement consists of using numerical measurements. Key performance indicators (KPIs), for example, are quantitative measurements. Qualitative measurement is the process of accessing the opinions and beliefs about a brand and primarily uses sentiment analysis to categorize what is being said about a company.

 Explain the meaning of e-business.

e-Business, or electronic business, can be defined as the organized effort of individuals to produce and sell, for a profit, the goods and services that satisfy society's needs *through the facilities available on the Internet.* The human, material, information, and financial resources that any business requires are highly specialized for e-business. In an effort to reduce the cost of e-business resources, many firms have turned to outsourcing.

Using e-business activities, it is possible to satisfy new customer needs created by the Internet as well as traditional ones in unique ways. Meeting customer needs is especially important when an e-business is trying to earn profits by increasing sales and reducing expenses. Each source of revenue flowing into the firm is referred to as a revenue stream.

 Understand the fundamental models of e-business.

e-Business models focus attention on the identity of a firm's customers. Firms that use the Internet mainly to conduct business with other businesses generally are referred to as having a business-to-business, or B2B, model. When examining B2B firms, two clear types emerge. In the first type of B2B, the focus is simply on facilitating sales transactions between businesses. A second, more complex type of the B2B model involves a company and its suppliers. In contrast to the focus of the B2B model, firms such as Amazon or eBay clearly are focused on individual buyers and are thus referred to as having a business-to-consumer, or B2C, model. In a B2C situation, understanding how consumers behave online is critical to the firm's success. Successful B2C firms often make a special effort to build long-term relationships with their customers. While B2B and B2C models are the most popular e-business models, there are other models that perform specialized e-business activities to generate revenues (see Table 16.2).

 Identify the factors that will affect the future of the Internet, social media, and e-business.

Since the beginning of commercial activity on the Internet, developments in computer technology, social media, and e-business have been rapid and formidable. Although a number of technology companies struggled or even failed during the recent economic crisis, most firms involved in computer technology, social media, and e-business today use a more intelligent approach to development. The long-term view held by the vast majority of analysts is that use of the Internet will continue to expand along with related technologies. Because approximately 77 percent of Americans now have access to the Internet, potential growth is limited in the United States. On the other hand, only 2.3 billion of the nearly 7 billion people in the world use the Web. Clearly, the number of Internet users in the world's developing countries is expected to increase dramatically.

The future of computer technology and the Internet will be influenced by advances in technology, the increasing popularity of social media, and the increasing use of e-business. Other factors including ethics, social responsibility, and Internet crime will all impact the way that businesses and consumers use computer technology and the Internet. Although the environmental forces at work are complex, it is useful to think of them as either internal or external forces that affect how businesses use computer technology. Internal environmental forces are those that are closely associated with the actions and decisions taking place within a firm. In contrast, external environmental forces are those factors affecting an e-business originating outside an organization.

You should now be able to define and give an example relevant to each of the following terms:

social media (458)
social content sites (460)
blog (460)
media sharing sites (461)
podcasts (461)
social game (461)
social media
    communities (462)
forum (462)
wiki (462)

Millennials (463)
social media marketing (464)
inbound marketing (464)
crowdsourcing (465)
quantitative social media
    measurement (469)
key performance indicators
    (KPIs) (469)
qualitative social media
    measurement (470)

sentiment analysis (470)
e-business (electronic
    business) (470)
outsourcing (471)
revenue stream (472)
business model (473)
business-to-business (or B2B)
    model (474)
business-to-consumer (or
    B2C) model (475)

cookie (476)
data mining (476)
malware (477)
computer virus (477)
cloud computing (477)
green IT (478)

REVIEW QUESTIONS

1. According to material in this chapter, what are the reasons why people use social media?
2. How is using social media to connect with other businesses and consumers different from the top-down traditional advertising approach used with television and magazine ads?
3. What is a blog? How can a business use blogs to develop relationships with customers?
4. What types of content can be used on a media sharing site? What factors should be considered when developing content for a media sharing site?
5. Describe the two ways that businesses can use "gamification" to generate sales revenue.
6. In your own words, describe how social media can help businesses to connect with other businesses and consumers.
7. For a business, why are crisis and reputation management and listening to stakeholders important activities?
8. How can social media be used to segment the market for a firm's products or services and target specific types of customers?

9. Why do you think companies are shifting their advertising monies from traditional advertising (television and newspapers) to social media (Internet search engines and social media)?
10. How can social media help companies generate new product ideas and recruit employees?
11. What are the steps required to develop a social media plan?
12. What is the difference between quantitative and qualitative measurement? Which type of measurement do you think is the most reliable when measuring the effectiveness of a company's social media plan?
13. What are the four major factors contained in the definition of e-business?
14. How do e-businesses generate revenue streams?
15. What are the two fundamental e-business models?
16. Give an example of an unethical use of computer technology by a business.
17. What is the difference between internal and external forces that affect an e-business? How do they change the way an e-business operates?

DISCUSSION QUESTIONS

1. Given the fast pace of everyday life, most people often feel there is not enough time to do everything that needs to be done. Yet, people do find time to post personal information, photos, etc., on Facebook, Twitter, blogs, and other social media sites. Why do you think people are so fascinated with social media?
2. Assume you are the owner of a small company that produces a line of barbeque grills. Describe how you could use social media to connect with customers, improve customer service, increase sales, and reduce expenses.

3. Can advertising provide enough revenue for an e-business to succeed in the long run? What other sources of revenue can an e-business use to generate revenue?
4. Is outsourcing good for an e-business firm? The firm's employees? Explain your answer.
5. What distinguishes a B2B from a B2C e-business model?
6. Experts predict that the Internet, social media, and e-business will continue to expand along with related computer technologies. What effect will this expansion have on how businesses connect with customers in the future?

When Luke Holden decided to open up a restaurant in 2009, using social media to promote it seemed like a no-brainer. "Word-of-mouth from friends is stronger than any other form of advertising in my opinion," says the 27-year-old.

Holden didn't start out in the restaurant business, though. After graduating from Georgetown University, he went to work on Wall Street as a financial analyst. A couple of years later, the banking crisis hit. When many of his coworkers started getting laid off, he began thinking about a backup plan for himself.

One thing Holden had noticed about New York City was that there were no restaurants serving good lobster rolls for a decent price: "They were all selling for $24, but you got only a little lobster, a lot of mayo, and more filler," he says. The Maine native sensed an opportunity. Plus, he knew where to find a good lobster supplier: his dad, Jeff Holden, who owns a seafood processing company in Portland, Maine. Luke had worked for his father when he was younger. If he purchased seafood directly from his father, rather than through a wholesaler, he figured he could offer a big lobster roll for a small price.

Because the restaurant business in New York City is very competitive, Holden figured he better not quit his day job right away. Instead, he posted an ad on Craigslist to find a partner who could help him get the business up and running. That's how he came across Ben Conniff. Conniff was fresh out of Yale and looking to get into the restaurant business, too. After coming up with a business plan and raising some money, he and Holden hired some employees and opened Luke's Lobster, a tiny eatery in New York City's East Village. Conniff worked the day shift. Holden worked nights and weekends.

Fortunately, Luke's Lobster quickly found a following. Better yet, customers got online to rave about the restaurant's generously portioned rolls as well as their $15 price. Health- and environmentally-conscious diners who want to know where their food is coming from were also attracted to the eatery. "We know the exact source of all our food," Holden says. "We can trace it from the bottom of the ocean to the East Village."

To further spread the word out about the restaurant, Holden and Conniff signed up with the social networking site Foursquare. Foursquare has a GPS-enabled, mobile-phone app that recommends businesses in the area where you're located based on what you and your friends in your network have said they like. People with the app can automatically "check in" with a business on Foursquare. They can let their friends know where they are and comment on their experience. When customers accumulate enough check-ins, they qualify for discounts and freebies. "Forget about loyalty cards and coupons. This makes it so it's more digital and virtual," Holden says about Foursquare. "It's a digital wallet that you can carry around, and it's constantly rewarding you."

In addition to using Foursquare to get customers in the door, Holden and Conniff use it to help manage Luke's. The data they get from Foursquare allows them to categorize their customers by gender, age, and arrival time. Analyzing the arrival times of customers helps the restaurant ramp up for busy periods and offer specials when business is slow.

The entrepreneurs didn't limit their social networking to Foursquare, however. They use a combination of Facebook, Twitter, Tumblr, Pinterest, and Vimeo to post photos and videos about Luke's, make announcements about specials and contests, and provide links to the restaurant's Web site and blog. The crew at Luke's also "listens" to what people on the Web are saying about the restaurant and replies to them. "Responding to folks who mention us is our way of bringing them into the family and incorporating their feedback into our business," Holden says.

Six months after setting up shop in the East Village, business was so good that Holden and Conniff were able to open up a second location. At that point, Holden felt comfortable enough to leave the banking business. Since then, the men have opened up two more Luke's Lobster restaurants in New York City, and one in Washington, D.C., which Holden's brother, Bryan, operates. In 2011, the Luke's chain rolled out a food truck in the New York area. The employees who work the truck use Twitter to update customers on its whereabouts.

Thanks to a good product and social networking strategy, New York City has been awash with information about Luke's Lobster. HauteLiving.com even named it the city's best lobster restaurant. What's interesting is that without doing any traditional advertising whatsoever, Holden and Conniff have achieved so much success—including landing a spot on the *Today Show* with Kathie Lee Gifford. With a little more angling, it's looking like they could net some cookbook or reality TV offers.[33]

Questions

1. What factors have contributed to the success of Luke's Lobster?
2. Why have Holden and Conniff shunned traditional advertising? Is that a good idea? Why or why not?
3. Pick another type of business and describe how it could use social media networking to promote its products or services?

In February of 2004, Harvard University sophomore Mark Zuckerberg cofounded a Web site as a "facebook" (formerly the term for a physical photo album provided to a student body) where he and his classmates could post their photos and basic profile information. It caught on so quickly that just a month later, Zuckerberg opened it to students at other colleges and universities. By summer, Facebook had become a national phenomenon. Zuckerberg moved the company from his dorm room to California's high-tech Silicon Valley, and he hired more engineers to write software for new features like the "wall," where users post messages, photos, and videos.

Year after year, millions of new users logged on to "friend" friends, acquaintances, family, and classmates. Businesses also created pages to promote themselves and their products. Facebook's rapid growth soon attracted the attention of Microsoft, which in 2007 invested $240 million to buy a tiny stake in the feisty firm. Zuckerberg and his team were already hard at work on a new round of upgrades to make Facebook even more social.

In early 2008, Facebook Chat went live. Although engineers had argued for a chat feature to allow private, real-time typed conversations between users, top managers weren't enthusiastic. Engineers continued development and demonstrated its use again and again until they finally won Zuckerberg's approval. Today, it remains one of the site's most popular features. By 2009, Facebook had more users worldwide than it primary competitor, MySpace. A year later, Jesse Eisenberg starred as Mark Zuckerberg in *The Social Network,* an Academy Award–winning movie about the legal battles embroiled in Facebook's financial bonanza.

Most of the company's revenues come from advertising. Facebook knows a lot about its users, so it can help advertisers like Domino's Pizza reach highly targeted audiences, such as people in certain age groups and people who have "liked" a particular brand or product. Now, with nearly 1 billion users, Facebook earns more than $3 billion every year from advertising revenues alone. Because the majority of Facebook users in the United States, Brazil, India, and other large markets access their accounts via smartphone, the company is working on ways to sell more mobile advertising.

Facebook is also trying to find an appropriate balance between its advertisers' need for marketing data and its users' need for privacy. A few years ago, it violated its own privacy policy by allowing advertisers access to some individually identifiable user data and by sharing some user data with outside software developers. After a public uproar and a government investigation, Facebook agreed in a settlement with the Federal Trade Commission that it would obtain the consent of users before making changes to their privacy settings. Under this settlement, Facebook must allow independent auditors to check its privacy controls and activities every other year for the next 20 years.

Facebook became a publicly traded corporation in 2012 by selling $16 billion worth of common stock. The money it raised will fuel its global expansion and pay for the next generation of social media services to meet users' needs now and into the future. "We don't build services to make money," CEO Mark Zuckerberg says. "We make money to build better services."[34]

Questions

1. Every day, millions of people use Facebook to connect with friends, relatives, and businesses. As a result, Facebook is now the world's leading social media company. In your opinion, what factors have led to Facebook's success?
2. What is Facebook's e-business model, and how does this model fit its customers' social media needs and interests? How does this social media company generate revenues and profits?
3. Because Facebook is a public corporation, it is now accountable to shareholders. If you owned Facebook shares, how would you react to the CEO's statement about making money to build better services, not building services to make money?

Building Skills for Career Success

❶ SOCIAL MEDIA EXERCISE

The purpose of the first part of this chapter is to introduce you to social media and its importance to business. After reading the chapter, choose a business that you either know something about, want to start, or is the company you already work for.

Assignment

1. Develop a social media plan for that business using what you learned in this chapter.
2. What are the objectives of your social media plan?

3. What social media tools would you choose and why? How would you measure success?
4. Prepare a report that describes how this exercise has helped you understand the material in this chapter.

❷ JOURNALING FOR SUCCESS

Today, more and more people use the Internet to purchase products or services. And yet, many people are reluctant to make online purchases because of identity and privacy issues. Still others are "afraid" of the technology.

Assignment

1. Have you ever used the Internet to purchase a product or service? If you answered yes, why did you purchase online as compared with purchasing the same product or service in a traditional retail store?
2. In your own words, describe whether the online shopping experience was a pleasant one. What factors contributed to your level of satisfaction or dissatisfaction?
3. If you answered no, describe why you prefer to shop in a traditional retail store as compared with shopping on the Web.

❸ DEVELOPING CRITICAL-THINKING SKILLS

Millions of people around the world belong to social networks. And yet, you may want to consider the following facts before joining or sharing personal information on a social site.

- Prospective or current employers often use the information you post on social sites to learn more about you.
- People who you do not know (or want to know) often can view your personal information.
- Although social sites have revised or improved their privacy policies, there are still too many reports of serious privacy abuses that affect too many users.

Today, the two most popular social sites are Facebook and Twitter. Both sites have privacy statements and attempt to protect users.

Assignment

1. Go to the Facebook Web site (www.facebook.com) and the Twitter Web site (www.twitter.com) and examine each site's privacy policy. (Hint: Scroll down to the bottom of the home page and look for the link marked "Privacy.")
2. Read each site's privacy policy. Note any concerns that you feel could restrict the type of information you might want to share or lead to a violation of your personal privacy.
3. In a two-page report, answer at least the following questions.
   a. What specific actions has each site taken to protect your privacy?
   b. Are there weaknesses in the policies that could lead to abuses of your personal privacy?
   c. Based on your research, which site do you think has the most effective privacy policy? Why?
   d. How has this exercise changed the type of information you would share on the Facebook or Twitter Web site? Explain your answer.

❹ BUILDING TEAM SKILLS

After graduating from college with a degree in marketing, your first job was working in the marketing department for a fast-food chain located in the southwestern part of the United States. After three years, you were promoted and became director of the chain's social media program. While monitoring posts about the company on Facebook and Twitter, you notice the following post from one of the firm's former employees.

> "Got fired today, but I was tired of serving low-quality food with expired expiration dates. Don't eat there or any of the chain's restaurants unless you want to get deathly ill."

To make matters worse, a couple of other employees who had recently been fired chimed in and made posts of a similar nature.

Assignment

1. Working in small teams, create a response that can be used to convince consumers that your company is committed to food freshness and quality and that these posts were made by employees who had been terminated.
2. Choose a spokesperson that will read your response to the rest of the class.
3. As a class, discuss the pros and cons of each response developed by each team.
4. Ask all members of the class to vote on the best response.
5. Finally, each team should prepare a report for the company's management that describes what happened and the response that was made to tell the company's side of this issue and restore consumer confidence in the firm's food products.

❺ RESEARCHING DIFFERENT CAREERS

Today, there are a wide assortment of career opportunities in companies that are involved in technology, social media, and e-business. In addition to existing business, there are new technology companies springing up every day. In many cases, these firms want people with a fresh outlook on how technology, social media, and e-business companies can differentiate their products or services from those of other companies in the same industry. They often prefer individuals without preconceived notions about how to proceed. Web site managers, designers, creative artists, and content specialists are just a few of the positions available. Many large online job sites, such as Monster.com, can help you to find out about employment opportunities and the special skills required for various jobs.

Assignment

1. Identify a Web site that provides information about careers in technology, social media, or e-business.
2. Summarize the positions that appear to be in high demand.
3. What are some of the special skills required to fill these jobs?
4. What salaries and benefits typically are associated with these positions?
5. Which job seems most appealing to you personally? Why?

ENDNOTES

1. Sources: Based on information in Dean Takahashi, "Angry Birds Space Introduces the Age of the Mobile Game Blockbuster," *Washington Post,* March 27, 2012, www.washingtonpost.com; Maeghan Ouimet, "Can This Company Become the New Disney?" *Inc.,* March 26, 2012, www.inc.com; Sherman So, "Angry Birds Head for China," *China Business,* January 18, 2012, www.atimes.com; Carter Dotson, "How Mobile Games Leapt from Cult to Cultural Phenomenon," *Mashable,* January 30, 2012, www.mashable.com; Chris Reidy, "Shipments Rise for Angry Birds Merchandise," *Boston Globe,* July 19, 2011, www.boston.com; Jenna Wortham, "Angry Birds, Flocking to Cellphones Everywhere," *New York Times,* December 11, 2010, www.nytimes.com; and the Rovio Entertainment Web site at www.rovio.com, accessed April 22, 2012.

2. Smith, Aaron, "Why Americans Use Social Media, Pew Internet and American Life Project," the Pew Web site at www.pewinternet.org, accessed November 14, 2011.
3. The Facebook Web site at www.facebook.com, accessed April 23, 2012.
4. The Coca-Cola Facebook Web site at www.facebook.com/cocacola, accessed April 23, 2012.
5. Williams, Kim, "Dell Hell: The Impact of Social Media on Corporate Communication" at https://learningspaces.njit.edu/elliot/content/dell-hell-impact-social-media-corporate-communication, accessed March 12, 2009.
6. Michael Miller, *The Ultimate Web Marketing Guide* (Indianapolis: QUE, 2011), 315.
7. Vipin Mayar and Geoff Ramsey, *Digital Impact: The Two Secrets to Online Marketing Success* (Hoboken, New Jersey: John Wiley & Sons, 2011), 147.
8. Tracy L. Tuten and Michael R. Solomonm, *Social Media Marketing* (Upper Saddle River, New Jersey: Pearson Publishing, 2013), 147.
9. Dave Chaffey, "2011 Marketing Trends," the Smart Insights Web site at www.smart-insights.com/digital-p.marketing-strategy/online-marketing-mix/2011-digital-marketing-trends/, accessed March 1, 2012.
10. Jessi Hempel, "Why Bing Loves Farmville," the CNNMoney Web site at http://tech.fortune.cnn.com/2010/03/09/why-bing-loves-farmville/, accessed March 9, 2010.
11. Tracy L. Tuten and Michael R. Solomonm, *Social Media Marketing* (Upper Saddle River, New Jersey: Pearson Publishing, 2013), 5.
12. Michael Norton and Jill Avery, "The Pepsi Refresh Project: A Thirst for Change," *Harvard Business School*, November 14, 2011, 1–24.
13. Stephanie Rosendahl, "Top 5 Tips for Reputation Management through Social Media," the Articlebase Web site at http://articlebase.com/internet-marketing-articles/top-5-tips-for-reputation-managmenet-through-social-media-4997832.html, accessed July 7, 2011.
14. John Deighton and Leora Kornfeld, "United Breaks Guitars" *Harvard Business School*, August 11, 2011, p. 1–13.
15. Emily Bryson York, "Domino's Reports 14 Percent Same-Store Sales Hike for First Quarter," the Advertising Age Web site at www.advertisingage.com, accessed April 1, 2012.
16. John Deighton and Leora Kornfeld, "The Ford Fiesta," *Harvard Business School*, June 20, 2011, 1–24.
17. Todd Wasserman, "How Old Spice Revived a Campaign that No One Wanted to Touch" the Mashable Social Media Web site at http://mashable.com/2011/11/01/old-spice-campaign, accessed November 1, 2011.
18. Vipin Mayar and Geoff Ramsey, *Digital Impact: The Two Secrets to Online Marketing Success* (Hoboken, New Jersey: John Wiley & Sons, 2011), p. 141–43.
19. Tracy L. Tuten and Michael R. Solomon, *Social Media Marketing* (Upper Saddle River, New Jersey: Pearson Publishing, 2013), 5.
20. "US Interactive Marketing Forecast 2011 to 2016," the Forrester Research Web site at wwwforrester.com, accessed August 24, 2011.
21. "Consumers Spend Less Time with Traditional Media: US Interactive Marketing Forecast 2011 to 2016," the Forrester Research Web site at www.forrester.com, accessed August 24, 2011.
22. Thomas Steenburgh, Jill Avery, and Naseem Dahoud, "Hubspot: Inbound Marketing and Web 2.0," *Harvard Business School*, January 24, 2011, 1–21.
23. Adam Ostrow (2009, December 8) "Dell Rides Twitter to $6.5 Million in Sales," the Mashable Social Media Web site at www.mashable.com, accessed April 1, 2012.
24. The Dorito's Crash the Super Bowl Web site at www.crashthesuperbowl.com, accessed May 2, 2012.
25. The Starbucks Idea Web site at www.mystarbucksidea.com, accessed April 27, 2012.
26. Melissa Barker, Donald Barker, Nicholas Bormann, and Krista E. Neher, *Social Media Marketing: A Strategic Approach* (Mason, OH: Cengage Publishing, 2103), 29.
27. Melissa Barker, Donald Barker, Nicholas Bormann, and Krista E. Neher, *Social Media Marketing: A Strategic Approach* (Mason, OH: Cengage Publishing, 2013), 31.
28. The Internet World Stats Web site at www.internetworldstats.com, accessed April 29, 2012.
29. Ibid.
30. Ibid.
31. Ibid.
32. The Javelin Strategy and Research Web site at www.idsafety.net, accessed April 29, 2012.
33. Based on information in "Foursquare: Social Media for Small Businesses," *CBSNews*, June 13, 2011, www.cbsnews.com; Katy Finneran, "Food Trucks' Tasty Tweets," *FOXBusiness*, May 13, 2011, http://foxbusiness.com; Dana Schuster, "On a Roll!" *New York Post*, May 11, 2011, www.nypost.com; Alexandra Wolfe, "Luke Holden's Luke's Lobster," *Businessweek*, October 14, 2010, www.businessweek.com; Benjamin Wallace, "On a Roll," *New York Magazine*, June 20, 2010, http://nymag.com.
34. Based on information in Bill Shea, "Advertisers Still Fans of Facebook," *Crain's Detroit Business*, May 20, 2012, www.crainsdetroit.com; "Road to IPO: Milestones in Facebook's History," *Associated Press*, May 18, 2012, www.businessweek.com; Somini Sengupta, "Facebook's Prospects May Rest on Trove of Data," *New York Times*, May 14, 2012, www.nytimes.com; Evelyn Rusli, Nicole Perlroth, and Nick Bilton, "The Education of Zuck," *New York Times*, May 13, 2012, BU1–BU5; Miguel Helft and Jessi Hempel, "Inside Facebook," *Fortune*, March 19, 2012, 113–122; Somini Sengupta, "FTC Settles Privacy Issue at Facebook," *New York Times*, November 29, 2011, www.nytimes.com.

©SERGEI KHAKIMULLIN/SHUTTERSTOCK

17

Using Management and Accounting Information

LEARNING OBJECTIVES

Once you complete this chapter, you will be able to:

1 Examine how information can reduce risk when making a decision.

2 Discuss management's information requirements.

3 Outline the five functions of an information system.

4 Explain why accurate accounting information and audited financial statements are important.

5 Read and interpret a balance sheet.

6 Read and interpret an income statement.

7 Describe business activities that affect a firm's cash flow.

8 Summarize how managers evaluate the financial health of a business.

PricewaterhouseCoopers Innovates Through PowerPitch

How do you get accounting and consulting specialists to think creatively about future business possibilities? With 766 offices in 158 nations, New York–based PricewaterhouseCoopers (now known as PwC) is one of the industry-leading "Big Four" accounting firms. It offers a wide range of accounting, auditing, consulting, and tax services—all designed to provide information to clients in many industries, including almost 90 percent of the *Fortune Global 500* companies. From a one-person operation in 1849, PwC has grown into a multinational giant with more than 169,000 employees.

To keep annual revenue growing beyond $30 billion, the company is looking for cutting-edge ideas as the foundation of future multimillion-dollar businesses. It recently held a contest called "PowerPitch," inviting teams of U.S. employees to pitch their best ideas for new businesses. The reward: $100,000 to the winning team, bragging rights, and the opportunity to shepherd the idea through the development process.

During the contest's first stage, hundreds of PwC teams submitted a grand total of 779 business proposals. Then all U.S. employees and a panel of PwC partners reviewed and voted on them. Of those proposals, 25 were chosen as semifinalists, and the five most promising moved on to become finalists. The finalist teams traveled to New York City to pitch to PwC's top executives (with thousands of colleagues watching via live webcast). After some discussion, the judges chose a grand prize winner. In a surprise move, they also backed all five of the finalist proposals for further development and sent the semifinalist proposals to an incubation group for further study. Just as important, PowerPitch proved that PwC welcomes and rewards bold new ideas—"the kind of program that becomes a talent magnet," says the U.S. chairman.

Meanwhile, PwC is already expanding into new services that will help corporate clients achieve their goals. For example, it now conducts "green" audits, examining a client's environmental activities at regular intervals. The audits show how much progress the client is making toward long-term sustainability targets such as conserving natural resources and energy, reducing emissions, and making products and processes as eco-friendly as possible.[1]

*I*nformation—that's what this chapter is all about! We begin this chapter with information about PricewaterhouseCoopers—the company profiled in the Inside Business feature. For this multinational accounting firm, one of its most important goals is to provide information to business clients so that managers and employees can increase sales, reduce expenses, and improve a firm's operating procedures. This same information is often shared with people outside the company—its lenders, suppliers, and investors. The "bottom line" is that without management and accounting information, managers can't make decisions, investors can't evaluate potential investments, and lenders and suppliers can't extend credit to a business firm.

We begin this chapter by describing why employees need information. The first three major sections in this chapter answer the following questions:

- How can information reduce risk when making a decision?
- What is a management information system?
- How do employees use a management information system?

Next, we look at why accounting information is important, attempts to improve financial reporting, and careers in the accounting industry. Then we examine the basic accounting equation and the three most important financial statements: the balance sheet, the income statement, and the statement of cash flows. Finally, we take a look at how managers evaluate the firm's financial health.

Examine how information can reduce risk when making a decision.

HOW CAN INFORMATION REDUCE RISK WHEN MAKING A DECISION?

As we noted in Chapter 1, information is one of the four major resources (along with material, human, and financial resources) managers must have to operate a business. Although a successful business uses all four resources efficiently, it is information that helps managers reduce risk when making a decision.

Information and Risk

To improve the decision-making process and reduce risk, the information used by individuals and business firms must be relevant or useful to meet a specific need. Using relevant information results in better decisions.

Relevant information → Better intelligence and knowledge → Better decisions

For businesses, better intelligence and knowledge that lead to better decisions are especially important because they can provide a *competitive edge* over competitors and improve a firm's *profits*.

Theoretically, with accurate and complete information, there is no risk whatsoever. On the other hand, a decision made without any information is a gamble. These two extreme situations are rare in business. For the most part, business decision makers see themselves located someplace between the extremes. As illustrated in Figure 17.1, when the amount of available information is high, there is less risk; when the amount of available information is low, there is more risk.

Suppose that a marketing manager for Procter & Gamble (P&G) responsible for the promotion of a well-known shampoo such as Pantene Pro-V has called a meeting of key people within her department to consider the selection of a new magazine advertisement. The company's advertising agency has submitted two new advertisements in sealed envelopes. Neither the manager nor any of her team has seen them before. Only one selection will be made for the new advertising campaign. Which advertisement should be chosen?

Without any further information, the team might as well make the decision by flipping a coin. If, however, team members were allowed to open the envelopes and examine the advertisements, they would have more information. If, in addition to allowing them to examine the advertisements, the marketing manager circulated a report containing the reactions of a group of target consumers to each of the two advertisements, the team would have even more information with which to work. Thus, information, when understood properly, produces knowledge and empowers managers and employees to make better decisions.

data numerical or verbal descriptions that usually result from some sort of measurement

information data presented in a form that is useful for a specific purpose

| FIGURE 17.1 | The Relationship Between Information and Risk |

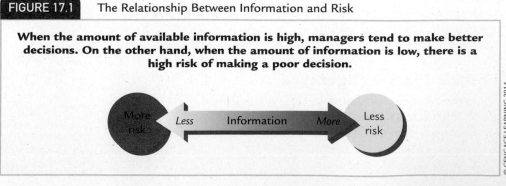

When the amount of available information is high, managers tend to make better decisions. On the other hand, when the amount of information is low, there is a high risk of making a poor decision.

© CENGAGE LEARNING 2014

Information Rules

Marketing research continues to show that discounts influence almost all car buyers. Simply put, if dealers lower their prices, they will sell more cars. This relationship between buyer behavior and price can be thought of as an information rule that usually will guide the marketing manager correctly. An information rule emerges when research confirms the same results each time that it studies the same or a similar set of circumstances.

Because of the volume of information they receive each day and their need to make decisions on a daily basis, businesspeople try to accumulate information rules to shorten the time they spend analyzing choices. Information rules are the "great simplifiers" for all decision makers. Business research is continuously looking for new rules that can be put to good use and looking to discredit old ones that are no longer valid. This ongoing process is necessary because business conditions rarely stay the same for very long.

The Difference Between Data and Information

Many people use the terms *data* and *information* interchangeably, but the two differ in important ways. **Data** are numerical or verbal descriptions that usually result from some sort of measurement. (The word *data* is plural; the singular form is datum.) Your current wage level, the amount of last year's after-tax profit for ExxonMobil Corporation, and the current retail prices of Honda automobiles are all data. Most people think of data as being numerical only, but they can be nonnumerical as well. A description of an individual as a "tall, athletic person with short, dark hair" certainly would qualify as data.

Information is data presented in a form that is useful for a specific purpose. Suppose that a human resources manager wants to compare the wages paid to male and female employees over a period of five years. The manager might begin with a stack of computer printouts listing every person employed by the firm, along with each employee's current and past wages. The manager would be hard pressed to make any sense of all the names and numbers. Such printouts consist of data rather than information.

Now suppose that the manager uses a computer to graph the average wages paid to men and to women in each of the five years. The result is information because the manager can use it for the purpose at hand—to compare wages paid to men with those paid to women over the five-year period. For a manager, information presented in a practical, useful form such as a graph simplifies the decision-making process.

Knowledge Management

The average company maintains a great deal of data that can be transformed into information. Typical data include records pertaining to personnel, inventory, sales, and accounting. Often each type of data is stored in individual departments within an organization. However, the data can be used more effectively when they are organized into a

Personal APPS

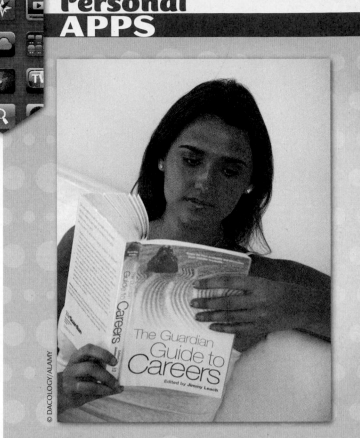

You can reduce the risk in any decision you make—a decision about school, a decision about work, or a decision about buying something expensive—by doing your homework. The more you know about the situation and your alternatives, the better your decision will be.

Technology giant! Cisco Systems is a company known for transforming how people connect, communicate, and collaborate. The technology giant is also a respected innovator that develops state-of-the-art equipment needed by employees, managers, *and* individuals to manage knowledge and information.

database. A **database** is a single collection of data and information stored in one place that can be used by people throughout an organization to make decisions. Although databases are important, the way the data and information are used is even more important—and more valuable to the firm. As a result, management information experts now use the term **knowledge management (KM)** to describe a firm's procedures for generating, using, and sharing the data and information. Typically, data, information, databases, and KM all become important parts of a firm's management information system.

WHAT IS A MANAGEMENT INFORMATION SYSTEM?

A **management information system (MIS)** is a system that provides managers and employees with the information they need to perform their jobs as effectively as possible. The purpose of an MIS (sometimes referred to as an information technology system or simply IT system) is to distribute timely and useful information from both internal and external sources to the managers and employees who need it (see Figure 17.2). Today, most medium-sized to large business firms have an information technology (IT) officer. An **information technology (IT) officer** is a manager at the executive level who is responsible for ensuring that a firm has the equipment necessary to provide the information the firm's employees and managers need to make effective decisions.

Today's typical MIS is built around a computerized system of record-keeping and communications software so that it can provide information based on a wide variety of data. After all, the goal is to provide needed information to all employees and managers.

A Firm's Information Requirements

Employees and managers have to plan for the future, implement their plans in the present, and evaluate results against what has been accomplished in the past. Of course, the specific types of information they need depend on their work area and on their level within the firm.

Today, many firms are organized into five areas of management: *finance, operations, marketing, human resources,* and *administration.* Managers in each of these areas need specific information in order to make decisions.

database a single collection of data and information stored in one place that can be used by people throughout an organization to make decisions

knowledge management (KM) a firm's procedures for generating, using, and sharing the data and information

management information system (MIS) a system that provides managers and employees with the information they need to perform their jobs as effectively as possible

information technology (IT) officer a manager at the executive level who is responsible for ensuring that a firm has the equipment necessary to provide the information the firm's employees and managers need to make effective decisions

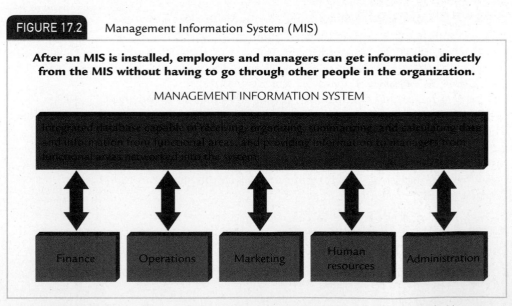

FIGURE 17.2 Management Information System (MIS)

After an MIS is installed, employers and managers can get information directly from the MIS without having to go through other people in the organization.

MANAGEMENT INFORMATION SYSTEM

Integrated database capable of receiving, organizing, summarizing, and calculating data and information from functional areas, and providing information to managers from functional areas networked into the system

Finance | Operations | Marketing | Human resources | Administration

Source: Adapted from Ricky W. Griffin, *Management* (Mason, OH: Cengage Learning, 2013). Reprinted with permission.

- *Financial managers* are obviously most concerned with a firm's finances. They must ensure that the firm's managers and employees, lenders and suppliers, stockholders and potential investors, and government agencies have the information they need to measure the financial health of the firm. Along with the firm's accountants, financial managers study its debts and receivables, cash flow, future capitalization needs, financial statements, and other accounting information. Of equal importance to financial managers is information about the present state of the economy, interest rates, and predictions of business conditions in the future.
- *Operations managers* are concerned with present and future sales levels, current inventory levels of work in process and finished goods, and the availability and cost of the resources required to produce products and services. They also must keep abreast of any innovative production technology that might be useful to the firm.
- *Marketing managers* need to have detailed information about a firm's products and services and those offered by competitors. Such information includes pricing strategies, new promotional campaigns, and products that competitors are test marketing. Information concerning the firm's customers, current and projected market share, and new and pending product legislation is also important to marketing managers.
- *Human resources managers* must be aware of anything that pertains to a firm's employees. Key examples include current wage levels and benefits packages both within the firm and in firms that compete for valuable employees, current legislation and court decisions that affect employment practices, union activities, and the firm's plans for growth, expansion, or mergers.
- *Administrative managers* are responsible for the overall management of the organization. Thus, they are concerned with the coordination of information—just as they are concerned with the coordination of material, human, and financial resources.

Administrators must ensure that all employees have access to the information they need to do their jobs. Administrative managers must also ensure that the information is used in a consistent manner throughout the firm. Suppose, for example, that General Electric (GE) is designing a new plant that will open in five years. GE's management will want answers to many questions: Is the capacity of the plant consistent with marketing plans based on sales projections? Will human resources managers be able to staff the plant on the basis of employment forecasts? And do sales projections indicate enough income to cover the expected cost of the plant? Next, administrative managers must make sure that all managers and employees are able to use the IT that is available. Certainly, this requires that all employees receive the skills training required to use the firm's MIS. Finally, administrative managers must commit to the costs of updating the firm's MIS and providing additional training when necessary.

Size and Complexity of the System

An MIS must be tailored to the needs of the organization it serves. In some firms, a tendency to save on initial costs may result in a system that is too small or overly simple. Such a system generally ends up serving only one or two management levels or a single department. Managers in other departments "give up" on the system as soon as they find that it cannot process their data.

Almost as bad is an MIS that is too large or too complex for the organization. Unused capacity and complexity do nothing but increase the cost of owning and operating the system. In addition, a system that is difficult to use probably will not be used at all.

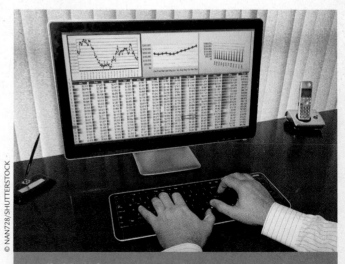

© NAN728/SHUTTERSTOCK

Is all this information really necessary? Today, we live in an information society—that is, a society in which large groups of individuals, employees, and managers generate or depend on information to perform everyday tasks. As a result, all three groups often complain that they have too much information. For many, the problem is not lack of information, but how to determine what information is really needed?

HOW DO EMPLOYEES USE A MANAGEMENT INFORMATION SYSTEM?

To provide information, a management information system (MIS) must perform five specific functions. It must (1) collect data, (2) store the data, (3) update the data, (4) process the data into information, and (5) present the information to users (see Figure 17.3).

Step 1: Collecting Data

A firm's employees, with the help of an MIS system, must gather the data and information needed to establish the firm's *database*. The database should include all past and current data that may be useful in managing the firm. Clearly, the data entered into the system must be *relevant* to the needs of the firm's managers. And perhaps most important, the data must be *accurate*. Irrelevant data are simply useless; inaccurate data can be disastrous. There are two data sources: *internal* and *external*.

Internal Sources of Data Typically, most of the data gathered for an MIS come from internal sources. The most common internal sources of information are managers and employees, company records and reports, and minutes of meetings.

Past and present accounting data can also provide information about the firm's transactions with customers, creditors, and suppliers. Sales reports are a source of data on sales, pricing strategies, and the effectiveness of promotional campaigns. Human resources records are useful as a source of data on wage and benefits levels, hiring patterns, employee turnover, and other personnel variables.

FIGURE 17.3　Five Management Information System Functions

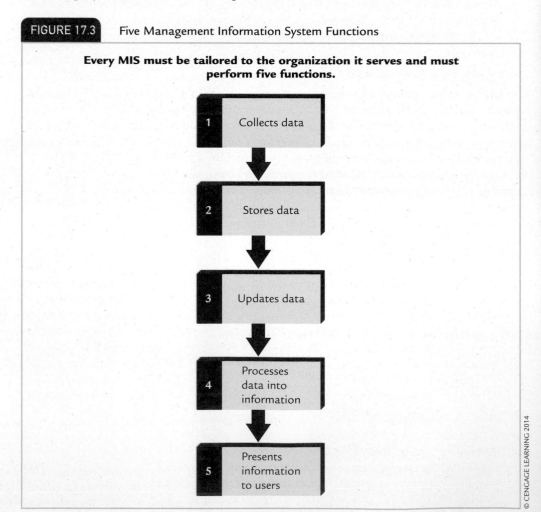

Every MIS must be tailored to the organization it serves and must perform five functions.

1. Collects data
2. Stores data
3. Updates data
4. Processes data into information
5. Presents information to users

© CENGAGE LEARNING 2014

Present and past production forecasts also should be included in the firm's database, along with information indicating how well these forecasts predicted actual events. Specific plans and management decisions—regarding capital expansion and new product development, for example—should also be incorporated into the MIS system.

External Sources of Data External sources of data include customers, suppliers, financial institutions and banks, trade and business publications, industry conferences, online computer services, lawyers, government sources, and firms that specialize in gathering data for organizations. For example, a marketing research company may acquire sales forecasts pertaining to product demand, consumer tastes, and other marketing variables. Suppliers are also an excellent source of information about the future availability and costs of raw materials and component parts. Bankers can often provide valuable economic insights and projections. The information furnished by trade and business publications and industry conferences is usually concerned as much with future projections as with present conditions. Legal issues and court decisions that may affect a firm are discussed occasionally in local newspapers and, more often, in specialized publications such as the *Wall Street Journal, Fortune,* and *BusinessWeek.* Government publications such as the *Monthly Labor Review* and the *Federal Reserve Bulletin* are also quite useful as sources of external data, as are a number of online computer services.

Whether the source of the data is internal or external, always remember the following three cautions:

1. The cost of obtaining data from some external sources, such as marketing research firms, can be quite high.
2. Outdated or incomplete data usually yield inaccurate information.
3. Although computers generally do not make mistakes, the people who use them can make or cause errors. When data (or information) and your judgment disagree, always check the data.

Step 2: Storing Data

An MIS must be capable of storing data until they are needed. Typically, the method chosen to store data depends on the size and needs of the organization. Small businesses may enter data and then store them directly on the hard drive inside an employee's computer. Generally, medium-sized to large businesses store data in a larger computer system and provide access to employees through a computer network. Today, networks take on many configurations and are designed by specialists who work with a firm's IT personnel to decide on what's best for the company.

Step 3: Updating Data

Today, an MIS must be able to update stored data regularly to ensure that the information presented to managers and employees is accurate, complete, and up-to-date. The frequency with which the data are updated depends on how fast they change and how often they are used. When it is vital to have current data, updating may occur as soon as the new data are available. For example, Giant Food Stores, a grocery store chain operating in the eastern part of the United States, has cash registers that automatically transmit data on each item sold to a central computer. The computer adjusts the store's inventory records accordingly. In some systems, the computer may even be programmed to reorder items whose inventories fall below some specified level. Data and information may also be entered into a firm's data bank at certain intervals—every 24 hours, weekly, or monthly.

Step 4: Processing Data

Some data are used in the form in which they are stored, whereas other data require processing to extract, highlight, or summarize the information they contain. **Data processing** is the transformation of data into a form that is useful for a specific purpose.

data processing the transformation of data into a form that is useful for a specific purpose

For verbal data, this processing consists mainly of extracting the pertinent material from storage and combining it into a report. Most business data, however, are in the form of numbers—large groups of numbers, such as daily sales totals or production costs for a specific product. Fortunately, computers can be programmed to process such large volumes of numbers quickly. While such groups of numbers may be difficult to handle and to comprehend, their contents can be summarized through the use of statistics. A **statistic** is a measure that summarizes a particular characteristic of an entire group of numbers.

Step 5: Presenting Information

An MIS must be capable of presenting information in a usable form. That is, the method of presentation—reports, tables, graphs, or charts, for example—must be appropriate for the information itself and for the uses to which it will be put.

Business Reports Verbal information may be presented in list or paragraph form. Employees often are asked to prepare formal business reports. A typical business report includes (1) an introduction, (2) the body of the report, (3) the conclusions, and (4) the recommendations.

The *introduction*, which sets the stage for the remainder of the report, describes the problem to be studied in the report, identifies the research techniques that were used, and previews the material that will be presented in the report. The *body* of the report should objectively describe the facts that were discovered in the process of completing the report. The body also should provide a foundation for the conclusions and the recommendations. The *conclusions* are statements of fact that describe the findings contained in the report. Conclusions should be specific, practical, and based on the evidence in the report. The *recommendations* section presents suggestions on how the problem might be solved. Like the conclusions, the recommendations should be specific, practical, and based on the evidence.

Visual Displays and Tables A visual display can also be used to present information and may be a diagram that represents several items of information in a manner that makes comparison easier. Figure 17.4 illustrates examples of visual displays generated by a computer. Typical visual displays include

- graphs;
- bar charts; and
- pie charts.

A tabular display is used to present verbal or numerical information in columns and rows. It is most useful in presenting information about two or more related variables. A table, for example, can be used to illustrate the number of salespeople in each region of the country, sales for different types of products, and total sales for all products (see Table 17.1). Information that is to be manipulated—for example, to calculate loan payments—is usually displayed in tabular form.

Tabular displays generally have less impact than visual displays. However, displaying the information that could be contained in a multicolumn table such as the one shown in Table 17.1 would require several bar or pie charts.

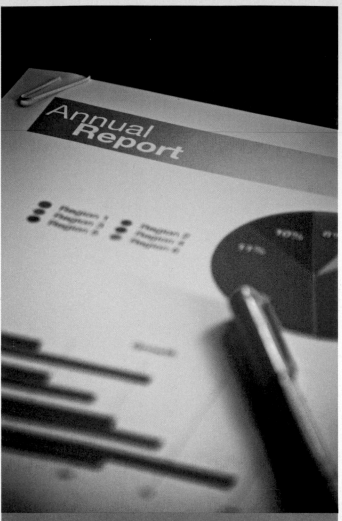

Who are the people who use information? Although the primary users of information are a firm's managers and employees, parties outside the organization—lenders, suppliers, stockholders, and government agencies—are also interested in the firm's information. In fact, both managers and employees and outside groups often examine a firm's annual report to determine the financial health of a firm.

statistic a measure that summarizes a particular characteristic of an entire group of numbers

FIGURE 17.4   Typical Visual Displays Used in Business Presentation

Visual displays help businesspeople present information in a form that can be understood easily.

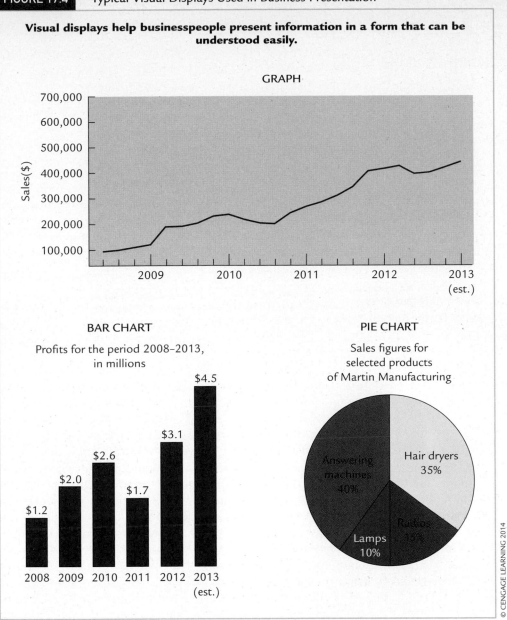

GRAPH

BAR CHART

Profits for the period 2008–2013, in millions

PIE CHART

Sales figures for selected products of Martin Manufacturing

© CENGAGE LEARNING 2014

TABLE 17.1   Typical Three-Column Table Used in Business Presentations

Tables are most useful for displaying information about two or more variables.

All-Star Technology Projected Sales

Section of the Country	Number of Salespeople	Consumer Products ($)	Industrial Products ($)
Eastern territory	15	1,500,000	3,500,000
Midwestern territory	20	2,000,000	5,000,000
Western territory	10	1,000,000	4,000,000
TOTAL	45	4,500,000	12,500,000

Going for SUCCESS

Information Technology and the Tablet

From factory floors to jetliner cockpits to corporate boardrooms, tablet computers have changed the way some businesses manage information—and created new challenges along the way. Jackson Kayak, a Tennessee-based kayak manufacturer, put iPads into the hands of 65 employees with the goal of improving efficiency and enhancing marketing. Until the company located and installed fully-functional apps for production management and other specific uses, it had to substitute iPhone apps and enlarge the images to fit the roomier iPad screen. Knowing that many kayak buyers are also adopting iPads, the company created its own app to introduce itself and its products.

Alaska Airlines is reducing weight and saving time and trees by giving every pilot a tablet computer equipped with aviation apps and digital flight manuals. Pilots can leave pounds of printed materials at home, and they gain fast touch-screen access to critical information. "When you need to make a decision in the cockpit, three to four minutes fumbling with paper is an eternity," says one pilot.

Top managers at the car-guide company Edmunds.com all carry tablet computers. The president, Avi Steinlauf, takes his tablet everywhere, loaded with custom apps to track and analyze data about the business. Whether he's on the road or in the boardroom, Steinlauf likes being able to monitor Web site traffic patterns and dig deep for details during meetings with staff and clients.

Sources: Based on information in Shara Tibken, "Here Come Tablets. Here Come Problems," *Wall Street Journal*, April 2, 2012, www.wsj.com; Alex Konrad, "Tablets Storm the Corner Office," *Fortune*, October 13, 2011, http://tech.fortune.cnn.com; Kate Murphy, "The Paperless Cockpit," *New York Times*, July 4, 2011, www.nytimes.com.

Making Smart Decisions

How do managers and employees sort out relevant and useful information from the spam, junk mail, and useless data? In addition to the steps described in the last section (collecting data, storing data, updating data, processing data, and presenting information) three different software applications can actually help to improve and speed the decision-making process for people at different levels within an organization. First, a **decision-support system (DSS)** is a type of software program that provides relevant data and information to help a firm's employees make decisions. It also can be used to determine the effect of changing different variables and answer "what if" type questions. For example, a manager at Michigan-based Pulte Homes may use a DSS to determine prices for new homes built in an upscale, luxury subdivision. By entering the number of homes that will be built along with different costs associated with land, labor, materials, building permits, promotional costs, and all other costs, a DSS can help to determine a base price for each new home. It is also possible to increase or decrease the building costs and determine new home prices for each set of assumptions with a DSS. Although similar to a DSS, an **executive information system (EIS)** is a computer-based system that facilitates and supports the decision-making needs of top managers and senior executives by providing easy access to both internal and external information.

An **expert system** is a type of computer program that uses artificial intelligence to imitate a human's ability to think. An expert system uses a set of rules that analyze information supplied by the user about a particular activity or problem. Based on the information supplied, the expert system then provides recommendations or suggests specific actions in order to help make decisions. Expert systems, for example, have been used to schedule manufacturing tasks, diagnose illnesses, determine credit limits for credit-card customers, evaluate loan applications, and develop electronic games.

decision-support system (DSS) a type of software program that provides relevant data and information to help a firm's employees make decisions

executive information system (EIS) a computer-based system that facilitates and supports the decision-making needs of top managers and senior executives by providing easy access to both internal and external information

expert system a type of computer program that uses artificial intelligence to imitate a human's ability to think

WHY ACCOUNTING INFORMATION IS IMPORTANT

④ Explain why accurate accounting information and audited financial statements are important.

In today's competitive business environment, all successful firms use information to make decisions. In order to obtain needed information, firms use a management information system like the one described in the first part of this chapter. Executives, managers, and employees also rely on the firm's accounting system to provide needed financial information. **Accounting** is the process of systematically collecting, analyzing, and reporting financial information. Just for a moment, think about the following three questions:

1. How much profit did a business earn last year?
2. How much tax does a business owe the Internal Revenue Service?
3. How much cash does a business have to pay lenders and suppliers?

In each case, the firm's accountants and its accounting system provide the answers to these questions and many others. Although accounting information can be used to answer questions about what has happened in the past, it can also be used to help make decisions about the future.

Because the information provided by a firm's accountants and its accounting system is so important, managers and other groups interested in a business firm's financial records must be able to "trust the numbers." To improve the accuracy of a firm's accounting information and its financial statements, businesses rely on audits conducted by accountants employed by public accounting firms.

Why Audited Financial Statements Are Important

An **audit** is an examination of a company's financial statements and the accounting practices that produced them. The purpose of an audit is to make sure that a firm's financial statements have been prepared in accordance with **generally accepted accounting principles (GAAPs)**. GAAPs have been developed to provide an accepted set of guidelines and practices for U.S. companies reporting financial information and the accounting profession. At the time of publication, the Financial Accounting Standards Board (FASB), which establishes and improves accounting standards for U.S. companies, is working toward establishing a new set of standards that combines GAAPs with the International Financial Reporting Standards (IFRS) to create one set of accounting standards that can be used by both U.S. and multinational firms. Created by the International Accounting Standards Board, IFRS are now used in more than 100 different countries around the world. For multinational firms, the benefits of global accounting standards are huge because preparing financial statements and accounting records that meet global standards saves both time and money. According to many accounting experts, it's not a question of whether IFRS guidelines will be adopted in the United States, but when.[2]

If an accountant determines that a firm's financial statements present financial information fairly and conform to GAAPs, then he or she will issue the following statement:

> *In our opinion, the financial statements . . . present fairly, in all material respects . . . in conformity with generally accepted accounting principles.*

Although an audit and the resulting report do not *guarantee* that a company has not "cooked" the books, it does imply that, on the whole, the company has followed GAAPs. Bankers, creditors,

accounting the process of systematically collecting, analyzing, and reporting financial information

audit an examination of a company's financial statements and the accounting practices that produced them

generally accepted accounting principles (GAAPs) an accepted set of guidelines and practices for companies reporting financial information and for the accounting profession

Two large accounting scandals! Many experts believe that top executives at home mortgage lenders Fannie Mae and Freddie Mac used fraudulent accounting tactics to enhance each firm's financial information. Unfortunately, these two firms were not the only companies involved in accounting scandals in recent years—there were many more. As a result, the demands for improved accounting procedures made by lenders, investors, employees, government agencies, and other interested groups led to the passage of the Sarbanes-Oxley Act.

investors, and government agencies are willing to rely on an auditor's opinion because of the historically ethical reputation and independence of auditors and accounting firms. Finally, it should be noted that without the audit function and GAAPs, there would be very little oversight or supervision. The validity of a firm's financial statements and its accounting records would drop quickly, and firms would find it difficult to obtain debt financing, acquire goods and services from suppliers, find investor financing, or prepare documents requested by government agencies.

Reform: The Sarbanes–Oxley Act of 2002

According to John Bogle, founder of Vanguard Mutual Funds, "Investing is an act of faith. Without that faith—that reported numbers reflect reality, that companies are being run honestly, that Wall Street is playing it straight, and that investors aren't being hoodwinked—our capital markets simply can't function."[3] In reality, what Mr. Bogle says is true. To help ensure that corporate financial information is accurate and to prevent the type of accounting scandals that have occurred in the past, Congress enacted the Sarbanes–Oxley Act in 2002. Key components include the following:[4]

- The Securities and Exchange Commission (SEC) is required to establish a full-time five-member federal oversight board that will police the accounting industry.
- Chief executive and financial officers are required to certify periodic financial reports and are liable for intentional violations of securities reporting requirements.
- Accounting firms are prohibited from providing many types of non-audit and consulting services to the companies they audit.
  - Auditors must maintain financial documents and audit work papers for five years.
  - Auditors, accountants, and employees can be imprisoned for up to 20 years and subject to fines for destroying financial documents and willful violations of the securities laws.
  - A public corporation must change its lead auditing firm every five years.
  - There is added protection for whistle-blowers who report violations of the Sarbanes–Oxley Act.

Although most people welcome the Sarbanes–Oxley Act, complex rules make compliance more expensive and time-consuming for corporate management and more difficult for accounting firms. Yet, most people agree that the cost of compliance is justified.

Different Types of Accounting

Although many people think that all accountants do the same tasks, there are special areas of expertise within the accounting industry. In fact, accounting is usually broken down into two broad categories: managerial and financial.

Managerial accounting provides managers and employees within the organization with the information needed to make decisions about a firm's financing, investing, marketing, and operating activities. By using managerial accounting information, both managers and employees can evaluate how well they have done in the past and what they can expect in the future. **Financial accounting**, on the other hand, generates financial statements and reports for interested people outside of an organization. Typically, stockholders, financial analysts, bankers, lenders, suppliers, government agencies, and other interested groups use the information provided by financial accounting to determine how well a business firm has achieved its goals. In

managerial accounting provides managers and employees with the information needed to make decisions about a firm's financing, investing, marketing, and operating activities

financial accounting generates financial statements and reports for interested people outside an organization

COURTESY OF AICPA

Information you can use to become a CPA. The American Institute of CPAs (AICPA) is an excellent source of information about the educational requirements and experience required to become a certified public accountant and also the CPA examination. In addition, the site provides information about current issues that affect the accounting industry and continuing education requirements for CPAs. If you're interested in a career in accounting, why not take a look at www.aicpa.org.

addition to managerial and financial accounting, additional special areas of accounting include the following:

- *cost accounting*—determining the cost of producing specific products or services;
- *tax accounting*—planning tax strategy and preparing tax returns for firms or individuals;
- *government accounting*—providing basic accounting services to ensure that tax revenues are collected and used to meet the goals of state, local, and federal agencies; and
- *not-for-profit accounting*—helping not-for-profit organizations to account for all donations and expenditures.

Careers in Accounting

According to the *Occupational Outlook Handbook,* published by the Department of Labor, job opportunities for accountants, as well as auditors in the accounting area, are expected to experience a 16 percent increase or about average employment growth between now and the year 2020.[5] And more good news: Starting salaries for employees in the accounting industry are often higher than the starting salaries for other entry-level positions.

Accounting can be an exciting and rewarding career. To be successful in the accounting industry, employees must

- Be responsible, honest, and ethical.
- Have a strong background in financial management.
- Know how to use a computer and software to process data into accounting information.
- Be able to communicate with people who need accounting information.

Today, accountants generally are classified as either private accountants or public accountants. A *private accountant* is employed by a specific organization. On the other hand, a *public accountant* works on a fee basis for clients and may be self-employed or be the employee of an accounting firm. Accounting firms range in size from one-person operations to huge international firms with hundreds of accounting partners and thousands of employees. Today, the largest accounting firms, sometimes referred to as the "Big Four," are PricewaterhouseCoopers (PwC), Ernst & Young, KPMG, and Deloitte Touche Tohmatsu.

Typically, public accounting firms include on their staffs at least one **certified public accountant (CPA),** an individual who has met state requirements for accounting education and experience and has passed a rigorous accounting examination. More information about general requirements and the CPA profession can be obtained by contacting the American Institute of CPAs (AICPA) at www.aicpa.org. State requirements usually include a college degree or a specified number of hours of college course work and generally from one to three years of on-the-job experience. Details regarding specific state requirements for practice as a CPA can be obtained by contacting the state's board of accountancy.

Certification as a CPA brings both status and responsibility. Publicly traded corporations must hire an independent certified public accountant to audit their financial statements. In addition to auditing a corporation's financial statements, typical services performed by CPAs include planning and preparing tax returns, determining the true cost of producing and marketing a firm's goods or services, and compiling the financial information needed to make major management decisions. Fees for the services provided by CPAs generally range from $50 to $300 an hour.

Social MEDIA

The Big Four Go Social

Why does a CPA tweet? All of the Big Four accounting firms are active on Twitter, as well as posting messages, contents, and photos on Facebook, listing job opening on LinkedIn, and posting videos and commercials on YouTube. The idea is to connect with potential job candidates, interact with clients and potential clients, engage employees, showcase the firms' expertise, and polish their reputations.

For example, PricewaterhouseCoopers, Ernst & Young, KPMG, and Deloitte Touche Tohmatsu recruit new graduates and experienced professionals by posting job openings on Facebook. They also use Twitter and LinkedIn to publicize studies they've conducted, comment on business conditions, and have special Facebook pages just for "alumni"—former staff members—to network.

Source: Luis Gallardo, "Fueling the Social Media Engine," *Social Media Marketing Magazine,* January 17, 2011, www.smmmagazine.com; Karl Flinders, "How Deloitte is Using Facebook, Twitter, and Linkedin, to Recruit, "*Computerweekly,* July 2, 2010, www.computerweekly.com

certified public accountant (CPA) an individual who has met state requirements for accounting education and experience and has passed a rigorous accounting examination

THE ACCOUNTING EQUATION AND THE BALANCE SHEET

At the beginning of this chapter, *information* was defined as data presented in a form that is useful for a specific purpose. Now, we examine how financial *data* is transformed into financial *information* and reported on three very important financial statements—the balance sheet, income statement, and statement of cash flows. We begin by describing why the fundamental accounting equation is the basis for a firm's balance sheet.

The Accounting Equation

The accounting equation is a simple statement that forms the basis for the accounting process. This equation shows the relationship between a firm's assets, liabilities, and owners' equity.

- **Assets** are the resources a business owns—cash, inventory, equipment, and real estate.
- **Liabilities** are the firm's debts—borrowed money it owes to others that must be repaid.
- **Owners' equity** is the difference between total assets and total liabilities—what would be left for the owners if the firm's assets were sold and the money used to pay off its liabilities.

The relationship between assets, liabilities, and owners' equity is shown by the following **accounting equation**:

$$\text{Assets} = \text{Liabilities} + \text{Owners' equity}$$

The dollar total of all of a firm's assets cannot equal more than the total funds obtained by borrowing money (liabilities) and the investment of the owner(s). Whether a business is a small corner grocery store or a giant corporation such as General Mills, its assets must equal the sum of its liabilities and owners' equity. To use this equation, a firm's accountants must record raw data—that is, the firm's day-to-day financial transactions—using the double-entry system of bookkeeping. The **double-entry bookkeeping system** is a system in which each financial transaction is recorded as two separate accounting entries to maintain the balance shown in the accounting equation. All of the financial transactions can now be summarized in the firm's financial statements. This information is presented in a standardized format to make the statements as accessible as possible to the various people who may be interested in the firm's financial affairs—managers, employees, lenders, suppliers, stockholders, potential investors, and government agencies. In fact the form of the financial statements is pretty much the same for all businesses, from a neighborhood video store or small dry cleaner to giant conglomerates such as Home Depot, Boeing, and Bank of America. A firm's financial statements are prepared at least once a year and included in the firm's annual report. An **annual report** is a report distributed to stockholders and other interested parties that describes a firm's operating activities and its financial condition. Most firms also have financial statements prepared semiannually, quarterly, or monthly.

The Balance Sheet

Question: *Where could you find the total amount of assets, liabilities, and owners' equity for Hershey Foods Corporation?*

Answer: The firm's balance sheet.

A **balance sheet** (sometimes referred to as a **statement of financial position**) is a summary of the dollar amounts of a firm's assets, liabilities, and owners' equity accounts at the end of a specific accounting period. The balance sheet must demonstrate that assets are equal to liabilities plus owners' equity. Most people think of a balance

assets the resources that a business owns

liabilities a firm's debts and obligations

owners' equity the difference between a firm's assets and its liabilities

accounting equation the basis for the accounting process: *assets=liabilities+owners' equity*

double-entry bookkeeping system a system in which each financial transaction is recorded as two separate accounting entries to maintain the balance shown in the accounting equation

annual report a report distributed to stockholders and other interested parties that describes the firm's operating activities and its financial condition

balance sheet (or statement of financial position) a summary of the dollar amounts of a firm's assets, liabilities, and owners' equity accounts at the end of a specific accounting period

FIGURE 17.5   Personal Balance Sheet

Often individuals determine their net worth, or owners' equity, by subtracting the value of their liabilities from the value of their assets.

Marty Campbell
Personal Balance Sheet
December 31, 20XX

ASSETS		LIABILITIES	
Cash	$ 2,500	Automobile loan	$ 9,500
Savings account	5,000	Credit card balance	500
Automobile	15,000	TOTAL LIABILITIES	$10,000
Stereo	1,000		
Television	500		
Furniture	2,500	NET WORTH (Owners' Equity)	16,500
TOTAL ASSETS	$26,500	TOTAL LIABILITIES AND NET WORTH	$26,500

© CENGAGE LEARNING 2014

sheet as a statement that reports the financial condition of a business firm such as the Hershey Foods Corporation, but balance sheets apply to individuals, too. For example, Marty Campbell graduated from college three years ago and obtained a position as a sales representative for an office supply firm. After going to work, he established a checking and savings account and purchased an automobile, stereo, television, and a few pieces of furniture. Marty paid cash for some purchases, but he had to borrow money to pay for the larger ones. Figure 17.5 shows Marty's current personal balance sheet.

Marty Campbell's assets total $26,500, and his liabilities amount to $10,000. Although the difference between total assets and total liabilities is referred to as *owners' equity* or *stockholders' equity* for a business, it is normally called *net worth* for an individual. As reported on Marty's personal balance sheet, net worth is $16,500. The total assets ($26,500) and the total liabilities *plus* net worth ($26,500) are equal. Thus, the accounting equation (Assets = Liabilities + Owners' equity) is still in balance.

Figure 17.6 shows the balance sheet for Northeast Art Supply, a small corporation that sells picture frames, paints, canvases, and other artists' supplies to retailers in New England. Note that assets are reported on the left side of the statement, and liabilities and stockholders' equity are reported on the right side. Let's work through the different accounts in Figure 17.6.

liquidity the ease with which an asset can be converted into cash

current assets assets that can be converted quickly into cash or that will be used in one year or less

Assets

On a balance sheet, assets are listed in order from the *most liquid* to the *least liquid*. The **liquidity** of an asset is the ease with which it can be converted into cash.

Current Assets Current assets are assets that can be converted quickly into cash or that will be used in one year or less. Because cash is the most liquid asset, it is listed first. Next are *marketable securities*—stocks, bonds, and other investments—that can be converted into cash in a matter of days.

© NDOELJINDOEL/SHUTTERSTOCK

Checking it once, checking it twice. . . . Before determining the total value of a firm's assets, accountants must determine the value of each type of inventory a firm has on hand to meet customer demand. Accurate accounting procedures for inventory can also determine when it is time to order more inventory.

FIGURE 17.6 Business Balance Sheet

A balance sheet (sometimes referred to as a statement of financial position) summarizes a firm's accounts at the end of an accounting period, showing the various dollar amounts that enter into the accounting equation. Note that assets ($340,000) equal liabilities plus owners' equity ($340,000) and the accounting equation is still in balance.

NORTHEAST ART SUPPLY, INC.

Balance Sheet
December 31, 20XX

ASSETS

Current assets

Cash		$ 59,000
Marketable securities		10,000
Accounts receivable	$ 40,000	
Less allowance for doubtful accounts	2,000	38,000
Notes receivable		32,000
Merchandise inventory		41,000
Prepaid expenses		2,000
Total current assets		$182,000

Fixed assets

Delivery equipment	$110,000	
Less accumulated depreciation	20,000	$ 90,000
Furniture and store equipment	$62,000	
Less accumulated depreciation	15,000	47,000
Total fixed assets		137,000

Intangible assets

Patents		$ 21,000
Total intangible assets		21,000
TOTAL ASSETS		$340,000

LIABILITIES AND STOCKHOLDERS' EQUITY

Current liabilities

Accounts payable	$ 35,000	
Notes payable	25,675	
Salaries payable	4,000	
Taxes payable	5,325	
Total current liabilities		$ 70,000

Long-term liabilities

Mortgage payable on store equipment	$ 40,000	
Total long-term liabilities		$ 40,000
TOTAL LIABILITIES		$110,000

Stockholders' equity

Common stock (25,000×$6)	$ 150,000	
Retained earnings	80,000	
TOTAL OWNERS' EQUITY		230,000
TOTAL LIABILITIES AND OWNERS' EQUITY		$340,000

Next are the firm's receivables. Its *accounts receivable,* which result from allowing customers to make credit purchases, generally are paid within 30 to 60 days. However, the firm expects that some of these debts will not be collected. Thus, it has reduced its accounts receivables by a 5 percent *allowance for doubtful accounts.* The firm's *notes receivable* are receivables for which customers have signed promissory notes. They generally are repaid over a longer period of time than the firm's accounts receivable.

Northeast's *merchandise inventory* represents the value of goods on hand for sale to customers. Since Northeast Art Supply is a wholesale operation, the inventory listed in Figure 17.6 represents finished goods ready for sale to retailers. For a manufacturing firm, merchandise inventory also may represent raw materials that will become part of a finished product or work that has been partially completed but requires further processing.

Northeast Art's last current asset is *prepaid expenses,* which are assets that have been paid for in advance but have not yet been used. An example is insurance premiums. They are usually paid at the beginning of the policy year. The unused portion (say, for the last four months of the time period covered by the policy) is a prepaid expense. For Northeast Art, all current assets total $182,000.

Fixed Assets **Fixed assets** are assets that will be held or used for a period longer than one year. They generally include land, buildings, and equipment used in the continuing operation of the business. Although Northeast Art owns no land or buildings, it does own delivery equipment that originally cost $110,000. It also owns furniture and store equipment that originally cost $62,000.

fixed assets assets that will be held or used for a period longer than one year

Note that the values of both fixed assets are decreased by their *accumulated depreciation*. **Depreciation** is the process of apportioning the cost of a fixed asset over the period during which it will be used, that is, its useful life. The depreciation amount allotted to each year is an expense for that year, and the value of the asset must be reduced by the amount of depreciation expense. In the case of Northeast's delivery equipment, $20,000 of its value has been depreciated (or used up) since it was purchased. Its value at this time is thus $110,000 less $20,000, or $90,000. In a similar fashion, the original value of furniture and store equipment ($62,000) has been reduced by depreciation totaling $15,000. Furniture and store equipment now has a reported value of $47,000. For Northeast Art, all fixed assets total $137,000.

Intangible Assets **Intangible assets** are assets that do not exist physically but that have a value based on the rights or privileges they confer on a firm. They include patents, copyrights, trademarks, and goodwill. By their nature, intangible assets are long-term assets—they are of value to the firm for a number of years.

Northeast Art Supply lists a *patent* for a special oil paint that the company purchased from the inventor. The firm's accountants estimate that the patent has a current market value of $21,000. The firm's intangible assets total $21,000. Now it is possible to total all three types of assets for Northeast Art. As calculated in Figure 17.6, total assets are $340,000.

Liabilities and Owners' Equity

The liabilities and the owners' equity accounts complete the balance sheet. The firm's liabilities are separated into two categories—current and long-term liabilities.

Current Liabilities A firm's **current liabilities** are debts that will be repaid in one year or less. Northeast Art Supply purchased merchandise from its suppliers on credit. Thus, its balance sheet includes an entry for accounts payable. *Accounts payable* are short-term obligations that arise as a result of a firm making credit purchases.

Notes payable are obligations that have been secured with promissory notes. They are usually short-term obligations, but they may extend beyond one year. Only those that must be paid within the year are listed under current liabilities.

Northeast Art also lists *salaries payable* and *taxes payable* as current liabilities. These are both expenses that have been incurred during the current accounting period but will be paid in the next accounting period. For Northeast Art, current liabilities total $70,000.

Long-Term Liabilities **Long-term liabilities** are debts that need not be repaid for at least one year. Northeast lists only one long-term liability—a $40,000 *mortgage payable* for store equipment. As you can see in Figure 17.6, Northeast Art's current and long-term liabilities total $110,000.

Owners' or Stockholders' Equity For a sole proprietorship or partnership, the owners' equity is shown as the difference between assets and liabilities. In a partnership, each partner's share of the ownership is reported separately in each owner's name. For a corporation, the owners' equity usually is referred to as *stockholders' equity*. The

Personal APPS

Before you accept a company's job offer or buy its stock, check financials and its business situation. Are profits increasing or decreasing? How is it handling its debt? What are its plans for expansion?

depreciation the process of apportioning the cost of a fixed asset over the period during which it will be used

intangible assets assets that do not exist physically but that have a value based on the rights or privileges they confer on a firm

current liabilities debts that will be repaid in one year or less

long-term liabilities debts that need not be repaid for at least one year dollar amount reported on the balance sheet is the total value of stock plus retained earnings that have accumulated to date. **Retained earnings** are the portion of a business's profits not distributed to stockholders.

The original investment by the owners of Northeast Art Supply was $150,000 and was obtained by selling 25,000 shares at $6 per share. In addition, $80,000 of Northeast Art's earnings has been reinvested in the business since it was founded. Thus, owners' equity totals $230,000.

As the two grand totals in Figure 17.6 show, Northeast Art's assets and the sum of its liabilities and owners' equity are equal—at $340,000. The accounting equation (Assets = Liabilities + Owners' equity) is still in balance.

Read and interpret an income statement.

THE INCOME STATEMENT

Question: *Where can you find the profit or loss amount for Apple, Inc.?*

Answer: The firm's income statement.

An **income statement** is a summary of a firm's revenues and expenses during a specified accounting period—one month, three months, six months, or a year. The income statement is sometimes called the *earnings statement* or *the statement of income and expenses*. Let's begin our discussion by constructing a personal income statement for Marty Campbell. Having worked as a sales representative for an office supply firm for the past three years, Marty now earns $33,600 a year, or $2,800 a month. After deductions, his take-home pay is $1,900 a month. As illustrated in Figure 17.7, Marty's typical monthly expenses include payments for an automobile

FIGURE 17.7	Personal Income Statement

By subtracting expenses from income, anyone can construct a personal income statement and determine if he or she has a surplus or deficit at the end of each month.

Marty Campbell
Personal Income Statement
For the month ended December 31, 20XX

INCOME (Take-home pay)		$1,900
LESS MONTHLY EXPENSES		
Automobile loan	$ 250	
Credit card payment	100	
Apartment rent	500	
Utilities	200	
Food	250	
Clothing	100	
Recreation & entertainment	250	
TOTAL MONTHLY EXPENSES		1,650
CASH SURPLUS (or profit)		$ 250

retained earnings the portion of a business's profits not distributed to stockholders

income statement a summary of a firm's revenues and expenses during a specified accounting period

FIGURE 17.8 Business Income Statement

An income statement summarizes a firm's revenues and expenses during a specified accounting period. For Northeast Art Supply, net income after taxes is $30,175.

NORTHEAST ART SUPPLY, INC.

Income Statement
for the Year Ended
December 31, 20XX

Revenues			
Gross sales		$465,000	
Less sales returns and allowances	$ 9,500		
Less sales discounts	4,500	14,000	
Net sales			$451,000
Cost of goods sold			
Beginning inventory, January 1, 20XX		$ 40,000	
Purchases	$346,000		
Less purchase discounts	11,000		
Net purchases		335,000	
Cost of goods available for sale		$375,000	
Less ending inventory December 31, 20XX		41,000	
Cost of goods sold			334,000
Gross profit			$117,000
Operating expenses			
Selling expenses			
Sales salaries	$ 22,000		
Advertising	4,000		
Sales promotion	2,500		
Depreciation—store equipment	3,000		
Depreciation—delivery equipment	4,000		
Miscellaneous selling expenses	1,500		
Total selling expenses		$ 37,000	
General expenses			
Office salaries	$ 28,500		
Rent	8,500		
Depreciation—furniture	1,500		
Utilities expense	2,500		
Insurance expense	1,000		
Miscellaneous expense	500		
Total general expense		42,500	
Total operating expenses			79,500
Net income from operations			$ 37,500
Less interest expense			2,000
NET INCOME BEFORE TAXES			$ 35,500
Less federal income taxes			5,325
NET INCOME AFTER TAXES			$ 30,175

© CENGAGE LEARNING 2014

loan, credit card purchases, apartment rent, utilities, food, clothing, and recreation and entertainment.

Although the difference between income and expenses is referred to as *profit* or *loss* for a business, it is normally referred to as a *cash surplus* or *cash deficit* for an individual. Fortunately for Marty, he has a surplus of $250 at the end of each month. He can use this surplus for savings, investing, or paying off debts. It is also possible to use the information from a personal income statement to construct a personal budget. A *personal budget* is a specific plan for spending your income—over the next month, for example.

Figure 17.8 shows the income statement for Northeast Art Supply. For a business, revenues *less* cost of goods sold *less* operating expenses equals net income.

Revenues

Revenues are the dollar amounts earned by a firm from selling goods, providing services, or performing business activities. Like most businesses, Northeast Art Supply obtains its revenues solely from the sale of its products or services. The revenues section of its income statement begins with gross sales. **Gross sales** are the total dollar amount

revenues the dollar amounts earned by a firm from selling goods, providing services, or performing business activities

gross sales the total dollar amount of all goods and services sold during the accounting period of all goods and services sold during the accounting period. Deductions made from this amount are

- *sales returns*—merchandise returned to the firm by its customers;
- *sales allowances*—price reductions offered to customers who accept slightly damaged or soiled merchandise; and
- *sales discounts*—price reductions offered to customers who pay their bills promptly.

The remainder is the firm's net sales. **Net sales** are the actual dollar amounts received by the firm for the goods and services it has sold after adjustment for returns, allowances, and discounts. For Northeast Art, net sales are $451,000.

Cost of Goods Sold

net sales the actual dollar amounts received by a firm for the goods and services it has sold after adjustment for returns, allowances, and discounts

cost of goods sold the dollar amount equal to beginning inventory *plus* net purchases *less* ending inventory

gross profit a firm's net sales *less* the cost of goods sold

operating expenses all business costs other than the cost of goods sold

net income occurs when revenues exceed expenses

net loss occurs when expenses exceed revenues

The standard method of determining the **cost of goods sold** by a retailing or a wholesaling firm can be summarized as follows:

Cost of goods sold = Beginning inventory + Net purchases – Ending inventory

According to Figure 17.8, Northeast Art Supply began its accounting period on January 1 with a merchandise inventory that cost $40,000. During the next 12 months, the firm purchased merchandise valued at $346,000. After deducting *purchase discounts*, however, it paid only $335,000 for this merchandise. Thus, during the year, Northeast had total *goods available for sale* valued at $40,000 plus $335,000, for a total of $375,000.

Twelve months later, at the end of the accounting period on December 31, Northeast had sold all but $41,000 worth of the available goods. The cost of goods sold by Northeast was therefore $375,000 less ending inventory of $41,000, or $334,000. It is now possible to calculate gross profit. A firm's **gross profit** is its net sales *less* the cost of goods sold. For Northeast Art Supply, gross profit was $117,000.

Operating Expenses

A firm's **operating expenses** are all business costs other than the cost of goods sold. Total operating expenses generally are divided into two categories: selling expenses or general expenses.

Selling expenses are costs related to the firm's marketing activities. For Northeast Art Supply, selling expenses total $37,000. *General expenses* are costs incurred in managing a business, in this case, a total of $42,500. Now it is possible to total both selling and general expenses. As Figure 17.8 shows, total operating expenses for the accounting period are $79,500.

Net Income

When revenues exceed expenses, the difference is called **net income**. When expenses exceed revenues, the difference is called **net loss**. As Figure 17.8 shows, Northeast Art's *net income from operations* is computed as gross profit ($117,000) less total operating expenses ($79,500). For Northeast Art, net income from operations is $37,500. From this amount, *interest expense* of $2,000 is deducted to obtain a *net income before taxes* of $35,500. The interest expense is deducted in this section of the income statement because it is not an operating expense. Rather, it is an expense that results from financing the business.

Northeast Art's *federal income taxes* are $5,325. Although these taxes may or may not be payable immediately, they are definitely an expense that must be deducted from income. This leaves Northeast Art with a *net income after taxes* of $30,175. This amount may be used to pay a dividend to stockholders, it may be retained or reinvested in the firm, it may be used to reduce the firm's debts, or all three.

Would you like to drive one of these to college or work? Although not your typical commuter vehicle, these trucks represent a necessary investment for an electric utility company. Without these "bucket trucks," a utility company would be unable to repair existing electric transmission lines or build new ones. In fact, dollar values for all equipment purchases are reported on a firm's statement of cash flows.

© TOM MCNEMAR/SHUTTERSTOCK

Entrepreneurial SUCCESS

Accounting for First-Time Entrepreneurs

How can a firm be profitable but have no cash? The founder of a small soap-making supply firm was spending money to develop profitable new products more quickly than she was generating cash from sales. She needed to focus on her *statement of cash flows* and on her *cost of goods sold*. She did, and within a few years, she had built the company into a million-dollar business. Entrepreneurs in her situation need to control expenses and have sufficient cash flow to get through occasional unprofitable periods.

What about being so busy selling to new customers that the firm doesn't do much to collect on outstanding invoices? A partner in a commercial tile company was pleased that he had more than $100,000 in accounts receivable—until he learned that some unpaid bills were so old that those customers had gone out of business. Now he pays more attention to his *accounts receivables,* and he doesn't sell to customers until they settle their outstanding balances. Some experts advise entrepreneurs to collect receivables within 30 days of making the sale.

Finally, record *revenues* at the proper time. One entrepreneur booked revenues in December when customers left deposits for custom-made furniture. Because he didn't deliver the items until January, the full sales should have been recorded in that month. Correcting this changed his firm's revenues and profitability for both years.

Sources: Based on information in Deanna Pogorelc, "Accounting 101 for the First-Time Entrepreneur," *Entrepreneurship.org,* March 22, 2012, www.entrepreneurship.org; Darren Dahl, "Basics of Accounting Are Vital to Survival for Entrepreneurs," *New York Times,* August 3, 2011, www.nytimes.com; Don Sadler, "It's All in the Numbers," *Costco Connection,* April 2012, p. 43; "Pay Yourself First," *SCORE,* July 28, 2011, www.score.org.

THE STATEMENT OF CASH FLOWS

 7 Describe business activities that affect a firm's cash flow.

Cash is vital to any business. In 1987, the SEC and the Financial Accounting Standards Board required all publicly traded companies to include a statement of cash flows, along with their balance sheet and income statement, in their annual report. The **statement of cash flows** illustrates how the company's operating, investing, and financing activities affect cash during an accounting period. Whereas a firm's balance sheet reports dollar values for assets, liabilities, and owners' equity and an income statement reports the firm's dollar amount of profit or loss, the statement of cash flows focuses on how much cash is on hand to pay the firm's bills. Executives and managers can also use the information on a firm's statement of cash flows to determine how much cash is available to pay dividends to stockholders. Finally, the information on the statement of cash flows can be used to evaluate decisions related to a firm's future investments and financing needs. Outside stakeholders including investors, lenders, and suppliers are also interested in a firm's statement of cash flows. Investors want to know if a firm can pay dividends in the future. Before extending credit to a firm, lenders and suppliers often use the information on the statement of cash flows to evaluate the firm's ability to repay its debts.

A statement of cash flows for Northeast Art Supply is illustrated in Figure 17.9. It provides information concerning the company's cash receipts and cash payments and is organized around three different activities: operating, investing, and financing.

- *Cash flows from operating activities.* This is the first section of a statement of cash flows. It addresses the firm's primary revenue source—providing goods and services. Typical adjustments include adding the amount of depreciation to a firm's net income. Other adjustments for increase or decrease in amounts for accounts receivable, inventory, accounts payable, and income taxes payable are also required to reflect a true picture of cash flows from operating activities.
- *Cash flows from investing activities.* The second section of the statement is concerned with cash flow from investments. This includes the purchase and sale of land, equipment, and other assets and investments.
- *Cash flows from financing activities.* The third and final section deals with the cash flow from all financing activities. It reports changes in debt obligation and owners'

statement of cash flows a statement that illustrates how the company's operating, investing, and financing activities affect cash during an accounting period

FIGURE 17.9   Statement of Cash Flows

A statement of cash flows summarizes how a firm's operating, investing, and financing activities affect its cash during a specified period—one month, three months, six months, or a year. For Northeast Art Supply, the amount of cash at the end of the year reported on the statement of cash flows is $59,000—the same amount reported for the cash account on the firm's balance sheet.

NORTHEAST ART SUPPLY, INC.

Statement of Cash Flows
for the Year Ended
December 31, 20XX

Cash flows from operating activities

Net Income		$30,175
Adjustments to reconcile net income to net cash flows		
Depreciation	$ 8,500	
Decrease in accounts receivable	1,000	
Increase in inventory	(5,000)	
Increase in accounts payable	6,000	
Increase in income taxes payable	3,000	13,500
Net cash provided by operating activities		$43,675
Cash flows from investing activities		
Purchase of equipment	$ (2,000)	
Purchase of investments	(10,000)	
Sale of investments	20,000	
Net cash provided by investing activities		8,000
Cash flows from financing activities		
Payments on debt	$(23,000)	
Payment of dividends	(5,000)	
Net cash provided by financing activities		(28,000)
NET INCREASE IN CASH		$23,675
Cash at beginning of year		35,325
CASH AT END OF YEAR		$59,000

equity accounts. This includes loans and repayments, the sale and repurchase of the company's own stock, and cash dividends.

The totals of all three activities are added to the beginning cash balance to determine the ending cash balance. For Northeast Art Supply, the ending cash balance is $59,000. Note that this is the same amount reported for the cash account on the firm's balance sheet. Together, the statement of cash flows, balance sheet, and income statement illustrate the results of past business decisions and reflect the firm's ability to pay debts and dividends and to finance new growth.

Summarize how managers
evaluate the financial health
of a business.

8

EVALUATING FINANCIAL STATEMENTS

All three financial statements—the balance sheet, the income statement, and the statement of cash flows—can provide answers to a variety of questions about a firm's ability to do business and stay in business, its profitability, and its value as an investment. Often the first step is to compare a firm's financial data with other firms in similar industries and with its own financial results over recent accounting periods.

Comparing Financial Data

Many firms compare their financial results with those of competing firms, with industry averages, and with their own financial results. Comparisons are possible as long as accountants follow GAAPs. Except for minor differences in format and terms, the balance sheet, income statement, and statement of cash flows of Procter & Gamble, for example, will be similar to those of other large corporations, such as Nestle, Clorox, Colgate-Palmolive, and Unilever, in the consumer goods industry. Comparisons among firms give managers a general idea of a firm's relative effectiveness and its standing within the industry. Competitors' financial statements can be obtained from their annual reports—if they are public corporations. Industry averages are published by reporting services such as D&B (formerly Dun & Bradstreet) and Standard & Poor's, as well as by some industry trade associations. Today, most corporations include in their annual reports comparisons of the important elements of their financial statements for recent years. For example, Figure 17.10 shows such comparisons—of revenue, research and development (R&D), operating income, and sales and marketing expenses—for Microsoft Corporation, a world leader in the computer software industry. By examining these data, an operating manager can tell whether R&D expenditures have been increasing or decreasing over the past three years. The vice president of marketing can determine if the total amount of sales and marketing expenses is changing. Stockholders and potential investors, on the other hand, may be more concerned with increases or decreases in Microsoft's revenues and operating income over the same time period. Still another

FIGURE 17.10 Comparisons of Present and Past Financial Statements for Microsoft Corporation

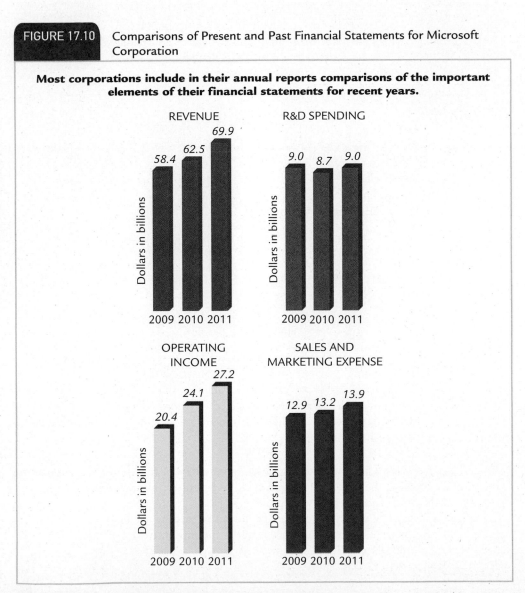

Most corporations include in their annual reports comparisons of the important elements of their financial statements for recent years.

Source: Adapted from the Microsoft Corporation 2011 Annual Report, www.microsoft.com (accessed April 10, 2012).

type of analysis of a firm's financial health involves computation of financial ratios.

Financial Ratios

A **financial ratio** is a number that shows the relationship between two elements of a firm's financial statements. While it is possible to calculate many different financial ratios, we'll only discuss three different ratios that are used to measure a firm's profitability, its ability to pay its debts, and how often it sells its inventory. Like the individual elements in financial statements, these ratios can be compared with those of competitors, with industry averages, and with the firm's past ratios from previous accounting periods. The information required to form these ratios is found in a firm's balance sheet, income statement, and statement of cash flows (in our examples for Northeast Art Supply, Figures 17.6, 17.8, and 17.9).

Measuring a Firm's Ability to Earn Profits A firm's net income after taxes indicates whether the firm is profitable. It does not, however, indicate how effectively the firm's resources are being used. For this latter purpose, a return on sales ratio can be computed. **Return on sales (or profit margin)** is a financial ratio calculated by dividing net income after taxes by net sales. For Northeast Art Supply,

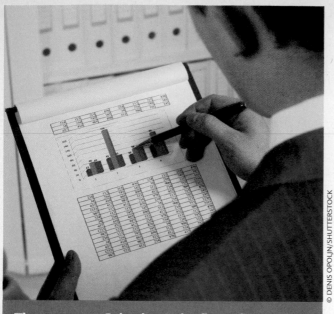

The next step: Going beyond a firm's financial statements. Often accountants must calculate financial ratios to determine the financial "health" of a firm. Among the most useful (and informative) are ratios that measure a firm's profitability, its ability to pay its debts, and how well it manages its inventory and receivables.

© DENIS OPOLJN/SHUTTERSTOCK

$$\text{Return on sales} = \frac{\text{net income after taxes}}{\text{net sales}} = \frac{\$30,175}{\$451,000}$$
$$= 0.067, \text{ or } 6.7 \text{ percent}$$

The return on sales indicates how effectively the firm is transforming sales into profits. A higher return on sales is better than a low one. Today, the average return on sales for all business firms is between 4 and 5 percent. With a return on sales of 6.7 percent, Northeast Art Supply is above average. A low return on sales can be increased by reducing expenses, increasing sales, or both.

Measuring a Firm's Ability to Pay Its Debts A current ratio can be used to evaluate a firm's ability to pay its current liabilities. A firm's **current ratio** is computed by dividing current assets by current liabilities. For Northeast Art Supply,

$$\text{Current ratio} = \frac{\text{current assets}}{\text{current liabilities}} = \frac{\$182,000}{\$70,000} = 2.6$$

This means that Northeast Art Supply has $2.60 of current assets for every $1 of current liabilities. The average current ratio for all industries is 2.0, but it varies greatly from industry to industry. A high current ratio indicates that a firm can pay its current liabilities. A low current ratio can be improved by repaying current liabilities, by reducing dividend payments to stockholders to increase the firm's cash balance, or by obtaining additional cash from investors.

Measuring How Well a Firm Manages Its Inventory A firm's **inventory turnover** is the number of times the firm sells its merchandise inventory in one year. It is approximated by dividing the cost of goods sold in one year by the average value of the inventory.

The average value of the inventory can be found by adding the beginning inventory value and the ending inventory value (given on the income statement) and dividing the sum by 2. For Northeast Art Supply, average inventory is $40,500. Thus

$$\text{Inventory turnover} = \frac{\text{cost of goods sold}}{\text{average inventory}} = \frac{\$334,000}{\$40,500}$$
$$= 8.2 \text{ times per year}$$

financial ratio a number that shows the relationship between two elements of a firm's financial statements

return on sales (or profit margin) a financial ratio calculated by dividing net income after taxes by net sales

current ratio a financial ratio computed by dividing current assets by current liabilities

inventory turnover a financial ratio calculated by dividing the cost of goods sold in one year by the average value of the inventory

Northeast Art Supply sells its merchandise inventory 8.2 times each year, or about once every 45 days. The average inventory turnover for all firms is about 9 times per year, but turnover rates vary widely from industry to industry. For example, supermarkets may have inventory turnover rates of 20 or higher, whereas inventory turnover rates for furniture stores are generally well below the national average. The quickest way to improve inventory turnover is to order merchandise in smaller quantities at more frequent intervals.

Like the three ratios described in this section, the calculations for other financial ratios, including return on owners' ratio, earnings per share, working capital, and debt-to-equity, are based on the information contained in a firm's balance sheet, income statement, and statement of cash flows. For more detailed information on ratio analysis, you may want to read more on the topic in an accounting or finance textbook or use an Internet search engine.

This chapter ends our discussion of management and accounting information. In Chapter 18, we begin our examination of business finances by discussing money, banking, and credit.

return to **Inside**
BUSINESS

PricewaterhouseCoopers

The 21st-century PwC is nothing like the small accounting practice that Samuel Lowell Price set up in London during the mid-19th century. Relying on the knowledge and experience of its global workforce, PwC offers a wide variety of auditing, accounting, and tax services. Its industry specialists also provide expert advice and guidance to banks, law firms, retailers, hospitals, energy firms, travel companies, and many other types of companies, as well as educational institutions, government agencies, and nonprofit groups.

PwC has some very glamorous clients, although its role is behind the scenes rather than on the red carpet. For example, PwC collects and counts the votes for the Academy Awards. Thanks to the firm's extreme

measures to ensure secrecy, nobody knows who won until the famous presenters step into the spotlight and make their announcements to the world.

Questions

1. When an accounting firm like PwC has been hired to examine and sign off on a public corporation's annual report, should it limit its consulting work to avoid being influenced by financial ties to the client? Explain your answer.

2. Why would the Academy of Motion Picture Arts and Sciences hire PwC instead of having its own employees count votes for the Academy Awards?

SUMMARY

Looking for Success?
Get Flashcards, Quizzes, Games, Crosswords, and more @ www.cengagebrain.com.

1 **Examine how information can reduce risk when making a decision.**

The more information a manager has, the less risk there is that a decision will be incorrect. Information produces knowledge and empowers managers and employees to make

better decisions. Because of the volume of information they receive each day and their need to make decisions on a daily basis, businesspeople use information rules to shorten the time spent analyzing choices. Information rules emerge when business research confirms the same results each time it studies the same or a similar set of circumstances. Although many people use the terms *data* and *information* interchangeably, there is a difference. Data are numerical or verbal descriptions that usually result from some sort of measurement. Information is data presented in a form that is useful for a specific purpose. A database is a single collection of data and information stored in one place that can be used by people throughout an organization to make decisions. Although databases are important, the way the data and information are used is even more important. As a result, management information experts now use the term *knowledge management* (KM) to describe a firm's procedures for generating, using, and sharing the data and information.

 Discuss management's information requirements.

A management information system (MIS) is a means of providing managers with the information they need to perform their jobs as effectively as possible. The purpose of an MIS (sometimes referred to as an information technology system or simply IT system) is to distribute timely and useful information from both internal and external sources to the decision makers who need it. The specific types of information managers need depend on their area of management and level within the firm. The size and complexity of an MIS must be tailored to the information needs of the organization it serves.

 Outline the five functions of an information system.

The five functions performed by an MIS system are collecting data, storing data, updating data, processing data into information, and presenting information. Data may be collected from such internal sources as company records, reports, and minutes of meetings, as well as from the firm's managers and employees. External sources include customers, suppliers, financial institutions and banks, trade and business publications, industry conferences, online computer services, and information-gathering organizations. An MIS must be able to store data until they are needed and to update them regularly to ensure that the information presented to managers and employees is accurate, complete, and timely. Data processing is the MIS function that transforms stored data into a form useful for a specific purpose. Finally, the processed data (which now can be called information) must be presented for use. Verbal information generally is presented in the form of a report. Numerical information most often is displayed in graphs, charts, or tables. In addition to the five basic functions performed by an MIS, managers and employees can use a decision-support system, an executive information system, and expert system to help improve the decision-making process.

 Explain why accurate accounting information and audited financial statements are important.

Accounting is the process of systematically collecting, analyzing, and reporting financial information. It can be used to answer questions about what has happened in the past; it also can be used to help make decisions about the future. In fact, the firm's accountants and its accounting system often translate goals, objectives, and plans into dollars and cents to help determine if a decision or plan of action makes "financial sense." The purpose of an audit is to make sure that a firm's financial statements have been prepared in accordance with generally accepted accounting principles. To help ensure that

corporate financial information is accurate and in response to the accounting scandals that surfaced in the last few years, the Sarbanes–Oxley Act was signed into law. This law contains a number of provisions designed to restore public confidence in the accounting industry.

 Read and interpret a balance sheet.

A balance sheet (sometimes referred to as a statement of financial position) is a summary of a firm's assets, liabilities, and owners' equity accounts at the end of an accounting period. This statement must demonstrate that the accounting equation is in balance. On the balance sheet, assets are categorized as current, fixed, or intangible. Similarly, liabilities can be divided into current liabilities and long-term liabilities. For a sole proprietorship or partnership, owners' equity is shown as the difference between assets and liabilities. For corporations, the owners' equity section reports the values of stock and retained earnings.

 Read and interpret an income statement.

An income statement is a summary of a firm's financial operations during the specified accounting period. On the income statement, the company's gross profit is computed by subtracting the cost of goods sold from net sales. Operating expenses and interest expense then are deducted to compute net income before taxes. Finally, income taxes are deducted to obtain the firm's net income after taxes.

 Describe business activities that affect a firm's cash flow.

Since 1987, the Securities and Exchange Commission (SEC) and the Financial Accounting Standards Board have required all publicly traded companies to include a statement of cash flows in their annual reports. This statement illustrates how the company's operating, investing, and financing activities affect cash during an accounting period. Together, the cash flow statement, balance sheet, and income statement illustrate the results of past decisions and the business's ability to pay debts and dividends as well as to finance new growth.

 Summarize how managers evaluate the financial health of a business.

The firm's financial statements and its accounting information become more meaningful when compared with information for competitors, for the industry in which the firm operates, and corresponding information for previous years. Such comparisons permit managers, employees, lenders, investors, and other interested people to pick out trends in growth, borrowing, income, and other business variables and to determine whether the firm is on the way to accomplishing its long-term goals. A number of financial ratios can be computed from the information in a firm's financial statements. These ratios provide a picture of a firm's profitability, its ability to pay its debts, and how often it sells its inventory. Like the information on the firm's financial statements, these ratios can and should be compared with information for competitors, for the industry in which the firm operates, and corresponding information for previous years.

KEY TERMS

You should now be able to define and give an example relevant to each of the following terms:

data (488)
information (488)
database (490)
knowledge management
    (KM) (490)
management information
    system (MIS) (490)
information technology (IT)
    officer (490)
data processing (493)
statistic (494)
decision-support system
    (DSS) (496)
executive information system
    (EIS) (496)

expert system (496)
accounting (497)
audit (497)
generally accepted accounting
    principles (GAAPs) (497)
managerial accounting (498)
financial accounting (498)
certified public accountant
    (CPA) (499)
assets (500)
liabilities (500)
owners' equity (500)
accounting equation (500)
double-entry bookkeeping
    system (500)

annual report (500)
balance sheet (or statement of
    financial position) (500)
liquidity (501)
current assets (501)
fixed assets (502)
depreciation (503)
intangible assets (503)
current liabilities (503)
long-term liabilities (503)
retained earnings (504)
income statement (504)
revenues (505)
gross sales (505)
net sales (506)

cost of goods sold (506)
gross profit (506)
operating expenses (506)
net income (506)
net loss (506)
statement of cash flows (507)
financial ratio (510)
return on sales (or profit
    margin) (510)
current ratio (510)
inventory turnover (510)

REVIEW QUESTIONS

1. In your own words, describe how information reduces risk when you make a personal or work-related decision.
2. What are information rules? How do they simplify the process of making decisions?
3. What is the difference between data and information? Give one example of accounting data and one example of accounting information.
4. List the five functions of an MIS.
5. What are the components of a typical business report?
6. Describe the three types of computer applications that help employees, managers, and executives make smart decisions.
7. What purpose do audits and GAAPs serve in today's business world?
8. How do the major provisions of the Sarbanes–Oxley Act affect a public company's accounting procedures?
9. What is the difference between a private accountant and a public accountant? What are certified public accountants?

10. State the accounting equation, and list two specific examples of each term in the equation.
11. What is the principal difference between a balance sheet and an income statement?
12. How are current assets distinguished from fixed assets? Why are fixed assets depreciated on a balance sheet?
13. Explain how a retailing firm would determine the cost of goods sold during an accounting period.
14. How does a firm determine its net income after taxes?
15. What is the purpose of a statement of cash flows?
16. Explain the calculation procedure for and significance of each of the following:
    a. Return on sales
    b. The current ratio
    c. Inventory turnover

DISCUSSION QUESTIONS

1. Do managers really need all the kinds of information discussed in this chapter? If not, which kinds can they do without?
2. How can confidential data and information (such as the wages of individual employees) be kept confidential and yet still be available to managers who need them?
3. Bankers usually insist that prospective borrowers submit audited financial statements along with a loan application. Why should financial statements be audited by a CPA?
4. What can be said about a firm whose owners' equity is a negative amount? How could such a situation come about?

5. Do the balance sheet, income statement, and statement of cash flows contain all the information you might want as a potential lender or stockholder? What other information would you like to examine?
6. Why is it so important to compare a firm's current financial statements with those of previous years, those of competitors, and the average of all firms in the industry in which the firm operates?

Video Case 17.1 — Information Helps Level the Playing Field for The Little Guys

As the "leading supplier of exclusive, high-end audio and video electronics for homes, businesses, educational institutions, and other organizations in greater Chicagoland," The Little Guys has built an enviable reputation since its founding in 1994. The Little Guys sells and installs top-brand home audio and theater equipment and does it well. The company prides itself on its highly knowledgeable salespeople and outstanding customer service, and these have helped it survive strong competition from both "big guys" like the Best Buy electronics chain, which has a store not far away, and economic downturns that have cut consumers' buying power. "We have the best employees," says the company's Web site, and "how we treat our customers makes us great."

David Wexler, the store's co-owner, describes how one of the firm's award-winning salespeople deals with his customers, for instance: "If a guy comes in to buy a $50 DVD player, Ed treats him the same as the guy who's spending $500,000 with us. I think that's what keeps people coming back over and over and over. He fights for them. Frankly, sometimes he fights too much for them. But he's their advocate, and they know it."

In response to recession-slowed sales, the company was recently forced to lay some people off and has reorganized departments from advertising to payroll (the latter is a major and complex expense for The Little Guys because its salespeople earn base pay plus a percentage of their sales). In another cost-cutting move, the company also recently moved to a new location not far from its original store, and it's keeping close track of its cash flows in and out. Salespeople are careful about customers' change orders, too, which often cost the company money. Now, as the economy begins to improve and consumers begin to spend more on electronics, these same cost-cutting measures will help improve the firm's bottom-line profit amount.

With the help of QuickBooks accounting software and a professional accountant who visits regularly, David Wexler and co-owner Evie Wexler have deepened their knowledge of accounting and finance as the business has grown. In the beginning, for instance, they checked sales figures every day, but David quickly realized that this practice created instant information overload.

Now he looks at the numbers about every week or ten days, comparing each set with past results, and the accountant comes in at least once each quarter to help with more complex issues like depreciation of assets and equipment for tax purposes. Taxes are a big concern. As Evie Wexler points out, sometimes the firm has to make a special push to sell off inventory in order to generate extra cash flow when taxes are due, or when it wants to purchase new merchandise that customers are asking for and that will therefore sell faster. Keeping warehoused inventory low saves money, too.

One reason cash flow can be slow is that customers often negotiate prices and repayment terms at The Little Guys, so that an expensive system might not only be sold at a discount, but the customer may also be given extra time to pay. That certainly helps make customers happy, but if it means the company is paying its own suppliers on time while customers lag in their payments, cash can get tight. As David explains, that's partly why The Little Guys limits the number of brands it sells and works with only a few suppliers. Establishing good relationships with these suppliers, largely by ordering regularly and paying on time, allows the company to ask them for special discounts or improved payment terms—even when other retailers aren't getting them—and find yet another way to earn a little more profit on the same volume of sales.[6]

Questions

1. Do you think a fairly small company like The Little Guys still needs a professional accountant after its owners have had so much experience running a successful business? Why or why not?
2. Do you think The Little Guys is doing a good job of using information to manage the business? If so, why, and if not, how can the company improve this function?
3. What are some of the factors that contribute to The Little Guys' cash-flow problems? How might the owners better manage its cash flow?

Case 17.2 — Making the Numbers or Faking the Numbers?

Will sales and profits meet the expectations of investors and Wall Street analysts? Managers at public corporations must answer this important question quarter after quarter, year after year. In an ideal world—one in which there is never an economic crisis, expenses never go up, and customers never buy competing products—the corporation's price for a share of its stock would soar, and investors would cheer as every financial report showed ever-higher sales revenues, profit margins, and earnings.

In the real world, however, many uncontrollable and unpredictable factors can affect a corporation's performance. Customers may buy fewer units or postpone purchases, competitors may introduce superior products, expenses may rise, interest rates may climb, and buying power may plummet. Faced with the prospect of releasing financial results that fall short of Wall Street's expectations, managers may feel intense pressure to "make the numbers" using a variety of accounting techniques.

For example, some executives at the telecom company WorldCom made earnings look better by booking billions of dollars in ordinary expenses as capital investments. The company was forced into bankruptcy a few weeks after the $11 billion accounting scam was exposed. As another example, top managers at the drug retailer Rite Aid posted transactions improperly to inflate corporate earnings. Later, when Rite Aid had to lower its earnings by $1.6 billion, investors fled and the share price fell.

Under the Sarbanes–Oxley Act, the CEO and CFO now must certify the corporation's financial reports. (For more information about Sarbanes–Oxley, visit www.aicpa.org, the Web site of the American Institute of Certified Public Accountants.) Immediately after this legislation became effective, hundreds of companies restated their earnings, a sign that stricter accounting controls were having the intended effect. "I don't mean to sugarcoat the figure on restatements," says Steve Odland, the former CEO of Office Depot, "but I think it is positive—it shows a healthy system." Yet not all earnings restatements are due to accounting irregularities. "The general impression of the public is that accounting rules are black and white," he adds. "They are often anything but that, and in many instances the changes in earnings came after new interpretations by the chief accountant of the SEC."

Now that stricter regulation has been in force for some time, fewer and fewer corporations are announcing restatements. In fact, the number of corporations restating earnings has declined since it peaked in 2006. The chief reason for the decline is that corporations and their accounting firms have learned to dig deeper and analyze the process used to produce the figures for financial statements, as well as checking the numbers themselves.

Because accounting rules are open to interpretation, managers sometimes find themselves facing ethical dilemmas when a corporation feels pressure to live up to Wall Street's expectations. Consider the hypothetical situation at Commodore Appliances, a fictional company that sells to Home Depot, Lowe's, and other major retail chains. Margaret, the vice president of sales, has told Rob, a district manager, that the company's sales are down 10 percent in the current quarter. She points out that sales in Rob's district are down 20 percent and states that higher-level managers want him to improve this month's

figures using "book and hold," which means recording future sales transactions in the current period.

Rob hesitates, saying that the company is gaining market share and that he needs more time to get sales momentum going. He thinks "book and hold" is not a good business practice, even if it is legal. Margaret hints that Rob will lose his job if his sales figures don't look better and stresses that he will need the book-and-hold approach for one month only. Rob realizes that if he doesn't go along, he won't be working at Commodore for very much longer.

Meeting with Kevin, one of Commodore's auditors, Rob learns that book and hold meets GAAPs. Kevin emphasizes that customers must be willing to take title to the goods before they're delivered or billed. Any book-and-hold sales must be real, backed by documentation such as e-mails to and from buyers, and the transactions must be completed in the near future.

Rob is at a crossroads: His sales figures must be higher if Commodore is to achieve its performance targets, yet he doesn't know exactly when (or if) he actually would complete any book-and-hold sales he might report this month. He doesn't want to mislead anyone, but he also doesn't want to lose his job or put other people's jobs in jeopardy by refusing to do what he is being asked to do. Rob is confident that he can improve his district's sales over the long term. However, Commodore's executives are pressuring Rob to make the sales figures look better right now. What should he do?[7]

Questions

1. What are the ethical and legal implications of using accounting practices such as the book-and-hold technique to inflate corporate earnings?
2. Why would Commodore's auditor insist that Rob document any sales booked under the book-and-hold technique?
3. If you were in Rob's situation, would you agree to use the book-and-hold technique this month? Justify your decision.
4. Imagine that Commodore has taken out a multimillion-dollar loan that must be repaid next year. How might the lender react if it learned that Commodore was using the book-and-hold method to make revenues look higher than they really are?

Building Skills for Career Success

❶ USING SOCIAL MEDIA

The Security and Exchange Commission (SEC) regulates accounting practices and has pretty specific rules about endorsements and testimonials. Yet, much of the content on social media sites deals with both endorsements and testimonials. For example, Facebook "likes" can be considered a type of endorsement. Recently the SEC weighed in on this. Read a summary of what they had to say at www.accountingtoday.com/news/SEC-Social-Media-Guidelines-61964-1.html.

1. What do you think of these rules? Do you agree or disagree? Why?

2. Can you think of other industries that may have to contend with the transparency of social media?

❷ JOURNALING FOR SUCCESS

More and more people are using computers and personal finance and accounting software to provide the information they need to manage their finances. To complete this journal entry, use the Internet to research the Quicken software package or a software package offered by a local bank or financial institution. Then answer the following questions.

Assignment

1. Today, personal finance and accounting software packages are used by millions of people. Based on your initial research, would you prefer to purchase Quicken software or use a free software package available from a bank or financial institution? Why?
2. Why do you think these money-management software packages have become so popular? Do you think either type of software package could help you manage your finances?

❸ DEVELOPING CRITICAL-THINKING SKILLS

According to the experts, you must evaluate your existing financial condition before establishing an investment plan. As pointed out in this chapter, a personal balance sheet provides a picture of your assets, liabilities, and net worth. A personal income statement will tell you whether you have a cash surplus or cash deficit at the end of a specific time period.

Assignment

1. Using your own financial information from last month, construct a personal balance sheet and personal income statement.
2. Based on the information contained in your personal financial statements, answer the following:
    a. What is your current net worth?
    b. Do you have a cash surplus or a cash deficit at the end of the month?
    c. What specific steps can you take to improve your financial condition?
3. Based on your personal financial information, prepare a plan for improving your financial condition over the next six months.

❹ BUILDING TEAM SKILLS

This has been a bad year for Miami-based Park Avenue Furniture. The firm increased sales revenues to $1,400,000, but total expenses ballooned to $1,750,000. Although management realized that some of the firm's expenses were out of control, including cost of goods sold ($700,000), salaries ($450,000), and advertising costs ($140,000), it could not contain expenses.

As a result, the furniture retailer lost $350,000. To make matters worse, the retailer applied for a $350,000 loan at Fidelity National Bank and was turned down. The bank officer, Mike Nettles, said that the firm already had too much debt. At that time, liabilities totaled $420,000; owners' equity was $600,000.

Assignment

1. In groups of three or four, analyze the financial condition of Park Avenue Furniture.
2. Discuss why you think the bank officer turned down Park Avenue's loan request.
3. Prepare a detailed plan of action to improve the financial health of Park Avenue Furniture over the next 12 months.

❺ RESEARCHING DIFFERENT CAREERS

To improve productivity, employers expect employees to use computers and computer software. Typical business applications include e-mail, word processing, spreadsheets, and graphics. By improving your skills in these areas, you can increase your chances not only of being employed but also of being promoted once you are employed.

Assignment

1. Assess your computer skills by placing a check in the appropriate column in the following table:

Software	None	Low	Average	High
e-Mail				
Word processing				
Desktop publishing				
Accounting				
Database management				
Graphics				
Spreadsheet				
Internet Research				

2. Describe your self-assessment in a written report. Specify the skills in which you need to become more proficient, and outline a plan for doing this.

Running a Business   PART 6   Graeter's

Adding MIS and Social Media to Graeter's Recipe for Success

Graeter's still makes ice cream by hand, just like the founders did in 1870. But in every other respect, it's a very different business from the mom-and-pop firm founded by the great-grandparents of Richard, Robert, and Chip Graeter. The founders greeted their customers in person, mixed and packed every batch of ice cream

by hand, and added up the cash in the till after hours to find out how much they had made.

In contrast, today's fourth generation of family owners runs a $30 million company with a workforce of nearly 800 and three factories capable of producing, in total, well over a million pints of ice cream every year. Graeter's now sells premium ice cream through supermarkets and grocery stores in 43 states, and receives thousands of orders through its Web site every year. It would be impossible for the owners to keep this business running smoothly—let alone keep up their fast-paced growth strategy—using only the basic information systems that served Graeter's earlier in its history.

NEW GROWTH, NEW SYSTEMS

Paul Porcino, a consultant working with the Graeter family, observes that small, entrepreneurial firms often have only "a very small amount of information, and . . . it hasn't been pulled together in any meaningful way." In fact, the Graeter's stores were collecting some useful sales data, but "not really enough to run the company of the future," he notes. Therefore, the first step in implementing an updated information system was to define what Graeter's executives needed to know to run the business. For example, they needed to be able to track unit sales online, in each store, and to each wholesale customer, and to measure both costs and profitability by product and channel. Without timely, accurate, and detailed data, they couldn't determine how far they were progressing toward their goals, nor could they coordinate the efforts of every business function for maximum efficiency.

With the new management information system, Graeter's owners would have "some of the same powerful decision-making tools available to managers in much larger companies," Porcino says. "We are going to be . . . bringing in probably a variety of different information systems . . . so we fully have an understanding of what we are selling, as well as some other financial systems, and probably some human resources information systems."

Despite some technical challenges during implementation, Graeter's has already experienced some of the benefits of collecting better information, particularly about store-level sales. When management noticed that overall bakery sales weren't up to par, "we had to adjust," comments Porcino. The remedy was surprising: "We actually reduced the number of products we were selling in the store . . . . It wasn't very clear exactly how much we were selling, but at least [we had] the good-enough gut sense in terms of the ones that were not selling, and we . . . adjusted the total inventory line." With the MIS in place, Graeter's managers have the data they need to fine-tune production, inventory, and shipments to meet demand in each channel.

COUNTING ON ACCOUNTING

Graeter's controller, David Blink, is responsible for preparing "all financial statements, all reports, payroll, [and] any ad hoc reports that any of the managers would need. I handle a lot of the reporting for the retail side as well as the manufacturing side," he says. Although an outside payroll company actually prints the employees' checks, Blink's department collects and analyzes payroll data as input for management decisions.

Blink and his staff are also in charge of accounts receivable, accounts payable, and financial reporting. They check and record financial details about revenues and expenses, and then send the data to an outside accounting firm, which prepares financial statements for top management use. With these reports in hand, the Graeter's team can make informed decisions about how many seasonal employees to hire, which products to keep, how much to invest in new equipment, and other issues that arise day by day.

GRAETER'S SOCIAL SIDE

Even a small business can have a big presence in social media. Graeter's has designated an employee to manage all of the company's activities on Facebook, Twitter, and YouTube. With 150,000 Facebook "likes," Graeter's engages its brand fans in conversations about new or favorite flavors, the size of its chocolate chunks, special celebrations featuring ice cream, and more. It posts a new message or photo every few days, and reveals the names of mystery flavors on Facebook in advance of other publicity. As a result, fans return to its Facebook page often and they enjoy commenting on what other customers post, as well. In addition, Graeter's tweets frequently and periodically posts videos on its YouTube channel.

Graeter's also monitors mentions of its brand on other social-media sites. For example, hundreds of consumers have shared images of Graeter's ice cream and its logo on the Pinterest site. As other people add their comments and click to "like," the conversation continues and the word of mouth builds more buzz for the Graeter's brand. Similarly, whenever a customer uses Foursquare to "check in" at a Graeter's shop while buying a sundae or another treat, others can see the activity. The social competition aspect of Foursquare encourages others to join the fun by vying to become "mayor" of a particular location (such as a Graeter's shop) by gaining the highest number of check-ins during the month. No matter who's the Foursquare mayor, Graeter's is always the brand winner.[8]

Questions

1. Suppose you were writing a social media plan for Graeter's, with two objectives: to improve brand awareness in markets where the ice cream is just becoming available and to build online orders during holiday periods. What quantitative and qualitative measurements would you plan to use to evaluate the results of your plan?

2. Graeter's uses information to track cash, sales revenue, and expenses on a daily basis. How does this type of accounting system facilitate effective decision-making and discourage store-level theft?

3. As a small but fast-growing, privately-owned company, which of the financial ratios should Graeter's track especially closely? Why?

Now that you have a marketing plan, the next big and important step is to prepare a financial plan. One of the biggest mistakes an entrepreneur makes when faced with a need for financing is not being prepared. Completing this section will show you that if you are prepared and provide accurate and relevant management and accounting information, the task may be easier than you think. Chapter 16 "Exploring Social Media and e-Business" and Chapter 17, "Using Management and Accounting Information," should help you to answer the questions in this part of the business plan.

THE INFORMATION AND ACCOUNTING PLAN COMPONENT

Information and accounting systems are important if your business is to succeed. Your information plan should answer at least the following questions.

6.1. How will you gather information about competitors, their products, and the prices that they charge for their products and services?

6.2. Explain how you will develop a management information system to collect, store, update, and process data, and present information?

6.3. Will your business have an e-business component? If so, explain how you will sell your products or services online.

6.4. Are there ways that you can use social media to promote products and services and reach out to your customers?

6.5. Who will create and maintain the accounting system that you will use to record routine business transactions for your business?

6.6. Will you hire an accountant to prepare financial statements for your firm?

THE FINANCIAL PLAN COMPONENT

Your financial plan should answer at least the following questions about the investment needed, sales and cash-flow forecasts, breakeven analysis, and sources of funding.

6.7. What is the actual amount of money you need to open your business (start-up budget) and the amount needed to keep it open (operating budget)? Prepare a realistic budget.

6.8. How much money do you have, and how much money will you need to start your business and stay in business?

6.9. Prepare a projected income statement by month for the first year of operation and by quarter for the second and third years.

6.10. Prepare projected balance sheets for each of the first three years of operation.

6.11. Prepare a breakeven analysis. How many units of your products or service will have to be sold to cover your costs?

6.12. Reinforce your final projections by comparing them with industry averages for your chosen industry.

REVIEW OF BUSINESS PLAN ACTIVITIES

Throughout this project you have been investigating what it takes to open and run a business, and now you are finally at the bottom line: What is it going to cost to open your business, and how much money will you need to keep it running for a year? Before tackling the last part of the business plan, review your answers to the questions in each part to make sure that all your answers are consistent throughout the entire business plan. Then write a brief statement that summarizes all the information for this part of the business plan.

ENDNOTES

1. Sources: Based on information from the PwC Web site at www.pwc.com, accessed April 12, 2012; Alison Overholt, "American Idol: Accounting Edition," *Fortune*, October 17, 2011, pp. 101–106; Dena Aubin, "Going Green, Big Business Hires Auditors for Proof," *Reuters*, November 23, 2011, www.reuters.com; Alex Spence, "PwC Reclaims the Lead in Global Consulting's Four-Horse Race," *The Times (London)*, October 4, 2011, www.thetimes.co.uk.

2 John Smith, "Financial Reporting in a Changing World," The International Accounting Standards Board Web site at www.iasb.org, accessed May 8, 2009.

3. Joseph Nocera, et al. "System Failure Corporate America Has Lost Its Way," *Fortune*, June 24, 2002, 64.

4. "Summary of the Provisions of the Sarbanes–Oxley Act of 2002," the AICPA Web site at www.aicpa.org, accessed April 9, 2012.

5. *Occupational Outlook Handbook*, The U.S. Bureau of Labor Statistics Web site at www.bls.gov/oco/ocos001.htm, accessed April 9, 2012.

6. Based on information found at The Little Guys Web site at www.thelittleguys.com/home.asp, accessed April 12, 2012; Alan Wolf, "The Little Guys Get New Home, Amended Name," *TWICE*, April 19, 2010, 6, 22; Audrey Gray, "Perfecting a Soft Sell," *Dealerscope*, March 2009, 82; and information from interviews with company staff and the video, "The Little Guys."

7. Based on information from The Office Depot Web site at www.officedepot.com, accessed April 12, 2012; Matt Krantz, "Companies Are Making Fewer Accounting Mistakes," *USA Today*, March 1, 2010, www.usatoday.com; Jane Sasseen, "White-Collar Crime: Who Does Time?" *BusinessWeek*, February 6, 2006, www.businessweek.com; Stephen Labaton, "Four Years Later, Enron's Shadow Lingers as Change Comes Slowly," *New York Times*, January 5, 2006, C1; *Making the Numbers at Commodore Appliance* (Cengage video).

8. Based on information from Kimberly L. Jackson, "Graeter's Premium Chocolate Chip Ice Cream Lands at Stop & Shop," *Newark Star-Ledger (NJ)*, April 4, 2012, www.nj.com; "Graeter's Ice Cream Debuts in Bay Area," *Tampa Bay Times (St. Petersburg, FL)*, January 10, 2012, p. 4B; Jim Carper, "Graeter's Runs a Hands-on Ice Cream Plant," *Dairy Foods*, August 2011, pp. 36+; Jim Carper, "The Greater Good," *Dairy Foods*, August 2011, pp. 95+; "Graeter's Unveils New 'Mystery Flavor,'" *Dayton Daily News*, March 29, 2012, www.daytondailynews.com; Bob Driehaus, "A Cincinnati Ice Cream Maker Aims Big," *New York Times*, September 11, 2010, www.nytimes.com; Lucy May, "Graeter's Northern Kentucky Franchisee Puts Stores on the Block," *Business Courier*, August 6, 2010, http://cincinnati.bizjournals.com; www.graeters.com; interviews with company staff and Cengage videos about Graeter's.

Finance and Investment

PART 7

In this part, we look at another business resource—money.
First, we discuss the functions of money and the financial institutions that are part of our banking system. Then we examine the concept of financial management and investing for both business firms and individuals.

© AP PHOTO/RICHARD DREW

18 Understanding Money, Banking, and Credit

LEARNING OBJECTIVES

Once you complete this chapter, you will be able to:

1 Identify the functions and characteristics of money.

2 Summarize how the Federal Reserve System regulates the money supply to maintain a healthy economy.

3 Describe the organizations involved in the banking industry.

4 Identify the services provided by financial institutions.

5 Understand how financial institutions are changing to meet the needs of domestic and international customers.

6 Explain how deposit insurance protects customers.

7 Discuss the importance of credit and credit management.

How Umpqua Bank Became "The World's Greatest Bank"

Umpqua Bank, based in Roseburg, Oregon, doesn't operate traditional bank branches. Instead, its 184 "stores" serve as community hubs, "providing banking services plus events and amenities to share with our neighbors," says executive vice-president Lani Hayward. Customers meet with bank employees at concierge desks, relax in easy chairs when opening new accounts, and enjoy a free cup of coffee and free Wi-Fi access whenever they stop in. Some Umpqua stores offer yoga classes, wine tastings, trivia contests, even conference rooms for impromptu business meetings. Customers can also sign up to see the world by joining the bank's travel club. Why all the extras? Because Umpqua wants customers to think of it as "the world's greatest bank," a good neighbor, and a force for positive change in the communities it serves.

Umpqua began with six employees and a single branch in 1953, growing through a combination of new branches, new markets, and bank mergers. Today, the branch system stretches through four states, from the Pacific Northwest through Northern California, serving customers with a mix of full-service branches, commercial bank offices, residential mortgage offices, and ATM-only locations.

In addition to its unique community store concept, Umpqua has a number of unique banking offers. One example is the GreenStreet Lending program, which provides loans to homeowners and businesses for installation of solar panels and other "green" building improvements. As another example, small businesses can borrow $10,000 to $100,000 through the MainStreet Lending program, which supplements the bank's regular business lending services.

Although Umpqua recently celebrated its 60th birthday, it thinks young when it comes to banking technology. Through online banking, mobile banking, and other high-tech systems, the bank can give its customers easy access to their money and information about their money at any hour. And as customers' needs change, Umpqua will be ready with a range of financial services for each new stage of their personal and professional lives.[1]

FYI

Did You Know?

Founded in 1953, Umpqua has grown from one small Oregon branch with six employees to 184 branches with over 2,200 employees in four states.

Most people regard a bank like Umpqua Bank—the financial institution profiled in the Inside Business feature for this chapter—as a place to deposit or borrow money. When you deposit money in a bank like Umpqua, you *receive* interest. When you borrow money from this bank or any financial institution or lender, you must *pay* interest. You may borrow to buy a home, a car, or some other high-cost item. In this case, the resource that will be transformed into money to repay the loan is the salary you receive for your labor.

Businesses also transform resources into money. A business firm (even a new one) may have a valuable asset in the form of an idea for a product or service. If the firm (or its founder) has a good credit history and the idea is a good one, a bank like Umpqua or other lenders may lend it the money to develop, produce, and market the product or service. The loan—with interest—will be repaid out of future sales revenue. In this way, both the firm and the lender will earn a reasonable profit.

In each of these situations, the borrower needs the money now and will have the ability to repay it later. Although the decision to borrow money from a bank or other financial institution should always be made after careful deliberation, the fact is that responsible borrowing enables both individuals and business firms to meet specific needs.

In this chapter, we begin by outlining the functions and characteristics of money that make it an acceptable means of payment for products, services, and resources. Then we consider the role of the Federal Reserve System in maintaining a healthy economy. Next, we describe the banking industry—commercial banks, savings and loan associations, credit unions, and other institutions that offer banking services. Then we turn our attention to how banking practices meet the needs of customers. We also describe the safeguards established by the federal government to protect depositors against losses. In closing, we examine credit transactions and sources of credit information.

Identify the functions and characteristics of money.

barter system a system of exchange in which goods or services are traded directly for other goods or services

money anything a society uses to purchase products, services, or resources

medium of exchange anything accepted as payment for products, services, and resources

measure of value a single standard or "yardstick" used to assign values to, and compare the values of, products, services, and resources

store of value a means of retaining and accumulating wealth

WHAT IS MONEY?

The members of some societies still exchange goods and services through barter, without using money. A **barter system** is a system of exchange in which goods or services are traded directly for other goods or services. The trouble with the barter system is that the two parties in an exchange must need each other's products at the same time, and the two products must be roughly equal in value. Thus, even very isolated societies soon develop some sort of money to eliminate the inconvenience of trading by barter.

Money is anything a society uses to purchase products, services, or resources. Historically, different groups of people have used all sorts of objects as money—whales' teeth, stones, beads, copper crosses, clamshells, and gold and silver, for example. Today, the most commonly used objects are metal coins and paper bills, which together are called *currency*.

The Functions of Money

Money aids in the exchange of goods, services, and resources. However, this is a rather general (and somewhat theoretical) way of stating money's function. Let's look instead at three *specific* functions money serves in any society.

Money as a Medium of Exchange A **medium of exchange** is anything accepted as payment for products, services, and resources. This definition looks very much like the definition of money. It is meant to, because the primary function of money is to serve as a medium of exchange. The key word here is *accepted*. As long as the owners of products, services, and resources *accept* money in an exchange, it is performing this function. For example, if you want to purchase a Hewlett-Packard Photosmart printer that is priced at $149 in a Best Buy store, you must give the store the correct amount of money. In return, the store gives you the product.

Money as a Measure of Value A **measure of value** is a single standard or "yardstick" used to assign values to, and compare the values of, products, services, and resources. Money serves as a measure of value because the prices of all products, services, and resources are stated in terms of money. It is thus the "common denominator" we use to compare products and decide which we will buy.

Money as a Store of Value Money received by an individual or firm need not be used immediately. It may be held and spent later. Hence, money serves as a **store of value**, or a means of retaining and accumulating wealth. This function of money comes into play whenever we hold onto money—in a pocket, a cookie jar, a savings account, or whatever.

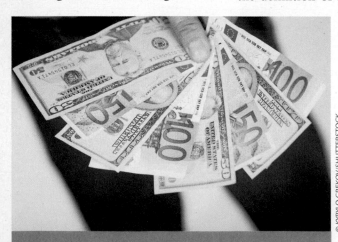

It's all money! Although it's easy for U.S. citizens to think their currency is the only currency in the world, there are many different currencies used throughout the world. Regardless of what their money looks like, people around the world know that their currency must serve as a medium of exchange, a measure of value, and a store of value.

© KYRYLO GREKOV/SHUTTERSTOCK

Value that is stored as money is affected by *inflation*. Remember from Chapter 1 that *inflation* is a general rise in the level of prices. Suppose that you can buy a Bose home theater system for $1,000. Your $1,000 has a value equal to the value of that home theater system. However, suppose that you wait and do not buy the home theater system immediately. If the price goes up to $1,025 in the meantime because of inflation, you can no longer buy the same home theater system with your $1,000. Your money has *lost* purchasing power because it is now worth less than the home theater system. To determine the effect of inflation on the purchasing power of a dollar, economists often refer to a consumer price index such as the one illustrated in Figure 18.1. The consumer price index measures the changes in prices of a fixed basket of goods purchased by a typical consumer, including food, transportation, housing, clothing, medical care, recreation, education, communication, and other goods and services. The base amount for the consumer price index is 100 and was established by averaging the cost of the items included in the consumer price index over a 36-month period from 1982 to 1984. In February 2012, it took approximately $228 to purchase the same goods that could have been purchased for $100 in the base period 1982 to 1984.

FIGURE 18.1   The Consumer Price Index and the Purchasing Power of the Consumer Dollar (Base Period 1982–1984 = 100)

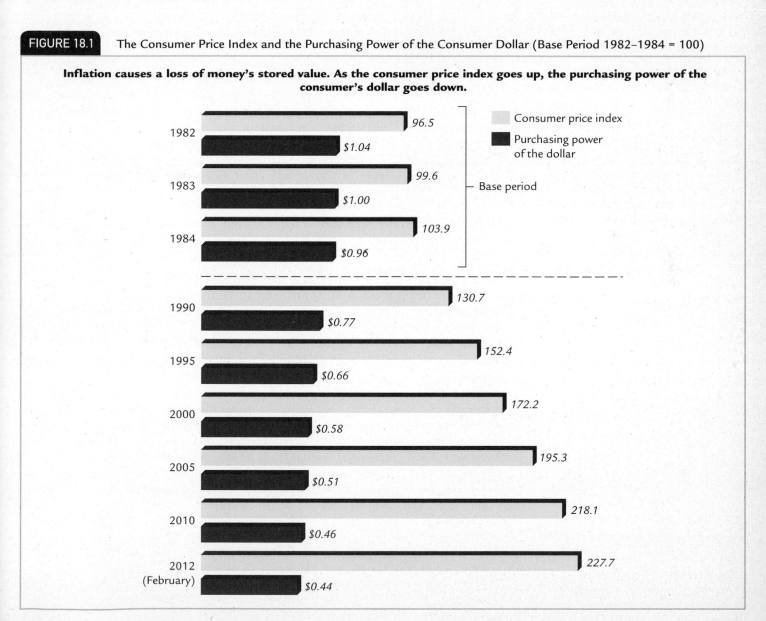

Source: The U.S. Bureau of Labor Statistics Web site, www.bls.gov (accessed March 22, 2012).

Inflation isn't just an economic indicator—it means that you'll pay more for many goods and services. If you're saving to buy a car or a home, the money you put aside won't go as far when prices are on the rise.

Important Characteristics of Money

Money must be easy to use, trusted, and capable of performing the three functions just mentioned. To meet these requirements, money must possess the following five characteristics.

Divisibility The standard unit of money must be divisible into smaller units to accommodate small purchases and large ones. In the United States, our standard is the dollar, and it is divided into pennies, nickels, dimes, quarters, and half-dollars.

Portability Money must be small enough and light enough to be carried easily. For this reason, paper currency is issued in larger denominations—5-, 10-, 20-, 50-, and 100-dollar bills.

Stability Money should retain its value over time. When it does not, people tend to lose faith in their money. When money becomes extremely unstable, people may turn to other means of storing value, such as gold and jewels, works of art, and real estate.

Durability The objects that serve as money should be strong enough to last through reasonable use. To increase the life expectancy of paper currency, most nations use special paper with a high fiber content.

Difficulty of Counterfeiting If a nation's currency were easy to counterfeit—that is, to imitate or fake—its citizens would be uneasy about accepting it as payment. In an attempt to make paper currency more difficult to counterfeit, the U.S. government periodically redesigns its paper currency and uses watermarks and intricate designs to discourage counterfeiting.

The Supply of Money: M_1 and M_2

How much money is there in the United States? Before we can answer this question, we need to define a couple of concepts. A **demand deposit** is an amount on deposit in a checking account. It is called a *demand* deposit because it can be claimed immediately—that is, on-demand—by presenting a properly made out check, withdrawing cash from an automated teller machine (ATM), or transferring money between accounts.

A **time deposit** is an amount on deposit in an interest-bearing savings account or certificate of deposit. Financial institutions generally permit immediate withdrawal of money from savings accounts. However, they can require advance **written notice** before withdrawal of money from savings accounts or certificates of deposit. The time between notice and withdrawal is what leads to the name *time* deposit.

There are two main measures of the supply of money: M_1 and M_2. The M_1 *supply of money* is a narrow definition and consists only of currency, demand deposits and other checkable deposits. The M_2 *supply of money* consists of M_1 (currency and demand deposits) plus savings accounts, certain money-market securities, and certificates of deposit (CDs) of less than $100,000. The M_2 definition of money is based on the assumption that time deposits can be converted to cash for spending. Figure 18.2 shows the elements of the M_1 and M_2 supply of money.

Therefore, the answer to our original question is that the amount of money in the United States depends very much on how we measure it. Generally, economists, politicians, and bankers tend to focus on M_1 or some variation of M_1.

demand deposit an amount on deposit in a checking account

time deposit an amount on deposit in an interest-bearing savings account or certificate of deposit

FIGURE 18.2 The Supply of Money

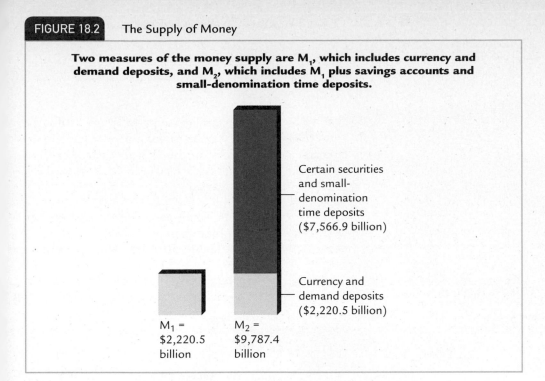

Two measures of the money supply are M₁, which includes currency and demand deposits, and M₂, which includes M₁ plus savings accounts and small-denomination time deposits.

Certain securities and small-denomination time deposits ($7,566.9 billion)

Currency and demand deposits ($2,220.5 billion)

M₁ = $2,220.5 billion

M₂ = $9,787.4 billion

Source: The Federal Reserve Web site, www.federalreserve.gov (accessed March 26, 2012).

THE FEDERAL RESERVE SYSTEM

Summarize how the Federal Reserve System regulates the money supply to maintain a healthy economy.

How do Federal Reserve actions affect me? What is the Federal Reserve System? These are both good questions. First, Federal Reserve Board (often referred to as the Fed) activities have an impact on the interest rates you pay for loans and credit cards. Although many people became aware of the Federal Reserve's actions during the recent economic crisis, the Fed's lending programs have been used since the early 1900s to maintain a healthy economy. Here's how it works. The Fed lowers the interest rates that banks pay to borrow money from the Fed in an effort to shore up a sagging economy. When the Fed lowers rates, banks pay less to borrow money from the Fed. In turn, they often lower the interest rates they charge for business loans, home mortgages, car loans, and even credit cards. Lower rates often provide an incentive for both business firms and individuals to buy goods and services, which, in turn, helps to restore the economic health of the nation. On the other hand, rate increases are designed to sustain economic growth while controlling inflation. When the Fed raises rates, banks must pay more to borrow money from the Fed. And the banks, in turn, charge higher rates for both consumer and business loans.

Now let's answer the second question. The **Federal Reserve System** is the central bank of the United States and is responsible for regulating the banking industry. Created by Congress on December 23, 1913, its mission is to maintain an economically healthy and financially sound business environment in which banks can operate.

The Federal Reserve System is controlled by its seven-member board of governors, who meet in Washington, D.C. Each governor is appointed by the president and confirmed by the Senate for a 14-year term. The president also selects the chairman and vice chairman of the board from among the board members for four-year terms.

The Federal Reserve System consists of 12 district banks located in major cities throughout the United States, as well as 24 branch banks (see Figure 18.3). All national (federally chartered) banks must be members of the Fed. State banks may join if they meet membership requirements. For more information about the Federal Reserve System, visit its Web site at www.federalreserve.gov.

Federal Reserve System the central bank of the United States responsible for regulating the banking industry

FIGURE 18.3 Federal Reserve System

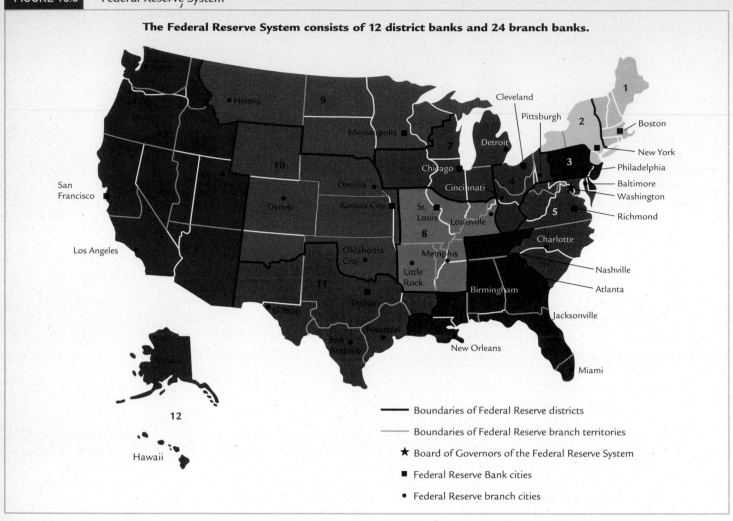

The Federal Reserve System consists of 12 district banks and 24 branch banks.

Boundaries of Federal Reserve districts

Boundaries of Federal Reserve branch territories

★ Board of Governors of the Federal Reserve System

■ Federal Reserve Bank cities

• Federal Reserve branch cities

Source: The Federal Reserve Board Web site at www.federalreserve.gov (accessed March 28, 2012).

Economic Crisis and the Fed's Response

Lately, it seems like the Federal Reserve Board has been in the news more than usual. The reason for all the news coverage is quite simple: The Fed was responsible for maintaining the health of the U.S. economy during the recent economic crisis. To maintain a healthy economy, the Federal Reserve Board took a number of specific steps to minimize the effects of the crisis for both business and individuals. Specifically, the Fed[2]

- **Provided liquidity.** The Fed allowed banks in need of cash to borrow money from the Federal Reserve System. If they could not have borrowed money from the Fed, banks would have tightened lending requirements or stopped funding loans to both businesses and individuals.
- **Supported troubled financial markets.** During the first part of the crisis, investors feared that many commercial paper issues would become worthless and they stopped investing in money-market funds that held commercial paper. **Commercial paper** is a short-term promissory note issued by a large corporation. At the same time, many investors were withdrawing money from money-market funds. In order to restore the commercial paper market and lower the cost of this type of short-term financing for businesses, the Federal Reserve provided secured loans to the financial institutions that sell this type of investment; as a result, the commercial paper market is now functioning well.

commercial paper a short-term promissory note issued by a large corporation

- **Supported important financial institutions.** The failure of investment bank Lehman Brothers and the commercial bank Washington Mutual fueled fears that other large financial institutions could fail. The resulting panic threatened to lead to a full-scale "run" on banks and lenders that could have caused the entire financial system to break down. To restore faith in the system, the Fed agreed to provide non-recourse loans to large banks. The ability to borrow money from the Fed and other government agencies helped to calm investors and avoid an even larger financial meltdown.
- **Conducted stress tests of major banks.** In the spring of 2009, the Federal Reserve, along with other federal agencies, conducted an unprecedented review of the financial condition of the 19 largest U.S. banks. This "stress" test measured how well these banks could weather the economic crisis. Banks that failed the test were required to obtain new capital by selling stock or bonds or accept federal government funds. Today, the nation's largest banks still must undergo the Fed's rigorous stress tests to determine if they are able to withstand another economic crisis.

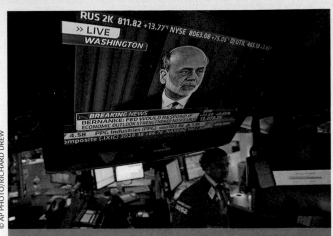

Is Ben Bernanke the nation's most important banker? If you ask that question to bankers, corporate executives, and politicians, the answer would be yes. Simply put: When Mr. Bernanke talks, the financial world listens. Over the last few years, it has been his decisions and the actions taken by the Federal Reserve Board that are responsible for reducing the effects of the recent economic crisis.

The Fed's actions did help to restore confidence in the financial system, to encourage continued lending, to stabilize an unstable economy, and to provide additional time to create a financial rescue plan to restore the nation's economy. At the time of publication, although the health of the banking and financial industry has improved, there are still concerns about the long-term effects of the Federal Reserve's actions, what future actions may be needed to ensure continued economic growth, and the cost of the Fed's actions.

The most important function of the Fed is to use monetary policy to regulate the nation's supply of money in such a way as to maintain a healthy economy. In Chapter 1, *monetary policy* was defined as the Federal Reserve's decisions that determine the size of the supply of money in the nation and the level of interest rates. The goals of monetary policy are continued economic growth, full employment, and stable prices. Three methods—controlling bank reserve requirements, regulating the discount rate, and running open-market operations—are used to implement the Fed's monetary policy.

Regulation of Reserve Requirements

When money is deposited in a bank, the bank must retain a portion of it to satisfy customers who may want to withdraw money from their accounts. The remainder is available to fund loans. By law, the Federal Reserve sets the reserve requirement for financial institutions. The **reserve requirement** is the percentage of its deposits a bank *must* retain, either in its own vault or on deposit with its Federal Reserve district bank. For example, if a bank has *new* deposits of $20 million and the reserve requirement is 10 percent, the bank must retain $2 million. The present reserve requirements range from 0 to 10 percent depending on such factors as the type of account and the total amount individual banks have on deposit.[3]

Once reserve requirements are met, banks can use the remaining funds to create more money and make more loans through a process called *deposit expansion*. In the preceding example, the bank must retain $2 million in a reserve account. It can use the remaining $18 million to fund consumer and business loans. Assume that the bank lends all $18 million to different borrowers and also assume that before using any of the borrowed funds, all borrowers deposit the $18 million in their bank accounts at the lending institution. Now the bank's deposits have increased by an additional $18 million. Because these deposits are subject to the same reserve requirement described earlier, the bank must maintain $1.8 million in a reserve account, and the bank can lend the additional $16.2 million to other bank customers. Of course, the bank's lending

reserve requirement the percentage of its deposits a bank *must* retain, either in its own vault or on deposit with its Federal Reserve district bank potential becomes steadily smaller and smaller as it makes more loans. Moreover, we should point out that as bankers are usually very conservative by nature; they will not use deposit expansion to maximize their lending activities. Instead, they will take a more middle-of-the-road approach.

The Fed's board of governors sets the reserve requirement. *When it increases the requirement, banks have less money available for lending.* Fewer loans are made, and the economy tends to slow. On the other hand, *by decreasing the reserve requirement, the Fed can make additional money available for lending to stimulate a slow economy.* Although the Fed may change the amount of deposits subject to the reserve requirement from year to year, the Fed seldom changes the reserve requirement because this means of controlling the money supply is so very potent.

Regulation of the Discount Rate

Member banks may borrow money from the Fed to satisfy the reserve requirement. The interest rate the Federal Reserve charges for loans to member banks, called the **discount rate**, is set by the board of directors of each Federal Reserve District bank. For the period from January 2003 to June 2006, the discount rate has been as low as 2 percent and as high as 6.25 percent.[4] In August 2007, in an attempt to stabilize the economy and encourage lending, the Federal Reserve began lowering the discount rate. By February 2010, the discount rate reached its lowest level and remains at 0.75 percent at the time of publication.[5]

When the Fed *lowers* the discount rate, it is easier and cheaper for banks to obtain money. Member banks feel free to make more loans and to charge lower interest rates. This action generally stimulates the nation's economy. When the Fed *raises* the discount rate, banks begin to restrict loans, increase the interest rates they charge for loans, and tighten their own loan requirements. The overall effect is to slow the economy. Although the discount rate has decreased to 0.75 percent, you should remember that the Fed can increase rates in an effort to maintain a healthy economy.

Open-Market Operations

The federal government finances its activities partly by buying and selling government securities issued by the U.S. Treasury. These securities, which pay interest, may be purchased by any individual, firm, or organization—including the Fed. **Open-market operations** are the buying and selling of U.S. government securities by the Federal Reserve System for the purpose of controlling the supply of money.

The Federal Open Market Committee (FOMC) is charged with carrying out the Federal Reserve's open-market operations by buying and selling U.S. Treasury securities through the trading desk of the Federal Reserve Bank of New York. To reduce the nation's money supply, the FOMC simply *sells* government securities. The money it receives from purchasers is taken out of circulation. Thus, less money is available for investment, purchases, or lending. To increase the money supply, the FOMC *buys* government securities. The money the FOMC pays for securities goes back into circulation, making more money available to individuals and firms.

Because the major purchasers of government securities are banking and financial institutions, open-market operations tend to have an immediate effect on lending and investment.

Of the three tools used to influence monetary policy, the use of open-market operations is the most important. When the Federal Reserve buys and sells securities, the goal is to change the federal funds rate. The **federal funds rate** is the interest rate at which a bank lends immediately available funds on deposit at the Fed to another bank overnight to meet the borrowing bank's reserve requirements. Because the Fed funds rate is what banks pay when they borrow, it affects the rates they charge when they lend. Although the FOMC sets a target for the federal funds rate, it does not actually set the rate because it is determined by the open market.[6] (*Note:* There is a difference between the federal funds rate and the discount rate discussed earlier in this section. The *federal funds rate* is the interest rate paid by a bank to borrow funds from other

discount rate the interest rate the Federal Reserve System charges for loans to member banks

open-market operations the buying and selling of U.S. government securities by the Federal Reserve System for the purpose of controlling the supply of money

federal funds rate the interest rate at which a bank lends immediately available funds on deposit at the Fed to another bank overnight to meet the borrowing bank's reserve requirements

TABLE 18.1 Methods Used by the Federal Reserve System to Control the Money Supply and the Economy

Method Used	Immediate Result	End Result
Regulating Reserve Requirement		
Fed *increases* reserve requirement	Less money for banks to lend to customers—reduction in overall money supply	Economic slowdown
Fed *decreases* reserve requirement	More money for banks to lend to customers—increase in overall money supply	Increased economic activity
Regulating the Discount Rate		
Fed *increases* the discount rate	Less money for banks to lend to customers—reduction in overall money supply	Economic slowdown
Fed *decreases* the discount rate	More money for banks to lend to customers—increase in overall money supply	Increased economic activity
Open-Market Operations		
Fed *sells* government securities	Reduction in overall money supply	Economic slowdown
Fed *buys* government securities	Increase in overall money supply	Increased economic activity

© Cengage Learning 2014

banks. The *discount rate* is the interest rate paid by a bank to borrow funds from the Federal Reserve.) Table 18.1 summarizes the effects of open-market operations and the other tools used by the Fed to regulate the money supply and control the economy.

Other Fed Responsibilities

In addition to its regulation of the money supply, the Fed is also responsible for serving as the government's bank, clearing checks and electronic transfers, inspecting currency, and applying selective credit controls.

Serving as Government Bank The Federal Reserve is the bank for the U.S. government. As the government's bank, it processes a variety of financial transactions involving trillions of dollars each year. For example, the Federal Reserve provides financial services for the U.S. Treasury, including accounts through which incoming tax deposits and outgoing government payments are handled.

Clearing Checks and Electronic Transfers Although not as popular as they once were, many people still use checks to pay their monthly bills and pay for purchases. A check written by a customer of one bank and presented for payment to another bank in the same town may be processed through a local clearinghouse. The procedure becomes more complicated, however, when the banks are not in the same town. Although at one point the Fed was responsible for the prompt and accurate collection of 15 to 17 billion checks each year, today the number of paper checks cleared through the Federal Reserve System is decreasing because of improved automation and electronic equipment.[7] Banks that use the Fed to clear checks are charged a fee for this service. Through the use of automation and electronic equipment, most checks can be cleared within two or three days.

Inspection of Currency As paper currency is handled, it becomes worn or dirty. The typical $1 bill has a life expectancy of less than two years. Most $50 and $100 bills usually last longer because they are handled less. When member banks deposit their surplus cash in a Federal Reserve Bank, the currency is inspected. Bills unfit for further use are separated and destroyed.

Selective Credit Controls The Federal Reserve System (along with the Consumer Financial Protection Bureau that was created in 2010) has the responsibility for enforcing the Truth-in-Lending Act, which Congress passed in 1968. This act requires lenders to state clearly the annual percentage rate and total finance charge for a consumer loan.

The Federal Reserve System is also responsible for setting the margin requirements for securities transactions. The *margin* is the minimum amount (expressed as a percentage) of the purchase price that must be paid in cash or eligible securities. (The investor may borrow the remainder.) The current initial margin requirement is 50 percent. Thus, if an investor purchases $4,000 worth of stock, he or she must pay at least $2,000 in cash or its equivalent in securities. The remaining $2,000 may be borrowed from the brokerage firm. Although the minimum margin requirements are regulated by the Federal Reserve, margin requirements and the interest charged on the loans used to fund margin transactions may vary among brokerage firms and different security exchanges.

Describe the organizations involved in the banking industry.

THE AMERICAN BANKING INDUSTRY

Most bankers will tell you that the last few years have been frustrating for the American banking industry, to say the least. Furthermore, it's not just bankers who felt the impact. Almost everyone has been affected in one way or another by the nation's economic crisis.

Banks, savings and loan associations, credit unions, and other financial institutions were at the center of the nation's economic problems. Aggressive lending practices that led to record numbers of home foreclosures and nonperforming loans caused a financial meltdown. As the economic problems within the banking and financial industry became larger, the ability to borrow money became more difficult for both individuals and business firms—a very serious problem for both borrowers and lenders. In fact, the nation's economic problems (and the world's) became so severe that the government needed to take action. Both the Bush and the Obama administrations developed financial stimulus plans to rescue the economy. In addition, both the Federal Reserve Board and the U.S. Treasury took action. Eventually, the rescue plans did help relieve at least some of the financial problems associated with the economic crisis. Still, there was need for more changes in the way that banks and financial institutions operate.

Banking and Financial Reform: New Regulations

Although there are many critics of increased regulation, it was apparent that something needed to be done to prevent the type of economic problems the nation experienced during the economic crisis. According to President Barack Obama, the goals of new government banking and financial regulations are more than justified in the wake of the crisis and include the following:[8]

- Protect American families from unfair and abusive financial and banking practices.
- Close the gaps in our financial system that allowed large banks and financial firms to avoid strong, comprehensive federal oversight. To accomplish these goals, the Dodd–Frank Wall Street Reform and Consumer Protection Act was passed in 2010. This act addressed many of the issues that led to the economic crisis. Specifically, the act
  - Creates a new Consumer Financial Protection Bureau.
  - Gives the government the power to seize and close down large failing financial firms in an orderly fashion.
  - Increases government regulation of firms in the financial and banking industry.
  - Curbs the high-risk investment strategies that led to the financial problems at some major financial institutions and the nation's economic crisis.
  - Creates a Financial Stability Oversight Council that serves as an early warning system of potential risks and problems in the financial system.

To provide this type of comprehensive reform, it will be necessary to make sure banks and financial institutions are complying with the new regulations. As a result, future regulations will subject banks and financial institutions to more in-depth evaluations to determine their financial health and to spot signs of trouble before they affect individuals, the American economy, and the world economy.

For more information about existing regulations and proposed new regulations, go to the Federal Reserve Board's Web site at www.federalreserve.gov, the U.S. Treasury Web site at www.ustreas.gov, or use a search engine like Google or Yahoo! and enter "banking reform" or "financial reform."

In addition to the nation's economic problems, competition among banks, savings and loan associations, credit unions, and other business firms that want to perform banking activities has never been greater. In fact, many financial institutions are using social media sites like Facebook and Twitter, as well as blogs and their own Web sites, to attract new customers and retain old ones. Let's begin this section with some information about one of the major players in the banking industry—the commercial bank.

When will the sun begin to shine on American banking? Good question. It seems that since the economic crisis began in the fall of 2007, banks have been at the center of the nation's economic problems. For most banks and many financial institutions, aggressive lending practices, record numbers of home foreclosures, and a large number of nonperforming loans caused a financial meltdown and created a situation where it was difficult for both businesses and individuals to borrow money.

© BLOOMBERG VIA GETTY IMAGES

Commercial Banks

A **commercial bank** is a profit-making organization that accepts deposits, makes loans, and provides related services to its customers. Like other businesses, the bank's primary goal—its mission—is to meet its customers' needs while earning a profit.

Because they deal with money belonging to individuals and other business firms, banks must meet certain requirements before they receive a charter, or permission to operate, from either federal or state banking authorities. A **national bank** is a commercial bank chartered by the U.S. Comptroller of the Currency. There are approximately 1,400 national banks.[9] These banks must conform to federal banking regulations and are subject to unannounced inspections by federal auditors.

A **state bank** is a commercial bank chartered by the banking authorities in the state in which it operates. State banks outnumber national banks by about four to one, but they tend to be smaller than national banks. They are subject to unannounced inspections by both state and federal auditors. Table 18.2 lists the seven largest banks in the United States. All are classified as national banks.

Other Financial Institutions

In addition to commercial banks, at least eight other types of financial institutions perform either full or limited banking services for their customers.

commercial bank a profit-making organization that accepts deposits, makes loans, and provides related services to its customers

national bank a commercial bank chartered by the U.S. Comptroller of the Currency

state bank a commercial bank chartered by the banking authorities in the state in which it operates

TABLE 18.2	The Seven Largest U.S. Banks, Ranked by 2011 Total Revenues		
Rank	Company	Revenues ($ millions)	Profits ($ millions)	Employees
1	Bank of America Corp.	134,194	−2,238	288,122
2	JPMorgan Chase & Co.	115,475	17,370	239,831
3	Citigroup	111,055	10,602	260,000
4	Wells Fargo	93,249	12,362	272,200
5	Goldman Sachs Group	45,967	8,354	38,700
6	Morgan Stanley	39,320	4,703	62,542
7	American Express	30,242	4,057	61,000

Source: From Fortune Magazine, "Fortune 500: Industries: Commercial Banks," May 23, 2011 © 2011 Time Inc. Used under license. Fortune and Time Inc. are not affiliated with, and do not endorse products or services of, Licensee.

Savings and Loan Associations A savings and loan association (S&L) is a financial institution that offers checking and savings accounts and CDs and that invests most of its assets in home mortgage loans and other consumer loans. Originally, S&Ls were permitted to offer their depositors *only* savings accounts. However, since Congress passed legislation regarding S&Ls in the 1980s, they have been able to offer other services to attract depositors.

Today, there are approximately 1,050 S&Ls in the United States insured by the Federal Deposit Insurance Corporation.[10] Federal associations are supervised by the U.S. Comptroller of the Currency, a branch of the U.S. Treasury. State-chartered S&Ls are subjected to unannounced audits by state authorities.

Credit Unions The United States currently has an estimated 7,300 credit unions.[11] A **credit union** is a financial institution that accepts deposits from, and lends money to, only those people who are its members. Usually, the membership consists of employees of a particular firm, people in a particular profession, or those who live in a community served by a local credit union. Credit unions may pay higher interest on deposits than commercial banks and S&Ls, and they may provide loans at lower cost. The National Credit Union Administration regulates federally chartered credit unions. State authorities regulate credit unions with state charters.

Organizations that Perform Banking Functions Six other types of financial institutions are involved in banking activities. Although not actually full-service banks, they offer customers some banking services.

- *Mutual savings banks* are financial institutions that are owned by their depositors and offer many of the same services offered by banks, S&Ls, and credit unions, including checking accounts, savings accounts, and CDs. Like other financial institutions, they also fund home mortgages, commercial loans, and consumer loans. Unlike other types of financial institutions, the profits of a mutual savings bank go to the depositors, usually in the form of dividends or slightly higher interest rates on savings. Today, most mutual savings banks are located in the Northeast.
- *Insurance companies* provide long-term financing for office buildings, shopping centers, and other commercial real estate projects throughout the United States. The funds used for this type of financing are obtained from policyholders' insurance premiums.
- *Pension funds* are established by employers to guarantee their employees a regular monthly income on retirement. Contributions to the fund may come from the employer, the employee, or both. Pension funds earn additional income through generally conservative investments in corporate stocks, corporate bonds, and government securities, as well as through financing real estate developments.
- *Brokerage firms* offer combination savings and checking accounts that pay higher-than-usual interest rates. Many people have switched to these accounts because they are convenient and to get slightly higher rates.
- *Finance companies* provide financing to individuals and business firms that may not be able to get financing from banks, S&Ls, or credit unions. Firms such as Ford Motor Credit and GE Capital provide loans to both individuals and business firms. Lenders such as Ace Cash Express, Inc., provide short-term loans to individuals. The interest rates charged by these lenders may be higher than the interest rates charged by other financial institutions.
- *Investment banking firms* are organizations that assist corporations in raising funds, usually by helping sell new issues of stocks, bonds, or other financial securities. Although these firms do not accept deposits or make loans like traditional banking firms, they do help companies raise millions of dollars. More information about investment banking firms and the role they play in American business is provided in Chapter 19.

savings and loan association (S&L) a financial institution that offers checking and savings accounts and CDs and that invests most of its assets in home mortgage loans and other consumer loans

credit union a financial institution that accepts deposits from, and lends money to, only the people who are its members

Careers in the Banking Industry

Take a second look at Table 18.2. The seven largest banks in the United States employ approximately 1,200,000 people. If you add to this amount the people employed by smaller banks not listed in Table 18.2 and those employed by S&Ls, credit unions, and other financial institutions, the number of employees grows dramatically. According to the *Occupational Outlook Handbook,* published by the U.S. Department of Labor, a number of different positions in the banking industry are projected to have average growth between now and the year 2020.[12]

To be successful in the banking industry, employees for a bank, S&L, credit union, or other financial institution must possess the following traits:

1. *You must be honest.* Because you are handling other people's money, many financial institutions go to great lengths to discover dishonest employees.
2. *You must be able to interact with people.* A number of positions in the banking industry require that you possess the interpersonal skills needed to interact not only with other employees but also with customers.
3. *You need a strong background in accounting.* Many of the routine tasks performed by employees in the banking industry are basic accounting functions. For example, a teller must post deposits or withdrawals to a customer's account and then balance out at the end of the day to ensure accuracy.
4. *You need to appreciate the relationship between banking and finance.* Bank officers must interview loan applicants and determine if their request for money is based on sound financial principles. Above all, loan officers must be able to evaluate applicants and their loan requests to determine if the borrower will be able to repay a loan.
5. *You should possess basic computer skills.* Almost all employees in the banking industry use a computer for some aspect of their work on a daily basis.

Depending on qualifications, work experience, and education, starting salaries generally are between $18,000 and $30,000 a year, but it is not uncommon for college graduates to earn $35,000 a year or more.

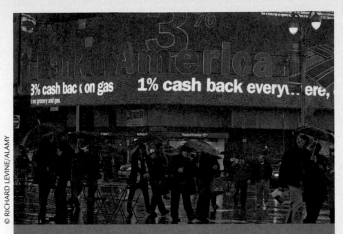

Even "big" banks want more customers. Bank of America, the largest bank in the United States, still wants your business. Like many competitors, the bank offers cash back, competitive rates for savings and loans, online banking, and many other services to attract new customers. Check out the latest promotions at www.bankofamerica.com.

TRADITIONAL SERVICES PROVIDED BY FINANCIAL INSTITUTIONS

 4 Identify the services provided by financial institutions.

To determine how important banking services are to you, ask yourself just three simple questions:

- How many checks did you write last month?
- Do you have a credit or debit card? If so, how often do you use it?
- How many times did you visit an ATM last month?

If you are like most people and business firms, you would find it hard to live a normal life without the services provided by banks and other financial institutions. Typical services provided by a bank or other financial institution are illustrated in Figure 18.4.

The most important traditional banking services for both individuals and businesses are described in this section. Online banking, electronic transfer of funds, and other significant and future developments are discussed in the next section.

Checking Accounts

Firms and individuals deposit money in checking accounts (demand deposits) so that they can write checks to pay for purchases. A **check** is a written order for a bank or

check a written order for a bank or other financial institution to pay a stated dollar amount to the business or person indicated on the face of the check

Banking services can be divided into three broad categories: traditional services, electronic services, and international services.

TRADITIONAL	ELECTRONIC	INTERNATIONAL
• Checking • Savings • Loans • Credit and debit cards • Financial advice • Payroll service • Certified checks • Trust services • Safe-deposit boxes	• Automatic teller machines • Electronic transfer of funds • Automated clearing-houses • Point-of-sale terminals • Electronic check conversion	• Letter of credit • Banker's acceptance • Currency exchange

© CENGAGE LEARNING 2014

other financial institution to pay a stated dollar amount to the business or person indicated on the face of the check. Today, some financial institutions offer free checking; others charge activity fees (or service charges) for checking accounts. Fees and charges generally range from $5 to $20 per month for individuals. For businesses, monthly charges are based on the average daily balance in the checking account, the number of checks written, or both. Charges for business checking accounts are often higher than those for individual accounts.

Most financial institutions offer interest-paying accounts called NOW (negotiable order of withdrawal) accounts that allow customers to write checks. A **NOW account** is an interest-paying checking account. For these accounts, the usual interest rate is between 0.05 percent and 0.25 percent. Typically, online Internet banks pay slightly higher interest rates. However, individual banks often impose certain restrictions on their NOW accounts.

Although banks and other financial institutions may pay low interest rates on checking accounts, even small earnings are better than no earnings. In addition to interest rates, be sure to compare monthly fees before opening a checking account for your personal use or a business.

Savings Accounts

Savings accounts (time deposits) provide a safe place to store money and a very conservative means of investing. At the time of publication, *passbook savings accounts* earned between 0.05 percent and 0.50 percent in commercial banks and S&Ls and slightly more in credit unions or online Internet banks.

A depositor who is willing to leave money on deposit with a bank for a set period of time can earn a higher rate of interest. To do so, the depositor buys a certificate of deposit. A **certificate of deposit (CD)** is a document stating that the bank will pay the depositor a guaranteed interest rate on money left on deposit for a specified period of time. At the time of publication, interest rates have ranged from 0.50 to 2 percent. The rate always depends on how much is invested and for how long. Generally, the rule is: The longer the period of time until maturity, the higher is the rate. Depositors are penalized for early withdrawal of funds invested in CDs.

Short- and Long-Term Loans

Banks, S&Ls, credit unions, and other financial institutions provide short- and long-term loans to both individuals and businesses. *Short-term business loans* must be repaid within one year or less. Typical uses for the money obtained through short-term loans include solving cash-flow problems, purchasing inventory, monthly expenses, and meeting unexpected emergencies.

NOW account an interest-paying checking account; *NOW* stands for *negotiable order of withdrawal*

certificate of deposit (CD) a document stating that the bank will pay the depositor a guaranteed interest rate on money left on deposit for a specified period of time

Entrepreneurial SUCCESS

Kiva.org Connects Microloan Borrowers and Lenders

Kiva.org is a non-profit organization that connects individual lenders—anyone who can lend at least $25—with borrowers who need a bit of cash to go into business or keep a business running. Microloans are much too small for traditional lenders, but large enough to make a big difference to low-income entrepreneurs who need to buy a fishing net, a box of merchandise for resale, or a bicycle to make deliveries.

Working through local organizations in 61 nations, Kiva posts borrowers' photos and stories on its Web site. Lenders determine which borrowers will receive their money, and Kiva's local partners manage the disbursement and repayment of the loans. As little as $200 can start a borrower in Peru or Kenya on the road to becoming a self-sufficient small business owner. Kiva has arranged loans of up to $10,000, helping entrepreneurs in New Orleans and elsewhere upgrade business equipment or branch out into new services.

Since Kiva was founded in 2005, it has arranged more than $300 million in microloans with money from 740,000 lenders in 218 countries. Nearly 99 percent of all loans are repaid, an extremely high percentage. Once a loan is repaid, the lender can reloan the money to another borrower, starting the cycle over again. "It's a different kind of financing opportunity," says the CEO. "It's personal."

Sources: Based on information in The Kiva Web site (www.kiva.org), accessed April 1, 2012; Joann Pan, "725,000 Loans Granted by Kiva, 2.6 Billion to Go," *Mashable*, March 15, 2012, www.mashable.com; Josh Constine, "Visit Kiva.org to Microlend $1 Million of Reid Hoffman's Money," *TechCrunch*, March 12, 2012, www.techcrunch.com; Matt Silverman, "How Kiva.org's CEO Uses Social Media to Spark a Dialogue of Change," *Mashable*, September 20, 2011, www.mashable.com; Kimberly Quillen, "Kiva CEO Says Entrepreneurial Community Should Include High-Growth and Traditional Firms," *Times-Picayune (New Orleans)*, March 12, 2012, www.nola.com.

To help ensure that short-term money will be available when needed, many firms establish a line of credit. A **line of credit** is a loan that is approved before the money is actually needed. Because all the necessary paperwork is already completed and the loan is pre-approved, the business can obtain the money later without delay, as soon as it is required. Even with a line of credit, a firm may not be able to borrow money if the bank does not have sufficient funds available. For this reason, some firms prefer a **revolving credit agreement**, which is a guaranteed line of credit.

Long-term business loans are repaid over a period of years. The average length of a long-term business loan is generally three to seven years but sometimes as long as 15 years or in a few cases even longer periods of time. Long-term loans are used most often to finance the expansion of buildings and retail facilities, mergers and acquisitions, replacement of equipment, or product development.

Most lenders require some type of collateral for long-term loans. **Collateral** is real estate or property (stocks, bonds, equipment, or any other asset of value) pledged as security for a loan. For example, when an individual obtains a loan to pay for a new Chevrolet Malibu, the automobile is the collateral for the loan. If the borrower fails to repay the loan according to the terms specified in the loan agreement, the lender can repossess the car.

Repayment terms and interest rates for both short- and long-term loans are arranged between the lender and the borrower. For businesses, repayment terms may include monthly, quarterly, semiannual, or annual payments. Repayment terms and interest rates for personal loans vary depending on how the money will be used and what type of collateral, if any, is pledged. However, individuals typically make monthly payments to repay personal loans. Borrowers always should "shop" for a loan, comparing the repayment terms and interest rates offered by competing financial institutions.

line of credit a loan that is approved before the money is actually needed

revolving credit agreement a guaranteed line of credit

collateral real estate or property pledged as security for a loan

How do you pay for your purchases? Today more and more people are using credit and debit cards to pay for their purchases. For consumers, "plastic cards" are convenient and fast. For the merchant, credit and debit card transactions can be converted to cash and improve a firm's cash flow.

Social MEDIA

Outsmart the Scam Artists

You may be able to friend your bank on Facebook, but watch out for scam artists who use social media to steal identities. If your full birth date, address, or e-mail is in your public Facebook profile, fraudsters can take those details, dig up other information about you, and apply for credit using your identity. Another scam is an application that offers something free (such as Facebook credits) if you will complete a survey or send in friends' e-mail addresses. Once you click, this application accesses your complete profile and your posts—and posts messages on friends' walls about this new "opportunity." But by keeping your data private, you can outsmart the scam artists.

Sources: Christina Tynan-Wood, "Facebook Con Artists on the Rise," *Infoworld*, January 17, 2011, www.infoworld.com; Matt Liebowitz, "Facebook Scam Targets Users with '150 Free Credits,'" *Security News Daily*, December 15, 2010. www.securitynewsdaily.com.

© MKABAKOV/SHUTTERSTOCK

Credit Card and Debit Card Transactions

By the end of 2012, 160 million Americans will use credit cards to pay for everything from tickets on American Airlines to Zebco fishing gear.[13] Why have credit cards become so popular?

For a merchant, the answer is obvious. By depositing charge slips in a bank or other financial institution, the merchant can convert credit card sales into cash. In return for processing the merchant's credit card transactions, the financial institution charges a fee that generally ranges between 1.5 and 4 percent. Let's assume that you use a Visa credit card to purchase a microwave oven for $300 from Gold Star Appliance, a retailer in Richardson, Texas. At the end of the day, the retailer deposits your charge slip, along with other charge slips, checks, and currency collected during the day, at its bank. If the bank charges Gold Star Appliance 4 percent to process each credit card transaction, the bank deducts a processing fee of $12 ($300 $\times$ 0.04 = $12) for your credit card transaction and immediately deposits the remainder ($288) in Gold Star Appliance's account. Typically, small businesses pay more than larger businesses. The number of credit card transactions, the total dollar amount of credit sales, and how well the merchant can negotiate the fees the bank charges determine actual fees.

Do not confuse debit cards with credit cards. Although they may look alike, there are important differences. A **debit card** electronically subtracts the amount of your purchase from your bank account at the moment the purchase is made. (By contrast, when you use your credit card, the credit card company extends short-term financing, and you do not make payment until you receive your next statement.) Debit cards are used most commonly to obtain cash at ATMs and to purchase products and services from retailers.

Understand how financial institutions are changing to meet the needs of domestic and international customers.

INNOVATIVE BANKING SERVICES

Today, many individuals, financial managers, and business owners are finding it convenient to do their banking electronically. Let's begin by looking at how banking will change in the future.

Changes in the Banking Industry

While the experts may not be able to predict with 100 percent accuracy the changes that will affect banking, they all agree that banking *will* change. The most obvious changes the experts do agree on are as follows:

- More emphasis on evaluating the credit-worthiness of loan applicants as a result of the recent economic crisis
- An increase in government regulation of the banking industry
- A reduction in the number of banks, S&Ls, credit unions, and financial institutions because of consolidation and mergers
- Globalization of the banking industry as the economies of individual nations become more interrelated
- The importance of customer service as a way to keep customers from switching to competitors
- Increased use of credit and debit cards and a decrease in the number of written checks
- Continued growth in online and mobile banking

debit card a card that electronically subtracts the amount of your purchase from your bank account at the moment the purchase is made

Going for SUCCESS

Vying to Run Your Digital Wallet

Cash isn't going away any time soon, but Google, PayPal, Visa, and other big companies are already competing to run the digital wallet that could replace your leather wallet in the future. The idea is to speed up transactions and make them as convenient as the one-click payments many online businesses accept. Instead of handing bills and coins to a cashier or waiting for change, you use your digital wallet (typically, your cell phone) to transfer money electronically to the business you're buying from. Your digital wallet might even alert you to special deals or earn you rewards for certain purchases.

The Google Wallet, for example, uses a wireless technology called near field communication to let your cell phone app "talk" to a cash register and arrange payment (charged to your credit card or another card) with just a tap of the phone. Subway sandwich shops and Macy's were among the first businesses to accept Google Wallet payments. PayPal's system, which works as an app and online, has an interesting feature: After you pay, you have several days to decide where the money will come from—a store credit card or a bank debit card, for example. Billions of dollars in cash transactions are going cashless every year. Is a digital wallet in your future?

Sources: Based on information in Olga Kharif, "Google Said to Rethink Wallet Strategy," *Bloomberg*, March 21, 2012, www.bloomberg.com; Edward C. Baig, "Mobile Wallet Competition Heats Up," *USA Today*, February 28, 2012, www.usatoday.com; Deirdre van Dyk, "The End of Cash," *Time*, January 9, 2012, pp. 48–49.

Online, Mobile, and International Banking

Online banking allows you to access your bank's computer system from home, the office, or even while you are traveling. For the customer, online banking offers a number of advantages, including the following:

- The ability to obtain current account balances
- The capability to deposit checks without leaving your home or office
- The convenience of transferring funds from one account to another
- The ability to pay bills
- The convenience of seeing which checks have cleared
- Simplified loan application procedures

Online banking provides a number of advantages for the financial institution. Probably the most important advantage is the lower cost of processing large numbers of transactions. As you learned in Chapter 17, lower costs often lead to larger profits. In addition to lower costs and increased profits, financial institutions believe that online banking offers increased security because fewer people handle fewer paper documents.

In addition to online banking, many banks now offer mobile banking via text message or apps (software applications) downloaded to cell phones and other electronic devices. The goal is to let customers use technology to check account balances, transfer money, and track deposits at any time, from anywhere. This is especially convenient for busy businesspeople who don't live or work next door to a bank branch and can't always get to a computer to use online banking.

electronic funds transfer (EFT) system a means of performing financial transactions through a computer terminal or telephone hookup

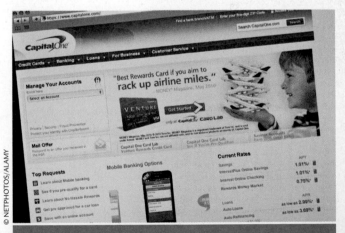

Now you can bank with a click of a computer's mouse. With improved technology, bank customers can now deposit checks without leaving their office or home, obtain current account balances, and pay bills online. In fact, many of the traditional banking services that used to require a trip to the bank can now be completed online. Why not take a look at your bank's Web site to see how online banking can help you manage your finances?

Electronic Funds Transfer (EFT)

An **electronic funds transfer (EFT) system** is a means of performing financial transactions through a computer terminal or telephone hookup. The following four EFT applications are changing how banks do business:

1. *Automatic teller machines (ATMs).* An ATM is an electronic bank teller—a machine that provides almost any service a human teller can provide. Once the customer is properly identified, the machine dispenses cash from the customer's checking or savings account or makes a cash advance charged to a credit card. ATMs are located in bank parking lots, supermarkets, drugstores, and even gas stations. Customers have access to them at all times of the day or night. There may be a fee for each transaction.

2. *Automated clearinghouse (ACH).* Designed to reduce the number of paper checks, an automated clearinghouse processes Social Security benefits, tax payments, recurring bill payments, payments for Internet sales, and employee salaries. For example, many large companies use the ACH network to transfer wages and salaries directly into their employees' bank accounts, thus eliminating the need to make out individual paychecks.

3. *Point-of-sale (POS) terminals.* A POS terminal is a computerized cash register located in a retail store and connected to a bank's computer. Assume you want to pay for purchases at a Walmart Supercenter. You begin the process by pulling your credit or debit card through a magnetic card reader. A central processing center notifies a computer at your bank that you want to make a purchase. The bank's computer immediately adds the amount to your account for a credit card transaction. In a similar process, the bank's computer deducts the amount of the purchase from your bank account if you use a debit card. Finally, the amount of your purchase is added to the retailer's account. The Walmart store then is notified that the transaction is complete, and the cash register prints out your receipt.

4. *Electronic check conversion (ECC).* Electronic check conversion is a process used to convert information from a paper check into an electronic payment for merchandise, services, or bills. When you give your completed check to a cashier at a Best Buy store, the check is processed through an electronic system that captures your banking information and the dollar amount of the check. Once the check is processed, you are asked to sign a receipt, and you get a voided (canceled) check back for your records. Finally, the funds to pay for your transaction are transferred into the Best Buy store's account. ECC also can be used for checks you mail to pay for a purchase or to pay on an account.

letter of credit a legal document issued by a bank or other financial institution guaranteeing to pay a seller a stated amount for a specified period of time

Why is a French bank in the United States? Because it makes perfect business sense in a world where national boundaries blur and multinational firms operate in many different countries. Actually, the number of U.S. banks that operate overseas and the number of foreign banks that operate in the United States are both increasing. For banks, the world is becoming smaller and much more competitive.

© RICHARD B. LEVINE/ALAMY

Bankers and business owners generally are pleased with online banking and EFT systems. Both online banking and EFT are fast, and they eliminate the costly processing of checks. However, many customers are reluctant to use online banking or EFT systems. Some simply do not like "the technology," whereas others fear that the computer will garble their accounts. Early on, in 1978, Congress responded to such fears by passing the Electronic Funds Transfer Act, which protects the customer in case the bank makes an error or the customer's account information is stolen.

International Banking Services For international businesses, banking services are extremely important. Depending on the needs of an international firm, a bank can help by providing a letter of credit or a banker's acceptance.

A **letter of credit** is a legal document issued by a bank or other financial institution guaranteeing to pay a seller a stated amount for a specified period of time—usually 30 to 60 days. With a letter of credit, certain conditions, such as delivery of the merchandise, may be specified before payment is made.

A **banker's acceptance** is a written order for a bank to pay a third party a stated amount of money on a specific date. With a banker's acceptance, no conditions are specified. It is simply an order to pay guaranteed by a bank without any strings attached.

Both a letter of credit and a banker's acceptance are popular methods of paying for import and export transactions. For example, imagine that you are a business owner in the United States who wants to purchase some leather products from a small business in Florence, Italy. You offer to pay for the merchandise with your company's check drawn on an American bank, but the Italian business owner is worried about payment. To solve the problem, your bank can issue either a letter of credit or a banker's acceptance to guarantee that payment will be made. In addition to a letter of credit and a banker's acceptance, banks also can use EFT technology to speed international banking transactions.

One other international banking service should be noted. Banks and other financial institutions provide for currency exchange. If you place an order for merchandise valued at $50,000 from a company in Japan, how do you pay for the order? Do you use U.S. dollars or Japanese yen? To solve this problem, you can use a bank's currency-exchange service. To make payment, you can use either currency. If necessary, the bank will exchange one currency for the other to complete your transaction.

banker's acceptance a written order for a bank to pay a third party a stated amount of money on a specific date

THE FDIC AND NCUA

6 Explain how deposit insurance protects customers.

During the Great Depression, which began in 1929, a number of banks failed, and their depositors lost all their savings. To make sure that such a disaster did not happen again and to restore public confidence in the banking industry, the U.S. Congress enacted legislation that created the *Federal Deposit Insurance Corporation (FDIC)* in 1933. The primary purpose of the FDIC is to insure deposits against bank failures.

Today, the FDIC provides basic deposit insurance of $250,000 per depositor. Deposits maintained in different categories of legal ownership are insured separately. Thus, you can have increased coverage for different categories of ownership in a single institution. The most common categories of ownership are single (or individual) ownership and joint ownership. A depositor also may obtain additional coverage by opening separate accounts in different financial institutions. To determine if your deposits are insured or if your bank or financial institution is insured, visit the FDIC Web site at www.fdic.gov or call 1-877-ASK-FDIC.

To obtain coverage, banks and S&Ls must pay insurance premiums to the FDIC. In a similar manner, the National Credit Union Administration (NCUA) insures deposits in member credit unions for up to $250,000 per depositor. Like FDIC coverage, increased coverage is provided for accounts with different categories of ownership.

The FDIC and NCUA have improved banking in the United States. When either of these organizations insures a financial institution's deposits, they reserve the right to examine that institution's operations periodically. If a bank, S&L, savings bank, or credit union is found to be poorly managed, it is reported to the proper banking authority.

COURTESY OF FDIC

Ever wonder how safe your money is when you make deposits at a bank? It's easy to find out if your deposits are insured by the FDIC. Just go to the FDIC Web site at www.fdic.gov, and take a look. While you're there, explore the Web site. There are many topics that describe what the FDIC is doing to regulate and improve banking in the United States.

EFFECTIVE CREDIT MANAGEMENT

One of the most important activities of any financial institution or business is making wise decisions regarding to whom it will extend credit. **Credit** is immediate purchasing power that is exchanged for a promise to repay borrowed money, with or without interest, at a later date. For example, suppose that you obtain a bank loan to buy a $150,000 home. You, as the borrower, obtain immediate purchasing power. In return, you agree to certain terms imposed by the lender. Generally, the lender requires that you make a down payment, make monthly payments, pay interest, and purchase insurance to protect your home until the loan is paid in full.

Banks and other financial institutions lend money because they are in business for that purpose. The interest they charge is what provides their profit. Other businesses extend credit to their customers for at least three reasons.

Some customers simply cannot afford to pay the entire amount of their purchase immediately, but they *can* repay credit in a number of smaller payments stretched out over some period of time. Some firms are forced to sell goods or services on credit to compete effectively when other firms offer credit to their customers.

Finally, firms can realize a profit from interest charges that a borrower pays on some credit arrangements.

credit immediate purchasing power that is exchanged for a promise to repay borrowed money, with or without interest, at a later date

Personal APPS

No one likes to pay more than they have to for anything. And yet, many consumers often pay more for loans than necessary. Factors that increase the amount of interest you pay for credit cards, an auto loan, or a home mortgage include how well you have paid your bills in the past, the amount of debt you currently have, and your credit score. It also helps to compare rates for different types of consumer credit. Even a one percent lower interest rate for a home mortgage, for example, can save you thousands of dollars over the life of a home loan.

Getting Money from a Bank or Lender after the Economic Crisis

While lenders need interest from loans to help pay their business expenses and earn a profit, they also want to make sure that the loans they make will be repaid. As a borrower, your job is to convince the lender that you are able and willing to repay the loan.

After the recent economic crisis, bankers, lenders and suppliers, and credit card companies are much more careful when evaluating credit applications.

For individuals, the following suggestions may be helpful when applying for credit:

• Obtain a loan application and complete it at home. At home, you have the information needed to answer *all* the questions on the loan application.
• Be prepared to describe how you will use the money and how the loan will be repaid.
• For most loans, an interview with a loan officer is required. Here again, preparation is the key. Think about how you would respond to questions a loan officer might ask.
• If your loan request is rejected, try to analyze what went wrong. Ask the loan officer why you were rejected. If the rejection is based on incorrect information, supply the correct information and reapply.

Business owners in need of financing may find the following additional tips helpful:

• It is usually best to develop a relationship with your banker before you need financing.
• Help the banker understand what your business is and how you may need future financing for expansion, cash-flow problems, or unexpected emergencies.

- Apply for a pre-approved line of credit or revolving credit agreement even if you do not need the money. View the application as another way to showcase your company and its products or services.
- In addition to the application, supply certified public accountant (CPA)-prepared financial statements and business tax returns for the last three years. If your business is small, you may want to supply your own personal financial statements and tax returns for the same period.
- Update your business plan in case the lender wants to review your plan. Be sure the sales estimates and other projections are realistic.
- Write a cover letter describing how much experience you have, whether you are operating in an expanding market, or any other information that would help convince the banker to provide financing.

The Five C's of Credit Management

When a business extends credit to its customers, it must face the fact that some customers will be unable or unwilling to pay for their credit purchases. To help determine if an individual or business is a good credit risk, lenders often examine a business firm's financial statements. Individuals may be asked to complete a credit application like the one illustrated in Figure 18.5. Most lenders will also consider the five C's of credit, described in Table 18.3.

Checking Credit Information

The five C's of credit are concerned mainly with information supplied by the applicant. But how can a lender determine whether this information is accurate? This depends on whether the potential borrower is a business or an individual consumer.

Credit information concerning businesses can be obtained from the following four sources:

- *Global credit-reporting agencies.* D&B (formerly Dun & Bradstreet) is the world's leading credit-reporting agency. Their reports present detailed credit information about specific companies. For more information on D&B services, visit the company's Web site at www.dnb.com.
- *Local credit-reporting agencies.* These agencies may require a monthly or yearly fee for providing information on a continual basis.
- *Industry associations.* These associations may charge a service fee.
- *Other firms.* This refers to other firms that have given the applicant credit.

TABLE 18.3 The Five C's of Credit	
Lenders often use the five C's of credit to determine which credit or loan requests will be approved and which will be rejected.	
Factor to Consider	Description of Why This Factor Is Important
Character	The borrower's attitude toward credit obligations
Capacity	The financial ability to meet credit obligations—that is, to make regular loan payments.
Capital	The term *capital* as used here refers to the borrower's assets or the net worth of the individual or business applying for a loan.
Collateral	Real estate or property including stocks, bonds, equipment, or any other asset pledged as security for a loan.
Conditions	General economic conditions that can affect a borrower's ability to repay a loan or other credit obligation.

© Cengage Learning 2014

FIGURE 18.5   Credit Application Form

Lenders use the information on credit application forms to help determine which customers should be granted credit.

Apply today! Just complete this application or call 1-800-438-9222.

Citizens Bank Customer Credit Card Application

Branch # _____

This offer is for existing Citizens Bank Customers applying for a new credit card account

Existing Citizens Bank cardholders should call 1-800-438-9222 for special cardholder rate information.

Citizens Bank VISA® (Code: BVCFNU)

Please tell us about yourself

_____

First Name   Middle Initial   Last Name

_____

Address (street)

_____

(City, state, zip)

_____   ___ — ___ — _____

Date of Birth   Social Security Number

❑ Own   ❑ Rent   ❑ Live with Parents

Years/Months at Present Address

$ _____   (____) _____

Monthly Housing Payment   Home Telephone

_____

Previous Address   Years/Months There
(if less than 2 years at present address)

_____

Mother's Maiden Name

Citizens Bank Account Information

❑ Checking   ❑ Savings   ❑ Loan   ❑ Citizens Circle℠ Checking

account # _____

Please tell us about your employment

_____   _____

Present Employer   Position

_____   (____) _____

Years/Months Employed There   Business Telephone

_____   _____

Previous Employer   Years/Months There
(if less than 2 years at present employer)

$ _____ $ _____

Gross Monthly Household Income   Other Monthly Income*

*Alimony, child support, or separate maintenance income need not be revealed if you do not wish it to be considered as a basis for repaying this obligation.

24-hour banking convenience

Your card(s) can be encoded with a four-digit personal identification number (PIN) to obtain cash advances at automated teller machines. This four-digit PIN will be known only to you. So that we may properly encode your card(s), please select the four digits of your choice and enter them in the spaces below:

_____   _____   _____   _____

Please send a second card at no cost for

_____

First Name   Middle Initial   Last Name

Please read and sign

_____   _____

Your Signature   Date

All information on this application is true and complete, and Citizens Bank of Rhode Island, the card issuer, is authorized to obtain further credit and employment information from any source. I understand that you will retain this application whether or not it is approved. You may share with others, only for valid business reasons, any information relating to me, this application, and any of my banking relationships with you. I request issuance of a Citizens credit card and agree to be bound by the terms and conditions of the Agreement received with the card(s). I understand that Citizens Bank of Rhode Island will assign a credit line based on information provided and information obtained from any other source; and the issuance of a Gold card is subject to a minimum annual income of $35,000 and qualification for a minimum $5,000 credit line.

Transfer balances and save

Citizens will transfer your high interest rate balances to your new Citizens Bank VISA Card at no extra charge. Use the form below to indicate the amount(s) to be transferred in order of priority. (Citizens Bank will not transfer balances from existing Citizens Bank accounts.) (see reverse side for balance transfer disclosure)

Creditor Name	Account Number	Amount
		$
		$
		$

Bank Use Only   Bank Code: ❑ CBMA ❑ CBRI ❑ CBCT   Sales ID# _____   Application code: 1122

Source: Courtesy of Citizens Financial Group, Inc., Providence, Rhode Island.

Various credit bureaus provide credit information concerning individuals. The following are the three major consumer credit bureaus:

- Experian—at www.experian.com or toll-free at 888-397-3742
- TransUnion—at www.transunion.com or toll-free at 800-888-4213
- Equifax Credit Information Services—at www.equifax.com or toll-free at 800-685-1111

Protection for Consumers

Consumer credit bureaus are subject to the provisions of the Fair Credit Reporting Act. This act safeguards consumers' rights in two ways. First, you have the right to know what information is contained in your credit bureau file. Second, if you feel that some information in the file is inaccurate, misleading, or vague you have the right to request that the credit bureau verify it. If the disputed information is found to be correct, you can provide a brief explanation, giving your side of the dispute. If the disputed information is found to be inaccurate, it must be deleted or corrected. Furthermore, you may request that any lender or prospective employer that has been supplied an inaccurate credit report in the last six months be sent a corrected credit report.

The Fair and Accurate Credit Transactions Act requires each of the nationwide credit reporting companies—Equifax, Experian, and TransUnion—to provide you with a free copy of your credit report, at your request, once every 12 months. To obtain your free credit report, go to www.annualcreditreport.com. (*Note*: Beware of other sites that may look and sound similar to this site but may charge for information or require that you spend money on credit monitoring.[14])

The Credit Card Act of 2009, which was enacted on February 22, 2010, also provides additional protection for credit card customers. This new federal law is designed to level the playing field between credit card customers and financial institutions that issue credit cards. This act encourages disclosures written in plain language that include more information about due dates, late fees, and the amount of time required to pay off card balances if only minimum monthly payments are made.[15] If you want more information about provisions in the Credit Card Act of 2009, contact the financial institution that issued your credit card, the Federal Reserve Board (www.federalreserve.gov), or conduct a Web search.

In the next chapter, you will see why firms need financing, how they obtain the money they need, and how they ensure that funds are used efficiently, in keeping with their organizational objectives.

return to Inside BUSINESS

Umpqua Bank

How many bank CEOs invite customers to call them with questions, compliments, or complaints? Every Umpqua Bank store (its preferred term for branches) has a direct phone line to the CEO's office, part of the bank's personalized, community-oriented customer service. At a time when so many companies are moving away from face-to-face service, Umpqua Bank is encouraging people to drop in and chat, even when they don't have any transactions to conduct. The bank also connects with customers via Facebook and Twitter, as well as through its own Web site.

Employees go to the World's Greatest Bank University (its in-house training facility) for classes on customer-service techniques and product knowledge. They are also paid for up to 40 hours of volunteer work each year because of the bank's commitment to community involvement. No wonder Umpqua has been named six times to *Fortune*'s list of "100 Best Companies to Work For."

Questions

1. Why would Umpqua go out of its way to make each branch a community hub?
2. Would you like to work for a commercial bank like Umpqua, which serves consumers, small businesses, and corporations? Explain your answer.

Identify the functions and characteristics of money.

Money is anything a society uses to purchase products, services, or resources. Money must serve as a medium of exchange, a measure of value, and a store of value. To perform its functions effectively, money must be divisible into units of convenient size, light and sturdy enough to be carried and used on a daily basis, stable in value, and difficult to counterfeit. The M_1 supply of money is made up of coins and bills (currency) and deposits in checking accounts (demand deposits). The M_2 supply includes M_1 plus savings accounts, certain money-market securities, and certificates of deposits.

 Summarize how the Federal Reserve System regulates the money supply to maintain a healthy economy.

The Federal Reserve System is responsible for regulating the U.S. banking industry and maintaining a sound economic environment. Banks with federal charters (national banks) must be members of the Fed. State banks may join if they can meet the requirements for membership. Twelve district banks and 24 branch banks compose the Federal Reserve System, whose seven-member board of governors is headquartered in Washington, D.C. During the recent economic crisis, it was necessary for the Federal Reserve to take actions in order to reduce the effects of the recent economic crisis. Specifically, the Fed provided liquidity to the banking and financial industry, supported troubled financial markets, supported troubled financial institutions, and conducted stress tests of major banks.

To control the supply of money, the Federal Reserve System regulates the reserve requirement, or the percentage of deposits a bank must keep on hand. It also regulates the discount rate, or the interest rate the Fed charges member banks for loans from the Federal Reserve. It also engages in open-market operations, in which it buys and sells government securities. When the Federal Reserve buys and sells securities, the goal is to increase or decrease the federal funds rate. The federal funds rate is the interest rate at which a bank lends immediately available funds on deposit at the Fed to another bank overnight in order to meet the borrowing bank's reserve requirements. The Fed serves as the government's bank and is also responsible for clearing checks and electronic transfers, inspecting currency, enforcing the Truth-in-Lending Act, and setting margin requirements for securities transactions.

 Describe the organizations involved in the banking industry.

Most everyone has been affected in one way or another by the nation's economic problems. To help resolve the major problems that led to the economic crisis, Congress passed and the president signed the Dodd–Frank Wall Street Reform and Consumer Protection Act that provides new protection for consumers and increased regulation of the financial industry.

A commercial bank is a profit-making organization that accepts deposits, makes loans, and provides related services to customers. Commercial banks are chartered by the federal government or state governments. Savings and loan associations and credit unions offer the same basic services that commercial banks provide. Mutual savings banks, insurance companies, pension funds, brokerage firms, finance companies, and investment banking firms provide some limited banking services. A large number of people work in the banking industry because of the number of banks and other financial institutions.

 Identify the services provided by financial institutions.

Banks and other financial institutions offer today's customers a tempting array of services. Among the most important banking services for both individuals and businesses are checking accounts, savings accounts, short- and long-term loans, and processing credit card and debit card transactions. Other traditional services include financial advice, payroll services, certified checks, trust services, and safe-deposit boxes.

 Understand how financial institutions are changing to meet the needs of domestic and international customers.

Competition among banks, brokerage firms, insurance companies, and other financial institutions has increased. The use of technology will also increase as financial institutions continue to offer online and mobile banking. Increased use of electronic funds transfer systems (automated teller machines, automated clearinghouses, point-of-sale terminals, and electronic check conversion) also will change the way people bank. For firms in the global marketplace, a bank can provide letters of credit and banker's acceptances that will reduce the risk of nonpayment for sellers. Banks and financial institutions also can provide currency exchange to reduce payment problems for import or export transactions.

 Explain how deposit insurance protects customers.

The Federal Deposit Insurance Corporation (FDIC) and the National Credit Union Association (NCUA) insure accounts in member financial institutions for up $250,000. Deposits maintained in different categories of legal ownership are insured separately. The most common ownership categories are single ownership and joint ownership. It is also possible to obtain additional coverage by opening separate accounts in different banks, S&Ls, or credit unions. When either the FDIC or NCUA insures a financial institution's deposits, they reserve the right to examine that institution's operations periodically. If a bank, S&L, or credit union is found to be poorly managed, it is reported to the proper banking authority.

 Discuss the importance of credit and credit management.

Credit is immediate purchasing power that is exchanged for a promise to repay borrowed money, with or without interest, at a later date. Banks lend money because they are in business for that purpose. Businesses sell goods and services on credit because some customers cannot afford to pay cash and because they must keep pace with competitors who offer credit. Businesses also may realize a profit from interest charges.

Decisions on whether to grant credit to businesses and individuals usually are based on the five C's of credit: character, capacity, capital, collateral, and conditions. Credit information can be obtained from various credit-reporting agencies, credit bureaus, industry associations, and other firms. A number of federal regulations even the playing field between consumers and credit card companies and lenders.

KEY TERMS

You should now be able to define and give an example relevant to each of the following terms:

barter system (522)
money (522)
medium of exchange (522)
measure of value (522)
store of value (522)
demand deposit (524)
time deposit (524)
Federal Reserve System (525)
commercial paper (526)

reserve requirement (527)
discount rate (528)
open-market operations (528)
federal funds rate (528)
commercial bank (531)
national bank (531)
state bank (531)
savings and loan association (S&L) (532)

credit union (532)
check (533)
NOW account (534)
certificate of deposit (CD) (534)
line of credit (535)
revolving credit agreement (535)
collateral (535)

debit card (536)
electronic funds transfer (EFT) system (537)
letter of credit (538)
banker's acceptance (539)
credit (540)

REVIEW QUESTIONS

1. How does the use of money solve the problems associated with a barter system of exchange?
2. What are three functions money must perform in a sound monetary system?
3. Explain why money must have each of the following characteristics:
   a. Divisibility
   b. Portability
   c. Stability
   d. Durability
   e. Difficulty of counterfeiting
4. What is included in the definition of the M_1 supply of money? Of the M_2 supply?
5. What is the Federal Reserve System? How is it organized?
6. Describe the actions the Federal Reserve took to maintain a healthy economy during the recent economic crisis. In your opinion, were the actions necessary? Were the Fed's actions effective?
7. Explain how the Federal Reserve System uses each of the following to control the money supply:
   a. Reserve requirements
   b. The discount rate
   c. Open-market operations

8. The Federal Reserve and the Consumer Financial Protection Bureau are responsible for enforcing the Truth-in-Lending Act. How does this act affect you?
9. What is the difference between a national bank and a state bank? What other financial institutions compete with national and state banks?
10. Describe the major banking services provided by financial institutions today.
11. For consumers, what are the major advantages of online banking?
12. How do automated teller machines, automated clearinghouses, point-of-sale terminals, and electronic check conversion affect how you bank?
13. How can a bank or other financial institution help American businesses to compete in the global marketplace?
14. What is the basic function of the FDIC and NCUA? How do they perform this function?
15. How would you check the information provided by an applicant for credit at a department store? By a business applicant at a heavy-equipment manufacturer's sales office?

DISCUSSION QUESTIONS

1. Based on what you know at the time you are answering this question, how would you describe the financial health of the U.S. economy? Of the global economy?
2. It is said that financial institutions use a process called deposit expansion to "create" money when they make loans to firms and individuals. Explain what this means.
3. Why does the Fed use indirect means of controlling the money supply instead of simply printing more money or removing money from circulation when necessary?
4. Why would banks pay higher interest on money left on deposit for longer periods of time (e.g., on CDs)?
5. How could an individual get in financial trouble by using a credit card? If you were in trouble because of credit card debt, what steps could you take to reduce your debts?
6. Assume that you want to borrow $10,000. What can you do to convince the loan officer that you are a good credit risk?

Video Case 18.1 — Chase Bank Helps Small Business Owners

JPMorgan Chase & Co. is a global financial holding company formed in 2000 by a merger of the financial institutions that today are its two major brands: Chase (formerly Chase Manhattan Corp.) and J.P. Morgan (formerly J.P. Morgan & Co.). In 2004, the company also acquired Bank One Corp.; later, in 2008, it added both Bear Stearns Companies, Inc., and Washington Mutual, in the process creating the second-largest branch network in the United States and bringing its banking services within the reach of 42 percent of the U.S. population. The bank, which operates in more than 60 countries and employs almost 240,000 people worldwide, holds assets estimated to be worth about $2 trillion and is included in the widely watched stock index, the Dow Jones Industrial Average (DJIA). Despite an economic downturn, the bank still posted profits for the last four years in a row. And now that the nation's economy is improving, the bank is poised for more growth and increased profits.

Most people are probably more familiar with the functions performed on the Chase side of the operation. These operations include conducting everyday banking via branch offices, ATMs, telephone, and online; issuing consumer credit cards; serving small businesses with financing and banking services; offering home mortgages and home equity loans; helping customers with personal retirement and investment planning; and making auto and educational loans.

In its small-business banking operations, Chase exemplifies the words of J.P. Morgan, who told a Senate subcommittee in 1933 that "Another very important use of the banker is to serve as a channel whereby industry may be provided with capital to meet its needs for expansion and development." Providing capital to small businesses is one of the most important functions the bank fulfills for these business clients. Whether small companies need short-term loans to expand their operations or to bridge the time gap between manufacturing a product and collecting money for the sale, a line of credit to ease their cash flow during a tough period, or a commercial mortgage loan to buy a new factory or warehouse, Chase is ready to lend the necessary funds. The bank also offers several kinds of business credit cards, which small-business owners can use for everyday needs when cash is tight. These cards offer different incentives such as no annual fee, cash back for purchases, bonus points, or no interest on balances paid in full each month. Business debit cards are another option, backed by fraud monitoring and account alerts.

Chase is also there to help firms hang on to their money—not only by providing all those branch offices for making deposits but also by handling the safe collection of payments through its lock-box service (through which consumers send bill payments to a post-office box for collection). Chase makes it easier for its small-business customers to deposit checks, too. Now firms can scan paper checks right in their own offices, transforming them into electronic payments so that they can take advantage of online banking's convenience, safety, and speed. Business checking accounts are available as well, with a wide range of specially tailored features and overdraft protection. Business savings accounts and CDs are offered, and business customers can link their accounts to Chase Business Packages to earn additional benefits, such as waived fees and reduced interest rates on borrowing. The bank even offers payroll processing.

Retail firms that accept credit cards like Visa, American Express, MasterCard, and Discover can rely on Chase for payment processing, and they can use the processed funds the very next day. Free technical support is available 24/7, and monthly statements and online reports help firms manage their credit card operations. Business owners can even pay bills, transfer funds, view account balances and transaction history, and send wire transfers by texting the bank from their mobile phones. Additionally, Chase makes it possible for small businesses to conduct transactions globally, whether that means buying goods abroad or accepting orders from international customers.[16]

Questions

1. If you were a small-business owner, would you take advantage of any of Chase's or another bank's small-business banking services? Why or why not?
2. Can you think of any additional financial or banking services that banks could offer to small-business owners?
3. Chase prides itself on its ability to know many of its business customers personally and to keep up-to-date on the industries in which they operate. Why would this familiarity be an advantage for the bank?

Established 62 years before Hawaii became a state, Bank of Hawaii is now one of the top-ranked independent banks in America, known as much for its community involvement as for its financial strength. With 81 branches spread across six Hawaiian islands, American Samoa, Saipan, Guam, and Palau, Bank of Hawaii provides a full range of financial services for corporations, small businesses, and individuals. From traditional checking and savings accounts to loans, mobile banking, online bill payment, and even international trade finance, Bank of Hawaii offers all the services its customers need to achieve their financial goals.

The Honolulu-based bank briefly experimented with an expansion on the mainland before refocusing on its home state, where its heritage and market share are competitive advantages. "The industry recognizes that Hawaii is a challenging place to do business," says CEO Peter Ho. "It's the most ethnically diverse state in the country in many ways." With this diversity in mind, Bank of Hawaii offers customers the choice of communicating in Japanese, Korean, French, Tagalog, Vietnamese, or any of three Chinese dialects. Also, the bank has arranged for the growing number of Chinese tourists who visit Hawaii to use their China UnionPay debit cards at any of Bank of Hawaii's ATMs.

Two-thirds of Hawaiian households use at least one of the bank's services, and it enjoys high customer loyalty within the business community, as well. Bank of Hawaii gave the founder of Yummy's Restaurant Group his first business loan more than 25 years ago. Today, the chain has grown to more than 40 restaurants, and both the company and its founder remain loyal customers. Maui Soda and Ice Works, a family-owned firm that makes ice cream sold throughout the Hawaiian islands, appreciates the bank's professionalism and its expertise in matters such as local economic forecasting. The bank was recently named Small Business Association lender of the year in Hawaii, reflecting its strength in providing financial services for entrepreneurs and growing businesses.

To help customers learn to better manage their money, Bank of Hawaii offers monthly seminars on topics such as buying a home, saving for retirement, developing a business plan, and making investment decisions. More than 2,000 of the bank's employees participate in community projects such as Junior Achievement, the Hawaii Book and Music Festival, and environmental cleanup programs. The annual "employee giving" campaign raises $500,000 every year to benefit local nonprofit groups, and the bank donates tens of thousands of dollars for scholarships and other community needs.

Bank of Hawaii remained profitable even during the recent recession, thanks in large part to its sound lending practices and its ability to adapt to changing economic and technological conditions. As customers began using iPhones and other digital devices, the bank expanded its mobile and online banking services to provide instant, on-the-go access to financial information. Bank representatives tweet and also post on the bank's Facebook page to stay in touch with customers who like to use social media. For added convenience, the bank is opening new branches inside popular stores, allowing customers to bank where they shop. Finally, bank officials have created a "business dashboard" to track performance on key measures of customer service and identify any areas for improvement.[17]

Questions

1. Do you agree with Bank of Hawaii's decision to open branches in stores while it continues to invest in new technology for electronic and mobile banking? Explain your answer.

2. How might Bank of Hawaii adjust its credit policies if the area experiences a sudden or dramatic economic downturn? Suggest at least two adjustments the bank should make when applying the five C's of credit in such a situation.

3. In addition to the many languages spoken throughout the islands, what other challenges do you think banks face in serving the financial needs of individuals and businesses in Hawaii? What are the implications for Bank of Hawaii?

Building Skills for Career Success

① SOCIAL MEDIA EXERCISE

As more and more people have smartphones, it is becoming quite clear that products like Google Wallet will soon become popular electronic money-management tools, especially for Millennials—people born after 1980. Google Wallet is a new way to use your smartphone to pay for things both in store and online. Google says you can "Save time and money by shopping with Google Wallet—a smart, virtual wallet that stores your payment cards, offers, and more on your phone and online." Take a look at Google Wallet to see how it works. www.google.com/wallet.

1. For the consumer, what are the advantages and disadvantages of Google Wallet (and similar services)?

2. For merchants, what are the advantages and disadvantages of Google Wallet (and similar services)?

3. Would you use Google Wallet? Why or why not?

② JOURNALING FOR SUCCESS

You could be one of the 11 million Americans who fall victim to the crime of identity theft every year. Crooks who steal your name, birth date, credit card numbers, bank account numbers, and Social Security number can withdraw money from your bank accounts, charge merchandise in your name, or contract for cell-phone service.

Assignment

1. Use the Internet to obtain information about how to prevent identity theft. Then, according to the professionals, describe the steps someone should take to protect his or her identity.
2. Complete a "security audit" of your personal information and financial records. Based on your audit and the recommendations from professionals, what should you do now to protect your identity?
3. It always helps to have a plan in case your identity is stolen. Based on the information you obtained from your Internet research, what immediate steps should you take if your identity is stolen?

③ DEVELOPING CRITICAL-THINKING SKILLS

Assumption: There are banks, savings and loan associations, credit unions, and other financial institutions that want your business. Therefore, it pays to shop around for the lowest interest rates for loans needed to purchase a home mortgage or an automobile. It's also easy to compare interest rates when investing in certificates of deposit (CDs) or savings accounts. A logical place to start is with the financial institution where you do your banking. You can also compare interest rates at other local banks and financial institutions located close to where you live or work. Finally, you can use the Internet and Web sites like www.bankrate.com or www.interest.com to determine interest rates for loans and CD investments.

Assignment

To answer each of the following questions, contact at least three different financial institutions in your city or town or three different Internet Web sites. *Hint*: If you use the Internet, use a search engine like Google or Yahoo! and enter "interest rates" in the search window.

1. What is the lowest rate you found for a 30-year $150,000 home mortgage?
2. Based on your research, what is the difference between the lowest interest rate and the highest interest rate for a home mortgage? Assuming you pay back the loan in 30 years, how could the difference in interest rates affect the total amount you will pay for your home?
3. What is the highest interest rate you found for a one-year certificate of deposit?
4. Based on your research, what is the difference between the highest rate and the lowest rate for a one-year CD? How could this affect the amount of money you would earn for the 12-month period?

5. In a one- to two-page report, summarize what you have learned from this critical-thinking exercise.

④ BUILDING TEAM SKILLS

Three years ago, Ron and Ginger were happy to learn that, upon graduation, Ron would be teaching history in a large high school, making $35,000 a year, and Ginger would be working in a public accounting firm, starting at $38,000. They married immediately after graduation and bought a new home for $110,000. Since Ron had no personal savings, Ginger used her savings for the down payment. They soon began furnishing their home, charging their purchases to three separate credit cards, and that is when their debt began to mount. When the three credit cards reached their $10,000 limits, Ron and Ginger signed up for one additional credit card with a $10,000 limit. Soon all their monthly payments were more than their combined take-home pay. To make their monthly payments, Ron and Ginger began to obtain cash advances on their credit cards. When they reached the credit ceilings on their four credit cards, they could no longer get the cash advances they needed to cover their monthly bills. Stress began to mount as creditors called and demanded payment. Ron and Ginger began to argue over money and just about everything else. Finally, things got so bad they considered filing for personal bankruptcy; ironically, they could not afford the legal fees. What options are available to this couple?

Assignment

1. Working in teams of three or four, use your local library, the Internet, and personal interviews to investigate the following:
   a. Filing for personal bankruptcy.
      - What is involved in filing for personal bankruptcy?
      - How much does it cost?
      - How does bankruptcy affect individuals?
   b. Review the Money Management International Web site at www.cccsintl.org.
      - What services does this organization provide?
      - How might this organization help Ron and Ginger?
      - What will it cost?
2. Prepare a specific plan for repaying Ron and Ginger's debt.
3. Outline the advantages and disadvantages of credit cards, and make the appropriate recommendations for Ron and Ginger concerning their future use of credit cards.
4. Summarize what you have learned about credit card misuse.

⑤ RESEARCHING DIFFERENT CAREERS

It has long been known that maintaining a good credit record is essential to obtaining loans from financial institutions, but did you know that employers often check credit records before offering an applicant a position? This is especially true of firms that handle financial accounts for others. Information contained in your credit report can tell an employer a lot about how responsible you are with money and how well you manage it. Individuals have the right to know what is in their credit bureau files and to have the credit bureau verify any inaccurate, misleading, or vague information. Before you apply for a job or a loan, you should check with a credit bureau to learn what is in your file.

Assignment
1. Using information in this chapter, use the Internet or call a credit bureau and ask for a copy of your credit report. A small fee may be required depending on the bureau and circumstances.
2. Review the information.

3. Have the bureau verify any information that you feel is inaccurate, misleading, or vague.
4. If the verification shows that the information is correct, prepare a brief statement explaining your side of the dispute, and send it to the bureau.
5. Prepare a statement summarizing what the credit report says about you. Based on your credit report, would a firm hire you as its financial manager?

ENDNOTES

1. Sources: Based on information in Charles Passy, "Banks Branch into Yoga," *Smart Money*, March 13, 2012, www.smartmoney.com; "100 Best Companies to Work For: No. 69, Umpqua Bank," *Fortune*, February 6, 2012, www.fortune.com; Michael Sisk, "Umpqua Keeps Testing New Ideas," *Bank Technology News*, July 1, 2011, p. 18; www.umpquabank.com.
2. "The Economy: Crisis & Response," The Federal Reserve Board of San Francisco Web site at www.frsb.org, accessed April 1, 2012.
3. The Federal Reserve Board Web site at www.federalreserve.gov, accessed March 30, 2012.
4. Ibid.
5. Ibid.
6. The Investopedia.com Web site at www.investopedia.com, accessed March 30, 2012.
7. The Federal Reserve Board at www.federalreserve.gov, accessed March 30, 2012.
8. "Wall Street Reform," the White House Web site at www.whitehouse.gov, accessed June 20, 2010.
9. The Office of the Comptroller of the Currency Web site at www.occ.gov, accessed March 31, 2012.
10. "The Quarterly Banking Profile for December 31, 2011," The Federal Deposit Insurance Corporation Web site at www.fdic.gov, accessed March 31, 2012.
11. U.S. Census Bureau, *Statistical Abstract of the United States, 2012* (Washington, DC: U.S. Government Printing Office), table 1183.
12. "The Occupational Outlook Handbook," the Bureau of Labor Statistics Web site at www.bls.gov, accessed March 31, 2012.
13. U.S. Census Bureau, *Statistical Abstract of the United States, 2012* (Washington, DC: U.S. Government Printing Office), table 1188.
14. The Federal Trade Commission Web site at www.ftc.gov, accessed March 27, 2012.
15. The United States Senate Committee on Banking, Housing, and Urban Affairs Web site at banking.senate.gov, accessed June 15, 2010.
16. Company Web sites www.chase.com and www.jpmorganchase.com, accessed March 31, 2012; "JPMorgan Chase Discloses Results," *American Banking and Market News*, July 15, 2010, www.americanbankingnews.com; Eric Dash, "JPMorgan Chase Easily Exceeds Estimates," *New York Times*, July 15, 2010, www.nytimes.com; and the video, "Chase Bank Helps Small Business Owners."
17. Based on information in Jackie Stewart, "Bank of Hawaii to Shift Some Branches to Grocery Stores," American Banker, February 7, 2012, www.americanbanker.com; Wang Kaihao, "Ready to Say 'Aloha,'" *China Daily*, June 6, 2011, www.chinadaily.com; Kurt Badenhausen, "America's Best and Worst Banks," *Forbes*, December 13, 2011, www.forbes.com; Rachel Witkowski, "Two Hawaiian Banks Find There's No Place Like Home," *American Banker*, May 18, 2011, p. 3; www.boh.com; *Bank of Hawaii Annual Report 2011*.

19 Mastering Financial Management

LEARNING OBJECTIVES

Once you complete this chapter, you will be able to:

1 Understand why financial management is important in today's uncertain economy.

2 Identify a firm's short- and long-term financial needs.

3 Summarize the process of planning for financial management.

4 Describe the advantages and disadvantages of different methods of short-term debt financing.

5 Evaluate the advantages and disadvantages of equity financing.

6 Evaluate the advantages and disadvantages of long-term debt financing.

Inside BUSINESS

How J. M. Smucker Manages Its Money

With a name like Smucker, financial management has to be good. The company is named for its founder, Jerome Monroe Smucker, who began selling apple cider and apple butter in 1897. Today, the Smucker family continues to be involved in running the Orrville, Ohio, firm, which employs 4,500 people and rings up $4.8 billion in food sales every year. Its well-known consumer brands include Smucker's (jams and jellies), Jif (peanut butter), Martha White (baking mixes), and many more that provide tasty food products to customers in both the United States and the global marketplace.

With an eye toward financing faster growth, the J. M. Smucker Co. first sold shares of its common stock to the public in 1959. In recent years, it has made a number of major acquisitions to diversify its product mix and expand its geographical reach. It bought Jif and Crisco from Procter & Gamble in 2002 and then acquired International Multifoods Corporation in 2004. In 2008, Smucker purchased Folgers, the largest U.S. coffee company, from parent Procter & Gamble. In 2011, it purchased Florida-based Rowland Coffee Roasters and folded its $110 million in annual revenues into the corporation's finances. In 2012, the company completed its acquisition of Sara Lee's Douwe Egberts liquid coffee concentrate brand for wholesaling to restaurants and institutions.

Multimillion-dollar acquisitions such as these require excellent financial management. For example, when Smucker bought Douwe Egberts from Sara Lee, it paid $350 million in cash when the deal closed and promised an additional $50 million in payments over the next ten years. The company had funds on hand for this and other acquisitions because it had arranged to borrow money by selling $400 million in bonds during 2010 and another $750 million in bonds during 2011. Although Smucker knew it would have to repay the money to bondholders in the future, it was able to take advantage of promising acquisition opportunities in the short term.

Some of the money is also being spent on investments that will take the company far beyond its Ohio roots. For instance, Smucker paid $35 million to buy a stake in Guilin Seamild Biologic Technology Development Company, a Chinese manufacturer of oatmeal products. "Seamild's portfolio of quality, trusted products aligns with Smucker's strategy of owning and marketing leading food brands," says a Smucker official.[1]

Unfortunately, the J. M. Smucker Co. mentioned in this chapter's opening Inside Business case was the exception when compared to many cash-strapped businesses that struggled to find the funds they needed to operate during the recent economic crisis. In fact, the crisis was a wake-up call for most corporate executives, managers, and business owners because one factor became obvious. The ability to borrow money (debt capital) or obtain money from the owners of a business (equity capital) is necessary for the efficient operation of a business firm *and* our economic system.

In this chapter we examine why financial management is important in an uncertain economy. Then, we discuss how firms find the financing required to meet two needs of all business organizations: the need for money to start a business and keep it going, and the need to manage that money effectively. We also look at how firms develop financial plans and evaluate financial performance. Then we compare various methods of obtaining short-term and long-term financing.

Understand why financial management is important in today's uncertain economy.

①

WHY FINANCIAL MANAGEMENT?

Question: How important is financial management for a business firm?

To answer that question, consider the recent financial problems of the "Big Three" U.S. automakers. Both General Motors and Chrysler filed for bankruptcy protection during the recent economic crisis, but Ford had the financial fuel to keep going, despite sagging sales and worldwide economic turmoil. Executives at Ford used aggressive financial planning to anticipate the automaker's need for financing. To avoid the same fate as General Motors and Chrysler—bankruptcy—Ford's financial managers borrowed money in anticipation of a downturn in the company's sales and profits. Ford also sold both stocks and bonds to raise the money it needed to keep the company operating during the crisis and even build for the future. Did that financial plan work? The answer: A definite yes! Today, Ford is selling more cars, developing environmentally friendly engines, creating concept cars for the future, and has returned to profitability. Although there are many factors that account for Ford's success, most experts agree that the firm's financial planning enabled it to weather the economic storm and build for the future.

Although most managers and employees have been affected by the economic crisis, the years since the end of 2007 have been especially difficult for financial managers. After all, they are the ones that must be able to raise the money needed to pay bills and expenses to keep a company's doors open. During the recent economic crisis, many financial managers and business owners found it was increasingly difficult to use many of the traditional sources of short- and long-term financing described later in this chapter. In some cases, banks stopped making loans even to companies that had always been able to borrow money. For example, both GE and AT&T—two premier names in corporate America—could not get the financing they needed.[2] Furthermore, the number of corporations selling stock for the first time to the general public decreased because investors were afraid to invest in new companies. The worst-case scenario: There was an increase in the number of businesses that filed for bankruptcy during the crisis, as illustrated in Figure 19.1. Fortunately, there were many more business firms that were able to weather the economic storm and keep operating because of their ability to manage their finances. And now that the nation's economy is improving, the number of bankruptcies is beginning to decline.

financial management all the activities concerned with obtaining money and using it effectively

How do managers decide how much inventory is needed? One of the most perplexing problems financial managers must deal with is the amount of inventory a retail store needs. If a retailer has too much inventory, then too much money is tied up in merchandise that is not selling. If a retailer has too little inventory, it may not have enough merchandise to meet consumer demand.

The Need for Financial Management

Financial management consists of all the activities concerned with obtaining money and using it effectively. To some extent, financial management can be viewed as a two-sided problem. On one side, the uses of funds often dictate the type or types of financing needed by a business. On the other side, the activities a business can undertake are determined by the types of financing available. Financial managers must ensure that funds are available when needed, that they are obtained at the lowest possible cost, and that they are used as efficiently as possible. In addition, proper financial management must also ensure that:

- Financing priorities are established in line with organizational goals and objectives.
- Spending is planned and controlled.
- Sufficient financing is available when it is needed, both now and in the future.
- A firm's credit customers pay their bills on time, and the number of past due accounts is reduced.
- Bills are paid promptly to protect the firm's credit rating and its ability to borrow money.

© CHRIS HOWES/WILDPLACESPHOTOGRAPHY/ALAMY

FIGURE 19.1   Business Bankruptcies in the United States

The number of businesses that filed for bankruptcy increased during the economic crisis. (*Note*: At the time of publication, 2011 was the most recent year for which complete statistics were available.)

2007   28,322
2008   43,546
2009   60,837
2010   56,282
2011   47,806

Source: Based on The American Bankruptcy Institute Web site at www.abiworld. org (accessed February 24, 2012).

- The funds required for paying the firm's taxes are available when needed to meet tax deadlines.
- Excess cash is invested in certificates of deposit (CDs), government securities, or conservative, marketable securities.

Financial Reform After the Economic Crisis

The job of financial managers became a bit easier as the economy stabilized. Still, it became apparent that something needed to be done to stabilize the financial system and prevent future economic meltdowns. In the wake of the crisis that affected both business firms and individuals, a cry for more regulations and reforms became a high priority. To meet this need, President Obama signed the Dodd–Frank Wall Street Reform and Consumer Protection Act into law on July 21, 2010. Even with the new regulations, some experts say the law did not go far enough while others argue it went too far. Although the U.S. Senate and House of Representatives debate additional regulations, the goals are to hold Wall Street firms accountable for their actions, end taxpayer bailouts, tighten regulations for major financial firms, and increase government oversight. There has also been debate about limiting the amount of executive pay and bonuses, limiting the size of the largest financial firms, and curbing speculative investment techniques that were used by banks before the crisis.

As mentioned in Chapter 18, new regulations will protect American families from unfair, abusive financial and banking practices. For business firms, the impact of new regulations could increase the time and cost of obtaining both short- and long-term financing.

Careers in Finance

After reading the material in the last section, you might be thinking why anyone would want a job in finance. And yet, a career in finance can be rewarding. As an added bonus, the Bureau of Labor Statistics projects there will be an 8 percent increase in the number of jobs in the financial sector of the economy between now and 2018.[3]

Today, there are many different types of positions in finance. At the executive level, most large business firms have a chief financial officer for financial management. A **chief financial officer (CFO)** is a high-level corporate executive who manages a firm's finances and reports directly to the company's chief executive officer or president. Some firms prefer to use the titles vice president of financial management, treasurer, or controller instead of the CFO title for executive-level positions in the finance area.

Although some executives in finance do make $300,000 a year or more, many entry-level and lower-level positions that pay quite a bit less are available. Banks,

chief financial officer (CFO) a high-level corporate executive who manages a firm's finances and reports directly to the company's chief executive officer or president

Did actions by politicians and government officials ease the economic crisis? While people still debate if the government's actions to reduce the effects of the economic crisis were justified, both politicians and government officials did take steps to stabilize the economy. In this photo, Senate majority leader Harry Reid tells reporters—and the nation—about the government's plan to improve the nation's economy.

insurance companies, and investment firms obviously have a need for workers who can manage and analyze financial data. So do businesses involved in manufacturing, services, and marketing. Colleges and universities, not-for-profit organizations, and government entities at all levels also need finance workers.

People in finance must have certain traits and skills. One of the most important priorities for someone interested in a finance career is honesty. Be warned: Investors, lenders, and other corporate executives expect financial managers to be above reproach. Moreover, both federal and state government entities have enacted legislation to ensure that corporate financial statements reflect the "real" status of a firm's financial position. In addition to honesty, managers and employees in the finance area must:

1. Have a strong background in accounting or mathematics.
2. Know how to use a computer to analyze data.
3. Be an expert at both written and oral communication.

Typical job titles in finance include bank officer, consumer credit officer, financial analyst, financial planner, loan officer, insurance analyst, and investment account executive. Depending on qualifications, work experience, and education, starting salaries generally begin at $25,000 to $35,000 a year, but it is not uncommon for college graduates to earn higher salaries. In addition to salary, many employees have attractive benefits and other perks that make a career in financial management attractive.

THE NEED FOR FINANCING

Identify a firm's short- and long-term financial needs.

Money is needed both to start a business and to keep it going. The original investment of the owners, along with money they may have borrowed, should be enough to open the doors. After that, ideally sales revenues should be used to pay the firm's expenses and provide a profit as well.

This is exactly what happens in a successful firm—over the long run. However, income and expenses may vary from month to month or from year to year. Temporary financing may be needed when expenses are high or sales are low. Then, too, situations such as the opportunity to purchase a new facility or expand an existing plant may require more money than is currently available within a firm.

Short-Term Financing

Short-term financing is money that will be used for one year or less. As illustrated in Table 19.1, there are many short-term financing needs, but three deserve special

TABLE 19.1	Comparison of Short- and Long-Term Financing
Whether a business seeks short- or long-term financing depends on what the money will be used for.	
Corporate Cash Needs	
Short-Term Financing Needs	**Long-Term Financing Needs**
Cash-flow problems	Business start-up costs
Speculative production	Mergers and acquisitions
Current inventory needs	New product development
Monthly expenses	Long-term marketing activities
Short-term promotional needs	Replacement of equipment
Unexpected emergencies	Expansion of facilities

© Cengage Learning 2014

short-term financing money that will be used for one year or less attention. First, certain business practices may affect a firm's cash flow and create a need for short-term financing. **Cash flow** is the movement of money into and out of an organization. The goal is to have sufficient money coming into the firm in any period to cover the firm's expenses during that period. This goal, however, is not always achieved. For example, California-based Callaway Golf offers credit to retailers and wholesalers that carry the firm's golf clubs, balls, clothing, and golf accessories. Credit purchases made by Callaway's retailers generally are not paid until 30 to 60 days (or more) after the transaction. Callaway therefore may need short-term financing to pay its bills until its customers have paid theirs.

A second major need for short-term financing is speculative production. **Speculative production** refers to the time lag between the actual production of goods and when the goods are sold. Consider what happens when a firm such as Connecticut-based Stanley Black & Decker begins to manufacture electric tools and small appliances for sale during the Christmas season. Manufacturing begins in February, March, and April, and the firm negotiates short-term financing to buy materials and supplies, to pay wages and rent, and to cover inventory costs until its products eventually are sold to wholesalers and retailers later in the year. Take a look at Figure 19.2. Although Stanley Black & Decker manufactures and sells finished products all during the year, expenses peak during the first part of the year. During this same period, sales revenues are low. Once the firm's finished products are shipped to retailers and wholesalers and payment is received (usually within 30 to 60 days), sales revenues are used to repay short-term financing.

A third need for short-term financing is to increase inventory. Retailers that range in size from Walmart to the neighborhood drugstore need short-term financing to build up their inventories before peak selling periods. For example, Dallas-based Bruce Miller Nurseries must increase the number of shrubs, trees, and flowering plants that it makes available for sale during the spring and summer growing seasons. To obtain this merchandise inventory from growers or wholesalers, it uses short-term financing and repays the loans when the merchandise is sold.

Business success often begins with a financial plan. Before the merchandise in this IKEA warehouse can be sold, it must be purchased from manufacturers or suppliers and then stored until it is needed in the retailer's stores. *Successful* businesses often use sound financial planning built on the firm's goals and objectives, different types of budgets, and available sources of funds to make sure financing is available to purchase inventory and other necessities needed to operate a business.

cash flow the movement of money into and out of an organization

speculative production the time lag between the actual production of goods and when the goods are sold

FIGURE 19.2   Cash Flow for a Manufacturing Business

Manufacturers such as Stanley Black & Decker often use short-term financing to pay expenses during the production process. Once goods are shipped to retailers and wholesalers and payment is received, sales revenues are used to repay short-term financing.

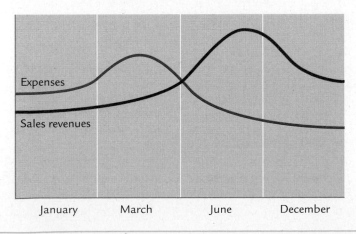

Expenses

Sales revenues

January   March   June   December

© CENGAGE LEARNING 2014

Personal APPS

Take a moment to write down your short-term and long-term financing needs. Paying for college is a long-term need, for example, as is buying a home. What kinds of short-term financing needs do you have? What can you do to meet your short- and long-term needs in the coming months and years.

long-term financing money that will be used for longer than one year

Summarize the process of planning for financial management. ③

risk–return ratio a ratio based on the principle that a high-risk decision should generate higher financial returns for a business and more conservative decisions often generate lower returns

financial plan a plan for obtaining and using the money needed to implement an organization's goals and objectives

Long-Term Financing

Long-term financing is money that will be used for longer than one year. Long-term financing obviously is needed to start a new business. As Table 19.1 shows, it is also needed for business mergers and acquisitions, new product development, long-term marketing activities, replacement of equipment that has become obsolete, and expansion of facilities.

The amounts of long-term financing needed by large firms can seem almost unreal. The 3M Company—a large multinational corporation known for research and development—has invested more than $7 billion over the last five years to develop new products designed to make people's lives easier and safer.[4]

The Risk–Return Ratio

According to financial experts, business firms will find it more difficult to raise both short- and long-term financing in the future for two reasons. First, financial reform and increased regulations will lengthen the process required to obtain financing. Second, both lenders and investors are more cautious about who receives financing. As a result of these two factors, financial managers must develop a strong financial plan that describes how the money will be used and how it will be repaid. When developing a financial plan for a business, a financial manager must also consider the risk–return ratio when making decisions that affect the firm's finances.

The **risk–return ratio** is based on the principle that a high-risk decision should generate higher financial returns for a business. On the other hand, more conservative decisions (with less risk) often generate lesser returns. Although financial managers want higher returns, they often must strive for a balance between risk and return. For example, Ohio-based American Electric Power may consider investing millions of dollars to fund research into new solar technology that could enable the company to use the sun to generate electrical power. Yet, financial managers (along with other managers throughout the organization) must determine the potential return before committing to such a costly research project.

PLANNING—THE BASIS OF SOUND FINANCIAL MANAGEMENT

In Chapter 6, we defined a *plan* as an outline of the actions by which an organization intends to accomplish its goals and objectives. A **financial plan**, then, is a plan for obtaining and using the money needed to implement an organization's goals and objectives.

Developing the Financial Plan

Financial planning (like all planning) begins with establishing a set of valid goals and objectives. Financial managers must then determine how much money is needed to accomplish each goal and objective. Finally, financial managers must identify available sources of financing and decide which to use. The three steps involved in financial planning are illustrated in Figure 19.3.

FIGURE 19.3   The Three Steps of Financial Planning

After a financial plan has been developed, it must be monitored continually to ensure that it actually fulfills the firm's goals.

1 Establish organizational goals and objectives

2 Budget the money needed to accomplish the goals and objectives

3 Identify the sources of funds

Sales revenue	Equity capital	Debt capital	Sale of assets
• Revenue projections for this planning period	• Money from sole proprietor or partners • Common stock • Preferred stock	• Short-term borrowing • Long-term borrowing	• For profit • To raise cash

Monitor and evaluate

© CENGAGE LEARNING 2014

Establishing Organizational Goals and Objectives As pointed out in Chapter 6, a *goal* is an end result that an organization expects to achieve over a one- to ten-year period. An *objective* was defined in Chapter 6 as a specific statement detailing what an organization intends to accomplish over a shorter period of time. If goals and objectives are not specific and measurable, they cannot be translated into dollar costs, and financial planning cannot proceed. For large corporations, both goals and objectives can be expensive. For example, have you ever wondered how much McDonald's spends on advertising? Well, to reach the nearly 68 million customers it serves each day, the world's most famous fast-food restaurant chain spends over $685 million each year.[5]

Budgeting for Financial Needs Once planners know what the firm's goals and objectives are for a specific period—say, the next calendar year—they can construct a budget that projects the costs the firm will incur and the sales revenues it will receive. Specifically, a **budget** is a financial statement that projects income, expenditures, or both over a specified future period.

Usually, the budgeting process begins with the construction of departmental budgets for sales and various types of expenses. Financial managers can easily combine each department's budget for sales and expenses into a company-wide cash budget. A **cash budget** estimates cash receipts and cash expenditures over a specified period. Notice in the cash budget for Stars and Stripes Clothing, shown in Figure 19.4, sales receipts and collections are listed at the top for each calendar quarter. Payments for purchases and routine expenses are listed in the middle section. Using this information, it is possible to calculate the anticipated cash gain or loss at the end of each quarter for this retail clothing store.

Most firms today use one of two approaches to budgeting. In the *traditional* approach, each new budget is based on the dollar amounts contained in the budget for the preceding year. These amounts are modified to reflect any revised goals, and managers are required to justify only new expenditures. The problem with this approach is that it leaves room for padding budget items to protect the (sometimes selfish) interests

budget a financial statement that projects income, expenditures, or both over a specified future period

cash budget a financial statement that estimates cash receipts and cash expenditures over a specified period of the manager or his or her department. This problem is essentially eliminated through zero-base budgeting. **Zero-base budgeting** is a budgeting approach in which every expense in every budget must be justified.

To develop a plan for long-term financing needs, managers often construct a capital budget. A **capital budget** estimates a firm's expenditures for major assets, including new product development, expansion of facilities, replacement of obsolete equipment, and mergers and acquisitions. For example, Berkshire Hathaway, a company known for purchasing well-managed and innovative companies, constructed a capital budget to determine the best way to finance the $9 billion acquisition of the highly successful Lubrizol Corporation in 2011.[6]

Identifying Sources of Funds The four primary sources of funds, listed in Figure 19.3, are sales revenue, equity capital, debt capital, and proceeds from the sale of assets. Future sales revenue generally provides the greatest part of a firm's financing. Figure 19.4 shows that for Stars and Stripes Clothing, sales for the year are expected to cover all expenses and to provide a cash gain of $106,000. However, Stars and Stripes has a problem in the first quarter, when sales are expected to fall short of expenses by $7,000. In fact, one of the primary reasons for financial planning is to provide management with adequate lead time to solve this type of cash-flow problem.

A second type of funding is **equity capital**. For a sole proprietorship or partnership, equity capital is provided by the owner or owners of the business. For a corporation, equity capital is money obtained from the sale of shares of ownership in the business. Equity capital is used almost exclusively for long-term financing.

A third type of funding is **debt capital**, which is borrowed money. Debt capital may be borrowed for either short- or long-term use—and a short-term loan seems made to order for Stars and Stripes Clothing's shortfall problem. The firm probably would borrow the needed $7,000 (or perhaps a bit more) at some point during the first quarter and repay it from second-quarter sales revenue.

Proceeds from the sale of assets are the fourth type of funding. Selling assets is a drastic step. However, it may be a reasonable last resort when sales revenues are declining and equity capital or debt capital cannot be found. Assets also may be sold to increase a firm's cash balance or when they are no longer needed or do not "fit" with the company's core business. In 2011, Pfizer, the world's biggest drug maker, agreed

zero-base budgeting a budgeting approach in which every expense in every budget must be justified

capital budget a financial statement that estimates a firm's expenditures for major assets and its long-term financing needs

equity capital money received from the owners or from the sale of shares of ownership in a business

debt capital borrowed money obtained through loans of various types

---

© CENGAGE LEARNING 2014

FIGURE 19.4 Cash Budget for Stars and Stripes Clothing

A company-wide cash budget projects sales, collections, purchases, and expenses over a specified period to anticipate cash surpluses and deficits.

STARS AND STRIPES CLOTHING
Cash Budget   From January 1, 2012 to December 31, 2012

	First Quarter ($)	Second Quarter ($)	Third Quarter ($)	Fourth Quarter ($)	Total ($)
Cash sales and collections	150,000	160,000	150,000	185,000	645,000
Less payments					
Purchases	110,000	80,000	90,000	60,000	340,000
Wages/salaries	25,000	20,000	25,000	30,000	100,000
Rent	10,000	10,000	12,000	12,000	44,000
Other expenses	4,000	4,000	5,000	6,000	19,000
Taxes	8,000	8,000	10,000	10,000	36,000
Total payments	157,000	122,000	142,000	118,000	539,000
Cash gain or (loss)	(7,000)	38,000	8,000	67,000	106,000

to sell its Capsugel manufacturing unit to KKR (Kohlberg Kravis Roberts), a world leading investment company, for $2.4 billion. The cash Pfizer receives from the Capsugel sale will be used to repurchase shares of its own stock.[7]

Monitoring and Evaluating Financial Performance

It is important to ensure that financial plans are implemented properly and to catch potential problems before they become major ones. Despite efforts to raise additional financing, reduce expenses, and increase sales to become profitable, retail and online bookseller Borders filed for bankruptcy protection in 2011. Eventually, the firm was forced to liquidate its inventory and close all its stores because a buyer could not be found for the bankrupt firm.

To prevent such problems, financial managers should establish a means of monitoring financial performance. Interim budgets (weekly, monthly, or quarterly) may be prepared for comparison purposes. These comparisons point up areas that require additional or revised planning—or at least areas calling for a more careful investigation. Budget comparisons can also be used to improve the firm's future budgets.

© OMNITERRA IMAGES

Borders bookstores—no more! After 40 years, Borders closed all of its stores. The firm filed for bankruptcy in early 2011 and was forced to close a large number of stores in order to reorganize. Then in the summer of 2011, the bookseller was forced to liquidate its inventory and remaining stores despite revised financial plans, new financial goals, and its reorganizational efforts. Simply put: A buyer could not be found for the bankrupt firm.

SOURCES OF SHORT-TERM DEBT FINANCING

Describe the advantages and disadvantages of different methods of short-term debt financing.

Typically, short-term debt financing is money that will be repaid in one year or less. During the economic crisis, many business firms found that it was much more difficult to borrow money for short periods of time to purchase inventory, buy supplies, pay salaries, and meet everyday expenses. Today the amount of available short-term financing has increased.

The decision to borrow money does not necessarily mean that a firm is in financial trouble. On the contrary, astute financial management often means regular, responsible borrowing of many different kinds to meet different needs. In this section, we examine the sources of *short-term debt financing* available to businesses. In the next two sections, we look at long-term financing options: equity capital and debt capital.

Sources of Unsecured Short-Term Financing

Short-term debt financing is usually easier to obtain than long-term debt financing for three reasons:

1. For the lender, the shorter repayment period means less risk of non-payment.
2. The dollar amounts of short-term loans are usually smaller than those of long-term loans.
3. A close working relationship normally exists between the short-term borrower and the lender.

Most lenders do not require collateral for short-term financing. If they do, it is usually because they are concerned about the size of a particular loan, the borrowing firm's poor credit rating, or the general prospects of repayment. Remember from Chapter 18 that *collateral* was defined as real estate or property pledged as security for a loan.

Unsecured financing is financing that is not backed by collateral. A company seeking unsecured short-term financing has several options.

unsecured financing financing that is not backed by collateral; unsecured short-term financing offers several options

Entrepreneurs can always use more capital. Even though Body Rest Mattress Company in St. Petersburg, Florida was successful, Carl and Emma Calhoun found that obtaining short-term financing was difficult during the economic crisis. Traditional sources of financing—banks and other financial institutions—tightened the requirements for obtaining unsecured loans or in many cases rejected loan requests.

Trade Credit Manufacturers and wholesalers often provide financial aid to retailers by allowing them 30 to 60 days (or more) in which to pay for merchandise. This delayed payment, known as **trade credit**, is a type of short-term financing extended by a seller who does not require immediate payment after delivery of merchandise. It is the most popular form of short-term financing, because most manufacturers and wholesalers do not charge interest for trade credit. In fact, from 70 to 90 percent of all transactions between businesses involve some trade credit.

Let us assume that Discount Tire Stores receives a shipment of tires from a manufacturer. Along with the merchandise, the manufacturer sends an invoice that states the terms of payment. Discount Tire now has two options for payment. First, the retailer may pay the invoice promptly and take advantage of any cash discount the manufacturer offers. Cash-discount terms are specified on the invoice. For instance, "2/10, net 30" means that the customer—Discount Tire—may take a "2" percent discount if it pays the invoice within ten days of the invoice date. Let us assume that the dollar amount of the invoice is $200,000. In this case, the cash discount is $4,000 ($200,000 × 0.02 = $4,000). If the cash discount is taken, Discount Tire only has to pay the manufacturer $196,000 ($200,000 − $4,000 = $196,000).

A second option is to wait until the end of the credit period before making payment. If payment is made between 11 and 30 days after the date of the invoice, Discount Tire must pay the entire amount. As long as payment is made before the end of the credit period, the retailer maintains the ability to purchase additional merchandise using the trade-credit arrangement.

Promissory Notes Issued to Suppliers A **promissory note** is a written pledge by a borrower to pay a certain sum of money to a creditor at a specified future date. Suppliers uneasy about extending trade credit may be less reluctant to offer credit to customers who sign promissory notes. Unlike trade credit, however, promissory notes usually require the borrower to pay interest. Although repayment periods may extend to one year, most short-term promissory notes are repaid in 60 to 180 days.

A promissory note offers two important advantages to the firm extending the credit.

1. A promissory note is legally binding and an enforceable contract.
2. A promissory note is a negotiable instrument.

Because a promissory note is negotiable, the manufacturer, wholesaler, or company extending credit may be able to discount, or sell, the note to its own bank. If the note is discounted, the dollar amount received by the company extending credit is slightly less than the maturity value because the bank charges a fee for the service. The supplier recoups most of its money immediately, and the bank collects the maturity value when the note matures.

Unsecured Bank Loans Banks and other financial institutions offer unsecured short-term loans to businesses at interest rates that vary with each borrower's credit rating. The **prime interest rate** is the lowest rate charged by a bank for a short-term loan. Figure 19.5 traces the fluctuations in the average prime rate charged by U.S. banks from 1990 to January 2012. This lowest rate generally is reserved for large corporations with excellent credit ratings. Organizations with good to high credit ratings may pay the prime rate plus "2" percent. Firms with questionable credit ratings may have to pay the prime rate plus "4" percent. (The fact that a banker charges a higher interest rate for a higher-risk loan is a practical application of the risk–return ratio

trade credit a type of short-term financing extended by a seller who does not require immediate payment after delivery of merchandise

promissory note a written pledge by a borrower to pay a certain sum of money to a creditor at a specified future date

prime interest rate the lowest rate charged by a bank for a short-term loan

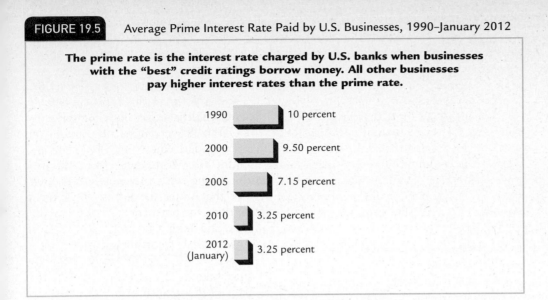

FIGURE 19.5 Average Prime Interest Rate Paid by U.S. Businesses, 1990–January 2012

The prime rate is the interest rate charged by U.S. banks when businesses with the "best" credit ratings borrow money. All other businesses pay higher interest rates than the prime rate.

1990	10 percent
2000	9.50 percent
2005	7.15 percent
2010	3.25 percent
2012 (January)	3.25 percent

Source: Federal Reserve Bank Web site, www.federalreserve.gov (accessed June 6, 2012).

discussed earlier in this chapter.) Of course, if the banker believes that loan repayment may be a problem, the borrower's loan application may well be rejected.

When a business obtains a short-term bank loan, interest rates and repayment terms may be negotiated. As a condition of the loan, a bank may require that a *compensating balance* be kept on deposit at the bank. Compensating balances, if required, are typically 10 to 20 percent of the borrowed funds. The bank may also require that every commercial borrower *clean up* (pay off completely) its short-term loans at least once each year and not use it again for a period of 30 to 60 days.

Commercial Paper Large firms with excellent credit reputations like Microsoft, Procter & Gamble, and Caterpillar can raise large sums of money quickly by issuing commercial paper. As defined in Chapter 18, commercial paper is a short-term promissory note issued by a large corporation. The maturity date for commercial paper is normally 270 days or less.

Commercial paper is secured only by the reputation of the issuing firm; no collateral is involved. The interest rate a corporation pays when it sells commercial paper is tied to its credit rating and its ability to repay the commercial paper. In most cases, corporations selling commercial paper pay interest rates slightly below the interest rates charged by banks for short-term loans. Thus, selling commercial paper is cheaper than getting short-term financing from a bank.

Although it is possible to purchase commercial paper in smaller denominations, larger amounts—$100,000 or more—are quite common. Money obtained by selling commercial paper is most often used to purchase inventory, finance a firm's accounts receivables, pay salaries and other necessary expenses, and solve cash-flow problems.

Sources of Secured Short-Term Financing

If a business cannot obtain enough money through unsecured financing, it must put up collateral to obtain additional short-term financing. Almost any asset can serve as collateral. However, *inventories* and *accounts receivable* are the assets most commonly pledged for short-term financing. Even when it is willing to pledge collateral to back up a loan, a firm that is financially weak may have difficulty obtaining short-term financing.

Loans Secured by Inventory Normally, manufacturers, wholesalers, and retailers have large amounts of money invested in finished goods. In addition, manufacturers carry raw materials and work-in-process inventories. All three types of inventory may be pledged as collateral for short-term loans. However, lenders prefer the much more salable finished merchandise to raw materials or work-in-process inventories.

A lender may insist that inventory used as collateral be stored in a public warehouse. In such a case, the receipt issued by the warehouse is retained by the lender. Without this receipt, the public warehouse will not release the merchandise. The lender releases the warehouse receipt—and the merchandise—to the borrower when the borrowed money is repaid. In addition to paying the interest on the loan, the borrower must pay for storage in the public warehouse. As a result, this type of loan is more expensive than an unsecured short-term loan.

Loans Secured by Receivables As defined in Chapter 17, *accounts receivable* are amounts owed to a firm by its customers. A firm can pledge its accounts receivable as collateral to obtain short-term financing. A lender may advance 70 to 80 percent of the dollar amount of the receivables. First, however, it conducts a thorough investigation to determine the *quality* of the receivables. (The quality of the receivables is the credit standing of the firm's customers, coupled with the customers' ability to repay their credit obligations when they are due.) If a favorable determination is made, the loan is approved. When the borrowing firm collects from a customer whose account has been pledged as collateral, generally it must turn the money over to the lender as partial repayment of the loan. An alternative approach is to notify the borrowing firm's credit customers to make their payments directly to the lender.

Factoring Accounts Receivable

Accounts receivable may be used in one other way to help raise short-term financing: They can be sold to a factoring company (or factor). A **factor** is a firm that specializes in buying other firms' accounts receivable. The factor buys the accounts receivable for less than their face value; however, it collects the full dollar amount when each account is due. The factor's profit thus is the difference between the face value of the accounts receivable and the amount the factor has paid for them. Generally, the amount of profit the factor receives is based on the risk the factor assumes. Risk, in this case, is the probability that the accounts receivable will not be repaid when they mature. In the aftermath of the economic crisis and because of the reluctance of some banks to provide short-term financing, some large financial firms, including CIT Group and GE Capital, are providing additional factoring services to both old and new firms that sell their accounts receivables.[8]

Even though the firm selling its accounts receivable gets less than face value, it does receive needed cash immediately. Moreover, it has shifted both the task of collecting and the risk of non-payment to the factor, which now owns the accounts receivable. Generally, customers whose accounts receivable have been factored are given instructions to make their payments directly to the factor.

Cost Comparisons

Table 19.2 compares the various types of short-term financing. As you can see, trade credit is the least expensive. Factoring of accounts receivable is typically the highest-cost method shown.

For many purposes, short-term financing suits a firm's needs perfectly. At other times, however, long-term financing may be more appropriate. In this case, a business may try to raise equity capital or long-term debt capital.

factor a firm that specializes in buying other firms' accounts receivable

TABLE 19.2 Comparison of Short-Term Financing Methods

Type of Financing	Cost	Repayment Period	Businesses That May Use It	Comments
Trade credit	Low, if any	30–60 days	All businesses with good credit	Usually no finance charge
Promissory note issued to suppliers	Moderate	One year or less	All businesses	Usually unsecured but requires legal document
Unsecured bank loan	Moderate	One year or less	All businesses	Promissory note is required and compensating balance may be required
Commercial paper	Moderate	270 days or less	Large corporations with high credit ratings	Available only to large firms
Secured loan	High	One year or less	Firms with questionable credit ratings	Inventory or accounts receivable often used as collateral
Factoring	High	None	Firms that have large numbers of credit customers	Accounts receivable sold to a factor

© Cengage Learning 2014

SOURCES OF EQUITY FINANCING

Sources of long-term financing vary with the size and type of business. As mentioned earlier, a sole proprietorship or partnership acquires equity capital (sometimes referred to as *owners' equity*) when the owner or partners invest money in the business. For corporations, equity-financing options include the sale of stock and the use of profits not distributed to owners. All three types of businesses can also obtain venture capital and use long-term debt capital (borrowed money) to meet their financial needs.

⑤ Evaluate the advantages and disadvantages of equity financing.

initial public offering (IPO) occurs when a corporation sells common stock to the general public for the first time

Selling Stock

Some equity capital is used to start every business—sole proprietorship, partnership, or corporation. In the case of corporations, stockholders who buy shares in the company provide equity capital.

Initial Public Offering and the Primary Market An **initial public offering (IPO)** occurs when a corporation sells common stock to the general public for the first time. To raise money, the social networking site Groupon used a 2011 IPO to raise $700 million that it could use to fund expansion and other business activities.[9] In another 2011 IPO, LinkedIn—one of the world's largest social media companies—raised over $350 million.[10] In mid-2012, Facebook used an IPO to raise capital, and it was one of the largest IPOs in recent history. And at the time of the publication of your text, there are more social media and technology IPOs planned for 2012. Corporations in other industries also use IPOs to raise money. In fact, as illustrated in Figure 19.6, the largest IPOs—Visa, General Motors, AT&T Wireless, Kraft Foods, and United Parcel Service—for U.S. companies involve companies from a number of different industries.

© TUPUNGATO/SHUTTERSTOCK

Just a piece of paper—or is it? In fact, a piece of paper can be worth a lot of money when it is a stock certificate. A corporation sells stock to raise needed financing for expansion and to pay for other long-term financial needs. On the other hand, investors purchase stock because they can profit from their investment if the price of the corporation's stock increases and a corporation pays dividends.

Angie's List is now a public company. Angie's List—the company that provides members with information about local professionals for home, health care, and automotive services—sold stock to the public in late 2011 and raised over $100 million. After the initial public offering (IPO), the company's stock was listed on the Nasdaq stock exchange where it can be bought and sold by investors in the secondary market.

Established companies that plan to raise capital by selling subsidiaries to the public can also use IPOs. In 2011, Sunoco sold shares in its metallurgical division and raised over $185 million. The new corporation—SunCoke Energy—will be a separate company and will produce metallurgical coke—a necessary component for manufacturing steel. Monies from the IPO will be used to increase the parent company's cash balance and provide funding for growth opportunities and expansion.[11] In addition to using an IPO to increase the cash balance for the parent company, corporations often sell shares in a subsidiary when shares can be sold at a profit or when the subsidiary no longer fits with its current business plan. Finally, some corporations will sell a subsidiary that is growing more slowly than the rest of the company's operating divisions.

When a corporation uses an IPO to raise capital, the stock is sold in the primary market. The **primary market** is a market in which an investor purchases financial securities (via an investment bank) directly from the issuer of the securities. An **investment banking firm** is an organization that assists corporations in raising funds, usually by helping to sell new issues of stocks, bonds, or other financial securities.

Although a corporation can have only one IPO, it can sell additional stock after the IPO, assuming that there is a market for the company's stock. Even though the cost of selling stock (often referred to as *flotation costs*) is high, the *ongoing* costs associated with this type of equity financing are low for two reasons. First, the corporation does not have to repay money obtained from the sale of stock because the corporation is under no legal obligation to do so. If you purchase corporate stock and later decide to sell your stock, you may sell it to another investor—not the corporation.

A second advantage of selling stock is that a corporation is under no legal obligation to pay dividends to stockholders. As noted in Chapter 4, a *dividend* is a distribution of earnings to the stockholders of a corporation. For any reason (e.g., if a company has a bad year), the board of directors can vote to omit dividend payments. Earnings then are retained for use in funding business operations. Of course, corporate management may hear from unhappy stockholders if expected dividends are omitted too frequently.

primary market a market in which an investor purchases financial securities (via an investment bank) directly from the issuer of those securities

investment banking firm an organization that assists corporations in raising funds, usually by helping to sell new issues of stocks, bonds, or other financial securities

FIGURE 19.6   The All-Time Largest Initial Public Offerings for U.S. Companies

These five corporations raised billions of dollars by selling stock. Visa—the record holder for U.S. companies—raised over $17 billion when it sold stock for the first time in 2008.

Visa — Financial	$17.9 billion
General Motors — Automotive	$15.8 billion
AT&T Wireless — Communications	$10.6 billion
Kraft Foods — Consumer Goods	$8.7 billion
United Parcel Service — Transportation	$5.5 billion

Source: Renaissance Capital, Greenwich, CT (www.renaissancecapital.com), accessed February 28, 2012.

Going for SUCCESS

Investor Relations in the Social Media Era

Tweeting about earnings? Increasingly, public corporations are communicating with their investors via Twitter, Facebook, YouTube, LinkedIn, and other social media. Companies still publish annual reports (in print and online) and hold annual meetings (in person and via webcast). In addition, because stockholders and potential investors want easy access to the latest financial news, companies like Alcoa, Dell, and eBay now use social media to provide official updates. Although the timing and content of these messages must comply with regulatory requirements, the ability to connect quickly and directly with investors is vital at a time when rumors can fly around the world at the click of a mouse.

Alcoa, for example, uses its Facebook page to announce quarterly earnings figures and link to executive webcasts. It also uses its Twitter account to call attention to specific results and invite comments from its followers. For investors who want to dig deeper into quarterly or annual financial reports, the investor relations department shares its electronic presentations on SlideShare.

Thanks to Twitter, YouTube, a dedicated investor relations blog, and other social media, Dell reaches more than five million people when it presents its quarterly financial results. And the online auction site eBay live-tweets earnings results as the CEO announces them. Watch for corporate investor relations departments to become even more social in the years ahead.

Sources: Based on information in Rachel Koning Beals, "Investors Increasingly Tap Social Media for Stock Tips," *U.S. News & World Report*, January 31, 2012, http://money.usnews.com/money; Dominic Jones, "Social Media Investor Relations Reaches Tipping Point," *IR Web Report*, April 14, 2011, http://irwebreport.com; Dave Hogan, "Investor Relations and Social Media: Together at Last," *PR News Online*, May 9, 2011, www.prnewsonline.com; Jennifer Van Grove, "Investor Relations Tool Helps Fortune 500 Companies Get Social," *Mashable*, June 8, 2011, www.mashable.com.

The Secondary Market Although a share of corporate stock is only sold one time in the primary market, the stock can be sold again and again in the secondary market. The **secondary market** is a market for existing financial securities that are traded between investors. Although a corporation does not receive money each time its stock is bought or sold in the secondary market, the ability to obtain cash by selling stock investments is one reason why investors purchase corporate stock. Without the secondary market, investors would not purchase stock in the primary market because there would be no way to sell shares to other investors. Usually, secondary-market transactions are completed through a securities exchange or the over-the-counter (OTC) market.

A **securities exchange** is a marketplace where member brokers meet to buy and sell securities. Generally, securities issued by larger corporations are traded at the New York Stock Exchange (NYSE) (now owned by the NYSE Euronext holding company), or at regional exchanges located in different parts of the country. The securities of very large corporations may be traded at more than one of these exchanges. Securities of firms also may be listed on foreign securities exchanges—in Tokyo or London, for example.

Stocks issued by several thousand companies are traded in the OTC market. The **over-the-counter (OTC) market** is a network of dealers who buy and sell the stocks of corporations that are not listed on a securities exchange. The term *over-the-counter* was coined more than 100 years ago when securities actually were sold "over the counter" in stores and banks. Most OTC securities today are traded through an *electronic exchange* called the Nasdaq (pronounced "nazzdack"). The term Nasdaq stands for National Association of Securities Dealers Automated Quotations. The Nasdaq is now one of the largest securities markets in the world. Today, the Nasdaq is known for its forward-looking, innovative, growth companies, including Intel, Microsoft, Cisco Systems, and Dell Computer.

There are two types of stock: common and preferred. Each type has advantages and drawbacks as a means of long-term financing.

secondary market a market for existing financial securities that are traded between investors

securities exchange a marketplace where member brokers meet to buy and sell securities

over-the-counter (OTC) market a network of dealers who buy and sell the stocks of corporations that are not listed on a securities exchange

Talk to Chuck

Founded in 1971, the Charles Schwab Corporation is a brokerage firm and banking company with extensive product lines including checking accounts, mortgages, brokerage and retirement accounts, mutual funds, stocks and bonds, and more.

While some financial service firms have been slow to adopt social media, due in part to the risk of violating the rules of the Financial Industry Regulatory Authority (FINRA), Schwab has long been viewed as a leader in the use of social media. The Schwab promotional campaign "Talk to Chuck" invited investors to check out the company as an option to more traditional investment companies. Take a look at www.charlesschwab.com. You can also find Schwab on Facebook, Twitter, and YouTube.

Common Stock A share of **common stock** represents the most basic form of corporate ownership. In return for the financing provided by selling common stock, management must make certain concessions to stockholders that may restrict or change corporate policies. Every corporation must hold an annual meeting, at which the holders of common stock may vote for the board of directors. Often, stockholders are also asked to approve or disapprove of major corporate actions by voting on the following:

1. Amendments to the corporate charter or corporate by-laws
2. Sale of certain assets
3. Mergers and acquisitions
4. New issues of preferred stock or bonds
5. Changes in the amount of common stock issued

Few investors will buy common stock unless they believe that their investment will increase in value. Information on the reasons why investors purchase stocks and how to evaluate stock investments is provided in Chapter 20, "Understanding Personal Finances and Investments."

Preferred Stock As noted in Chapter 4, the owners of **preferred stock** must receive their dividends before holders of common stock receive theirs. Also, preferred stockholders know the dollar amount of their dividend because it is stated on the stock certificate. When compared to common stockholders, preferred stockholders also have first claim (after creditors) on assets if the corporation is dissolved or declares bankruptcy. Even so, as with common stock, the board of directors must approve dividends on preferred stock, and this type of financing does not represent a debt that must be legally repaid. In return for preferential treatment, preferred stockholders generally give up the right to vote at a corporation's annual meeting.

Although a corporation usually issues only one type of common stock, it may issue many types of preferred stock with varying dividends or dividend rates. For example, New York–based Consolidated Edison has one common-stock issue but three preferred-stock issues.

Retained Earnings

Most large corporations distribute only a portion of their after-tax earnings to stockholders. The portion of a corporation's profits *not* distributed to stockholders is called **retained earnings**. Because they are undistributed profits, retained earnings are considered a form of equity financing.

The amount of retained earnings in any year is determined by corporate management and approved by the board of directors. Most small and growing corporations pay no cash dividend—or a very small dividend—to their stockholders. All or most earnings are reinvested in the business for research and development, expansion, or the funding of major projects. Reinvestment tends to increase the value of the firm's stock while it provides essentially cost-free financing for the business. More mature corporations may distribute 40 to 60 percent of their after-tax profits as dividends. Utility companies and other corporations with very stable earnings often pay out as much as 80 to 90 percent of what they earn. For a large corporation, retained earnings can amount to a hefty bit of financing. For example, in 2011, the total amount of retained earnings for General Electric was over $137 billion.[12]

common stock stock whose owners may vote on corporate matters but whose claims on profits and assets are subordinate to the claims of others

preferred stock stock whose owners usually do not have voting rights but whose claims on dividends and assets are paid before those of common-stock owners

retained earnings the portion of a corporation's profits not distributed to stockholders

Entrepreneurial SUCCESS

Looking for Venture Capital from Corporations

Why would General Electric (GE), Dell, Google, and other major corporations set aside hundreds of millions of dollars as venture capital for small businesses? One reason is to work with entrepreneurs who have cutting-edge ideas. "It allows us to connect to these incredible, innovative companies," explains a GE executive. With venture-capital partners, GE has invested in small businesses that are in the early stages of developing and commercializing environmentally friendly technology and products.

Another reason is to identify potential partners that are active in fast-growing markets. Dell, for example, has reactivated its venture capital group and is planning investments in entrepreneurial firms that are working on software for business use and pushing the limits of cloud computing. Because Dell is diversifying beyond computer equipment, venture capital allows it to gain entry into emerging technology services.

Finally, long-term profit drives corporations to make capital venture available. Google Ventures, the search company's investment arm, provides money as well as assistance to technology entrepreneurs in a wide range of industries, including life sciences, energy, and digital entertainment. Google Ventures has already helped 70 businesses with recruiting, engineering, design, and marketing, with an eye toward future financial return. "When cash is a commodity, you need to do other things to show an entrepreneur how you'll help them," says the managing partner.

Sources: Based on information in Lizette Chapman, "Venture Firms Offer More than Just Cash," *Wall Street Journal*, April 4, 2012, www.wsj.com; Deborah Gage, "Dell Resurrects Venture Capital Arm," *Wall Street Journal*, December 16, 2011, www.wsj.com; Evelyn M. Rusli, "GE Invests in 10 Home Energy Start-Ups," *New York Times*, June 23, 2011, www.nytimes.com.

Venture Capital and Private Placements

To establish a new business or expand an existing one, an entrepreneur may try to obtain venture capital. In Chapter 5, we defined *venture capital* as money invested in small (and sometimes struggling) firms that have the potential to become very successful. Most venture capital firms do not invest in the typical small business—a neighborhood convenience store or a local dry cleaner—but in firms that have the potential to become extremely profitable. Today, most venture capital firms are investing in companies that build the nation's infrastructure, develop computer software, or provide consumer information or social media services. For example, Zynga—the fast-growing company behind such popular games as FarmVille and Words with Friends—received venture capital before selling stock to the public.[13]

Generally, a venture capital firm consists of a pool of investors, a partnership established by a wealthy family, or a joint venture formed by corporations with money to invest. In return for financing, these investors generally receive an equity or ownership position in the business and share in its profits. Venture capital firms vary in size and scope of interest. Some offer financing for start-up businesses, whereas others finance only established businesses. Although venture capital firms are willing to take chances, they have also been more selective about where they invest their money after the recent economic crisis.

Another method of raising capital is through a private placement. A **private placement** occurs when stock and other corporate securities are sold directly to insurance companies, pension funds, or large institutional investors. When compared with selling stocks and other corporate securities to the public, there are often fewer government regulations and the cost is generally less when the securities are sold through a private placement. Typically, terms between the buyer and seller are negotiated when a private placement is used to raise capital.

private placement occurs when stock and other corporate securities are sold directly to insurance companies, pension funds, or large institutional investors

© RYAN ANSON/BLOOMBERG VIA GETTY IMAGES

One smart venture capitalist! Venture capital firms make no secret of where they're looking to invest, and these days they're investing heavily in information technology. Venture capitalist, Marc Andreessen, is a partner in California-based Andreessen Horowitz—one of the best venture capitalist firms in the world. Since the venture capital firm was founded, his firm has invested money in many very recognizable and profitable firms including Facebook, Twitter, and Pinterest.

SOURCES OF LONG-TERM DEBT FINANCING

As pointed out earlier in this chapter, businesses borrow money on a short-term basis for many valid reasons other than desperation. There are equally valid reasons for long-term borrowing. In addition to using borrowed money to meet the long-term needs listed in Table 19.1, successful businesses often use the financial leverage it creates to improve their financial performance. **Financial leverage** is the use of borrowed funds to increase the return on owners' equity. The principle of financial leverage works as long as a firm's earnings are larger than the interest charged for the borrowed money.

To understand how financial leverage can increase a firm's return on owners' equity, study the information for Texas-based Cypress Springs Plastics presented in Table 19.3. Pete Johnston, the owner of the firm, is trying to decide how best to finance a $100,000 purchase of new high-tech manufacturing equipment.

- He could borrow the money and pay 7 percent annual interest.
- He could invest an additional $100,000 in the firm.

Assuming that the firm earns $95,000 a year and that annual interest for this loan totals $7,000 ($100,000 × 0.07 = $7,000), the return on owners' equity for Cypress Springs Plastics would be higher if the firm borrowed the additional financing. Return on owners' equity is determined by dividing a firm's net income by the dollar amount of owners' equity. Based on the calculations illustrated in Table 19.3, Cypress Springs Plastics' return on owners' equity equals 17.6 percent if Johnston borrows the additional $100,000. The firm's return on owners' equity would decrease to 15.8 percent if Johnston invests an additional $100,000 in the business.

The most obvious danger when using financial leverage is that the firm's earnings may be lower than expected. If this situation occurs, the fixed interest charge actually works to reduce or eliminate the return on owners' equity. Of course, borrowed money eventually must be repaid.

For a small business, long-term debt financing is generally limited to loans. Large corporations have the additional option of issuing corporate bonds.

Long-Term Loans

financial leverage the use of borrowed funds to increase the return on owners' equity

Many businesses satisfy their long-term financing needs, such as those listed in Table 19.1, with loans from commercial banks, insurance companies, pension funds, and other financial institutions. Manufacturers and suppliers of heavy machinery may also provide long-term debt financing by granting credit to their customers.

TABLE 19.3 Analysis of the Effect of Additional Capital from Debt or Equity for Cypress Springs Plastics, Inc.

Additional Debt		Additional Equity	
Owners' equity	$ 500,000	Owners' equity	$ 500,000
Additional equity	+ 0	Additional equity	+100,000
Total owner's equity	$ 500,000	Total owner's equity	$ 600,000
Loan (@ 7%)	+100,000	No loan	+ 0
Total capital	$ 600,000	Total capital	$ 600,000
Year-End Earnings			
Gross profit	$95,000	Gross profit	$ 95,000
Less loan interest	− 7,000	No interest	− 0
Operating profit	$88,000	Operating profit	$ 95,000
Return on owners' equity	17.6%	Return on owners' equity	15.8%
($88,000 ÷ $500,000 = 17.6%)		($95,000 ÷ $600,000 = 15.8%)	

Term-Loan Agreements A **term-loan agreement** is a promissory note that requires a borrower to repay a loan in monthly, quarterly, semiannual, or annual installments. Although repayment may be as long as 15 to 20 years, long-term business loans normally are repaid in 3 to 7 years.

Assume that Pete Johnston, the owner of Cypress Springs Plastics, decides to borrow $100,000 and take advantage of the principle of financial leverage illustrated in Table 19.3. Although the firm's return on owners' equity does increase, interest must be paid each year and, eventually, the loan must be repaid. To pay off a $100,000 loan over a three-year period with annual payments, Cypress Springs Plastics must pay $33,333 on the loan balance plus $7,000 annual interest, or a total of $40,333 the first year. Although the amount of interest decreases each year because of the previous year's payment on the loan balance, annual payments of this amount are still a large commitment for a small firm such as Cypress Springs Plastics.

The interest rate and repayment terms for term loans often are based on factors such as the reasons for borrowing, the borrowing firm's credit rating, and the value of collateral. Although long-term loans occasionally may be unsecured, the lender usually requires some type of collateral. Acceptable collateral includes real estate, stocks, bonds, equipment, or any asset with value. Lenders may also require that borrowers maintain a minimum amount of working capital.

The Basics of Getting a Loan According to many financial experts, preparation is the key when applying for a long-term business loan. In reality, preparation begins before you ever apply for the loan. To begin the process, you should get to know potential lenders before requesting debt financing. Although there may be many potential lenders that can provide the money you need, the logical place to borrow money is where your business does its banking. This fact underscores the importance of maintaining adequate balances in the firm's bank accounts. Before applying for a loan, you may also want to check your firm's credit rating with a national credit bureau such as D&B (formerly known as Dun & Bradstreet).

Typically, business owners will be asked to fill out a loan application. In addition to the loan application, the lender will also want to see your current business plan. Be sure to explain what your business is, how much funding you require to accomplish your goals, and how the loan will be repaid. Most lenders insist that you submit current financial statements that have been prepared by an independent certified public accountant. Then compile a list of references that includes your suppliers, other lenders, or the professionals with whom you are associated. You may also be asked to discuss the loan request with a loan officer. Hopefully, your loan request will be approved. If not, try to determine why your loan request was rejected. Think back over the loan process and determine what you could do to improve your chances of getting a loan the next time you apply.

Corporate Bonds

In addition to loans, large corporations may choose to issue bonds in denominations of $1,000 to $50,000. Although the usual face value for corporate bonds is $1,000, the total face value of all the bonds in an issue usually amounts to millions of dollars. In fact, one of the reasons why corporations sell bonds is so that they can borrow a lot of money from a lot of different bondholders and raise larger amounts of money than could be borrowed from one lender. A **corporate bond** is a corporation's written

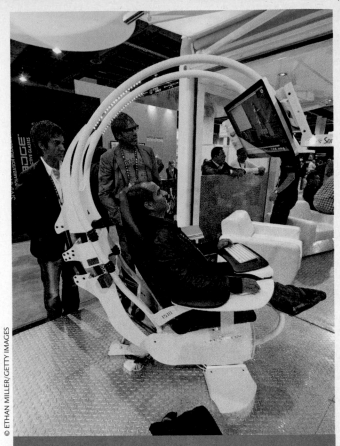

© ETHAN MILLER/GETTY IMAGES

The office of the future. While this product may look like something that should be on the next spaceship to the moon, it is a state-of-the-art office chair designed for people who spend long hours in front of computer monitors. The chair was created by Modern Work Environment (MWE) Lab. Companies that develop innovative products like this one need financing, and they generally have two choices. They can obtain financing from owners and investors or they can borrow money.

term-loan agreement a promissory note that requires a borrower to repay a loan in monthly, quarterly, semiannual, or annual installments

corporate bond a corporation's written pledge that it will repay a specified amount of money with interest

As CFO of your life, you should put your financial house in order before you apply for any loan. Be sure to check your credit report in advance to see how it looks, and think about how you'll repay the loan. Apply only when you know your finances are ready for the spotlight.

maturity date the date on which a corporation is to repay borrowed money

registered bond a bond registered in the owner's name by the issuing company

debenture bond a bond backed only by the reputation of the issuing corporation

mortgage bond a corporate bond secured by various assets of the issuing firm

convertible bond a bond that can be exchanged, at the owner's option, for a specified number of shares of the corporation's common stock

pledge that it will repay a specified amount of money with interest. Interest rates for corporate bonds vary with the financial health of the company issuing the bond. Specific factors that increase or decrease the interest rate that a corporation must pay when it issues bonds include

- The corporation's ability to pay interest each year until maturity.
- The corporation's ability to repay the bond at maturity.

For bond investors, the interest rate on corporate bonds is an example of the risk–return ratio discussed earlier in this chapter. Simply put: Investors expect more interest if there is more risk with more speculative bond issues—see Figure 19.7.

The **maturity date** is the date on which the corporation is to repay the borrowed money. Today, most corporate bonds are registered bonds. A **registered bond** is a bond registered in the owner's name by the issuing company. Many corporations do not issue actual bonds. Instead, the bonds are recorded electronically, and the specific details regarding the bond issue, along with the current owner's name and address, are maintained by computer. Computer entries are safer because they cannot be stolen, misplaced, or destroyed, and make it easier to transfer when a bond is sold.

Until a bond's maturity, a corporation pays interest to the bond owner at the stated rate. For example, owners of American & Foreign Power Company bonds that mature in 2030 receive 5 percent per year for each bond. For each $1,000 bond issued, the corporation must pay bondholders $50 ($1,000 × 0.05 = $50). Because interest for corporate bonds is usually paid semiannually, the owner of an American & Foreign Power bond will receive a $25 payment every six months for each bond they own. On the maturity date, a registered owner will receive cash equaling the face value of the bond.

Types of Bonds Corporate bonds are generally classified as debentures, mortgage bonds, or convertible bonds. Most corporate bonds are debenture bonds. A **debenture bond** is a bond backed only by the reputation of the issuing corporation. To make its bonds more appealing to investors, a corporation may issue mortgage bonds. A **mortgage bond** is a corporate bond secured by various assets of the issuing firm. Typical corporate assets that are used as collateral for a mortgage bond include real estate, machinery, and equipment that is not pledged as collateral for other debt obligations. The corporation can also issue convertible bonds. A **convertible bond** can be

| FIGURE 19.7 | The Risk–Return Ratio for Corporate Bond Investors |

High-quality corporate bonds pay less interest when compared to bonds that are more speculative.

LESS RISK Bonds with less risk have lower interest rates

lower Interest rates *higher*

MORE RISK Bonds with more risk have higher interest rates

© CENGAGE LEARNING 2014

exchanged, at the owner's option, for a specified number of shares of the corporation's common stock. An Advanced Micro Devices (AMD) bond that matures in 2015 is convertible: Each bond can be converted to 35.6125 shares of AMD common stock.[14] A corporation can gain in three ways by issuing convertible bonds. First, convertibles usually carry a lower interest rate than nonconvertible bonds. Second, the conversion feature attracts investors who are interested in the speculative gain that conversion to common stock may provide. Third, if the bondholder converts to common stock, the corporation no longer has to redeem the bond at maturity.

Repayment Provisions for Corporate Bonds Maturity dates for bonds generally range from 10 to 30 years after the date of issue. Some bonds are callable before the maturity date; that is, a corporation can buy back, or redeem, them. For these bonds, the corporation may pay the bond owner a call premium. The amount of the call premium, if any, is specified, along with other provisions, in the bond indenture. The **bond indenture** is a legal document that details all the conditions relating to a bond issue.

Before deciding if bonds are the best way to obtain corporate financing, managers must determine if the company can afford to pay the interest on the corporate bonds. It should be obvious that the larger the bond issue, the higher the dollar amount of interest that must be paid each year. For example, assume that American Express issues bonds with a face value of $100 million. If the interest rate is 4.875 percent, the interest on this bond issue is $4,875,000 ($100 million $\times$ 0.04875 = $4,875,000) each year until the bonds are repaid. In addition, the American Express corporate bonds must all be redeemed for their face value ($100 million) at maturity. If the corporation defaults on (does not pay) either interest payments or repayment of the bond at maturity, owners of bonds can force the firm into bankruptcy and their claims take precedence over the claims of both common and preferred stockholders.

A corporation may use one of three methods to ensure that it has sufficient funds available to redeem a bond issue. First, it can issue the bonds as **serial bonds**, which are bonds of a single issue that mature on different dates. For example, a company may use a 25-year $50 million bond issue to finance its expansion. None of the bonds mature during the first 15 years. Thereafter, 10 percent of the bonds mature each year until all the bonds are retired at the end of the 25th year. Second, the corporation can establish a sinking fund. A **sinking fund** is a sum of money to which deposits are made each year for the purpose of redeeming a bond issue. When Union Pacific Corporation sold a $275 million bond issue, the company agreed to contribute to a sinking fund until the bond's maturity in the year 2025.[15] Third, a corporation can pay off an old bond issue by selling new bonds. Although this may appear to perpetuate the corporation's long-term debt, a number of utility companies and railroads use this repayment method.

A corporation that issues bonds must also appoint a **trustee**, an individual or an independent firm that acts as the bond owner's representative. A trustee's duties are handled most often by a commercial bank or other large financial institution. The corporation must report to the trustee periodically regarding its ability to make interest payments and eventually redeem the bonds. In turn, the trustee transmits this information to the bond owners, along with its own evaluation of the corporation's ability to pay.

Cost Comparisons

Table 19.4 compares some of the methods that can be used to obtain long-term equity *and* debt financing. Although the initial flotation cost of issuing stock is high, selling common stock is generally a popular option for most financial managers. Once the stock is sold and upfront costs are paid, the *ongoing* costs of using stock to finance a business are low. The type of long-term financing that generally has the highest *ongoing* costs is a long-term loan (debt).

To a great extent, firms are financed through the investments of individuals—money that people have deposited in banks or have used to purchase stocks, mutual funds, and bonds. In Chapter 20, we look at how securities markets help people invest their money in business.

bond indenture a legal document that details all the conditions relating to a bond issue

serial bonds bonds of a single issue that mature on different dates

sinking fund a sum of money to which deposits are made each year for the purpose of redeeming a bond issue

trustee an individual or an independent firm that acts as a bond owner's representative

TABLE 19.4   Comparison of Long-Term Financing Methods

Type of Financing	Repayment	Repayment Period	Cost/Dividends Interest	Businesses That May Use It
Equity				
Common stock	No	None	High initial cost; low ongoing costs because dividends not required	All corporations that sell stock to investors
Preferred stock	No	None	Dividends not required but must be paid before common stockholders receive any dividends	Large corporations that have an established investor base of common stockholders
Debt				
Long-term loan	Yes	Usually 3–7 years	Interest rates between 3.25 and 12 percent depending on economic conditions and the financial stability of the company requesting the loan	All firms that can meet the lender's repayment and collateral requirements
Corporate bond	Yes	Usually 10–30 years	Interest rates between 3 and 9 percent depending on the financial stability of the company issuing the bonds and economic conditions	Large corporations that are financially healthy

return to Inside BUSINESS

The J. M. Smucker Company

More than a century after Jerome Monroe Smucker founded his company, Smucker family members are still making smart financial decisions. Going public in 1959 provided money for growth through investments in product development and other activities. More recently, the firm issued corporate bonds during periods when interest rates were low, keeping long-term borrowing costs low while building Smucker's cash position so that it could make timely acquisitions whenever it spotted good opportunities.

Looking ahead to expansion in China, Smucker has made an equity investment in a leading local oatmeal company. What Smucker learns from this company's knowledge of the market will pave the way for higher sales of its North American products in Asia, as well as the possibility of developing and manufacturing new foods specifically for China.

Questions

1. Why would Smucker prefer to issue more than $1 billion in bonds over 18 months, rather than issuing common or preferred stock?
2. What do you think of Smucker's deal to spread $50 million in payments to Sara Lee over 10 years after paying $350 up front for the liquid coffee concentrate business? Explain your answer.

Understand why financial management is important in today's uncertain economy.

The last few years have been especially difficult for financial managers. Financial managers have had to deal with a downturn in sales and profits. In some cases, banks stopped making loans even to companies that had always been able to borrow money. And the number of companies selling stock for the first time to the general public decreased. The worst-case scenario: There was an increase in the number of businesses that filed for bankruptcy during the crisis. Fortunately, there were many more business firms that were able to weather the economic storm and keep operating because of their ability to manage their finances.

Financial management consists of all activities concerned with obtaining money and using it effectively. Financial management can be viewed as a two-sided problem. On one side, the uses of funds often dictate the type or types of financing needed by a business. On the other side, the activities a business can undertake are determined by the types of financing available. Financial managers must ensure that funds are available when needed, that they are obtained at the lowest possible cost, and that they are used as efficiently as possible. In the wake of the economic crisis, the Dodd–Frank Wall Street Reform and Consumer Protection Act was signed into law. And today, there is an ongoing debate if more regulations are needed. Still, there are a number of rewarding jobs in finance for qualified job applicants.

 Identify a firm's short- and long-term financial needs.

Short-term financing is money that will be used for one year or less. There are many short-term needs, but cash flow, speculative production, and inventory are three for which financing is often required. Long-term financing is money that will be used for more than one year. Such financing may be required for a business start-up, for a merger or an acquisition, for new product development, for long-term marketing activities, for replacement of equipment, or for expansion of facilities. According to financial experts, business firms will find it more difficult to raise both short- and long-term financing in the future because of increased regulations and more cautious lenders. Financial managers must also consider the risk–return ratio when making financial decisions. The risk–return ratio is based on the principle that a high-risk decision should generate higher financial returns for a business. On the other hand, more conservative decisions generate lesser returns.

 Summarize the process of planning for financial management.

A financial plan begins with an organization's goals and objectives. Next, a firm's goals and objectives are "translated" into departmental budgets that detail expected income and expenses. From these budgets, which may be combined into an overall cash budget, the financial manager determines what funding will be needed and where it may be obtained. Whereas departmental and cash budgets emphasize short-term financing needs, a capital budget can be used to estimate a firm's expenditures for major assets and its long-term financing needs. The four principal sources of financing are sales revenues, equity capital, debt capital, and proceeds from the sale of assets. Once the needed funds have been obtained, the financial manager is responsible for monitoring and evaluating the firm's financial activities.

 Describe the advantages and disadvantages of different methods of short-term debt financing.

Most short-term financing is unsecured; that is, no collateral is required. Sources of unsecured short-term financing include trade credit, promissory notes issued to suppliers, unsecured bank loans, and commercial paper. Sources of secured short-term financing include loans secured by inventory and accounts receivable. A firm may also sell its receivables to factors. Trade credit is the least-expensive source of short-term financing. The cost of financing through other sources generally depends on the source and on the credit rating of the firm that requires the financing. Factoring is generally the most expensive approach.

⑤ Evaluate the advantages and disadvantages of equity financing.

A corporation can raise equity capital by selling either common or preferred stock. The first time a corporation sells stock to the general public is referred to as an initial public offering (IPO). With an IPO, the stock is sold in the primary market. Once sold in the primary market, investors buy and sell stock in the secondary market. Usually, secondary market transactions are completed through a securities exchange or the over-the-counter market. Common stock is voting stock; holders of common stock elect the corporation's directors and often must approve changes to the corporate charter. Holders of preferred stock must be paid dividends before holders of common stock are paid any dividends. Another source of equity funding is retained earnings, which is the portion of a business's profits *not* distributed to stockholders. Venture capital—money invested in small (and sometimes struggling) firms that have the potential to become very successful—is yet another source of equity funding. Finally, a private placement can be used to sell stocks and other corporate securities.

Evaluate the advantages and disadvantages of long-term debt financing.

For a small business, debt financing is generally limited to loans. Large corporations have the additional option of issuing corporate bonds. Regardless of whether the business is small or large, it can take advantage of financial leverage. Financial leverage is the use of borrowed funds to increase the return on owners' equity. The rate of interest for long-term loans usually depends on the financial status of the borrower, the reason for borrowing, and the kind of collateral pledged to back up the loan. Long-term business loans are normally repaid in 3 to 7 years but can be as long as 15 to 20 years.

Money realized from the sale of corporate bonds must be repaid when the bonds mature. In addition, the corporation must pay interest on that money from the time the bonds are sold until maturity. The interest rate the corporation must pay often depends on the financial health of the firm issuing bonds. Maturity dates for bonds generally range from 10 to 30 years after the date of issue. Three types of bonds—debentures, mortgage bonds, and convertible bonds—are sold to raise debt capital. When comparing the cost of equity and debt long-term financing, the ongoing costs of using stock (equity) to finance a business are low. The most expensive is a long-term loan (debt).

KEY TERMS

You should now be able to define and give an example relevant to each of the following terms:

financial management (552)
chief financial officer (CFO) (553)
short-term financing (554)
cash flow (555)
speculative production (555)
long-term financing (556)
risk–return ratio (556)
financial plan (556)
budget (557)
cash budget (557)

zero-base budgeting (558)
capital budget (558)
equity capital (558)
debt capital (558)
unsecured financing (559)
trade credit (560)
promissory note (560)
prime interest rate (560)
factor (562)
initial public offering (IPO) (563)

primary market (564)
investment banking firm (564)
secondary market (565)
securities exchange (565)
over-the-counter (OTC) market (565)
common stock (566)
preferred stock (566)
retained earnings (566)
private placement (567)
financial leverage (568)

term-loan agreement (569)
corporate bond (569)
maturity date (570)
registered bond (570)
debenture bond (570)
mortgage bond (570)
convertible bond (570)
bond indenture (571)
serial bonds (571)
sinking fund (571)
trustee (571)

REVIEW QUESTIONS

1. For a business firm, what type of activities does financial management involve?
2. How does short-term financing differ from long-term financing? Give two business uses for each type of financing.
3. In your own words, describe the risk–return ratio.
4. What is the function of a cash budget? A capital budget?
5. What is zero-base budgeting? How does it differ from the traditional concept of budgeting?
6. What are four general sources of funds?
7. How does a financial manager monitor and evaluate a firm's financing?
8. How important is trade credit as a source of short-term financing?
9. Why would a supplier require a customer to sign a promissory note?

10. What is the prime rate? Who gets the prime rate?
11. Explain how factoring works. Of what benefit is factoring to a firm that sells its receivables?
12. What are the advantages of financing through the sale of stock?
13. From a corporation's point of view, how does preferred stock differ from common stock?
14. Where do a corporation's retained earnings come from? What are the advantages of this type of financing?
15. For a corporation, what are the advantages of corporate bonds over long-term loans?
16. Describe the three methods used to ensure that funds are available to redeem corporate bonds at maturity.

1. During the recent economic crisis, many financial managers and corporate officers have been criticized for (a) poor decisions, (b) lack of ethical behavior, (c) large salaries, (d) lucrative severance packages worth millions of dollars, and (e) extravagant lifestyles. Is this criticism justified? Justify your opinion.
2. If you were the financial manager of Stars and Stripes Clothing, what would you do with the excess cash that the firm expects in the second and fourth quarters? (See Figure 19.4.)
3. Develop a *personal* cash budget for the next six months. Explain what you would do if there are budget shortfalls or excess cash amounts at the end of any month during the six-month period.
4. Why would a lender offer unsecured short-term loans when it could demand collateral?
5. How can a small-business owner or corporate manager use financial leverage to improve the firm's profits and return on owners' equity?
6. In what circumstances might a large corporation sell stock rather than bonds to obtain long-term financing? In what circumstances would it sell bonds rather than stock?

Video Case 19.1

Financial Planning Equals Profits for Nederlander Concerts

Nederlander Concerts is in the business of booking, promoting, and producing live music shows in the western United States. The company presents artists ranging from James Taylor to Flogging Molly, Bruce Springsteen, Bonnie Raitt, and the Allman Brothers Band. But, says CEO Adam Friedman, "We're not trying to be necessarily a national player or an international player. We seek out opportunities that fit within and leverage our existing portfolio of small- to mid-size venues. . . . It's one of the few remaining family-run entertainment enterprises worldwide. . . . What this means for us on a day-to-day basis is that we can focus on running the business. We're not as guided by Wall Street, we don't have the same constraints, we don't have the same reporting responsibilities, and it allows us to focus on . . . our business strategy for development."

Of course, being a privately owned company and not needing to respond to shareholders (Wall Street) doesn't mean that Nederlander has *no* reporting responsibilities. As the CEO explains, "We assess at the beginning of the year not only concert revenue and expenses but also special event revenue." Nederlander owns some theaters, amphitheaters, and arenas, and it sometimes rents space for concerts and events along the West Coast. "When we rent the facilities to, for example, movie premieres here in Los Angeles, what kind of revenue are we going to see? What kind of expenses are attended to generating that revenue? What's our fixed overhead for the year? Who's on the payroll, whether full-time, or part-time, or seasonal, and how much does it cost us to run the business on a day-to-day basis in order to secure those revenues and pay those expenses? That's wrapped up into an annual budget at the beginning of every year, which is kind of a guideline for me to know how we achieve growth. It also allows me to communicate to our owners what our growth orientation is for that given year. . . . Every event has its own profit and loss statement . . . which is a mini version of that annual plan," says the CEO.

In addition to daily, weekly, and quarterly event reports, Nederlander's financial team generates daily and weekly reports of ticket sales. Monthly reports on company-wide performance feed into quarterly and annual reports. Each annual report is compared to that year's budget. The finance department tallies hundreds of transactions in order to arrive at some of these annual numbers, which are reported to the company's owners to ensure that the company is running as profitably as it can be.

Nederlander's managers say growth in the concert industry must be measured in the long term because the business is cyclical and the cost of real estate is so high that short-term profit is hard to generate. Still, the company is in a strong financial position (it is part of a profitable global theater-ownership company called the Nederlander Organization), so it can afford to fund its own growth and expansion, or it can borrow on favorable terms. "We're very fortunate to have an ownership that is very well capitalized with over 80 years in the business," says the CEO. "Our balance sheet is so strong that we have the ability to tap into debt financing if it makes the most sense. . . . or [use] the corporate treasury. . . . If it makes more sense to borrow the money, we will, and we're typically able to do that on very favorable rates because of very long-term banking relationships."

It can be thrilling to meet some of the artists the company books. "But at the end of the day, it's a business," the CEO points out. "If we're not successful in growing our revenue and managing our expense, ultimately we won't be profitable, and our ownership will not be happy with those results."[16]

Questions

1. Here's what Nederlander's chief operating officer has to say about its business model: "A show has a short lifetime. You go and sell two months out, and the tickets have no value on any day but the day of the show. So it's a very interesting model in that sense." How do you think the short life of the company's products affects its financial planning?
2. The company uses its own arenas and theaters about 90 percent of the time. What are some of the possible advantages and disadvantages of owning its own venues?
3. Why would Nederlander choose to sometimes borrow funds for expansion if it has capital of its own?

Growth has been on the menu ever since Bill Darden opened his first Red Lobster restaurant in Florida in 1968. The combination of fresh seafood and casual dining caught on quickly—and quickly caught the eye of General Mills, which bought the fast-growing company in 1970. In 1995, General Mills renamed the company after its founder and spun it off in a public offering. Once it went public, Darden Restaurants used the proceeds to chart a new financial path to long-term growth.

Today, Darden employs 180,000 people and serves more than 400 million meals each year across North America in 1,900 casual, full-service restaurants. The company's seven restaurant brands are: Red Lobster (seafood), Olive Garden (Italian menu), LongHorn Steakhouse (Western-theme steaks and more), The Capital Grille (premium steak house), Bahama Breeze (Caribbean-theme casual dining), Seasons 52 (fresh-grilled foods), and Eddie V's (prime seafood and steaks). In all, Darden's yearly revenue tops $7.5 billion.

Healthy cash flow is definitely on the menu. The average Capital Grille unit rings up $6.5 million in annual sales, the average Olive Garden rings up $4.8 million in annual sales, the average Red Lobster rings up $3.6 million, and the average LongHorn Steakhouse rings up $2.9 million. With the cash generated from restaurant revenue, Darden has been reinvesting in its businesses by opening new units, remodeling existing units, and greening its restaurants with eco-friendly materials and energy-saving touches. Because of its size, it can take advantage of economies of scale in buying foods and beverages from global sources, which in turn helps keep costs under control and supports good profit margins.

Over the years, the company has fueled its continued expansion with a combination of debt and equity. The company can draw on a revolving credit agreement of almost $500 million, which helps smooth out the financial bumps of its seasonal business. Typically, Darden's revenue spikes in the spring and descends to a low point in the fall, although sales are definitely affected by weather conditions, economic circumstances, holidays, and other uncontrollable elements. Having revolving credit in place provides the flexibility to borrow if and when needed.

Darden has also raised money by issuing corporate bonds, some of which mature in 5 years, some in 10 years, some in 20 years, and some with even longer maturities. Twice a year, the company pays interest to its bondholders. On the equity side, Darden's common stock trades on the New York Stock Exchange, and it pays cash dividends to its shareholders. Its

cash flow has been so strong, in fact, that Darden increased its dividend not long ago and has focused on paying down debt even as it invests in business.

Looking ahead, Darden expects to continue its growth spurt, despite an unpredictable economy and intense competition from big names in fast food and casual dining. It avoided the heavy, broad-based discounting that some chains used to attract customers during the recent economic crisis. Instead, it used occasional, selective price promotions to heighten its message of affordability. The company's financial stability means that it has money available for making acquisitions, building new restaurants, developing new menu items, training new staff members, and launching new advertising campaigns.

Within the past decade, Darden has used its financial strength to buy and expand the Capital Grill and LongHorn Steakhouse restaurant chains. And Darden acquired the Eddie V's and Wildfish Seafood Grill restaurant chain in 2011. It is also responding to increased consumer interest in healthy dining by opening more of its Seasons 52 restaurants, which feature only steamed, baked, or grilled dishes. As its name implies, Seasons 52 adds new menu items regularly, depending on what's in season. The ever-changing menu brings customers back again and again to try seasonal specialties and enjoy old favorites.

Sometimes Darden closes underperforming units or sells entire chains so that it can put its money and management attention into other growth opportunities. A few years ago, Darden divested its Smokey Bones Barbecue & Grill chain after determining that this restaurant concept did not have the potential for nationwide expansion and profit potential that Darden required. What will Darden do next in its quest for profitable, long-term growth?[17]

Questions

1. Darden is spending heavily to upgrade the interior of many of its Red Lobster and LongHorn Steakhouse restaurants. How would you suggest that the company measure the financial results of this remodeling program?

2. Why would Darden issue corporate bonds with maturities of 5, 10, 20 years or even longer maturities?

3. If Darden needs cash to remodel existing restaurants and open new restaurants, as well as to pay down debt, why would it increase its cash dividend that is paid to its stockholders?

① SOCIAL MEDIA EXERCISE

Turbo Tax is probably one of the best-known tax preparation services in the world. One of the reasons for its popularity is that it provides tax software that people really need. Another reason for its popularity is the company's use of social media through various platforms that include building an online community of users, using Twitter, and developing a YouTube channel. Each video on the TurboTax channel illustrates how a company can use social media to provide valuable information to customers. You can check out Turbo Tax videos at www.youtube.com/user/TurboTax/videos.

1. Visit the YouTube channel for Turbo Tax (www.youtube.com/user/TurboTax/videos). Do you think social media is an effective method of obtaining the tax information you might need to prepare your taxes?
2. Can you think of other companies that could use videos on a YouTube channel to share information that their customers could use?

② JOURNALING FOR SUCCESS

Because many people spend more than they make on a regular basis, they often use credit cards to make routine daily purchases. As a result, the amount they owe on credit cards increases each month and there is no money left to begin a savings or investment program. This exercise will help you to understand (1) how you manage your credit cards and (2) what steps you can take to improve your personal finances.

Assignment

1. How many credit cards do you have?
2. Based on the information on your monthly credit card statements, what types of credit card purchases do you make?
3. Do you pay your balance in full each month or make minimum payments on your credit cards?
4. Most experts recommend that you have one or two credit cards that you use only if you are in an emergency situation. The experts also recommend that you avoid using credit cards to make inexpensive purchases on a daily basis. Finally, the experts recommend that you pay your balance in full each month.
5. Based on the preceding information, what steps can you take to better manage your personal finances?

③ DEVELOPING CRITICAL-THINKING SKILLS

Financial management involves preparing a plan for obtaining and using the money needed to accomplish a firm's goals and objectives. To accomplish your own goals and objectives, you should prepare a *personal* financial plan. You must determine what is important in your life and what you want to accomplish, budget the amount of money required to obtain your goals, and identify sources for acquiring the funds. You should monitor and evaluate the results regularly and make changes when necessary.

Assignment

1. Using the three steps shown in Figure 19.3, prepare a personal financial plan.
2. Prepare a three-column table to display your plan.
   a. In column 1, list at least two goals or objectives under each of the following areas: Financial (savings, investments, retirement), Education (training, degrees, certificates), Career (position, industry, location), and Family (children, home, education, trips, entertainment).
   b. In column 2, list the amount of money it will take to accomplish your goals or objectives.
   c. In column 3, identify the sources of funds for each goal or objective.
3. Describe what you learned from doing this exercise in a comments section at the bottom of the table.

④ BUILDING TEAM SKILLS

Suppose that for the past three years you have been repairing lawn mowers in your garage. Your business has grown steadily, and you recently hired two part-time workers. Your garage is no longer adequate for your business; it is also in violation of the city code, and you have already been fined for noncompliance. You have decided that it is time to find another location for your shop and that it also would be a good time to expand your business. If the business continues to grow in the new location, you plan to hire a full-time employee to repair small appliances. You are concerned, however, about how you will get the money to move your shop and get it established in a new location.

Assignment

1. With all class members participating, use brainstorming to identify the following:
   a. The funds you will need to accomplish your business goals
   b. The sources of short-term financing available to you
   c. Problems that might prevent you from getting a short-term loan
   d. How you will repay the money if you get a loan
2. Have a classmate write the ideas on the board.
3. Discuss how you can overcome any problems that might hamper your current chances of getting a loan and how your business can improve its chances of securing short-term loans in the future.
4. Summarize what you learned from participating in this exercise.

⑤ RESEARCHING DIFFERENT CAREERS

Financial managers are responsible for determining the best way to raise funds, for ensuring that the funds are used to accomplish their firm's goals and objectives, and for developing and implementing their firm's financial plan. Their decisions have a direct impact on the firm's level of success.

Assignment

1. Investigate the job of financial manager by searching the library or Internet, by interviewing a financial manager, or both.

2. Find answers to the following questions:
   a. What skills do financial managers need?
   b. How much education is required?
   c. What is the starting salary? Top salary?
   d. What will the job of financial manager be like in the future?
   e. What opportunities are available?
   f. What types of firms are most likely to hire financial managers? What is the employment potential?

3. Prepare a report on your findings.

ENDNOTES

1. Sources: Based on information from the J. M. Smucker Co. Web site at www .smucker.com, accessed April 15, 2012; Betty Lin-Fisher, "Smucker Spreads into China Market," *Akron Beacon Journal Online*, March 26, 2012, www.ohio.com; "Smucker Completes Deal for Sara Lee Coffee Unit," *Columbus Business First (Ohio)*, January 4, 2012, www.bizjournals.com/Columbus/news; Cecile Vannucci, "J.M. Smucker Completes Acquisition of Rowland Coffee," *Bloomberg News*, May 17, 2011, www.bloomberg.com; Robert Schoenberger, "J.M. Smucker to Buy Sara Lee's Coffee and Tea Business for $400 Million," *Cleveland Plain Dealer*, October 24, 2011, www.cleveland.com; Joseph Ciolli, "Smucker Plans Biggest Bond Offering to Help Finance Acquisitions," *Akron Beacon Journal Online*, October 13, 2011, www.ohio.com.

2. Maria Bartiromo, "BlackRock's Peter Fisher on When the Pan Will End," the *BusinessWeek* Web site, accessed October 8, 2008.

3. The U.S. Bureau of Labor Statistics at http://bls.gov, accessed February 29, 2012.

4. The 3M Corporation Web site at www.3m.com, accessed February 24, 2012.

5. The McDonald's Corporate Web site at www.aboutmcdonalds.com, accessed February 27, 2012.

6. Lubrizol Corporate Web site at www.lubrizol.com, accessed March14, 2011.

7. Tom Randall, "Pfizer Sells Capsugel Pill Unit to KKR for $2.4 Billion," the Bloomberg Web site at wwwbloomberg.com, accessed April 4, 2011.

8. "CIT, GE Capital Add to Factoring Businesses," the Reuters Web site at www.reuters .com, accessed March 29, 2010.

9. Julianne Pepitone, "Groupon IPO Opens at $28," the Fidelity.com Web site at https://fidelity.com/news, accessed November 4, 2011.

10. Ari Levy and Lee Spears, "LinkedIn Retains Most Gains Second Day After Surging in Initial Offering," the Bloomberg Web site at www.bloomberg.com, accessed May 20, 2011.

11. Ginger Crist, "Sun Coke Energy IPO Shares Soar," the Dayton Business Journal Web site at www.bizjournals.com, accessed July 21, 2011.

12. "The GE 2011 Annual Report," the General Electric Web site at www.ge.com, accessed August 20, 2012.

13. Russ Garland, "Zynga Inc: Venture Capital Investment Up Despite Fund-Raising Constraints," the 4-Traders.com Web site at www.4-traders.com, accessed January 20, 2012.

14. The Advanced Micro Devices corporate Web site at www.amd.com, accessed February 25, 2012.

15. *Mergent Transportation Manual* (New York: Mergent, Inc., 2009), 64.

16. Based on information from the company Web site www.nederlanderconcerts. com, accessed February 29, 2012; Nederlander Organization company overview, *BusinessWeek*, www.businessweek.com, accessed August 20, 2010; Hannah Heineman, "Moving Forward on Capital Improvement Projects," *Santa Monica Mirror*, July 28, 2010, www.smmirror.com; Steve Knopper, "Tour Biz Strong in Weak Economy," *Rolling Stone*, October 2, 2008, 11–12; Ray Waddell, "Nederlander/Viejas Deal Offers Touring Opportunities," *Billboard*, January 10, 2008, www.billboard .com; interviews with Nederlander employees and the video "Financial Planning and Budgets Equal Profits for Nederlander Concerts."

17. Based on information from the company Web site at www.darden.com, accessed February 29, 2012; Jason Daley, "The 500 Calorie Smack Down," *Entrepreneur*, May 2010, 85ff; Jim Johnson, "Darden Plans Eco Eateries," *Waste & Recycling News*, March 29, 2010, 6; Ron Ruggless, "Darden Says No to Discounting," *Nation's Restaurant News*, March 25, 2010, www.nrn.com; Jonathan Birchall, "Darden Claws Back Custom of US Diners," *Financial Times*, March 25, 2010, 18; "Darden 3Q Profit Rises 25 Percent," *BusinessWeek*, March 23, 2010, www.businessweek.com; Michael Sanson, "Darden Restaurants," *Restaurant Hospitality*, August 2009, 28.

Understanding Personal Finances and Investments

20

Once you complete this chapter, you will be able to:

1 Explain why you should manage your personal finances and develop a personal investment program.

2 Describe how the factors of safety, risk, income, growth, and liquidity affect your investment program.

3 Recognize how you can reduce investment risk and increase investment returns.

4 Explain the reasons people choose conservative investments including bank accounts and bonds.

5 Identify the advantages and disadvantages of stocks, mutual funds, real estate, and more speculative investments.

6 Use financial information to evaluate investment alternatives.

7 Understand how different investments are bought and sold.

The Vanguard Group Thinks Low-Cost and High-Tech

The Vanguard Group helps investors make the most of their money by offering low-cost investments and high-tech access. From its early days, the company focused not on individual stocks or bonds but on selling shares in mutual funds, pools of money invested in a select group of stocks or bonds. Vanguard was a pioneer in establishing mutual funds tied to a specific group of common stocks or bonds in a particular financial index. Before Vanguard launched its Vanguard 500 Index Fund, individual investors had no way to buy this type of indexed mutual fund directly from an investment company. Today, Vanguard offers hundreds of mutual funds and many other securities for every type of investor and every investment goal, short- and long-term.

Because the Vanguard Group is owned by the different funds it manages, it has a long tradition of operating mutual funds "at cost." As a result, investors pay lower mutual fund fees, and more of their money remains invested to earn returns year after year. Exactly how low is low? By Vanguard's calculations, its average expense ratio is, on average, one-fifth of the industry average. To dramatize this difference, Vanguard recently sent an "At-Cost Café" food truck on tour selling coffee at 28 cents per cup—just one-fifth of the usual price. "The concept of at-cost investing can be difficult to explain," says a Vanguard spokesperson, "so we are trying to help investors 'experience' it through something tangible, such as a routine daily purchase like coffee."

Vanguard also uses the latest technology to let customers check on their accounts and investigate new investment possibilities at any hour, from any place. In addition to its Web site, which offers detailed financial information, online trading, and much more, the company provides downloadable apps for cell phones and tablet computers. Whether investors are just starting out or have a lot of investing experience, they can use the technology of their choice to see their recent transactions, analyze investment performance, buy or sell securities, read Vanguard's research reports, subscribe to its electronic newsletter, and watch its educational videos—all at the touch of a finger or the click of a mouse.[1]

As the saying goes, "I've been rich and I've been poor, but believe me, rich is better." Yet, just dreaming of being rich does not make it happen. Although being rich does not guarantee happiness, managing your personal finances and beginning an investment program are both worthy goals. Firms such as Vanguard Group—the company profiled in the Inside Business feature for this chapter—offer an array of services to help people manage their personal finances, research investments, and buy and sell stocks, bonds, mutual funds, and other securities. Nevertheless, you must be willing to invest the time and effort required to manage your personal finances and become a good investor. Furthermore, do not underestimate how important you are when it comes to managing your money. No one is going to make you manage your money. No one is going to make you save the money you need to fund an investment program. These are your decisions—important decisions that literally can change your life.

Many people ask the question: Why begin an investment program now? To answer that question, you must understand that personal finance experts agree that the best investment program is one that stresses long-term growth over a 20- to 40-year period. As you will see later in this chapter, the dollar value of your investments may decrease over a short time period, but historically the value of quality securities has usually increased over a long time period.

A second compelling reason to start an investment program is that the sooner you start an investment program, the more time your investments have to work for you. So why do people wait to begin investing? In most cases, there are two reasons. First, they do not have the money needed to fund an investment program. However, once you begin managing your personal finances and get your spending under control, you will be able to save the money needed to fund an investment program. The second reason people do not begin investing is because they do not know anything about investing. Again, this chapter provides the basics to get you started.

We begin this chapter by examining everyday money management activities and outlining the reasons for developing a personal investment plan. Next we discuss important factors to consider when choosing investments and describe both traditional and high-risk (or speculative) investments. Then, we explain how to use information to evaluate potential investments. Finally, we examine the methods used to buy and sell investments.

It is time! Take the first step, and begin managing your personal finances.

MANAGING YOUR PERSONAL FINANCES

 Explain why you should manage your personal finances and develop a personal investment program.

Although it would be nice if you could accumulate wealth magically, it is not magic. Most people begin by making sure that their "financial house" is in order. In this section, we examine several steps for effective money management that will help you to prepare for an investment program.

Step 1: Tracking Your Income, Expenses, Assets, and Liabilities

Many personal finance experts recommend that you begin the process of managing your money by determining your current financial condition. Often the first step is to construct a personal income statement and balance sheet. (*Note*: Both personal income statements and balance sheets were examined in more detail in Chapter 17.) A *personal income statement* lists your income and your expenses for a specific period of time—usually a month. By subtracting expenses from income, you can determine if you have a surplus or a deficit at the end of the time period. Surplus funds can be used for savings, investing, or for any purpose that you feel is important. On the other hand, if you have a deficit, you must take actions to reduce spending and pay down any debts you may have that will keep you from starting an investment program.

To get another picture of your current financial condition, you should construct a personal balance sheet. A *personal balance sheet* lists your assets and liabilities on a specific date. By subtracting your total liabilities from your total assets, you can determine your net worth. For an individual, **net worth** is the difference between the value of your total assets and your total liabilities. Over time, the goal is to increase the value of your assets (items of value that you own) and decrease liabilities (your debts).

Based on the information contained in these two statements, you can determine your current financial condition and where you spend your money. You can also take the next step: Construct a personal budget.

Step 2: Developing a Budget that Works

A **personal budget** is a specific plan for spending your income. You begin by estimating your income for a specific period—for example, next month. For most people, their major source of income is their salary. The second step is to list expenses for the same time period. Typical expenses include savings and investments, housing, food, transportation, entertainment, and so on. For most people, this is the area where you can make choices and increase or decrease the amount spent on different items listed in your budget. For example, you may decide to reduce the dollar amount spent on entertainment to increase the amount for savings. Above all, it is important to balance

net worth the difference between the value of your total assets and your total liabilities

personal budget a specific plan for spending your income your budget so that your income is equal to the money you spend, save, or invest each month. For help managing your money and constructing a realistic budget, you may want to visit the Mint.com Web site (www.mint.com), the Motley Fool Web site (www.fool.com), or similar sites on the Internet. Both of these Web sites provide free help and advice that can help you take the necessary steps to improve your personal finances.

After you have constructed your personal budget, you will need to compare the amounts included in your budget with your actual income and expenses. The goal is that the estimated income and expenses are correct and that you have a surplus at the end of the budgeting period. If income is less than anticipated or expenses are more than budgeted, then you will need to take corrective actions to get your budget back on track. Often one change will affect other areas of your budget as well. An increase in your monthly rent payment, for instance, may mean that you have to reduce the amount spent on entertainment to balance your budget. *Caution*: Avoid the temptation to spend more than you make by using credit cards or borrowing money.

Step 3: Managing Credit Card Debt

Unfortunately, many individuals spend more than they make. They purchase items on credit and then make monthly payments and pay finance charges ranging from 10 to 21 percent or more. It makes no sense to start an investment program until payments for credit card and installment purchases, along with the accompanying finance charges, are reduced or eliminated.

Although all cardholders have reasons for using their credit cards, the important point to remember is that it is *very easy* to get in trouble by using your credit cards. Watch for the following five warning signs.

1. Don't fall behind on payments. One of the first warning signs is the inability to pay your entire balance each month.
2. Do not use your credit cards to pay for many small purchases during the month. This can often lead to a "real surprise" when you open your credit card statement at the end of the month.
3. Do not use the cash advance provision that accompanies most credit cards. The reason is simple: The interest rate is usually higher for cash advances.
4. Think about the number of cards you really need. Most experts recommend that an individual have one or two cards and use these cards for emergencies.
5. Get help if you think you are in trouble. Organizations like Consumer Credit Counseling Service (www.cccs.net) or the National Foundation for Credit Counseling (www.nfcc.org) can often help you work out a plan to pay off credit card debt.

By reducing or eliminating credit purchases, eventually the amount of cash remaining after the bills are paid will increase and can be used to start a savings and investment program that will help you obtain your investment goals.

Investment Goals

Personal investment is the use of your personal funds to earn a financial return. Thus, in the most general sense, the goal of investing is to earn money with money. However, such a goal is completely useless for the individual because it is so vague and so easily attained.

In reality, an investment goal must be specific and measurable. It must be tailored to you so that it takes into account your particular financial needs. It must also be oriented toward the future because investing is usually a long-term undertaking. By investing small amounts of money each year over a 20- to 40-year period, you can accumulate money for emergencies and retirement. In addition, if you choose quality investments, the value of your investments will grow over a long period of time. Finally, an investment goal must be realistic in terms of current economic conditions and available investment opportunities.

Some financial planners suggest that investment goals should be stated in terms of money: "By January 1, 2022, I will have total assets of $80,000." Others believe that

personal investment the use of your personal funds to earn a financial return people are more motivated to work toward goals that are stated in terms of the particular things they desire: "By May 1, 2024, I will have accumulated enough money so that I can take a year off from work to travel around the world." Like the goals themselves, the way they are stated depends on you. The following questions can be helpful in establishing valid investment goals:

1. What financial goals do you want to achieve?
2. How much money will you need, and when?
3. What will you use the money for?
4. Is it reasonable to assume that you can obtain the amount of money you will need to meet your investment goals?
5. Do you expect your personal situation to change in a way that will affect your investment goals?
6. What economic conditions could alter your investment goals?
7. Are you willing to make the necessary sacrifices to ensure that your investment goals are met?

Keep in mind the investment goals you develop may be affected by your career choice. If you choose a career that provides above-average financial rewards, you can develop more challenging investment goals. If you choose a career that provides average or below-average financial rewards, it is still possible to develop an investment program by carefully managing your personal finances. Simply put: You must control spending and manage debt regardless of how much money you make.

What are your personal, professional, and investment goals? Just like a successful business, you should be looking ahead to what you want to achieve in the next few years and writing down specific goals for yourself. If one goal is to start an investment program, for example, it will help to think about how much you'll need to start investing and how much you will want to accumulate by a specific date.

A Personal Investment Program

Once you have formulated specific goals and have some money to invest, investment planning is similar to planning for a business. It begins with the evaluation of different investment opportunities—including the potential return and risk involved in each. At the very least, this process requires some careful study and maybe some expert advice. Investors should beware of people who call themselves "financial planners" but who are in reality nothing more than salespersons for various financial investments, tax shelters, or insurance plans.

A true **financial planner** has had at least two years of training in investments, insurance, taxation, retirement planning, and estate planning and has passed a rigorous examination. As evidence of training and successful completion of the qualifying examination, the Certified Financial Planner (CFP) Board of Standards (www.cfp.net) in Washington, D.C., allows individuals to use the designation CFP. Similarly, the American College (www.theamericancollege.edu) in Bryn Mawr, Pennsylvania, allows individuals who have completed the necessary requirements to use the designation Chartered Financial Consultant (ChFC). Most CFPs and ChFCs do not sell a particular investment product or receive commissions for their investment recommendations. Instead, they charge consulting fees that range from $100 to $250 an hour.

Many financial planners suggest that you accumulate an "emergency fund"—a certain amount of money that can be obtained quickly in case of immediate need—before beginning an investment program. The amount of money that should be salted away in a savings account varies from person to person. Most financial planners agree that an amount equal to at least three months' living expenses is reasonable. However, you may want to increase your emergency fund in anticipation of a crisis.

financial planner an individual who has had at least two years of training in investments, insurance, taxation, retirement planning, and estate planning and has passed a rigorous examination

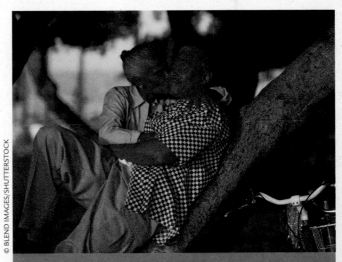

Managing your personal finances can improve a relationship! Often money problems can cause relationships to sour and can even lead to divorce for some couples. On the other hand, managing your personal finances can lead to financial stability, peace of mind, and a more stable personal relationship.

TABLE 20.1	Suggestions to Help You Accumulate the Money Needed to Fund an Investment Program

1. *Pay yourself first.* Many financial experts recommend that you (1) pay your monthly bills, (2) save a reasonable amount of money, and (3) use whatever money is left over for personal expenses.

2. *Take advantage of employer-sponsored retirement programs.* Many employers will match part or all of the contributions you make to a 401(k) or 403(b) retirement account.

3. *Participate in an elective savings program.* Elect to have money withheld from your paycheck each payday and automatically deposited in a savings or investment account.

4. *Make a special savings effort one or two months each year.* By cutting back to the basics, you can obtain money for investment purposes.

5. *Take advantage of gifts, inheritances, and windfalls.* During your lifetime, you likely will receive gifts, inheritances, salary increases, year-end bonuses, or federal income tax returns. Instead of spending these windfalls, invest these funds.

Source: Jack R. Kapoor, Les R. Dlabay, and Robert J. Hughes, *Focus on Personal Finance*, 3rd ed. Copyright © 2010 by The McGraw Hill Companies Inc. Reprinted with permission of The McGraw Hill Companies Inc.

After the emergency account is established, you may invest additional funds according to your investment program. Some additional funds may already be available, or money for further investing may be saved out of earnings. For suggestions to help you obtain the money needed to fund your investment program, see Table 20.1.

Monitoring the Value of Your Investment Program

In fall 2007, the stock market, as measured by the Dow Jones Industrial Average, reached an all-time high at 14,000. The **Dow Jones Industrial Average** is an average of 30 leading U.S. corporations that reflect the U.S. stock market as a whole. By March 2009, the same average had declined to 6,600. What happened? The simple answer is that the United States (and most of the world) experienced an economic meltdown. This economic crisis had many causes, including a banking and financial crisis, a downturn in home sales, lower consumer spending, and high unemployment rates. Although the economy shows signs of improving at the time of publication, and the Dow Jones Industrial Average is just over 13,000 at the time of publication, a crisis could happen again.

Although monitoring your investment program and re-evaluating your investment choices are always important, the recent economic crisis underscores the importance of managing your personal finances *and* your investment program. Because of the nation's economic problems, many people were caught off guard. Moreover, some individuals were forced to sell some or all of their investments at depressed prices just to pay for everyday necessities.

To avoid the type of problems just described, you must monitor your investment program and, if necessary, modify it. Always keep in mind your circumstances and economic conditions are both subject to change.

Describe how the factors of safety, risk, income, growth, and liquidity affect your investment program.

IMPORTANT FACTORS IN PERSONAL INVESTMENT

How can you (or a financial planner) tell which investments are "right" for your investment program and which are not? One way to start is to match potential investments with your investment goals in terms of safety, risk, income, growth, and liquidity.

Safety and Risk

Dow Jones Industrial Average an average of 30 leading U.S. corporations that reflect the U.S. stock market as a whole

Safety and risk are two sides of the same coin. *Safety* in an investment means minimal risk of loss; *risk* in an investment means a measure of uncertainty about the outcome. If you want a steady increase in value over an extended period of time, choose safe investments, such as certificates of deposit (CDs), highly rated government and corporate bonds, and the stocks of highly regarded corporations—sometimes called blue-chip stocks. A **blue-chip stock** is a safe investment that generally attracts conservative investors. Blue-chip stocks are generally issued by corporations that are industry leaders and have provided their stockholders with stable earnings and dividends over a number of years. Selected mutual funds and real estate may also be very safe investments.

If you want higher dollar returns on investments, you must generally give up some safety. In general, *the potential return should be directly related to the assumed risk*. That is, the greater the risk you assume, the higher the potential monetary reward. As you will see shortly, there are a number of speculative—and potentially profitable—investments.

Often beginning investors are afraid of the risk associated with many investments. However, it helps to remember that without risk, it is impossible to obtain larger returns that really make your investment program grow. In fact, some investors often base their investment decision on projections for rate of return. You can also use the same calculation to determine how much you actually earn on an investment over a specific period of time. To calculate **rate of return**, the total dollar amount of return you receive on an investment over a specific period of time is divided by the amount invested. For example, assume that you invest $5,000 in Home Depot stock, you receive $108 in dividends, and the stock is worth $5,300 at the end of one year. Your rate of return is 8.2 percent, as illustrated here.

Purchasing stocks is one way to invest. Since 1926, stocks have returned just below 10 percent a year—a larger return than most other investment alternatives. So why not just pick a bunch of stocks and begin investing? The truth is that an investment program should begin with a financial checkup to make sure that you are ready to invest and the creation of investment goals before you purchase any investment.

Step 1: Subtract the investment's initial value from the investment's value at the end of the year.

$$\$5,300 - \$5,000 = \$300$$

Step 2: Add the dividend amount to the amount calculated in step 1.

$$\$108 + \$300 = \$408$$

Step 3: Divide the total dollar amount of return calculated in step 2 by the original investment.

$$\$408 \div \$5,000 = 0.082 = 8.2 \text{ percent}$$

Note: If an investment decreases in value, the steps used to calculate the rate of return are the same, but the answer is a negative number. With this information, it is possible to compare the rate of return for different investment alternatives that offer more or less risk.

Investment Income

Investors sometimes purchase certain investments because they want a predictable source of income. For example, CDs, corporate and government bonds, and certain stocks pay interest or dividends each year. Some mutual funds and real estate may also offer steady income potential. Such investments are generally used by conservative investors or retired individuals who need a predictable source of income.

When purchasing investments for income, most investors are concerned about the issuer's ability to continue making periodic interest or dividend payments. Investors in CDs and bonds know exactly how much income they will receive each year. The dividends paid to stockholders can and do vary, even for the largest and most stable corporations. As with dividends from stock, the income from mutual funds and real estate may also vary from one year to the next.

Investment Growth

To investors, *growth* means that their investments will increase in value. For example, growing corporations such as Monster Beverage, Adobe Systems, Questcor Pharmaceuticals, and Silicon Motion Technology usually pay a small cash dividend or no dividend at all. Instead, profits are reinvested in the business (as retained earnings)

blue-chip stock a safe investment that generally attracts conservative investors

rate of return the total dollar amount of return you receive on an investment over a specific period of time divided by the amount invested

© STEPHEN COBURN/SHUTTERSTOCK

to finance additional expansion. In this case, the value of the stock increases as the corporation expands.

Other investments that may offer growth potential include selected mutual funds and real estate. For example, many mutual funds are referred to as growth funds or aggressive growth funds because of the growth potential of the individual securities included in the fund.

Investment Liquidity

Liquidity is the ease with which an investment can be converted into cash. Investments range from cash or cash equivalents (such as investments in government securities or money-market accounts) to the other extreme of frozen investments, which you cannot convert easily into cash.

Although you may be able to sell stock, mutual-fund, and corporate-bond investments quickly, you may not regain the amount of money you originally invested because of market conditions, economic conditions, or many other reasons. It may also be difficult to find buyers for real estate. Furthermore, finding a buyer for investments in certain types of collectibles may also be difficult.

FACTORS THAT CAN IMPROVE YOUR INVESTMENT DECISIONS

Recognize how you can reduce investment risk and increase investment returns.

We begin this section with an overview of how portfolio management can reduce investment risk and factors that you should consider to choose "just the right" investments. Then in the next two sections, we describe how the investments listed in Table 20.2 can help you to reach your investment goals.

TABLE 20.2 Investment Alternatives
Traditional investments involve less risk than speculative or high-risk investments.
Traditional Investments
Bank accounts
Corporate and government bonds
More Speculative Investments
Common stock
Preferred stock
Mutual funds
Real estate
The Most Speculative Investments
Short transactions
Margin transactions
Stock options
Derivatives
Commodities
Precious metals
Gemstones
Coins
Antiques
Collectibles

© CENGAGE LEARNING 2014

liquidity the ease with which an investment can be converted into cash

Portfolio Management

"How can I choose the right investment?" That's a good question! Unfortunately, there are no easy answers because your investment goals, age, tolerance for risk, and financial resources are different from those of the next person. To help you to decide what investment is right for you, consider the following: Since 1926, as measured by the Standard and Poor's 500 Stock Index, stocks have returned on average just below 10 percent a year. The **Standard & Poor's 500 Stock Index** is an index that contains 500 different stocks that reflect increases or decreases in value for the U.S. stock market as a whole. During the same period, U.S. government bonds have returned about 6 percent.[2] Therefore, why not just invest all your money in stocks or mutual funds that invest in stocks? After all, they offer the largest potential return. In reality, stocks may have a place in every investment portfolio, but there is more to investing than just picking a bunch of stocks or stock mutual funds.

Asset Allocation, the Time Factor, and Your Age

Asset allocation is the process of spreading your money among several different types of investments to lessen risk. Although the term *asset allocation* is a fancy way of saying it, simply put, it really means that you need to diversify and avoid the pitfall of putting all of your eggs in one basket—a common mistake made by investors. Asset allocation is often expressed in percentages. For example, what percentage of my assets do I want to put in stocks and mutual funds? What percentage do I want to put in more conservative investments such as CDs and government bonds? In reality, the answers to these questions are determined by:

- The time your investments have to work for you
- Your age
- Your investment objectives
- Your ability to tolerate risk
- How much you can save and invest each year
- The dollar value of your current investments
- The economic outlook for the economy
- Several other factors

Two factors—the time your investments have to work for you and your age—are so important they deserve special attention.

The Time Factor The amount of time you have before you need your investment money is crucial. If you can leave your investments alone and let them work for five to ten years or more, then you can invest in stocks, mutual funds, and real estate. On the other hand, if you need your investment money in two years, you probably should invest in short-term government bonds, highly rated corporate bonds, or CDs. By taking a more conservative approach for short-term investments, you reduce the possibility of having to sell your investments at a loss because of depressed market value or a staggering economy. For example, during the recent economic crisis, many retirees who were forced to sell stocks and mutual funds to pay for everyday living expenses lost money. On the other hand, many young investors with long-term investment goals could afford to hold their investments until the price of their securities recovered.

Your Age You also should consider your age when developing an investment program. Younger investors tend to invest a large percentage of their nest egg in growth-oriented investments. On the other hand, older investors tend to choose more conservative investments. As a result, a smaller percentage of their nest egg is placed in growth-oriented investments. While no investor regardless of age likes to lose money on an investment, the fact is that younger investors have more time for an investment to recover its original value and even increase in value.

How much of your portfolio should be in growth-oriented investments? Well-known personal financial expert Suze Orman suggests that you subtract your age

Standard & Poor's 500 Stock Index an index that contains 500 different stocks that reflect increases or decreases in value for the U.S. stock market as a whole

asset allocation the process of spreading your money among several different types of investments to lessen risk from 110, and the difference is the percentage of your assets that should be invested in growth investments. For example, if you are 30 years old, subtract 30 from 110, which gives you 80. Therefore, 80 percent of your assets should be invested in growth-oriented investments, whereas the remaining 20 percent should be kept in safer conservative investments.[3]

Your Role in the Investment Process

Investors want large returns, yet they are often unwilling to invest the time required to become a good investor. They would not buy a car without a test drive or purchase a home without comparing different homes, but for some unknown reason they invest without doing their homework. The suggestions given here will help you choose investments that will increase in value.

- *Evaluate potential investments.* Keep in mind that successful investors evaluate their investments before making investment decisions. Often, it is useful to keep copies of the material you used to evaluate each investment. Then, when it is time to re-evaluate an existing investment, you will know where to begin your search for current information. Much of the information in this chapter in the section "Sources of Financial Information" will help you learn how to evaluate different investment opportunities.
- *Monitor the value of your investments.* Would you believe that some people invest large sums of money and do not know what their investments are worth? They do not know if their investments have increased or decreased in value and if they should sell their investments or continue to hold them. A much better approach is to monitor the value of your investments.
- *Keep accurate and current records.* Accurate record keeping can help you spot opportunities to maximize profits, reduce dollar losses when you sell your investments, and help you decide whether you want to invest additional funds in a specific investment. For tax purposes, you should keep purchase records for each of your investments that include the actual dollar cost of the investment, plus any commissions or fees you paid, along with records of dividends, interest income, or rental income you received.

Explain the reasons people choose conservative investments including bank accounts and bonds.

CONSERVATIVE INVESTMENT ALTERNATIVES

Typically investors who are afraid of the risk associated with stocks, mutual funds, and other investment alternatives, beginning investors, investors that need a predictable source of income, or people worried about a downturn in the economy will often invest their money in bank accounts, government bonds, or corporate bonds.

Bank Accounts

Bank accounts that pay interest—and therefore are investments—include passbook savings accounts, money-market accounts, CDs, and other interest-bearing accounts. These investments were discussed in Chapter 18. The interest paid on bank accounts can be withdrawn to serve as income, or it can be left on deposit and increase the value of the bank account and provide for growth. At the time of this publication, one-year CDs were paying between 0.50 and 1 percent. Although CDs and other bank accounts are risk-free for all practical purposes, many investors often choose other investments because of the potential for larger returns.

Corporate and Government Bonds

In Chapter 19, we discussed why corporations issue bonds to obtain financing. The U.S. government and state and local governments also issue bonds for the same reason. Investors generally choose bonds because they provide a predictable source of income.

Ethical
SUCCESS OR FAILURE?

Invest in Green Bonds?

Should investors choose green bonds? The World Bank issues green bonds to pay for sustainability projects such as water purification, solar installations, and reforestation. Since 2008, it has issued $3.3 billion worth of green bonds, in 17 currencies, with a range of maturities from 2 to 10 years. For example, Bank of America Merrill Lynch offers World Bank green bonds with 10-year maturities starting with a $1,000 investment. Because repayment is not tied to the performance of the projects they finance, these bonds are rated as low-risk and carry relatively low interest rates.

Nobody questions the need to fund sustainability projects. In fact, some institutional investors see green bonds as a way to support environmental action while diversifying their portfolios. One issue, however, is that the money goes into a World Bank account designated for environmental projects—and investors don't know which project they're supporting. As a result, money from an investor who hopes to preserve the rainforest may actually be used for mass transportation improvements that reduce pollution. Another issue is liquidity. Demand for green bonds is unproven, and they aren't traded as widely or as often as, say, U.S. Treasury bonds. In fact, lack of liquidity may be a real problem for investors who have to sell prior to maturity. So should investors choose green bonds?

Sources: Based on information in Sally Bakewell, "Green Bond Bankers in Japan, Sweden Beat U.S. to $7 Billion," *Bloomberg*, January 24, 2012, www.bloomberg.com; "A Modest, But Important, Addition to Climate Finance," *Economist*, October 29, 2011, www.economist.com; Sonia Kolesnikov-Jessop, "A Change of Heart on Investing in the Climate," *New York Times*, November 27, 2011, www.nytimes.com; Elizabeth O'Brien, "Now Bonds Are Going Green Too," *Smart Money*, October 25, 2011, www.smartmoney.com; www.worldbank.org.

Government Bonds Despite concerns about the increasing dollar amount of national debt for the United States, most investors still consider the nation's government bonds to be risk-free. The other side of the coin is that these bonds pay lower interest than most other investments. Interest paid on U.S. government securities is taxable for federal income tax purposes, but is exempt from state and local taxation. Generally, investors choose from the five different types of U.S. government bonds and securities described in Table 20.3. With the exception of savings bonds, the minimum purchase for each type of U.S. government security is $100 with additional increments of $100 above the minimum. For more information about U.S. government securities, go to www.treasurydirect.gov.

Like the federal government, state and local governments sell bonds to obtain financing. A **municipal bond**, sometimes called a *muni*, is a debt security issued by a state or local government. Municipal bonds are especially attractive to wealthy investors because interest income from municipal bonds may be tax exempt from federal taxes. Whether or not the interest on municipal bonds is tax-exempt often depends on how the funds obtained from their sale are used. *Caution: It is your responsibility, as an investor, to determine whether or not the interest paid by municipal bonds is taxable. It is also your responsibility to evaluate municipal bonds.* Although most municipal bonds are relatively safe, defaults have occurred in recent years.

municipal bond sometimes called a *muni,* a debt security issued by a state or local government

Corporate Bonds Because they are a form of long-term debt financing that must be repaid, investment-grade corporate bonds are generally considered a more conservative investment than either stocks or mutual funds that invest in stocks. One of the principal advantages of corporate bonds is that they are primarily long-term, income-producing investments. Between the time of purchase and the maturity date, the bondholder will receive interest payments— usually semiannually, or every six months. For example, assume that you purchase a $1,000 bond—the usual face value for a corporate bond—issued by the rail-based transportation giant CSX

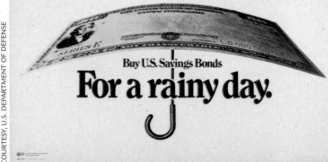

COURTESY, U.S. DEPARTMENT OF DEFENSE

Can U.S. savings bonds provide an umbrella for a rainy day? Despite concerns about the increasing dollar amount of the national debt for the United States, most investors still consider the nation's savings bonds and securities issued by the U.S. Treasury to be risk-free because they are backed by the full faith and credit of the U.S. government. But be warned: When you invest in these conservative investments, you must accept smaller returns on your investments.

TABLE 20.3 Information about U.S. Government Securities

Type of Security	Maturity	Interest	Notes
Treasury bill (T-bills)	4, 13, 26, or 52 weeks	T-bills are sold at a discount and the actual purchase price is less than $100.	When T-bills mature, you receive the maturity value.
Treasury notes	2, 3, 5, 7, or 10 years	Interest is paid every six months until maturity.	Interest is slightly higher than T-bills because of the longer maturity.
Treasury bonds	30-year	Interest is paid every six months until maturity.	Interest rate is slightly higher than T-bills and Treasury notes because of the longer maturity.
Treasury inflation-protected securities (TIPS)	5, 10, or 30 years. At maturity, you are paid the adjusted principal or original principal, whichever is greater.	Interest is paid every six months until maturity at a fixed rate applied to the adjusted principal.	The principal of TIPS securities increases with inflation and decreases with deflation.
Savings bonds	Pay interest for up to 30 years.	Interest is added to bonds monthly and paid when you redeem savings bonds.	Minimum purchase is $25. Note: If interest is used to pay qualified college expenses, it may be exempt from federal taxation.

© CENGAGE LEARNING 2014

Corporation and that the interest rate for this bond is 6 percent. In this situation, you receive interest of $60 ($1,000 × 0.06 = $60) a year from the corporation. For corporate bonds, interest is usually paid semiannually or every six months. In the case of the CSX bond just described, a bondholder will receive two $30 interest payments each year.

Most beginning investors think that a $1,000 bond is always worth $1,000. In reality, the price of a bond may fluctuate until its maturity date. Changes in the overall interest rates in the economy are the primary cause of most bond price fluctuations. When overall interest rates in the economy increase, the market value of existing bonds with a fixed interest rate typically declines. For example, the value of the CSX bond with a fixed 6 percent interest rate will decline if interest rates in the economy or interest rates for comparable bonds increase. When a bond's price declines, it may be purchased for less than its face value. By holding the bond until maturity, bond owners can redeem the bond for more than they paid for it.

A corporate bond with a fixed interest rate can also increase in value if overall interest rates in the economy decline. In this situation, a bond like the CSX bond with a 6 percent fixed interest rate will increase in value. The difference between the purchase price and the selling price is profit and is in addition to annual interest income.

Before you invest in bonds, remember that the price of a corporate bond can decrease and that interest payments and eventual repayment may be a problem for a corporation that encounters financial difficulty. To compare potential risk and return on corporate bond issues, many investors rely on the bond ratings provided by Moody's Investors Service, Inc., Fitch Ratings, and Standard & Poor's Corporation.

Convertible Corporate Bonds Some corporations prefer to issue convertible bonds because they carry a lower interest rate than nonconvertible bonds—by about 1 to 2 percent. In return for accepting a lower interest rate, owners of convertible bonds have the opportunity for increased investment growth. For example, assume that you purchase an Advanced Micro Devices $1,000 corporate bond that is convertible to 35.6125 shares of the company's common stock. This means that you could convert the bond to common stock whenever the price of the company's stock is $28.08 ($1,000 ÷ 35.6125 = $28.08) or higher.[4] However, owners may opt not to convert their bonds to common stock even if the market value of the common stock does increase to $28.08 or more. The reason for not exercising the conversion feature is quite simple. As the market value of the common stock increases, the price of the convertible bond also increases. By not converting to common stock, bondholders enjoy interest income from the bond in addition to the increased bond value caused by the price movement of the common stock.

MORE SPECULATIVE INVESTMENTS

5 Identify the advantages and disadvantages of stocks, mutual funds, real estate, and more speculative investments.

Earlier in this chapter, we discussed the concepts of safety and risk. Before you examine more speculative investment alternatives, it may help to review the basic rule: *The potential return should be directly related to the assumed risk.* While all investors want larger returns, you must consider the risk involved with each of the following investments. Above all, keep in mind that dollar returns for the more speculative investments described in this section are not guaranteed.

Common Stock

stock dividend a dividend in the form of additional stock

capital gain the difference between a security's purchase price and its selling price

market value the price of one share of a stock at a particular time

As mentioned in Chapter 19, corporations issue common stock to finance their business start-up costs and help pay for expansion and their ongoing business activities. Before investing in stock, keep in mind that corporations do not have to repay the money a stockholder pays for stock. Usually, a stockholder may sell her or his stock to another individual.

How do you make money by buying common stock? Basically, there are three ways: through dividend payments, through an increase in the value of the stock, or through stock splits.

Dividend Payments One of the reasons why many stockholders invest in common stock is *dividend income.* Generally, dividends are paid on a quarterly basis. At the time of publication, Kraft Foods paid its stockholders an annual dividend of $1.16 per share in quarterly payments of $0.29 every three months. Although corporations are under no legal obligation to pay dividends or can reduce dividends if the company experiences financial difficulties, most corporate board members like to keep stockholders happy (and prosperous). A corporation may pay stock dividends in place of—or in addition to—cash dividends. A **stock dividend** is a dividend in the form of additional stock. It is paid to shareholders just as cash dividends are paid—in proportion to the number of shares owned.

© RICHARD LEVINE/ALAMY

Should you invest in Cheerios? While most everyone in the United States recognizes the Cheerios brand, did you know that the famous cereal is manufactured and marketed by General Mills? Often you have to dig deeper if you want to invest in a corporation that produces a famous product or service to determine if the "parent" company is a quality investment that will help you obtain your financial goals.

Increase in Dollar Value Another way to make money on stock investments is through a capital gain that occurs when you sell stock. A **capital gain** is the difference between a security's purchase price and its selling price. To earn a capital gain, you must sell when the market value of the stock is higher than the original purchase price you paid for the stock. The **market value** is the price of one share of a stock at a particular time. Let's assume that on March 8,

TABLE 20.4 Sample Common-Stock Transaction for Kellogg

Assumptions: 100 shares of common stock purchased on March 8, 2009, for $37 a share; 100 shares sold on March 8, 2012, for $52 a share; dividends for three years total $4.75 a share.

Cost when Purchased		Return when Sold	
100 shares @ $37	$3,700	100 shares @ $52	$5,200
Plus commission	+25	Minus commission	−25
Total investment	$3,725	Total return	$5,175
Transaction Summary			
Total return	$5,175		
Minus total investment	−3,725		
Profit from stock sale	$1,450		
Plus total dividends (three years)	+475		
Total return for this transaction	$1,925		

Source: Price data and dividend amounts were taken from the Yahoo Finance Web site, http://finance.yahoo.com (accessed March 8, 2012).

2009, you purchased 100 shares of Kellogg common stock at a cost of $37 a share and that you paid $25 in commission charges, for a total investment of $3,725. Let's also assume that you held your 100 shares until March 8, 2012, and then sold the Kellogg stock for $52. Your total return on investment is shown in Table 20.4. You realized a profit of $1,925 because you received dividends totaling $4.75 a share during the three-year period and because the stock's market value increased by $15 a share. Of course, if the stock's market value had decreased, or if the firm's board of directors had voted to reduce or omit dividends, your return would have been less than the total dollar return illustrated in Table 20.4.

Stock Splits Directors of many corporations feel that there is an optimal price range within which their firm's stock is most attractive to investors. When the market value increases beyond that range, they may declare a *stock split* to bring the price down. A **stock split** is the division of each outstanding share of a corporation's stock into a greater number of shares.

The most common stock splits result in one, two, or three new shares for each original share. For example, in November 2011, the board of directors of Estée Lauder, the company known for skin care, cosmetics, fragrances, and hair-care products, approved a two-for-one stock split. After this split, a stockholder who originally owned 100 shares owned 200 shares. The value of an original share was proportionally reduced. In the case of Estée Lauder, the market value per share was reduced to half the stock's value before the two-for-one stock split. There is no evidence to support that a corporation's long-term performance is improved by a stock split; however, some investors do profit from stock splits on a short-term basis. *Be warned: There are no guarantees that the stock will increase in value after a split.* However, the stock may be more attractive to the investing public because of the potential for a rapid increase in dollar value. This attraction is based on the belief that most corporations split their stock only when their financial future is improving and on the upswing.

Preferred Stock

As we noted in Chapter 19, a firm's preferred stockholders must receive their dividends before common stockholders are paid any dividends. Moreover, the preferred-stock dividend amount is specified on the stock certificate. In addition, the owners of preferred stock have first claim, after bond owners and general creditors, on corporate assets if the firm is dissolved or enters bankruptcy. These features make preferred stock

stock split the division of each outstanding share of a corporation's stock into a greater number of shares a more conservative investment with an added degree of safety and a more predictable source of income when compared with common stock.

In addition, owners of preferred stock may gain through special features offered with certain preferred-stock issues. Owners of *cumulative* preferred stocks are assured that omitted dividends will be paid to them before common stockholders receive any dividends. Owners of *convertible* preferred stock may profit through growth as well as dividends. When the value of a firm's common stock increases, the market value of its convertible preferred stock also increases. Convertible preferred stock thus combines the lower risk of preferred stock with the possibility of greater speculative gain through conversion to common stock.

Mutual Funds and Exchange-Traded Funds

For many investors, mutual funds are the investment of choice. There are plenty of funds from which to choose. In 1970, there were only about 400 mutual funds. In January 2012, there were over 10,000 funds.[5]

According to the Mutual Fund Education Alliance (www .mfea.com), a **mutual fund** pools the money of many investors—its shareholders—to invest in a variety of different securities.[6] The major advantages of a mutual fund are its *professional management* and its *diversification*, or investment in a wide variety of securities. Most investment companies do everything possible to convince you that they can do a better job of picking securities than you can. In reality, mutual funds are managed by professional fund managers who devote large amounts of time to picking just the "right" securities for their funds' portfolios. *Be warned:* Even the best portfolio managers make mistakes. So you, the investor, must be careful and evaluate different funds before investing. Diversification spells safety because an occasional loss incurred with one security is usually offset by gains from other investments.

Mutual-Fund Basics There are basically three types of mutual funds: (1) open-end funds, (2) closed-end funds, and (3) exchange-traded funds (ETFs). The investment company sponsoring an *open-end fund* issues and sells new shares to any investor who requests them. It also buys back shares from investors who wish to sell all or part of their holdings. A *closed-end fund* sells shares in the fund to investors only when the fund is originally organized. Once all the shares are sold, an investor must purchase shares from some other investor who is willing to sell them. The investment company is under no obligation to buy back shares from investors.

An **exchange-traded fund (ETF)** is a fund that generally invests in the stocks or securities contained in a specific stock or securities index. Although most investors think of an ETF as investing in the stocks contained in the Standard & Poor's 500 Stock Index, there are many different types of ETFs available that attempt to track all kinds of indexes including different types of stocks, bonds, and even commodities. Exchange-traded funds tend to mirror the performance of a specific index, moving up or down as the individual stocks or securities contained in the index move up or down.

Like a closed-end fund, shares of an exchange-traded fund are traded on a securities exchange or in the over-the-counter market at any time during the business day. Although exchange-traded funds are similar to closed-end funds, there is an important difference. Most closed-end funds are actively managed, with portfolio managers making the selection of stocks and other securities contained in a closed-end fund. Almost

Sustaining the PLANET

Green Investing

Interested in earning some green (backs) while you're saving the planet? Maybe green investing is for you! Green investing involves choosing to invest in companies that are involved in operations aimed at improving the environment, such as alternative energy sources, clean air and water projects, or companies that provide environmentally friendly products. Socially Responsible Investing is an organization that provides information about green investing, including green stock investment choices, green mutual funds, and tips for investors. Take a look at http://yesinvesting.com/.

COURTESY OF HTTP://YESINVESTING.COM

mutual fund pools the money of many investors—its shareholders—to invest in a variety of different securities

exchange-traded fund (ETF) a fund that generally invests in the stocks or other securities contained in a specific stock or securities index all exchange-traded funds, on the other hand, normally invest in the stocks, bonds, or securities included in a specific index. Therefore, there is less need for a portfolio manager to make investment decisions. Because of passive management, fees associated with owning shares are generally less when compared to both closed-end and open-end funds. Although increasing in popularity, there are only about 1,100 exchange-traded funds.[7]

The share value for any mutual fund is determined by calculating its net asset value. **Net asset value (NAV)** per share is equal to the current market value of the mutual fund's portfolio minus the mutual fund's liabilities divided by the number of outstanding shares. For most mutual funds, NAV is calculated once a day and is reported in newspapers and financial publications and on the Internet. Because ETFs and closed-end funds trade like stocks, their shares trade at the current market value, which can be more or less than a closed-end fund's or ETF's NAV.

Mutual-Fund Sales Charges and Fees With regard to costs, there are two types of mutual funds: load and no-load funds. An individual who invests in a *load fund* pays a sales charge every time he or she purchases shares. This charge may be as high as 8.5 percent. Although many exceptions exist, the average load charge for mutual funds is between 3 and 5 percent. Instead of charging investors a fee when they purchase shares in a mutual fund, some funds charge a *contingent deferred sales fee*. Generally, this fee ranges from 1 to 5 percent of the amount withdrawn during the first five to seven years. Typically, the amount of the contingent deferred sales fee declines each year that you own the fund until there is no withdrawal fee.

The purchaser of shares in a *no-load fund* pays no sales charges at all. Although some fund salespeople claim that load funds outperform no-load funds, there is no significant performance difference between funds that charge load charges (commissions) and those that do not.[8] Because no-load funds offer the same type of investment opportunities as load funds, you should investigate them further before deciding which type of mutual fund is best for you.

Mutual funds also collect a yearly management fee of about 0.25 to 1.5 percent of the total dollar amount of assets in the fund. Although fees vary considerably, the average management fee is between 0.50 and 1 percent of the fund's assets. Finally, some mutual funds charge a 12b-1 fee (sometimes referred to as a *distribution fee*) to defray the costs of advertising and marketing the mutual fund. Annual 12b-1 fees are calculated on the value of a fund's assets and cannot exceed 1 percent of the fund's assets. Unlike the one-time sales fees that some mutual funds charge to purchase *or* sell mutual-fund shares, the management fee and the 12b-1 fee are ongoing fees charged each year.

Together, all the different management fees; 12b-1 fees, if any; and additional operating costs for a specific fund are referred to as an **expense ratio**. As a guideline, many financial planners recommend that you choose a mutual fund with an expense ratio of 1 percent or less. To learn more about different mutual fund charges and fees, you should visit the Securities and Exchange Commission Web site at www.sec.gov.

Today, mutual funds can also be classified as A, B, or C shares. With A shares, investors pay commissions when they purchase shares in the mutual fund. With B shares, investors pay commissions when money is withdrawn or shares are sold during the first five to seven years. With C shares, investors often pay no commissions to buy or sell shares but usually must pay higher ongoing management and 12b-1 fees.

Managed Funds Versus Indexed Funds Most mutual funds are managed funds. In other words, there is a professional fund manager (or team of managers) who chooses the securities that are contained in the fund. The fund manager also decides when to buy and sell securities in the fund.

net asset value (NAV) current market value of a mutual fund's portfolio minus the mutual fund's liabilities divided by the number of outstanding shares

expense ratio all the different management fees; 12b-1 fees, if any; and additional operating costs for a specific fund

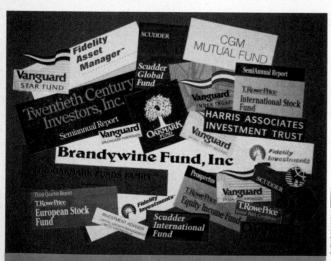

© SUSAN VAN ETTEN

How do you choose the right investment and financial company to help you obtain your financial goals? Beginning investors often see the investment world as a jungle because of the different investment alternatives and the large number of companies that want to help you invest. In reality, all investments *and* the companies that want to help you should be evaluated before you make any decisions on how and where to invest.

Instead of investing in a managed fund, some investors choose to invest in an index fund. Why? The answer to this question is simple: Over many years, index funds have outperformed managed funds. The exact statistics vary depending on the year and the specific fund, but a common statistic is that the Standard & Poor's 500 Stock Index outperforms 80 percent of all mutual funds.[9] Simply put: It is hard to beat an index such as the Standard & Poor's 500. If the individual securities included in an index increase in value, the index goes up. Because an index fund contains the same securities as the index, the dollar value of a share in an index fund also increases when the index increases. Unfortunately, the reverse is also true. A second reason why investors choose index funds is the lower fees charged by these passively managed funds. (*Note:* Various indexes are discussed later in this chapter.)

Types of Mutual-Fund Investments Based on the type of securities they invest in, mutual funds generally fall into three broad categories: stocks, bonds, and other. The majority of mutual funds are *stock funds* that invest in stocks issued by small, medium-size, and large corporations that provide investors with income, growth, or a combination of income and growth. *Bond funds* invest in corporate, government, or municipal bonds that provide investors with interest income. The third category includes funds that stress asset allocation and money-market investments or strive for a balance between stocks and bonds. In most cases, the name of the category gives a pretty good clue to the type of investments included in the fund. Typical fund names include:

- Aggressive growth stock funds
- Balanced funds
- Global stock funds
- Growth stock funds
- High-yield (junk) bond funds
- Income stock funds
- Index funds
- Life cycle funds
- Long-term U.S. bond funds
- Regional funds
- Sector stock funds
- Socially responsible funds
- Small-cap stock funds

To help investors obtain their investment objectives, most investment companies now allow shareholders to switch from one fund to another fund within the same family of funds. A **family of funds** exists when one investment company manages a group of mutual funds. For example, shareholders, at their option, can change from the Fidelity International Growth Fund to the Fidelity Small-Cap Discovery Fund. Generally, investors may give instructions to switch from one fund to another fund within the same family either in writing, over the telephone, or via the Internet. Charges for exchanges, if any, are small for each transaction.

Real Estate

Real estate ownership represents one of the best hedges against inflation, but like all investments it has its risks. A piece of property in a poor location, for example, can actually decrease in value. Table 20.5 lists some of the many factors you should consider before investing in real estate.

There are, of course, disadvantages to any investment, and real estate is no exception. If you want to sell your property, you must find an interested buyer with the ability to obtain enough money to complete the transaction. Finding such a buyer can be difficult if loan money is scarce, the real estate market is in a decline, or you overpaid for a piece of property. For example, many real estate investors were forced to hold some properties longer than they wanted because buyers could not obtain financing

family of funds a group of mutual funds managed by one investment company

TABLE 20.5 Real Estate Checklist

Although real estate offers one of the best hedges against inflation, not all property increases in value. Many factors should be considered before investing in real estate.

Evaluation of Property	Inspection of the Surrounding Neighborhood	Other Factors
Is the property priced competitively with similar property?	What are the present zoning requirements?	Why are the present owners selling the property?
What type of financing, if any, is available?	Is the neighborhood's population increasing or decreasing?	How long will you have to hold the property before selling it to someone else?
How much are the taxes?	What is the average income of people in the area?	How much profit can you reasonably expect to obtain?
How much will it cost to repair or remodel a property?	What is the state of repair of surrounding property? Do most of the buildings and homes need repair?	Is there a chance that the property value will decrease?

© CENGAGE LEARNING 2014

during the recent economic crisis. If you are forced to hold your investment longer than you originally planned, taxes, interest, and installment payments can be a heavy burden. As a rule, real estate increases in value and eventually sells at a profit, but there are no guarantees. The degree of your success depends on how well you evaluate different alternatives.

The Most Speculative Investment Techniques

A **high-risk investment** is one made in the uncertain hope of earning a relatively large profit in a short time. (See the most speculative investments category in Table 20.2.) Although all investments have some risk, some investments become high-risk because of the methods used by investors to earn a quick profit. These methods can lead to large losses as well as to impressive gains. They should not be used by anyone who does not fully understand the risks involved. We begin this section with a discussion of selling short. Then we examine margin transactions and other high-risk investments.

Selling Short Normally, you buy stocks expecting that they will increase in value and then can be sold at a profit. This procedure is referred to as **buying long**. However, many securities decrease in value for various reasons. The market value for a share of a corporation's stock, for example, can decrease when sales and profits are lower than expected. When this type of situation occurs, you can use a procedure called selling short to make a profit when the price of an individual stock is falling. **Selling short** is the process of selling stock that an investor does not actually own but has borrowed from a brokerage firm and will repay at a later date. The idea is to sell at today's higher price and then buy later at a lower price. To make a profit from a short transaction, you must proceed as follows:

1. Arrange to borrow a certain number of shares of a particular stock from a brokerage firm.
2. Sell the borrowed stock immediately, assuming that the price of the stock will drop in a reasonably short time.
3. After the price drops, buy the same number of shares that were sold in step 2.
4. Give the newly purchased stock to the brokerage firm in return for the stock borrowed in step 1.

high-risk investment an investment made in the uncertain hope of earning a relatively large profit in a short time

buying long buying a stock with the expectation that it will increase in value and then can be sold at a profit

selling short the process of selling stock that an investor does not actually own but has borrowed from a brokerage firm and will repay at a later date

Your profit is the difference between the amount received when the stock is sold in step 2 and the amount paid for the stock in step 3. For example, assume that you think Barnes & Noble stock is overvalued at $18 a share. You also believe that the stock will decrease in value over the next three to four months. In this example, you can make money with a short transaction—*if the stock's value does decline*. On the other hand, if the market value for a share of Barnes & Noble increases, you lose.

Buying Stock on Margin An investor buys stock *on margin* by borrowing part of the purchase price, usually from a stock brokerage firm. The **margin requirement** is the portion of the price of a stock that cannot be borrowed. This requirement is set by the Federal Reserve Board.

Today, the current margin requirement is 50 percent, which means you can borrow up to 50 percent of the cost of a stock purchase. Some securities exchanges and brokerage firms may impose other restrictions and require that you deposit more cash, which reduces the percentage that can be borrowed. However, why would investors want to buy stock on margin? Simply because they can buy up to twice as much stock that way. Suppose that an investor expects the market price of a share of common stock of American Electric Power Corporation—a U.S. energy company—to increase in the next three to four months. Assume you have enough money to purchase 200 shares of the stock. However, if you buy on margin, you can purchase an additional 200 shares for a total of 400 shares. If the price of American Electric Power's stock increases by $8 per share, your profit will be $1,600 ($8 × 200 = $1,600) if you pay cash. But it will be $3,200 ($8 × 400 = $3,200) if you buy the stock using margin. By buying more shares on margin, you will earn more profit (less the interest you pay on the borrowed money and customary commission charges).

Note that the stock purchased on margin serves as collateral for the borrowed funds. Before you become a margin investor, you should consider two factors. First, if the market price of the purchased stock does not increase as quickly as expected, interest costs mount and eventually drain your profit. Second, if the price of the margined stock falls, your dollar loss will be greater because you own more shares.

If the value of a stock you bought on margin decreases to approximately 60 percent of its original price, you may receive a *margin call* from the brokerage firm. You then must provide additional cash or securities to serve as collateral for the borrowed money. If you cannot provide additional collateral, the stock is sold, and the proceeds are used to pay off the loan and commissions. Any funds remaining after the loan and commissions are paid off are returned to you.

margin requirement the portion of the price of a stock that cannot be borrowed

Other High-Risk Investments We have already discussed two high-risk investments—selling short and margin transactions. Other high-risk investments include the following:

- Stock options
- Derivatives
- Commodities
- Precious metals
- Gemstones
- Coins
- Antiques and collectibles

Without exception, investments of this kind are normally referred to as high-risk investments for one reason or another. For example, the gold market has many unscrupulous dealers who sell worthless gold-plated lead coins to unsuspecting, uninformed investors. It pays to be careful. *Although investments in this category can lead to large dollar gains, they should not be used by anyone who does not fully understand all the potential risks involved.*

© ANAKENM2012/SHUTTERSTOCK

Is gold a conservative or a high-risk investment? Good question. When purchased from reputable dealers, gold can be a conservative investment—especially in troubled economic times. And yet, there are many unscrupulous dealers who sell worthless gold-plated coins to unsuspecting investors who want to make a fast buck. The final answer: Consider the potential risks for a conservative or high-risk investment before investing your money.

SOURCES OF FINANCIAL INFORMATION

A wealth of information is available to investors. Sources include the Internet, professional advisory services, newspapers, brokerage firm reports, business periodicals, corporate reports, and securities averages.

The Internet

By using the Internet, investors can access a wealth of information on most investment and personal finance topics. For example, you can obtain interest rates for CDs; current price information for stocks, bonds, and mutual funds; and experts' recommendations to buy, hold, or sell an investment. You can even trade securities online.

Because the Internet makes so much information available, you need to use it selectively. One of the Web search engines such as Yahoo! (www.yahoo.com) or Google (www.google.com) can help you locate the information you really need. These search engines allow you to do a word search for the personal finance topic or investment alternative you want to explore. Why not take a look? To access a search engine, enter the Web site address and then type in a key term such as *personal finance* or *financial planning* and see the results. In addition to using a search engine to locate information, you can also obtain information from a number of investment sites. For example, the Web sites described in Table 20.6 are often used by successful investors.

Corporations; brokerage firms; investment companies that sponsor mutual funds; real estate brokers and agents; and federal, state, and local governments also have Web sites where you can obtain valuable investment information. You may want to explore the information available on the Internet for two reasons. First, these sites are easily accessible. All you have to do is type in the Web address or use a search engine to locate the site. Second, the information on these sites may be more up-to-date than printed material obtained from published sources. Today, many of the above sources of information also use social media to connect with investors. Charles Schwab, for example, uses Facebook, Twitter, and YouTube to reach existing and potential clients.

In addition, you can access professional advisory services—a topic discussed in the next section—for information on stocks, bonds, mutual funds, and other investment alternatives. Although some of the information provided by these services is free, there is a charge for the more detailed information you may need to evaluate an investment.

TABLE 20.6	Five Popular Web Sites to Help You Establish a Successful Investment Program
Sponsor and Web Address	**Description**
The Motley Fool Web (www.fool.com)	Light-hearted financial advice and step-by-step activities to help you start an investment program
CNN/Money (www.money.cnn.com)	Current financial news and investment information that can help investors sharpen their investment skills
Market Watch (www.marketwatch.com)	Price information about stocks and funds along with information about investing, the economy, and personal financial planning
Yahoo! Finance (http://finance.yahoo.com)	Current price information and general research information for stocks, mutual funds, and bonds
Smart Money (http://smartmoney.com)	Information about how to save, invest, and spend along with easy-to-use financial calculators

© CENGAGE LEARNING 2014

Professional Advisory Services

For a fee, various professional advisory services provide information about investments. Information from these services may also be available at university and public libraries.

As discussed earlier in this chapter, Moody's, Standard & Poor's, and Fitch Ratings provide information that can be used to determine the quality and risk associated with bond issues. Standard & Poor's, Mergent, Inc., and Value Line also rate the companies that issue stock. Each investor service provides detailed financial reports. Take a look at the Mergent's research report for Dollar Tree, Inc., illustrated in Figure 20.1. Notice that there are main sections that provide financial data, summary information about the company's business operations, recent developments, prospects, and other valuable information. Research reports published by Standard & Poor's and Value Line are like the Mergent's report and provide similar information.

A number of professional advisory services provide detailed information on mutual funds. Morningstar, Inc., Standard & Poor's, Lipper Analytical Services, and Value Line are four widely tapped sources for such information. Although some information may be free, a fee is generally charged for more detailed research reports. In addition, various mutual-fund newsletters supply financial information to subscribers for a fee.

Financial Coverage of Securities Transactions

Many local newspapers carry several pages of business news, including reports of securities transactions. The *Wall Street Journal* (published on weekdays) and *Barron's* (published once a week) are devoted almost entirely to financial and economic news. Both include coverage of transactions on major securities exchanges.

Because transactions involving stocks, bonds, and mutual funds are reported differently, we examine each type of report separately.

Common and Preferred Stocks Stock transactions are reported in tables that usually look like the top section of Figure 20.2. Stocks are listed alphabetically. Your first task is to move down the table to find the stock you are interested in. To read the stock quotation, you read across the table. The highlighted line in Figure 20.2 gives detailed information about common stock issued by Aflac—the insurance company with the talking duck.

Bonds Although some newspapers and financial publications provide limited information on certain corporate and government bond issues, it is usually easier to obtain more detailed information on a greater number of bond issues by accessing the Internet. Regardless of the source, bond prices are quoted as a percentage of the face value, which is usually $1,000. Thus, to find the current price, you must multiply the face value ($1,000) by the quotation. For example, a price quoted as 84 translates to a selling price of $840 ($1,000 × 84% = $840). Detailed information obtained from the Yahoo! Finance Web site for a $1,000 AT&T corporate bond, which pays 5.50 percent interest and matures in 2018, is provided in Figure 20.3.

Mutual Funds Purchases and sales of shares of mutual funds are reported in tables like the one shown in Figure 20.4. As in reading stock quotations, your first task is to move down the table to find the mutual fund you are interested in. Then, to find the mutual-fund price quotation, read across the table. The first line in Figure 20.4 gives information for the Vanguard 500 Index mutual fund.

Personal APPS

There is more to successful investing than just luck! In fact, you must "invest" the time needed to research stocks, bonds, mutual funds, and other alternatives before you invest your money. And in order to be a "best" investor, you'll need to continue to evaluate each investment. Continued evaluation can help you decide if you want to hold, sell, or buy more of each investment in your investment portfolio.

FIGURE 20.1   Mergent's Research Report for Dollar Tree, Inc.

A research report from Mergent's is divided into main parts that describe not only the financial condition of a company but also its history and outlook for the future.

*7 Year Price Score 220.86 *NYSE Composite Index = 100   *12 Month Price Score 134.45

Interim Earnings (Per Share)

Qtr.	Apr	Jul	Oct	Jan
2008–9	0.32	0.28	0.31	0.77
2009–10	0.44	0.42	0.51	1.01
2010–11	0.49	0.61	0.73	1.26
2011-12	0.82	0.77	0.87	

nterim Dividends (Per Share)

No Dividends Paid

Valuation Anaylsis		Institutional Holding	
Forecast EPS	$4.01	No of Institutions	
	(12/10/2011)	545	
Market Cap	$9.7 Billion	Shares	
Book Value	$1.4 Billion	124,758,872	
Price Book	6.70	% Held	
Price/Sales	1.51	N/A	

Business Summary: Retail - General Merchandise/Department Stores (MIC: 2.1.1 SIC: 5331 NAIC: 452990)
Dollar Tree is an operator of discount variety stores providing merchandise at the fixed price of $1.00. Co.'s merchandise mix consists of consumable merchandise, which includes candy and food, health and beauty care, and household consumables; variety merchandise, which includes toys, housewares, gifts, party goods, greeting cards, softlines, and other items; and seasonal goods, which include Easter, Halloween and Christmas merchandise. At Jan 29 2011, Co. operates 4.015 stores in 48 states and the District of Columbia, as well as 86 stores in Canada under the Dollar Tree, Deal$, Dollar Tree Deal$, Dollar Giant and Dollar Bills names.

Recent Developments: For the quarter ended Oct 29 2011, net income increased 12.1% to US$104.5 million from US$93.2 million in the year-earlier quarter. Revenues were US$1.60 billion, up 11.9% from US$1.43 billion the year before. Operating income was US$164.9 million versus US$140.9 million in the prior-year quarter, an increase of 17.0%. Direct operating expenses rose 12.5% to US$1.04 billion from US$920.6 million in the comparable period the year before. Indirect operating expenses increased 8.4% to US$395.7 million from US$365.1 million in the equivalent prior-year period.

Prospects: Our evaluation of Dollar Tree Inc. as of Dec. 11, 2011 is the result of our systematic analysis on three basic characteristics; earnings strength, relative valuation, and recent stock price movement. The company has produced a positive trend in earnings per share over the past 5 quarters and while recent estimates for the company have been raised by analysts, DLTR has posted better than expected results. Based on operating earnings yield, the company is about fairly valued when compared to all of the companies in our coverage universe. Share price changes over the past year indicates that DLTR will perform well over the near term.

Financial Data

(US$ in Thousands)	9 Mos	6 Mos	3 Mos	01/29/2011	01/30/2010	01/31/2009	02/02/2008	02/03/2007
Earning Per Share	3.74	3.60	3.44	3.10	2.37	1.69	1.39	1.23
Cash Flow Per Share	5.53	5.10	5.21	4.09	4.34	2.98	2.56	2.62
Tang Book Value Per Share	10.70	11.55	10.73	10.42	9.87	8.23	6.24	6.83
Income Statement								
Total Revenue	4,684,900	3,088,300	1,545,900	5,882,400	5,231,200	4,644.900	4,242,600	3,969,400
EBITDA	600,100	394,200	201,600	795,200	670,600	526,900	488,800	469,800
Depn & Amortn	119,900	78,800	39,200	159,700	157,800	161,100	158,500	159,600
Income Before Taxes	478,000	313,800	161,500	629,900	507,600	359,100	319,800	302,900
Income Taxes	177,600	117,900	60,500	232,600	187,100	129,600	118,500	110,900
Net Income	300,400	195,900	101,000	397,300	320,500	229,500	201,300	192.000
Average Shares	120,700	123,000	123,500	128,000	135,000	136,200	144,600	155,700
Balance Sheet								
Current Assets	1,332,500	1,408,300	1,325,500	1,333,300	1,305,600	1,073,200	788,800	959,000
Total Assets	2,431,200	2,478,900	2,381,300	2,380,500	2,289,700	2,035,700	1,787,700	1,873,300
Current Liabilities	587,100	495,800	504,700	532,800	475,900	409,900	405,900	383,300
Long-Term Obligations	250,000	250,000	250,000	250,000	250,000	250,000	250,000	250,000
Total Liabilities	984,300	891,200	894,600	921,500	860,500	782,500	799,300	705,600
Stockholders' Equity	1,446,900	1,587,700	1,486,700	1,459,000	1,429,200	1,253,200	988,400	1,167,700
Share Outstanding	119,000	122,300	122,277	123,393	131,284	136,157	134,677	149,495
Statistical Record								
Return on Assets %	19.31	19.07	19.22	17.06	14.86	12.04	11.03	10.29
Return on Equity %	32.38	30.42	31.28	27.59	23.96	20.53	18.72	16.15
EBITDA Margin %	12.81	12.76	13.04	13.52	12.82	11.34	11.52	11.84
Net Margin %	6.41	6.34	6.53	6.75	6.13	4.94	4.74	4.84
Asset Turnover	2.67	2.64	2.69	2.53	2.43	2.44	2.32	2.13
Current Ratio	2.27	2.84	2.63	2.50	2.74	2.62	1.94	2.50
Debt to Equity	0.17	0.16	0.17	0.17	0.17	0.20	0.25	0.21
Price Range	81.74-48.58	70.21-41.04	58.12-39.15	57.36-31.41	34.22-22.45	29.17-19.39	30.38-14.20	21.40-16.30
P/E Ratio	21.86-12.99	19.50-11.40	16.90-11.38	18.50-10.13	14.44-9.47	17.26-9.70	21.86-10.22	17.40-13.25

FIGURE 20.2 Reading Stock Quotations

Reproduced at the top of the figure is a portion of the stock quotations listed in the *Wall Street Journal*. At the bottom is an enlargement of the same information. The numbers above each of the enlarged columns correspond to the numbered entries in the list of explanations that appears in the middle of the figure.

STOCK	(SYM)	CLOSE	NET CHG
ABB ADS	ABB	18.33	−0.45
ACE Ltd	ACE	68.41	−0.96
AES Cp	AES	11.72	−0.14
Aflac	AFL	42.89	−0.89

1. Name (often abbreviated) of the corporation: Aflac
2. Ticker symbol or letters that identify a stock for trading: AFL
3. Close is the price paid in the last transaction of the day: $42.89
4. Difference between the price paid for the last share sold today and the price paid for the last share sold on the previous day: −0.89 (in Wall Street terms, Aflac "closed down $0.89" on this day).

1	2	3	4
STOCK	(SYM)	CLOSE	NET CHG
ABB ADS	ABB	18.33	−0.45
ACE Ltd	ACE	68.41	−0.96
AES Cp	AES	11.72	−0.14
Aflac	AFL	42.89	−0.89

Source: The *Wall Street Journal*, December 13, 2011, C8.

FIGURE 20.3 Reading Bond Quotations

Reproduced at the top of the figure is bond information obtained from the Yahoo! Finance Web site. The numbers beside each line correspond to numbered entries in the list of explanations that appears at the bottom of the figure.

AT&T INC

OVERVIEW	
1. Price	112.28
2. Coupon (%)	5.500
3. Maturity Date	1-Feb-2018
4. Yield to Maturity (%)	3.447
5. Current Yield (%)	4.899
6. Fitch Ratings	A
7. Coupon Payment Frequency	Semi-annual
8. First Coupon Date	1-Aug-2008
9. Type	Corporate
10. Callable	No

1. Price quoted as a percentage of the face value: $1,000 × 112.28% = $1,122.80
2. Coupon (%) is the rate of interest: 5.500 percent
3. Maturity Date is the date when bondholders will receive repayment: February 1, 2018
4. Yield to Maturity (%) takes into account the relationship among a bond's maturity value, the time to maturity, the current price, and the amount of interest: 3.447 percent
5. Current Yield (%) is determined by dividing the dollar amount of annual interest by the current price of the bond: ($55 ÷ $1,122.80 ÷ 0.04899 = 4.899 percent)
6. Fitch Ratings is used to assess risk associated with this bond: A
7. Coupon Payment Frequency tells bondholders how often they will receive interest payments: Semi-annual
8. First Coupon Date: August 1, 2008
9. Type: Corporate
10. Callable: No

Source: The Yahoo! Finance bond Web site at http://bonds.yahoo.com (accessed March 12, 2012).

FIGURE 20.4   Reading Mutual-Fund Quotations

Reproduced at the top of the figure is a portion of the mutual-fund quotations as reported by the _Wall Street Journal_. At the bottom is an enlargement of the same information. The numbers above each of the enlarged columns correspond to numbered entries in the list of explanations that appears in the middle of the figure.

FUND	NAV	NET CHG	YTD %RET
Vanguard 500 Index	126.74	+0.46	9.4
TotBd	11.01	–	0.6
TotIntl	14.60	-0.04	11.8
TotSt	34.44	+0.16	10.1

1. The name of the mutual fund: Vanguard 500 Index
2. The net asset value (NAV) is the value of one share of the Vanguard 500 Index Fund: $126.74
3. The difference between the net asset value today and the net asset value on the previous trading day: +0.46 (in Wall Street terms, the "Vanguard 500 Index fund closed up $0.46" on this day)
4. The YTD% RET gives the total return for the Vanguard 500 Index fund for the year to date: 9.4%

1	2	3	4
FUND	NAV	NET CHG	YTD %RET
Vanguard 500 Index	126.74	+0.46	9.4
TotBD	11.01	–	0.6
TotIntl	14.60	-0.04	11.8
TotSt	34.44	+0.16	10.1

Source: The _Wall Street Journal_, March 10, 2012, B14.

Other Sources of Financial Information

In addition to the Internet, professional advisory services, and financial and newspaper coverage, other sources, which include brokerage firm reports, business periodicals, corporate reports, and securities averages offer information about investment alternatives.

Brokerage Firm Analysts' Reports Brokerage firms employ financial analysts to prepare detailed reports on individual corporations and their securities. Such reports are based on the corporation's sales, profits or losses, management, and planning, plus other information on the company, its industry, demand for its products, its efforts to develop new products, and the current economic environment. The reports, which may include buy or sell recommendations, are usually provided free to the clients of full-service brokerage firms. Brokerage firm reports may also be available from discount brokerage firms, although they may charge a fee.

Business Periodicals Business magazines such as _Bloomberg Businessweek_, _Fortune_, and _Forbes_ provide not only general economic news but also detailed financial information about individual corporations. Trade or industry publications such as _Advertising Age_ include information about firms in a specific industry. News magazines such as _U.S. News & World Report, Time_, and _Newsweek_ feature financial news regularly. _Money, Kiplinger's Personal Finance Magazine, Smart Money_, and similar magazines provide information and advice designed to improve your investment skills. These periodicals are available at libraries and are sold at newsstands and by subscription. Many of these same periodicals sponsor an online Web site that may contain all or selected articles that are contained in the print version.

Career SUCCESS

You'll Need a License to Trade

Thinking about a career in the securities industry? You'll need a license (or more than one) to work with investors and place trades on their behalf—which means taking challenging tests prepared by the Financial Industry Regulatory Authority (FINRA). The higher you move in a brokerage firm, the more licenses you'll need to offer a broader range of securities and to supervise other employees who work with investors and investment accounts.

As an entry-level account executive with a firm like Charles Schwab or Raymond James, you'll need to pass the Series 7 exam for General Securities Representatives. The good news: The two-part test contains only multiple-choice questions. The bad news: Each part is three hours long, which means you'll sit through six hours of testing to complete the entire exam. You'll need to answer at least 72 percent of the questions correctly to earn a passing grade.

Although the exact questions differ from year to year, one set of questions typically covers securities such as stocks, bonds, and mutual funds. Another set tests your understanding of various accounts, including individual retirement accounts (IRAs) and employer-sponsored retirement accounts like 401(k) accounts. A third set of questions focuses on regulatory rules, such as the disclosures you're required to provide to investors. Finally, you'll have to answer questions that test what you know about securities markets and financial management—big-picture information you will need to help your clients choose the right investments to meet their particular needs.

Sources: Based on information in "General Securities Representative Qualification Examination: Series 7 Content Outline," Financial Industry Regulatory Authority, Inc. (2011); Financial Industry Regulatory Agency Web site (www.finra.org); Joan Quigley, "MSRB Wants to Pick Up Ball from FINRA," *The Bond Buyer*, September 14, 2011, p. 1; Danielle Reed, "Asked and Answered: Deadline Looms for Comments on BrokerCheck Changes," *Financial Planning*, March 19, 2012, www.financial-planning.com.

Corporate Reports Publicly held corporations must publish annual reports which include a description of the company's performance, information about the firm's products or services, and detailed financial statements that readers can use to evaluate the firm's actual performance. There should also be a letter from the accounting firm that audited the corporation. As mentioned in Chapter 17, an audit does not guarantee that a company has not "cooked" the books, but it does imply that the company has followed generally accepted accounting principles to report revenues, profits, assets, liabilities, and other financial information.

In addition, a corporation issuing a new security must—by law—prepare a prospectus and ensure that copies are distributed to potential investors. A **prospectus** is a detailed, written description of a new security, the issuing corporation, and the corporation's top management. A corporation's prospectus and its annual reports are available to the general public. You can request both an annual report and a prospectus by mail or telephone. In addition you can obtain an annual report, prospectus, or other financial information online. It's simple: Go to the corporation's Web site and click on "Investor Relations."

Security Averages

Investors often gauge the stock market through the security averages reported in newspapers and on television news programs. A **security average (or security index)** is an average of the current market prices of selected securities. For example, the Dow Jones Industrial Average and the Standard & Poor 500 Stock Index are both used by investors to track the U.S. stock market. Today, there are averages for not only stocks, but also averages for bonds, U.S. Treasury securities, mutual funds, real estate, commodities, natural resources, and many popular investments. Over a period of time, these averages indicate price trends, but they do not predict the performance of individual investments. At best, they can give the investor a "feel" for what is happening to investment prices.

HOW INVESTMENTS ARE BOUGHT AND SOLD

Think back over the material that was covered in this chapter. We began by discussing why it is important to examine your current financial situation and the need to manage your money. Next we talked about the factors that influence your choice of investments,

prospectus a detailed, written description of a new security, the issuing corporation, and the corporation's top management

security average (or security index) an average of the current market prices of selected securities

Understand how different investments are bought and sold.

how successful investors are involved in their investment program, and conservative and speculative investment alternatives. Then, in the last section, we discussed how you can evaluate different investment alternatives in order to make an informed decision to buy or sell an investment. Once you understand the information in the previous sections and have researched a potential investment, you can use the options described in this section to buy or sell an investment.

Purchasing Stocks and Bonds

To purchase a Geoffrey Beene sweater, you simply walk into a store that sells these sweaters, choose one, and pay for it. To purchase stocks and bonds, you work through a brokerage firm. In turn, an employee of the brokerage firm buys or sells securities for you.

Brokerage Firms and Account Executives An **account executive**—sometimes called a *stockbroker* or *registered representative*—is an individual who buys and sells securities for clients. Before choosing an account executive, you should have already determined your investment goals. Then you must be careful to communicate these goals to the account executive so that she or he can do a better job of advising you. You must also decide whether you need a *full-service* broker or a *discount* broker. A full-service broker usually charges higher commissions when compared to a discount broker. To help decide if you should use a full-service or a discount brokerage firm, you should consider how much help you need when making an investment decision. Many full-service brokerage firms argue that you need a professional to help you make important investment decisions. Although this may be true for some investors, most account executives employed by full-service brokerage firms are too busy to spend unlimited time with you on a one-on-one basis, especially if you are investing a small amount. On the other side, many discount brokerage firms argue that you alone are responsible for making your investment decisions. Furthermore, they argue that discount brokerage firms have both the personnel and research materials to help you to become a better investor.

The Mechanics of a Transaction Once you decide on a particular stock or bond, you can telephone your account executive or use the Internet to place a market or limit order. A **market order** is a request that a security be purchased or sold at the current market price. Figure 20.5 illustrates one method of executing a market order to sell a stock listed on the New York Stock Exchange (NYSE) at its current market value. It is also possible for a brokerage firm to match a buy order for a security for one of its

account executive an individual, sometimes called a *stockbroker* or *registered representative,* who buys and sells securities for clients

market order a request that a security be purchased or sold at the current market price

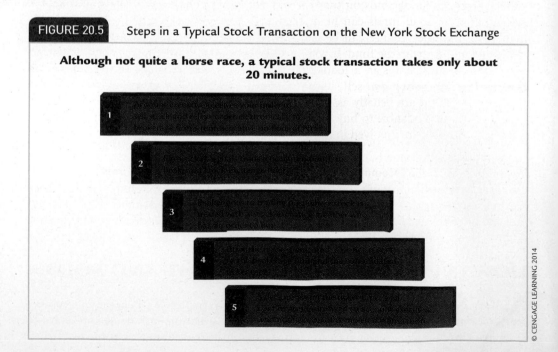

FIGURE 20.5   Steps in a Typical Stock Transaction on the New York Stock Exchange

Although not quite a horse race, a typical stock transaction takes only about 20 minutes.

© CENGAGE LEARNING 2014

customers with a sell order for the same security from another of its customers. Matched orders are not completed through a security exchange or the over-the-counter market. Regardless of how the security is bought or sold, payment for stocks, bonds, and many other financial securities generally is required within three business days of the transaction.

A **limit order** is a request that a security be bought or sold at a price equal to or better than (lower for buying, higher for selling) some specified price. Suppose that you place a limit order to *sell* Coca-Cola common stock at $70 per share. Your broker's representative sells the stock only if the price is $70 per share or *higher*. If you place a limit order to *buy* Coca Cola at $70, the representative buys it only if the price is $70 per share or *lower*. Usually, a limit order is good for one day, one week, one month, or good until canceled.

Commissions Most brokerage firms have a minimum commission ranging from $7 to $25 for buying and selling stock. Additional commission charges are based on the number of shares and the value of stock bought and sold.

Table 20.7 shows typical commission fees charged by online brokerage firms. Generally, online transactions are less expensive when compared with the costs of trading securities through a full-service brokerage firm. As a rule of thumb, full-service brokerage firms charge as much as 1 to 2 percent of the transaction amount. Commissions for trading bonds, commodities, and options are usually lower than those for trading stocks.

Purchasing Mutual Funds, Real Estate, and Other Investments

The method used to buy or sell mutual funds depends on the type of fund you choose. Open-end funds, for example, can be purchased or sold directly from the investment company that sponsors the fund on any business day. Both closed-end funds and exchange-traded funds can be purchased or sold on any business day through a securities exchange or the over-the-counter market. The amount of sales charge also depends on the type of fund you purchase. The sales charge for load funds can be as high as 8 1/2 percent. For a load fund, the sales charge can be charged when you make a purchase or when you withdraw money from the fund. If you purchase a no-load fund, there is no sales charge. When purchasing shares in a load fund, you usually pay commission to buy *or* sell shares—but not to buy *and* sell shares. Reminder: For fund investments, you will also pay other fees that are usually assessed each year.

Although it is possible to buy or sell real estate without a real estate agent or broker, these professionals are involved in most transactions. Finding an agent or broker that can

© AP PHOTO/DAVID KARP

Case closed—150 years in prison. The common phrase "Don't do the crime if you can't do the time," explains why Bernard "Bernie" Madoff looks so unhappy in this photo. Mr. Madoff was found guilty of securities fraud when the Ponzi scheme he managed collapsed and investors lost almost $65 billion. Perhaps another common phrase, "Crime doesn't pay," is applicable to Bernie Madoff who will spend the rest of his life in prison.

TABLE 20.7	Typical Commission Costs Charged by Online Brokerage Firms		
	Internet ($)	Interactive Voice-Response Telephone System ($)	Broker-Assisted ($)
TD Ameritrade	$9.99	$34.99	$49.99
Charles Schwab	$8.95	13.95	33.95
Fidelity	7.95	12.95	32.95
Scottrade	7.00	17.00	27.00

Source: The Brokerage-Review.com Web site at www.brokerage-review.com (accessed March 13, 2012).

limit order a request that a security be bought or sold at a price that is equal to or better than some specified price help you to either buy or sell an investment is especially important because she or he can provide professional advice, realistic market values for different properties, and help completing the transaction. You should expect to pay commissions when you sell a property.

A broker (or account executive) is usually involved in the purchase or sell of the most speculative investment alternatives listed in Table 20.2. For example, brokers can help you purchase commodities and precious metals. It is especially important to "know" the person you are dealing with when purchasing many of the speculative investments because of the potential for fraud and misrepresentation. It pays to be careful.

It should be apparent that vast sums of money are involved in securities trading. In an effort to protect investors from unfair treatment, both federal and state governments have acted to regulate securities trading.

Regulation of Securities Trading

Government regulation of securities was begun as a response to abusive and fraudulent practices in the sale of stocks, bonds, and other financial securities. Today, with so many news reports of banks with a portfolio of bad loans and of corporations that are in "hot water" over financial reporting problems that range from simple mistakes to out-and-out fraud, the concerns of both government officials and investors have grown.

Today, a regulatory pyramid consisting of four different levels exists to make sure that investors are protected. The U.S. Congress is at the top of the pyramid. Early on, Congress passed the Securities Act of 1933 (sometimes referred to as the Truth in Securities Act). This act provides for full disclosure. **Full disclosure** means that investors should have access to all important facts about stocks, bonds, and other securities so that they can make informed decisions. This act also requires that corporations issuing new securities file a registration statement and publish a prospectus. Since 1933, Congress has passed additional legislation that includes creating the Securities Investor Protection Corporation to protect investors. Congress also has passed legislation to curb insider-trading abuses. **Insider trading** occurs when insiders—board members, corporate managers, and employees—buy and sell a corporation's stock. Although insiders can buy and sell a corporation's stock, they must disclose their trading activities to the public. More recently, Congress passed the Sarbanes–Oxley Act to improve corporate accountability and financial reporting (see Chapter 17).

On the next level of the regulatory pyramid is the Securities and Exchange Commission (SEC), created in 1934 by the Securities Exchange Act of 1934. The SEC is the agency that enforces federal securities regulations. The SEC also supervises all national exchanges, investment companies, the OTC market, brokerage firms, and just about every other organization involved in trading securities.

On the next level of the regulatory pyramid are individual states. Today, most states require that new security issues be registered with a state agency and that brokerage firms, brokers, and investment advisors operating within the state be licensed. Most state regulations also provide for the prosecution of individuals accused of the fraudulent sale of stocks, bonds, and other securities.

The foundation and most important level of the regulatory pyramid is self-regulation by securities exchanges and brokerage firms. According to the NYSE, self-regulation—the way the securities industry monitors itself to create a fair and orderly trading environment—begins here.[10] To provide guidelines of ethical behavior, the NYSE has published rules, policies, and standards of conduct. These standards are applied to every member in the NYSE's investment community. The NYSE also conducts a thorough examination of each member firm that does business with the public at least once a year.[11] In addition, there are more than 300 brokerage firms that buy and sell securities for their customers. These firms are responsible for ensuring that their employees are highly trained and meet rigorous ethical standards.

Before they can start investing, most people have to decide on a career and obtain a job that will provide the money needed to finance an investment program. To help you find the right job (and the money needed to fund an investment program), read Appendix A where we provide information that can help you to explore different career options (see text Web site @ www.cengagebrain.com).

full disclosure requirement that investors should have access to all important facts about stocks, bonds, and other securities so that they can make informed decisions

insider trading the practice of board members, corporate managers, and employees buying and selling a corporation's stock

The Vanguard Group

Whether investors call the Vanguard Group, visit one of its offices, log onto its Web site, or use its apps, they'll find a wealth of information, tools, and advice to help them manage their investments and achieve their financial goals. Best-known for its low-cost index funds, Vanguard also offers brokerage services, retirement planning services, college investment accounts, and research and educational information for individuals. In addition, it manages pension funds for companies and for nonprofit organizations such as colleges and hospitals.

Because of Vanguard's long-time focus on mutual funds, it didn't begin offering exchange-traded funds (ETFs) until 2001, again keeping costs low as it does with its mutual funds. Now the company has become the third-largest U.S. provider of ETFs, and more than 45 percent of the funds it receives from clients flow into its ETFs—adding up to more than $200 billion in EFT assets.

Questions

1. When investing for a long-term goal such as retirement, how are the costs associated with your investments likely to affect your results? Explain your answer in terms of this chapter's concepts.
2. As an investor, what questions would you like to ask a Vanguard representative? How do these questions relate to your financial goals?

SUMMARY

Looking for Success?
Get Flashcards, Quizzes, Games, Crosswords, and more @ www.cengagebrain.com.

 Explain why you should manage your personal finances and develop a personal investment program.

Many personal finance experts recommend that you begin the process of managing your money by determining your current financial condition. The first step often is to construct a personal income statement sheet and a personal balance sheet. You can also construct a personal budget. Before you begin investing, you must manage your credit card debts. For most people, the next step is to formulate realistic investment goals. A personal investment program then is designed to implement these goals. Many financial planners also suggest that the investor should establish an emergency fund equivalent to at least three months' living expenses. However, you may want to increase your emergency fund in anticipation of a crisis. Then additional funds may be invested according to the investment program. Finally, all investments should be monitored carefully, and if necessary, the investment program should be modified.

 Describe how the factors of safety, risk, income, growth, and liquidity affect your investment program.

Depending on their particular investment goals, investors seek varying degrees of safety, risk, income, growth, and liquidity from their investments. Safety is, in essence, freedom from the risk of loss. Generally, the greater the risk, the greater should be the potential return on an investment. To determine how much risk you are willing to assume, many investors calculate the rate of return. It is also possible to compare the rate of return for different investments that offer more or less risk. Income is the periodic return from an investment. Growth is an increase in the value of the investment. Liquidity is the ease with which an asset can be converted to cash.

 Recognize how you can reduce investment risk and increase investment returns.

The investments in your investment portfolio should be tailored to your goals, age, tolerance for risk, and financial resources. Asset allocation is the process of spreading your money among several different types of investments to lessen risk. Two other factors—the time your investments have to work for you and your age—should also be considered before deciding where to invest your money. To reduce investment risk and increase the returns on your investments, you should evaluate potential investments before investing your money, monitor the value of your investments on a regular basis, and keep accurate and current records.

 Explain the reasons people choose conservative investments including bank accounts and bonds.

In this section, we examined traditional investments that include bank accounts, government bonds, and corporate bonds. Although bank accounts and bonds can provide investment growth, they are generally purchased by investors who seek a predictable source of income. There are a number of different types of bonds and securities issued by both the U.S. government (see Table 20.3) and local governments. There are also a number of different types of corporate bonds. Both government and corporate bonds are a form of debt financing. As a result, bonds are generally considered a more conservative investment than stocks, mutual funds, or other more speculative investments.

 Identify the advantages and disadvantages of stocks, mutual funds, real estate, and more speculative investments.

With stock investments, investors can make money through dividend payments, an increase in the market value of the stock, or stock splits. The major advantages of mutual-fund investments are professional management and diversification. Today, there are mutual funds to meet just about any conceivable investment objective. The success of real estate investments is often tied to how well each investment alternative is evaluated. High-risk investment techniques can provide greater returns, but they also entail greater risk of loss. You can make money by selling short when the market value of a financial security decreases. An investor can also buy stock on margin by borrowing part of the purchase price, usually from a stock brokerage firm. Because you can purchase up to twice as much stock by using margin, you can increase your return on investment as long as the stock's market value increases. Other high-risk investments include stock options, derivatives, commodities, gemstones, precious metals, antiques, coins, and collectibles.

 Use financial information to evaluate investment alternatives.

Today, there is a wealth of information on stocks, bonds, and other securities and the firms that issue them. There is also a wealth of investment information on other types of investments, including mutual funds, real estate, and high-risk investment alternatives. Two popular sources—the Internet and newspapers—report daily securities transactions.

The Internet can also be used to obtain detailed research information about different investment alternatives. Often, the most detailed research information about securities—and the most expensive—is obtained from professional advisory services. In addition, brokerage firm reports, business periodicals, and corporate reports can also be used to evaluate different investment alternatives. Finally, there are a number of security indexes or averages that indicate price trends but reveal nothing about the performance of individual securities.

 Understand how different investments are bought and sold.

If you invest in stocks and bonds, chances are that you will use the services of an account executive who works for a brokerage firm. It is also possible to use a discount broker or trade securities online with a computer. Both a market order and a limit order can be used to purchase stocks on a securities exchange or in the over-the-counter market. Full-service brokerage firms usually charge higher commissions than discount brokerage firms. With the exception of mutual funds and real estate, you generally pay a commission to buy *and* sell stocks, bonds, commodities, and most other investments.

The method used to buy or sell mutual funds depends on the type of fund you choose. Open-end funds, for example, can be purchased or sold directly from the investment company that sponsors the fund on any business day. Both closed-end funds and exchange-traded funds can be purchased or sold on any business day through a securities exchange or the over-the-counter market. While it is possible to buy or sell real estate without the help of an agent or broker, most investors rely on the professional advice provided by agents and brokers to help complete a real estate transaction.

Today, a regulatory pyramid consisting of four different levels exists to make sure that investors are protected. The U.S. Congress, the Securities and Exchange Commission (SEC), individual states, and securities exchanges and brokerage firms are all involved in regulating the securities industry.

KEY TERMS

You should now be able to define and give an example relevant to each of the following terms:

net worth (581)	Standard & Poor's 500 Stock Index (587)	exchange-traded fund (ETF) (593)	prospectus (603)
personal budget (581)	asset allocation (587)	net asset value (NAV) (594)	security average (or security index) (603)
personal investment (582)	municipal bond (589)	expense ratio (594)	account executive (604)
financial planner (583)	stock dividend (591)	family of funds (595)	market order (604)
Dow Jones Industrial Average (584)	capital gain (591)	high-risk investment (596)	limit order (605)
blue-chip stock (585)	market value (591)	buying long (596)	full disclosure (606)
rate of return (585)	stock split (592)	selling short (596)	insider trading (606)
liquidity (586)	mutual fund (593)	margin requirement (597)	

1. How could developing a personal budget help you obtain the money needed to fund your investment program?
2. What is an "emergency fund," and why is it recommended?
3. What is the trade-off between safety and risk? How do you calculate rate of return?
4. In general, what kinds of investments provide income? What kinds provide growth?
5. How do you think that asset allocation, the time your investments have to work for you, and your age affect the choice of investments for someone who is 25 years old? For someone who is 59 years old?
6. Characterize the purchase of corporate and government bonds as an investment in terms of safety, risk, income, growth, and liquidity.
7. Describe the three methods by which investors can make money with stock investments.
8. An individual may invest in stocks either directly or through a mutual fund. How are the two investment methods different?
9. What are the risks and rewards of selling short and purchasing stocks on margin?
10. How could the Internet help you to research an investment?
11. In addition to the Internet, what other sources of financial information could help you to obtain your investment goals?
12. Would you use a full-service or a discount brokerage firm? Explain your answer.
13. What is the difference between a market order and a limit order?
14. Describe how the securities industry is regulated.

1. For the time period between 2007 and 2009 people experienced dramatic declines in the market value of stocks, mutual funds, and other investments. Then, the market began to rebound. Based on the current state of the economy and the investment markets at the time you answer this question, do you think that it is a good time to begin an investment program? Justify your answer.
2. What personal circumstances might lead investors to emphasize income rather than growth in their investment planning? What might lead them to emphasize growth rather than income?
3. In this chapter, it was apparent that stocks have outperformed other investment alternatives over a long period of time. With this fact in mind, why would investors choose to use asset allocation to diversify their investments?
4. What type of individual would invest in government bonds? In growth mutual funds? In real estate?
5. Suppose that you have just inherited 500 shares of IBM common stock. What would you do with it, if anything?
6. What kinds of information would you like to have before you invest in a particular common stock or mutual fund? From what sources can you get that information?
7. Take another look at Figure 20.1 (Mergent's research report for Dollar Tree, Inc.). Based on the research provided by Mergent's, would you buy stock in Dollar Tree? Justify your decision by providing specific examples from Figure 20.1.

Video Case 20.1

Taming the Debt Monster One Budget at a Time

Danny Kofke and his family have purchased some pretty nice things for themselves over the years. They own a lovely home that is about half paid for and have taken nice vacations to places like Europe. He and his wife, Tracy, recently bought a new washer, dryer, refrigerator, and 50-inch flat-screen TV. For the past seven years, Tracy has been able to stay at home to raise their children.

How have the Kofkes, who are only in their thirties, managed to live so well—especially in today's tough economy? Are they members of the 1 percent? Is Danny a highly paid executive or a Wall Street banker, perhaps?

Not hardly. Danny is actually a special-needs teacher who earns just a little over $40,000 a year. That's about $10,000 less than the average family in the United States makes. He and Tracy have figured out how to live well by paying careful attention to their finances. If the Kofkes stick to their financial plan, they are on track to retire with a million dollars or more.

Having a budget has been critical to their success. "The biggest mistake people make when it comes to their money is that they don't keep track of it, and they don't know how they are spending it," Danny explains. Sticking to the budget is also important. The Kofkes carefully prioritize their spending. They don't buy things they don't really want or need just because other people have them. "Don't worry about what your neighbors think," he says. "I know that's hard today when everybody feels like they have to keep up with the Joneses."

Trevor Thomas and his wife, Michelle, are good managers of their money as well. Like the Kofkes, they are diligent budgeters. "A budget can help keep you from overspending during any particular income period or in any particular area," says Trevor. It can help you plan for non-regular expenses, such as car repairs, and help you plan for your financial future." The rising price of gas and food are two areas the Thomases' budget has helped with. "We are a family of six, so these increases have hit us hard," he says. But by examining their budget, he and Michelle were able to figure out how to adjust their spending. As a result, they haven't run up debt on their credit cards like other people without a budget might have done.

In fact, not only do the Thomases have no credit card debt, they don't even have a mortgage on their home. After paying off all of their consumer debt, they regularly saved as much money as they could. They then built an impressive two-story home bit-by-bit over the course of a three-and-a-half-year period. "We built it from the ground up, contracting it and financing it completely by ourselves," Trevor says.

The difference between people who carry credit card debt and those who don't is that the people without it don't feel deprived when they can't have everything they want right away, says Bedda D'Angelo, a certified financial planner. "They're not cheap. They're just not willing to pay for things they don't need and

haven't saved for." They also don't lie awake at night wondering how they are going to pay their bills.

The Kofkes admit they have been teased a time or two by people who think they are tightwads. They don't let it get them down, though. In today's debt-addicted world, where so many people, businesses, and even governments are broke, they're happy not to be under a monster-load of debt. "Do what's right for you and your family," Danny advises. "If people who don't do well managing their money—if they are laughing at you and telling you to change—then you must be doing something right."[12]

Questions

1. Is all debt bad? When does going into debt make sense?
2. Why is it so important for people to save and invest when they are young?
3. What steps can you take now to improve your financial outlook?

Case 20.2

Fidelity Helps Investors Prepare for Their Financial Future

Boston-based Fidelity Investments wants its 20 million customers to be able to manage their money and receive responsive assistance from anywhere at any time. Whether customers use an iPad or Android app, tweet for customer service, transfer money electronically, use online chat for service, call a broker, or place orders through the company's Web site, Fidelity is ready to help around the clock.

Founded in 1946, Fidelity now has 39,000 employees worldwide and offers 524 mutual funds that hold a total of $3.6 trillion in assets from individuals and institutional investors. Its mutual funds fall into four main categories: money market, stocks, bonds, and international securities. Fidelity is best known for its managed funds, such as the Contrafund and the Magellan Fund, although it also offers many indexed stock and bond funds. Over the years, it has expanded into a wide range of other financial services, including discount brokerage services, college savings accounts, credit cards, checking accounts, and online bill payment. Fidelity is also the country's largest administrator of 401(k) retirement accounts, handling retirement plans for more than 19,000 corporations, educational institutions, and nonprofit groups.

When the financial markets are open, Fidelity completes 345,000 securities trades per day for its customers. More than 3 million customers click on its user-friendly Web site every day to read analysts' reports, learn about investment and account options, view market update webinars, monitor their portfolios, or place a trade. For in-person service and advice, customers can visit one of the 168 Fidelity Investor Centers around the United States or attend a local seminar featuring Fidelity's investment experts.

Technology has always been one of Fidelity's strengths, so it's not surprising that the company has a Facebook page with 55,000 "likes" and a Twitter account with 48,000 followers. "Our expectation is that over time, we'll be interacting with not tens of thousands, but millions of people on these channels," says Fidelity's head of digital distribution. On the company's Web site, customers

are invited to rate brokerage products and services for convenience, value, and features on a scale of one to five stars. In addition, they can write detailed reviews of what they like and don't like. This allows investors to see what other investors think, as well as giving Fidelity vital feedback and fresh ideas for new products.

Given Fidelity's diverse menu of offerings, "The time has arrived when a lot of people can do very well with a firm like Fidelity for all of their cash management [needs]," says a senior executive. For example, customers can deposit checks to non-retirement accounts using a smart phone app, and withdraw money from any local bank's ATM—Fidelity pays the ATM fee. In fact, customers now click to make 7 million transfers of money to or from Fidelity accounts every year, a number that is growing as customers shift more of their personal finances to Fidelity.

Are young people going to have the money they need to enjoy retirement decades in the future? Fidelity's research shows that, thanks to new U.S. laws, more employees are being automatically enrolled in their employers' retirement plans. The earlier people begin to build their savings, the more money they will have when they reach retirement age. Among the plans that Fidelity administers, more than half of company employees now participate in the plan—triple the number of employees who participated in 2006. When these people need help with other financial matters, Fidelity will be ready.[13]

Questions

1. Why would Fidelity offer 524 mutual funds? What are the advantages to the company and to investors?
2. What are the pros and cons of having a checking account with Fidelity rather than with a local bank or credit union?
3. If you were trying to evaluate a specific mutual fund, where would you obtain the research information needed to choose the right fund? Assuming that you have found the right fund, would you prefer to invest online or talk with a Fidelity broker to complete the transaction?

① SOCIAL MEDIA EXERCISE

A growing number of personal finance- and investment-related ventures are starting to take advantage of the power of social media by connecting people beyond the boundaries of Facebook and Twitter. Peer-to-peer collaboration is now part of a new reality in the personal finance and investment fields. Online investor communities like Investorvillage (http://investorvillage.com), Covestor (http://covestor.com), and SocialPicks (http://social-picks.com) allow people to compare their investment ideas and their investment portfolio's performance to those of peers, professional analysts, and financial bloggers. According to SocialPicks, the site is "a trusted online investing community where investors and traders invest smarter together."

1. Do you think peer-to-peer investment and personal finance Web sites like these are valuable? Why or why not?
2. Do you trust peer-to-peer collaboration when it comes to investing and personal finance? Why or why not?

② JOURNALING FOR SUCCESS

According to many financial experts, the logical place to begin the search for a quality investment is to examine the products and services you use on a regular basis—products and services that provide a high level of consumer satisfaction.

The preceding statement is based on the assumption that if you like the product or service and you feel that you got excellent value for your money, other consumers will too. And while it may be obvious, a satisfied, growing customer base can mean increased sales, profits, and ultimately higher stock values for the company that manufactured the product or provided the service.

Assignment

1. To begin this journal exercise, think about purchases you made over the last month. Describe one product or service that you feel "was worth the money."
2. For the product or service you chose, describe the attributes or features that impressed you.
3. Determine if the company that made the product or provided the service is a public company that has issued stock.* Then use the Internet or go to the library to research the investment potential for this company. Finally, describe why you feel this would be a good or bad investment at this time.

    *If the company that manufactured the product or service you chose is not a public company, choose another product or service.

③ DEVELOPING CRITICAL-THINKING SKILLS

One way to achieve financial security is to invest a stated amount of money on a systematic basis. This investment strategy is called *dollar-cost averaging*. When the cost is lower, your investment buys more shares. When the cost is higher, your investment buys fewer shares. A good way to begin investing is to select a mutual fund that meets your financial objectives and to invest the same amount each month or each year.

Assignment

1. Select several mutual funds from the financial pages of the *Wall Street Journal* or a personal finance periodical such as *Money, Kiplinger's Personal Finance,* or *SmartMoney* that provides information about mutual funds. Call the toll-free number for each fund and ask about its objectives. Furthermore, request that the company send you a prospectus and an annual report.
2. Select one fund that meets your financial objectives.
3. Prepare a table that includes the following data:
    a. An initial investment of $2,000 in the mutual fund you have selected
    b. The net asset value (NAV)
    c. The number of shares purchased
4. Record the investment information on a weekly basis. Look in the *Wall Street Journal* or on the Internet to find the NAV for each week.
5. Determine the value of your investment until the end of the semester.
6. Write a report describing the results. Include a summary of what you learned about investments. Be sure to indicate if you think that dollar-cost averaging (investing another $2,000 next year) would be a good idea.

④ BUILDING TEAM SKILLS

Investing in stocks can be a way to beat inflation and accumulate money. Traditionally, stocks have earned just below 10 percent per year since 1926. Bonds and certificates of deposit, on the other hand, often earn little more than the inflation rate, making it very difficult to accumulate enough money for retirement.

Assignment

1. Form teams of three people. The teams will compete against each other, striving for the largest gain in investments.
2. Assume that you are buying stock in three companies; some should be listed on the NYSE, and some should be traded in the Nasdaq over-the-counter market.
    a. Research different investments, and narrow your choices to three different stocks.
    b. Divide your total investment of $25,000 into three amounts.
    c. Determine the number of shares of stock you can purchase in each company by dividing the budgeted amount by the price of the stock. Allow enough money to pay for the commission. To find the cost of the stock, multiply the number of shares you are going to purchase by the closing price of the stock.

d. Assume that the commission is 1 percent. Calculate it by multiplying the cost of the stock by 0.01. Add the dollar amount of commission to the cost of the stock to determine the total purchase price.

3. Set up a table to reflect the following information:
   a. Name of the company
   b. Closing price per share
   c. Number of shares purchased
   d. Amount of the commission
   e. Cost of the stock

4. Record the closing price of the stock on a weekly basis. Prepare a chart to use for this step.

5. Before the end of the semester, assume that you sell the stock.
   a. Take the closing price on the day you sell your stocks and multiply it by the number of shares; then calculate the commission at 1 percent.
   b. Deduct the amount of commission from the selling price of the stock. This is the total return on your investment.

6. Calculate your profit or loss. Subtract the total purchase price of the stock from the total return. If the total return is less than the total purchase price, you have a loss.

7. Prepare a report summarizing the results of the project. Include the table and individual stock charts, as well as a statement describing what you learned about investing in stocks.

⑤ RESEARCHING DIFFERENT CAREERS

Today many people choose a personal financial advisor to help develop an investment program that will help them achieve their financial goals. Not only is this career choice an opportunity to help others, it is also one of the fastest growing career fields in the United States. According to the *Occupational Outlook Handbook*, the job opportunities for personal financial advisors are expected to increase by 32 percent between now and the year 2020. For help completing this exercise, use the *Occupational Outlook Handbook* in your college's library or career center or go to www.bls.gov/ooh.

Assignment

1. Answer the following questions based on information obtained in the *Occupational Outlook Handbook*.
   a. What is the nature of the work performed by personal financial advisors?
   b. What type of training or qualifications is required for a career in financial planning?
   c. Where are the job opportunities for personal financial advisors?
   d. What are typical annual wages for a personal financial advisor?

2. Summarize your findings in a report. Be sure to include if you would choose this career and why.

Running a Business   PART 7   Graeter's

Plans for Financing Growth

Almost as soon as Richard, Chip, and Robert Graeter became fourth-generation owners of the business their family had built, they started talking about expansion. They worked with Kroger, now their largest distribution partner, to put pints of Graeter's ice cream on store shelves many miles from the company's Cincinnati headquarters. Year by year, they increased their distribution reach with new retail partners—which meant they would need sufficient production capacity to fill all their orders, especially during months of peak demand.

Graeter's Reading Road factory, opened in 1934, was a printing plant before its conversion to ice-cream production. But it was bursting at the seams, and despite dramatic improvements in production efficiency, the Graeters recognized the increasingly urgent need to construct a new facility to support ongoing expansion.

FROM ONE FACTORY TO TWO

The economic situation was less than ideal for obtaining financing for a new factory, because the country—and the world—was in the grip of a severe and prolonged financial crisis. After scouting possible locations and exploring various options, Graeter's signed a 20-year deal with the city of Cincinnati. It paid the city a token amount for land in the Bond Hill neighborhood and borrowed $10 million from the city to pay for construction of a new 28,000-square-foot factory. The loan carried low interest rates and would be repaid over 20 years. In turn, Cincinnati issued $10 million in bonds to provide Graeter's with this funding.

Graeter's received a total package of financial incentives worth $3.3 million toward its new Bond Hill factory. In exchange, Graeter's committed to "stay and grow" in Cincinnati for at least 20 years, creating new jobs when the facility opened and even more as Graeter's growth continued.

Following months of construction, the new facility officially opened in 2010, during Graeter's landmark 140th anniversary year. "As a Cincinnati-based, family-run company, we are proud of our association with this wonderful city and look forward to new generations of success," said Richard Graeter II, Graeter's CEO. "We are incredibly grateful [for the City's assistance], because not only will their support help us expand nationally, but it is also helping us create jobs locally."

FROM TWO FACTORIES TO THREE

Even as the Bond Hill facility was nearing opening day, Graeter's was presented with an unexpected opportunity. Its largest franchisee wanted to sell the franchise operation, complete with stores and an ice-cream factory, and Graeter's had the right to buy the franchise back. The timing was almost perfect for its growth strategy, giving Graeter's not one, not two, but three production facilities to fuel expansion. On the other hand, how would the company pay for this unanticipated acquisition?

"That was not planned, not part of our strategic vision," explains Richard Graeter, "but the opportunity came up, and we had to look at it." If the Graeters decided to move ahead with the acquisition, "we had to come up with several millions of dollars in additional financing over and above what we had borrowed to build our new plant. So that means working with the bankers and lawyers and accountants to model how the business would look after the acquisition to determine if it makes financial sense, and then going out and raising the investment that you need to make the acquisition."

In the end, after looking at what the business had done in the past and where it was going in the future, the three great-grandsons of Graeter's founders decided that this unexpected acquisition would be a good move. They put together the financing needed to buy the stores and factory from the franchisee. Now Graeter's has the added strength of a sizable retail chain as well as three factories equipped to make the company's signature French-pot ice cream, one small batch after another—the right combination of ingredients for expanding from coast to coast and beyond.[14]

Questions

1. What kinds of questions do you think Cincinnati officials asked Graeter's owners before agreeing to loan the company $10 million? Why would Graeter's go with this financing arrangement rather than borrowing from a bank to pay for the Bond Hill factory?
2. One of the financing strategies Graeter's has not used is to sell common stock to the general public. Why would Graeter's hesitate to go public? Do you agree with its decision to use debt rather than equity financing?
3. As an investor, would you be willing to buy shares in Graeter's if it decided to go public through an IPO? Explain why the company's stock would or would not be a good investment for you.

Building a Business Plan   PART 7

In this last section, provide some information about your exit strategy, and discuss any potential trends, problems, or risks that you may encounter. These risks and assumptions could relate to your industry, markets, company, or personnel. Make sure to incorporate important information not included in other parts of the business plan in an appendix. Now is also the time to go back and prepare the executive summary, which should be placed at the beginning of the business plan.

THE EXIT STRATEGY COMPONENT

Your exit strategy component should at least include answers to the following questions:

7.1 How do you intend to get yourself (and your money) out of the business?
7.2 Will your children take over the business, or do you intend to sell it later?
7.3 Do you intend to grow the business to the point of an IPO?
7.4 How will investors get their money back?

THE CRITICAL RISKS AND ASSUMPTIONS COMPONENT

Your critical risks and assumptions component should answer at least the following questions:

7.5 What will you do if your market does not develop as quickly as you predicted? What if your market develops too quickly?
7.6 What will you do if your competitors underprice or make your product obsolete?

7.7 What will you do if there is an unfavorable industry-wide trend?
7.8 What will happen if trained workers are not available as predicted?
7.9 What will you do if there is an erratic supply of products or raw materials?

THE APPENDIX COMPONENT

Supplemental information and documents are often included in an appendix. Here are a few examples of some documents that can be included:

- Résumés of owners and principal managers
- Advertising samples and brochures
- An organization chart
- Floor plans of a retail facility or factory

REVIEW OF BUSINESS PLAN ACTIVITIES

As you have discovered, writing a business plan involves a long series of interrelated steps. As with any project involving a number of complex steps and calculations, your business plan should be reviewed carefully and revised before you present it to potential investors or lenders.

Remember, there is one more component you need to prepare after your business plan is completed: The executive summary should be written last, but because of its importance, it appears after the introduction.

THE EXECUTIVE SUMMARY COMPONENT

In the executive summary, give a one- to two-page overview of your entire business plan. This is the most important part of the business plan and is of special interest to busy bankers, investors, and other interested parties. Remember, this section is a summary; more detailed information is provided in the remainder of your business plan.

Make sure that the executive summary captures the reader's attention instantly in the first sentence by using a key selling point or benefit of the business.

Your executive summary should include answers to at least the following:

7.10 *Company information.* What product or service do you provide? What is your competitive advantage? When will the company be formed? What are your company objec-

tives? What is the background of you and your management team?

7.11 *Market opportunity.* What is the expected size and growth rate of your market, your expected market share, and any relevant market trends?

Once again, review your answers to all the questions in the preceding parts to make sure that they are all consistent throughout the entire business plan.

Although many would-be entrepreneurs are excited about the prospects of opening their own business, remember that it takes a lot of hard work, time, and in most cases a substantial amount of money. Though the business plan provides an enormous amount of information about your business, it is only the first step. Once it is completed, it is now your responsibility to implement the plan. Good luck in your business venture.

ENDNOTES

1. Sources: Based on information in Chris Flood, "Vanguard ETF Assets Surge to Top $200 bn," *Financial Times*, March 25, 2012, www.ft.com; Jackie Noblett, "Vanguard Drives Home Low-Cost Mantra, in a Mobile Café," *Financial Times*, March 21, 2012, www.ft.com; Jason Kephart, "Vanguard Steps Up Efforts to Woo Advisers," *Investment News*, March 12, 2012, p. 2; Robert Steyer, "Providers Going Big with Technology," *Pensions & Investments*, October 31, 2011, p. 2; www.vanguard.com.
2. "Money 101 Lesson 4: Basics of Investing," the CNN/Money Web site at www.money.cnn.com, accessed March 8, 2012.
3. Suze Orman, *The Road to Wealth* (New York: Riverbend Books, 2001), 371.
4. The 2010 Advanced Micro Devices Annual Report, the Advanced Micro Devices Web site at www.amd.com, accessed March 8, 2012.
5. The Investment Company Institute Web site at www.ici.org, accessed August 21, 2012.
6. The Mutual Fund Education Alliance Web site at www.mfea.com, accessed March 8, 2012.
7. The Investment Company Institute Web site at www.ici.org, accessed August 21, 2012.
8. Bill Barker, "Loads," the Motley Fool Web site at www.fool.com, accessed March 8, 2012.
9. "The Low Down on Index Funds," the Investopedia Web site at www.investopedia.com, accessed October 23, 2009.
10. "The Regulatory Pyramid," the New York Stock Exchange Web site, accessed March 10, 2012.
11. Ibid.
12. Based on information in Julia Gabriel, "Little Money? Live Rich on Simple Financial Wisdom," *CBN News*, October 30, 2011, www.cbn.com; Trevor Thomas, "Living Debt Free," *American Thinker*, July 24, 2011, www.americanthinker.com; Shelly K. Schwartz, "You Can Live Debt Free," *CNBC*, August 12, 2008, www.cnbc.com.
13. Based on information in John McCrank, "E-Brokerages Tap Social Media for Faster Service," *Reuters*, April 5, 2012, www.reuters.com; Stephen Miller, "Pension Protection Act Changes Plan Design, Motivates Saving," *HR Magazine*, February 2012, p. 14; Dan McCrum, "Original US Fidelity Business Thrives," *Financial Times*, April 11, 2012, www.ft.com; Ari I. Weinberg, "Coming to Your 401(k): Fidelity ETFs?" *Wall Street Journal*, January 3, 2012, www.wsj.com; William Baldwin, "Who Needs Bank Branches?" *Forbes*, August 3, 2011, www.forbes.com; www.fidelity.com.
14. Sources: Based on information from Kimberly L. Jackson, "Graeter's Premium Chocolate Chip Ice Cream Lands at Stop & Shop," *Newark Star-Ledger (NJ)*, April 4, 2012, www.nj.com; "Graeter's Ice Cream Debuts in Bay Area," *Tampa Bay Times (St. Petersburg, FL)*, January 10, 2012, p. 4B; Jim Carper, "Graeter's Runs a Hands-on Ice Cream Plant," *Dairy Foods*, August 2011, pp. 36+; Jim Carper, "The Greater Good," *Dairy Foods*, August 2011, pp. 95+; "Graeter's Unveils New 'Mystery Flavor,'" *Dayton Daily News*, March 29, 2012, www.daytondailynews.com; Bob Driehaus, "A Cincinnati Ice Cream Maker Aims Big," *New York Times*, September 11, 2010, www.nytimes.com; Lucy May, "Graeter's Northern Kentucky Franchisee Puts Stores on the Block," *Business Courier*, August 6, 2010, http://cincinnati.bizjournals.com; "Cincinnati Officials Help Dedicate New Graeter's Plant," *Cincinnati Economic Development*, September 2010, www.choosecincy.com; www.graeters.com; interviews with company staff and Cengage videos about Graeter's.

GLOSSARY

A

absolute advantage the ability to produce a specific product more efficiently than any other nation (71)

accessory equipment standardized equipment used in a firm's production or office activities (360)

accountability the obligation of a worker to accomplish an assigned job or task (195)

account executive an individual, sometimes called a *stockbroker* or *registered representative*, who buys and sells securities for clients (604)

accounting the process of systematically collecting, analyzing, and reporting financial information (497)

accounting equation the basis for the accounting process: *assets = liabilities + owners' equity* (500)

ad hoc committee a committee created for a specific short-term purpose (204)

administrative manager a manager who is not associated with any specific functional area but who provides overall administrative guidance and leadership (175)

advertising a paid nonpersonal message communicated to a select audience through a mass medium (426)

advertising agency an independent firm that plans, produces, and places advertising for its clients (435)

advertising media the various forms of communication through which advertising reaches its audience (428)

affirmative action program a plan designed to increase the number of minority employees at all levels within an organization (55)

agency shop a workplace in which employees can choose not to join the union but must pay dues to the union anyway (317)

agent a middleman that expedites exchanges, represents a buyer or a seller, and often is hired permanently on a commission basis (403)

alien corporation a corporation chartered by a foreign government and conducting business in the United States (116)

analytical process a process in operations management in which raw materials are broken into different component parts (215)

analytic skills the ability to identify problems correctly, generate reasonable alternatives, and select the "best" alternatives to solve problems (176)

annual report a report distributed to stockholders and other interested parties that describes the firm's operating activities and its financial condition (500)

arbitration the step in a grievance procedure in which a neutral third party hears the two sides of a dispute and renders a binding decision (318)

asset allocation the process of spreading your money among several different types of investments to lessen risk (587)

assets the resources that a business owns (500)

audit an examination of a company's financial statements and the accounting practices that produced them (497)

authority the power, within an organization, to accomplish an assigned job or task (195)

autocratic leadership task-oriented leadership style in which workers are told what to do and how to accomplish it; workers have no say in the decision-making process (177)

automatic vending the use of machines to dispense products (410)

automation the total or near-total use of machines to do work (233)

B

balance of payments the total flow of money into a country minus the total flow of money out of that country over some period of time (74)

balance of trade the total value of a nation's exports minus the total value of its imports over some period of time (73)

balance sheet (or statement of financial position) a summary of the dollar amounts of a firm's assets, liabilities, and owners' equity accounts at the end of a specific accounting period (500)

banker's acceptance a written order for a bank to pay a third party a stated amount of money on a specific date (539)

bargaining unit the specific group of employees represented by a union (312)

barter an exchange in which goods or services are traded directly for other goods or services without using money (25)

barter system a system of exchange in which goods or services are traded directly for other goods or services (522)

behavior modification a systematic program of reinforcement to encourage desirable behavior (288)

benchmarking a process used to evaluate the products, processes, or management practices of another organization that is superior in some way in order to improve quality (181)

bill of lading document issued by a transport carrier to an exporter to prove that merchandise has been shipped (86)

blog a Web site that allows a company to share information in order to not only increase the customer's knowledge about its products and services, but also to build trust (460)

blue-chip stock a safe investment that generally attracts conservative investors (585)

board of directors the top governing body of a corporation, the members of which are elected by the stockholders (117)

bond indenture a legal document that details all the conditions relating to a bond issue (571)

boycott a refusal to do business with a particular firm (320)

brand a name, term, symbol, design, or any combination of these that identifies a seller's products as distinct from those of other sellers (369)

brand equity marketing and financial value associated with a brand's strength in a market (371)

brand extension using an existing brand to brand a new product in a different product category (373)

brand loyalty extent to which a customer is favorable toward buying a specific brand (371)

brand mark the part of a brand that is a symbol or distinctive design (369)

brand name the part of a brand that can be spoken (369)

breakeven quantity the number of units that must be sold for the total revenue (from all units sold) to equal the total cost (of all units sold) (379)

broker a middleman that specializes in a particular commodity, represents either a buyer or a seller, and is likely to be hired on a temporary basis (403)

budget a financial statement that projects income, expenditures, or both over a specified future period (557)

bundle pricing packaging together two or more complementary products and selling them for a single price (384)

business the organized effort of individuals to produce and sell, for a profit, the goods and services that satisfy a society's needs (10)

business buying behavior the purchasing of products by producers, resellers, governmental units, and institutions (348)

business cycle the recurrence of periods of growth and recession in a nation's economic activity (20)

business ethics the application of moral standards to business situations (37)

business model represents a group of common characteristics and methods of doing business to generate sales revenues and reduce expenses (473)

business plan a carefully constructed guide for the person starting a business (144)

business product a product bought for resale, for making other products, or for use in a firm's operations (359)

business service an intangible product that an organization uses in its operations (360)

business-to-business (or B2B) model a model used by firms that conduct business with other businesses (474)

business-to-consumer (or B2C) model a model used by firms that focus on conducting business with individual consumers (475)

buying allowance a temporary price reduction to resellers for purchasing specified quantities of a product (441)

buying behavior the decisions and actions of people involved in buying and using products (348)

buying long buying stock with the expectation that it will increase in value and then can be sold at a profit (596)

C

capacity the amount of products or services that an organization can produce in a given time (221)

capital budget a financial statement that estimates a firm's expenditures for major assets and its long-term financing needs (558)

capital gain the difference between a security's purchase price and its selling price (591)

capital-intensive technology a process in which machines and equipment do most of the work (222)

capitalism an economic system in which individuals own and operate the majority of businesses that provide goods and services (14)

captioned photograph a picture accompanied by a brief explanation (442)

captive pricing pricing the basic product in a product line low, but pricing related items at a higher level (384)

carrier a firm that offers transportation services (414)

cash budget a financial statement that estimates cash receipts and cash expenditures over a specified period (557)

cash flow the movement of money into and out of an organization (555)

catalog marketing a type of marketing in which an organization provides a catalog from which customers make selections and place orders by mail, telephone, or the Internet (408)

catalog showroom a retail outlet that displays well-known brands and sells them at discount prices through catalogs within the store (404)

category killer a very large specialty store that concentrates on a single product line and competes on the basis of low prices and product availability (407)

caveat emptor a Latin phrase meaning "let the buyer beware" (48)

centralized organization an organization that systematically works to concentrate authority at the upper levels of the organization (196)

certificate of deposit (CD) a document stating that the bank will pay the depositor a guaranteed interest rate on money left on deposit for a specified period of time (534)

certified public accountant (CPA) an individual who has met state requirements for accounting education and experience and has passed a rigorous accounting examination (499)

chain of command the line of authority that extends from the highest to the lowest levels of an organization (191)

chain retailer a company that operates more than one retail outlet (404)

channel of distribution (or marketing channel) a sequence of marketing organizations that directs a product from the producer to the ultimate user (396)

check a written order for a bank or other financial institution to pay a stated dollar amount to the business or person indicated on the face of the check (533)

chief financial officer (CFO) a high-level corporate executive who manages a firm's finances and reports directly to the company's chief executive officer or president (553)

closed corporation a corporation whose stock is owned by relatively few people and is not sold to the general public (115)

closed shop a workplace in which workers must join the union before they are hired; outlawed by the Taft–Hartley Act (317)

cloud computing a type of computer usage in which services stored on the Internet are provided to users on a temporary basis (477)

code of ethics a guide to acceptable and ethical behavior as defined by the organization (41)

collateral real estate or property pledged as security for a loan (535)

collective bargaining the process of negotiating a labor contract with management (313)

command economy an economic system in which the government decides what goods and services will be produced, how they will be produced, for whom available goods and services will be produced, and who owns and controls the major factors of production (16)

commercial bank a profit-making organization that accepts deposits, makes loans, and provides related services to its customers (531)

commercial paper a short-term promissory note issued by a large corporation (526)

commission a payment that is a percentage of sales revenue (258)

commission merchant a middleman that carries merchandise and negotiates sales for manufacturers (403)

common stock stock owned by individuals or firms who may vote on corporate matters but whose claims on profits and assets are subordinate to the claims of others (116, 566)

communication skills the ability to speak, listen, and write effectively (176)

community shopping center a planned shopping center that includes one or two department stores and some specialty stores, along with convenience stores (411)

comparable worth a concept that seeks equal compensation for jobs requiring about the same level of education, training, and skills (257)

comparative advantage the ability to produce a specific product more efficiently than any other product (71)

comparison discounting setting a price at a specific level and comparing it with a higher price (385)

compensation the payment employees receive in return for their labor (256)

compensation system the policies and strategies that determine employee compensation (256)

competition rivalry among businesses for sales to potential customers (21)

component part an item that becomes part of a physical product and is either a finished item ready for assembly or a product that needs little processing before assembly (360)

computer-aided design (CAD) the use of computers to aid in the development of products (233)

computer-aided manufacturing (CAM) the use of computers to plan and control manufacturing processes (233)

computer-integrated manufacturing (CIM) a computer system that not only helps to design products but also controls the machinery needed to produce the finished product (234)

computer virus a software code designed to disrupt normal computer operations (477)

conceptual skills the ability to think in abstract terms (175)

consumer buying behavior the purchasing of products for personal or household use, not for business purposes (348)

consumer price index (CPI) a monthly index that measures the changes in prices of a fixed basket of goods purchased by a typical consumer in an urban area (19)

consumer product a product purchased to satisfy personal and family needs (359)

consumerism all activities undertaken to protect the rights of consumers (51)

consumer sales promotion method a sales promotion method designed to attract consumers to particular retail stores and to motivate them to purchase certain new or established products (439)

convenience product a relatively inexpensive, frequently purchased item for which buyers want to exert only minimal effort (359)

convenience store a small food store that sells a limited variety of products but remains open well beyond normal business hours (405)

convertible bond a bond that can be exchanged, at the owner's option, for a specified number of shares of the corporation's common stock (570)

contingency plan a plan that outlines alternative courses of action that may be taken if an organization's other plans are disrupted or become ineffective (171)

continuous process a manufacturing process in which a firm produces the same product(s) over a long period of time (234)

controlling the process of evaluating and regulating ongoing activities to ensure that goals are achieved (172)

cookie a small piece of software sent by a Web site that tracks an individual's Internet use (476)

cooperative an association of individuals or firms whose purpose is to perform some business function for its members (123)

cooperative advertising an arrangement whereby a manufacturer agrees to pay a certain amount of a retailer's media cost for advertising the manufacturer's product (441)

core competencies approaches and processes that a company performs well that may give it an advantage over its competitors (168)

corporate bond a corporation's written pledge that it will repay a specified amount of money with interest (569)

corporate culture the inner rites, rituals, heroes, and values of a firm (201)

corporate officers the chairman of the board, president, executive vice presidents, corporate secretary, treasurer, and any other top executive appointed by the board of directors (118)

corporation an artificial person created by law with most of the legal rights of a real person, including the rights to start and operate a business, to buy or sell property, to borrow money, to sue or be sued, and to enter into binding contracts (115)

cost of goods sold the dollar amount equal to beginning inventory *plus* net purchases *less* ending inventory (506)

countertrade an international barter transaction (89)

coupon an offer that reduces the retail price of a particular item by a stated amount at the time of purchase (440)

craft union an organization of skilled workers in a single craft or trade (304)

creative selling selling products to new customers and increasing sales to present customers (436)

credit immediate purchasing power that is exchanged for a promise to repay borrowed money, with or without interest, at a later date (540)

credit union a financial institution that accepts deposits from, and lends money to, only the people who are its members (532)

cross-functional team a team of individuals with varying specialties, expertise, and skills that are brought together to achieve a common task (200, 293)

crowdsourcing outsourcing tasks to a group of people in order to tap into the ideas of the crowd (465)

cultural (or workplace) diversity differences among people in a workforce owing to race, ethnicity, and gender (6, 249)

currency devaluation the reduction of the value of a nation's currency relative to the currencies of other countries (76)

current assets assets that can be converted quickly into cash or that will be used in one year or less (501)

current liabilities debts that will be repaid in one year or less (503)

current ratio a financial ratio computed by dividing current assets by current liabilities (510)

customary pricing pricing on the basis of tradition (384)

customer lifetime value a measure of a customer's worth (sales minus costs) to a business over one's lifetime (333)

customer relationship management (CRM) using information about customers to create marketing strategies that develop and sustain desirable customer relationships (333)

D

data numerical or verbal descriptions that usually result from some sort of measurement (488)

database a single collection of data and information stored in one place that can be used by people throughout an organization to make decisions (490)

data mining the practice of searching through data records looking for useful information (476)

data processing the transformation of data into a form that is useful for a specific purpose (493)

debenture bond a bond backed only by the reputation of the issuing corporation (570)

debit card a card that electronically subtracts the amount of your purchase from your bank account at the moment the purchase is made (536)

debt capital borrowed money obtained through loans of various types (558)

decentralized organization an organization in which management consciously attempts to spread authority widely in the lower levels of the organization (195)

decision making the act of choosing one alternative from a set of alternatives (179)

decision-support system (DSS) a type of computer program that provides relevant data and information to help a firm's employees make decisions (496)

delegation assigning part of a manager's work and power to other workers (194)

deflation a general decrease in the level of prices (18)

demand the quantity of a product that buyers are willing to purchase at each of various prices (22, 376)

demand deposit an amount on deposit in a checking account (524)

departmentalization the process of grouping jobs into manageable units (193)

departmentalization by customer grouping activities according to the needs of various customer populations (193)

departmentalization by function grouping jobs that relate to the same organizational activity (193)

departmentalization by location grouping activities according to the defined geographic area in which they are performed (193)

departmentalization by product grouping activities related to a particular product or service (193)

department store a retail store that (1) employs 25 or more persons and (2) sells at least home furnishings, appliances, family apparel, and household linens and dry goods, each in a different part of the store (404)

depreciation the process of apportioning the cost of a fixed asset over the period during which it will be used (503)

depression a severe recession that lasts longer than a typical recession and has a larger decline in business activity when compared to a recession (21)

design planning the development of a plan for converting an idea into an actual product or service (220)

directing the combined processes of leading and motivating (171)

direct-mail advertising promotional material mailed directly to individuals (429)

direct marketing the use of the telephone, Internet, and nonpersonal media to introduce products to customers, who can then purchase them via mail, telephone, or the Internet (408)

direct-response marketing a type of marketing in which a seller advertises a product and makes it available, usually for a short time period, through mail, telephone, or online orders (409)

direct selling the marketing of products to customers through face-to-face sales presentations at home or in the workplace (407)

discount a deduction from the price of an item (386)

discount rate the interest rate the Federal Reserve System charges for loans to member banks (528)

discount store a self-service general-merchandise outlet that sells products at lower-than-usual prices (404)

discretionary income disposable income *less* savings and expenditures on food, clothing, and housing (349)

disposable income personal income *less* all additional personal taxes (349)

dividend a distribution of earnings to the stockholders of a corporation (117)

domestic corporation a corporation in the state in which it is incorporated (116)

domestic system a method of manufacturing in which an entrepreneur distributes raw materials to various homes, where families process them into finished goods to be offered for sale by the merchant entrepreneur (25)

double-entry bookkeeping system a system in which each financial transaction is recorded as two separate accounting entries to maintain the balance shown in the accounting equation (500)

Dow Jones Industrial Average an average of 30 leading U.S. corporations that reflect the U.S. stock market as a whole (584)

draft issued by the exporter's bank, ordering the importer's bank to pay for the merchandise, thus guaranteeing payment once accepted by the importer's bank (86)

dumping exportation of large quantities of a product at a price lower than that of the same product in the home market (75)

E

e-business (electronic business) the organized effort of individuals to produce and sell *through the Internet,* for a profit, the products and services that satisfy society's needs (26, 470)

economic community an organization of nations formed to promote the free movement of resources and products among its members and to create common economic policies (83)

economic model of social responsibility the view that society will benefit most when business is left alone to produce and market profitable products that society needs (49)

economics the study of how wealth is created and distributed (13)

economy the way in which people deal with the creation and distribution of wealth (13)

electronic funds transfer (EFT) system a means of performing financial transactions through a computer terminal or telephone hookup (537)

embargo a complete halt to trading with a particular nation or of a particular product (75)

employee benefit a reward in addition to regular compensation that is provided indirectly to employees (259)

employee ownership a situation in which employees own the company they work for by virtue of being stockholders (291)

employee training the process of teaching operations and technical employees how to do their present jobs more effectively and efficiently (260)

empowerment making employees more involved in their jobs by increasing their participation in decision making (291)

entrepreneur a person who risks time, effort, and money to start and operate a business (14)

entrepreneurial leadership personality-based leadership style in which the manager seeks to inspire workers with a vision of what can be accomplished to benefit all stakeholders (178)

Equal Employment Opportunity Commission (EEOC) a government agency with the power to investigate complaints of employment discrimination and the power to sue firms that practice it (56)

equity capital money received from the owners or from the sale of shares of ownership in a business (558)

equity theory a theory of motivation based on the premise that people are motivated to obtain and preserve equitable treatment for themselves (282)

esteem needs our need for respect, recognition, and a sense of our own accomplishment and worth (278)

ethics the study of right and wrong and of the morality of the choices individuals make (37)

everyday low prices (EDLPs) setting a low price for products on a consistent basis (384)

exchange-traded fund (ETF) a fund that generally invests in the stocks or other securities contained in a specific stock or securities index (593)

exclusive distribution the use of only a single retail outlet for a product in a large geographic area (398)

executive information system (EIS) a computer-based system that facilitates and supports the decision-making needs of top managers and senior executives by providing easy access to both internal and external information (496)

expectancy theory a model of motivation based on the assumption that motivation depends on how much we want something and on how likely we think we are to get it (283)

expense ratio all the different management fees; 12b-1 fees, if any; and additional operating costs for a specific fund (594)

expert system a type of computer program that uses artificial intelligence to imitate a human's ability to think (496)

Export-Import Bank of the United States an independent agency of the U.S. government whose function is to assist in financing the exports of American firms (91)

exporting selling and shipping raw materials or products to other nations (72)

express warranty a written explanation of the producer's responsibilities in the event that a product is found to be defective or otherwise unsatisfactory (375)

external recruiting the attempt to attract job applicants from outside an organization (252)

F

factor a firm that specializes in buying other firms' accounts receivable (562)

factors of production resources used to produce goods and services (13)

factory system a system of manufacturing in which all the materials, machinery, and workers required to manufacture a product are assembled in one place (25)

family branding the strategy in which a firm uses the same brand for all or most of its products (373)

family of funds a group of mutual funds managed by one investment company (595)

feature article a piece (of up to 3,000 words) prepared by an organization for inclusion in a particular publication (442)

federal deficit a shortfall created when the federal government spends more in a fiscal year than it receives (21)

federal funds rate the interest rate at which a bank lends immediately available funds on deposit at the Fed to another bank overnight to meet the borrowing bank's reserve requirements (528)

Federal Reserve System the central bank of the United States responsible for regulating the banking industry (525)

financial accounting generates financial statements and reports for interested people outside an organization (498)

financial leverage the use of borrowed funds to increase the return on owners' equity (568)

financial management all the activities concerned with obtaining money and using it effectively (552)

financial manager a manager who is primarily responsible for an organization's financial resources (173)

financial plan a plan for obtaining and using the money needed to implement an organization's goals and objectives (556)

financial planner an individual who has had at least two years of training in investments, insurance, taxation, retirement planning, and estate planning and has passed a rigorous examination (583)

financial ratio a number that shows the relationship between two elements of a firm's financial statements (510)

first-line manager a manager who coordinates and supervises the activities of operating employees (173)

fiscal policy government influence on the amount of savings and expenditures; accomplished by altering the tax structure and by changing the levels of government spending (21)

fixed assets assets that will be held or used for a period longer than one year (502)

fixed cost a cost incurred no matter how many units of a product are produced or sold (379)

flexible benefit plan compensation plan whereby an employee receives a predetermined amount of benefit dollars to spend on a package of benefits he or she has selected to meet individual needs (260)

flexible manufacturing system (FMS) a single production system that combines electronic machines and computer-integrated manufacturing (234)

flextime a system in which employees set their own work hours within employer-determined limits (288)

foreign corporation a corporation in any state in which it does business except the one in which it is incorporated (116)

foreign-exchange control a restriction on the amount of a particular foreign currency that can be purchased or sold (76)

form utility utility created by converting production inputs into finished products (215, 333)

forum an interactive version of a community bulletin board and focuses on threaded discussions (462)

franchise a license to operate an individually owned business as though it were part of a chain of outlets or stores (151)

franchisee a person or organization purchasing a franchise (151)

franchising the actual granting of a franchise (151)

franchisor an individual or organization granting a franchise (151)

free enterprise the system of business in which individuals are free to decide what to produce, how to produce it, and at what price to sell it (4)

frequent-user incentive a program developed to reward customers who engage in repeat (frequent) purchases (441)

full disclosure requirement that investors should have access to all important facts about stocks, bonds, and other securities so that they can make informed decisions (606)

full-service wholesaler a middleman that performs the entire range of wholesaler functions (402)

functional middleman a middleman that helps in the transfer of ownership of products but does not take title to the products (396)

G

Gantt chart a graphic scheduling device that displays the tasks to be performed on the vertical axis and the time required for each task on the horizontal axis (228)

General Agreement on Tariffs and Trade (GATT) an international organization of 153 nations dedicated to reducing or eliminating tariffs and other barriers to world trade (81)

generally accepted accounting principles (GAAPs) an accepted set of guidelines and practices for companies reporting financial information and for the accounting profession (497)

general-merchandise wholesaler a middleman that deals in a wide variety of products (402)

general partner a person who assumes full or shared responsibility for operating a business (110)

generic product (or brand) a product with no brand at all (370)

goal an end result that an organization is expected to achieve over a one- to ten-year period (168)

goal-setting theory a theory of motivation suggesting that employees are motivated to achieve goals that they and their managers establish together (284)

grapevine the informal communications network within an organization (204)

green IT a term used to describe all of a firm's activities to support a healthy environment and sustain the planet (478)

grievance procedure a formally established course of action for resolving employee complaints against management (317)

gross domestic product (GDP) the total dollar value of all goods and services produced by all people within the boundaries of a country during a one-year period (18)

gross profit a firm's net sales *less* the cost of goods sold (506)

gross sales the total dollar amount of all goods and services sold during the accounting period (505)

H

hard-core unemployed workers with little education or vocational training and a long history of unemployment (56)

high-risk investment an investment made in the uncertain hope of earning a relatively large profit in a short time (596)

hostile takeover a situation in which the management and board of directors of a firm targeted for acquisition disapprove of the merger (124)

hourly wage a specific amount of money paid for each hour of work (258)

human resources management (HRM) all the activities involved in acquiring, maintaining, and developing an organization's human resources (246)

human resources manager a person charged with managing an organization's human resources programs (174)

human resources planning the development of strategies to meet a firm's future human resources needs (247)

hygiene factors job factors that reduce dissatisfaction when present to an acceptable degree but that do not necessarily result in high levels of motivation (279)

I

import duty (tariff) a tax levied on a particular foreign product entering a country (75)

import quota a limit on the amount of a particular good that may be imported into a country during a given period of time (75)

importing purchasing raw materials or products in other nations and bringing them into one's own country (72)

inbound marketing a marketing term that describes new ways of gaining attention and ultimately customers by creating content on a Web site that pulls customers in (464)

incentive payment a payment in addition to wages, salary, or commissions (258)

income statement a summary of a firm's revenues and expenses during a specified accounting period (504)

independent retailer a firm that operates only one retail outlet (404)

individual branding the strategy in which a firm uses a different brand for each of its products (373)

industrial union an organization of both skilled and unskilled workers in a single industry (305)

inflation a general rise in the level of prices (18)

infomercial a program-length televised commercial message resembling an entertainment or consumer affairs program (430)

informal group a group created by the members themselves to accomplish goals that may or may not be relevant to an organization (204)

informal organization the pattern of behavior and interaction that stems from personal rather than official relationships (204)

information data presented in a form that is useful for a specific purpose (488)

information technology (IT) officer a manager at the executive level who is responsible for ensuring that a firm has the equipment necessary to provide the information the firm's employees and managers need to make effective decisions (490)

initial public offering (IPO) occurs when a corporation sells common stock to the general public for the first time (563)

injunction a court order requiring a person or group either to perform some act or to refrain from performing some act (310)

insider trading the practice of board members, corporate managers, and employees buying and selling a corporation's stock (606)

inspection the examination of the quality of work-in-process (230)

institutional advertising advertising designed to enhance a firm's image or reputation (427)

intangible assets assets that do not exist physically but that have a value based on the rights or privileges they confer on a firm (503)

integrated marketing communications coordination of promotion efforts to ensure their maximal informational and persuasive impact on customers (425)

intensive distribution the use of all available outlets for a product (398)

intermittent process a manufacturing process in which a firm's manufacturing machines and equipment are changed to produce different products (234)

internal recruiting considering present employees as applicants for available positions (253)

international business all business activities that involve exchanges across national boundaries (71)

International Monetary Fund (IMF) an international bank with 188 member nations that makes short-term loans to developing countries experiencing balance-of-payment deficits (93)

International Organization for Standardization (ISO) a network of national standards institutes and similar organizations from over 160 different countries that is charged with developing standards for quality products and services that are traded throughout the globe (231)

interpersonal skills the ability to deal effectively with other people (176)

inventory control the process of managing inventories in such a way as to minimize inventory costs, including both holding costs and potential stock-out costs (226)

inventory management the process of managing inventories in such a way as to minimize inventory costs, including both holding costs and potential stock-out costs (412)

inventory turnover a financial ratio calculated by dividing the cost of goods sold in one year by the average value of the inventory (510)

investment banking firm an organization that assists corporations in raising funds, usually by helping to sell new issues of stocks, bonds, or other financial securities (564)

invisible hand a term created by Adam Smith to describe how an individual's personal gain benefits others and a nation's economy (14)

J

job analysis a systematic procedure for studying jobs to determine their various elements and requirements (251)

job description a list of the elements that make up a particular job (251)

job enlargement expanding a worker's assignments to include additional but similar tasks (287)

job enrichment a motivation technique that provides employees with more variety and responsibility in their jobs (287)

job evaluation the process of determining the relative worth of the various jobs within a firm (257)

job redesign a type of job enrichment in which work is restructured to cultivate the worker–job match (288)

job rotation the systematic shifting of employees from one job to another (192)

job security protection against the loss of employment (316)

job sharing an arrangement whereby two people share one full-time position (289)

job specialization the separation of all organizational activities into distinct tasks and the assignment of different tasks to different people (192)

job specification a list of the qualifications required to perform a particular job (251)

joint venture an agreement between two or more groups to form a business entity in order to achieve a specific goal or to operate for a specific period of time (123)

jurisdiction the right of a particular union to organize particular groups of workers (313)

just-in-time inventory system a system designed to ensure that materials or supplies arrive at a facility just when they are needed so that storage and holding costs are minimized (227)

K

key performance indicators (KPIs) measurements that define and measure the progress of an organization toward achieving its objectives (469)

knowledge management (KM) a firm's procedures for generating, using, and sharing the data and information (490)

L

labeling the presentation of information on a product or its package (375)

labor-intensive technology a process in which people must do most of the work (222)

labor union an organization of workers acting together to negotiate their wages and working conditions with employers (303)

leadership the ability to influence others (177)

leading the process of influencing people to work toward a common goal (171)

lean manufacturing a concept built on the idea of eliminating waste from all of the activities required to produce a product or service (232)

letter of credit a legal document issued by a bank or other financial institution guaranteeing to pay a seller a stated amount for a specified period of time (86, 538)

liabilities a firm's debts and obligations (500)

licensing a contractual agreement in which one firm permits another to produce and market its product and use its brand name in return for a royalty or other compensation (85)

lifestyle shopping center an open-air-environment shopping center with upscale chain specialty stores (411)

limited liability a feature of corporate ownership that limits each owner's financial liability to the amount of money that he or she has paid for the corporation's stock (119)

limited-liability company (LLC) a form of business ownership that combines the benefits of a corporation and a partnership while avoiding some of the restrictions and disadvantages of those forms of ownership (121)

limited-line wholesaler a middleman that stocks only a few product lines but carries numerous product items within each line (403)

limited partner a person who contributes capital to a business but has no management responsibility or liability for losses beyond the amount he or she invested in the partnership (110)

limited-service wholesaler a middleman that assumes responsibility for a few wholesale services only (403)

limit order a request that a security be bought or sold at a price that is equal to or better than some specified price (605)

line-and-staff structure an organizational structure that utilizes the chain of command from a line structure in combination with the assistance of staff managers (198)

line extension development of a new product that is closely related to one or more products in the existing product line but designed specifically to meet somewhat different customer needs (364)

line manager a position in which a person makes decisions and gives orders to subordinates to achieve the organization's goals (198)

line of credit a loan that is approved before the money is actually needed (535)

line structure an organizational structure in which the chain of command goes directly from person to person throughout the organization (198)

liquidity the ease with which an asset can be converted into cash (501, 586)

lockout a firm's refusal to allow employees to enter the workplace (320)

long-term financing money that will be used for longer than one year (556)

long-term liabilities debts that need not be repaid for at least one year (503)

lump-sum salary increase an entire pay raise taken in one lump sum (258)

M

macroeconomics the study of the national economy and the global economy (13)

maintenance shop a workplace in which an employee who joins the union must remain a union member as long as he or she is employed by the firm (317)

major equipment large tools and machines used for production purposes (359)

Malcolm Baldrige National Quality Award an award given by the President of the United States to organizations judged to be outstanding in specific managerial tasks that lead to improved quality for both products and services (229)

malware a general term that describes software designed to infiltrate a computer system without the user's consent (477)

management the process of coordinating people and other resources to achieve the goals of an organization (165)

management by objectives (MBO) a motivation technique in which managers and employees collaborate in setting goals (285)

management development the process of preparing managers and other professionals to assume increased responsibility in both present and future positions (260)

management information system (MIS) a system that provides managers and employees with the information they need to perform their jobs as effectively as possible (490)

managerial accounting provides managers and employees with the information needed to make decisions about a firm's financing, investing, marketing, and operating activities (498)

manufacturer (or producer) brand a brand that is owned by a manufacturer (370)

manufacturer's sales branch essentially a merchant wholesaler that is owned by a manufacturer (403)

manufacturer's sales office essentially a sales agent owned by a manufacturer (403)

margin requirement the portion of the price of a stock that cannot be borrowed (597)

market a group of individuals or organizations, or both, that need products in a given category and that have the ability, willingness, and authority to purchase such products (336)

market economy an economic system in which businesses and individuals decide what to produce and buy, and the market determines quantities sold and prices (15)

marketing the activity, set of institutions, and processes for creating, communicating, delivering, and exchanging offerings that have value for customers, clients, partners, and society at large (334)

marketing concept a business philosophy that a firm should provide goods and services that satisfy customers' needs through a coordinated set of activities that allow the firm to achieve its objectives (334)

marketing information system a system for managing marketing information that is gathered continually from internal and external sources (344)

marketing manager a manager who is responsible for facilitating the exchange of products between an organization and its customers or clients (174)

marketing mix a combination of product, price, distribution, and promotion developed to satisfy a particular target market (337)

marketing plan a written document that specifies an organization's resources, objectives, strategy, and implementation and control efforts to be used in marketing a specific product or product group (342)

marketing research the process of systematically gathering, recording, and analyzing data concerning a particular marketing problem (344)

marketing strategy a plan that will enable an organization to make the best use of its resources and advantages to meet its objectives (337)

market order a request that a security be purchased or sold at the current market price (604)

market price the price at which the quantity demanded is exactly equal to the quantity supplied (23)

market segment a group of individuals or organizations within a market that share one or more common characteristics (339)

market segmentation the process of dividing a market into segments and directing a marketing mix at a particular segment or segments rather than at the total market (339)

market value the price of one share of a stock at a particular time (591)

markup the amount a seller adds to the cost of a product to determine its basic selling price (379)

Maslow's hierarchy of needs a sequence of human needs in the order of their importance (277)

mass production a manufacturing process that lowers the cost required to produce a large number of identical or similar products over a long period of time (215)

master limited partnership (MLP) a limited partnership that has units of ownership that can be traded on security exchanges much like shares of ownership in a corporation (111)

materials handling the actual physical handling of goods, in warehouses as well as during transportation (414)

materials requirements planning (MRP) a computerized system that integrates production planning and inventory control (227)

matrix structure an organizational structure that combines vertical and horizontal lines of authority, usually by superimposing product departmentalization on a functionally departmentalized organization (199)

maturity date the date on which a corporation is to repay borrowed money (570)

measure of value a single standard or "yardstick" used to assign values to, and compare the values of, products, services, and resources (522)

media sharing sites allow users to upload multimedia content including photos, videos, and podcasts (461)

mediation the use of a neutral third party to assist management and the union during their negotiations (320)

medium of exchange anything accepted as payment for products, services, and resources (522)

merchant middleman a middleman that actually takes title to products by buying them (396)

merchant wholesaler a middleman that purchases goods in large quantities and then sells them to other wholesalers or retailers and to institutional, farm, government, professional, or industrial users (402)

merger the purchase of one corporation by another (124)

microeconomics the study of the decisions made by individuals and businesses (13)

middleman (or marketing intermediary) a marketing organization that links a producer and user within a marketing channel (396)

middle manager a manager who implements the strategy and major policies developed by top management (173)

Millennials tech-savvy digital natives born after 1980 (463)

minority a racial, religious, political, national, or other group regarded as different from the larger group of which it is a part and that is often singled out for unfavorable treatment (55)

mission a statement of the basic purpose that makes an organization different from others (167)

missionary salesperson a salesperson—generally employed by a manufacturer—who visits retailers to persuade them to buy the manufacturer's products (436)

mixed economy an economy that exhibits elements of both capitalism and socialism (15)

monetary policies Federal Reserve decisions that determine the size of the supply of money in the nation and the level of interest rates (21)

money anything a society uses to purchase products, services, or resources (522)

monopolistic competition a market situation in which there are many buyers along with a relatively large number of sellers who differentiate their products from the products of competitors (23)

monopoly a market (or industry) with only one seller, and there are barriers to keep other firms from entering the industry (24)

morale an employee's feelings about his or her job and superiors and about the firm itself (275)

mortgage bond a corporate bond secured by various assets of the issuing firm (570)

motivating the process of providing reasons for people to work in the best interests of an organization (171)

motivation the individual internal process that energizes, directs, and sustains behavior; the personal "force" that causes you or me to behave in a particular way (275)

motivation factors job factors that increase motivation, although their absence does not necessarily result in dissatisfaction (279)

motivation–hygiene theory the idea that satisfaction and dissatisfaction are separate and distinct dimensions (279)

multilateral development bank (MDB) an internationally supported bank that provides loans to developing countries to help them grow (93)

multinational enterprise a firm that operates on a worldwide scale without ties to any specific nation or region (89)

multiple-unit pricing the strategy of setting a single price for two or more units (383)

municipal bond sometimes called a *muni,* a debt security issued by a state or local government (589)

mutual fund pools the money of many investors—its shareholders—to invest in a variety of different securities (593)

N

National Alliance of Business (NAB) a joint business–government program to train the hard-core unemployed (57)

national bank a commercial bank chartered by the U.S. Comptroller of the Currency (531)

national debt the total of all federal deficits (21)

National Labor Relations Board (NLRB) the federal agency that enforces the provisions of the Wagner Act (309)

natural monopoly an industry requiring huge investments in capital and within which any duplication of facilities would be wasteful and thus not in the public interest (24)

need a personal requirement (277)

negotiated pricing establishing a final price through bargaining (383)

neighborhood shopping center a planned shopping center consisting of several small convenience and specialty stores (411)

net asset value (NAV) current market value of a mutual fund's portfolio minus the mutual fund's liabilities divided by the number of outstanding shares (594)

net income occurs when revenues exceed expenses (506)

net loss occurs when expenses exceed revenues (506)

net sales the actual dollar amounts received by a firm for the goods and services it has sold after adjustment for returns, allowances, and discounts (506)

network structure an organizational structure in which administration is the primary function, and most other functions are contracted out to other firms (201)

net worth the difference between the value of your total assets and your total liabilities (581)

news release a typed page of about 300 words provided by an organization to the media as a form of publicity (442)

non-price competition competition based on factors other than price (377)

nonstore retailing a type of retailing whereby consumers purchase products without visiting a store (407)

nontariff barrier a nontax measure imposed by a government to favor domestic over foreign suppliers (75)

not-for-profit corporation a corporation organized to provide a social, educational, religious, or other service rather than to earn a profit (122)

NOW account an interest-paying checking account; *NOW* stands for *negotiable order of withdrawal* (534)

O

objective a specific statement detailing what an organization intends to accomplish over a shorter period of time (168)

odd-number pricing the strategy of setting prices using odd numbers that are slightly below whole-dollar amounts (383)

off-price retailer a store that buys manufacturers' seconds, overruns, returns, and off-season merchandise for resale to consumers at deep discounts (407)

oligopoly a market (or industry) in which there are few sellers (24)

online retailing retailing that makes products available to buyers through computer connections (409)

open corporation a corporation whose stock can be bought and sold by any individual (115)

open-market operations the buying and selling of U.S. government securities by the Federal Reserve System for the purpose of controlling the supply of money (528)

operating expenses all business costs other than the cost of goods sold (506)

operational plan a type of plan designed to implement tactical plans (171)

operations management all the activities required to produce goods and services (213)

operations manager a manager who manages the systems that convert resources into goods and services (174)

order-getter a salesperson who is responsible for selling a firm's products to new customers and increasing sales to present customers (436)

order processing activities involved in receiving and filling customers' purchase orders (413)

order-taker a salesperson who handles repeat sales in ways that maintain positive relationships with customers (436)

organization a group of two or more people working together to achieve a common set of goals (190)

organization chart a diagram that represents the positions and relationships within an organization (190)

organizational height the number of layers, or levels, of management in a firm (197)

organizing the grouping of resources and activities to accomplish some end result in an efficient and effective manner (171)

orientation the process of acquainting new employees with an organization (256)

out-of-home advertising short promotional messages on billboards, posters, signs, and transportation vehicles (430)

outsourcing the process of finding outside vendors and suppliers that provide professional help, parts, or materials at a lower cost (471)

over-the-counter (OTC) market a network of dealers who buy and sell the stocks of corporations that are not listed on a securities exchange (565)

overtime time worked in excess of 40 hours in one week (under some union contracts, time worked in excess of eight hours in a single day) (316)

owners' equity the difference between a firm's assets and its liabilities (500)

P

packaging all the activities involved in developing and providing a container with graphics for a product (373)

participative leadership leadership style in which all members of a team are involved in identifying essential goals and developing strategies to reach those goals (177)

partnership a voluntary association of two or more persons to act as co-owners of a business for profit (110)

part-time work permanent employment in which individuals work less than a standard work week (289)

penetration pricing the strategy of setting a low price for a new product (382)

perfect (or pure) competition the market situation in which there are many buyers and sellers of a product, and no single buyer or seller is powerful enough to affect the price of that product (22)

performance appraisal the evaluation of employees' current and potential levels of performance to allow managers to make objective human resources decisions (262)

periodic discounting temporary reduction of prices on a patterned or systematic basis (383)

personal budget a specific plan for spending your income (581)

personal income the income an individual receives from all sources *less* the Social Security taxes the individual must pay (349)

personal investment the use of your personal funds to earn a financial return (582)

personal selling personal communication aimed at informing customers and persuading them to buy a firm's products (426)

PERT (Program Evaluation and Review Technique) a scheduling technique that identifies the major activities necessary to complete a project and sequences them based on the time required to perform each one (228)

physical distribution all the activities concerned with the efficient movement of products from the producer to the ultimate user (412)

physiological needs the things we require for survival (277)

picketing marching back and forth in front of a place of employment with signs informing the public that a strike is in progress (320)

piece-rate system a compensation system under which employees are paid a certain amount for each unit of output they produce (276)

place utility utility created by making a product available at a location where customers wish to purchase it (333)

plan an outline of the actions by which an organization intends to accomplish its goals and objectives (170)

planning establishing organizational goals and deciding how to accomplish them (167)

planning horizon the period during which an operational plan will be in effect (223)

plant layout the arrangement of machinery, equipment, and personnel within a production facility (223)

podcasts digital audio or video files that people listen to or watch online on tablets, computers, MP3 players, or smartphones (461)

point-of-purchase display promotional material placed within a retail store (441)

pollution the contamination of water, air, or land through the actions of people in an industrialized society (57)

positioning the development of a product image in buyers' minds relative to the images they have of competing products (444)

possession utility utility created by transferring title (or ownership) of a product to a buyer (334)

preferred stock stock whose owners usually do not have voting rights but whose claims on dividends and assets are paid before those of common-stock owners (116, 566)

premium a gift that a producer offers a customer in return for buying its product (441)

premium pricing pricing the highest-quality or most-versatile products higher than other models in the product line (385)

press conference a meeting at which invited media personnel hear important news announcements and receive supplementary textual materials and photographs (442)

price the amount of money a seller is willing to accept in exchange for a product at a given time and under given circumstances (375)

price competition an emphasis on setting a price equal to or lower than competitors' prices to gain sales or market share (377)

price leaders products priced below the usual markup, near cost, or below cost (385)

price lining the strategy of selling goods only at certain predetermined prices that reflect definite price breaks (385)

price skimming the strategy of charging the highest possible price for a product during the introduction stage of its life-cycle (382)

primary-demand advertising advertising aimed at increasing the demand for all brands of a product within a specific industry (427)

primary market a market in which an investor purchases financial securities (via an investment bank) directly from the issuer of those securities (564)

prime interest rate the lowest rate charged by a bank for a short-term loan (560)

private placement occurs when stock and other corporate securities are sold directly to insurance companies, pension funds, or large institutional investors (567)

problem the discrepancy between an actual condition and a desired condition (179)

problem-solving team a team of knowledgeable employees brought together to tackle a specific problem (292)

process material a material that is used directly in the production of another product but is not readily identifiable in the finished product (360)

producer price index (PPI) an index that measures prices that producers receive for their finished goods (19)

product everything one receives in an exchange, including all tangible and intangible attributes and expected benefits; it may be a good, a service, or an idea (358)

product deletion the elimination of one or more products from a product line (365)

product design the process of creating a set of specifications from which a product can be produced (221)

product differentiation the process of developing and promoting differences between one's products and all competitive products (23, 377)

product life-cycle a series of stages in which a product's sales revenue and profit increase, reach a peak, and then decline (360)

product line a group of similar products that differ only in relatively minor characteristics (220, 363)

product mix all the products a firm offers for sale (363)

product modification the process of changing one or more of a product's characteristics (364)

productivity the average level of output per worker per hour (18)

profit what remains after all business expenses have been deducted from sales revenue (11)

profit-sharing the distribution of a percentage of a firm's profit among its employees (258)

promissory note a written pledge by a borrower to pay a certain sum of money to a creditor at a specified future date (560)

promotion communication about an organization and its products that is intended to inform, persuade, or remind target-market members (424)

promotional campaign a plan for combining and using the four promotional methods—advertising, personal selling, sales promotion, and publicity—in a particular promotion mix to achieve one or more marketing goals (443)

promotion mix the particular combination of promotion methods a firm uses to reach a target market (424)

prospectus a detailed, written description of a new security, the issuing corporation, and the corporation's top management (603)

proxy a legal form listing issues to be decided at a stockholders' meeting and enabling stockholders to transfer their voting rights to some other individual or individuals (117)

proxy fight a technique used to gather enough stockholder votes to control a targeted company (124)

publicity communication in news-story form about an organization, its products, or both (442)

public relations communication activities used to create and maintain favorable relations between an organization and various public groups, both internal and external (426)

purchasing all the activities involved in obtaining required materials, supplies, components, and parts from other firms (225)

Q

qualitative social media measurement the process of accessing the opinions and beliefs about a brand and primarily uses sentiment analysis to categorize what is being said about a company (470)

quality circle a team of employees who meet on company time to solve problems of product quality (230)

quality control the process of ensuring that goods and services are produced in accordance with design specifications (230)

quantitative social media measurement using numerical measurements, such as counting the number of Web site visitors, number of fans and followers, number of leads generated, and the number of new customers (469)

R

random discounting temporary reduction of prices on an unsystematic basis (383)

rate of return the total dollar amount of return you receive on an investment over a specific period of time divided by the amount invested (585)

ratification approval of a labor contract by a vote of the union membership (314)

raw material a basic material that actually becomes part of a physical product; usually comes from mines, forests, oceans, or recycled solid wastes (359)

rebate a return of part of the product's purchase price (359, 439)

recession two or more consecutive three-month periods of decline in a country's GDP (20)

recruiting the process of attracting qualified job applicants (252)

reference pricing pricing a product at a moderate level and positioning it next to a more expensive model or brand (383)

regional shopping center a planned shopping center containing large department stores, numerous specialty stores, restaurants, movie theaters, and sometimes even hotels (411)

registered bond a bond registered in the owner's name by the issuing company (570)

reinforcement theory a theory of motivation based on the premise that rewarded behavior is likely to be repeated, whereas punished behavior is less likely to recur (281)

relationship marketing establishing long-term, mutually satisfying buyer–seller relationships (333)

replacement chart a list of key personnel and their possible replacements within a firm (248)

research and development (R&D) a set of activities intended to identify new ideas that have the potential to result in new goods and services (219)

reserve requirement the percentage of its deposits a bank must retain, either in its own vault or on deposit with its Federal Reserve district bank (527)

reshoring a situation in which U.S. manufacturers bring manufacturing jobs back to the United States (214)

responsibility the duty to do a job or perform a task (195)

retailer a middleman that buys from producers or other middlemen and sells to consumers (396)

retained earnings the portion of a business's profits not distributed to stockholders (504, 566)

return on sales (or profit margin) a financial ratio calculated by dividing net income after taxes by net sales (510)

revenues the dollar amounts earned by a firm from selling goods, providing services, or performing business activities (505)

revenue stream a source of revenue flowing into a firm (472)

revolving credit agreement a guaranteed line of credit (535)

risk–return ratio a ratio based on the principle that a high-risk decision should generate higher financial returns for a business and more conservative decisions often generate lower returns (556)

robotics the use of programmable machines to perform a variety of tasks by manipulating materials and tools (233)

S

safety needs the things we require for physical and emotional security (277)

salary a specific amount of money paid for an employee's work during a set calendar period, regardless of the actual number of hours worked (258)

sales forecast an estimate of the amount of a product that an organization expects to sell during a certain period of time based on a specified level of marketing effort (343)

sales promotion the use of activities or materials as direct inducements to customers or salespersons (426)

sales support personnel employees who aid in selling but are more involved in locating prospects, educating customers, building goodwill for the firm, and providing follow-up service (436)

sample a free product given to customers to encourage trial and purchase (440)

Sarbanes–Oxley Act of 2002 provides sweeping new legal protection for employees who report corporate misconduct (41)

savings and loan association (S&L) a financial institution that offers checking and savings accounts and CDs and that invests most of its assets in home mortgage loans and other consumer loans (532)

S-corporation a corporation that is taxed as though it were a partnership (121)

scheduling the process of ensuring that materials and other resources are at the right place at the right time (227)

scientific management the application of scientific principles to management of work and workers (275)

secondary market a market for existing financial securities that are traded between investors (565)

secondary-market pricing setting one price for the primary target market and a different price for another market (383)

securities exchange a marketplace where member brokers meet to buy and sell securities (565)

security average (or security index) an average of the current market prices of selected securities (603)

selection the process of gathering information about applicants for a position and then using that information to choose the most appropriate applicant (253)

selective-demand (or brand) advertising advertising that is used to sell a particular brand of product (427)

selective distribution the use of only a portion of the available outlets for a product in each geographic area (398)

self-actualization needs the need to grow and develop and to become all that we are capable of being (278)

self-managed teams groups of employees with the authority and skills to manage themselves (292)

selling short the process of selling stock that an investor does not actually own but has borrowed from a brokerage firm and will repay at a later date (596)

seniority the length of time an employee has worked for an organization (316)

sentiment analysis a measurement that uses technology to detect the moods, attitudes, or emotions of people who experience a social media activity (470)

serial bonds bonds of a single issue that mature on different dates (571)

Service Corps of Retired Executives (SCORE) a group of businesspeople who volunteer their services to small businesses through the SBA (148)

service economy an economy in which more effort is devoted to the production of services than to the production of goods (26, 217)

shopping product an item for which buyers are willing to expend considerable effort on planning and making the purchase (359)

shop steward an employee elected by union members to serve as their representative (317)

short-term financing money that will be used for one year or less (554)

sinking fund a sum of money to which deposits are made each year for the purpose of redeeming a bond issue (571)

Six Sigma a disciplined approach that relies on statistical data and improved methods to eliminate defects for a firm's products and services (231)

skills inventory a computerized data bank containing information on the skills and experience of all present employees (248)

slowdown a technique whereby workers report to their jobs but work at a slower pace than normal (320)

small business one that is independently owned and operated for profit and is not dominant in its field (135)

Small Business Administration (SBA) a governmental agency that assists, counsels, and protects the interests of small businesses in the United States (147)

small-business development centers (SBDCs) university-based groups that provide individual counseling and practical training to owners of small businesses (149)

small-business institutes (SBIs) groups of senior and graduate students in business administration who provide management counseling to small businesses (149)

small-business investment companies (SBICs) privately owned firms that provide venture capital to small enterprises that meet their investment standards (150)

social audit a comprehensive report of what an organization has done and is doing with regard to social issues that affect it (62)

social content sites allow companies to create and share information about their products and services (460)

social game a multiplayer, competitive, goal-oriented activity with defined rules of engagement and online connectivity among a community of players (461)

social media the online interactions that allow people and businesses to communicate and share ideas, personal information, and information about products and services (27, 458)

social media communities social networks based on the relationships among people (462)

social media marketing the utilization of social media technologies, channels, and software to create, communicate, deliver, and exchange offerings that have value for an organization (464)

social needs the human requirements for love and affection and a sense of belonging (278)

social responsibility the recognition that business activities have an impact on society and the consideration of that impact in business decision making (44)

socioeconomic model of social responsibility the concept that business should emphasize not only profits but also the impact of its decisions on society (49)

sole proprietorship a business that is owned (and usually operated) by one person (106)

span of management (or span of control) the number of workers who report directly to one manager (196)

special-event pricing advertised sales or price cutting linked to a holiday, season, or event (385)

specialization the separation of a manufacturing process into distinct tasks and the assignment of the different tasks to different individuals (25)

specialty-line wholesaler a middleman that carries a select group of products within a single line (403)

specialty product an item that possesses one or more unique characteristics for which a significant group of buyers is willing to expend considerable purchasing effort (359)

speculative production the time lag between the actual production of goods and when the goods are sold (555)

staff manager a position created to provide support, advice, and expertise within an organization (198)

stakeholders all the different people or groups of people who are affected by the policies and decisions made by an organization (12)

Standard & Poor's 500 Stock Index an index that contains 500 different stocks that reflect increases or decreases in value for the U.S. stock market as a whole (587)

standard of living a loose, subjective measure of how well off an individual or a society is, mainly in terms of want satisfaction through goods and services (24)

standing committee a relatively permanent committee charged with performing some recurring task (204)

state bank a commercial bank chartered by the banking authorities in the state in which it operates (531)

statement of cash flows a statement that illustrates how the company's operating, investing, and financing activities affect cash during an accounting period (507)

statistic a measure that summarizes a particular characteristic of an entire group of numbers (494)

stock the shares of ownership of a corporation (115)

stock dividend a dividend in the form of additional stock (591)

stockholder a person who owns a corporation's stock (115)

stock split the division of each outstanding share of a corporation's stock into a greater number of shares (592)

store (or private) brand a brand that is owned by an individual wholesaler or retailer (370)

store of value a means of retaining and accumulating wealth (522)

strategic alliance a partnership formed to create competitive advantage on a worldwide basis (88)

strategic plan an organization's broadest plan, developed as a guide for major policy setting and decision making (170)

strategic planning process the establishment of an organization's major goals and objectives and the allocation of resources to achieve them (167)

strike a temporary work stoppage by employees, calculated to add force to their demands (304)

strikebreaker a non-union employee who performs the job of a striking union member (320)

supermarket a large self-service store that sells primarily food and household products (406)

superstore a large retail store that carries not only food and nonfood products ordinarily found in supermarkets but also additional product lines (406)

supply the quantity of a product that producers are willing to sell at each of various prices (22, 376)

supply an item that facilitates production and operations but does not become part of a finished product (360)

supply-chain management long-term partnership among channel members working together to create a distribution system that reduces inefficiencies, costs, and redundancies while creating a competitive advantage and satisfying customers (399)

sustainability meeting the needs of the present without compromising the ability of future generations to meet their own needs (27)

SWOT analysis the identification and evaluation of a firm's strengths, weaknesses, opportunities, and threats (168)

syndicate a temporary association of individuals or firms organized to perform a specific task that requires a large amount of capital (123)

synthetic process a process in operations management in which raw materials or components are combined to create a finished product (215)

T

tactical plan a smaller scale plan developed to implement a strategy (170)

target market a group of individuals or organizations, or both, for which a firm develops and maintains a marketing mix suitable for the specific needs and preferences of that group (337)

task force a committee established to investigate a major problem or pending decision (204)

team two or more workers operating as a coordinated unit to accomplish a specific task or goal (292)

technical salesperson a salesperson who assists a company's current customers in technical matters (437)

technical skills specific skills needed to accomplish a specialized activity (176)

telecommuting working at home all the time or for a portion of the work week (290)

telemarketing the performance of marketing-related activities by telephone (409)

television home shopping a form of selling in which products are presented to television viewers, who can buy them by calling a toll-free number and paying with a credit card (409)

tender offer an offer to purchase the stock of a firm targeted for acquisition at a price just high enough to tempt stockholders to sell their shares (124)

term-loan agreement a promissory note that requires a borrower to repay a loan in monthly, quarterly, semiannual, or annual installments (569)

Theory X a concept of employee motivation generally consistent with Taylor's scientific management; assumes that employees dislike work and will function only in a highly controlled work environment (281)

Theory Y a concept of employee motivation generally consistent with the ideas of the human relations movement; assumes responsibility and work toward organizational goals, and by doing so they also achieve personal rewards (280)

Theory Z the belief that some middle ground between type A and type J practices is best for American business (281)

time deposit an amount on deposit in an interest-bearing savings account or certificate of deposit (524)

time utility utility created by making a product available when customers wish to purchase it (334)

top manager an upper-level executive who guides and controls the overall fortunes of an organization (172)

total cost the sum of the fixed costs and the variable costs attributed to a product (379)

total quality management (TQM) the coordination of efforts directed at improving customer satisfaction, increasing employee participation, strengthening supplier partnerships, and facilitating an organizational atmosphere of continuous quality improvement (181)

total revenue the total amount received from sales of a product (379)

trade credit a type of short-term financing extended by a seller who does not require immediate payment after delivery of merchandise (560)

trade deficit a negative balance of trade (73)

trademark a brand name or brand mark that is registered with the U.S. Patent and Trademark Office and thus is legally protected from use by anyone except its owner (369)

trade name the complete and legal name of an organization (370)

trade sales promotion method a sales promotion method designed to encourage wholesalers and retailers to stock and actively promote a manufacturer's product (439)

trade salesperson a salesperson—generally employed by a food producer or processor—who assists customers in promoting products, especially in retail stores (437)

trade show an industry-wide exhibit at which many sellers display their products (441)

trading company provides a link between buyers and sellers in different countries (89)

traditional specialty store a store that carries a narrow product mix with deep product lines (406)

transfer pricing prices charged in sales between an organization's units (386)

transportation the shipment of products to customers (414)

trustee an individual or an independent firm that acts as a bond owner's representative (571)

U

undifferentiated approach directing a single marketing mix at the entire market for a particular product (337)

unemployment rate the percentage of a nation's labor force unemployed at any time (19)

union–management (labor) relations the dealings between labor unions and business management both in the bargaining process and beyond it (303)

union security protection of the union's position as the employees' bargaining agent (317)

union shop a workplace in which new employees must join the union after a specified probationary period (317)

unlimited liability a legal concept that holds a business owner personally responsible for all the debts of the business (108)

unsecured financing financing that is not backed by collateral; unsecured short-term financing offers several options (559)

utility the ability of a good or service to satisfy a human need (215)

V

variable cost a cost that depends on the number of units produced (379)

venture capital money that is invested in small (and sometimes struggling) firms that have the potential to become very successful (150)

vertical channel integration the combining of two or more stages of a distribution channel under a single firm's management (399)

vertical marketing system (VMS) a centrally managed distribution channel resulting from vertical channel integration (399)

virtual team a team consisting of members who are geographically dispersed but communicate electronically (293)

W

wage survey a collection of data on prevailing wage rates within an industry or a geographic area (257)

warehouse club a large-scale members-only establishment that combines features of cash-and-carry wholesaling with discount retailing (406)

warehouse showroom a retail facility in a large, low-cost building with a large on-premises inventory and minimal service (405)

warehousing the set of activities involved in receiving and storing goods and preparing them for reshipment (413)

whistle-blowing informing the press or government officials about unethical practices within one's organization (42)

wholesaler a middleman that sells products to other firms (396)

wiki a collaborative online working space that enables members to contribute content that is then sharable with other people (462)

wildcat strike a strike not approved by the strikers' union (320)

World Trade Organization (WTO) powerful successor to GATT that incorporates trade in goods, services, and ideas (82)

Y

Yellow Pages advertising simple listings or display advertisements presented under specific product categories appearing in print and online telephone directories (429)

Z

zero-base budgeting a budgeting approach in which every expense in every budget must be justified (558)

NAME INDEX

McFollum, Tim, 226
McGregor, Douglas, 279–280
McGuinness, Joe, 153
McMillion, Denver, 149
Meany, George, 306
MediaBistro, 252
Mercedes-Benz, 230, 333
Merck & Co., Inc., 47
Mergent,Inc., 599
Merkle, 344
Merrill Lynch, 124
Michael and Susan Dell Foundation, 45
Michelin tires, 371
Mickelson ExxonMobil Teachers Academy, 46
Microsoft Corporation, 115, 371, 483, 509, 561, 565
Midvale Steel Company, 275
Mills, Karen, 141, 150, 151
Minnesota Twins, 380
Minority Business Development Agency, 148
Mint.com, 109
Minute Maid, 358
Missoni, 398
Modern Work Environment (MWE) Lab, 569
Money, 602
Monopoly game, 361
Monster Beverage, 585
Monster.com, 6, 175, 252
Mont Blanc pens, 339
Montgomery Ward, 408
Monthly Labor Review, 493
Moody's Investors Service, Inc., 590, 599
Morgan, J.P., 546
Morgan Stanley, 124, 531
Morningstar, Inc., 599
Motley Fool Web site, 582, 598
Motorola, 229, 230, 231, 399, 444
Mozilla, 293
MSN, 431
Murray's Cheese, 158–159
Mustafa, Isaiah, 424, 446
Mutual Fund Education Alliance, 593
MySpace, 207, 483

N

Nabisco, 365
Nader, Ralph, 52
Nanigian, Daniel J., 156
Nanmac Corporation, 156
NASDAQ (National Association of Securities Dealers Automated Quotations), 565
National Alliance of Business (NAB), 57
National Basketball Association (NBA), 303, 321
National Black McDonald's Operators Association, 153
National Center for Employee Ownership, 291
National Consumers' League, 52
National Credit Union Administration (NCUA), 532, 539
National DCP (NDCP), 399
National Football League, 32
National Foundation for Credit Counseling, 582
National Highway Safety Administration, 364
National Labor Relations Board (NLRB), 309
National Nurses United, 324
National Public Radio (NPR), 461
National Whistle Blower Center, 42
Nature Valley, 444

Nature Valley Trail View Web site, 444
Nautica, 370
NCR, 214
Nebraska Furniture Mart, 130, 131
Nederlander Concerts, 31, 575
Nederlander Organization, 575
Nespresso, 331, 350
Nestlé, 96, 99, 212, 222, 331, 509
Nestlé Purina, 229
Netapp, 275
Netflix, 185, 341, 409
NetJets, 130–131
New Scientist magazine, 346
New United Motor Manufacturing, Inc. (NUMMI), 88
New York Stock Exchange (NYSE), 565, 604, 606
New York Times, 461
Newport News, 408
Newsweek, 602
New-Wave Fashions, Inc., 194
Nielsen marketing research, 347
Nielsen Media Research, 461
Nike, 189, 199, 333, 369, 370, 414, 431
Nisource (Columbia Gas), 149
Nissan, 24, 337
Nixon, Richard, 38
NLRB, 312, 313
Nortel Networks Corporation, 39
North American Free Trade Agreement (NAFTA), 84
Northeast Art Supply, 501, 502, 503, 504, 505–506, 507–508, 510–511
Northrop Grumman Corporation, 230
Noxema, 369
Numi Organic Tea, 207–208
NYSE Euronext holding company, 565

O

Obama, Barack, 85, 90, 92, 150–151, 432, 530, 553
Occupational Safety and Health Administration (OSHA), 266
Ocean Spray Cranberries, Inc., 123
Odland, Steve, 515
Office Depot, 407, 408, 515
OfficeMax, 339–340
Office of the U.S. Trade Representative, 84
Old Spice, 424, 446, 464
Oliberte, 226
Olive Garden, 218, 576
Olyai, Nikki, 137
Omnicon Group, 332
Online Women's Business Center, 149
Oovoo, 254
OPEC (Organization of Petroleum Exporting Countries), 85
Open Pantry, 406
Oracle Corporation, 124, 399, 466
Orbitz, 475
Organization of Petroleum Exporting Countries (OPEC), 85
Orman, Suze, 587–588
Ouchi, William, 280–281
Outback Steakhouse, 150
Oxley, Michael J., 41

P

PA Live Bait Vending, 410
Packard, Dave, 208

Page, Brandt, 145
Page, Larry, 177
Palm, 208
Pampered Chef, 130, 408
Panasonic, 221
Panera Bread, 36
Panera Cares, 36, 63
Papa John's Pizza, 118
Parham, Victoria, 461
Parker Brothers, 361
Patek Philippe watches, 398
Pateer, Aaron, 109
Patient Assistance Program, 47
Pattillo, Aaron, 366
PayPal, 537
Pencil Makers Association, 75
Pennsylvania Association of Staff Nurses and Allied Professionals, 324
People's United Bank, 435
Pepsi, 378, 425, 462–463
PepsiCo, 106, 152, 155, 194, 353–354, 358, 387, 390, 432
Perdue chicken products, 435
Perry, Herman, 153
Perry, Katy, 430
PERT (Program Evaluation and Review Technique), 228–229
Petcare, 229
Pfizer, 434, 558–559
Philip Morris, 51, 89
Phillips Petroleum, 44
Pier 1 Imports, 70
Piggyback Consolidators, 416
Pincus, Mark, 3, 28
Pinterest, 462, 475, 476, 482, 567
Pixar, 32
Pizza Hut, 220, 370
Plains All American Pipeline, 416
Planned Parenthood, 463
Plumbing Warehouse, 405
Polaroid, 141
Polman, Paul, 66
Polo, 370
Pomerantz, Carrie Schwab, 46
Porcino Paul, 517
Prevot, Corinne, 145
Price, Samuel Lowell, 511
PricewaterhouseCoopers (PwC), 38, 250, 487, 499, 511
Prius, 428
Private Label Manufacturer's Association, 370
Procter, William, 114
Procter & Gamble (P&G), 27, 39, 106, 114, 115, 140, 148, 191, 203, 208, 212, 214, 292, 363, 367, 369, 373, 384, 398, 400, 424, 433, 434, 446, 488, 509, 551, 561
Providence Sacred Heart Medical Center, 324
Puck, Wolfgang, 105
Pulte Homes, 496
Putin, Vladimir, 125

Q

Qantas Airways, 315
Quaker Oats, 260, 390
Qualified Resources, Inc., 149
Questcor Pharmaceuticals, 585
Questor Corporation, 86

SUBJECT INDEX

processing, 493–494
  storing, 493
  updating, 493
data mining, 476–477
data processing, 493–494
database, 346, 490, 492
debenture bond, 570
debit card, 536
debt capital, 551, 558
debt financing, sources of short-term, 559–563
decentralized organization, 195
decision making, 179
decision on where to incorporate, 115–116
decision-support system (DSS), 496
decline stage, of the product life-cycle, 362–363
Deepwater Horizon
  explosion of, 58
  oil leak, 426
deferred compensation, 315
deflation, adjusting for, 18
deforestation, preventing, 168
delegation, 194
  of authority, 194–195
  barriers to, 195
  steps in, 195, 196
deleting, products, 365
"Dell Hell," series of rants called, 460
demand
  defined, 22
  matching personnel supply with, 248
  for a product, 376
demand curve, 376
demand deposit, 524
demand-based pricing, 379–381
democratic leaders, 177
Democrats, preferring smaller more affordable
      cars, 345
dense smog, geographic conditions for creating, 59
department stores, 404
departmentalization, 193–194
dependability, of transportation, 415
deposit expansion, 527
depreciation, 503
depression, defined, 21
depth, of product mix, 363
derivatives, new rules for, 181
design planning, 220
desired behavior, reward for, 288
determinants, regarding benefits, 316
devaluation, increasing cost of foreign goods, 76
development and implementation, 219
Dewmocracy campaign, 353
differential pricing, 382–383
differentiated market segmentation, 338, 339
difficulty of counterfeiting, 524
digital marketing, areas of, 465
digital media, higher use among teenagers and young
      adults, 353
digital merit badges, 6
digital native, 458
digital wallet, 537
direct channel, 396, 397
direct compensation, 315
direct investment, 87–88
direct marketing, 408
direct selling, 407–408
directing, 171
direct-mail advertising, 429
direct-response marketing, 408–409

discount, 386
discount broker, 604
discount rate, 528, 529
discount stores, 404
discounting, in business pricing, 386
discretionary income, 349
disposable income, 349
dissatisfaction, of employees, 278–279
dissatisfiers, 279
distribution, of Chobani yogurt, 395
distribution fee, 594
distribution industries, 136–137
distribution ingredients, of the marketing mix,
      340–341
distributors, 362, 402
"Diverse by Design" teams, 250
diversification, of a mutual fund, 593
Diversity and Inclusion Advisory Board, 250
diversity training programs, 250
dividend payments, 591
dividends, 117, 564
divisibility, of money, 524
Do Not Call Implementation Act (2003), 54
Dodd-Frank Wall Street Reform and Consumer
      Protection Act (2010), 54, 530, 553
Doha Round (2001), 82
dollar value, increase in, 591–592
domestic corporation, 116
domestic jobs, protecting, 77
domestic system, 25
do-not-call registries, 409
door-to-door selling, 407
double taxation, of corporations, 120
double-entry bookkeeping system, 500
Dow Jones Industrial Average (DJIA), 546,
      584, 603
draft, from a bank, 86
dual role, by leader of a team, 294
dual-branded franchises, 153
dumping, 75
durability, of money, 524

E

early retirement, 248
earnings statement, 504
e-business, 25–26
  challenges for, 477–478
  creating profit, 472–473
  defined, 470
  fundamental models of, 473–475
  organizing resources, 470–471
  satisfying new needs, 471
e-commerce, 470
economic benefits, of higher education, 5
economic community, 83
economic crisis (2007), 3–4
economic crisis (2009), 584
  Federal Reserve Board response and, 526–527
  financial reform after, 553
  getting money from a bank or lender after,
      540–541
economic environment, 27
economic forces, in the marketing
      environment, 342
economic indicators, measuring a nation's economy,
      19–20
economic model, of social responsibility, 49, 50
economic performance, measuring, 17–20

economic systems
  differences in, 13
  key issues challenging, 28
  types of, 12–17
economics, defined, 12
economies, economic indicators measuring,
      19–20
economy, 13
  effect of productivity growth, 18
  methods used to control, 529
efficiency, provided by an intermediary, 400
e-learning, Internet-based, 260
electronic business, defined, 470
electronic check conversion (ECC), 538
electronic communities, 462
Electronic Funds Transfer Act (1978), 538
electronic funds transfer (EFT) system, 537–538
electronic transfers, 529
embargo, 75
emergency fund, 583
emissions, cutting, 414
employee benefits, 259
employee empowerment, 291
employee ownership, 291–292
employee participation, 181, 230–231
employee pay, central to union-management
      relations, 315–316
employee relations, 246
employee stock ownership plans (ESOPs), 291–292
employee training, 260
employees
  being successful, 6–7
  characteristics of, 7
  concerns of, 37
  difficulty in hiring by sole proprietors, 109
  joining unions, 311
  recruiting, 466
  resolving customer problems, 298
employer-sponsored retirement programs, 584
employment, small businesses providing, 141–142
employment applications, 253, 254
employment practices, 55–57
Employment Retirement Income Security Act (1974),
      265, 266
employment tests, administered to job
      candidates, 253
empowerment, 291
enforcement, of company policies, procedures, and
      ethical codes, 41
enterprise resource planning (ERP), 227
entertainment empire, 32
entrepreneurial leadership, 178
entrepreneurs, 14, 137–140
  accounting for first-time, 507
  average age of, 138
  selling a small business to a big business, 109
entrepreneurship self-tests, 139
environment, concern for, 57–61
environmental impact, minimizing, 235
environmental laws, summary of major, 58
environmental legislation, effects of, 57–60
environmental responsibility, in developing
      packages, 374
environments, affecting business, 26–27
Equal Credit Opportunity Act (1974), 54
Equal Pay Act (1963), 258, 264, 265
equilibrium (market) price, 22–23
equilibrium price, 377
equity, defined, 282